BELIEVER

BELIEVER

MY FORTY YEARS IN POLITICS

DAVID AXELROD

PENGUIN PRESS

New York

2015

PENGUIN PRESS
Published by the Penguin Group
Penguin Group (USA) LLC
375 Hudson Street
New York, New York 10014

USA • Canada • UK • Ireland • Australia
New Zealand • India • South Africa • China

penguin.com
A Penguin Random House Company

First published by Penguin Press, a member of Penguin Group (USA) LLC, 2015

Photograph credits appear on page 511.

ISBN 978-1-59420-587-3

Printed in the United States of America
1 3 5 7 9 10 8 6 4 2

DESIGNED BY AMANDA DEWEY

Penguin is committed to publishing works of quality and integrity.
In that spirit, we are proud to offer this book to our readers;
however, the story, the experiences, and the words
are the author's alone.

For **SUSAN, LAUREN, MICHAEL,** and **ETHAN,**
whose love and sacrifice made all things possible.

"The future is not a gift. It is an achievement."

ROBERT F. KENNEDY

CONTENTS

PART FOUR

PART FIVE

PART SIX

BELIEVER

INTRODUCTION

NOT EVERYONE CAN POINT to a moment, the exact time and place, when a lifelong passion began. I can.

It was 1960, twelve days before the presidential election. John F. Kennedy, locked in a dead-even race with Richard Nixon, was barnstorming the neighborhoods of New York City. And on the afternoon of October 27, he came to mine.

Stuyvesant Town, a forest of redbrick high-rises on Manhattan's Lower East Side, was built after World War II to house the flood of returning GIs and their families. Now, in the final, frantic days of his campaign, Kennedy had come there to summon a new generation of leadership.

I was, no doubt, a little newer than he had in mind. I was five.

An inspiring woman named Jessie Berry, who all but raised me while my mother was at work, took me to see JFK that day. Jessie, an African American, had come to New York from South Carolina as a young woman during the Great Migration. She had spent her days taking care of other people's kids, scraping together what she could to help support her own two daughters. Yet she was determined that the future be better, if not for her, then for her children and her grandchildren.

Maybe that's why she took me to see this promising young leader, a Catholic, whose election would break down a historic barrier. Maybe she saw in him hope for the future. (Looking back, I see that she might also have viewed the outing as a way to occupy her maddeningly hyperactive little charge.)

So when Jessie heard that Kennedy was coming to Stuyvesant Town, and would be just two blocks from my family's apartment at 622 East Twentieth Street, she took me by the hand and we headed to the rally. There, she sat me on top of a mailbox to give me a better view. From that perch, I watched in awe as Twentieth Street (at that section, a wide boulevard) filled up with people instead of the usual, ceaseless parade of cars. Near the front of the crowd, close enough to shake hands with the candidate, I spotted my sister, Joan, and her friends heading home from the junior high across First Avenue.

I wasn't the only young kid in the crowd. Stuyvesant Town and the adjoining Peter Cooper Village were built and designed for young families, with a network of playgrounds on greened, tree-lined campuses. So when JFK came, many mothers turned out, babies in tow, eager to catch a glimpse of the dashing young senator. It was, as the advance people who plan such rallies say, a built-in audience.

They listened in rapt attention as he delivered his call to action.

It was just fifteen years after the end of World War II. Every adult there had endured that ordeal and, before it, the Great Depression. Now a Cold War hovered over their everyday lives, carrying with it the threat of nuclear annihilation. They had played a role in saving the nation, and were accustomed to sacrifice, not the pain-free succor that would become the coin of the realm of future political campaigns.

So Kennedy, himself a war hero, didn't come bearing lavish promises. In a harbinger of the inaugural address he would deliver three months later, he came with a challenge.

"I don't run on the presidential program of saying that if I am elected, life will be easy," Kennedy declared, his voice booming off the surrounding highrise buildings. "I think to be a citizen of the United States in the 1960s is a hazardous occupation. But it is also one that offers challenge and hope, and I believe the choice lies with you on November 8."

"Whether I am the candidate for the presidency, or president, or stay in the Senate, I regard our obligation not to please you but to serve you, and in my judgment, in 1960, a candidate for the presidency should be willing to give the truth to the people, and the truth is that what we are now doing is not good enough."

I was too young to understand the full meaning of his speech or the magnitude of the moment. I recovered his words only years later, from one of those online archives no one back then could have imagined. I might not have understood exactly why the crowd cheered when it did, or that Kennedy was desperately seeking votes, locked in what would be one of the closest presidential contests ever. Yet to this five-year-old, the scene was pure magic, electric and important. Though I couldn't grasp the nuances, I somehow absorbed the larger message: we are the masters of our future, and politics is the means by which we shape it. From that moment on, I was hooked. I wanted to be a part of the action.

Fifty-two years later, on November 5, 2012, I stood at the foot of the stage at another huge, outdoor rally, on the eve of another presidential election. It was 10:00 p.m. in Des Moines. A crowd of twenty thousand stretched from the podium on Locust Street four blocks east toward the glistening gold dome of the Iowa state capitol. They waited for hours, on that chilly November night, to watch President Barack Obama deliver the final speech at the final campaign stop of his political career—and mine.

For Team Obama, it was a homecoming. Four years earlier, Iowans had breathed life into his audacious candidacy for president. Obama had virtually taken up residence there, spending eighty-nine days in the state during the run-up to Iowa's critical, first-in-the-nation presidential caucuses, as he made his case for change. Along the way, he developed strong bonds with the folks he met in countless living rooms, diners, and union halls across the state.

While the pundits and political insiders in Washington were smugly writing him off as a political shooting star, Obama placed his bet on Iowa and the army of idealistic young people who descended upon the state, hell-bent on changing the course of history. And without Iowa's embrace, his candidacy almost certainly would have died a quick, snowy death.

Iowa was the beginning of everything. Now, steeled by a thousand battles, Obama had returned there to plead his case, seeking the chance to finish what he had started. He had taken bold and controversial steps to revive a wounded economy, but the work of redeeming an embattled middle class was far from done. He had ended our war in Iraq and, having brought Osama bin Laden and many of Al Qaeda's leaders to justice, was on the path to ending another war in Afghanistan. Yet it would take a continued commitment to bring those troops home, and the world would only become more complex and challenging. After a lengthy and bruising fight to pass historic health care reform, it would take his next term to implement and undergird it against continuing opposition efforts at subversion and repeal. He felt an urgency to deal with the great, unresolved problems of climate change and immigration reform. And maybe, just maybe, a second, resounding victory would pave the way for more comity and cooperation in Washington, which was the great, unfulfilled promise of his presidency.

A year earlier, following a devastating standoff with Congress over the nation's debt limit, Obama's standing with the public had hit a new low. Some polls showed his approval ratings sinking perilously below 40 percent. Trial heats with Mitt Romney, the likely Republican nominee, showed the president running well below the majority he would need to win. Nate Silver, the whiz kid political handicapper who later would win plaudits for accurately calling the outcome of the election, had written a provocative and, for our team, thoroughly depressing magazine piece for the *New York Times* with a pointed headline: "Is Obama Toast?"

And while Obama remained publicly defiant back then, he was privately resigned to the prospect of defeat. "I'm realistic about this. We have an uphill fight," he said, during one of our conversations in the dark days of 2011. "Michelle and I have talked about it—about where we would live if we lose. The girls are settled here now, so we really need to think about that."

But whatever doubts Obama harbored were matched by a preternatural sense of competitiveness. This man hated to lose a game of H-O-R-S-E, much less an election that would define his presidency. So he fought his way back, knowing what defeat would mean for his programs, his legacy, and for the millions of young black Americans for whom his election had opened new vistas. And he believed the stakes for the country were large.

Now, seven hours before the first polling places opened out east, he stood inside a security tent in Des Moines, waiting to be introduced to the rapturous crowd and shuffling from foot to foot like an athlete champing at the bit to get into the game. Michelle Obama, who had been crisscrossing the nation on her own, had joined up with her husband for the final stop and was making the introductory remarks onstage.

It had been remarkable to watch Michelle's evolution, from reluctant conscript in 2007 to a buoyant and beloved campaigner five years later.

Thrown out on the campaign trail without adequate staffing or preparation in 2007, she quickly became fodder for the right-wing noise machine, which seized on every opportunity to cast her as the angry, militant black woman behind the affable candidate. Michelle, an accomplished lawyer who had given up her career to make her husband's dream possible, never expected to become fodder for his opposition. She was stung by the nasty characterizations and skittish about putting herself out there for more abuse.

But over the years, she had made peace, if sometimes an uneasy one, with her role as a public figure, using her platform to promote child nutrition and fitness, the welfare of military families, and other vital causes about which she felt deeply. She had become an extraordinarily evocative speaker as well as a charming and witty guest on late-night talk shows. Still, if the First Lady was willing to put herself out there, she was adamant that her splendid daughters, Malia and Sasha, be shielded from the public stage.

Whenever there was a potential scheduling conflict between her public role and her parental obligations, everyone in the White House knew which priority would win. Anyone brave (or dumb) enough to question that rule invariably emerged with scorched ears.

Buoyed by a deep and abiding belief in her husband, Michelle had become his most effective surrogate and, privately, his fiercest defender. Though she had little direct contact with the White House staff, word would spread quickly if Michelle felt the president had been let down. She could be tough, even on his supporters, sharing her frustration over the frequent friendly fire from the Left that always seems unhappy with any compromise. "I'm tired of all the complaining," she told a small fund-raising luncheon in New York City a few weeks before the election, upbraiding a group of women who had paid twenty thousand dollars a plate for the privilege. "My husband has worked his heart out to get a lot of things done for this country, up against a bunch of folks on the other side who will do anything to get in the way. So just stop it! He needs your help, not your complaints!"

But now the election was just hours away, and Michelle warmed up the Des Moines crowd with one last impassioned plea for support.

"While we have come so far, we know that there is so much more to do. And what we really, truly know is that we cannot turn back now. We need to keep moving this country forward," she said. "So that means that we need to re-elect the man who has been fighting for us every single day—my husband, the love of my life, the President of the United States . . . Barack Obama!"

On cue, Obama burst out of the tent and sprinted up a set of stairs onto the makeshift stage and into a warm embrace with his wife.

We tend to idealize political families, but the Obamas deserve any admiration they get. As they stood there together and waved to the crowd, at this last rally of their last campaign, they both understood the many sacrifices that Michelle and the family had endured to make Obama's career possible.

For twelve years as a state legislator, U.S. senator, and presidential candidate, Obama had spent much of his time away from home. Though he was a doting father who pined for his kids when he was on the road, most of the responsibility for raising them fell to Michelle. Their years in the White House, living above his office, were the first in which Barack could regularly and reliably share dinner with the family and spend time with his girls. Yet the presidency also placed extraordinary constraints on their lives.

Maybe it was that knowledge, or Michelle's proud words, or the sight of so many old Iowa friends at the end of this long gauntlet, but the normally unflappable president was quickly moved to tears.

"Right behind these bleachers is the building that was home to our Iowa headquarters in 2008," he said, pointing to a rambling storefront that was, five years earlier, our littered, frenzied nerve center. (Today it's the pristine headquarters of a New Age church.)

"This was where some of the first young people who joined our campaign set up shop, willing to work for little pay and less sleep because they believed that people who love their country can change it."

"And when the cynics said we couldn't, you said 'Yes, we can!'"

The crowd picked up the chant. "Yes, we can!"

"You said, 'Yes, we can!'—and we did. Against all odds, we did! We didn't know what challenges would come when we began this journey. We didn't know how deep the crisis would turn out. But we knew we would get through those challenges the same way this nation always has—with that determined, unconquerable American spirit that says no matter how bad the storm gets, no matter how tough times are, we're all in this together. We rise or fall as one nation and as one people."

"Yes We Can." It was the tag line I had written for the first TV ad of our first, long-shot campaign together just eight years earlier, when Obama, a largely unknown and seriously underfunded state legislator, set out to win a seat in the U.S. Senate. And it became our mantra when, in 2007, he enlisted millions of Americans to the cause of change.

As Obama spoke almost wistfully about those heady, hopeful days of 2008, they seemed like a distant dream. He had first come to Iowa as an apostle of change. Now it was impossible to ignore how much the intervening years had changed *him*. His faced lined and his hair flecked with gray, Obama had been tested through four of among the most challenging years any American president has faced, and they had taken their toll. He had major accomplishments to his credit, achievements that would help people and advance the nation.

In his first two years in office, Obama had passed more substantive legislation than any president since Lyndon Johnson. But when, in 2010, he lost the gaudy Democratic majorities he had helped sweep in, progress was hard to find.

Washington was more bitterly divided and gridlocked than ever. And, now faced with an implacable Republican opposition in control of the House and numerous enough to tie up the Senate, Obama himself had taken on a more partisan edge. The White House operator called me a few weeks before the election and asked if I was available for the president. When Obama got on the line, I asked him if anyone ever said, "No, I'm not available for the president." He laughed. "Only John Boehner," he said. The president had once viewed Boehner as a prospective partner. "He reminds me of a lot of the guys I used to serve with in Springfield," Obama said, recalling his days as a state senator, when he worked easily across party lines. But that proved to be wishful thinking; the two never found a groove. Boehner would be hemmed in by the Tea Party contingent (who helped propel him to the Speakership in 2011), antigovernment absolutists for whom compromise was tantamount to treason. And Obama, burned too many times, grew increasingly dark about the prospects for reconciliation in Washington.

By denying Obama the collaboration for which he had hoped, the Republican leaders had shrewdly forced him into a partisan corner if he wanted to get anything done. And while the slow recovery and continued economic anxieties presented a challenge to his reelection, the president's failure to tame Washington and build bipartisan bridges was the most often-stated disappointment among the movable independent voters who had decisively tilted his way in 2008.

So 2012 had to be a different kind of campaign, more modest in its ambitions and more pointed in drawing out the deficiencies of our opponent. In 2008 we had built a once-in-a-generation movement for change. In 2012 we simply ran a very proficient political campaign.

As I stood together with my colleagues, and watched the president's emotional closing argument in Des Moines, I was tearing up as well. I was proud of Obama and what we had accomplished. I knew this amazing band of ours would never be together again, and I was moved by the sea of people, many with kids on their shoulders, who had come out on this cool election eve.

Gazing at young kids on their parents' shoulders, I was transported back in time. I knew that those kids were *me*, the wide-eyed little boy on the mailbox. And I felt the same excitement I had that fateful day in Stuyvesant Town more than half a century before.

For all the division, rancor, and tawdriness in our politics, the enduring ritual of Americans coming together to choose their leader and chart their course still moved me—as noble and inspiring to a weathered political warrior as it had been to a five-year-old child in New York City.

After a lifetime of the rough-and-tumble, I still believed: in politics as a calling; in campaigns as an opportunity to forge the future we imagine; in government as an instrument for that progress.

Throughout those years, I had seen our democracy at its best and its worst. I had represented great men and women who had made me proud of my chosen path, and some who had left me disappointed, appalled, and, worst of all, ashamed. My childhood idealism was more measured and mature, shaped by the realization that even great leaders are human and, therefore, imperfect. I had lived the life I imagined as a little boy. Now this period of it was over.

For just as the president had run his last race, I had run my own. Our decade-long partnership was an impossible act to follow. He was an incomparable client—not perfect by a long shot; but brilliant and honorable and motivated by the best intentions; a good friend and a fellow idealist. I had been spoiled. The thought of starting over with someone new—and almost certainly somebody who would fall short of Obama—was unappealing.

Moreover, after more than 150 campaigns, I had to acknowledge the physical and emotional toll they had taken. Campaigns are at once exhilarating and exhausting. For the campaign "guru" (the driver of the strategy), they require the projection of utter assurance, even as you constantly wrestle with uncertainty. They dominate your life and infiltrate your mind, even when you're sleeping (which is rare). Wisdom and experience have their place, but campaigns demand the energy and mental acuity of youth.

I had spent a good deal of my life on the campaign trail, as a newspaper reporter and strategist, and two glorious but draining years working twenty feet from the Oval Office at a time of seemingly perpetual crisis. And while I had lived my dreams, my valiant wife, Susan, and our three children had paid a high price. I was often away, even when I was home; too frequently an absentee father, leaving Susan and the family to cope with the impact of our oldest child's debilitating, lifelong battle with epilepsy.

It was enough. So I knew even before the 2012 campaign began that it would be my last. And I relished every moment—the combat, camaraderie, and satisfaction of, to paraphrase Teddy Roosevelt, spending myself in a worthy cause.

Now, in Des Moines, as the president made his final, fervent appeal, I thought about the many colorful characters, famous and obscure, I had covered as a reporter and conspired with (and against) as a political operative for nearly four decades.

And I thought about Jessie Berry, the wonderful woman, now long gone, who looked after me as a child and took me to see John F. Kennedy that fateful October day. What would she have thought if she knew that the little boy she put on the mailbox to catch a glimpse of the next president would one day work twenty feet from the Oval Office? Twenty feet from the Oval Office where a black man sat as president of the United States.

In 1960, in South Carolina, where Jessie was born and raised, the Negro's right to vote was still being contested by literacy tests and white-robed mobs. This was the withering reality from which she fled.

How would she have felt if she had stood with me now, watching President Barack Obama make his case for reelection?

The half century between the campaign rallies that bracket my life has been one of revolutionary change—changes in our society; changes in our politics and our campaigns, the way they are waged and the way they are covered; changes both in government and in public attitudes toward it, as the boundless faith of the postwar years has often surrendered to the cynicism and gridlock endemic to our politics today.

I've seen those changes from many vantage points—as a youthful campaigner in New York City in the tumultuous 1960s; as a Chicago newspaperman in the 1970s and '80s, chronicling the waning days of America's last great urban political machine and the emergence of a black independent political movement that laid the foundation for Barack Obama's rise; as a political strategist for nearly three decades, working on campaigns rife with drama and change; and as a top aide to a trailblazing president facing epic challenges and impossible expectations. This book is the story of that journey, from my seat on the mailbox in more innocent times to the inner sanctums of historic campaigns and the White House.

PART ONE

ONE

ROOTS

ON JULY 6, 2009, I stood with an American delegation near Red Square as a Russian military band struck up a stirring rendition of our national anthem. Wherever I traveled with the president, I found this rite moving. There was something about hearing "The Star-Spangled Banner" on foreign soil that caused my chest to swell with pride. For me, that day in Moscow also triggered a lifetime of memories.

Ninety years earlier, my father, Joseph Axelrod, had fled eastern Europe with his family, routed from their small village by the pogroms, the officially sanctioned wave of mob violence targeting Jews. Now, on the eve of what would have been my dad's ninety-ninth birthday, I arrived in Moscow as an honored guest, senior adviser to the president of the United States.

My dad didn't share many memories of those difficult early years. Once, he told me about walking with his dad, Morris, through a street strewn with bodies, to try to buy some bread. Mostly, though, he stored those searing memories in some dark recess of his mind, too painful a burden to inflict on a child.

Only after Dad died did I learn more of the story, from a cousin, Jack Biederman, who had fled with the family.

They lived in a shtetl in the south of what was then Bessarabia, a region that has since been divided. Most of it formed what today is the Republic of Moldova, but the area from which my dad came is now a part of Ukraine. By 1921 the entire region was engulfed by anti-Semitic violence. My grandparents' home was bombed, and the family was forced to flee. My dad, an only child, was eleven at the time. His cousins Jack and Jack's brother, Don, were younger. The scene was chaotic, and the boys were separated from their parents, who, as a precaution, had given them a prearranged meeting point on the Black Sea. "We were so little," Jack told me, sobbing, a few days after my father died. "But somehow, Joe got us there. I don't know how he did it, but we got there and found our parents."

The family sailed from the Black Sea, along with many other Jewish refugees. They settled briefly in Montreal, but within the year, when my dad was turning twelve, they'd crossed into America and settled in the Bronx. It wasn't long before my father had adopted the great American pastime as an enduring passion. Lean and athletic, he quickly excelled at baseball. He spent his days playing sandlot games with neighborhood kids, including a tall, young slugger named Hank Greenberg, who would go on to become one of the game's immortals.

Within a few years, my dad had become a noted schoolboy pitcher. A crumbling, yellowed clipping saved by my grandmother from a New York newspaper touted the pitching exploits of the "elongated" Joe Axelrod, which struck me as odd, as my father was no more than five foot ten. It was either a commentary on the diminutive stature of athletes at the time or, more likely, a clumsy effort at embellishment by a rewrite man half in the bag.

"Elongated" or not, Dad was good enough to win a scholarship to pitch for Long Island University. After college, he played for semipro teams around the New York City area, until he severely injured his pitching arm in a fall on an ice-skating rink.

For years after, he was a young man in search of direction. He attended art school, where he sketched a dark, haunting self-portrait that still sits on my desk. He studied philosophy for a time at Columbia University.

In keeping with this bohemian lifestyle, when Dad registered to vote at the height of the Depression, he listed his party affiliation as "Communist." Years later, when a friend used my dad as a reference for a promotion in the military, Dad's youthful act of defiance came up.

"They figured if I had really been a member of the Communist Party, I would have registered as a Republican, to throw everyone off the scent," my dad told me, recounting the drama. And of course, they were right. Dad wasn't much of a joiner, unless you count baseball teams.

Into his early thirties, Dad earned a living, or at least his keep, mostly by helping out at the little shoe store my grandfather had started under the elevated train tracks in Brooklyn. The family had, by then, moved from the Bronx to a small, second-floor apartment in a house at Sea Gate, an oceanfront community near Coney Island. Sea Gate was a summer destination for Jewish families looking for relief from the heat. The beaches were filled with young people, and there, my dad met Myril Davidson, a student ten years his junior, who was visiting with her family from Jersey City.

The two could not have been more different. If my dad was easygoing, without great ambition or direction, my mother was as driven as a freight train.

Her father, Louis, was an immigrant from Russia who worked as a butcher to put himself through dental school. Writhing in his dental chair as a kid, I often thought Grandpa had never quite shed the brutal techniques of his old vocation. Outside the office, though, he was a gentle soul, an Orthodox Jew who lived for his family and faith.

Mom's mother, Gertrude, a first-generation American, was my grandfather's cousin before she became his wife—not unusual in those days. Grandma was a cold, hard woman. When my mother was in grammar school, she came home one day and proudly presented a report card that included a grade of "Perfect" for penmanship. Grandma looked the report card over, grabbed my mom by the hand, and marched her back to the school. When they found my mother's teacher, my grandmother insisted that she change the grade. "No one's perfect," she huffed.

My mother was the proverbial middle child. Her older brother, Bill, was a great student who ran track and field for New York University. My uncle went on to become a noted war correspondent for *Yank*, an award-winning magazine writer, and the author of thirteen books. He was the apple of his parents' eyes. And little sister Sally was their baby, leaving my mother the odd child out, craving approval and determined to achieve.

I'll never know what caused my parents to get together, the driven woman and the drifter. Willful as she was, perhaps Myril saw in this bright, gentle man someone she could mold. Maybe Joe saw in this ambitious, attractive woman someone who would bring needed ballast to his life. Whatever the source of the attraction, in 1942, they married.

By then, World War II was raging. Dad was drafted into the army, and the newlyweds shipped off to Omaha—the town in Nebraska, not the beach in France where D-day began—and then Florida. After the war, they returned to New York City, where my dad used the GI Bill to pursue a doctorate in psychology while my mother landed a coveted reporting job at *PM*, a short-lived but celebrated New York daily. The paper, funded by Chicago newspaper magnate Marshall Field III, had a decidedly leftist bent. To ensure its independence, it accepted no advertising, and its roster of writers was a veritable Who's Who of progressive literati. I. F. Stone was the Washington correspondent. Dorothy Parker and Ben Hecht were contributors. Theodor Geisel, better known later in life as Dr. Seuss, was the paper's cartoonist.

My mother wasn't an ideologue, but *PM* was a great gig for an aspiring young reporter. In those days, women were scarce in the nation's newsrooms, and those women who did get jobs were generally assigned to the society beat. Not Mom. She covered education and worked her way onto the City Desk. While at *PM*, she also was detailed to Stone to assist on a series of stories that became his 1946 classic, *Underground to Palestine*, which chronicles the harrowing journey of European refugees who defied a British blockade to return to the Jewish homeland. It was a great assignment, but not entirely won on the merits. Mom explained that she got it, in part, because Stone's hearing was failing, and she had a high-pitched voice. "He could hear me," she said.

In 1948, *PM* closed after less than a decade, buried under the weight of its unsustainable business model and growing pressures over its left-leaning editorial bent. My mother turned to freelance magazine writing. My father got his PhD and went to work at a Veterans Administration hospital in Westchester, New York. The couple, now contemplating a family, settled in Stuyvesant Town, the mammoth new housing development that hugged the East River and divided the Lower East Side from Midtown Manhattan.

My sister, Joan, was born in 1949. After my mother suffered a miscarriage, I came along on George Washington's Birthday, February 22, 1955. Everyone likes to believe they chart their own life's course, but it's hard to ignore my mother's role in mine, considering that she gave me a name she said would "look good in a byline" and insisted on decking our apartment with red, white, and blue bunting on my birthdays. If I couldn't be the next Walter Lippmann, she figured, maybe I could be a congressman or senator.

In 1956 my mother made the transition from journalism to the emerging field of qualitative research. She began with a few freelance projects for advertising agencies, interviewing consumers about their attitudes toward various products. Within a couple of years this led to full-time work conducting focus groups. The objective was to get small, homogenous groups of people together to explore their feelings about issues and products. And with the probing instincts of a reporter, my mother was a natural, eliciting valuable insights for ads and marketing campaigns. Within a decade, she became director of qualitative research and, later, a vice president for Young and Rubicam, one of the nation's largest ad agencies. Mom was hardly a feminist, but in both journalism and advertising, she surely was a trailblazer.

As Mom's career took off, my parents' marriage crumbled. She was frustrated by my dad's lack of ambition. He was content with a small psychotherapy practice and insisted on charging his patients modest fees. "These people have enough problems," he would explain when she pushed. Never a great pairing, Mom and Dad now increasingly lived in different worlds. Many of their friends in the 1950s were psychologists and intellectuals. Always sensitive to slights, Mom felt they looked down on her and viewed the crassly commercial world of Madison Avenue with scorn. Now her circle included the martini-loving *Mad Men* crowd, with whom my dad had little in common. They separated, tried to reconcile, and by the time I was eight, split for good—though they didn't get divorced for another five years. When we were all together, the tension was palpable and painful. My mother was as subtle as a sledgehammer. When she was unhappy, her face dissolved into what my dad would call her "hangdog look." My sister often had to play mediator, and deal with Mom's demanding moods.

The wounds of childhood never fully heal and often cut across generations. Driven by the ravenous need for the recognition and approval she seldom got growing up, my mother was so preoccupied by the demands of her career that she had little time or emotional space for me. Mom also saw her kids mostly as a reflection on her. When we did well in the eyes of others, she was thrilled. When we did not, she was horrified. "What did they say?" she would ask when talk turned to school or work or whatever venture I was involved in at the time. I never exactly knew who "they" were. They could be teachers, bosses, or, when I became more visible, elite commentators or the public. When I worked for popular candidates or causes, my mother bragged. When I worked for controversial or, God forbid, losing campaigns, she would keep it to herself like a dark family secret.

We think that we can escape the pathologies of our past, but too often that turns out not to be true. My mother was scarred by her upbringing, and without malice or the least trace of self-awareness, she passed the virus on to me. On the one hand, I credit much of my professional success to the drive and skills I drew from her. On the other, I have spent my life fighting off the same debilitating self-doubt, too often fretting over the very same questions that obsessed her: "What did *they* say? What did *they* think?" It's painful to acknowledge that my own children also paid a price, often losing out to my career in the battle for my attention.

If my mother didn't have the time or emotional bandwidth for me, I have to confess that I also wasn't the easiest child to parent. In the parlance of today, I was a "hyperactive kid," filled with maddening, unfocused energy. My mother called me "the Monster," only half in jest. I couldn't sit still, and even when I was sitting, my legs would be pumping, shaking everything within a hundred-yard radius—a habit that rattles my family and friends to this day. My handwriting was as far from "perfect" as one could imagine. As for reading, I could rip through a newspaper but had a hard time concentrating on anything long enough to finish my homework. I was a handful, salvaged, in part, by a few extraordinary (and extraordinarily patient) public school teachers.

My dad, Joan, and Jessie, our caretaker, filled in the gap, providing the love and support I was missing. Stuyvesant Town also was a safe haven, yielding a community of loyal, lifelong friends. As kids, we would hang out at the playgrounds until it was too dark to see. Later, we shared the raptures and torments of adolescence in a wild 1960s New York City scene. With numerous temptations and very few limits, we hung together and guided one another through many storms. Maybe that's why I have always found comfort in community. Whether in newsrooms, campaigns, or the White House, I have thrived in communal settings, finding emotional nourishment in the friendships and camaraderie of the team.

Mine was the first generation raised on TV, and John F. Kennedy was the first president truly of the television age. He was suave, handsome, cool, and witty, with a picture-perfect family and the aura of a war hero. When I could, I watched his televised news conferences. I watched his stirring speech calling for the Civil Rights Act. I followed the drama of the Cuban missile crisis, my interest aroused by the absurd duck-and-cover exercises we would routinely hold at school to prepare for a nuclear attack.

My mom's brother, Bill, had collaborated with JFK on a children's version of his Pulitzer Prize–winning *Profiles in Courage*, which at the age of seven, I labored mightily to digest. I tried to imitate Kennedy's signature Boston accent (albeit badly) and could name the key players in his cabinet as readily as I could tick off the top ten home run hitters of all time.

Then, on November 22, 1963, Kennedy became the first American president to be assassinated in the television age. When the shocking news came, we were dismissed from school. I ran home, turned on the TV, and watched for days, in horror and morbid fascination, as the grim history unfolded. Yet the assassination and stormy years to follow did nothing to diminish my interest in politics. If anything, they underscored the stakes.

When JFK's younger brother Bobby moved to New York to run for the U.S. Senate in 1964, I went to the local Democratic club to volunteer. Bobby had picked up JFK's torch, and I wanted to march behind him. At the age of nine, I was more mascot than warrior, though, and was assigned an appropriately nominal task. I was thrilled when Bobby upset the Republican incumbent. Ironically, Bobby was swept to victory in the wake of a man he despised, Lyndon Johnson, who carried New York and the nation in a landslide.

In January 1965, I was invited to attend Johnson's inauguration. My mother's cousin Joan Kushnir had been a cochair of JFK's 1960 campaign in Colorado and had come to Washington, along with thousands of other New Frontiersmen, at the dawning of the Kennedy presidency. Joan, a tiny woman with an outsize personality, never did take a government job, but she had forged connections all over town, and she used them to show me a side of Washington not visible from a tour bus. She introduced me to Supreme Court justice Byron "Whizzer" White, who had been her fellow cochair in Colorado in 1960. He brought me into his chambers and talked about his work. He also shared memorabilia from his years as an All-American running back for the University of Colorado. Joan took me to meet Senator Abe Ribicoff of Connecticut, a former member of President Kennedy's cabinet, who humored me by asking about my political aspirations. "Maybe you'll work here someday," he said warmly. "We could use you." If only, I thought to myself then. Wouldn't that be something? And then there was the inaugural ceremony itself. The indefatigable cousin Joan hustled a perch on a riser so I could get a better look. Some kids dreamed of a trip to Disneyland. For me, this was Disneyland.

Later that year, Democrats in New York City nominated an uninspiring hack for mayor—or, at least, that's how their candidate, Abe Beame, seemed to me. So one day after school, I walked over to the Liberal Party headquarters a few blocks from my home and volunteered for John Lindsay. Lindsay was a charismatic, young reformist congressman from our area who had big dreams for New York and inspired comparisons to the Kennedys. He was a Republican, but he also ran on the Liberal Party line, which was then common in New York. In the context of New York City politics in 1965, Lindsay represented bold, progressive change. Even at the age of ten, I knew that his was the side on which I wanted to be. So, after school and on weekends, I stood on street corners in Stuyvesant Town distributing his campaign literature.

One afternoon, when I was manning my post, a woman stopped to chat, intrigued as to why a ten-year-old boy would be electioneering on a perfect day for stickball. I gave my pitch for Lindsay and, perhaps getting a head start on my career as a campaign consultant, landed a few shots on his opponent. The woman laughed at my thorough and earnest presentation, and handed me a white pastry box she had been carrying. "Here," she said. "You've earned this!" After handing out my last brochure, I went back to the local Liberal Party office, where the district leader opened the box. Inside were the promised goodies—and an unanticipated stack of ten-dollar bills. "Here, kid, you take the donuts and I'll take the cash," the district leader said, patting me on the back as he walked me out the door.

The age of thirteen is an important rite of passage in the Jewish faith, and that year, under my mother's incessant prodding, I fulfilled my bar mitzvah mandate. Yet I will always remember 1968 for a different rite of passage, in which my still relatively idealistic view of politics was tempered by ugly and tragic events as well as experience.

The year was one of the most momentous in U.S. history: a president driven from office over a disastrous, costly war; two stunning political assassinations; America's inner cities aflame; and a calamitous Democratic National Convention, marked by chaos in the hall and rioting, by protesters and police, on the streets of Chicago. It was a year that both ignited, and tested, my youthful idealism. And there were two central characters in my process of self-discovery—a tragic hero, Robert F. Kennedy; and a feckless newcomer named Andrew Stein.

I worked for both in 1968. Bobby was running what would be his last campaign, driven by a relentless sense of urgency and mission. Andrew, a twenty-three-year-old heir to a local publishing fortune, was running his first campaign, simply hoping to buy himself a starter office. Together, these campaigns taught me lasting lessons about politics at its best and worst.

From that day on the mailbox, I was obsessed with all things Kennedy. Even as a small child, I heard JFK's call. I believed him when he said that, together, we Americans could chart our future and change the world, and that we each had a role to play. I was intrigued from the start by the game of politics and the larger-than-life players it attracted. I also sensed that it was about big, noble ideals. It was about history and historic change.

JFK embodied that spirit, and when he was killed, there was a sense of things coming apart. His assassination was the first in a series of societal shock waves—unfortunately with many more to follow—that came to define the decade. There were deadly clashes in the South and elsewhere over civil rights, even as Lyndon Johnson advanced Kennedy's civil rights agenda in Washington. And just two decades after the Greatest Generation had united to save the world from fascism, deep discord over the escalating war in Vietnam divided Americans by age and class.

The generation that had triumphed over war and the Depression had a firm belief in itself, the country, and our institutions. Still, our generation, at least the one I knew in New York City in the '60s, was filled with growing skepticism and moral outrage over the war and social injustice amid historic postwar affluence. For many, Bobby Kennedy had become the voice of that outrage, and the best hope for change within the existing system.

Part of the hope, to be sure, was rooted in memories of Camelot, as if restoring another Kennedy to the White House would make things right. But it was more than that. Once viewed as his brother's coldhearted political enforcer, Bobby Kennedy had emerged from a period of mourning and reflection as a fierce and fearless advocate for change and reform. He toured the darkest corners of America to shine a light on suffering and injustice. He turned against the war that had begun in earnest under JFK but was now raging and tearing at the fabric of the country. He challenged the worn ideas and shibboleths of both parties. Steeled by his personal loss and the recognition of his own mortality, Kennedy communicated a sense of urgency as he called to action a new generation. With his longish, tousled hair, perpetually disheveled look, and penchant for speaking blunt truths, he was also an authentic tribune for the young.

So when Bobby announced his candidacy for president in 1968, quickly driving Lyndon Johnson from the race for reelection, I eagerly volunteered and monitored every aspect of his campaign.

On April 4, Dr. King was killed in Memphis. Grieving with an almost entirely black audience in an Indianapolis ghetto later that night, Bobby gave a moving plea for constructive action rather than mindless violence, and thus helped avert the riots that erupted in many other cities. I cheered as he won a series of hard-fought primaries, turning back another antiwar candidate, Eugene McCarthy, and providing a growing challenge to the candidacy of Johnson's vice president, Hubert Humphrey.

On June 4, Bobby won the California primary, and I went to bed thrilled, and confident in my belief that he would almost certainly be the Democratic nominee and, very likely, the next president. When I woke up the next morning, however, I learned that after delivering the victory speech at a Los Angeles hotel, Bobby had been mortally wounded as he exited the room through the hotel's kitchen. It was an absolutely crushing blow in a convulsive and violent year punctuated by the riots at the convention in Chicago and the dark presidency of Richard Nixon.

Bobby Kennedy had challenged a failed status quo, mobilizing millions behind an inspiring campaign for American renewal to which he had given his all. Had he lived, I am convinced he would have defeated Nixon, and changed the course of history for the better.

Nearly forty years later, when Barack Obama was considering his candidacy for president, I talked with him about Bobby and the campaign of '68. "Bobby inspired, and spoke for, a whole generation that believed we could do better," I told Obama, another young senator poised to challenge an unpopular war and the established political order. "If you run, we need to be as bold, and rekindle that kind of hope."

But if the lessons of the Kennedy campaign and 1968 have stuck with me for a lifetime, so has the memory of the much less celebrated (or elevated) campaign I had participated in that year.

The father of a school friend had signed on to help a wealthy and powerful newspaper publisher and entrepreneur named Jerry Finkelstein elect his son, Andrew Stein—his name presumably shortened for ballot appeal—to the New York State Assembly. I'm sure I have seen less qualified candidates for public office over the years, though none immediately springs to mind.

Stein challenged a Republican incumbent, William Larkin, who was a thoroughly acceptable and competent, moderate Republican assemblyman. Under normal circumstances, Larkin would easily have turned back the challenge, but Stein's dad was willing to spend whatever it took to buy his son the seat. By all accounts (on the books and off), they ran what was then the most expensive assembly campaign in New York State history. Among the advantages all this money afforded young Andrew was an army of teenage mercenaries whom the campaign enlisted to penetrate the secure high-rises of Stuyvesant Town and Peter Cooper Village and place his campaign literature under every door.

I'm sure some pamphlets wound up in trash cans before they ever reached the doors, but most of us dutifully fulfilled our assignments and reported back to the campaign for more tasks. There weren't many other gigs that paid thirteen-year-olds the then-princely sum of three dollars an hour.

On Election Night, my friend's dad, who had recruited us to work for Stein, walked into a satellite campaign office on East Fourteenth Street with a big smile on his face. "Andrew won by five thousand votes," he reported. My friends jumped up and down, cheering and pumping their fists in celebration. I did not. I couldn't shake this nagging feeling that, for a few bucks, we had just helped install an unworthy nitwit in public office.

If the Kennedy campaign inspired me to believe what politics could be, my mercenary assignment as a foot soldier for young Andrew Stein opened my eyes to what politics would increasingly become. With unlimited resources and contacts—he received the endorsements of national Democratic luminaries, from Humphrey on down—an ambitious but wholly unqualified twenty-three-year-old won a seat in the New York State Assembly. Bobby was an authentic crusader, fighting for things larger than himself. Andy was ambitious *for* himself, not for a cause—a synthetic candidate saying and doing whatever it took to win.

It was my first exposure to politics as a business rather than a calling.

That year, 1968, was noteworthy for another reason. My parents, who had been separated for years, finally made their split official, and were divorced the following year. Soon after, my mother married Abner Bennett, a marketing executive for a liquor importer, with whom I had a frosty relationship. So I spent as little time as I had to at home, and as much as I could with my father, who lived nearby, and with my treasured friends from the cloistered world of Stuyvesant Town.

Growing up in the hive of protest, drugs, and rock and roll that was New York City in the late 1960s and early '70s made for a lot of fun, but not exceptionally good grades. At Stuyvesant High School, one of New York's elite specialized public schools, I was a student leader and edited the literary magazine, but I graduated in the middle of the pack. Still, when the time came to choose a college, I managed to parlay those credentials, and a gift of gab, into acceptance at a few good schools, including Columbia University and the University of Chicago.

I wanted to stay in New York to be close to my dad, whose company I cherished and whose guidance I sorely needed. Warm, caring, and funny, he was always there for me. I relished our time together, which often was at Shea or Yankee stadiums, taking in ball games. But he felt that I needed to get far enough away from home to temper the contentious relationship I had with my mother and stepfather. "I'd love you to stay, boy," he told me, "but it would be good for you to get away from New York."

The University of Chicago was a highly regarded institution, and far enough from home, a teacher reminded me, that my parents would never surprise me with a visit. For me, there was another attraction: Chicago had the most interesting politics of any major American city. It was home to the last of the big-city machines, whose boss, Mayor Richard J. Daley, had played a critical role in electing John F. Kennedy president. But his roughhouse tactics in dealing with unrest in Chicago's black community, and fallout from the calamitous 1968 convention, had thrown a serious wrench in the Daley machine.

With politics as a big lure, I packed my bags and headed off to Chicago.

I would never return.

TWO

CITY OF THE BIG SHOULDERS

MY FIRST DAY as a student at the University of Chicago was almost my last.

The incoming college class had gathered in an ornate auditorium on the impressive, imposing Gothic campus. Yet the message from the university's president, Edward Levi, seemed far from welcoming, much less comforting. In fact, he scared the hell out of me.

"Four years from now, forty percent of you won't be here," said Levi, as sober and austere as the institution he led. There were hundreds of students in the freshman class, but, somehow I felt that Levi was speaking directly to me when he said, "The University of Chicago is not for everyone," as if he had already spotted the B student poseur in the crowd.

As it turned out, Levi would be gone before *me*. Three years after my frightening initiation, he was recruited by President Gerald Ford to serve as attorney general and restore integrity to a Department of Justice shaken to its foundations by the Watergate scandal.

The U of C, then as now, had distinguished graduate schools, known for their erudition and Nobel Prize–winning scholars, but the undergraduate college at that time was more of an afterthought, with scant campus life. It was a wonderful school for highly motivated students who were not looking for much more than great professors and an outstanding syllabus, and many of my classmates came eager to settle into the monastic life of the scholar. I did not. I was not the typical U of C freshman. I was still very much the hyper kid, smart enough to get by, but too distracted to sit still for hours contemplating Aristotle.

Much of what we were required to study, particularly in our first years, was rooted in ancient history. The classes I enjoyed most were the few (such as those offered by sociologists Morris Janowitz and Richard Taub) about contemporary Chicago and its byzantine politics. (Okay, maybe some of that ancient history, for example, that of the Byzantine Empire, was relevant.)

As interesting as those courses were, what really fascinated me was the community that surrounded the campus, starting with the Hyde Park home of the university. Nestled in the heart of the South Side, the U of C was an island, largely cut off from the low-income areas around it through the creative use of "urban renewal" and the visible presence of a robust security force. Mike Nichols, who attended the college in the 1950s before attaining fame as a comic and a film director, described the Hyde Park community of his day as "black and white together, shoulder to shoulder, against the lower classes." Yet Hyde Park also had a rich history as the seat of liberal, anti-machine politics in Chicago. From the beginning of the twentieth century, Hyde Park sent to the City Council aldermen who stood up, often alone, for government reform and racial integration. Hyde Park was a world apart from that of the antiquated, rough-and-tumble machine politics that still ruled the city.

Chicago was a parochial town, divided into fifty wards with strong, ethnic identities and politics that could best be described as tribal. There were the black wards of the South and West Sides; the heavily Jewish wards on the lakefront in the North Side; small but growing Hispanic enclaves (Mexican in the South, Puerto Rican in the North); and the white ethnic strongholds of the Northwest and Southwest Sides, mostly Irish, Italian, and Polish. At times these tribes had warred over political spoils. Richard J. Daley's great genius was to forge them into a cohesive political whole. Seizing two powerful positions, as party chair and mayor, Daley used the vast patronage at his disposal to harmonize the disparate parts of the machine, and keep it humming. It was a system of interlocking mutual obligations.

To maintain that system, the mayor relied on the Democratic committeemen, who reigned over their ward organizations like rough-hewn feudal lords.

Each ward had its chieftain, and Daley would ply them with patronage in exchange for their political fealty to the party's ticket and, by extension, his public programs. The committeemen, in turn, would build ward organizations made up of an army of patronage workers, who owed their public jobs to their more important work in their precincts on behalf of the local party and its candidates.

The precinct captains would essentially become customer service representatives, using their clout and connections to deliver "favors" to residents: a new trash can or a curb repair; help with a job; or running interference with some government bureaucracy. In exchange, the captains expected loyalty from grateful voters for the party's entire slate of candidates.

Congressman Dan Rostenkowski, who went on to become chairman of the House Ways and Means Committee, was one of the most powerful men in Washington before he went to prison for chiseling a few extra bucks by cashing in government-issued stamps. He was also a local Democratic committeeman, and he would come home to Chicago from Washington every week to tend to his ward duties. When his precinct captains gathered, they often opened their meetings with a polka in his honor. "Danny Boy, oh Danny Boy, oh Danny Rostenkowski," the faithful would sing in praise of their leader, whose dad, Joe, had preceded him as the ward's committeeman. "He's our Ways, he's our Means . . . that's Danny Rostenkowski!"

Of course, when public workers were evaluated on the basis of votes in their precincts rather than their performance (or even attendance) at their public jobs, it didn't exactly guarantee quality government. It did, however, guarantee lopsided vote totals that, in some precincts, occasionally defied common sense and even the rules of arithmetic. Some voters found it galling that they were required to pledge their ballots in exchange for "favors," or basic public services that they already paid for through their taxes. In any case, they had little recourse. Many accepted it as the way Chicago worked.

At its zenith, in the late 1950s and early '60s, Daley's power was enormous. He had wielded it to build and modernize Chicago, earning cover boy treatment in *Time* magazine as America's leading mayor. And he amplified it by providing the critical votes for Jack Kennedy in 1960, delivering enough late-breaking ballots to tip the state and the election to his fellow Irish Catholic—a favor Kennedy would never forget.

Even as his power and health waned, his organization began to fracture, and voters increasingly balked at the old arrangements, Daley remained the Man. When he suffered a stroke in 1974, and disappeared for months, reporters asked Ed Vrdolyak, one of the young turks on the City Council, how he and other committeemen would choose their slate of candidates for the upcoming election.

"Well, Daley will tell us who we're for and we'll be for 'em, just like always," he said.

"But Ed," one scribe responded. "We don't even know if he can speak!"

Vrdolyak was unfazed. "He can point, can't he?"

Still, by the time I arrived in Chicago in the fall of '72, things were changing rapidly. Once-quiescent voters, many in the long-neglected African American community, were rumbling with discontent. Dan Walker, a corporate lawyer who had issued a blistering official report on police misconduct at the '68 convention, stunned the political world by defeating Daley's candidate for governor, Lieutenant Governor Paul Simon. A Republican would unseat the local Democratic prosecutor who had orchestrated a police raid that resulted in the deaths of two unarmed leaders of the Black Panthers, and a crusading young U.S. attorney named James R. Thompson, appointed by President Nixon, was rattling cages with corruption investigations that would eventually put several of Daley's lieutenants in the federal penitentiary.

Chicago's four newspapers covered this raucous scene with side-of-the-mouth verve, led by Mike Royko of the *Chicago Daily News*. The Pulitzer Prize–winning columnist had just published his book *Boss*, a brilliant takedown of Daley and his machine. In DC, two young investigative reporters, Bob Woodward and Carl Bernstein of the *Washington Post*, had begun to unravel the Watergate scandal. And in 1973, Timothy Crouse published *The Boys on the Bus*, which depicted life on the campaign trail for some of the great national political reporters.

I was transfixed by both the Chicago political scene and the growing Watergate saga in Washington. Journalism seemed like a great way to sate my thirst for politics. Yet while I was a voracious reader of newspapers, I had no experience writing for them, and the University of Chicago's predilection for the intellectual meant there weren't many campus outlets that provided a grittier experience. So when my summer break came, I returned to New York, sat down with the Yellow Pages, and visited just about any newspaper or magazine I could find, asking for a chance.

After dozens of rejections, I walked into the nearly empty offices of a down-on-its-luck weekly called the *Villager*, in Greenwich Village. The paper had enjoyed a great run, until a snappy, irreverent rival more suited to the times, the *Village Voice*, stole many of its readers and most of its advertising base. The *Villager*'s misfortune was my opportunity. Desperate for help, they offered me a fifty-dollar-a-week internship to augment their bare-bones operation.

"You're going to have to do a little of everything, because we're a bit thin on staff," said the paper's wiry young editor, Reed Ide, as we sat in a barren office. "You'll have to learn as you go."

He was as good as his word. During six months at the *Villager*—a stint I stretched into the fall by delaying my return to school—I got great, early grounding as a newspaperman. Crime, zoning, community festivals—I covered it all. And aware of my interest in politics, they threw me plenty of that as well. I covered a walking tour of the Village by my childhood hero John Lindsay, now an embittered, outgoing incumbent whose promising career had never reached the heights he imagined. I represented the paper at a small luncheon briefing with Abe Beame, who would succeed Lindsay. I was in heaven.

The long summer also gave me a chance to spend more time with my dad, who, for the first time, hinted that he was struggling financially. One night, when we were out to dinner, he asked if the paper needed an advice columnist. "You know, it would be really helpful if I could pick up a few extra bucks," he explained, with a trace of embarrassment. "You think they might have any interest?"

My dad was paying my tuition, and I knew he was helping to support my grandmother and her sister. Yet it was only then that I began to understand that he was really stretched. Later, I learned that he also had taken on a part-time job administering psychological tests at a local settlement house, though he hadn't done such work since his early days at the Veterans Administration.

For all our years together, my father was always the one who provided a listening ear and loving support. Even throughout the stormy relationship with my mom, he never shared with us kids his pain, disappointments, or burdens. So this conversation was striking. I didn't ask my bosses, who could barely pay me, if there was a slot for my dad. I simply told him, a few days later, that there was nothing available. He never spoke to me about his financial difficulties again.

When I returned to Chicago, I walked into the offices of the *Hyde Park Herald*, another weekly community newspaper. Armed with a stack of clippings from my stint at the *Villager*, I was hoping that the *Herald* would be willing to take the same leap of faith. The general manager was a big, garrulous man named Murvin Bohannan. "Everyone calls me Bo," he said, extending a big hand across his desk when I walked into his office. With a jaunty smile and an ever-present Tiparillo clenched between his teeth, he looked like an African American version of Franklin D. Roosevelt.

Bo listened to my pitch, skimmed my portfolio, and looked me over for a long moment. "So you say you know something about politics?" he asked.

I nodded enthusiastically. "Yes, sir. It's what really interests me."

"Well, you showed up at the right time. I had a guy who wrote a column on local politics, but he just quit. You think you can do that?"

I had no doubt, I told him. Just give me a shot.

"Okay. Fifteen dollars a column, and we'll see how you do," he said. "You work out, maybe you can do some other stuff for us, too."

Looking back, I see that it was kind of crazy on both our parts—crazy of Bo for entrusting a political column to an unproven eighteen-year-old kid after maybe a half hour of conversation; and of me for unreservedly accepting the assignment. Still, I was too young to know what I didn't know, and I plunged into political reporting with an enthusiasm I rarely demonstrated for my academic work.

My first column, published on December 19, 1973, and entitled "The Mayor, Metcalfe and Police Brutality," examined the growing gulf between Mayor Daley and his top African American lieutenant, Congressman Ralph Metcalfe, over the treatment of black residents by the Chicago Police Department.

Metcalfe became a local hero after running alongside Jesse Owens at the 1936 Olympics in Hitler's Berlin and returned home to become a cog in the Democratic machine. But in 1972, he broke from Daley after one of Metcalfe's constituents, a respected South Side dentist, was stopped and grievously mistreated by police officers for the apparent crime of being black, a not-infrequent occurrence in Chicago. Metcalfe was soon calling for an independent civilian agency with the power to investigate alleged incidents of misconduct. In the column, I analyzed a recent speech by the mayor condemning police brutality and subsequently calling for a civic committee to review the problem—a proposal that fell well short of the civilian agency with investigative power that Metcalfe's panel had demanded.

Their relationship deteriorated, and in 1975, Metcalfe refused to endorse the mayor for reelection. A year later, Daley tried to purge Metcalfe, but the defiant congressman defeated Daley's candidate by an overwhelming margin, a harbinger of dramatic changes ahead in Chicago's politics.

The Daley-Metcalfe split ignited the black, independent political movement that would ultimately bring down the Democratic machine—though only after both Daley and Metcalfe had died. It would also lead to the election of Chicago's first black mayor, Harold Washington, and provide the base for the meteoric rise in Illinois politics of Barack Obama.

Hyde Park was a great beat; its Fifth Ward was a hotbed of liberal activism and anti-machine dissent, rich with crackling politics and vivid characters.

My favorites were the colorful lead actors in the ward's ongoing political drama: Alderman Leon M. Despres, the irrepressible dean of the City Council's small, vocal independent bloc; and Marshall Korshak, the wily Democratic ward committeeman and patronage dispenser who had the unenviable task of trying to tame this bastion of anti-Daleyism. Each of them was Jewish. Each was a lawyer. They were contemporaries in age, and lived blocks apart. Yet Despres and Korshak could not have been more different.

Despres was an erudite labor and civil liberties lawyer with deep roots in the left-wing politics of the 1930s. For years he was a fearless, lone dissenting voice on the City Council, using his mastery of parliamentary rules to try to frustrate Daley's maneuvers. With oratorical talents more suited for the U.S. Senate than the Chicago City Council, Despres would, on occasion, bewilder his less lettered colleagues with passages from Shakespeare. More often, he would infuriate them by shining an unforgiving light on corruption and racial discrimination in Chicago.

"There is not one bit of evidence to support the charge that Alderman Marzullo and his transportation committee are taking pay-offs from the taxi industry . . . not one bit," Despres said one day, his tongue firmly planted in cheek, as he railed against a proposed taxi fare hike. "But if each and every member of the transportation committee were on the payrolls of the Yellow and Checker Cab companies, they wouldn't behave any differently than they do right now."

The target of Despres's attack, a crusty, old ward boss named Vito Marzullo, shook his fist in rage, uttering expletives in two languages. A decade later, when Despres was shot in the leg while on his way home from a late night of work, Marzullo offered a tart observation that probably summed up the feeling of many council members: "They aimed too low."

Despres became a great resource as well as a mentor to me. By then, in his fifth term as alderman, he was an undisputed expert on the City Council and the labyrinthine workings of local government. He was always ready with a brilliant, biting quote. Yet I learned as much from Korshak, a wry, world-weary veteran of the Democratic machine, who migrated to Hyde Park from Chicago's notorious Twenty-Fourth Ward.

Once a Jewish ghetto on the city's West Side, the Twenty-Fourth Ward had become a seat of political power in Chicago thanks to its ability to deliver overwhelming margins for the Democratic ticket. The ward's longtime boss, Colonel Jacob Arvey, was the county Democratic chairman who, in 1948, pulled off an improbable trifecta by carrying Illinois for Harry Truman and two long-shot candidates, Adlai Stevenson II for governor and Paul Douglas for the U.S. Senate.

The tradition of tight organization and gaudy vote totals continued even after the ward's makeup turned from predominantly Jewish to black. The first African American alderman of the Twenty-Fourth Ward, Ben Lewis, won a special election in 1958, the handpicked designee of the ward's real power: a Democratic boss named Erwin "Izzy" Horwitz. In 1963, Lewis was shot to death in his ward office. His bodyguard, George Collins, who said he had gone out for a smoke when Lewis was murdered, succeeded him as alderman and later rose to Congress.

When Collins, in turn, perished in a plane crash in 1972, his grieving widow, Cardiss, visited Mayor Daley to propose herself as her husband's replacement. As the legend goes, Daley gently explained to Mrs. Collins that he had another candidate in mind. "Mr. Mayor," she purportedly replied, "did I mention that George kept a diary?" Whatever occurred in that meeting, Mrs. Collins emerged as the mayor's choice. Cardiss Collins went on to serve two decades in Congress. The Ben Lewis murder was never solved.

But if the Twenty-Fourth Ward was infamous for its politics, it had an even seamier history as home to the Jewish wing of organized crime in Chicago, which developed deep ties to labor racketeers and Las Vegas gambling interests. And Korshak maintained a foot in both traditions.

He had spent his life in service to the Democratic organization, and was rewarded with a series of public positions, from state legislator to the coveted patronage post of city treasurer. Under the friendly rules of Chicago politics, Korshak also developed a lucrative law practice, greatly enhanced by the clout he wielded.

But Marshall was not the most powerful Korshak. His brother Sidney rose through that other Twenty-Fourth Ward career path and became organized crime's lawyer in Vegas and Hollywood. Sidney oversaw the legal work for several mob-owned casinos, and through his ties to the Teamsters union, he had the power to bring film productions to a screeching halt until the "right people" got their cut. As such, he was a man the entertainment industry didn't cross.

Like Despres, Marshall Korshak became an invaluable resource to me, a tutor on the ins and outs of Chicago politics.

In 1974, when a local man drowned in the unsupervised swimming pool of a Hyde Park motel with reputedly shady management, I was assigned by the *Herald* to look into it. After a bit of investigation, I found that the motel had neither the required license nor a lifeguard to operate a public pool. I asked Korshak, as both the Democratic ward leader and city revenue director, for comment. "This is an outrage," he said. "We're going to throw the book at them!" But when the case was called a few weeks later, the promised reckoning never came. A city attorney stood up in court and sheepishly reported that the revenue department had simply "misfiled" the motel's license.

I called Korshak back. "How could this happen?" I asked. "Weeks later, this license suddenly 'turns up'? You had an open-and-shut case!"

"David, let me answer off the record," Korshak wearily responded. "If you're going to work in this town, there's one thing you need to know: in the city of Chicago, there's no such thing as an 'open-and-shut case.'"

Another early mentor was Don Rose, a local writer, newspaper publisher, and political activist from the Hyde Park area with deep roots in the civil rights and antiwar movements. By the time I met him, Rose's life had had many acts. As a young man in the 1950s, he was a jazz trumpeter and heroin addict. By the '60s, he had cleaned up, and served as Martin Luther King Jr.'s press secretary during the reverend's 1966 marches for open housing in Chicago. (King claimed that the racism he encountered in Chicago was more "hateful" than anything he had encountered in the South.) Rose had also served as the spokesman for the Chicago Seven, the eclectic crew of hippies, yippies, and leftist lawyers who led the antiwar protests at the 1968 Democratic National Convention. Don lays claim to the iconic line chanted by the protesters as the Chicago police advanced: "The whole world is watching!"

In the 1970s, Don took on yet another incarnation, this time as a part-time political consultant and ad maker. Outraged by the Black Panther slayings and committed to being a burr under Daley's saddle, he orchestrated the upset election of a former FBI agent, Bernard Carey, for state's attorney. Carey was a Republican, but in the topsy-turvy world of Daley's Chicago, liberals often supported reform-minded Republicans for local office. And Don was in the forefront of those fights.

The bearded, biting Rose also was a deft writer, with an encyclopedic knowledge of Chicago politics. He was a fixture at the preferred watering holes of Chicago's coolest journalists—Royko, Studs Terkel, and others—many of whom shared Don's political leanings, admired him as a talent, and revered him as a source.

Shortly after taking on the *Herald* column, I called Rose cold and asked him to critique my work and to offer guidance. He generously did so except during one period in 1975, when he felt I was insufficiently supportive of one of his candidates.

"You're letting yourself be used," he bellowed in fury over the phone one day. By the following year, though, Don had forgiven me. In fact, it was his letter of recommendation in which he pointedly recalled that we "had not always agreed" that, in 1976, helped secure me a coveted summer internship at the *Chicago Tribune.*

A City Council race to replace the venerated Despres, which was hotly contested, gave me the opportunity to earn my spurs with some original investigative reporting.

There were four candidates in the race, three African Americans and a white man named Ross Lathrop, who had no political involvement in the community prior to the race, but who nevertheless seemed to be gaining traction. Though Lathrop postured himself as an independent candidate, I began to suspect that Korshak and the machine Democrats had put him up for the seat, hoping to keep it in friendly hands if the African American candidates split the black vote. Korshak, of course, denied this.

Lathrop won the election, but when his campaign finance disclosure appeared months later, I became suspicious about a series of large contributions that had all come in during a five-day period from eight construction and engineering contractors, only one of whom listed an address in the ward. I suspected that the donations were procured by Mike Igoe, a Korshak lieutenant rumored to be in line to become the next ward committeeman. Igoe's day job was secretary of the Cook County Board of Commissioners, through whose office all county contracts passed before final approval.

I spent a day at the county building, looking for matches between Lathrop's donors and county contracts. After cutting through the red tape designed to discourage such foraging, I hit the mother lode. "Bingo," I muttered to myself. "Every single one."

Among them, Lathrop's donors had received nearly thirty million dollars in county contracts, all of which passed through Igoe. When I called them, a few even acknowledged that they could not have distinguished Lathrop from a bale of hay. Igoe fessed up that he had solicited the donations on Lathrop's behalf.

There was nothing illegal, or even unusual, about the donations—certainly not in the Wild, Wild West of Chicago and Cook County—but they called into question Lathrop's credentials as a self-styled reformer, and tied him to the Democratic organization. Though this wasn't an earthshaking story, it was thrilling for me to pursue a hunch, do the sometimes tedious reporting, and ultimately reveal something meaningful to the public.

Of course, the time I spent in a dark room reviewing records at the County Building was time I wasn't spending in class or at the library. I wish I could retake some of the courses I sprinted through then, doing only enough work to get by with decent grades. The education I was offered was far better than the one for which I settled. But I was a young man in a big hurry. I had found a calling, and the best preparation for it was on the street, not in the classroom.

I loved politics, and I loved reporting, but I pursued journalism relentlessly for another reason.

In the spring of 1974, I got an unusual call from my dad. We spoke relatively often, but almost always because I'd called him for advice or solace, or to ask for a few bucks to tide me over. He rarely phoned me, and his message had a strange, parting tone.

"Whatever happens, I know now that you and your sister are going to do very well in life," he said. "I want you to know I am so proud of you both, and the people you've become."

I didn't know what had prompted the call and, though pleased by his praise, didn't think much about it.

A few days later, there was a knock on the door of the shabby off-campus apartment I shared with two others. My roommate Daniel Nugent, a long-haired, guitar-playing anthropology student from Tucson, answered the door.

"My name is Gardner, Chicago Police," said the man on the other side of it. "I'm looking for David Axelrod. Is he home?"

Daniel hesitated. It was, after all, the '70s. The apartment we lived in was once known as Happy House, for some of the unwholesome frivolity that took place there, and such unannounced visits by police were rarely good news. The officer persisted. "Please, son," he said gently. "I have something I have to tell him."

I overheard the conversation and nodded at Daniel, who reluctantly opened the door and waved the officer into the darkened foyer. From the living room, I could hear the haunting guitar instrumental "Jessica," by the Allman Brothers, still playing on the turntable.

"Are you David?"

I said I was.

"Is your father Joseph Axelrod?"

The question itself hinted at something awful.

"David, we just got a call from New York City. The NYPD. They found your dad in his apartment. They think it was a suicide. They need you to go home to identify his body."

"Oh God," Daniel said softly.

The Allman Brothers continued to play as the three of us stood in silence for a long moment.

Officer Gardner gave me a contact at the NYPD, grasped my shoulder, and shook my hand. "I'm so sorry to have to bring you this news, son."

I thanked him, but I didn't cry. Not then. I don't remember saying much of anything at all. I didn't ask many questions. I heard his words but I couldn't quite grasp them. I was numb, dazed.

I called my mother because I didn't know what else to do.

"What?" she screamed into the phone. "Are they sure? I can't believe it. Are they sure, Dave?"

I asked her to tell my sister.

I hung up, and my thoughts turned to that last phone call, which suddenly made sense. My dad knew then that he was going to kill himself. When he said he was sure my sister and I would do well in life, he knew he would not be there to see it. He was calling to say good-bye.

Oh, how I wished I had had the chance to tell him how much he meant to me. There was no one I loved more. I hoped he knew that—but if he did, I thought, then why had he left me?

Whenever I was hurting or anxious and felt as if there were nowhere else to turn, Dad was there for me with soothing, sensible advice and a warm, loving, always comforting smile. "It'll be all right, boy," he would tell me. "It'll be better tomorrow." And it almost always was, but would it now? Would it ever?

I returned to New York and joined my sister to deal with the grim business of funeral arrangements. Mercifully, a family friend agreed to spare me by identifying the body. Many of Dad's patients and former patients came to his funeral, and more than a few told Joan and me how he had saved their lives and how much they would miss this warm, graceful man. I wished he could have heard their tearful tributes and the difference he had made in their lives.

He didn't leave a note, but there was no doubt that the financial burdens

Dad had hinted at the previous summer were a constant concern. He had taken on the extra work doing testing at the settlement house, but had performed badly and was fired, evidence that this bright, talented man was no longer quite himself. I'll never know the whole story, but I believe it was this desperation coupled with a sense of failure that drove Dad to hang himself in the sterile little studio apartment in Midtown where he and I had spent so many nights.

Dad left me seventeen thousand dollars, an old Plymouth Fury, and a broken heart. I was angry with myself for missing the clues, and angry with him for not seeking help. A mental health professional, he had saved the lives of others, but was apparently incapable of reaching out to save his own.

For years after his death, the anniversary announced itself to me through bouts of depression and self-doubt. What did it say about my fate that the man I so admired could end up broke and alone, overcome by feelings of failure?

In the sorrowful and confusing aftermath of my dad's death, however, the strongest sentiment I felt was that my childhood was over.

My father was dead. My mother, distant. I was completely on my own.

THREE

DEADLINE DAVE

Two days after I graduated from college, in June 1976, I stood on Michigan Avenue just north of the Chicago River, waiting anxiously for the massive clock on the Wrigley Building to strike nine. Across the street stood the imposing, neo-Gothic Tribune Tower, where I was about to begin my summer internship. Sporty in a brand-new suit—one of two I had bought to upgrade my threadbare student wardrobe—I leaned against a light pole, contemplating the whirlwind three months leading up to that moment.

It was an extraordinary break to win a *Tribune* internship, for which several hundred students from across the country had competed—but it was an absolute miracle that I had graduated in time to take advantage of it.

Years of neglecting my studies finally had caught up with me. The spring my father died, I was forced to take some incompletes so I could return to New York for the funeral and aftermath. And they wouldn't be the last.

All the writing and reporting I had done had earned me the shot at the *Tribune*, but in order to focus on journalism, I kept deferring classwork. By the time the final quarter rolled around, I had to finish five incompletes, along with four other courses, in order to graduate and get that chance to prove that I belonged in a newsroom.

At the start of my final quarter, the registrar, who, in my memory, was a misanthropic character worthy of Dickens, seemed to take perverse pleasure in telling me that there was no way I could complete the academic gauntlet in time.

"Mr. Axelrod," he said, "if I were you, I'd plan on summer school."

"Not a chance," I replied. "I have an internship waiting for me at the

Chicago Tribune, and I am not going to summer school. I'm finishing. Wait and see."

The next ten weeks were a blur. Little by little, I knocked off the load, but I literally worked around the clock. I remember having to negotiate with one professor who accused me of plagiarizing my final paper.

"Are you kidding me?" I asked, incredulous at the slander. I was bone tired, and final grades were due that day. "I could have plagiarized," I told him. "A lot of my friends who have taken your course offered me their papers. But I wanted to do my own work."

Still, he wouldn't budge. "No one who attended my class regularly could have written this paper," he said. "It's way off topic."

"Well," I replied slowly, "I confess I may not have been the most *regular* attendee. But this is my work. And, Professor, I have to graduate. I have an internship at the *Chicago Tribune* this summer. I can't go to summer school."

The professor stared hard at me, stroked his chin, and changed the F to a D—the only one I received during my four years at the university. It was just enough for me to get by.

I strode triumphantly into the registrar's office with my final grade. He looked over my transcript glumly, and then a small, sadistic smile curled up on his face.

"Wait one minute, Mr. Axelrod," he said, barely able to contain his joy. "It says here you never passed your freshman swimming requirement. If you don't pass the test by three p.m., you won't be graduating with your class."

I looked at the clock. It was almost one.

Now, I have never been a great swimmer, and the quarter when I entered the U of C, when one would customarily have done a stint in the pool, I was given a pass because I was recovering from mononucleosis.

So I sprinted across campus to the gym, found a coach who could administer the test, and explained my dilemma. "And if I start to drown, please let me go," I told him, without a trace of humor. "I just don't want to explain to my family and friends that I'm not graduating because I flunked the freshman swimming test." I stripped down and paddled my way through five laps in positions that were varied enough to qualify as separate "strokes"—at least in the eyes of a sympathetic coach. He called in the news to the registrar, and I staggered off to the main quadrangle of the campus and collapsed in a triumphant heap.

Four days later I was on Michigan Avenue, experiencing that adrenaline rush as I waited for the top of the hour to report to the City Desk for my first day at the *Trib*. I didn't want to be too early, and appear overeager, but I also didn't want to be late, and seem indifferent. So at nine sharp, I crossed the street, took an elevator to the fourth floor, and entered a time warp.

The cavernous, two-story *Tribune* newsroom was essentially the same as it had been for generations, a vast sea of desks, phones, and typewriters framed by heavy doors and trim of dark wood. On one wall hung a gigantic reproduction of "Injun Summer," an anachronistic tribute to autumn, drawn by famed *Tribune* cartoonist John T. McCutcheon in 1907, and then republished by the paper every fall from 1912 onward (until 1992, when political correctness and good taste relegated the once-celebrated but vaguely racist classic to the archives). On other walls, huge clocks marked the time in Chicago and in Washington and other world capitals. Above the newsroom was an observation window, from which visitors could look down on the frenzy. And by nine, the action was stirring, as dayside reporters checked in for their assignments.

I was greeted by Sheila Wolfe, the day city editor and intern coordinator, who had stuck her neck out by hiring me over a flood of impressive applicants from America's leading journalism schools. In an intern class of nine, I was the lowly claimer among highly trained thoroughbreds. Now, I thought, she looked slightly dyspeptic as she considered her long-shot bet. "You ready?" she asked as she led me over to the City Desk to introduce me around.

The first to extend his hand was Bernie Judge, the young, dark-haired city editor, who would become a great mentor and a lifelong friend. Bernie was a veteran of the City News Bureau, a local wire service with a grand history in Chicago's front-page lore. In fact, the playwright Charles MacArthur, who co-authored the hit Broadway comedy *The Front Page*, got his start there, as did Royko, Seymour Hersh, and a raft of other celebrated reporters and writers. On Bernie's wall hung a quote from A. A. Dornfeld, the longtime night city editor of City News, that summed up the wire service's gestalt: "If your mother says she loves you, check it out!" Translation: get it right!

Sheila turned me over to Don Agrella, the crusty assignment editor. Agrella had spent his entire career working for Chicago newspapers, as had his brothers Chris and Joe. Between them, they had more than a century of experience. I would quickly learn that when Agrella shouted your name—followed by a "hat and coat!"—it meant there was breaking news somewhere in the city, and you had better get a move on it.

In our first encounter, he looked a little bemused. "Nice suit," he said, with the smile of the veteran gently hazing a rookie. "But it's going to get a little dirty. There was a tornado in Lemont last night. Lots of damage. I'm sending you out with Jeff Lyon."

Lyon, a second-generation reporter and one of the paper's star writers, showed up a few minutes later, appropriately dressed in blue jeans and a Hawaiian print shirt. He was my Sherpa as we tromped through the muddy, littered streets of Lemont, and then visited a local hospital, looking for victims. After a few hours, we called our notes in, and a rewrite man turned those facts into a coherent narrative. Rewrite men, I learned, were the anonymous heroes in journalism's trenches. By the time we returned, there was a story with Jeff's and my bylines in the afternoon editions. Damn, I thought. Whole new world.

The next day, Agrella's hazing continued. That summer, Frank Fitzsimmons, the mobbed-up Teamsters president, had proposed obscenely large pay raises for himself and other top union officials. Agrella had an idea. "Hey, kid," he said, calling me over to the desk. "Why don't you go out and find some Teamsters and see how they feel about Fitzsimmons giving himself a raise."

I had no clue where to start, but also no inclination to ask. Agrella smelled my fear. He directed me to a set of loading docks on the Southwest Side, where he said I would find a bunch of Teamsters packing or unpacking trucks. What he didn't mention was the obvious: regardless of their feelings, Teamsters were not terribly eager to be quoted speaking disparagingly of the guy at the top. They were angry about the pay raise, but not enough to risk life and limb.

"Are you fucking nuts?" said one driver, pushing me off the running board of his truck, when I asked him for a reaction to the Fitzsimmons raise. "You trying to get me killed?" His was the standard response.

Still, the only thing scarier to me than an angry Teamster was the prospect of returning to Agrella from my first solo assignment without a story. Finally, I found a few guys bitter (or crazy) enough to challenge their corrupt and menacing union boss on the record.

Such were my days that summer, a steady and varied diet of challenges, each meant as a test and almost all of them an education. I loved the paper, and like the eight other aspiring reporters who worked as *Tribune* interns that summer, I desperately wanted to stay. History said the *Trib* would keep only a few of us, and I was bound and determined to be among them.

It was a diverse class, and everyone's assumption was that the paper's selections would reflect that diversity. So I found myself competing all summer with a bright, young Jewish guy named Paul Weingarten. We each quietly assumed that, between us, it would be one or the other, but not both. If Paul worked extra hours, I made sure I put in at least as many. Whenever there was a tough or odious assignment, and volunteers were requested, our hands shot up in unison. I read his excellent copy with a mixture of admiration and dread, and pushed myself that much harder. At summer's end, we were shocked to learn that we had *both* been hired. "I just couldn't choose between you guys," Bernie explained.

So began my formative years at the *Tribune*, which at the time still represented what was best about the journalism of that era. Though my colleagues were all different, most shared one quality: an unquenchable thirst for a good yarn. They viewed reporting as a calling. As products of one of America's most competitive newspaper towns, they lived to get it first and to get it right.

Our editors would be as enthusiastic about a good story as their reporters, often sending congratulatory notes and handing out small bonuses for scoops or simply a well-told story. They also were fearless, or so it seemed to me; always willing—maybe even delighting—in taking the high and mighty down a peg when they deserved it.

There were plenty of role models, but none more so than Bernie, the city editor, whose guidance meant everything to a kid still reeling from the loss of his dad and looking to find his way. When I joined the staff, he sat me down and explained the facts of life to a young man in a hurry.

"I know you love politics; that's what impressed us," he said. "And the truth is you probably already know more about the committeemen and aldermen and all that jazz than ninety-nine percent of the people in this newsroom. But there's a lot more to reporting and a lot more to life. So starting next week, you're on nights, six p.m. to two a.m."

Bernie was right. I would have loved simply to step into the political beat, but I was twenty-one years old, and a reporter at one of the biggest papers in the country. Who was I to gripe? And as it turned out, that nightside stint was exactly what he promised: another layer of my education. Murder, mayhem, and disasters, both man-made and the natural variety, became my beat, as that's pretty much the bread and butter of the late-night shift.

The night city editor was a former Green Beret named Frank Blatchford, who loved nothing more than a grisly crime or gruesome catastrophe because they would put him and his team to the test. The more horrific the disaster, the more blissful Frank would become. Around the *Tribune*, such calamities were known as Blatchford Brighteners. I had my share, each a learning experience about large notions such as evil, heroism, and the perils of life in the big city.

I covered an elevated train that overshot the tracks and fell twenty feet to the downtown street below, scattering bodies in its wreckage. Stunned pedestrians ran from person to person, trying to identify the living to offer help.

A massive fire broke out at a Commonwealth Edison facility, where wreckage pinned a fireman to the upper wall of a huge, burning plant. An elderly police surgeon climbed into a cherry picker, rose seventy feet, and amputated the fireman's pinned leg, in a vain effort to free him and save his life.

One night, early in my tenure, we heard a crackling bulletin on the newsroom police radio—"shots fired . . . officer down." It was a drug raid gone wrong. I raced to a South Side police district and waited with other reporters until two detectives dragged a suspect in, bloodied and bruised.

"What happened to him?" I shouted as the trio passed by.

One of the detectives turned around to see who had asked such a naïve question, and shot me a scowl. "He had a fall," he sneered, as they disappeared into the lockup. An older, streetwise reporter from City News grabbed me by the sleeve and pulled me close. "The kind of fall you take when you kill a cop," she whispered.

During my nearly three years on nights, I learned more about reporting, about Chicago, about people and life, than I ever could have imagined. Bernie's admonition had been right.

Yet Bernie also honored my long-term interest in politics by assigning me, in election season, to cover candidates—albeit almost always the sure losers. In that spirit, he gave me a reprieve from nights in early 1979 to cover the seemingly quixotic mayoral campaign of Jane Byrne. I didn't know it then, but a campaign that seemed like a welcome respite would become another watershed in my career—and in Chicago political history.

A slight, pugnacious Irishwoman from Chicago's Northwest Side, Byrne was one of Mayor Richard J. Daley's favorites. He appointed her as his consumer commissioner—a rare spot for a woman in Daley's all-male domain. When the mayor died in 1976, Byrne continued in her city post. The man who replaced Daley as mayor, a charismatically challenged former alderman named Michael Bilandic, failed to share the Old Man's appreciation for Byrne's feisty Celtic charms. Their relationship eroded, and by 1977, Byrne was accusing

Bilandic of having struck a corrupt bargain with the politically connected taxicab industry for another rate hike.

Byrne declared her candidacy for mayor with a full-throated call for reform. "A cabal of evil men has fastened itself onto the government of the city of Chicago," Byrne charged, inveighing against the "fast-buck artists" on the City Council—scheming lawyer-politicians who she claimed were running Bilandic and the city for their own gain. Suddenly, the woman who had been a stalwart defender of Daley and his organization had been transformed into the darling of the city's anti-machine liberals.

Her punchiest lines were provided by Jay McMullen, a longtime City Hall reporter for the *Chicago Daily News*, who first had covered Byrne, then married her. In between, the two had a racy affair that was the talk of the City Hall pressroom—with the loutish McMullen doing most of the talking.

Byrne soon joined forces with my clever, rabble-rousing friend and mentor Don Rose, who signed on as the campaign manager and chief strategist. Together, they took dead aim at Bilandic and the machine.

As the old saying goes, "Luck is where preparation meets opportunity." Byrne, McMullen, and Rose ran a smart campaign, but fate—or at least the weather gods—dealt them one hell of an opportunity when Chicago was hit with an epic snowstorm.

Day after day, for weeks before the primary election, the white stuff came down; and not just light dustings, but wet, heavy snow that clogged the streets and snarled traffic. Rose cut an ad with Byrne, speaking over images of an immobilized transit stop, vowing competent new government. As the public fumed, Bilandic, the hapless understudy thrust into the mayoralty after Daley's death, was a portrait of indifference, futility, and denial. Bilandic's tone-deafness was reflected in his emergency order to turn the city's rapid transit lines into express service from downtown to the suburbs, bypassing stops in the city's mostly black South and West Side neighborhoods.

In the midst of the snows, state senator Richard M. Daley, son of the late mayor, dropped by City Hall to urge Bilandic to take action. On the way home to Bridgeport, the neighborhood where both Bilandic and Daley lived, Daley dusted off an icy window and pointed to a group of freezing commuters. "You see those people, Mike? They're waiting for a bus that isn't coming. And they hate you!"

"They should walk, Richard," Bilandic replied. "It's good for them." Daley slumped in his seat, and resigned himself to disaster for Bilandic and the Democratic machine.

On primary night, the disaster came. Byrne stunned Bilandic, propelled by a two-to-one margin in some of the city's black wards. At her Election Night headquarters, Don Rose scrambled around frantically, almost in disbelief, as the numbers came in. He had realized his impossible dream of wresting from the machine its most coveted prize, City Hall.

In a stunning turn, Jane Byrne had been transformed from gadfly into a historic figure—the woman who toppled the mighty Chicago machine. But her good fortune would also transform my life. Byrne plucked one of the *Tribune*'s lead political writers for her mayoral staff, clearing the way for me to grab his spot on the political beat. Since I was the resident expert on this unexpected new mayor, Bernie decided my nightside apprenticeship was over. Instead of covering fires, plane crashes, and homicides, I was covering local, state, and national politics. I had just turned twenty-four. And within the next few years, I would add the titles of City Hall bureau chief and weekly political columnist to my growing portfolio.

The promotion came at a propitious time in my life. The previous fall, I had begun dating a raven-haired, blue-eyed beauty named Susan Landau, and it was becoming serious. We had met when I was still in college. Susan was raised in Hyde Park, the daughter of an eminent medical professor, and had come home after college to contemplate her next steps. In the interim, she had taken a job as a typesetter at the University of Chicago Press. A friend of mine who also worked there invited me to join a coed basketball game in which Susan was a regular. She was pleasant and bright, though painfully shy. She also was long, graceful, and athletic, and in every way out of my league. Besides, she had a steady boyfriend, who also was a member of the basketball group.

So Susan and I remained basketball acquaintances. I graduated and got a job. She moved to Madison, Wisconsin, to explore a graduate program, and then returned to enroll for a master's degree in the U of C's highly regarded business school. Emboldened by a regular paycheck and the news that she and her boyfriend had broken up, I mustered all the courage I needed—and it was a lot—to ask Susan out.

On our first date, we went to dinner at a Mexican restaurant called the Azteca, which had passable food but outstanding margaritas by the pitcher. We talked for hours, and she was lovely company. As we hopped in Susan's car for the ride back to mine at the *Tribune*, I blurted out something I instantly regretted: "I just want you to know, I'm not looking to get married." It was a supremely asinine remark, probably prompted by my dawning recognition, combined with fear, that I could fall head over heels in love with this woman.

Susan fired back, "Who the hell is asking?" It was right out of Katharine Hepburn, and only piqued my sense that this was the gal for me.

Happily, Susan didn't give up on me on the spot, and we began seeing each other more and more frequently. She was fun and easygoing, thoughtful and caring—and very independent. While she was interested in my work, it was very clear that Susan was going to pursue her own dreams, not live through mine.

We also shared profound setbacks in our lives. Susan had lost two brothers to illness. I had lost my dad. Few people our age had experienced that kind of grief, or felt comfortable talking about it. With Susan, I felt I could talk about anything. Shortly after the mayoral election that spring, Susan and I decided to move in together. By September, we were married.

Yet as we took our vows, I already had plunged into the daily work of charting how Byrne was flagrantly and repeatedly breaking her promises to the voters who had swept her into office. I had wondered during the campaign whether Byrne was for real or simply masquerading as a reformer to win the election. Now I had the answer. In the blink of an eye, Byrne made the transition from populist to potentate, shedding all reform pretensions and running City Hall like a parody of the old machine.

Her roguish husband in her ear, Byrne quickly cut deals with the "cabal of evil men" she had railed against just months earlier. Two cunning, young City Council operators who had been her frequent campaign targets, Ed Vrdolyak and Ed Burke, became her council floor leaders. She filled key positions with the favored appointees of the notorious First Ward, for generations the political arm of Italian organized crime in Chicago. She marginalized African Americans who served on key boards and commissions, inexplicably antagonizing the voting bloc that had propelled her into office. And in a Shakespearean twist, Byrne quickly moved to crush Richard M. Daley, namesake of her longtime patron, apparently fearful that Richard II might return to claim the throne.

It was a head-spinning reversal.

When Daley, seeking higher ground from which to defend his political franchise, announced that he would run for state's attorney in 1980, Byrne recruited Alderman Burke, once a stalwart Daley ally, to run against him in a Democratic primary. And with carrots in one hand and a big stick in the other, she lined up most of the old machine ward committeemen to back her man.

But Byrne's machinations weren't limited to local politics.

In the fall of 1979, she staged the largest fund-raiser in Chicago history and invited the president of the United States, Jimmy Carter, to be the evening's speaker. More than ten thousand people, most of whom had opposed Byrne earlier in the year but now were hoping to hang on to their patronage jobs and contracts, crammed into McCormick Place, the sprawling convention center on the banks of Lake Michigan, where the president and the mayor exchanged lavish praise.

Hailing Carter as the "savior of the nation's big cities," Byrne called for unity behind the president. If the convention were that night, she said, "I would vote in our party caucus without hesitancy to renominate our present leader for another four years." Carter sat beaming a few feet away. Of course, the convention *wasn't* that night, and two weeks later, Byrne endorsed Carter's rival, Senator Edward M. Kennedy, for president. Renominating Carter, she said, would be a "disaster" for the Democratic Party.

It might not have been the greatest betrayal in the history of American politics, but it certainly was one of the most public. Byrne had been a Young Democrat when Mayor Daley helped deliver Illinois and the presidency to John F. Kennedy. Now she apparently believed she could do the same for JFK's surviving brother. Only it wasn't 1960. Between the scars of Chappaquiddick—where, in 1969, a young woman drowned in Teddy's car after he drove off a small bridge and fled—and the growing sense of alienation from liberal Democrats among Chicago's ethnic Catholics, the youngest Kennedy brother was bound to face a tough road. And, as it turned out, Byrne's imprimatur became more an albatross than a boon.

By the time of the St. Patrick's Day Parade, a perennial showcase for candidates that falls just before the Illinois primary, Kennedy himself must have been questioning just how much of a blessing Byrne's endorsement was as noisy hecklers—many of them aggrieved firefighters battling Byrne for a new contract—greeted them along the parade route. Meanwhile, Daley, who already had close ties to Carter, seized on the opportunity created by Byrne's audacious gambit and tied his fortunes to the president and his delegate slates.

On primary day, both Carter and Daley rolled to victory, handing Byrne a humiliating defeat, though one she characteristically refused to accept.

That summer, when Kennedy made a last-ditch effort to change the rules at the Democratic National Convention and free Carter delegates to switch their votes, Byrne flew to New York City with Vrdolyak and other political muscle in tow. As the mayor set up a command post in a posh hotel suite, her henchmen invaded the floor of the convention at Madison Square Garden and headed for the Illinois delegation, dominated by Carter delegates. I was on the floor when they arrived, and watched in amazement as pandemonium ensued.

In one section, John Donovan, Byrne's sanitation commissioner, got into a scrap with state senator Jeremiah Joyce, a pugnacious former Chicago cop and ardent ally of Daley and Carter. Charlie Chew, a flamboyant, African American legislator and Carter supporter, sat on a nearby railing, urging Joyce on. "Hit him again," Chew bellowed, from under a festive straw hat. "Hit him again!"

In another section, Charles Swibel, Byrne's controversial housing authority czar and bagman, grabbed the pint-size Cook County treasurer Ed Rosewell by the collar and told him that salacious, career-ending revelations would be leaked about him unless he switched sides. Rosewell broke into tears. Sensing an opportunity, Mike Holewinski, a Carter floor whip, summoned the few Chicago reporters on site to survey the wreckage.

"Look what they've done to this fine, upstanding public official," said Holewinski, placing a consoling arm around the red-eyed, sniffling treasurer. "They have no shame!"

While the bedlam continued, I ran to the unguarded house phone by the Illinois stanchion, somehow reached the *Tribune* convention bureau, and began dictating. When the editors in the booth read what was going on, they ripped up the front page of the afternoon edition and made room for the story. You couldn't make this stuff up.

After Daley defeated Byrne's candidate in the primary for state's attorney, I asked her at every opportunity if she would be supporting Daley in the fall election. We both knew the answer, but then and for months after, she refused to give it. Two weeks before the election, Byrne summoned the City Hall press corps to her office for what we were told was a major announcement that had implications for the election.

In sorrowful tones, Byrne announced that she had uncovered a plot, concocted by Daley and others and carried out through his allies in the city's building department, to deny permits to developers that would provide minority housing in the predominantly white wards of Daley and his allies. She leveled a separate charge accusing an alderman, and Daley ally, of barring an African American developer from building homes in the alderman's ward. The charges were explosive, recalling a long legacy of racism in these neighborhoods. It threatened to drive a wedge between Daley and the black votes he would need to win, which, I presumed, was her intention.

"Mayor," I asked, when she opened the floor for questions, "given that you just implicated Senator Daley in a racist plot, can we now assume that you are not supporting him for state's attorney?"

If looks could kill, I would have been carried out of that press conference on a gurney. "Excuse me, David," she responded, in slow, deliberate tones. "If I respected you, I'd answer. But I don't respect you."

The mayor turned to one of my colleagues from the *Tribune* who had double-teamed the press conference.

"If his name appears on this story, you're not going to be allowed in this office again," Byrne said, vowing revenge against the entire paper.

A few minutes after I returned to my desk, I got a call from McMullen, the mayor's husband. "Uh, David," said the old reporter, "sorry about what happened there. The mayor's a little angry today."

When my editors heard about all this, Byrne's day became infinitely worse. They plastered the main story across page one, complete with analysis of the obvious political intent of Byrne's showy charges. They turned her blustery threat against the *Trib* into a sidebar story, placing that on the front page as well. And my byline was prominently displayed.

The next day, I was digging into Byrne's charge when a package of documents was dropped on my desk from an anonymous source. It turned out that one of the developers whose cause Byrne had championed was white, not black, as she had implied. Moreover, he had a long history of housing code violations and a youthful conviction for negligent homicide. My follow-up story, "'Black Victim of Racism' Is White," led the Sunday paper.

Despite all Byrne's machinations, and the opposition of the many Democratic committeemen who bowed to her will, Daley narrowly edged out his Republican opponent to become the county prosecutor. Through her desperate attempts to bury him, Byrne stirred a suburban backlash that lifted him, creating the future opponent she most feared.

The following year, 1981, brought big changes in my life.

On June 17, Susan and I welcomed our first child, Lauren, into the world. Everyone boasts that their baby is the cutest who ever lived. Lauren actually was. Small, at under six pounds, with blue, almond-shaped eyes, she was destined, I had no doubt, as I held her in my arms, to turn heads and break hearts. Yet when Lauren turned seven months old, it was our hearts that were broken.

Having just arrived at work, I was sitting at my desk in the newsroom when the phone rang. I could tell it was Susan, but I could barely make out what she was saying. Her voice was filled with a dread I had never heard before. "Something's wrong with the baby," she screamed. "I'm taking her to the hospital."

I raced after them. When I got there, Susan explained that she had found Lauren blue and limp in her crib. She thought, at first, that the baby had died. Then, she said, Lauren's arms snapped up, her eyes rolled back in her head, as she made strange, guttural sounds.

"She's had a seizure," the neurologist explained. "It was probably caused by a fever."

Lauren had been sick with a cold that had kept her awake for several nights. Susan, who was working on her MBA degree and was facing exams, had consulted a pediatrician, who prescribed a cold medication for the baby. Then she had the seizures. "She'll probably be fine in a couple of days," the neurologist assured us.

She wouldn't be all right. Not in a couple of days. Not ever. A month after we first arrived at the hospital, Lauren was released, still seizing as many as ten times a day. Susan stayed by her side every minute of that dreadful month, which was one of the coldest in Chicago history. Every day, I would walk the six blocks from our apartment across frozen, abandoned streets to be with them. It turns out, I thought, that hell is cold, not hot.

Susan and I had been married for less than two years when Lauren's epilepsy erupted. We were in our midtwenties, still trying to figure out how to be a couple. Now we had a chronically ill child who would require constant care, and for whom every seizure could have mortal consequences. It would test our relationship and launch Susan on a lifelong crusade for epilepsy research.

There were struggles at work as well. The economic pressures that later would visit newsrooms everywhere began to reshape the *Tribune*, even before the arrival of the Internet.

Dissatisfied with their diminishing margins, the *Tribune* board brought in new management to wring greater profits out of its newspapers. The muscular, irreverent tradition of Chicago journalism, where there was nothing more valued than "a good yarn," was becoming secondary to the bottom line.

Costly crusades against abuses by powerful public and private interests felt less welcome. Veteran reporters and writers became an expendable luxury when young, eager recruits would work for less. So, some of my closest friends began to leave the paper.

The new management regime installed its own editor, and rather than choosing a veteran of Chicago journalism, they picked a preening, ambitious son of the South, James D. Squires, to change the culture at the *Tribune*. Squires was a whiz kid who had made his name as a young political reporter for the Nashville *Tennessean*. He quickly rose to become the *Tribune*'s Washington bureau chief, then editor of the *Orlando Sentinel-Star*, a *Tribune* property. Before he took over as *Tribune* editor, Squires hadn't spent much time in Chicago, and hastened to make it clear that he had little regard for the way things had been done before his arrival.

Several of the key editors who were my mentors were replaced. Before long, the city editor who had hired me, Bernie Judge, would be gone.

One player who rose in the shake-up was F. Richard Ciccone, the paper's political editor, and one of the smartest people I've ever known. Quick-witted and knowledgeable, the ex-marine could write as fast as he could type. Even blind drunk, as he often was in those days, Dick could turn out brilliantly written copy on deadline without breaking a sweat. Yet his reporting was often based on the conventional thinking of the old-line pols with whom he frequently shared libations. Ciccone, who had spent a great deal of time with Squires covering campaigns, was named metropolitan and then managing editor. I moved up and acquired the title of political writer, but Squires and Ciccone also brought in another political reporter from Washington, Steve Neal, to share the beat and, I believed, compete with me.

Now, instead of nurturing mentors who valued my work, I was working for two men each of whom saw himself as the consummate political reporter and had little regard for the upstarts who followed. Where Bill and Bernie generally greeted my story ideas with enthusiasm, Squires and Ciccone more often received them with studied indifference.

The new dynamics made life at the *Tribune* less fun. Yet the dynamics at Byrne's City Hall still made it the greatest story around. Investigative stories in the Byrne years were ripe and easy to come by, given the antipathy she stirred within a city bureaucracy filled with eager tipsters.

One piece I wrote detailed how Byrne was larding the executive staff at O'Hare airport with the unqualified relatives of city commissioners, political allies, and other VIPs, including the son of *Sun-Times* columnist Mike Royko. My source challenged me to include all the names, suggesting that I might try to protect the child of a revered, reform-minded journalist.

I didn't know Royko well, but I had met him the previous year, when we were both covering the Republican primary in Wisconsin. In his prime, he turned out five, even six, columns a week. They were brilliantly written—often funny, sometimes poignant, and almost always filled with saucy, side-of-the-mouth wisdom. The H. L. Mencken of his time, Royko had a similarly prickly reputation, but when I told him the first time we met how much I admired his work, he seemed genuinely pleased—even surprised.

Why, I asked a mutual friend, would Royko even care what a twenty-five-year-old kid thought of his work? After all, he must hear it all the time. The Pulitzer committee had rendered its verdict years earlier.

"Mike lives every day in fear that he'll be found out," the friend said. "He lives in fear that people will look behind the curtain and find out that he's not as good as they thought."

I came to learn that Royko wasn't alone. Many of the successful, creative people in the public realm whom I have known have been driven, at least in part, by that same fear. I regularly battle it myself, my mother's nagging question "What did they say?" playing in my head.

Now, with the information about his son in hand, I met Royko at his favorite haunt, the Billy Goat Tavern, to ask for a comment. I could see the anguish in his face as he explained that his son had problems. He had dropped out of school, and Royko, a widower, told him that if he wasn't in school, he had to find a job. The boy approached one of Royko's friends, who, in turn, asked McMullen, the mayor's husband, for help.

"I didn't know anything about it," Royko said. "But when the kid came home, and was so proud that he had a job, I didn't have the heart to tell him no."

Today, with the benefit of years, I would have omitted Royko's son from the story. In my uncompromising, youthful zeal, however, I included it. It didn't matter. Before it could appear in print, Squires walked by and threw the copy on my desk, a line struck through the reference to Royko.

"We're not going to get into a pissing match with fucking Mike Royko," he harrumphed, saving me from adding to the pain of a single father coping with a troubled son. It was the right call, but for the wrong reason. Unbeknownst to me, Squires and the brass were intent on bringing Royko across the street to Tribune Tower, which they would do a few years later. Still, even though the item never saw the light of day, there were consequences. However warm Royko had been in our first encounter, he, understandably, was less so forever after.

Another tip led me to focus on Byrne's chief of police detectives, a storied department veteran highly regarded for, among other things, breaking up major cartage theft rings. My source said that William Hanhardt's success was not the product of good policing and his work was not aimed at fighting crime. Instead, the source said, Hanhardt was busting independent operators on behalf of the Chicago mob.

Almost as soon as I began investigating the story, however, the City Desk got a furious call from our beat reporter at police headquarters. "What is this kid doing?" the police reporter said. "He's maligning a hero cop. This story is ridiculous. You have to pull him off this before he embarrasses the paper!"

The editors yielded to the judgment of their longtime beat man. And who was I to question them?

Years later, Hanhardt was indicted for masterminding a national jewel theft ring, his mob ties exposed. I've often wondered what induced the police reporter, now deceased, to intervene. Was he simply protecting a source, or was our man at police headquarters, who was always dressed to the nines, working for a more tangible kind of tip? There was a history of this in Chicago. In a story that is part of the city's enduring journalistic lore, a *Tribune* reporter named Jake Lingle was shot to death on a crowded street by a mob hit man. Lingle was lionized as a martyr, until it was revealed that he had been doing business with Al Capone.

A looming showdown for City Hall between Daley and Byrne was the focus of a lot of attention in the summer of 1982. Yet as the '83 election approached, the wild card would be the African American community. Black voters had been the key to Byrne's victory in 1979, but now they felt betrayed. Community leaders were calling for a "plebiscite" to choose a black candidate for mayor. There was only one black candidate who might pose a real threat to the other Democratic candidates, and everyone knew it.

That summer, Ciccone asked me to write a four-part series on the upcoming mayoral race, and my first stop was a rundown storefront on the South Side, just off the Dan Ryan Expressway, that served as the headquarters of Congressman Harold Washington.

Washington was also a product of the Democratic machine, albeit a balky one. His father, Roy, had been a Democratic precinct captain, and Harold had risen through the ranks as a protégé of Congressman Ralph Metcalfe, when Metcalfe was still in Daley's good graces. Yet as a member of the legislature, Washington often tangled with his party's leaders over the issues of civil rights and police brutality.

A voracious reader, Washington also was a powerful speaker, for whom words were sometimes a stiletto and often a bludgeon. Harold—everyone in Chicago simply referred to him by his first name—could charm, amuse, or land on an opponent like a ton of bricks, often in the same rhetorical flight. And he did it with irresistible gusto.

When Metcalfe died in 1978, the ward committeemen in the district named a reliable political hack as his replacement. When he came up for reelection, Harold annihilated him in the primary and eventually took a seat in Congress. No one in politics felt, or articulated, the sense of alienation and injustice experienced by black residents of Chicago better than Harold Washington. Yet his rebellious nature and provocative speeches were tempered by shrewd political instincts, honed over a lifetime in the brawling wards of Chicago politics.

When I asked Harold if he was going to run, he settled back in his big leather desk chair and suggested we speak off the record.

"You know what it's like to be a congressman?" he asked. "They treat you like a king. You can come and go as you please. No one cares. Now, mayor? That's a real job, twenty-four/seven. Lots of headaches. Lots of problems. Why would I do that to myself?"

But what about the genuine draft that appeared to be gaining steam within the black community? How could he resist?

"So here's what I am going to do," he said. "I am going to say to those folks, 'Okay. You register another fifty thousand voters in the next three months.

You raise half a million dollars. Then I'll know this is for real.' They'll never make those goals.'"

The next time I saw Harold was a little more than three months later, as he announced his candidacy for mayor. Spotting me amid the throng of reporters and cameras, he pulled me aside and recalled our conversation of the previous summer.

"They hit every target I threw at them," he said, with a shrug and a smile, his hands spread. "What else could I do?"

Over time it became clear that Harold was anything but a reluctant candidate. As Byrne and Daley positioned themselves against each other, Harold aggressively worked the black and liberal lakefront wards, an ebullient campaigner sensing an opportunity to make history by becoming the city's first black mayor—or at least by transforming the black, independent political movement into an enduring force.

With three vivid personalities (Byrne, Daley, and Washington) waging battle, Chicagoans were riveted by the unusual spectacle of a wide-open mayor's race. The city's TV stations agreed to simulcast one of the debates in prime time, an event that would normally be relegated to a poorly watched weekend slot. The arrangement was tailor-made for Harold, an electric performer, who lacked the funds to compete with Byrne and Daley in thirty-second ads. Now he could use the platform the debates provided to reach many voters who hadn't seen him before.

It wasn't that Byrne and Daley were bad debaters. It's just that Harold was so much better. By turns funny, moving, and incisive, Harold thoroughly dominated his opponents and commanded the stage.

"I am running to end Jane Byrne's four-year effort to further institutionalize racial discrimination in this great city," Harold declared. He railed against patronage abuses and corruption, and attacked Byrne's police chief as "the top cop who's become a political prop," castigating him for endorsing the mayor in TV ads. "Then he compounded it by saying he had every right to do it," Harold thundered. "Well, every right should not be exercised. There's a question of judgment and discretion . . . the day I walk into that office, Superintendent Brzeczek will go."

It was a tour de force, and the impact among African American voters was seismic. Suddenly, it seemed that every black man, woman, and even kid was sporting the blue Washington button with the sunrise design, to signify the coming of a new day. (That button became my starting point when we were designing the iconic Obama logo in 2007.) Thanks to Harold's campaign, these Chicagoans felt that they were full participants in the civic life of the city. Their pride in that, and in him, was inspiring.

As the signs of this burgeoning, new movement became obvious, a growing sense of panic and foreboding was cresting in the other camps. Eager to cut into Daley's support, Byrne and her team played the race card, exploiting the fear of a black mayor among residents of the white ethnic neighborhoods where Daley was strong. In the final days of the campaign, I was chatting with Alderman Roman Pucinski, a voluble former congressman and old machine hand, who was backing Byrne. "Washington could win this thing," he said. "But I think the Ogilvie letter will help. Have you seen it?"

Pucinski cheerfully shared with me a copy of a Byrne direct mail piece—a letter from former Illinois governor Richard Ogilvie to voters on the Northwest Side of Chicago. Though Ogilvie was a Republican, he still held favor with voters in the conservative, all-white Northwest Side. And his message was blunt. Only two candidates were viable: Byrne and Washington. It was the smoking gun. I had picked up plenty of talk about race in private conversations with pols around town. Yet this was an official mailing, penned by a major figure in Byrne's camp, with a simple message: vote for Byrne or the black guy wins.

I pitched the story hard for page one, but when the next day's paper appeared, it had been cut in half and buried in the Metro section. Given the implications of the letter, and the election, I was livid at the dismissive way the story was treated by the editors. Their stunning misjudgment was one I would remember as I began to evaluate my future at the paper.

On the Sunday before the election, I was at the office, working and watching the evening news out of the corner of my eye. I saw a clip of Byrne at one of Chicago's notorious public housing developments. What made the scene unusual was that there were no security men in the picture. Her normally aggressive detail was nowhere to be seen, as an edgy crowd of black residents jostled the petite mayor.

"This is exactly the picture they want," I said to my colleagues. "The valiant mayor wading into the unruly black mob. They staged this!"

I made a small reference to it in my account of the day. Two months after the election, a documentary called *The Last Campaign of Lady Jane* showed Byrne's strategists watching the same news clip and high-fiving one another in response to the image of the mayor under siege.

Even so, it wasn't enough. The woman who had made history just four years earlier was now swept out in its tide.

On primary day, Harold hit the heady numbers he needed: an unheard-of 69 percent turnout among African Americans, with Washington claiming 82 percent of that vote overall. Along with a tiny sliver of support among white liberals, Harold Washington became the Democratic nominee for mayor of Chicago.

Normally, in a town where fifty of the fifty aldermen were Democrats, that would have been tantamount to election. Yet such a conclusion would defy the history of a city where race and ethnicity trumped party. So, rather than embrace the results of the primary, many of the city's Democratic committeemen gravitated to Harold's Republican opponent.

Bernard Epton, a balding, bearded Jew, was a state legislator from Hyde Park who looked and sounded more like a Talmudic scholar than a politician. A liberal on social issues, he was a wholly unlikely standard-bearer for the anti-Washington forces. But he was white, and that was good enough for them.

Sensing an opportunity to seize one of the Democratic Party's crown jewels, Chicago's City Hall, state and national Republicans rushed in to take over the Epton campaign. Their less-than-subtle slogan, "Epton Now, Before It's Too Late," misread the depth of racial antagonism in Chicago. The folks they were counting on needed no prodding or reminders.

When former vice president Walter Mondale, gearing up for his own campaign for the presidency, campaigned with Harold at Saint Pascal, a Northwest Side church, an angry mob greeted them. The iconic image of contorted faces shouting racial epithets came to symbolize the dismal contest and Chicago's enduring problem. But it also nudged enough liberal consciences to tip the balance.

With the nation watching, Washington captured a majority of Hispanic votes and just enough of the white vote to edge Epton, who was almost an apparition in his own campaign.

It was a once-in-a-lifetime campaign to cover, one that shone a bright light on the politics of race. And though the campaign ended, the struggle did not.

For decades under the elder Daley and his successors, the Chicago City Council was a docile charade, where aldermen, reliant on the patronage of the mayor, invariably fell in line. Yet almost as soon as Washington took the oath, a bloc of twenty-nine aldermen who opposed his election organized to thwart his agenda.

The situation was quickly dubbed the Council Wars. Its leaders were the two Eddies—Ed Vrdolyak, a cunning, smooth-talking tavern owner's son from the old, immigrant wards bordering the dying steel mills on the Southeast Side; and Ed Burke, a flamboyant second-generation alderman and ward boss from the Back of the Yards neighborhood, who joined the council at the age of twenty-five, after his father's sudden death.

Both lawyers, Vrdolyak and Burke had fastened themselves to the machine and became wealthy trading on their clout and the City Hall patronage that fueled their ward organizations. They began their careers as Daley loyalists, seamlessly transferred their allegiances to Bilandic, and then eventually cut a deal with Byrne, even though they were numbers one and two in her notorious "cabal of evil men."

Vrdolyak and Burke knew there would be no such deal forthcoming from Harold, who seemed more serious than Byrne about scrapping the old patronage system. So they hijacked the council using the most potent organizing tool available, race, to stymie the new mayor and preserve as much of their power as they could. The council meetings took on the aura of theater as Harold regularly locked horns with the Eddies in a battle of wits and parliamentary procedure.

I broke loose from the story long enough to head to Iowa to handicap the upcoming Democratic presidential caucuses. I would come to love the Iowa caucuses and the New Hampshire primary, the only stops on the presidential calendar where candidates genuinely interact with voters. The people in the early states poke and prod and comparison-shop in a way that simply isn't possible later in the process.

The conventional wisdom leading up to the 1984 campaign held that Mondale was the prohibitive favorite to win the nomination and the dubious honor of challenging Reagan. The Minnesotan would almost certainly win Iowa. The question was, who would finish second and earn the chance to stop Mondale down the line?

As I traveled the state, it became clear to me that Gary Hart, a young senator from Colorado, could be that guy, but he wasn't yet on many radar screens. The manager of George McGovern's ill-fated presidential campaign twelve years earlier, Hart was not a party insider or Washington schmoozer. He was running an insurgent campaign, offering a new vision for the Democratic Party.

The handsome, earnest Coloradan impressed Iowans—and me as well—with his message of reform, deftly positioning Mondale as the candidate of a Democratic vision badly in need of updating. The buzz on the ground was favorable. When I returned to the paper to write my piece, the editors were skeptical. On caucus night, however, Hart edged out all the other challengers to Mondale to place second, setting up a confrontation in independent-minded New Hampshire, where Hart had already laid siege.

Eight days later, Hart stung Mondale in the Granite State, scrambling a nomination fight that most had assumed a foregone conclusion. Covering Hart that night, I worked on a forward-looking piece about how he, as McGovern's manager and a strong liberal, would try to win votes in more conservative southern states with primaries that were next on the election calendar. It turned out that he had a well-conceived plan, keyed to his expansive work on military reform and his willingness to challenge organized labor on trade issues.

I was proud of the story, but when I returned to the *Trib* after a few days on the road, I found that it had been gutted. My reporting was combined with that of the reporter covering Mondale and mashed into a wire service–style campaign piece. The reporting and analysis were lost. I stormed over to the National Desk.

"You know, the AP does a fine job of covering what happened that day," I said to the editor on duty, my voice rising. "Why do you bother sending us?"

"Sorry," he said. "We just didn't have the space for two stories so we had to put them together."

In that instant, my frustrations boiled over. Change was happening at the paper, foreshadowing disturbing trends in the industry. The atmosphere of bonhomie and shared mission I cherished had yielded to a kind of bloodless grind. What drew me and many of my colleagues to journalism was a healthy skepticism of authority. Now, in Squires's more corporate, go-along-to-get-along newsroom, I had fallen out of place.

For months, Congressman Paul Simon, a progressive champion from downstate Illinois, had been urging me to leave the paper and join his campaign for the U.S. Senate. We had a good relationship, and he apparently felt my contacts and cachet as a political writer for the state's largest paper would redound to his benefit.

I deeply admired Simon and felt a kinship with him. At nineteen, he had dropped out of college and bought a little newspaper in Troy, Illinois. He used the paper to crusade against a local gambling syndicate. When he couldn't recruit others to challenge local officials beholden to the mob, Simon ran for the state legislature himself and won the seat.

In Springfield during the 1950s and '60s, he fought a courageous battle for civil rights, though the downstate district he represented was more like the rural South in its culture and politics than Chicago. Even as the amiable Simon maintained friendships with machine Democrats, he was a steadfast voice for reform in a legislature dominated by politicians who profited handsomely from the corrupt status quo.

With his big jug ears and horn-rim glasses, Paul was an authentic character— the Orville Redenbacher of Illinois politics. He was decent, honorable, and idealistic, and represented the kind of hopeful politics I believed in. If I jumped ship, I knew he would never embarrass me.

So when Simon and his wife, Jeanne, first came to my home to make the case to my wife and me, I was intrigued, if not yet convinced. Susan was deeply concerned about the implications for our family. Lauren was struggling with seizures and our son, Michael, had just been born.

"What is it like for the kids to have a father in politics?" Susan asked Jeanne, who had met her husband in Springfield when both were state legislators. "Well, it's a mixed bag," Jeanne said. "When our son was young he got to sit next to George McGovern and Fritz Mondale at a dinner. On the other hand, his dad wasn't home very much."

When the Simons left, Susan closed the door behind them and said, "That didn't sound like a great deal to me!"

So I put Simon on hold. Besides, I wasn't quite ready to give up on journalism. Despite my growing disenchantment, I had a coveted position at the *Tribune* at a relatively young age, and the prospect of bigger things to come. "Leaving would be a terrible mistake," one of the higher-ups lectured me sternly when he heard I was contemplating a move. "You could be the editor of this newspaper someday!"

By the spring of 1984, I was reconsidering Simon's offer. I loved reporting but not my bosses or the direction of the paper, and I increasingly felt as if I were doing my work by rote. More and more, I wondered if I could have a bigger impact by being in the arena than by simply writing about those who were. I recalled what an old political reporter who had made the jump from journalism to politics told me: "One day you're going to get tired of chasing people down hallways to ask questions you already know the answers to."

Perhaps that time had come.

Moreover, Simon's circumstances had changed. Since his visit to my home at the start of his campaign, he had won a competitive Democratic primary. Now, as he prepared to face Republican incumbent Charles Percy, in what promised to be a marquee national race in the fall of '84, Simon again asked me to join.

We had two small children, one of whom was seriously ill. Susan, who had quit her job to care for them, bore the brunt of the burden, while I far too often ditched my responsibilities as a husband and a father. Yet in an act of love— and more than a little weariness at hearing my constant complaints about the paper—Susan changed her mind.

Despite legitimate concerns about additional demands on my time and un- certainties about what would come after the campaign, she said that I should seriously consider making the move.

"You don't want to go through life unhappy," she told me. "If you think you'll be happier doing this, you should go ahead and do it. We'll make it work."

So, at twenty-nine, I left the security of the *Tribune* for a new adventure.

I was back in campaigns.

FOUR

BOW-TIE BRAVADO

IN THE BLINK OF AN EYE, I made the transition from chronicler to campaigner.

After a decade of studious public neutrality, I was now in the ring as the communications director for Paul Simon, in a race that already was drawing the eyes of the nation. At first I felt a bit odd applauding at campaign events. I was accustomed to having my hands filled with a reporter's notebook and pen. On the whole, though, I was surprised at how easy it had been to trade in those tools for a new career; how naturally I'd adjusted to my new role, and the colorful characters who would become my allies and friends.

On the first day I walked into Simon's bustling headquarters, just across from City Hall, I encountered an intense young fund-raiser sitting in an open cubicle, working his quarry over the phone.

Curious, I stopped to watch the spectacle.

"Five hundred bucks? Five hundred bucks! You know what you're telling me? You don't give a shit about Israel," the intense, wiry young man shouted at God knows which mover and shaker on the other end of the line. "I'd be embarrassed for you to take your five hundred bucks."

The kid hung up and stared at the phone, which rang an instant later. "Yeah, that's better," he said, in a markedly calmer tone. "Thanks."

Even at twenty-four, Rahm Emanuel had a gift for getting his point across, a quality I would see on display many times as we teamed up in the decades to come.

Rahm, who split his time between fund-raising and field duties, was part of an impressive kiddie corps of young political talent who found inspiration in

Simon's defiant liberalism. With his bow tie, horn-rim glasses, and ill-fitting suits—several bequeathed to him by a slightly shorter constituent—Simon was the antithesis of the blow-dried, finger-to-the-wind politicians who were increasingly in fashion. He was an authentic, unapologetic liberal in the Age of Reagan, and to the band of idealistic young men and women I was joining, that made Simon the coolest candidate around.

It also made him the perfect counterpoint to Charles Percy, a three-term incumbent whose rapid conversion from reliable moderate to Reagan cheerleader had given whiplash to voters across the political spectrum. Yet Percy, a senior member of the Senate and chair of the powerful Foreign Relations Committee, hadn't made that shift idly. After a rocky start following his election, Reagan was ascendant. Now the Gipper was a solid bet to carry his native Illinois in his race for a second term. Percy was determined to make peace with the conservatives he had battled in the past, and grab hold of Reagan's long coattails. And if that meant shifting positions on some hot-button issues such as school prayer or professing unbridled enthusiasm for the "miracle" of Reaganomics, so be it.

One irony was that Percy, so willing to subjugate his views to politics on other issues, had held firm on one topic, and it would cost him dearly. As the Foreign Relations Committee chairman, he had strayed from the American-Jewish community by supporting arms sales to Saudi Arabia and proclaiming that Yasser Arafat of the Palestine Liberation Organization, officially pledged to Israel's destruction, was a "relative moderate." This led to a furious campaign among the pro-Israel activists to oust him. Half of Simon's money would come from the community, which was critical to his chances. (We happily accepted those donations then. But, in retrospect, it foreshadowed an unhealthy trend toward the issue-driven funding that would increasingly cause public officials to look over their shoulders for fear of offending well-heeled interest groups.)

Simon had a base in conservative downstate Illinois. He had been a popular lieutenant governor in the late 1960s and early '70s, before eventually winning a seat in Congress. Yet the Reagan tide meant that, to win, Simon would have to swim upstream.

In addition to Rahm Emanuel, Simon's talented young team included many who would go on to hold public office, lead campaigns, or become noted policy experts. Among them was David Wilhelm, a wholesome twenty-seven-year-old field whiz from Ohio, who eight years later would manage Bill

Clinton's presidential campaign and then become chair of the Democratic National Committee.

For the primary, the communications role I assumed had been played by a gifted young lawyer whose rustic-sounding name pegged him as a product of small-town Illinois. It took me only a few minutes of conversation to see that Forrest Claypool was a special talent. Then just twenty-six, Forrest would become my lieutenant in the campaign, my business partner afterward, and, later, a brilliant, reform-minded public official in Chicago.

I would need his help, because my role would soon grow.

When I arrived at the campaign, I found that Simon had hired a new manager. Tom Pazzi, a fast-talking itinerant campaign operative, had served earlier in the 1984 election cycle, in the brief, unsuccessful presidential quest of Senator Alan Cranston of California. It quickly became apparent that Cranston had done Simon no favors by recommending his old aide as a prospective manager.

A short, stocky fireplug, Pazzi loved to talk, and talk, and talk. And he insisted that those of us in senior campaign positions had nothing more urgent to do than be there to listen to him. One thing Pazzi didn't talk much about was hiring and budget, both of which were growing well beyond the campaign's capacity to sustain them. Pazzi's mismanagement was compounded by a quirky personality, and after a staff insurrection, Simon decided to let him go.

Lacking any better options, Simon decided to install me as Pazzi's replacement.

Green as I was to campaigns, I was well known to the Chicago press corps and political community and, from this new perch, could handle the local politics and shepherd the message. Wilhelm, who was a master organizer, would act as executive director, overseeing the field, budget, and general operations.

When the time came to tell Pazzi he was out, he had already flown to San Francisco, site of the 1984 convention. He had hatched an absurdly elaborate plan to shepherd Congressman Simon through the city during the four-day event, and when we arrived at our hotel, Pazzi was outside, barking into a walkie-talkie: "Pazzi to base, Pazzi to base." If Simon had any misgivings about the sacking, they probably were allayed by the sight of his manager playing General Eisenhower on the streets of San Francisco.

The '84 convention was memorable for one more reason. The dispatching of Pazzi complete, I accompanied the Simons to the hall to hear the keynote speech by New York's governor, Mario Cuomo.

Cuomo had won an upset victory in 1982, after defeating New York City's popular mayor Ed Koch in the primary, and was emerging as the dynamic, new voice of American liberalism. His keynote didn't disappoint. In a muscular critique, Cuomo assailed Reagan's gauzy characterization of America as "a shining city on the hill."

"A shining city is perhaps all the President sees from the portico of the White House and the veranda of his ranch, where everyone seems to be doing well," said Cuomo, with the timing and cadence of a master orator. "But there's another city; another part to the shining city; the part where some people can't pay their mortgages, and most young people can't afford one; where students can't afford the education they need and middle-class parents watch the dreams they hold for their children evaporate."

Cuomo, the son of immigrants, went on to paint the Democratic alternative in hopeful, uplifting language that brought the hall to its feet and, at least for that one night, gave the party faithful the courage to believe.

I learned from his star turn how, overnight, a single, soaring convention speech, viewed by tens of millions, could instantly transform a relatively unknown politician into a potential presidential candidate. Though Cuomo never ran for president, his name stayed at the top of the Democratic wish list until he finally demurred.

Part of my job as campaign manager was to deal with the pols and press I knew so well from my days at the *Trib*. Once a scribe, now I was spending a good deal of time in front of cameras and mikes and working the phones. Though just in our twenties, Wilhelm and I also had the responsibility of keeping our equally young staff up and focused. My principal job, though, was as strategist, overseeing the development and execution of the campaign's message, that fundamental argument for Simon's election over Percy. I had studied campaign messaging since I was a kid. Now I had the chance to craft one.

I worked with our researchers to probe every aspect of Percy's record, however obscure. An abstruse technical vote he had cast in committee in 1980, for example, allowed us to say that Percy had cast the deciding vote in favor of President Carter's grain embargo against the Russians that Congressman Simon had opposed. This would become fodder for press hits, direct mail, and TV ads in normally Republican downstate Illinois, where grain farmers abounded. We charted several shifts of position Percy had made to retrofit himself to the liking of Reagan-era Republicans, a disturbing litany for the suburban swing voters who had prized his independence and moderation, and a counterpoint to

Simon, whose views were as constant and reliable as the classic old wristwatch he wore.

We looked for every opportunity to highlight how the economic policies Percy supported, and Simon opposed, had failed to benefit the state and its working people. No plant closing or round of layoffs escaped our radar. We eagerly foraged the monthly economic reports for evidence to support our case, and charted every speech or interview in which Percy, eager to latch on to Reagan, continued to tout economic policies that had done little for Illinois.

From early morning to after midnight, seven days a week, I would be anchored at the campaign headquarters. I would brief Simon for interviews, speeches, and debates; meet with press staff and field operatives to package messages; and sign off on the direct mail and phone calls the campaign employed. Most interesting to me, I worked closely with the campaign's media consultants, Bob Squier and Carter Eskew, to help fashion the television and radio ads. These two were at the top of the game when it came to campaign media, and it was a chance to learn from the best.

I loved the energy, pace, and camaraderie of the campaign, which was intense from start to finish, with a flood of negative ads and a series of no-holds-barred debates in which Percy, fighting for his political life, effectively pilloried the folksier Simon.

With the one major televised debate approaching, and the race polling close, Simon was determined not to let Percy push him around again. He summoned Squier, whose acid wit and vast campaign experience were invaluable assets, to lead the prep sessions and arm him with an arsenal of barbed lines.

The debate was ornery from the start, with words such as *sleazy* and *liar* flying freely. And for all of Squier's diabolically creative, scripted attacks, Simon wound up ad-libbing the single most memorable line of the evening. Accusing Percy of repeatedly mischaracterizing his positions, Simon noted that each of them was hard of hearing. "I'll make a deal with you, Chuck," he said. "I'll turn up my hearing aids if you'll turn up yours!"

Simon gave as good as he got in the final debate, which was punctuated by gasps and groans from the prim League of Women Voters audience, affronted by the rancorous and personal tone. Unfortunately, they weren't the only ones who took offense.

A few days later, and little more than two weeks before the election, I got a call in the middle of the night from our pollster. "We're in trouble," he said. "The bottom's dropped out. We were three down. Now it's eleven. It isn't all the debate, but that sure didn't help." In savaging Percy, Simon had undermined the aura of decency and character that had always been his greatest strength. Now less than 30 percent of Illinois voters expressed a positive view of either candidate.

The consultants reacted with the state-of-the art advice: go all negative, all the time. Squier had a few scathing spots ready to go. Yet it seemed to me that, in this rancid environment for which we bore some of the responsibility, we needed to get out of the mud bath and remind people why they liked Simon in the first place.

Squier, who was the reigning king of Democratic media consultants in Washington, with a large trophy case of victories attesting to his political acumen (or at least his shrewd choice of candidates) was skeptical of that direction—and of the young novice who was giving it—but we arrived at a compromise, splitting our buy between positive and negative ads.

My idea was simple: a direct-to-camera spot in which Simon returned to first principles, affirming his liberal views about the necessary and positive role of government, for which he had always stood, through high tide and low. Eskew and I collaborated on a script.

"There are a lot of pressures to sell out in politics, so you have to know what you believe and be ready to fight for it," Simon began. "I still believe in what America has always been about—hope; that we have an obligation to leave the next generation something better than what we found. Government must do its part—not just for the rich and powerful, but for all Americans. My opponent says that makes me old-fashioned. But I'd rather lose with principle than win by standing for nothing.

"I want to be a senator you can count on."

The last, unorthodox lines, which I added, stirred quite a debate among the consultants and within the campaign. Many were nervous about what would be Simon's public acknowledgment that fidelity to his principles could cost him the election. "I don't like it," Squier grumped. "Sends a bad signal."

But the message was bigger than that. By declaring that there were things for which he was willing to lose, Simon provided a welcome counterpoint to Percy, who was widely viewed as a political chameleon willing to change colors to win. Yet on Election Night, the early returns were ominous. Television exit polls showed Percy winning, and he even gave an interview claiming victory. Simon, honest to a fault, shrugged uncertainly as he entered our Election Night headquarters when waiting reporters asked him how he felt. Still, Wilhelm and his team felt we were hitting our marks, and they were right. Simon, the un-apologetic liberal, would win by eighty-nine thousand votes, even while Ronald Reagan swept Illinois in a landslide. One-fifth of Reagan's supporters split their votes, choosing Simon over Percy, and many of Paul's neighbors in Southern Illinois split their tickets, choosing Reagan and their local favorite.

Less than six months out of the newspaper business, I had survived my baptism of fire. Well, a lot more than survived. A campaign I led had defied the betting odds and campaign orthodoxies to elect a very good man and someone in whom I deeply believed. And for all the bashing back and forth, we won in the end by appealing to hope; by projecting the ideal of one American community in which everyone gets a fair shot. That's what Simon believed, and by forthrightly expressing it, he defeated not just an opponent on the ballot, but also the cynical political calculus of the day.

It was a heady moment, but one I couldn't share with the person closest to me. Susan was home with our two infants, Lauren and Michael, who had barely seen their dad in months—and they wouldn't for another two days. Lauren was struggling with the impact of her epilepsy; Mike, for his fair share of attention; and Susan was exhausted and ground down. Yet instead of going home for a long-planned, postelection dinner with my family, I stayed downtown and spent the next day and night celebrating with colleagues and taking media bows.

My memories of my exhilarating breakthrough in politics—the heady rookie-of-the-year notions I entertained—are tempered by my embarrassment and shame over how completely self-absorbed I was at that moment. I am sure that, that night, Susan was recalling Jeanne Simon's admonition about life in politics and wondering if our marriage would survive. It only did because of her forbearance and determination to make it work.

Now I had to decide what to do next.

I had agreed, when I joined the Simon campaign, to become the vice president of an up-and-coming Chicago public relations firm, Jasculca Terman and Associates, which had been founded by two good friends who were veterans of the Carter-Mondale administration. Their offer gave me the security to leave the *Tribune*, knowing I would have a job after the campaign. Yet when the campaign ended, I knew that corporate public relations was not the path for me—nor was becoming an aide to Simon. Campaigns held out more excitement for me than government. I loved their energy, communal spirit, and win-

or-go-home urgency. And now I saw the possibility of making a decent living doing them.

When a wealthy Simon donor offered to back me in a new political consulting firm, I was intrigued—until he told me the conditions: I couldn't work against any candidate, Republican or Democrat, who was a strong supporter of Israel, he said—even if the rest of their record was abysmal. I said thanks, but no thanks. If I started my own firm to produce campaign strategy and media, I wasn't going to hand anyone veto power over the candidates or causes we would represent.

So with Forrest Claypool as my junior partner, I borrowed a small room in the downtown law offices of one of Simon's ardent supporters, and Axelrod and Associates was born.

PART TWO

FIVE

STRATEGIST FOR HIRE

Of all the careers I imagined for myself, "businessman" would have ranked about 101st on my Top 100 countdown. Yet here I was at the helm of a start-up.

Encouraged by the Simon victory, I saw the chance to do well and do good at the same time. I knew there was a better living to be made in campaign consulting than I had enjoyed as a reporter. I believed in my capacity to design and execute winning campaign messages and advertising—a bold claim, since I had exactly one race under my belt. Still, I relished the chance to prove it at the highest levels.

Yet in January 1985, despite my auspicious debut, the "highest levels" still seemed a long way up. Forrest and I began by begging our way into long-shot races for small, local offices that were appropriate for a firm with no real track record, led by guys with no formal training.

Our first winning race was for one of those long shots. Chuck Bernardini was a reform-minded candidate for the Cook County Board of Commissioners, a legislative backwater traditionally dominated by machine candidates. To try to break through, I wrote a series of comedic radio ads to burnish Bernardini's name in the minds of voters. The playful ads starred a local improv actor named Dan Castellaneta, who would become famous a few years later as the voice of Homer Simpson.

We almost pulled off a much bigger upset in that first campaign cycle by nearly defeating future Speaker of the House Dennis Hastert, who was making his first bid for Congress in an overwhelmingly Republican, exurban district.

Riding a populist wave over high utility rates, we entered the remaining weeks with our candidate, a nurse and county coroner named Mary Lou Kearns, in a position to win. Yet on the final weekend, thousands of mailings landed on the district's doorsteps recounting salacious accusations against Kearns, who had been part of a messy divorce. Though the mailings were unsigned, and Hastert disavowed them, he advanced to Congress on the tide of this scurrilous, eleventh-hour smear effort.

Small-gauge though they were, these early races were fun and exciting, and gave us the chance to cut our teeth as political strategists and ad makers. I loved all of it: the creative challenge of scriptwriting; the long hours I spent directing actors in recording studios; choosing scenes in darkened film-editing suites. TV was a new medium for me, but a familiar challenge: tell stories in ways that are attention-grabbing and authentic. I had learned how to be a newspaperman by doing exactly that, and with the help of local producers, I would learn the ropes as a media consultant.

In making that leap, I found my background as a reporter enormously helpful. Obviously, that experience was useful in advising candidates on how to frame their stories and respond to the stories conceived by others. More than that, I had spent several years examining campaigns throughout this rich and diverse country, armed with questions aimed at understanding the unique dynamics of each race. I brought that same approach to my job as a consultant, probing to understand the critical and often shifting dynamics of the candidates, voters, and venues wherever I worked.

Every race is different, but the protocol is the same: Understand fully the array of arguments that could be made for and against your candidate, test them in polling, and cull the two or three that are most meaningful and that will have the greatest impact on the targeted voters you need to win. Then weave those arguments into a larger, authentic narrative that communicates who your candidate is and why he or she is running. In the end, campaigns are always a choice. Why should a voter choose Candidate A over Candidate B? The winning campaign is generally the one that dictates the terms of that choice by defining what the race is about.

A reporter's ability to listen, probe, and gather information served me well. The art of storytelling was indispensable. And my high profile in Chicago political circles, both from reporting and from Simon's victory, gave us a leg up on other fledgling firms in the competition for clients. While most of our early races were way down the ballot, we did find ourselves in the middle of one of the strangest governor's races in Illinois history.

In 1982, former U.S. senator Adlai Stevenson III, heir to one of the great names in Illinois political history, decided to challenge Governor James R. Thompson in what was to be a heavyweight match. Thompson, the former corruption-busting prosecutor, was widely considered a rising star in national Republican politics. Yet with Reagan in the White House and the economy still struggling, 1982 would be a tough year for the GOP, and the supremely confident Thompson underestimated Stevenson, who proved far more tenacious than his staid image suggested. What resulted was the closest governor's race in Illinois history. Thompson was declared the winner by just 5,074 votes out of more than 3.6 million ballots cast. Yet the Illinois Supreme Court refused Stevenson a recount. In a case of what goes around, comes around, the deciding vote was cast by a Democratic justice whom Senator Stevenson had refused to endorse for the federal bench.

As 1986 approached, Stevenson, now out of office, didn't appear to have the stomach for a rematch. The consensus Democratic candidate was the state attorney general, Neil Hartigan, son of an alderman and protégé of the late mayor Daley. In 1972, the handsome redheaded Hartigan had been elected lieutenant governor at the tender age of thirty-four, which marked him as a man to watch in Illinois politics. Yet fidelity to the party organization meant waiting his turn. In 1986, Hartigan's number came up.

Forrest and I were briefly contemplating a new partnership at the time, with David Doak, who had worked for Squier on the Simon race; Bob Shrum, a highly regarded speechwriter for Ted Kennedy and a legion of Democrats; and the pollster Pat Caddell. Part of the ante was to deliver a top Illinois race. I had misgivings about Hartigan. He was a thoroughly good and decent person, but he never struck me as particularly bold or incisive. Even so, he was going to be the nominee, and we signed on to the race. It wasn't long before I began to regret it. The final straw was a strategy meeting at which one of his advisers asked him where he stood on abortion.

"Well, I'm against abortion," replied Hartigan, a devout Catholic.

The aide persisted. "Yes, but is that in all cases? What about cases of rape and incest?"

"I don't know," Hartigan replied, turning to his brother, David, who was a lobbyist for the Chicago Archdiocese. "Dave, where is the pope on this?" We all burst out laughing, thinking Hartigan had meant this as a joke, but he wasn't laughing. "I'm not kidding, you guys," he shouted, his face reddening. "There may be some value in the answer." That Hartigan wanted guidance on where the pope stood on abortion was shocking, but no more so than that three years into his tenure as attorney general, he seemed to have given no thought to this timely and sensitive legal issue.

Convinced that Hartigan was fatally flawed, I withdrew from the campaign that day. This would be a tug-and-pull I would wrestle with for years to come, between the demands of running a business and my ideas about what politics should be. Signing on with Hartigan wouldn't be the last such compromise I would make, particularly early in my career, when I was struggling to establish our business. Still, it was unfair to him for me to have signed on halfheartedly and bad form to leave. Looking back, what was even more dubious was what I did next.

I began talking to Stevenson about the possibility of a rematch. This wasn't a business decision. I could have made more money by sticking with Hartigan. Yet I genuinely believed that a rematch was the difference between winning and losing, and that Adlai, quirky but smart and honorable, would be a far better governor than either Hartigan or Thompson.

In the Senate, Adlai had teamed with Gary Hart, Bill Bradley, and other New Democrats to begin to redefine liberalism for the modern era, departing from orthodoxy on trade and other issues. While I didn't agree with all of it, I had no doubt that Adlai would bring fresh thinking and integrity to the governor's office.

As it became known that Stevenson was exploring another race for governor, a local newscaster invited him and Hartigan to appear for an hour of debate on his public affairs show. The night before the show, I went to Stevenson's house to help him prepare. When I arrived, I found him sitting in a high-backed chair, a tumbler of whiskey in his hand. As soon as he spoke, it was clear that this had not been his first glass.

"I'm fine, I'm fine. We don't need to do much," he said, although the word sounded more like "mush," and the former senator's eyes appeared to be only half-open.

Holy crap, I thought. This guy has a debate in twelve hours, and he's shit-faced!

But Stevenson indulged us and, whatever state of consciousness he was in, apparently absorbed our discussion. The next day, the old pro showed up and executed about 95 percent of the strategy. When an exasperated Hartigan finally played what he considered his trump card, suggesting that Stevenson was coasting on his famous name, Adlai was locked and loaded:

"You know, Neil, when I first decided to run for office many years ago, I went to Dick Daley and asked for his advice," he began, a smile on his face. "And you know what he told me? He said, 'Adlai, don't ever change your name.' And I never will."

Hartigan dropped out shortly after the one-sided debate, and Adlai now had his rematch with Thompson. Before that contest was fully engaged, however, fate intervened. On the assumption that the entire party-endorsed state Democratic ticket would sail through the primary against nominal challengers, we hoarded our money for the general election and did little advertising. This was a dreadful mistake.

On primary night, two supporters of Lyndon LaRouche, the madcap neo-fascist, nabbed spots on the Democratic ticket in races that no one had bothered to poll because they were deemed uncompetitive. One of the winners, Mark Fairchild, defeated Adlai's candidate for lieutenant governor. Now Adlai was tied on the ballot with a LaRouchie, duly nominated and unwilling to resign. The only answer was for *Adlai* to quit the ticket and run as a third-party candidate.

It was an incredible break for Thompson, who had run ten years earlier as an anti-machine reformer and was a man with talent and intellect as big as his six-foot-six frame. Yet Thompson had settled comfortably into a familiar and dreary pattern—temporizing problems while dispensing and accepting goodies as the state's chief executive. Running as a Democrat, Stevenson could have taken Thompson. As the candidate of the newly constituted Solidarity Party, he had no chance.

But we did make Big Jim work, with a series of ads that got some attention. One featured a tap-dancing governor, shot from pin-striped knees down, highlighting Thompson's many switches of position and broken promises. Yet in the end, Thompson had the last laugh, dispatching Stevenson with 53 percent of the vote.

In the fall of 1986, I got a call from Mayor Washington, who asked me to drop by his office at City Hall. When I walked in, Harold was sitting behind his ornate desk, eating.

"You want half my lunch?" he asked, thrusting an overstuffed sandwich in my direction.

I didn't.

"Come on, look at me," said the mayor, who had quit smoking after taking office and had put on what looked to be a good forty or fifty additional pounds. "You think I need a whole sandwich?"

Harold quickly got to the point. He was running for reelection in 1987 and wanted my help. "This is going to be a brawl," he said. "These guys will do anything to beat me. They know if I win this one, it's over. That's the ball game."

For three years, Council Wars raged on as the white ethnic bloc, led by Vrdolyak and Burke, had engaged the mayor in an epic battle, seeking to bedevil him at every turn. With a special election in 1986, a Washington-backed candidate, Luis Gutiérrez, had taken an aldermanic seat from a Vrdolyak ally in a new Hispanic ward, tipping the council's balance of power in the mayor's favor. All the more reason Harold's foes were going to make one last run to take back the mayor's office and regain control of the machinery of city government.

Blessed with an unparalleled gift for rewriting history in her own mind, Jane Byrne had returned to the fray, posturing herself once again as the plucky challenger and outsider. The combination of continuing racist resistance to Harold and widespread weariness with the ceaseless strife between the council and mayor actually made her comeback plausible. In early polls, Byrne was beating Washington among Democratic voters.

Even if he turned back Byrne's challenge in the primary, Harold couldn't assume victory. In the past, the general election was merely a formality, the ritual sacrifice of whatever poor, hapless soul was willing to run on the Republican line in an overwhelmingly Democratic city. Yet for many Chicago voters, race still trumped party. Bernard Epton, Harold's last Republican opponent, had proven that. Now, with the city's first black mayor on the ballot, candidates were lining up to take a shot.

Thomas Hynes, the popular county assessor and Daley ally, had signaled his intention to challenge the winner of the primary as an independent candidate. So had Vrdolyak, Washington's council nemesis. And the Republicans would slate a credible candidate as well. If voters coalesced around one of them, the mayor knew it could be a close and competitive race.

"This is serious business," Harold told me, in grave tones. "I don't want to play around."

While I would be the point man on the Washington reelection campaign, I needed help in what promised to be a full-tilt rumble. So I recruited my friends Shrum and Doak, who had dropped Caddell and started their own media firm, to partner in what I saw as an important moment in the city's history. Fortunately, Washington had plenty to tout, having made good on his pledge to end the most egregious patronage abuses at City Hall and to refocus its efforts on improving the city's neighborhoods. Though Harold was plainly happier on the hustings than behind a desk, and though some of his appointees were more notable for their loyalty than their talent, he had made a solid impact.

Beyond that, he had the ebullient, larger-than-life quality that suited Carl Sandburg's "City of the Big Shoulders." Even if they didn't support him, Chicagoans delighted in Harold's joyful rants, such as when he took off after his "antediluvian dodohead" opponents. They loved his exuberant, if off-key, renditions of "My Kind of Town." They laughed when he only half-jokingly boasted of improving Chicago's image from the corrupt old days of Al Capone: "Now anywhere you go in the world . . . you know what they say to you? They ask, 'How's Harold?'"

As the mayor barnstormed the city, we mounted a dual media strategy, highlighting Washington as a "mayor for all of Chicago's neighborhoods," while reminding voters—two-thirds of whom had voted against Byrne in the last election—what life was like under Calamity Jane. Slowly but surely, we moved the needle. Chicago's newspapers backed Washington, giving a timely nudge to wavering white voters. On primary day, Washington defeated Byrne by 80,000 votes, or seven points, lifted by a familiar formula: the nearly unanimous support of the black community, a solid Hispanic majority, and more white votes than he needed to make the difference.

The next day, a few of us gathered at the mayor's office to help prepare him for a postprimary press conference. The group was gleeful, relieved to have put Byrne and the primary behind us, but the normally garrulous mayor was pensive.

"Say, what percentage of the white vote did I get?" he asked.

"About twenty-one percent," someone replied. "But that's a lot better than last time, when you only got eight percent!"

"Twenty-one percent?" Harold said. "You know, I've probably spent seventy percent of my time in those white neighborhoods. I think I've been a good mayor for those neighborhoods. I've reached out to everyone in this city. And I get twenty-one percent of the white vote, and we're all happy?"

Harold smiled and shook his head.

"Ain't it a bitch to be a black man in the land of the free and the home of the brave?"

Despite any disappointment, Harold attacked the general election like a pile driver, and with particular enthusiasm in the final days, when Vrdolyak emerged as the leading challenger. Though both Vrdolyak and Burke were ringleaders in the acrid Council Wars, it was only Vrdolyak whom the mayor loathed. I asked him why.

"Because I think Burke is the product of his upbringing and environment. He is an honest racist," said Harold, who didn't live to see Burke later adopt an African American son. "But Vrdolyak isn't a racist. He's an opportunist. He's *using* race, whipping people up for his own political purposes. And that I can't forgive. That's evil."

On Election Night, Harold polished off Vrdolyak and the field. He had run the gauntlet, and now a sense of calm settled over the city. Harold was the mayor and could no longer be dismissed as a historical accident. And Chicagoans seemed eager for an end to the constant strife at City Hall.

That night, at a boisterous postelection reception, we were confronted by a logistical problem. Two inveterate camera hogs, the Reverend Jesse Jackson and boxing impresario Don King, were on hand and would almost certainly try to flank Washington at the lectern for the "hero" shot in the morning papers. It wasn't the photo we wanted, as Harold worked to bring a diverse city together. So we decided to flood the stage with a multiracial crowd of supporters, who would provide the backdrop for Harold's acceptance speech. To ensure that Jackson and King were not in the picture, we would provide catnip by asking them to do out-of-town media interviews that would keep them busy almost right up to the moment Washington took to the stage.

It seemed like a good plan, but we underestimated the skills Jackson and King had in navigating their way to the limelight. Though the reverend and the impresario reached the stage after the backdrop crowd was in place, each worked his way to the lectern from opposite sides, like knives through butter. By the time Washington began speaking, they were, just as we feared, flanking him, nearly jostling the mayor's fiancée out of the way. When Washington finished his remarks, Reverend Jackson, who was planning a second race for president in 1988, grabbed the mayor's left arm to hoist it in the familiar victory salute. Yet Harold was a strong man, and his arm didn't budge. He kept it plastered to the lectern while he waved to the crowd with his other hand.

"I'll be damned if I was going to let that SOB lift my arm up," Harold whispered, as he left the stage. "This isn't *his* night."

Sadly, this victory night, which held out such promise, would be Harold's last.

Shortly before Thanksgiving, I was flying home to Chicago from New York. Upon landing, I found several urgent messages from Mike Holewinski, a former state legislator who was one of Harold's top aides. "The mayor collapsed at his desk," Holewinski said quietly. "They took him out of here on a stretcher, but it doesn't look good."

Seven months after his resounding victory, Harold Washington was dead, the victim of a massive heart attack.

Chicagoans formed long lines outside City Hall to view his body, reflecting a cross-section of the diverse city he led. For all the tumult Harold's ascension had provoked, Chicago appeared united in its grief. I felt the loss acutely. Harold was as interesting, authentic, and fearless a character as I have met in politics. I thoroughly enjoyed working with him and appreciated the historic role he played with such brass and verve. I miss him to this day.

When I got home the night of his funeral, my son, Michael, just four, had set up his own tribute, creating an open "casket" in which he placed a teddy bear to signify the mayor. He had been watching the news with Susan and, touchingly, had somehow sensed our loss.

Yet in the fall of 1987, I had little time to dwell on my feelings. My old boss Paul Simon was running for president. I wasn't crazy about the idea, and I told him so. In the little more than two years he had been in the Senate, Simon had gotten off to an admirable start, leading fights to address illiteracy and to combat influence peddling in Washington. He even worked with Reagan on a balanced-budget amendment, though they had vastly different ideas about *how* the budget should be balanced. He was having an impact. Yet I worried that a failed presidential race might jeopardize his reelection in 1990, and with it his chance to do more. Also, I frankly doubted America was ready for a jug-eared, bow-tied liberal as president.

Still, Simon's reasoning wasn't entirely crazy. Hart began as a front-runner, but was forced out by news of an alleged tryst. Reagan was retiring, and the field was open. The presidential race would begin in Iowa, a state with a huge Illinois border. And Paul's small-town, midwestern liberalism was well suited for a caucus that tilted left. If he could win there, he would have momentum and a legitimate shot at the nomination.

I loved Paul, and despite my concerns, once he decided to run, I was very much in the thick of the race. I produced an unusual two-minute biographical ad, a minidocumentary that told Paul's compelling story in his unscripted words and the words of others. The ad featured a valuable testimonial from Harold Hughes, the crusty former senator and governor of Iowa, revered by his state's party activists. "I look at Paul Simon," said Hughes, "I trust Paul Simon."

Authenticity is an indispensable requirement for any successful candidate, but particularly a candidate for president. Biography is foundational. More and more, I had become convinced that voters were inured to slick, highly produced media, and the antidote was this more genuine, documentary-style approach. Part of that might have been defensive, since I felt more comfortable, and proficient at, telling stories than I did creating the ads that were the state-of-the-art in Washington. The documentary style also particularly suited Simon, with his Orville Redenbacher looks and Capra-esque story.

I ended the ads with a silent challenge, words on the screen that went to Paul's authenticity and his defiant belief that government could still be a force for good: "Isn't it time to believe again?"

And for a while, Iowans did. After an early flurry of media, Simon vaulted into the lead. Yet leadership also makes you a target. Paul had an abundance of warmth and decency, but his heart sometimes led him to positions that were hard to square. He had insisted on including in his platform hefty new social spending as well as the balanced-budget amendment. What neither he nor we had entirely figured out was just how to square the two. Now that Simon had emerged as the putative front-runner in Iowa, this stubborn math problem was fodder for the news media and his opponents.

In a debate in early December, Congressman Dick Gephardt, a Missourian who also was banking on a shared border with Iowa to jump-start his own campaign, scored with a potent line comparing Paul's suspect plan to the dubious assumptions by Ronald Reagan's supply-side economics. In deeply cutting taxes, Reagan had said that dynamic growth would more than make up for the lost revenues. It hadn't.

"Simonomics is really Reaganomics with a bow tie," Gephardt said.

It was a killer line. Then, as Simon's poll numbers began to spiral, Gephardt launched new ads that delivered a hard, populist message on trade. Gephardt had introduced an amendment in Congress that would slap deep tariffs on imported Korean cars in retaliation for the prohibitive taxes placed on the sale of American-made autos in Korea.

"When that government's done, a ten-thousand-dollar Chrysler K car costs forty-eight thousand dollars in Korea," Gephardt said in a brilliantly manipulative ad. If the Koreans didn't relent under a Gephardt administration, he concluded, they would be "left asking themselves how many Americans are going to pay forty-eight thousand dollars for one of their Hyundais?"

The ad, tagged with a new slogan, "It's Your Fight, Too," struck an immediate chord in Iowa, where thousands of auto and factory workers feared losing their jobs to plants overseas. Gephardt surged, and we faced a dogfight. The lead shifted from day to day, but on caucus night, Gephardt barely edged out Simon—a murky result, which Simon privately disputed until the day he died. Still, a narrow loss on what was viewed as Simon's home turf was enough to doom his candidacy.

Even in defeat, I found the experience of producing media and strategy for a presidential contest heady stuff. I hoped I would get the chance again. The cost, at least in the short run, was my relationship with Simon. When Paul ran for reelection in 1990, he retained Gephardt's consultants—my old friends Bob Shrum and David Doak—to do the race, concluding that they had the secret sauce he had lacked in 1988. I was disappointed but not surprised. Candidates place their trust in their consultants and expect these highly paid geniuses to deliver, much as if they've retained a lawyer to win a big case. If you lose, they look for the next genius.

Still, I owe Paul a great deal. In the biggest race of his life, he entrusted his media to me and my fledgling firm. Just three years after we opened our doors, we got to play, albeit for a brief time, on the presidential stage.

In the end, Paul might not have been the best messenger, but there was power in his message. A lot of folks *did* want to believe again that we had a stake in one another as Americans. They wanted to believe again that we still could act together to build a better future in which everyone had a place. They wanted to believe again in a politics of conviction, and not just calculation. They wanted to believe again in hope.

Old-fashioned, maybe, but some ideas would never go out of style.

SIX

WHERE THE RUBBER HITS THE ROAD

CHICAGO IN THE LATE 1980S was unraveling. The newspapers called it "Beirut on the Lake."

After Harold Washington's death, the racial divisions and gridlock he had hoped his election would settle reemerged with a vengeance. It began a week after Harold died, at a raucous City Council meeting at which the white, anti-Washington bloc installed a reliable African American hack, Eugene Sawyer, to serve out the remainder of Washington's term. The vote came in the middle of the night, with thousands of protesters surrounding City Hall. Mild-mannered and easily manipulated, Sawyer was more figurehead than leader, a mayor under whom the connivers on the City Council would have their way.

As the old racial and ethnic divisions flared up, Chicago's problems multiplied. Although the city, with its more diverse economic base, was better fortified to withstand the pressures that were eating away at other big cities in the Midwest, we weren't immune to some of the same disturbing patterns. Our downtown was dying. The school system was floundering. The white middle class was fleeing.

With the city adrift, the 1989 mayoral election loomed as, possibly, the last chance to arrest the slide and resurrect the sense of community and basic decorum necessary to confront these pressing problems. It would take strong, smart leadership, and having covered the genial but feckless Sawyer for years on the City Council, I was sure he couldn't provide it. His installation as interim mayor was an inflection point for the city I had come to love. So I wasn't looking for just any client willing to take on a challenging race. I was looking for one who could unite the city and take on these festering problems.

Not that I could afford to be fussy. My third child, Ethan, had come along in 1987. Lauren's problems were growing more severe. Her seizures were coming relentlessly. The drug regimens were wreaking havoc with her moods, and as she grew, the developmental gap between her and her peers was becoming more obvious. It was heartbreaking, and placed a great strain on our family. Too often, I escaped, justifying my absences by the urgency of campaigns. Yet there was no escaping what had become obvious: we would need significant resources in the years to come to meet the challenges our daughter faced. Given the sorry state Chicago was in, I felt that our choice in the mayoral race had to be more than a business decision. Chicago was now my hometown. I wanted to work for someone who had the stature, the strength, and the savvy to save the city.

I talked to others, but to my mind, the obvious candidate was Richard M. Daley. It was odd to think that the son and namesake of a mayor remembered for his divisive leadership could be a force for reconciliation. Many Chicagoans—particularly black Chicagoans—still remembered Richard J. Daley's stunning "shoot to kill" order during the race riots of the 1960s, and his heavy-handed effort to purge his onetime loyalist Metcalfe for defiantly shining a bright light on the issue of police brutality.

The younger Daley was, in many ways, unmistakably his father's son: the same bulldog mien; the familiar running battle with the English language (Royko wrote of Daley's father that he would rarely "exit from the same paragraph he entered"); the innate sense of how to get things done; and a palpable, unshakable love for the city of Chicago. Yet on issues of race and tolerance, he was a new and different generation of Daley. He understood that love of city in 1989 meant rebuilding community, not tearing it apart.

More than a decade after Richard J. Daley died, the Daley name still carried the patina of competence and strength that Chicagoans yearned for in the midst of the prevailing chaos in Sawyer's City Hall. And Rich Daley's role as state's attorney, crusading against gangs and drugs, bolstered that image. Alongside those efforts, though, he had worked to build strong relationships with religious and civic leaders in the black community. While I knew there still would be some resistance from the lakefront liberals who, more than a decade after his death, still defined themselves in opposition to Daley's father, I didn't share their reservations. The son had proven broader-minded than his dad on an array of issues, and had strong support in the precincts where Richard J. was reviled. I had done a few ads for his reelection as state's attorney in 1988, and began joining strategy sessions chaired by his brother Bill as he and Daley's top aides contemplated a mayoral campaign.

By December 1988, three months before the mayoral primary, all the pieces were in place for a Daley candidacy. Bill and I went to brief the soon-to-be candidate at his home, where we sat down with him and his wife, Maggie.

"Here, Rich, is a draft of a script I've written for a kickoff ad," I said, shoving a piece of paper across the coffee table. Our plan was to get in with a bang. I'd written a simple, direct-to-camera message for Daley that would introduce his candidacy and frame the race. In it, he would wryly acknowledge the most frequent critique of those who questioned his credentials. "I may not be the best speaker in town," he would say, "but I know how to run a government and bring people together."

There was only one problem.

"Script? What script?" Maggie asked. "What are you talking about?"

"Uh, Mag," Rich said, a little sheepishly, his face flushing. "There's something I've been meaning to tell you."

Though the announcement was just a few days away, Daley had not yet shared with his wife his decision to run.

"Okay, then," Bill said nervously, gathering up his papers. "David, why don't you and I go out for a little walk? I'll show you around the neighborhood."

Rich had been reluctant to tell Maggie because he knew she was deeply scarred from the ugly, racial overtones of the last mayoral campaign. Though Daley had refused to play the race card against Washington, many white ethnic Chicagoans had viewed him as the spoiler who opened the doors to City Hall for Harold. Shortly after that election, Daley had gotten into a fistfight with one of his neighbors in a local toy store, after the man blistered him for paving the way for "a nigger" to win. Daley's seven-year-old son, Patrick, had witnessed the ugly scrap.

"I don't want to have any part of a racial thing," Maggie told us when Bill and I returned. "If that's what this is going to be, count me out."

I loved her for saying it. I was sure that most Chicagoans were, like me, desperately looking for a candidate who could heal Chicago by leading it past this racial maelstrom—and only Rich was positioned to be that leader. We had data to prove it. The only cards we would play were unity cards, I assured Maggie, who would go on to become one of Chicago's most beloved figures.

"Okay, then," she said, in the skeptical tone of a reproving schoolteacher. "I hope that's the case."

From day one that became the central theme of Daley's campaign: a mayor strong enough to lead Chicago beyond racial politics in order to tackle the many tangible challenges it faced.

We had no illusions about our ability to attract black votes in the primary. Although Sawyer wasn't the choice of the community, African Americans had fought hard to put one of their own in the mayor's office and were likely to cast their votes, however grudgingly, to keep a black man there, despite his limitations. This was the cynical calculation the white ward bosses had made when they installed him to replace Harold. Nonetheless, Daley spent much of his time campaigning in the predominantly African American wards. We wanted to send a strong signal that he would be a mayor for the entire city. While this gesture was the right thing to do, it also had the strategic virtue of reassuring white, liberal voters who would make the difference in the election.

Sawyer's campaign manager, Reynard Rochon, a wily operative from New Orleans, tried hard to embroil Daley in a controversy that would allow Sawyer's campaign to depict him as a closet racist and drive a wedge between him and those liberals. So Rochon pounced when Daley, addressing a rally on the city's Southwest Side, mangled a line in his standard stump speech.

For months, Daley had maintained extraordinary discipline, delivering the same stump speech about bringing the city together. At this stop, however, he got tangled up as he reached the crescendo, which always began with the phrase "What you want is a mayor who can sit down with everybody." On this night, he said, "*You want a what mayor* who can sit down with everybody." With this mixed-up construction, a campaign desperate to light a fire could make the argument that Daley was telling an all-white crowd that what they wanted was a "*white* mayor." Within hours of the tape's surfacing, Rochon publicly accused Daley of making a racial appeal.

Daley's wrestling match with the English language was hardly news, and any reporter who had covered his speeches had heard the line dozens of times and knew that he had simply mangled it. Besides, did it make any sense for a candidate who had pitched his whole campaign on healing the racial divide suddenly to change course weeks before the election, with a ham-handed, public appeal to elect a "white mayor"? It was preposterous. Yet a civic committee that had been formed to police the tone of Chicago's campaigns deliberated and sanctioned Daley for his remarks. As sometimes happens, the self-anointed good guys wound up inflaming rather than calming. I spent hours urging the group's leader not to enter the fray, and a few cathartic minutes lambasting him after he did. With one careless press conference, this group, with no doubt the best of intentions, threatened to undermine the premise of Daley's entire campaign and, to my mind, derail the city's best hope for bridging the racial divide.

But the people of Chicago were watching the race intensely, and taking their own measure of the candidates. I would see this often in high-profile races for sensitive offices like mayor or president. People watch the candidates carefully and form their judgments based on the totality of what they see. Some gaffes are dismissed as such, if they fly in the face of the impression voters have developed. Yet if a gaffe reflects what voters have come to believe is the true character of a candidate, it can be deadly. In this case, Chicagoans had sized up Daley and his campaign and dismissed the dustup for what it was: a verbal hiccup, not a racial call to arms.

Daley swept to the mayoralty with strong support from white liberals and Hispanic voters and, as we expected, only a sliver of black votes. Yet over his twenty-two years as mayor, he governed as promised, building strong ties to all the city's communities, working on local problems such as school reform and crime, and assiduously avoiding divisive language or politics. He would be rewarded in subsequent elections with a greater share (even majorities) of the black vote, forged not by a machine, but his own good works. Like his father, Rich Daley was a builder—of parks, schools, libraries, the community anchors that make a city and its neighborhoods strong. His tenure wasn't without controversy or scandal—and by the end, when the Great Recession hit, the due bills came in for the obligations Daley had pushed into the future. But one legacy no one can deny is that Rich Daley pulled Chicago back from the racial abyss.

Never one to sully or dishonor his legendary father's record, Daley would never admit it, but I always felt he took great pride in being the Mayor Daley who healed rather than divided.

The Chicago elections—Harold's and Daley's—gained a great deal of attention nationally, and made my consulting firm a go-to place for urban politics. Given my experiences as a child of the big city, and the years I spent patrolling Chicago's fabled City Hall as a newspaperman and consultant, these campaigns were a natural niche for me. They also were my special passion.

Urban politics is the most visceral and interesting, first, because of the ethnic and racial diversity you find in most cities. Chicago's phone book is like a United Nations directory, rife with names that have roots in every corner of the world. And while Chicago's ethnic communities are not as siloed as they once were—in homogenous wards commanded by party bosses with names such as Vito Marzullo, Izzy Horwitz, and Paddy Bauler—there still is a distinct ethnic flavor to many of its neighborhoods. Politics requires a general understanding of that vital and complex mosaic. When I was working mayoral races in Chicago, I was careful to use a neutral Colombian voice over talent on Spanish-language ads so as not to offend either the Puerto Rican voters on the city's North Side or the Mexicans on the South.

To this day, issues of race are still simmering just beneath the surface in Chicago and other big cities, where so many interact in relatively small spaces. Yet there also is a shared sense of community that, despite all the differences, ties people together. I was struck by this when Daley's wife, Maggie, died after a long bout with cancer shortly after he had left office in 2011. Maggie's wake was held at the Chicago Cultural Center, on Michigan Avenue, on a drizzly November day. Yet there was a long and continuing line of Chicagoans, from wealthy businessmen to cabbies to waitresses, waiting in the rain for hours to pay their respects. The crowd was as diverse as the city itself. The warm and gracious Maggie had been their First Lady for twenty-two years. She was family, and this was a loss they shared.

Local government is where the rubber hits the road. While state legislators and members of Congress are more remote, local officials are present and visible. They are the first responders of politics. They are held most accountable for fundamental problems, from the education of our kids and safety in the streets to the more mundane but still important issues of daily life. When a sidewalk buckles or you need a business permit or graffiti removed from your garage, the local politicians are the ones to whom you turn. I recall one Chicago alderman who fielded multiple calls from an irate constituent who was steaming because her neighbor's dog was barking incessantly. After trying several times to intervene, with no luck, the alderman came up with another idea. "I bought a box of dog biscuits, went over there, and threw them over the fence. I figured that would shut her up for a while," he said, leaving vague whether he was talking about the barking dog or the griping constituent.

There is no buffer between local officials and their constituents. That's why voters in big cities often relate to their mayors in a very personal way. They know them as people, their strengths and foibles. They watch them closely. They connect with them in much the way Americans do their presidents. No other position in the political galaxy promotes that kind of relationship, or affords an officeholder the chance to make as visible a difference, day by day.

At the height of Daley's popularity, his name periodically came up in connection with open governor and U.S. Senate races as well as for cabinet positions in Washington. He invariably laughed the rumors off. "Why would I give up this job for that?" said the man who would eclipse his father's record for longevity in the Chicago mayor's office. "Here you can actually do things without a bunch of bureaucrats standing between you and actually getting things done."

Harold and Daley gave our political consulting venture its start. Over the next two decades, we would help elect mayors in many of America's largest cities, including Cleveland, Detroit, Salt Lake City, Philadelphia, Houston, and Washington, DC. Some of these candidates broke racial and gender barriers, but all of them had to negotiate diverse constituencies. To win and then to govern, all had to find a way to reach across the sometimes enormous social and economic chasms that can divide one city neighborhood from the next.

Shortly after Daley's election, I got a call from the campaign manager for a long-shot candidate for mayor of Cleveland named Michael White. White had devoted himself to public service, as a City Council aide and then a councilman before winning a seat in the Ohio Senate. In 1989, at the age of thirty-seven, he joined a crowded field to replace George Voinovich, the popular if pallid outgoing mayor.

Like Chicago, Cleveland was racially divided, and the conventional wisdom was that the field would winnow down to a runoff between a black candidate, City Council president George Forbes, and one of the white candidates. Mike White was a talented and charismatic speaker, but was thought to lack the organization and money to challenge the favorites. He made up for that, in part, by roaming the streets of Cleveland, listening to the radio and driving to the scene of breaking news, particularly when the story gave him a platform to discuss crime, education, or some of the other central issues of his campaign. Yet there was one momentous event that turned the tide in his favor.

It was tradition in Cleveland that all mayoral candidates participate in a luncheon debate at the City Club. The city's flagship paper, the *Plain Dealer*, and local broadcast outlets would provide intensive coverage of the event. The debate in 1989 featured five candidates, almost all of them eager to praise the outgoing Voinovich, a low-key, moderate Republican who was highly regarded for restoring equilibrium to Cleveland after the brief and stormy reign of populist mayor Dennis Kucinich. George Forbes, an irascible and incendiary figure as City Council president, depicted himself as Voinovich's governing partner and the candidate of "continuity."

Mike White, once an aide to Forbes, had a starkly different message.

"One of my opponents talked about continuity, and I think in some respects we should and must have continuity between the Voinovich years . . . a continuity in conduct that says no matter how we disagree—business community, civic community, and City Council—we will find a way and we must find a way to get along," White said. "But I want to say to each and every one of you here, ladies and gentlemen, that I do not want continuity on the crucial issues affecting this town."

As White spoke, passionately and with few notes, about the challenges of the city—drugs, crime, and a shortage of police; population flight; poor schools and a politicized school board; and racial divisions that stood in the way of progress—he slowly rallied the crowd behind him. After each refrain, he punctuated his critique with the same message: "Continuity just won't do."

"I think we need a mayor who will say, yes, we must go forward. Yes, we must have a town that provides an opportunity for all of its citizens, black and white. And we must have a mayor who has the same understanding as Andrew Young, that while we all came over on different ships, ladies and gentlemen, we in Cleveland and our suburbs are in the same boat now. Continuity just won't do."

By the time he'd finished, even tables of people there to support opposing candidates were standing and cheering, especially when White called for unity and a shared vision for Cleveland's future.

It was one of those electric moments when a leader emerges by seizing an opportunity. Soon after his rousing performance, the *Plain Dealer* endorsed White. Voters, black and white, tipped his way. With his appeal for unity and change, White defied the dreary and conventional political calculus by unexpectedly winning a spot in the runoff with Forbes. Anticipating a ferocious contest, I quickly wrote and recorded a script to foreshadow the attacks we anticipated. "The experts said that our campaign was a dream that would end in the primary, but thanks to you, the dream is still alive," White told Clevelanders in the TV ad. "A dream of a Cleveland that rises above racial politics and name-calling. A dream of One City, working together to fight drugs, crime, poor schools and neighborhood decline. In these final weeks, the forces of division will launch their last stand. They will say or do anything to keep us from working together. But, you know, it's hard to stop a dream whose time has come!"

Indeed, it was. White's momentum proved unstoppable. He won in a landslide, driven by a multiracial coalition of Clevelanders drawn to the ideal of fighting problems instead of one another. White went on to become Cleveland's longest-serving mayor. I didn't keep in close touch with him after the election, though I knew his long tenure didn't entirely live up to its great promise. Still, he had some significant accomplishments, among them new sports stadiums and the Rock and Roll Hall of Fame, which would attract tourists and help revive a fraying downtown. Idealistic as his appeal was at the start, governing is always more difficult than campaigning. The problems of the city proved stubborn, and in the end, he would be tarnished by corruption charges against one of his closest friends and allies.

Nonetheless, White's 1989 election and the diverse coalition he built were inspiring. Its quixotic nature appealed to my idealism. Beyond that, it taught me a valuable lesson that has informed my understanding of mayoral and presidential elections ever since. When incumbents step down, voters rarely opt for a replica of what they have, even when that outgoing leader is popular. They almost always choose change over the status quo. They want successors whose strengths address the perceived weaknesses in the departing leader. Voinovich, a Republican, defeated the volatile Kucinich and was a well-regarded mayor. Still, after a decade of his placid leadership, Clevelanders were looking for a dynamic figure to usher in change, and they chose White.

I would store that lesson away. Though the places where I went on to work could appear, at least on the surface, entirely different, my underlying principles and understanding of urban politics would travel with me from campaign to campaign, from one city to the next.

Mayoral campaigns would be a staple of my work for many years, and the lens through which I would continue to confront the prominence of race in our politics.

In one election, I helped Fernando Ferrer, a longtime Puerto Rican officeholder in New York City, build an unprecedented multiracial coalition of black, Hispanic, and liberal voters at the end of Rudy Giuliani's reign as mayor.

For Ferrer to win, he would have to give voice to the millions of New Yorkers who weren't beneficiaries of the Giuliani years: middle-class families and those struggling just to get there, who were being squeezed by the high cost of living; parents vainly searching for good schools and for after-school programs for their kids; minorities clamoring for a balance between securing the streets and protecting their civil liberties. He needed to shine a bright light on the other New York. Grabbing these edgy issues was unnatural for Freddy, whose political instincts were decidedly mainstream and "go along to get along." Yet as the race wore on, he grew into this more contentious role of advocate, challenging the status quo on behalf of the forgotten New York—and became more genuine in identifying himself as part of it.

One day, as Ferrer began to move in the polls, a member of the city's business elite took him to lunch at an exclusive Midtown club. "You see these people," the man said quietly, gesturing to the well-heeled crowd absorbed in conversations around them. "These people will never let you become mayor, Freddy. You're not from here."

"What do you think he meant by that?" Freddy asked, recounting the story. "'You're not from here.' The hell with that. Let's win this thing."

We didn't. We were on the brink of victory on primary day, September 11, 2001, when planes struck the Twin Towers in Lower Manhattan and the world emphatically changed. By the time the rescheduled primary took place, Giuliani was leading the city through its darkest calamity, and our message lost a little of its efficacy. Ferrer was the candidate whose campaign focused on the two New Yorks at a time when New York had suddenly been united as one.

That conversation in the club that Ferrer reported sticks with me to this day. I'm sure there were similar conversations in generations past about the Irish, the Italians, and the Jews. My dad "wasn't from here," but he came because of the promise of America, and as its barriers fell, America grew stronger.

Redeeming that promise, expanding its reach, was a worthy cause.

SEVEN

GOING NATIONAL

IN THE EARLY 1990S, our Chicago campaigns had caught the attention of another voracious consumer of politics, the young governor of Arkansas. So when Bill Clinton came through town prospecting for money and talent in advance of his 1992 presidential bid, I was asked to say hello.

Like so many others, I was immediately taken with Clinton. He was palpably brilliant, but as a southerner with a great personal story, he spoke in a colloquial way folks could grasp. Moreover, Clinton shared my view that, to win, the Democratic Party had to update its vision and speak to (as well as for) an increasingly embattled middle class. I'll admit that I also sensed that Clinton probably left *everyone* he met with the feeling that he shared their view. That is a valuable, if not wholly admirable, asset in politics, and Clinton was so good at it that I didn't mind.

If his purpose was to corral me, Clinton succeeded halfway through that first meeting. Unseating the then popular incumbent, George H. W. Bush, would be a daunting task, I thought, but Clinton had what it would take to run a strong race. Later, I was among the many people Clinton invited to Little Rock to confer with him in the weeks leading up to his campaign launch, and the significant one-on-one time he gave me was flattering. After his announcement, I received a handwritten card thanking me for my help and noting that he had incorporated my thoughts on the middle class. His note was no more than a line or two, but it meant something to me, as he knew it would. Clinton understood this part of politics as well as anyone I would ever know. Even as I recognized that he had probably written hundreds of such cards and that my wisdom on the middle class was hardly original, I appreciated the gesture and was amazed by the effort.

Clinton's admiration for the Daley operation was apparent. In the fall of 1991, he hired David Wilhelm as his campaign manager. My old collaborator from the Paul Simon race, Wilhelm had gone on to manage Daley's campaign, winning plaudits for his work. He, in turn, recruited Rahm Emanuel, who had raised huge sums as Daley's finance director, to shake the money trees for Clinton. When salacious stories nearly capsized Clinton's campaign as the make-or-break New Hampshire primary approached, the millions that the relentless Rahm had raised for crucial TV ads would help keep it afloat.

A month after that primary, when the campaign moved to Illinois, Clinton had righted the ship and was the clear front-runner for the nomination. Since he already had a media consultant, my role in the campaign was limited. Still, Wilhelm asked me to be the campaign's point man on arrangements for a March 15 presidential debate that would be held in Illinois.

Before the debate, I had a beer with James Carville, Clinton's brilliant and colorful strategist, who was a bundle of raw nerve endings. Born and raised in Louisiana, the former marine had bounced around politics for years as an itinerant campaign manager, off the radar of Washington's political elite. He didn't win his first statewide race until 1986, at the age of forty-two, when he engineered the upset election of Bob Casey as governor of Pennsylvania. In 1991, Carville and his redoubtable sidekick, Paul Begala, returned to Pennsylvania to help Harris Wofford, the longest of long shots, defeat a popular former Republican governor, Dick Thornburgh, in a special election for the U.S. Senate. Wofford had pinned his entire election on one issue, national health care, and the stunning result was seen as a harbinger for the upcoming presidential race. It also made Carville and Begala the hottest consulting team in politics.

Clinton won the derby for their services, and Carville, with his serpentine looks and endless supply of memorable Bayou-isms, became an overnight celebrity. Beyond the amusing, Ragin' Cajun character he played on TV, James was a very shrewd strategist. Unlike many in Washington, he had a great gut for what working-class folks thought, and was more than willing to flout conventional wisdom. Now Carville, who had been broke and on his way out of politics a decade earlier, was on the cusp of winning the biggest campaign of his life—but he wasn't ready to claim victory.

"This guy is really, really good," Carville told me, as we huddled in a corner of the bar at the Chicago Hilton where Clinton's team was staying. "He's smart. He loves this shit. The only question is whether there is anything so important to him that he would be willing to risk losing for it. That's the big question he has to answer."

Little was expected from the Illinois debate. Then Jerry Brown, the pugnacious former California governor, making his third run for president, enlivened the evening by accusing Clinton of "funneling money to his wife's law firm for state business."

As Brown finished his broadside, Clinton erupted. "I don't care what you say about me," the red-faced Arkansan fired back, his pointed finger about two feet from Brown's face, "but you ought to be ashamed of yourself for jumping on my wife."

It was great TV, and in the short run, it redounded to Clinton's benefit. After weathering charges of marital infidelity, he welcomed the opportunity to stand up for Hillary's honor, and eagerly, deftly seized the moment. Still, the underlying charges Brown made would linger, and how to deal with the aftermath was the immediate postdebate concern. Wilhelm asked me to stop by Clinton's suite to chew it over.

By the time I arrived, the Clintons were casually dressed. Hillary lay on the couch gently resting her head on Bill's shoulder. What struck me then, and since, was the obvious affection there was between the couple. Whatever storms they had already endured and would endure again in the future, it was evident that they really did love each other. Clinton's indignation at Brown's attack had been more than just theater.

Now the question on the floor was what to do the following morning, when the Clintons were scheduled to campaign together at an El stop in the city. I was new to the group, but Wilhelm asked for my view.

"If it were me, I would not send Hillary out," I said. "If she's there, she and the debate confrontation with Brown will be front and center. I'd send the governor out on his own."

By now Hillary had left the room. Mickey Kantor, the campaign chairman, and Kevin O'Keefe, a Chicago attorney who was a childhood buddy of Hillary's, dismissed my concerns.

"Hillary can handle herself," Kantor assured me. O'Keefe confidently seconded that view. Being an outsider to the group, I nodded and shut up.

The next day, a throng of reporters descended on the Busy Bee, a café next to an El stop on the city's near Northwest Side. Looking for a way to keep the story alive, they were eager to follow up on the previous night's contretemps. Hillary took the bait.

"I suppose I could have stayed home and baked cookies and had teas," she said, when pressed on Brown's conflict-of-interest charge. "But what I decided to do was to fulfill my profession."

Whatever her intent, with that one comment, Hillary appeared to be demeaning every stay-at-home mom in America—I quickly heard from Susan, who was irate about it—and opened up a culture war that would dog both Clintons for a long time to come.

That dustup notwithstanding, Clinton handily won the Illinois primary, and all but secured the nomination. Wilhelm called me a few weeks later.

"We've got this thing pretty well nailed down," he said. "Governor Clinton wanted to know if you would come down here for the general and be his communications director."

I was overwhelmed by the prospect. Clinton was going to be the nominee. I believed in him, and felt close to my old comrades who were now key members of his team. It was the opportunity of a lifetime.

Then my thoughts turned to Susan and the kids. As it was, I was already an absentee father far too often, leaving my wife to manage our very challenging home. Lauren's struggles were only getting worse. The seizures were coming more frequently. The clusters were becoming harder to subdue, requiring that we blast her full of Ativan, a heavy sedative, to slow them down.

Lauren's episodes almost always began at night. Susan and I would sleep lightly, ears peeled to a baby monitor, so we could pick up the guttural sounds that foreshadowed a seizure. More than once, I would watch as Lauren seized again and again, coming around just long enough to grab Susan's hand and cry out, "Mommy, make them stop!" And Susan and I would cry together in the darkness because we could do nothing to make them stop.

Epilepsy took its toll on Lauren. After ten years of seizures, her developmental delays were much more evident, as the gap between her and her peers grew. It was painful to see other little girls begin to take the first turn into adolescence, with all that that foretold, while Lauren lagged behind, functioning more like a five- or six-year-old. Her life became increasingly lonely. Moreover, the many different drugs, diets, and procedures she had endured had contributed to sharp, sometimes violent mood swings. And many times, her younger brothers unfairly bore the brunt of her fury.

Michael was just nineteen months younger than Lauren. When he was a baby, we often would have to swaddle him in a blanket and hand him off to neighbors while we rushed Lauren to the hospital. He and little brother Ethan had sacrificed playdates, birthday parties, and vacations to Lauren's illness. And like most siblings of children with chronic illness, at times they were angry about what they had lost, and then angry at themselves for feeling angry about what they knew their sister could not control.

If I took the job working for Clinton, it would be seven months away from home. And if Clinton won, it would be hard to turn down the chance to serve in the White House. Would I move my family away from Lauren's doctors and all of Susan's support?

Wilhelm's offer was alluring—a chance to vault from my modestly successful campaign practice to the highest echelons of American politics. Who knew when, or if, such an opportunity would come again? Yet it took me just a day to say no. I recognized that this great opportunity would likely destroy my family. It was a watershed moment in my life. As driven as I was, I discovered that there was something more important to me than the job of my dreams. As imperfect a husband and father as I had been, I loved my wife and children. Leaving them at such a critical time would have been a shameful thing to do. I had been scarred by one driven parent who always put her career first, and by another who left me on my own when I was far too young. I wanted to do better for my kids. For someone bred to aspire, that recognition provided an oddly liberating moment.

I called Wilhelm back the next day and turned him down. "What are you going to do with that spot now?" I asked, out of curiosity.

"I guess we'll give it to George," Wilhelm said, referring to a plainly bright young refugee from Capitol Hill who had been a traveling aide to the candidate.

History would suggest that it all worked out well for Clinton, for George Stephanopoulos, and for me.

Beyond my family considerations, the prospect of landing in Washington also troubled me. I was all too familiar with the town's pathological focus on "who's up and who's down." It's a place where you are always being measured, which seemed like the worst possible environment for someone who was all too prone to his mother's compulsive need for approval. Moreover, I truly believed that I was a better political strategist living outside the Beltway, where the conversation and concerns are almost always starkly different from the self-involved chatter in that one-industry town. In DC, it's all about elections and power. Everywhere else, folks are focused on their day-to-day lives. It's why, as Gary Hart once wisely shared, "Washington is always the last to get the news."

This would come back to me with force years later, shortly after the Monica Lewinsky scandal first broke. Stephanopoulos, who had made a smart transition from politics to journalism after a tumultuous ride with Clinton, called to feel me out about the story. "Do you think he'll have to resign?" he asked, as talk of the president's tryst with an intern filled the airwaves. Several similar calls came in that morning from Washington, where the early betting was that Clinton was finished.

Later that day, I grabbed lunch at Manny's, a delicatessen on the Near South Side where I frequently go to clog my arteries and clear my head. When I reached the register to pay, an elderly cashier named Helen called me aside. "You know," she said, "I'm not here because I want to be. I'm here because I have to be. My husband's sick. Social Security and Medicare don't cover everything. So I have to keep working. And this guy, Clinton? I think he's trying to help us." Helen's eyes narrowed. She leaned forward and lowered her voice to make a final point, which was as salty as Manny's corned beef. "So why don't they get off his ass? I don't care about his sex life. That's his business. All I care about is that he's trying to help us." It was a jarring message, especially coming from the mouth of this blue-haired old lady. After lunch, I called George and the other reporters I'd heard from to relate my conversation with Helen. "Don't count this guy out," I told them. "I bet there are a lot of Helens out there."

Working outside the Center of the Political Universe meant Axelrod and Associates was not on the radar screen for many A-list candidates, who naturally turned to DC's big, brand-name firms for their political advice and media. We were more like the main character in *Jerry Maguire*, the plucky little guys fighting for our share. Still, you were less likely to bump into the Helens of the world in Washington, and my small, scrappy team and I were sharper for that. So, though we had to work harder than some of our Washington competitors to land campaigns, we pitched our outside-the-Beltway status as a virtue, indeed a difference maker. Our reputation, developed through our mayoral campaigns, helped open doors around the country.

In 1990 one of those doors opened in Nebraska, where we worked for a candidate for governor named Bill Hoppner. Hoppner, a longtime aide to Bob

Kerrey, that state's war hero senator and former governor, was a brilliant student of government, but lacked the charisma of his boss. And he faced a tough opponent in Ben Nelson, a wealthy insurance executive who had committed significant personal resources to the race.

Kerrey was deeply involved in the campaign strategy. We wanted to make abortion rights an issue in the primary, where, contrary to the state as a whole, a majority of voters were pro-choice. Yet the senator vetoed our recommendation. "The less said about abortion, the better," he told us, worried that such a tack could complicate the general-election campaign. Still, we went into the final week within hailing distance of Nelson, and were prepared to launch an endorsement ad we had taped with the wildly popular Kerrey, when the senator called. "I just spoke to Ben Nelson, and he reminded me that I had promised him I wouldn't do an ad. So we can't run it."

It was a stunning development. The Kerrey endorsement was always meant to be our closing pitch and would certainly have made a difference for his friend and protégé. Now we were left to scramble, while Kerrey's closest supporters privately hammered him for pulling the rug out from under Hoppner. At 5:00 p.m. on the Friday before the primary, Kerrey called back. "You know, I've been talking to folks back home, and I feel like I owe Bill more," he said. "Go ahead and run the ad." Yet Kerrey, an experienced politician, almost certainly knew when he placed the call that the state's TV stations had closed their advertising logs for the weekend. It would be very hard to place the ad at that hour. So, our fine young media buyer, Debra Schommer, went into overdrive hunting down and browbeating traffic managers at TV stations around the state, and somehow got half of them to reopen their logs to make room for our ad. Where it aired, Hoppner surged. It wasn't enough. After a long recount, Nelson was declared the winner by 42 votes—the closest gubernatorial contest in state history.

I thought about that episode when, the following year, Kerrey announced his candidacy for president, touting his political courage. This was one case, but certainly not the only, when, upon closer inspection, I found a political figure of some stature wanting. And often, the politicians—even the genuinely introspective ones like Kerrey—lacked a clear-eyed view of themselves.

Then there are those who are exactly as they appear to be, for better or worse.

The senior U.S. senator from Illinois, Alan Dixon, was a grinning, glad-handing pol from downstate. "Al the Pal" was the quintessential go-along-to-get-along politician. He had risen through the ranks of the party, from the legislature to statewide office to the Senate, by cutting deals and carefully calibrating his positions on issues. Over a decade in Washington, his votes seemed more about defusing potential Republican electoral challenges than advancing the public interest. In 1991, I felt that Dixon went too far by being one of the very few Democrats to vote for the confirmation of Clarence Thomas to the Supreme Court. If Dixon's position had been rooted in principle, it might have been palatable. Yet I suspected that "Al the Pal" had cut a deal with the White House, trading his critical support for Thomas's nomination in return for the promise of a weak Republican opponent in 1992. (Investigative reporters Jane Mayer and Jill Abramson later confirmed my hunch in their superb book on the Thomas nomination.) Outraged by Dixon's vote and his general approach to legislating, I was determined to find an opponent willing to take him on in a Democratic primary.

Months earlier, I had met with Al Hofeld, a wealthy Chicago trial lawyer and Daley supporter who wanted to explore the possibility of running for office. After a very general discussion, we agreed to stay in touch. Following the Clarence Thomas vote, I called Hofeld back and suggested that he consider challenging Dixon in the Democratic primary, which was just five months away. I didn't know Hofeld well, but he appeared to be perfectly cast for the job, an attractive political outsider with a good up-by-the-bootstraps story. Hofeld had made his living persuading juries. Now he could indict Dixon and the system of squalid horse trading that had come to characterize politics in Washington. Moreover, Hofeld had the personal wealth to underwrite his own campaign, which was the only way a challenger could overcome the incumbent's ample war chest. After a few weeks of contemplation, and some polling that confirmed Dixon's vulnerability, Hofeld jumped into the race. We launched with a simple, direct-to-camera ad that amounted to a declaration of war, on not just Dixon, but politics as usual.

"My name is Al Hofeld, and I'm about to break the rules," the shirtsleeved challenger began, speaking directly to voters, in an unadorned setting. "I'm running for the United States Senate, where the rules say you should be everyone's pal, sell yourself to the special interests, and tap dance around the tough issues."

The allusion to Dixon was unmistakable.

"Well, I refuse to take a dime of special interest PAC money because we won't get national health care until we're ready to take on the insurance lobby," Hofeld continued. "And we won't get guns off our streets until we're ready to take on the NRA. You see, Congress is all tied up in knots by the special interests, and they never get around to giving us what we need: tax relief for middle-income families; a shot at college for every kid; and a trade policy that's as fair to us as it is to them. So if you feel you're being heard in Washington, then I'm not your guy. But if you're fed up like I am, then let's break the rules."

The ad and others that followed struck an immediate chord with voters. Yet our opponents had done probing research on Hofeld that we, in our haste to find a candidate, had not. Eager to subject this deep-pocketed newcomer to a thorough hazing, the news media were willing consumers for that opposition research. Even before the ads began, stories surfaced that Hofeld had failed to vote in many critical elections. His depth of knowledge on public policy was suspect. His prodigious campaign spending became an issue. It was a learning experience for me. Instead of finding the ideal challenger, I had tried to take a flawed candidate and make him conform to my ideal. That rarely works. Meanwhile, another candidate seized the opening that the Dixon-Hofeld face-off created.

Carol Moseley Braun was the Cook County recorder of deeds—not your typical springboard to the U.S. Senate. She had burst on the local political scene in 1978, a bright, charismatic former federal prosecutor elected to the legislature from Hyde Park as an anti-machine Democrat. Yet Carol had never quite lived up to her promise, which once seemed as bright as her incandescent smile. Still, with two competitive white men in the race for the U.S. Senate, Carol had a chance to salvage her career. It turned out to be a good bet. While Hofeld and Dixon savaged each other in TV ads, Moseley Braun charmed voters who were looking for an alternative. She galvanized African Americans, liberals, and suburban women, who were thrilled by the opportunity to elect the first black woman to the U.S. Senate.

With 38 percent of the vote, Moseley Braun won the nomination, ending Dixon's forty-two-year political career. Hofeld was reduced to the role of blocking back, spending millions to create the hole through which Carol ran to history.

I had mixed feelings. The candidate I urged to run had lost, despite prodigious spending from which, it was widely noted, our firm had profited handsomely. Royko wrote a snarly column about me, armed with a couple of friendly letters I had written to Dixon's aides. One was written six years earlier, when I was hustling races to bring to the prospective partnership with Doak, Shrum, and Caddell. "I have great affection for Alan," I wrote then, seeking the Dixon campaign account. "It is a campaign I would feel good about doing." Royko also had been lagged a second letter I had written the Dixon aide in 1990—before the offensive Thomas vote—calling "nonsensical" the rumors that I was planning to field a candidate against him in '92. It hardly took a writer of Royko's rapier wit to carve me up as a shameless mercenary. Still, given our history, he warmed to it with special enthusiasm. My old *Tribune* colleague Steve Neal, now a *Sun-Times* columnist, called me "the Mr. Flexibility of Illinois politics."

It was the first really rough treatment I had received in the media. Yet I had set myself up for it with my disingenuous letter sucking up to Dixon years earlier, chasing business for Doak, Shrum, and Caddell. I had walked away from that union, in part, because I didn't want to treat campaigns simply as paydays, taking any candidate who could pay the freight. I wanted to work for candidates in whom I believed. Over the years, I can't say I never chose a clunker or allowed business considerations to creep in, but Mr. Flexibility? That's not who I was or wanted to be.

The greater fallout from the race was that I also got crosswise with my old friend and mentor Paul Simon, in whom I *did* believe. Dixon and Simon had been friends for nearly forty years, and Paul pulled out all the stops to try to save him. I never doubted Paul's honesty or integrity, but he always had a greater tolerance and affection for characters like Dixon than I thought he should. It bothered me that he would vouch for Dixon, and in a childish fit of pique, I told a reporter for the *National Journal* that Simon was "an aspiring hack trapped in a reformer's body." My understanding was that the comment was off the record, but I was sophisticated enough to know that it was too pungent not to find its way into print. In any case, it was a terrible thing to say about a guy to whom I owed so much. I regret it more than anything I have ever said to a reporter.

Ironically, by trading his Thomas vote for the weak Republican candidate he thought he would face, Dixon also made it almost impossible for Moseley Braun to lose in the fall—though it quickly became apparent that she was going to give it a try. With her primary victory, Moseley Braun had become an instant national sensation. Yet, as the months wore on, she continued to take victory laps while her Republican opponent, Rich Williamson, a conservative former State Department official, worked for the vote.

She had effectively entrusted the leadership of her team to her future fian-cée, a cantankerous South African named Kgosie Matthews. Together they seemed more eager to plunder the campaign than to win the election. By the fall, investigative reporters also had zeroed in on charges that Moseley Braun had conspired with her mother to commit Medicaid fraud, an accusation she heatedly denied. Suddenly, it was a horse race.

Moseley Braun and Matthews had a shrewd and experienced media consul-tant, Jerry Austin, who had done a good job for her in the primary. Still, they asked if I would help stop the bleeding, and I agreed. For her to lose now would be unthinkable. I hammered out a batch of scripts, some to remind people why they'd liked her in the first place; others to bring Williamson down to earth.

We set up a shoot in the Hyde Park home of my in-laws, just blocks from Carol's home. It was a Sunday, meaning double time for the crew. Yet this was when her schedule was free, and time was of the essence. We waited for hours, cameras at the ready, but the candidate was a no-show. Finally, an aide called to say she would not be coming. The fire drill cost her campaign twenty thou-sand dollars and, worse, valuable time.

When Moseley Braun finally deigned, days later, to sit for a shoot, she absolutely lit up the screen. We wanted to give voters a renewed stake in her success by offering her improbable rise as a parable about our country at its best. An ad we ran in the closing week reflected the strategy.

"When I began this race a year ago, I was called a hopeless underdog," Carol began. "But I was outraged about how they do business in Washington. It turned out a lot of you were outraged, too. And, together, we overcame the odds and sent a message of change and hope. On Tuesday, you can send more than a message. You can send a vote. For guaranteed health care. For policies that will create jobs and opportunity. For an America where we finally put people first . . . and where even an underdog can win."

Helped by spots like this as well as Bill Clinton's extra-long coattails and some hard-hitting ads targeting Williamson, we regained control of the race. Sadly, Carol never fully took control of her life. With the emotionally abusive Matthews in her ear, offering colossally bad advice, she would spend much of her short tenure in Washington mired in controversy. The first African American woman elected to the U.S. Senate, who would pave the way for another pathbreaking Illinois senator, was defeated after just one term.

Carol was the daughter of an abusive father. It's hard to know how much that factored into the drive that led her to a political career, or the erratic, self-destructive behavior that claimed it. In my experience, such struggles are not uncommon among men and women who are drawn to the great emotional risks and rewards of the public stage. So many are chasing ghosts—trying to live up to the legacies and demands of a parent, or compensating for one's absence.

In 1994, I worked for two such candidates, each tragic figures in his own way.

In Rhode Island, Patrick Kennedy, son of Ted, was seeking a seat in Congress. Just twenty-six, Patrick had already served five years in the Rhode Island legislature, helped by his famous name. The sweet, anxiety-ridden young Kennedy, however, had inherited little of the family's trademark charisma or campaign skills. Patrick, who struggled with addiction as a teenager and would again, so wanted to please his dad, but lived in constant fear of disappointing him.

"We have to win this race," moaned young Kennedy, who spent much of the campaign figuratively curled up in the fetal position. "In my family, you don't lose." It was curious, because his dad had in 1980. Propelled by the family legend, Patrick also was a prisoner of it.

We did win, mostly by annihilating a strong Republican opponent with a devastating negative ad.

Patrick served for sixteen years, a tenure marked by real accomplishment and periodic breakdowns. Yet shortly after his father died, he left Congress and politics, settled down, had a family, and lived a much happier life as an advocate for the mentally ill.

Dan Rostenkowski was a political prince, albeit of a less exalted domain. Elected to Congress at the age of thirty, he had served under nine presidents. As a member of the House Ways and Means Committee, he had helped fashion Medicare under LBJ. As its mighty chairman, Rostenkowski worked with President Reagan on landmark tax-reform legislation and with President Clinton on health care reform. He had been the go-to guy in Washington for two Mayor Daleys, and in Chicago, he was the unquestioned boss of the Thirty-Second Ward, where he and his father, Joe, had ruled as Democratic committeemen for half a century.

As a reporter, I had little relationship with Rosty, who might have hoisted a few with the Washington press types but who had little use for the ink-stained wretches in Chicago. At the behest of Rich Daley, I agreed to do a few radio ads for Rostenkowski in 1992, when he faced a minor primary challenge. By 1994 he was even more vulnerable, and for good reason. Rostenkowski had overcome his youthful image as an undeserving machine princeling to become a towering force in Washington. Now all that was threatened. Rosty was under siege—the subject of a federal investigation for the kind of two-bit chiseling one had come to expect from a Chicago alderman, not from the powerful chair of the House Ways and Means Committee. Having worked a lifetime to be seen as more than a Chicago ward heeler, he was in jeopardy of joining some of the hacks from back home in prison.

"Did you see them out there?" he demanded nervously one day when I visited him at his campaign headquarters. Both the White House and City Hall had asked me to help Rosty again, and despite the gathering storm clouds, I was eager to do what I could. Still, it was jarring to find this legislative powerhouse sitting at a small desk in the middle of a cavernous and largely empty headquarters, his eyes darting back and forth between me and the store-front window. "The G, the government—the FBI. They're out there. They're all over me."

Helped by a rousing endorsement ad from Clinton, Rosty survived a serious primary fight, but he would be indicted before the general election, and swept away by a political unknown on the Republican ticket.

While Clinton's endorsement might have been valuable to Rostenkowski in the Democratic precincts of Chicago, 1994 was a national disaster for the party. By 1996, though, Clinton's Republican foil, House Speaker Newt Gingrich, had overplayed his hand, the economy was improving, and the president was cruising to reelection.

Chicago would be the scene of the Democratic National Convention, which promised to be more harmonious than the last party confab in the Second City. Mayor Daley, who sat by his father's side when the '68 convention dissolved into chaos, was determined to supplant those bitter memories with happier images of his city.

In the spring of '96, I got a call from Doug Schoen, a New York-based pollster with whom I had worked, asking me to come to Washington to meet with Dick Morris, the politically ambidextrous Svengali whom Clinton had turned to for help in salvaging his presidency after the disastrous midterms.

"Dick wants to talk to you about Chicago," explained Schoen, who, with partner Mark Penn, had teamed up with Morris to take over the president's polling after Clinton cashiered the team that had helped elect him.

I had mixed feelings. I wanted to help Clinton, but I had deep suspicions about Morris, who had worked for liberal Democrats but also for arch-conservatives like Jesse Helms. To me, Dick seemed like an opportunist, often pushing the envelope—and always leaving with his own nicely stuffed. Still, I liked Schoen, and decided that if Morris was Clinton's guy, I should, at the very least, hear him out. We set up an appointment for the Jefferson Hotel, where Morris was living, just five blocks from the White House. Morris burst into the hotel lobby, forty-five minutes late, with an entourage of aides, including Penn. In his suite, he settled into a high-backed chair and summoned me over in the fashion of a Mafia don.

"I heard you were a smart guy," he began, "but I didn't call you, because I also heard you were a liberal. But Schoen says you're all right.

"You see, we're in a battle with Ickes and the liberals in the White House for the heart and soul of this administration," Morris said, referring to Harold Ickes, the president's deputy chief of staff and a progressive stalwart, who kept a close rein on Morris and his budget. "So you're either with us or you're with them."

As Morris talked, the disheveled, wild-haired Penn paced anxiously behind him, occasionally casting a wary eye in my direction.

"Well, gee, Dick," I replied. "I'm here because I am with the president. I just want to do what I can to help him."

Morris pondered my answer, and tried a different approach.

"Okay, okay. Fair enough. So how do you think the president's doing?"

"Very well," I said. "He's done some great things. The economy is picking up. The only thing is that there still are a lot of folks who aren't sharing in that recovery."

With that, Penn exploded.

"Come on, Dick, let's get out of here," he shouted. "He's one of them!"

Without looking at Penn, Morris waved him off and resumed our conversation.

"Look, it would be useful to me to have someone who really gets Chicago and could help me understand where the opportunities and problems might arise there," he said. "Let me try and get you on board with the campaign for that."

I never heard from Morris again; maybe my liberal leanings scared him off.

Nor did he get the chance to experience much of Chicago. Just as the convention opened, the story broke that Morris had been entertaining a prostitute in that same suite at the Jefferson, and that his guest had taken some positions that would prove far more distressing for Morris than mine. Morris was banished from the campaign, leaving Penn as the chief strategist.

Meanwhile, I was able to make a small contribution to the president's effort. I had watched the Republican convention, where their nominee, Senator Robert Dole, had spoken of being a bridge to the values of the past. This struck me as off-key, particularly coming from a candidate whose age and worldview already seemed retrograde. I wrote a memo to Rahm in the White House, suggesting that the president consider inverting Dole's reference in what would be the last acceptance speech of the twentieth century.

"The odd thing about Dole's speech is that rather than offer a vision for the future, he served up an ode to the past," I wrote. "Clearly, people yearn for the values and comforts—and sense of control—of an earlier time. But they also recognize that we can't put the genie back into the bottle. They want a President who confidently meets the challenges of changing times, not one who curses and shrinks from them, or pretends they aren't there." So, for Clinton's speech, I suggested a formulation: "We must build bridges to the future, not the past. Much as we might like to, we can't go back. As we enter a new century and a new millennium, wistful reflections about simpler times won't be enough to solve the challenges of today and tomorrow." I also proposed that the president pivot off the rancorous tone of the other convention, and challenge the Republicans to a "contest, not of insults, but ideas."

Michael Waldman, the president's speechwriter, generously credited my memo in his memoirs as a spark behind the "bridge to the twenty-first century" theme Clinton embraced, and when I ran into Stephanopoulos after the president's speech, he seemed familiar with it as well. "Ideas, not insults," he said, with a smile. "Highest-testing line in the speech."

The run-up to the convention presented me with another challenge.

The previous fall, I had signed on to help a spirited, young state legislator, Rod Blagojevich, who was angling to knock off the Republican who had lucked into Rostenkowski's seat the previous election.

I liked Rod. He was fun-loving, warm, and self-effacing. The son of a Serbian immigrant—his father had been a steelworker, his mother, a ticket taker for the Chicago Transit Authority—he seemed genuinely to identify with people who, in his words, had come from the "wrong side of the tracks." His thick helmet of black hair was an homage to Elvis Presley, his favorite working-class hero.

Rod's story was not entirely a Horatio Alger tale, however. His political career had taken off only after he began courting the daughter of Richard Mell, an influential Chicago alderman and ward boss. Still, Rod had voted a solid independent line in Springfield, bucking party leaders on some key votes.

In the midst of the congressional race, the *Tribune* decided that it would commit considerable space in its convention editions to a feature the paper dubbed "Lord of His Ward." The idea was to clue visiting delegates and media into the quaint, old ways of Chicago politics. Many of the most likely candidates to be profiled were close to reporters at the *Trib*, who lobbied to spare their sources the "honor" of this special recognition. So the editors chose Mell, in part because his effort to elect his son-in-law to Congress would provide a colorful backdrop for the story.

Seven months before the convention, the editors assigned a team to work on the series, including several investigative reporters. Soon they began asking unfriendly questions of Blagojevich's colleagues and associates. Freedom of Information requests were being dropped all over town, and it became clear that the *Trib*'s team was intent on painting the picture of an incompetent ghost payroller—an empty suit propelled up the ladder by his powerful father-in-law.

The series was mildly threatening to Blagojevich's chances, though it wouldn't appear in the newspaper until after the crucial Democratic primary. To me the exercise seemed a bit like bounty hunting. Having been cut loose for months to produce this opus, the reporters understood it would be bad form to come back empty-handed.

To counter, I dusted off my old skills as an investigative reporter and began tracking their inquiries. Anticipating their charge that Blagojevich had not worked for his paycheck when he was a part-time hire on Mell's aldermanic staff, I collected close to a hundred affidavits from people for whom Rod had been a caseworker. I looked into his law cases to rebut charges about his legal competence. As summer approached, I wrote a twelve-page memo to the *Trib*'s editor, rebutting the many lines of attack and arguing why the piece should not run. "Somewhere this project got off the rails," I wrote. "Instead of an honest and balanced profile, it became, at least for some involved, a search-and-destroy mission. And now, it seems, every negative inference is accepted as fact; every bit of positive information is deemed irrelevant." The piece I feared did not run. Ultimately, some of the material was used, but in a less prominent form.

Rod won. In Congress, he became known more for his elaborate pranks than his body of work. Still, he took on my son Michael as an unpaid intern for three summers, and helped lift the spirits of a boy who was burdened by many challenges. For that I will always be grateful.

When Rod went on to run for governor in 2002, however, it was without my help.

"Why do you want to be governor?" I asked him when he summoned me to talk about the race.

"You can help me figure that out," he said, an answer that was, for me, a conversation stopper.

"Look," I said, "if you can't tell me why you're running, I can't help you explain it to others."

I left the meeting, and our seven-year relationship was over.

I believed in Rod in 1996, and in what I was doing. Later, when he went to prison for corruption as governor, I revisited '96 in my head and wondered if, even then, he had conned me as he had so many others.

We racked up more victories in '98 and '99, and the firm's national reputation continued to grow. Forrest Claypool had left our firm to serve Daley as his chief of staff and had won great notices for his tenure as the reform-minded chief of the Chicago Park District. In 2002 he beat the Democratic organization for a seat on the Cook County Board of Commissioners. John Kupper, a skillful communications specialist with Capitol Hill experience, had now replaced Forrest, and would work at my side for two decades.

One of our most satisfying races of this period took place next door, in Iowa, familiar terrain for me after years of reporting and consulting on campaigns. We got a call from a little-known state senator, who was lagging far behind in his race for the Democratic nomination for governor in a state that hadn't elected a Democrat governor in thirty-two years. "Right up our alley," Kupper joked. "Buy low, sell high."

Tom Vilsack had a story straight out of Hollywood. Left on the doorstep of an orphanage in Pittsburgh, he was adopted by a dysfunctional family. His abusive mother wrestled with alcoholism and prescription drug abuse. His father struggled financially, and secretly sold much of what the family owned to send Tom to college. There, Tom met Christie Bell of Mount Pleasant, Iowa, an aspiring schoolteacher. The two would marry, and when Tom graduated from law school, they would move back to Mount Pleasant. Tom joined Christie's dad at his small law firm, and basked in the warm embrace of this quintessential small town, quickly becoming a pillar of the community. When Mount Pleasant's mayor was shot to death at a City Council meeting, the slain mayor's family and the traumatized town drafted Tom, then thirty-six, to replace him. When Tom tried to step down after two terms, 90 percent of Mount Pleasant's voters wrote his name on the ballot to ensure he continued in office. He went on to win a seat in the state senate from a predominantly Republican district in southeast Iowa and, in 1997, was pondering a race for governor when I met with him at his modest law offices. The odds were long, but Vilsack was the real deal, and I badly wanted the race.

"There were some pretty slick guys from Washington in to see me right before you," the slightly rumpled Vilsack would tell me later. "I hired you because your shirttail was sticking out, and I figured I could relate to you."

It turned out that Iowans were as impressed with Vilsack and his story as I was. He would go on to win two spirited, come-from-behind victories in the primary and general election. It helped that the Republican nominee, Jim Ross Lightfoot, had been a part of the Republican majority in Congress, which in four short years had fallen into disrepute. One of our ads pictured members of a fictional Iowa family standing in front of their home and disappearing from the screen one by one as we catalogued Lightfoot's votes for budget cuts. The ad slashed a fifteen-point lead in half, and Tom's momentum never waned.

While the Vilsacks were celebrating their victory, Susan and I were struggling with an increasingly bleak prognosis for Lauren. She was so hobbled by seizures and drugs that she could barely speak intelligibly, and struggled just to keep her head up. We tried a vagal nerve stimulator, implanted in her chest, to combat the seizures with electrical impulses, but it didn't help. We also tried a draconian 90 percent–fat diet, precisely measured to stimulate anti-epileptic ketones in her system. It failed. When she was fifteen, Lauren had brain surgery. A hole was drilled in her skull, and a strip of electrodes was laid on top of her brain to try to identify the source of her seizures. If the doctors could locate it, they would remove the tissue. After ten days of monitoring, though, during which her drugs were withdrawn to induce constant seizures, Lauren's neurologist glumly shared the results: "We couldn't find it," he said. "The focal point is too deep in her brain. I'm so sorry."

Delivering that news to a little girl who had eagerly submitted herself to a torturous medical hell in the hope of being freed from seizures would be one of the most painful days of our lives.

Susan could no longer contain her anger and grief. In 1998, she and two other moms of similarly impacted children founded Citizens United for Research in Epilepsy, or CURE, to promote cutting-edge research into the causes of epilepsy. Existing treatments were often ineffective and punishing. The mission of these moms, and the many others who would join: "No seizures. No side effects."

First Lady Hillary Clinton was the guest speaker at CURE's first fundraiser, in January 1999, and she bowled us over with the kindness she showed Lauren and the seriousness with which she plunged into the issue. Like many Americans, she told us, she, too, had a relative who had been devastated by seizures.

Our lives were still hostage to Lauren's unpredictable episodes. Yet when Al Gore called that spring and invited me to Washington to talk about joining his upcoming presidential campaign, Susan urged me to go. "The kids are older now," she said. "We can manage. If you miss another chance, you don't know when, or if, the next one will come along."

I didn't know Gore well, but I liked him. He was a serious guy, with big ideas, and a dry sense of humor that he rarely flashed in public. He asked me about my family. We each had a sixteen-year-old son. "Interesting age," he said, with the knowing smile of another dad who was dealing with the mercurial moods of an adolescent boy. We talked at length about the campaign, and Gore outlined the senior strategic communications role he wanted me to fill. I told him I would get back to him relatively soon.

Before I could accept, however, life dealt our family another blow. I was driving home from work when Susan called. Something clearly was wrong, and this time, it wasn't Lauren.

"I didn't want to tell you until I knew," Susan said, holding back sobs. "I really thought it was nothing. But I had a lump in my breast, and went to get it tested. The test came back today. I have cancer."

I nearly drove off the road. It was another unreal moment, like the one when I learned my dad had died, or when I witnessed my baby convulse for the first time. In such moments, you're at first gripped by the conviction that things like this don't happen to us, that they happen to other people. My life had already made a mockery of any such belief, and now it was doing so again.

Susan was just forty-six. She was extremely fit and seemed healthy in every way. Now she had cancer, and we wouldn't know for weeks just how severe a case. I thought about the worst. What if we lost her? I couldn't imagine my life without her. She was the rock of our family. She had held us together through all Lauren's trials. How could I possibly provide our kids with the constant measure of love and support that Susan did every day? These moments have a way of putting everything in perspective. A presidential campaign was suddenly the last thing on my mind.

When Susan's evaluation came, it was mildly encouraging. The tumor was small. Chances of survival were good. Yet she would need a regimen of chemotherapy and radiation that would sap her energy and jangle her spirits. Every session was an ordeal, and the recovery time after them agonizing. Still, despite private moments in which she questioned whether she could go on, Susan maintained a brave front for our kids and did everything she could to keep our family routines normal.

Our youngest, Ethan, then eleven, had signed up for ranch camp in Wyoming. It would be his first extended stay away from home, and Susan had promised him that she would take him there to get him settled. When the time came, she insisted on keeping her word, even though she had a chemo treatment just two days before. So at 4:00 a.m., Susan and Ethan set out for the airport and their long-planned trip to Jackson Hole. She did not let on how terribly sick she felt. I often recall her silent heroics that day and marvel at just how powerful a force is a mother's love.

Susan's illness was a wakeup call. We were mortal; we would not live forever. We thought hard about what would become of Lauren when we were gone, and began looking for a living arrangement for our child that would allow her some independence but provide her with the structure and support she needed. We found that place in Misericordia Home, a lovely, nurturing community for people with disabilities on Chicago's North Side, where Lauren would move in 2002. What would make that move possible would be nothing short of a miracle.

In the spring of 2000, when Lauren was hospitalized with seizures and was spiraling down, she was given an anti-epilepsy drug, Keppra, that was just emerging. Though twenty other drugs had failed her, Keppra, in concert with her other medications, shut her seizures down. The cocktail of drugs Lauren would take, probably for the rest of her life, were punishing in their own right. The brain damage brought on by constant seizures was irreversible. Still, for the first time in eighteen years, she was stable, without recurrent seizures.

Gore was gracious and understanding when I called to turn down his offer, and I was touched that he would phone occasionally in the midst of his campaign to ask about Susan's progress. Hillary also heard about Susan's illness and checked in. Since the benefit dinner in Chicago, she had become a critical ally in the quest for epilepsy research, and was the driving force behind the first White House conference on curing epilepsy, a watershed event in the movement to focus research on the underlying causes of epilepsy.

Hillary had been dealing with the aftermath of her own personal crisis, this one played out on the public stage. The Lewinsky scandal had dominated 1998, during which the eyes of the world were on the First Lady. As a result of a combination of sympathy for her ordeal and admiration for the strength and dignity with which she navigated it, Hillary's popularity had grown to new heights. Reports were swirling that she was contemplating a race for the U.S. Senate from New York. I was skeptical of such a move and told her so in a private meeting at the White House.

"Why would you want to squander your standing just to become one of a hundred senators?" I asked. "You could make an enormous impact without that when you leave here. You could be another Eleanor Roosevelt!" Yet it was clear that Hillary was well down the road in her thinking. "I think it's important to have a platform," she said, all but acknowledging the rumors of her plans. Daniel Patrick Moynihan, New York's senior senator, would be retiring, and Hillary was very much eying his seat.

The Hillary juggernaut was launched the following year, and our firm was on board. While she had her own talented media consultant, the sharp-edged Mandy Grunwald, we would produce ads on Hillary's behalf for the Democratic Senatorial Campaign Committee. In that role, I was part of a group that helped prepare her for the upcoming debates. Underscoring the unusual nature of her candidacy, our mock debates were held in the White House theater, where the president would drop by from time to time to observe. As a veteran of the news media, my job was to assume the role of a panelist asking the toughest, most provocative questions I could devise. "You're just mean," Hillary joked during a break from these sessions when I pressed her on some past comments. "I think you're enjoying this a little too much!" Still, Hillary clearly warmed to the task. After Robert Barnett, a Washington attorney standing in for her Republican opponent, Rick Lazio, tore into her in our first run-through, she came back with a vengeance in the next, her fierce, competitive instincts fully engaged.

Hillary was impressive, and so was her team, filled with young talents such as Howard Wolfson, Bill de Blasio, and Neera Tanden, who would later become stars in their own right. Yet hanging over the campaign was the dark, brooding presence of Mark Penn, who replaced Morris as the Clintons' resident pollster and strategist. True to the Morris creed, Penn saw his mission as quashing any liberal impulses of the candidate or the campaign, and he justified himself with fuzzy polling numbers and a smug self-assurance that made every discussion grating. I felt he spent as much time manipulating his clients as providing constructive counsel. On the night the Clintons were featured at the 2000 Democratic National Convention, Penn told me he would begin polling the Senate race the following day.

"Mark, is that methodologically sound?" I asked. "Given that the Clintons just dominated TV tonight, won't you get a false positive?"

"Listen, I know these people," he said, referring to the president and First Lady. "They're going on vacation. They're going to fulminate about this race. What harm does it do to give them a little good news?"

Bloodless and calculating, Penn was at the top of the heap in political consulting. My interactions with him only added to a growing feeling I had that maybe the time had come for me to move on. I relished campaigns, and was proud of many (though by no means all) of my clients. I loved my colleagues and the creative rush, and since opening my firm, I had made a better living than I'd ever imagined. Still, I hadn't gotten into politics as a business. The compromises required and the level of cynicism that seemed more pervasive than ever were beginning to wear me down.

Back home in Chicago, I would watch a cynical governor's race unfold in 2002 that only added to my dismay.

After I turned him down, Blagojevich hired Squier's old firm to honcho his gubernatorial campaign. (Squier himself passed away in 2000, at the age of sixty-five, offering me one more reason to get out of the high-stress world of political consulting.) Taking a candidate who had no compelling rationale to run other than ambition, the consultants skillfully molded him to specs dictated by polling and focus groups and then spent a fortune—and made a fortune themselves—selling a fiction.

The retiring Republican governor, George Ryan, was under federal investigation and, after a lifetime in politics, would wind up serving his next term at the Federal Correctional Complex in Terre Haute, Indiana. So Rod cast himself as a reformer, even as his team scooped up campaign contributions with a vigor that would make even the most hardened Chicago ward heeler blush. True to the polling, he pledged to hold the line on taxes, even as the state drifted into a deep budget morass.

By the summer of 2002, it was clear to me that Blagojevich was on his way to the statehouse.

I was happy for Rod personally, and grateful for the continuing kindness he had shown my family, even after I had declined to join his campaign. Weeks after his election, he would headline a Chicago event for Susan's CURE foundation. Yet his success also raised troubling questions.

The Blagojevich campaign was a masterpiece of modern political technique. Armed with incisive research, Rod's consultants had furnished him with a compelling rationale to match his boundless ambition. As a purely clinical matter, I admired their execution. They had deftly used the tools of our trade to propel into high office a man who would prove himself thoroughly ill-suited to hold it. Fickle and immature, he would rarely show up for work, and when he did, he often made impulsive decisions that proved costly to the state. Maybe his consultants had done what I had, more times than I cared to admit: convinced themselves that their candidate was actually the man they spent millions selling to voters. Or maybe they just thought he was the better of two bad choices. Or, then again, maybe it was just another lucrative gig.

I recalled a conversation I once had with one of my most successful peers, who, in discussing his work, offered a depressing analogy to another profession. "These candidates come in, one after another, and say, 'Write me a spot,' and they pay me a shitload of money to do it," he said. "But, Axe, the next day, I can't even remember their names."

The weight of all this—the demands of intense campaigns and needy, self-absorbed candidates—was mounting. I knew that I either had to find a way to recharge my batteries and renew my idealism or give up political consulting.

Then I got a perfectly timed and totally unexpected call from an old friend that would change my life.

"David, it's Barack. I'm thinking about what I want to do next, and was wondering if we could talk."

EIGHT

THE NATURAL

I FIRST MET BARACK OBAMA only as a favor to a friend.

It was 1992. Obama had recently graduated from Harvard Law School, where he made national news as the first African American editor of the extremely prestigious and equally stodgy *Harvard Law Review*. Now he had been hired to organize Project Vote, a registration drive focused on the large number of unregistered minority voters in the Chicago area. Bettylu Saltzman, a longtime Democratic activist, called to ask me to get together with Obama. "He's a really extraordinary young guy," she said. "I think it's important for you two to know each other."

"Happy to, Bettylu, but why?" I asked.

"Honestly?" she replied. "I think he could be the first black president."

Bettylu was a dear friend whose sensibilities about politics and taste in candidates tended to line up with mine. She had been one of Paul Simon's earliest supporters and had served as his first state director when he moved to the Senate. I wanted to meet this new wunderkind, if only because it was Bettylu who'd asked.

So Barack and I arranged to get together for lunch. While I didn't exactly leave that first meeting humming "Hail to the Chief," I could see why Bettylu was so enthused about this newcomer. Without displaying any arrogance, Barack spoke with the wisdom and earnest self-assurance of someone much older. Any law firm or corporation in America would have paid handsomely to recruit a guy like him, I thought. Instead, he had returned to Chicago to sign up voters in the neighborhoods where, before law school, he had worked as a community organizer. In a city where politics was too often treated as a business proposition, Obama's decision to turn down a private-sector windfall to lead a voter registration drive impressed me. He was clearly ambitious, but those ambitions seemed less about doing well than about doing good.

I didn't keep in close touch with Barack during the next few years, though I bumped into him at the occasional political event. I knew he had joined a small law firm, well known around town for its support of progressive causes. He was practicing civil rights and employment law and teaching at the University of Chicago Law School. He had married Michelle Robinson, another promising Harvard Law School grad, who had worked for Mayor Daley. The couple had settled in Hyde Park, which made sense because it was close to the university. It also was the perfect base for a brainy, reform-minded black man contemplating a run for office. To the extent that I thought about it, which wasn't much, it seemed to me that Barack was shrewdly and methodically preparing himself for a career in public life.

In late 1994, three years after Obama returned to Chicago, his opportunity came. State senator Alice Palmer, a fiery but flighty independent Democrat from Barack's South Side district, announced an exploratory campaign to challenge Congressman Mel Reynolds, who had been indicted for having sexual relations with a sixteen-year-old campaign volunteer. Palmer's seat had an illustrious history. Back in 1966, her predecessor, Richard Newhouse, had become one of two African Americans to successfully challenge the Daley machine for the state senate. For a quarter century, Newhouse, an attorney from Hyde Park, was a maverick voice in Springfield, and in 1975 he became the first African American to run for mayor of Chicago. His campaign, though unsuccessful, helped lay the foundation for Harold Washington's election as mayor eight years later.

Newhouse's seat would be a potential launching pad for Obama, who quickly became the choice of Palmer and key progressive leaders in the district. Yet as the filing date approached, Obama's glide path to office ran into unexpected turbulence. Reynolds's conviction forced a special election in the fall of 1995, which Palmer lost to Jesse Jackson Jr. Soon after, she rescinded her pledge to retire from the state senate and instead sought reelection. When Barack refused to defer to her wishes and step aside, Palmer chose to take him on in the March primary. Yet Barack, who stood a good chance of losing the primary to an established political figure, challenged Palmer's hastily prepared candidacy petitions, and she was thrown off the ballot for lack of sufficient signatures.

It was a controversial move—and a revealing one as well—to dispatch a popular incumbent and former ally on a technicality. Barack might have felt that Palmer had broken her commitment. Yet in effectively ending her career to launch his own, Barack had engaged in the bare-knuckle politics that they didn't teach at Harvard. I made a mental note. This thoughtful and polished young man had a competitive edge. Clearly he could be tough, unsentimental, and even bruising when the situation demanded. I would see that quality surface at critical junctures in future campaigns, when his will to win required something more than Marquess of Queensberry rules.

If some of his new constituents were dismayed by the way in which Obama reached the state capital of Springfield, most were pleased by his work once he arrived. In his first term, Obama—encouraged by my old mentor Paul Simon, who had just retired from the U.S. Senate—cosponsored and passed the state's first significant campaign finance reform law in a generation. It took dead aim at one of the perks most cherished by politicians and most despised by reformers. Under it, public officials were allowed to pocket campaign contributions for personal use as long as they paid the appropriate income taxes. Whatever you called it—tipping, or legalized bribery—it was an egregious practice, and Obama, bolstered by growing public outrage, persuaded his colleagues to grandfather out the tawdry loophole. I knew that anytime you could persuade Illinois politicians to forgo money, it was an impressive bit of work.

In this and other early initiatives, Barack demonstrated an uncanny ability to forge consensus, often mediating between the parties and among factions within his own. It was a skill he had honed as a community organizer and as editor of the law review at Harvard, where he harmonized a host of noisy intellectuals of varied philosophical stripes. Barack cleaved close to Emil Jones, a wily, old Chicago precinct captain and sewer inspector who had worked his way up to become the state senate's Democratic leader. The two had first met when Barack was a community organizer, prodding Jones and other local officials for action on a new school to give dropouts a second chance. In Obama's first year, Jones tapped him to lead the Democrats in complex negotiations with the Republican majority over how the state would adopt and implement the new national welfare reform law. The resulting Illinois version was still tough but more humane than the guidelines adopted by many other states. Obama quickly mastered the senate, earning the admiration of many of his colleagues and the resentment of only a few. Still, almost no one believed Springfield would contain Barack's interest or ambition for long. "He's too big a talent for this place," one of his colleagues told me.

In the summer of 1999, a little more than two years after joining the state senate, Obama asked to meet with me again. Earlier in the year, Daley had won a fourth term by crushing Bobby Rush, a South Side congressman, carrying 45 percent of the black vote citywide and even winning in Rush's home ward, an almost unimaginable rebuke in the parochial world of Chicago politics. Obama had little respect for Rush, who had risen to prominence as a leader of the Black Panthers in the late '60s, but had long since settled into a comfortable career as a run-of-the-mill Chicago politician. Eager to move up, Obama saw opportunity in Rush's stumble. "I think Bobby is vulnerable," he told me. "I'm going to take a shot."

Barack asked for my help, but I still was Daley's media consultant and, having just helped engineer his landslide, felt it would be overkill to work to purge Rush from Congress. It would have looked like old-school political revenge, which is exactly how Rush would have framed it. That would have been bad for Daley and me, and wouldn't have helped Barack. So I recommended some consultants and offered behind-the-scenes advice where I could.

Obama's calculation was that if he could run up the score among white voters, who constituted more than a quarter of the primary electorate, and hold his own among black voters, he could eke out a win. It turned out to be a very bad calculation. Rush was universally known within the black community and, despite his poor showing against Daley, generally well liked. That support only grew when, in October '99, Rush's twenty-nine-year-old son, Huey, was shot on a Chicago street and died four days later, a tragedy all too familiar to residents of Chicago's South Side. At the same time, Rush subtly positioned Obama as the effete candidate of outsiders: a Harvard-trained professor alien to the district and the community. Obama, who started the race as an unknown to most of the district's voters, was crushed in the black wards and lost the primary by thirty points.

For a man who had known so much success, the outcome was stinging. It was also costly. The race left Barack not only dispirited but broke. Between his legislative duties and the demands of the campaign, Obama, now the father of two small daughters, had sacrificed a good deal of his outside income to politics. It was money he could ill afford to forgo, given the cost of raising kids, covering the mortgage, and paying off the student loan debts he and Michelle had accrued. So when we spoke in the early summer of 2002, at a time when I was contemplating what direction my future should take, Barack was also at a crossroads, and thinking about a Hail Mary pass in the hope of regenerating his political career.

"I'm looking at the U.S. Senate in 2004," he said. "I promised Michelle that if I did it, this would be up or out for me. If it doesn't work, I'm going to have to go out and make a living."

If Barack was prepared to roll the dice on his career, it seemed like an audacious bet. The Republican incumbent, Senator Peter Fitzgerald, was indisputably vulnerable. A quirky conservative, Fitzgerald had won the Senate seat in 1998 primarily because of the baggage that Moseley Braun carried. Yet to face Fitzgerald, Obama would have to win a Democratic primary, and many Democrats wanted a crack at Fitzgerald, and several seemed to have more political advantages than Obama. After all, he had just failed badly in a House race in a largely black district. Now he wanted to aim higher—a black man from the South Side of Chicago with no money, no statewide organization, and precious little name recognition—and that's before you considered the problem that Obama's exotic surname rhymed with that of the hated terrorist who, one year earlier, had masterminded the horrific 9/11 attacks that killed three thousand Americans. How accepting would voters be of a black man with an alien-sounding name in the wake of that?

In our first conversations about the Senate race, I made these points to Obama, and suggested alternative paths. I was concerned that by aiming too high, Obama could gamble away his career. Why didn't he wait and run for mayor after Daley was done? Barack would be the perfect candidate to bridge the city's divides. That was years off, he said. He also rejected my suggestion that he consider running in a primary against Danny Davis, a thoroughly decent but hardly impactful U.S. congressman from the West Side. A few precincts of Obama's senate district extended into Davis's, giving him some rationale for running in the district, which included the upscale downtown and lakefront high-rises where Obama might find support. But Davis was a friend, Obama said. Besides, "If I am going to take one last shot, I have to take it soon and it should be for something I really want to do."

Our conversations continued into the fall, and the more we talked, the more I realized that, despite the odds and obstacles, this was exactly where I wanted to be. Barack personified the kind of politics and politician I believed in. He seemed motivated by a fundamental conviction, born of his own experience that, in America, everyone who's willing to work for it should get a fair chance to succeed. He was principled enough to stand alone when necessary, but pragmatic enough to make deals and get things done. Besides, I felt it was a disgrace that after Moseley Braun's defeat, there was not a single African American in the U.S. Senate. Barack's election would make the Senate a more representative body. Despite my words of caution, I was energized by the prospect of helping him.

Two other leading candidates had approached me about the race.

Dan Hynes, the Illinois state comptroller, was a thoughtful and serious young politician, well known to voters and well liked by Democratic officials across the state. His father, Tom, a former Cook County official, state senate president, and Chicago ward committeeman, had many friends within the state party and organized labor who would be active on Dan's behalf.

Blair Hull, a former Vegas card counter who made a fortune betting on commodities, had gotten a taste of politics backing Blagojevich. A diffident speaker with no public record, Hull was far from a natural, but a net worth of upward of half a billion dollars and a willingness to spend liberally would make him a player regardless. Underscoring that point, Hull had already hired Blagojevich's consultants, Squier, Knapp, and Dunn, but was willing to pay the freight to get us on board, too.

In a meeting with Hull, I warned him that politics could be a nasty business and that he needed to be prepared for every aspect of his life to be closely scrutinized. This was particularly true for a newcomer to the public arena, a lesson I painfully learned while working for Hofeld. I had heard gossip that Hull once had been treated for substance abuse. He unflinchingly acknowledged this. When I asked him about another rumor—that he had been accused of domestic violence—he shot me a long, icy stare. "There's no paper on that," he said. In the parlance of my old profession, it was a "nondenial denial."

Even without his obvious liabilities, I wouldn't have taken up Hull on his offer. Choosing one of the other candidates might have been a smarter business decision than signing on with Obama, but neither would have addressed my growing sense of alienation from politics. I loved the exhilarating back-and-forth of campaigns and the urgent challenge of framing messages and producing media to deliver them. It was certainly a better living than I had ever imagined. Yet I hadn't gotten into politics simply for the adrenaline rush of competition or for the comforts the money provided. After two decades, I felt worn down by the growing cynicism and acrimony of campaigns. I was tired of ministering to needy candidates and craven donors and wrestling with my own fears about living up to their expectations. Long shot that he might be—and perhaps even because he was a long shot—Obama offered a path back to the ideals that had drawn me to politics in the first place.

"You know, I could make a boatload of money doing one of these other guys," I told Susan. "And, I don't know, maybe one of them has a better chance. But if I could help elect Barack to the Senate, that would be something I could be proud of for the rest of my life."

Even after sitting out the Illinois governor's race, I found 2002 a busy year. With Blagojevich moving on, I got a call from an old friend who saw his own opportunity.

"I'm thinking of running for Rod's seat," said Rahm Emanuel, who had left the Clinton administration in 1998 and returned to Chicago to make money as an investment banker. "Do you think I can win?"

It was a fair question. Rahm was not a natural for the seat. Raised in the affluent northern suburbs, he was new to the district, which stretched from the liberal North Side lakefront across the Northwest Side that was still heavily populated with eastern Europeans. He had never run for office before. He was a Jew with an ethnic-sounding name, known for his profanity-laced tirades. In two short years as a corporate dealmaker, he had pocketed millions.

"I know you'll win," I said, without hesitation.

"What do you mean 'you know'?" he asked incredulously. "How do you know?"

"Because you're not allowed to lose," I told him. "It's against your nature. You're like a heat-seeking missile. You always hit your target."

For Rahm, failure of any kind was a terrifying prospect. His father, Ben, a physician, was an Israeli immigrant who demanded excellence from his children. Report cards were posted on the refrigerator, where anything less than an A was considered an unpardonable blemish. Dinners at home with Ben, and Rahm's mom, Marsha, were raucous affairs, in which each of the Emanuel boys competed for attention. Not surprisingly, they all grew up to be superachievers. Older brother Zeke became an oncologist and world-renowned bioethicist. Younger brother Ari became a Hollywood superagent so colorful and influential that HBO would build a hit show, *Entourage*, around a character based on him. Losing? That was not an option, and Rahm's allergy to it already was legendary.

After he raised a then-prodigious seventy-one million dollars for Clinton in 1992, Rahm was rewarded with the position of White House political director. Young and brash, he quickly antagonized people all over Washington—including, most damagingly, the First Lady. Hillary wanted Rahm gone, he was told. When he shared this with me, I told him to pack his things. "Come on home, man. It's over." Rahm refused. "I work for the president of the United States and until the president of the United States tells me to go, I'm not leaving. I didn't come here to get fired. I'm not going to let it end this way."

Rahm wasn't fired. Instead, he was relieved of his title and relegated to a windowless basement office from which he was assigned to provide assistance on unspecified "special projects." A few months of this purgatory, the pooh-bahs reasoned, and he would take the hint. Not Rahm. In 1994 he helped orchestrate the White House campaign for a crime bill that included hotly debated gun control measures and he spearheaded passage of the North American Free Trade Agreement, over the objections of organized labor and many progressive Democrats. By the second Clinton administration, he was sitting twenty feet from the Oval Office, an indispensable force with the lofty title of senior adviser to the president.

On paper, the congressional race would be no slam dunk. Nancy Kaszak, the former legislator who, in 1996, had waged a pitched battle against Blagojevich, was running again, with strong support from the liberal and women's communities. Kaszak had a valuable Polish surname and deeper roots in the district. Yet, as predicted, Rahm was relentless, outraising and out-organizing his opponent and rolling out all his assets, including a campaign visit from President Clinton. None of this was a surprise, of course. The question was how my ambitious friend would deal with the everyday people he was bidding to represent. Would he treat them as necessary irritants in his climb to power? Or would he warm to them and the task of serving them?

It was a revelation to watch Rahm grow into the role. He routinely began before dawn at El stations, camped out in supermarkets during the day, and finished late at night, talking to folks in diners, bowling alleys, and fire stations. I don't know whether Rahm had an impact on the voters just because he showed up everywhere, but they surely had an impact on him. He still had the win-at-all costs mentality, but politics for him had ceased to be a remote-control exercise. He was coming face-to-face with people, listening to their stories and, more important, hearing their stories. Even he was surprised how much those interactions moved him. "I like being out there with people," he told me.

During the race, I would hear from Rahm a half-dozen times a day. The conversations would almost always begin the same way: "What do you hear? What do you think?" Reassuring Rahm at all hours of the day and night was part of the service. So when the phone rang at 7:00 a.m. on February 18, a few weeks before his primary, Susan wasn't terribly surprised by the voice on the other end of the line. Yet this day was different. It was the day we were to take Lauren to live at Misericordia. We knew it would be good for Lauren, and she was eager for the move. She would have an active life and friendships there that we simply couldn't have provided at home. Misericordia was a short car ride away, but after twenty years in which she was our constant charge and companion, it was a heart-wrenching day.

I was out running a last-minute chore when Rahm called, but he sensed the heaviness in Susan's voice and asked her what was wrong. Later that day, he called my home again. "Sorry, Rahm, you keep missing him," Susan said. "Try the office." "I didn't call for David," he said. "I called for you. I just wanted to see how you were doing." That call, coming amid the frenzy of his own campaign, told me a lot about him. It was a kind and unexpected gesture that we would never forget.

Rahm's humanity—a phrase thought by some in Washington to be an oxymoron—was apparent also in an interview we filmed for the campaign during which he reflected on the children's health care law he had helped pass during the Clinton administration. Speaking as the parent of three small children, Rahm's eyes filled with tears when he talked about what the new law had meant to millions of children and families. We turned that interview into an ad. In another, a world-weary Chicago police sergeant named Les Smulevitz spoke approvingly of Rahm's work on Clinton's crime bill, and closed with a twist: "And I'd tell you that even if I weren't his uncle." The surprising fact that Rahm's uncle Les was a cop on the Northwest Side of Chicago was no small matter in a district that was home to thousands of police officers and firefighters.

In the end, the "heat-seeking missile" hit its target. Rahm won the primary by a comfortable margin, and went on to a landslide in the general election.

My central focus that year was Tom Vilsack's reelection campaign in Iowa.

Vilsack had been a fine governor. He had followed through on his commitments to expand early childhood education and to strengthen the state's community colleges. He had expanded health care for children and promoted the production of wind energy and biofuels, which meant jobs for Iowans and new opportunities for Iowa farmers. Yet like every governor elected in 1998, when the economy was booming, Vilsack was facing a serious challenge now that the country was mired in recession. So, five months before the election, Vilsack trailed the most likely Republican nominee, Doug Gross (former chief of staff to longtime governor Terry Branstad), by nine points in our polls. Gross had hired Mike Murphy, an incisive and creative Republican media consultant with whom I had tangled before, and lost. It was going to be a war.

I knew we couldn't play defense or simply tout Vilsack's accomplishments when far fewer than 50 percent of voters approved of his performance in our own polling. We had to shine a bright light on the alternative, and Gross was an inviting target. Since leaving government, he had become a leading lawyer-lobbyist in Des Moines. Among his clients were the widely reviled corporate hog confinements that were springing up, polluting local communities and putting family hog farmers out of business. Even before the Republican primary in June, we were hammering Gross with testimonials from Iowans who had been victimized by the hog confinements and Gross's heavy-handed advocacy for them. By August, we had begun to seize control of the race, but when I visited Vilsack at the governor's mansion to prep him for a film shoot, he seemed not to have gotten that news.

"You don't have to sugarcoat it," said the governor, who was given to bouts of gloominess, and was more apt to believe erroneous public polling that showed him behind than his own. "I've already told Christie and the boys that we're probably going to lose."

"Lose?" I said in disbelief. "Tom, we're kicking this guy's ass. We're not going to lose!"

On Election Day, Vilsack beat Gross by eight points. Of the eleven new Democratic governors elected in 1998, only Vilsack and California's Gray Davis survived—and Davis lost a recall vote the following year.

As the Iowa votes were being cast, I got an e-mail of surrender from my counterpart Murphy, who had become both a fierce competitor and a close friend. "Well, old buddy, it looks like you're going to win the Iowa Cup this year," read Murphy's gracious note. "It turns out that hog shit sticks to my guy like Velcro."

As I oversaw Iowa and our other 2002 races, I kept a close eye on the emerging 2004 U.S. Senate race in Illinois. It was still an uphill struggle for Obama, but

I could see a path to a primary victory if he forged the same black-liberal coalition that had propelled Carol Moseley Braun to the Senate in 1992. There was one major obstacle: Carol Moseley Braun.

After a brief stint as ambassador to New Zealand and a failed attempt at nut farming in Georgia, Moseley Braun had returned to Chicago to explore the possibility of seeking her old seat. While she lacked the support to win a general election, Moseley Braun still retained the loyalty of elements of her old coalition. If she were to run, Obama's path would be blocked, and he knew it.

A primary poll Obama had commissioned in the spring made this abundantly clear. In it, Moseley Braun led a crowded field with 31 percent of the vote, fueled by overwhelming support among African Americans. Obama was at a mere 6 percent, just outside the poll's margin of error. (Obama's pollster, Paul Harstad, had also probed whether Obama might have better luck campaigning under his childhood nickname of Barry, the theory being that one exotic name was enough of a challenge. While the poll bore this out, Obama laughed it off. "That's fine, but my name's Barack," he said.) The bottom line was clear, and Obama, having been schooled by Bobby Rush so recently, knew it. He was not about to take on another well-known icon of the black community. "The ball's pretty much in Carol's court," he said. "If she runs, I don't really have a shot."

I began offering Barack advice informally that fall as he positioned himself for a campaign that might not materialize. One of the first issues on which he sought my counsel would turn out to be pivotal to the Senate race and Obama's future—though neither of us realized it at the time. The U.S. Senate was about to consider the authorization of military action in Iraq. Days before the vote, Bettylu Saltzman invited Barack to speak at a small antiwar rally in front of a federal building in downtown Chicago. The question was, should he accept? Most of the other potential Democratic candidates were either silent or supporting President Bush's war resolution, which was polling well in the feverish, post-9/11 climate. Obama's inclination was to weigh in on the other side. He was convinced the war would be a mistake, yet he still wanted my read on the politics of an antiwar stance.

Pete Giangreco, a Chicago-based direct mail consultant and longtime collaborator of mine, was also on the call. Pete, one of the lead strategists for Blagojevich, knew the state well, and was no shrinking violet. Built like a bulldog, he had a personality to match. On this, however, he was nervous. "This Iraq thing is pretty popular," Giangreco said. "You'll fire up the Left, but long term, it's risky."

I argued that the long term didn't mean much if Obama didn't win the Democratic primary. "The folks we need to win this primary, the folks who would support you—they're going to strongly oppose this war," I said.

Barack took in the discussion, and made his decision. "Well, I don't believe this war is a good idea, and I'm very comfortable saying so," he said. "The folks who invited me are good friends and supporters we're going to be counting on. I think I should go."

The next day, Susan and my younger son, Ethan, now in high school, attended the rally with a few thousand others. I didn't show up, nor did I send a crew to tape it. Years later I would kick myself for that decision. "Boy, Barack made a great speech," Susan reported that evening. "I think he did really well."

Looking back, Obama had delivered one of the most cogent arguments offered anywhere against the resolution the Senate would overwhelmingly pass nine days later. Arguing that war sometimes was necessary and unavoidable, Obama told the crowd that the looming invasion of Iraq did not pass the test.

"I know that even a successful war against Iraq will require a U.S. occupation of undetermined length, at undetermined cost, with undetermined consequences," he told the crowd. "I know that an invasion of Iraq without a clear rationale and without strong international support will only fan the flames of the Middle East, and encourage the worst, rather than best, impulses of the Arab world, and strengthen the recruitment arm of Al Qaeda.

"I am not opposed to all wars. I'm opposed to dumb wars."

It was one of my early insights into the capabilities of this relatively green but promising candidate. Viewing the rally as more of a throwaway than a seminal event, I did not even ask to see his remarks beforehand. Overnight, he had produced a brilliantly reasoned, elegantly stated critique of the war strategy, and had delivered it with power and conviction. His declaration that he was not opposed to all wars, just "dumb" wars, was both genuine and shrewd. It reflected his thinking, but also prevented opponents, then and in the future, from disqualifying him as a knee-jerk pacifist.

As prescient and meaningful as Obama's analysis would prove to be, there was precious little at the time to mark its historical significance. All of fourteen seconds of his remarks made it to the evening news. Newspapers did little more than note his presence. For the activists who witnessed it, however, he had laid down a marker that would separate him from the other major Senate contenders.

Still, Obama was forced to play a waiting game. The mercurial Moseley Braun held his plans hostage as she pondered her options. All he could do was touch base with potential supporters, asking for their provisional backing.

Obama had spoken with Moseley Braun to try to assess her intentions, indicating that he would defer to her plans; he gleaned little. Also, while Carol's prospects of winning a general election were dim, I assumed her huge primary advantage would draw her into the race and bar an Obama candidacy. So I was shocked in January 2003 when the *Sun-Times* reported that Moseley Braun would not seek her old Senate seat. She had something bigger in mind: Carol was planning a race for president.

It seemed like a preposterous idea, but I was all for it. Now Obama had a shot. I called him to chew over the news.

"Game on," he said.

PART THREE

NINE

MAGIC CARPET RIDE

THERE WAS LITTLE TIME to waste.

Befitting her grand ambition, Moseley Braun timed her surprise announcement for the beginning of the Martin Luther King Jr. weekend. Though the Senate primary was more than a year away, Barack agreed that he should stake his claim quickly, before a more prominent African American filled the vacuum Carol's stunning decision had created. So the Tuesday after the King holiday, we gathered at my office, hammered out an announcement statement, and headed to a downtown hotel for a hastily called press conference.

Looking back, I find it quaint to think of pulling off such an important announcement without weeks of planning and deliberation. Yet in January 2003, Barack Obama was just a small speedboat trying to launch before some battleship came along and capsized his ambitions.

"Four years ago, Peter Fitzgerald bought himself a Senate seat, and he's betrayed Illinois ever since," Obama said. Fitzgerald came from a wealthy banking family, and had spent his millions on his '98 campaign. "But we are here to take it back on behalf of the people of Illinois."

The announcement took place in a cramped meeting room at the Allegro Hotel, just a block from City Hall, convenient enough to reporters to guarantee at least a little coverage. Flanking Barack were two of the city's three black congressmen, Danny Davis and Jesse Jackson Jr. Jackson's presence was particularly meaningful. He was a popular young officeholder, widely regarded as the black community leader with the most potential for higher office. It was noteworthy that the ambitious young heir to the most famous name in African American politics had deferred his ambitions to Obama, whom young Jackson would generously refer to in a subsequent ad as "the best our community has to offer."

Additionally, Obama was joined by his patron and the newly elected state senate president, Emil Jones Jr. Several white state senate colleagues from suburban and downstate Illinois surrounded Obama at the press conference, as did a handful of luminaries from Chicago's progressive and reform communities. All in all, it was an impressive tableau, especially given the short notice we'd had to pull it together.

One notable absentee was Michelle Obama. With a community relations position at the University of Chicago, and two small children at home, Michelle appeared rarely during this campaign—and certainly not at spur-of-the-moment events. It was clear that she and Barack had an understanding: she would tolerate one last political adventure with all the long absences that the campaign and his work in Springfield demanded of him, but he could not expect her to play a big role in it.

By April, Fitzgerald was out. Perhaps spooked by the polls, or disillusioned by the experience, he announced that he would quit the U.S. Senate after one term. Now that we were vying for an open seat, the prospects for Democrats were even better. It was a presidential year, which would bring out a big Democratic turnout in a state that had become solidly blue. Whoever won the Senate primary would be the odds-on favorite to win the seat. Our challenge was to persuade a skeptical political and donor community that a little-known black man with an alien name and unproven campaign skills—a man who just a few years earlier had been trounced by Bobby Rush—could topple a formidable primary field.

With his career on the line, Obama dedicated himself completely to the task at hand. When he wasn't in Springfield or on the road, he spent hour upon hour in his cramped, downtown campaign office, dialing for dollars and support. Maybe he drew inspiration from the iconic photo he had hanging on the wall behind him, showing a young and improbable heavyweight champion, Muhammad Ali, standing triumphantly over the once-indomitable Sonny Liston.

I would like to believe that Obama pursued me simply because he had a keen eye for talent and kindred spirits. Still, he also knew that I had credibility with the state's political players and press corps. If I were willing to bet on him, Obama bluntly acknowledged, others would give him a longer look. Obama wanted to use me, and I was more than willing to be used. For much of 2003, my job was to meet with potential supporters and make the case for how Barack could win and why I believed he could pull it off.

Another critical ally was Jones, the state senate president who had taken Obama under his wing. In many ways, they were an odd pair. Nearly seventy, Jones was a gruff, plainspoken ward heeler—which is how Obama refers to him in his memoirs of his days as a community organizer—who patiently rose through the ranks of the Democratic machine. Obama was the Hawaiian-born, Harvard-educated law school instructor, a young man in a hurry, audaciously trying to jump to the front of the line. Yet there grew between them a strong personal relationship. Jones took an almost filial pride in Obama, who, from day one, had shown the potential to be a great asset in the state senate. Obama found in the streetwise senate president a political guardian angel and father figure. When John Stroger, a powerful South Side committeeman, told Jones that he was committed to young Hynes over Obama because of his political debt to Hynes's father, Jones exploded. "How many generations do we have to pay off these debts, John?" Jones demanded. "What about our sons? Barack is like a son to me."

The senate president's zeal was not lost on those who would have to deal with him in Springfield. Obama had been a strong ally to the state's powerful public employee unions, and shared their progressive bent on the issues. Yet he was no sure bet, and the state AFL-CIO was tilting toward Hynes, whose father had long-standing ties to the mostly white building trades unions. Still, with strong encouragement from Jones, the SEIU and AFSCME would split with their labor brethren, giving Obama their endorsement and a bounty of campaign cash and foot soldiers.

I saw in these first months the two sides of Barack Obama. As he demonstrated years earlier when he shoved Palmer off the ballot, and as he had shown in Springfield, he was no dreamy reformer. He was idealistic in his aspirations, but pragmatic in pursuit of them—ready and willing to do what was necessary to advance his political and legislative goals. At the same time, as the campaign evolved, I saw the emergence of the inspiring tribune of hope for change in America and its relationship to the world. It was a preview of the man the nation would come to know and embrace.

For much of the U.S. Senate campaign, Barack's companion and traveling aide on the trail was David Katz, a kid from Hyde Park who had recently graduated from the University of Michigan. Katz had many virtues, but I think the one Obama most appreciated was his proficiency in golf. Once, during the spring, I called Barack in Springfield and caught him on the golf course. "I'm in the middle of a match with Katz and we're playing for money, can I call you back?" When he did, I told him he had worried me. "I backed you because I thought you were a smart guy. But now you tell me you're playing golf for money against a scratch golfer who was on the team at Michigan?" Barack was incredulous. "Don't be ridiculous," he said. "He was on my team. We just took a nice dinner from a couple of my colleagues."

In addition to his value as a ringer, Katz was a skilled photographer and had a good ear to go along with his keen eye. One day, I called him to check on the progress of Obama's swing through the small towns of Southern Illinois. We didn't expect to do well there, in what was akin to the rural South, but in a close contest, we couldn't afford to surrender that turf completely. Katz's report caught me by surprise.

"We've had a great day down here," he said. "Visited a veterans' hall. He did well. The reaction was really positive."

I scratched my head, and mentioned it to Obama when I spoke with him at the end of the day.

"Why do you sound so surprised?" he asked.

"Let me see," I said, "I guess because you're a black guy named Barack Obama in an all-white section of deep Southern Illinois. Maybe I'm nuts, but I thought it might be a little challenging."

"No, you don't get it," Obama said. "These folks? They're just like my grandparents from rural Kansas. I talk about my grandfather, and how he marched in Patton's army. And I talk about my grandmother, who was a Rosie the Riveter. And we have a great time."

Listening to Barack, I reflected on how comfortable he seemed with people wherever he found them. He moved as easily in a VFW hall downstate as he did in an inner-city church in Chicago or a tony suburban parlor. He had lived in so many different worlds that he felt comfortable in all of them. Born to an interracial couple in Hawaii, he was raised by a single mother, partly in Indonesia, but also by his white, working-class grandparents. He had won scholarships to exclusive schools, but spent three years working to lift impoverished communities. His ability to navigate all these worlds so seamlessly was a gift few politicians—few people, generally—shared. Also, at a time when our politics had grown so divisive, he was the rare politician who genuinely could transcend race and class divides with a remarkable ability to appeal to our common values, hopes, and dreams.

This was evident not just on the campaign trail but also in Springfield, the capital of our large, diverse state. Illinois spans from the quintessential big city and sprawling suburbs in the north to the farms and coal mine country of the south, the tip of which is closer to Little Rock than Chicago. In between are many small industrial towns that had been battered through the decades by drastic changes in the economy. The legislature reflects that diversity, which, in many ways, reflects our nation. Part of Obama's success in navigating this terrain, I learned, was rooted in another of his rare qualities that too many politicians lack: empathy.

"My mother drummed into me that I should always try to put myself in the other person's shoes," Obama told me. "I try to understand what people are saying, and where they're coming from."

It was not a quality he was taught in the classroom, but an innate virtue that he had honed in the hallowed halls of Harvard and on the gritty Chicago streets. So I was not surprised when I heard about a debate in Springfield over gun control in which Obama, whose inner-city district was ravaged by violence, engaged a colleague from a rural district, where guns were a cherished way of life. Instead of confronting his colleague, Barack sought common ground.

"I understand that, for you, hunting has been a tradition passed on from generation to generation," Obama said. "Your father probably took you out at dawn to hunt, like his dad did with him. And now, you're doing the same with your own kids. But where I come from, mothers sit by the window, anxiously waiting for their kids to come home from school, hoping they don't get shot in some gang crossfire. There has to be a way we can find to both preserve your traditions and save our children."

As president, he later would be criticized for valuing dinners with his family over socializing with politicians and donors. Yet, as a legislator stuck in Springfield, three hours from home, Obama made the most of dinners, golf outings, and poker games with colleagues from both parties, developing warm relationships that crossed the aisle and opened the door to constructive dialogue when it came time to do business.

In the spring of 2003, as he geared up for the Senate race, Obama had a new opportunity to bring those relationships to bear. For the first time in twenty-six years, Democrats held both the governor's office and a majority in the state senate. With an ally in the senate president's chair, Obama was determined to tackle legislation that he never could have contemplated under Republican control.

Among the dozens of bills he took up, two were potentially explosive. The death penalty and racial profiling were issues that could strengthen Obama as he sought to galvanize the black electorate. They also were knotty, emotional questions fraught with difficulty and political peril.

In 2000, then-governor George Ryan suspended the Illinois death penalty shortly after a death row inmate became the thirteenth person in Illinois to be acquitted or to have his charges dropped since the state reinstated the death penalty in 1977. Some were exonerated by DNA testing; a number were convicted on the basis of coerced confessions during police interrogations. In 2003, Obama convened a series of meetings between police and prosecutors, defense attorneys and civil libertarians to thrash out thorny issues surrounding the Illinois law before the death penalty would be reinstated. After months of negotiation, he passed a landmark bill with strong bipartisan support requiring police interrogations to be videotaped in all homicide cases.

Another bill Obama passed that spring dealt with racial profiling in traffic stops by police. "If you're a young black man behind the wheel, you're going to get stopped by the police at some point," Barack said. "Everyone in the community knows it." Yet, passionate as he was about rectifying this practice that stigmatized and, in some cases, traumatized young black men, he followed the same disciplined process as he had on the death penalty, bringing disparate interests together to hammer out a compromise. The final bill required police to keep records of every traffic stop, including the race of the motorists, and submit these to the state. It also mandated sensitivity training for police to reduce incidents of profiling and needless confrontations.

Neither bill fully satisfied either side of the debate. Death penalty opponents preferred an outright ban, which would come later. Police were wary of any taping at all. Some opponents of racial profiling wanted stronger proscriptions than the Obama bill would yield. Law enforcement feared that the new law would hamstring them. Yet Barack persuaded critics on the left that these laws, while imperfect, were a big step forward, and he argued to police and prosecutors that the laws would protect all those officers who were doing things by the book from being tarred by a few bad actors.

To be sure, it was shrewd and deft politics, yielding key achievements that we would tout in the campaign. Beyond those victories, however, was a larger portrait of Obama, who pursued progressive goals in a pragmatic way. He gave all sides a fair hearing and refused to allow the perfect solution to stand in the way of a good one. He was an idealist but not an ideologue. And while his openness to compromise occasionally annoyed the Left, he was a bridge builder at a time when so many were dismayed by the withering partisanship that had descended on Washington.

Just a year after Obama's antiwar speech, public opinion had caught up with his view on Iraq. The weapons of mass destruction we had invaded to secure proved illusory. Rather than being greeted as "liberators," as Vice President Dick Cheney had forecast, we were mired in the sectarian warfare of which Obama had warned. Also, partisan anger toward Bush, Cheney, and their entire bellicose crowd was on the rise. I saw it surface in an odd way in a heated race in the fall of 2003 in Philadelphia, where I was working to reelect an embattled client, Mayor John F. Street.

It's not that Street hadn't done a good job. He had greatly expanded after-school programs. He had pressured drug dealers off the street corners on which they had been loitering in crime-ridden neighborhoods. He'd launched an all-out war on the abandoned cars that littered the streets of Philadelphia, and won. It's just that Street, a black man who worked his way up from rural poverty to become mayor of one of America's largest cities, took pride in bending his knee to no one. He didn't romance voters in the way to which they had become accustomed. He spoke his mind to a fault, took positions that were impolitic, and generally operated under the assumption that if you won an election by more than a percentage point, you had probably wasted a lot of time and money. So, by the end of his first term, he had provoked a reaction that was highly unusual in politics. His job approval rating was higher than his popularity. Philadelphians liked what he was doing; they just didn't like *him*. So his race against a Republican challenger in an overwhelmingly Democratic city was no sure thing.

As we approached the final month of the campaign, I got a call from George Burrell, Street's savvy political deputy at City Hall.

"I think we have a problem."

"Problem?" I asked warily.

"Yes, it seems we've found a bug in the mayor's office."

"A bug?"

"Yes, a listening device."

"And who do we think this bug belongs to?" I said. I really didn't have to ask, but was hoping against hope for an unexpected explanation.

"It appears to belong to the United States government," Burrell said, slamming the door on my wishful thinking.

Four weeks before the election, the news would be filled with headlines about a federal investigation of the mayor and his administration. It struck me, as I thought about it, that this was our problem but also our opportunity. In an overwhelmingly Democratic town, a probe launched by the Republican Justice Department in Washington would surely be greeted with skepticism, perhaps even outrage. I called Burrell back. "We need to hold a press conference on the steps of City Hall and accuse John Ashcroft of trying to steal this election." (Attorney General Ashcroft, a well-known conservative ideologue, was highly unpopular among Democrats.) When Street confronted reporters, frantic over the news, he came armed with a line I had written for him: "I'm happy to speak into a microphone I can see!"

On Election Day, Street rolled to a crushing victory. The federal probe had thoroughly transformed the race in his favor. Liberal whites, traditionally resistant to Street, decided that any enemy of John Ashcroft's was a friend of theirs. Sensing a looming injustice, an outraged African American community came out in large numbers to support Street, who defeated the Republican by seventeen points. The headline of the *Philadelphia Daily News* the morning after the election said it all: "We Interrupt This Probe . . . for a Landslide!"

Back in Illinois, I was holding off Obama, who nervously eyed the TV ads of some of his rivals, and periodically asked if we weren't ceding too much ground. We didn't have a huge bankroll, however, and I wanted to make sure that when we hit, we hit with force and stayed on the air for the duration of the race. By our estimate, this meant three or four weeks before the primary in March.

I was eager, too. I was excited about the ads we had produced early in 2004 for the primary. The initial ad, narrated by Obama, wove his personal history of defying the odds—as the first black president of the *Harvard Law Review* and on issues such as death penalty reform—into a parable about breaking down barriers. It had strong appeal to the black and liberal voters on whom we were counting. The closing lines tied his personal history to a larger theme.

"Now they say we can't change Washington?" said the telegenic young legislator, stepping forward in the frame. "I'm Barack Obama, I'm running for the United States Senate and I approve this message to say, 'Yes We Can!'"

I loved the closing line because it gave voters a stake in making change happen. It wasn't just about him. It was about what we all could do together. After the first take, though, Obama wrinkled his face and expressed a concern. "'Yes we can.' Is that too corny?" he asked.

I made my case for the line. Still not convinced, Barack turned to Michelle, who had a spare hour and had come to watch him tape his first ad at the home of a neighbor. "Meesh, what do you think?"

Michelle, who was sitting on a staircase, chin in hand, slowly shook her head.

"Not corny," she said.

That was enough. My reassurance had left Obama still wondering, but he deeply trusted Michelle's instincts and connection with people. Her imprimatur immediately sealed the deal, preserving a tag line that would become our rallying cry in this and future campaigns.

A second ad featured Paul Simon, in absentia. Paul, with whom I had repaired my relationship, had been reluctant to endorse in a crowded primary. Yet, having spent his life fighting for civil rights and political reform, it was inconceivable to me that Simon would remain neutral. I wrote him a letter and said so. Two prominent supporters of Obama and longtime political allies of Simon, Newton Minow and Abner Mikva, joined in the lobbying. Finally, in October 2003, I picked up the phone to a familiar, countrified baritone voice.

"Dave, I'm ready to go anytime," Paul told me. "I've been watching and I'm really impressed with Barack. I decided I just can't sit this one out."

Paul's endorsement was a hugely valuable prize. He shared with Obama an approach to politics and a set of values that resonated with the liberal base of the party to whom Paul remained a hero. Yet voters weren't entirely focused on the race yet. Looking to maximize the impact of Paul's endorsement, I suggested that we delay it until closer to the primary. "Why don't we roll this out in a statewide tour with you and Barack after the first of the year?" I said. "It would be a great way to kick off the sprint to the primary." Simon cheerfully agreed.

It never happened. In early December, Paul went in to have a faulty heart valve repaired. The day before his surgery, he called me from the hospital with some thoughts on the campaign and said he was looking forward to the endorsement tour. He was confident he would be ready. Yet the next day, the surgery went tragically awry. Suddenly, shockingly, Paul Simon was dead at the age of seventy-five.

A month later, when we tested Obama's biography with focus groups of liberal Democrats in the northern suburbs, the value of the lost endorsement opportunity was apparent. When these folks heard that Obama was a protégé of the revered Senator Simon, the reaction was kinetic. "That's enough for me," one woman said, echoing a widely held sentiment in the room. "I loved Paul."

I was desperate to communicate to voters the link between Simon and Obama, but how do you tastefully imply the unstated support of a dead man?

To try, I produced an ad featuring the voice of a mystery female narrator, recalling Simon's history and character over archival scenes that I had shot of Paul in action. "State Senator Barack Obama is cut from that same cloth," she said, describing Barack's record as the video shifted to matching footage of Obama on the trail. "I know Barack Obama will be a U.S. senator in the Paul Simon tradition," the narrator declared, as the camera revealed a woman who bore an unmistakable resemblance to the late senator. "You see," she concluded with a sweet smile, "Paul Simon was my dad." We never got Paul's endorsement, but Democratic voters would be moved by this heartfelt testimonial from his daughter, Sheila.

In mid-January, two months before the primary, we trailed Hynes by six points in our internal polling, bunched with Hull and others in the teens. Still, we stuck to our plan, and in late February, just a week after the "Yes We Can" ads started airing, Obama vaulted into a clear lead. Almost overnight, support among African Americans and white liberals nearly doubled. The coalition we envisioned was coming together, but the growth was not limited to these groups. Wherever he traveled, Obama was now encountering warm and enthusiastic crowds, including many who had not been involved in campaigns before. In style and substance, he projected a new kind of politics, and a hungry electorate was catching on. The spirit was contagious.

Some public polls had shown Hull in the lead in early February, though our polls never did. Then, as Barack's campaign started surging, Hull's campaign took a huge hit when, three weeks before Election Day, news surfaced that his ex-wife had asked for an order of protection against him, alleging domestic violence. The rehab story soon followed. The Hull campaign suggested to reporters that I had leaked the stories, and I knew their suspicions traced back to my early conversation with Hull, when I had asked about some of these rumors. Yet I considered those discussions out of bounds, and hadn't leaked the stories. I was certain they had come from the Hynes camp. Hynes had strong support at the Chicago Board of Trade, where Hull had made his fortune over decades. In that hypercompetitive, insular world, the players knew a lot about one another, and particularly about the superstars among them. At the time the stories surfaced, Hynes and Hull were jousting for support downstate. The stories effectively ended Hull's chances.

Then, in late February, as we launched the Simon ad, the newspaper endorsements started coming through. Normally, even effusive newspaper endorsements were of limited value. Yet I had learned, through years of experience, that with minority candidates, editorial endorsements can be a welcome reassurance for white voters who are contemplating what for them would be a precedent-shattering act—voting for a minority candidate. It affirmed their instincts, made the leap less "risky." That certainly proved true for Obama, who won the enthusiastic endorsement of virtually every major newspaper in Illinois.

The *Sun-Times* weighed in first, calling Obama "a rising star" and a doer who "demonstrated an ability to forge partnerships across party lines." Two days later, the generally conservative *Tribune* was just as effusive. Obama, they said, "rises above this field as one of the strongest Democratic candidates Illinois has seen in some time. He richly deserves his party's nomination for the U.S. Senate."

A week after that, the major suburban newspaper, the *Daily Herald*, outdid the *Trib*, praising Obama as "refreshing" for his "evident sense of decency and justice when so many phonies and fools—if not felons—are giving governing a bad name."

"Very few candidates for public office have impressed us in this way," the *Herald* wrote. "Paul Simon comes to mind." We promptly featured each of these editorials in a TV ad.

A week after the launch of the Simon ad, Barack had stretched his lead to fifteen points over Hynes, 36 percent to 21 percent. Hull was a distant third. Blacks and liberals had solidly closed ranks behind Obama, but now he was showing some strength in other communities, swept up by the positive vibe surrounding his campaign. We had not run one negative ad. Obama's candidacy promised a commonsense politics of cooperation and progress, and Illinoisans were responding.

"We're rolling," I reported to the candidate, but he wasn't ready for good news. Barack was not given to giddiness or elation, even when things were going his way. When the game was on the line, he was all business. "Let's just finish it," he said.

We felt bullish enough in the final week to stop polling in order to put every last dime on the air, so we were flying blind. Still, there is a sense of rhythm in a campaign, a feeling that you acquire over time. Barack had the momentum, and you could sense it from the crowds and the media coverage. Yet even we were surprised on Election Night when the numbers began rolling in.

"Axe, our model calls for us to win with thirty-eight percent of the vote," Giangreco said as he scanned the early returns.

"Right. I know. And?"

"This is crazy, but I think we might bust fifty!"

I was thinking back to what a long shot Obama had been when we teamed up a year and a half earlier. We had run the race we hoped to wage, appealing to the best in people by describing what politics could be. We had defied the cynics and beaten the odds. It was as satisfying a moment as I had ever had in politics.

Obama would take an unimaginable 53 percent of the vote in a seven-way race. Hynes finished second, nearly thirty points behind. Even our Election Night crowd estimate was low. We expected hundreds of people at a hotel ballroom in downtown Chicago, but more than a thousand showed up, wanting to be part of it. If Obama was the symbol of a new, inclusive politics, the exultant crowd was the portrait of that vision: old, young, folks of every hue, from every background. Some were familiar faces, but many were new to campaigns. All of them felt as if they were stakeholders in this inspiring journey.

As the results poured in, I was stunned to see that Obama had carried all but one ward, on Chicago's Northwest Side, where two decades earlier white ethnic voters had almost unanimously rejected Harold Washington. I looked up the precinct that housed Saint Pascal Catholic Church, where those bitter protesters had greeted Washington and Walter Mondale. Obama had carried it.

After his rousing victory speech, which was punctuated by chants of "Yes, we can," I took Barack aside and shared this news. As a young community organizer, he had witnessed the ugliness of the Council Wars. He knew what this meant. He smiled broadly and put a hand on my shoulder.

"Harold is smiling down on us tonight," I said.

TEN

SHOT FROM A CANNON

WHEN I WAS A KID, my father and I would occasionally watch chess masters in the park, who silently moved from board to board as they took on multiple opponents at the same time.

Such is the life of a political consultant, and in the spring of 2003, I would add another challenging match to my lineup.

I got a call from Pete Giangreco on behalf of one of his other clients, Senator John Edwards of North Carolina. Edwards was a charismatic trial lawyer elected to the Senate in 1998 with great fanfare. Now he was running for president. I knew that Bob Shrum, who had done Edwards's Senate race, had recently left him to take over as media consultant for the presidential campaign of Edwards's Senate rival, John Kerry of Massachusetts. "Can you go to Washington and talk to Edwards?" Giangreco asked. "He needs a media consultant and is really interested in you."

I called my friend Mike Murphy, the Republican consultant who had masterminded the clever, insurgent presidential candidacy of John McCain in 2000. He urged me to take it slow.

"Don't make any judgments off your first meeting," he said. "Spend a few days traveling with the guy and get a sense of whether this will work."

But I was eager.

I didn't know Edwards, but I believed strongly that an economic populist, in times of growing economic inequality and stress, could pose the greatest challenge to Bush. Besides, the starting gun was about to sound for the Super Bowl of American politics, and I wanted to play on that big stage. I had passed on two previous presidential campaigns, and was champing at the bit to be involved in this one.

A few days later, I met with Edwards and his wife, Elizabeth, in his ornate office in the Dirksen Senate Office Building, a short walk from the Capitol. Mindful of Murphy's advice, I tried to center the conversation on Edwards's career, family, and the upcoming race, to better understand the man I was potentially following into the foxhole. When Edwards asked for my analysis, I told him that, with the middle class feeling besieged, a strong populist candidate had a real chance. "Those are the people I've been fighting for my entire life," he said, recalling his beginnings as the son of a millworker from Robbins, North Carolina, and his career as a trial lawyer. "That's really why I want to make this race."

A handsome guy with Ken-doll looks, Edwards was camera friendly from his laboriously coiffed brown hair right down to his broad, toothy grin.

And if Edwards seemed confident in his abilities, his wife was downright effusive.

"John connects with people like no one I know," said Elizabeth, her intense blue eyes locked on mine. "When they see him, they'll respond. I'm sure of it."

During this first meeting, John and Elizabeth talked about the death of their sixteen-year-old son Wade, from a car wreck in 1996. While he often shied away from this question in public for fear of injecting politics into their family tragedy, John told me that Wade's death had jarred him into considering a career in public service after amassing a fortune practicing law. The loss was obviously a painful memory with which the two were still struggling. While they had one other child at the time, their then-fourteen-year-old daughter, Cate, Elizabeth said Wade's death had left a "hole in our hearts." Since his death, they'd had two more children, Emma Claire and Jack, who were five and three.

"That's why we had more kids," she explained. "They helped fill that hole. They've brought our house back to life."

After two hours of conversation, we left it that we both would think about moving forward together, though he seemed interested and so was I. I was heartened by Edwards's professed sense of advocacy, and felt a bond with both of them. Though I hadn't lost a child, I knew what it was like to anguish over one.

When I got home, Susan asked me about the meeting. I related the sad story of Wade's death and the Edwards's struggle to cope with their loss. As I told the story, something caught her ear.

"Wait, they had these other children to fill this hole in their hearts?" Susan asked. "How did their daughter feel about that?"

It wasn't an idle question. Susan had lost two brothers in her life, one to meningitis and the other to heart disease. She knew what it was like to be the surviving child.

"How old is Elizabeth?"

"I think she's fifty-three," I replied.

"So they had these kids when she was forty-eight and fifty to fill the hole in their hearts?" Susan asked.

"That's what she said."

Susan, an expert on what campaigns do to families, was incredulous. "And now they're going to run for president and basically orphan them for the next couple of years? Dave, I don't think you should do this race. There's something wrong with this picture."

I hadn't really thought about the questions Susan was raising, and I was so eager to get in the game that I foolishly ignored her keen intuition and plunged headlong into the Edwards race.

It was troubled from the start. Having no prior relationship with Edwards, I lacked insight into the man or a bond or at least some basis for mutual trust, which you need to run a gauntlet together. I immediately clashed with his long-time pollster, Harrison Hickman, a cantankerous southerner who was deeply invested in preserving his preeminent place in the Edwards universe. I never felt as if he were dealing from the top of the deck with me. Yet the most difficult personality in this caustic stew was Elizabeth.

John and Elizabeth had met as law school students on the campus of the University of North Carolina. She was the beautiful, worldly child of a career military man and had lived in many places. He was the handsome, athletic son of a millworker and had barely seen the world beyond Robbins. "John was a hick in a plaid shirt when I met him," Elizabeth told me, in the manner of Professor Henry Higgins reflecting on Eliza Doolittle. "He's come a long way." If her attitude toward John was right out of My Fair Lady, her approach to the campaign bore a greater resemblance to The Manchurian Candidate.

Elizabeth, also an attorney, was clearly bright and even charming, often in public or social situations. Behind the scenes, though, she was always edgy and quite often unhappy, especially when she believed John's campaign was being harmed. Then she was prone to fits of rage, which often played out in nasty e-mails or late-night calls. One such call came my way when I was planning to shoot an interview with John's parents, Bobbie and Wallace, for possible use in ads and videos in Iowa. I felt their humble roots and small-town bearing would be embraced by many Iowans as a familiar image, and would help connect Edwards's story to his message.

"That's a waste of time and money," Elizabeth shouted through the phone. I assured her that nothing would go on the air without her knowledge and approval. I reasoned that it could help if John's parents, as well as Elizabeth and their daughter, filled out a portrait of John for voters, sharing insights into him that he could not. Finally, she relented and allowed the shoot to move forward.

Edwards's parents were as appealing as I had hoped, radiating the simple decency and small-town values I had seen in Iowa and all across rural America. They told their own stories, and spoke proudly of how far John had come while maintaining his identification with people who lived from paycheck to paycheck. I was thrilled.

To my mind, John's roots in Robbins were an important authentication of his message. Yet to Elizabeth, I learned, they were something of an embarrassment; a reminder of the unrefined "hick in a plaid shirt" her husband was before she orchestrated his transformation. Besides, Elizabeth had an almost messianic belief in John's communication skills and felt that any other messenger would be inferior and, thus, a waste of money.

"When they see John, they'll respond to him," she said with absolute confidence. "We don't need anyone else."

Elizabeth was unstinting in her criticisms and lashed out at anyone she felt was failing the candidate in any fashion, from senior staff and consultants to low-level volunteers. Once, on a conference call, she opined that a spot I had worked hard on "belonged in the circular file." The dismissive rebuke on a group call didn't sit well with me. Before long, Elizabeth was bypassing me altogether and communicating through Hickman and his team. They would then deliver unhelpful, sometimes conflicting translations of Elizabeth's input. Confused by the mixed signals and frustrated by the constant palace intrigue, I knew I wasn't doing my best work and wasn't the man driving the message, as I'd expected to be.

Not that there wasn't reason for tension within the campaign, which, in the fall of 2003, was languishing in also-ran territory, falling behind in the money race and ceding much of the populist support to Vermont governor Howard

Dean. Dean's strident opposition to the war in Iraq, and portrayal of DC Democrats who supported it as milquetoast accommodators, had fired up the Left and inspired young voters. And under the leadership of Dean's cyber-savvy manager, Joe Trippi, the campaign had, for the first time, turned the Internet into a potent fund-raising machine. Edwards had initially led the money race on the strength of his support from trial lawyers across the country, but by summer, Dean had shocked the political world, vastly outraising his opponents, largely through the collection of small donations online.

By October, polls showed Dean moving past Dick Gephardt in Iowa and surging into the lead in New Hampshire. Looking for a spark, Senator and Mrs. Edwards called a meeting in Washington to discuss an upcoming vote on the Bush administration's $87-billion proposal to fund the war in Iraq. Senator Edwards had voted to authorize the war, but with Dean riding the wave of discontent over Iraq to the top of the polls, Elizabeth saw a winning issue and was adamant that John oppose the funding. The senator and senior staff remained mostly silent as his wife hammered the point. "I didn't think authorizing the war was the right vote in the first place," she said, "but it would be suicidal to vote for this funding now."

I thought to oppose funding for the war Edwards had so recently voted to authorize would come off as politics at its worst, and I said so.

"Senator, if you had opposed the war in the first place, you could make an intellectually honest argument to oppose this funding now," I said, as others nervously toed the floor and averted their eyes. "I think this will look like a transparent reaction to Dean."

Elizabeth exploded with a combination of fury and disdain, and I could see clearly where this was heading. Edwards voted against the funding, as, in a similar reversal, did the ultimate Democratic nominee, John Kerry. Kerry's vote and his clumsy attempt to explain it gave the Bush campaign a huge opportunity to portray the Democratic ticket of Kerry and Edwards as craven opportunists who put party politics ahead of protecting the troops. Yet if this episode proved costly to Kerry and Edwards in the long run, it had an immediate cost to me, further aggravating my already uneasy relationship with Elizabeth.

I began to have less say in strategic decisions and even less control over the campaign's message, until ultimately the campaign ads that ran those final weeks in Iowa were not mine.

I was in New Hampshire observing focus groups when I got a message that

Edwards, who was campaigning in the area, wanted to see me. I met the candidate in the private room of a local restaurant. It was an awkward conversation, though not one that came as much of a surprise. Nonetheless, I felt as if I'd been punched in the gut.

"I feel like we need to add to our media team," Edwards said. "Harrison recommended a guy he knows who he thinks could help. You're still our guy, but we just want to bring another approach to the table."

That was a lie, and Edwards and I both knew it, but he was eager to avoid stories about a shake-up within his campaign. And while I was angry and bruised by the dismissive treatment, such stories weren't in my interest, either. So I agreed to stay on and continued to act as a principal media spokesperson for the duration of the campaign. We maintained the fiction that I was the chief media strategist, though I was no longer even in the loop. I did my nimble best, but in the end I would find myself simply bullshitting when called upon by reporters to explain ads that the new team hadn't had the courtesy to show me.

As Dean imploded, Edwards closed strong in Iowa but finished second to Kerry, who solidified his front-runner status with a follow-up win in New Hampshire. By Super Tuesday, on March 2, Edwards was gone. Looking back, I see that Susan's sight-unseen insights into Elizabeth and John were prescient. Mike Murphy's admonition to spend time with Edwards before signing on was wise. I ignored them both in favor of my ego, and it was a bracing learning experience. Sometime later, I read that Elizabeth didn't think I "got" John. Maybe she was right. I resolved that I would never again work on a presidential race unless I had a close, trusting relationship with the candidate.

While I was in Wisconsin for Edwards, just weeks before the Illinois primary, I had a drink in the bar of Milwaukee's Pfister Hotel with Dan Balz, the veteran political writer for the *Washington Post*, and talked to him about a candidate I strongly believed in.

"I'm working for a guy running in Illinois who's going to win and make a real impact nationally down the line," I told Balz, a thoughtful, thorough throwback to the golden age of political reporting. "His name is Barack Obama."

"Barack Obama?" Balz mused. "Interesting name. I've never heard of him. I'll keep an eye on him."

Barack might still have been a well-kept secret in Washington, but his talents were evident to all those who worked with him and, increasingly, to voters in Illinois.

It was a revealing experience to work with Obama and Edwards at the same time, as they wrestled with many of the same policy issues. Edwards was a stellar performer on the stump, but his one-on-one interactions with people were plastic, and out of the public eye, his interest in the substance of issues was thin. He wanted only as much information as he needed to glide by—and he was bright and glib enough to glide a long way. Once he locked in his lines, Edwards delivered them flawlessly, repeating on cue every word, every inflection, every catch of the throat, and every tearful eye. It reminded me of the old George Burns adage "The secret of acting is sincerity. If you can fake that, you've got it made."

Obama was just the opposite, drilling three and four levels deep on issues to hone his thinking, changing up his stump speech from stop to stop because he felt inauthentic sticking to a script. At one strategy meeting, he engaged my old partner, Forrest Claypool, on the issue of school vouchers. A strong believer in market solutions, Forrest was interested in vouchers as a means of improving educational opportunity for inner-city students.

"Forrest, I have supported charter schools, but not vouchers because I worry about siphoning off resources from public schools, where they're needed," Obama said. "But make the best case for that position. A lot of these students you're talking about are poor black kids, like the kids in my state senate district. I don't want to casually throw away good ideas if they can help."

For the next forty-five minutes, Barack and Forrest engaged in a riveting colloquy on school choice. It was thrilling to watch these two brilliant, passionate politicians earnestly exploring an issue they each cared deeply about. I, and the rest of Obama's campaign team, sat transfixed by their exchange. I could not have imagined John Edwards carrying on the same conversation or, indeed, wanting to. "Barack has a beautiful mind," Forrest said admiringly as we walked to our car after their "debate."

Still, Obama's interest in policy sometimes weighed him down. Susan and I held a fund-raiser for Barack at our apartment during the Senate primary. We raised about eleven thousand dollars, which was significant for Obama in those days. When Barack spoke, I thought his remarks were too elevated and lacked an emotional connection. I sensed he was talking up to what he thought was the level of the crowd. Afterward, I was honest with him. His speech should be consistent and connecting, not calibrated up or down depending upon an assessment of the audience.

"You call me every night from the road with these moving stories about the struggles people are facing," I said. "Why don't you share them in these speeches? They animate the things you're fighting for. It isn't an intellectual exercise."

Obama didn't enjoy my critique, but—to his credit—he took it to heart. As he developed his stump speech, he increasingly relied on the stories of the people he had met across the state. He became less the professor and more the advocate, standing up for folks who were fighting to join the middle class and the many who were struggling to stay there. And once he found that groove, Obama, a brilliant storyteller, was a natural in bringing others' stories to life. The narrative wasn't new. For Barack, the impact of a changing economy on everyday people had been an animating concern since his days as a community organizer.

One person who saw this firsthand was John Kerry, now the Democratic presidential nominee-in-waiting. He had come to Illinois shortly after our state's primary for a big fund-raising event and watched as Obama brought down the house. The next day, Kerry got a closer look at Obama as the two campaigned together at a job-training site on the city's West Side. Thinking ahead to the Democratic National Convention, Kerry made a mental note of this rising star.

Meanwhile, Obama's opponent and the Republican's rising star, Jack Ryan, collapsed after his own divorce file was released, detailing steamy allegations that he had forced his ex-wife to accompany him to sex clubs.

Obama's talent was beyond dispute, but his luck was beyond belief. Moseley Braun's improbable decision to seek the presidency instead of the Senate seat had made Obama's candidacy possible. Though he would have won the primary regardless, Hull's implosion surely didn't hurt. Now Obama's well-regarded Republican opponent was being forced to drop out, leaving the state GOP in disarray.

"This guy must sleep with a horseshoe under his pillow," I told my partners.

Not long after, Obama was on a campaign swing in Southern Illinois when his cell phone rang. It was Mary Beth Cahill, Kerry's campaign manager. Cell service being what it was downstate, it took three calls to complete one conversation, but the offer came through loud and clear—would Obama be the keynote speaker at the 2004 Democratic National Convention?

"Yes, that's great," Obama said quickly, before the call got dropped again. "I'd be honored to do it."

After acknowledging the magnitude of the role, Obama turned and said, "I know what I want to say." He clearly had been giving this serious thought, having heard weeks earlier that he was being considered for the coveted slot. "I want to talk about my own story as part of the larger American story. I want to talk about who we are at our best."

In the coming weeks, Barack worked on a draft whenever and wherever he could. He would write in longhand on car rides around the state. He would duck into the men's room off the state senate floor to jot down lines in between votes. One evening in July, he e-mailed me a first draft after having worked into the early morning hours.

Susan and I were on vacation in Italy, but my office faxed a copy to our hotel in Florence. As I read each page, I passed it on to Susan for her reaction. By the third page, we looked at each other with the same thought. "My God," I said. "This is going to be one of the greatest convention speeches ever."

I knew Barack was an exceptional writer. *Dreams from My Father*, the memoir he published at the age of thirty-three, was a powerful and poignant work, and when I finally got to see the written speech, I felt the same emotional tug. He had crafted something that contemplated America's promise and potential through the lens of his own extraordinary experience. Tracing the paths that brought together the son of a Kenyan goatherder and the daughter of small-town Kansas, Obama spoke not only of his parents' "improbable love," but of their "abiding faith in the possibilities of this nation."

"I stand here today, grateful for the diversity of my heritage, aware that my parents' dreams live on in my two precious daughters," he said. "I stand here knowing that my story is part of the larger American story, that I owe a debt to all of those who came before me, and that, in no other country on earth, is my story even possible."

Then he shared the stories of people he had met across Illinois, to ask if America today was living up to its promise. He spoke of the factory workers who saw their jobs shipped out of the country; the father struggling to afford the lifesaving medications his son needed; the student who "has the grades, has the drive, has the will, but doesn't have the money to go to college."

The language was fresh, honest, and suffused with enduring American values. Among its most memorable moments was his assault on the red state/blue state mind-set that had divided Washington and our nation's politics.

"The pundits like to slice and dice our country into red states and blue states; red states for Republicans, blue states for Democrats. But I've got news for them," he had written. "We worship an awesome God in the blue states, and we don't like federal agents poking around in our libraries in the red states. We coach Little League in the blue states and, yes, we've got some gay friends in the red states. There are patriots who opposed the war in Iraq and there are patriots who supported the war in Iraq. We are one people, all of us pledging allegiance to the stars and stripes, all of us standing up for the red, white and blue."

There were only two problems with this brilliant speech. The Kerry convention planners, in their desire to keep the program running on time, had allotted just eight minutes for the keynote, and Obama's draft clocked in at four times that long. "I can't do it," Obama grumbled. "It's ridiculous. If they insist, I don't think I should speak." After a great deal of haggling, we agreed to a seventeen-minute speech. And while Obama hated cutting the words he had so lovingly crafted, the edits made the speech tighter without sacrificing its power.

The second problem was that Obama had never spoken in an arena before and had it in his head that he wouldn't be heard unless he bellowed. One of the strengths of the speech was that it was at once elegant and conversational. It didn't sound like a political speech, but with Barack doing an imitation (and not even a very good imitation) of an old-time tub-thumper, his soaring prose didn't take flight.

We still had plenty of work to do when, less than seventy-two hours until his big moment, we took off from Springfield in a private plane bound for Boston: Barack, Michelle, me, and Robert Gibbs, the campaign's new communications director.

For Gibbs, the return to Boston was a satisfying redemption. He had quit the Kerry campaign in November during a messy shake-up. We had a big hole in communications to fill after the primary, and Giangreco and others who had worked with Robert were effusive about his talents. The tough, quick-witted Alabama native swiftly became a mainstay of our campaign.

Our mission on the flight was to brief Obama for his maiden appearance the next morning on *Meet the Press* with Tim Russert. Russert was a masterful interviewer with a well-earned reputation for using exhaustive research to confront his guests with their own past statements and deeds. Gibbs and I took turns firing questions at Obama, laying the traps we anticipated in Russert's signature prosecutorial style. As is often the case, Michelle kept Barack loose with good-natured ribbing, teasing him when he complained that his favorite drink was not on board. "Aww," she said, with mock compassion. "Poor Barack." He broke up in laughter.

The next morning, Obama aced the exam, handling Russert's crafty questions like a pro. Later that day, he began rehearsing his keynote with an expert speech coach, Michael Sheehan. Michael had studied as an actor to overcome a childhood stutter and transformed himself into one of the foremost media trainers in America. He was a fixture at Democratic conventions, setting up training booths beneath the rostrum where all the major speakers would prepare. I had known Michael for years and privately had confided Obama's habit of over-orating. "First lesson: Let the microphone do the work," he told Barack. "You don't have to shout. You'll be heard in the hall. But you're really speaking to twenty million people at home. Have a conversation with them."

With each repetition of the speech, Barack became more relaxed and conversational, adding pauses, nuanced phrasing, and natural gestures to accent his points. Soon his performance rivaled the quality of the words on the page. "This is really, really good," Gibbs whispered to me between takes. "He's definitely got it."

The only hiccup came when Kerry's team sent a crew-cutted young speechwriter to iron out a small turf problem. Jon Favreau, then just twenty-three, explained that Senator Kerry had a phrase in his speech that was similar to one in Obama's draft and they needed Obama to cut his version—or, in other words, to take one for the team. "Just get in there and tell him," Gibbs advised the doe-eyed rookie.

Unfortunately, the phrase in question was one of Obama's favorites—the crescendo of his red state/blue state passage in which he declared that we are one, "all of us standing up for the red, white, and blue."

When Favreau left, Obama was furious.

"You know they didn't have that in Kerry's speech," he said, his voice rising. "They saw it, they liked it, and now they're stealing it!"

No doubt he was right, but in the bigger scheme of things, it was a sacrifice worth making.

"Listen, Barack," I said. "They're giving you a chance to speak to millions of people. They want to steal a few words? Let 'em. It's a small price to pay."

"I guess," he said. "But damn, why did it have to be those words? I loved the way that worked!"

On Tuesday, the night of the speech, Obama ran into the Reverend Al Sharpton, who was scheduled to speak the next evening.

"How much time did they give you?" Obama asked Sharpton.

"Six minutes," the reverend replied. "But you never know how the Lord may move me!"

Obama was calm as he waited for his turn at the podium, chatting with Michelle and Illinois senator Dick Durbin, who would introduce him. Since the primary, Durbin had become one of Obama's most vocal and active supporters, without displaying any trace of the resentment that senior senators often feel toward highly touted newcomers invading their turf. Gibbs and I, on the other hand, were nervous wrecks. Obama must have sensed this as we walked him to the runway for his big national debut.

"Don't worry," he said, his hand on my shoulder. "I always make my marks."

With that, he strode off to await his cue, while Gibbs and I hustled to the floor of the arena. As Obama began to speak, there was the murmur of disinterest that greets most convention speakers. Delegates networked, stretched their legs, and sauntered to and from their various pit stops. But it didn't take long for Obama to capture the crowd. Gone was the wooden, labored delivery that had marred his speech in early run-throughs. For the first time, he was working with a teleprompter, though by now he could deliver this speech from memory. He had internalized the words and served them up with remarkable ease and considerable energy. In both language and delivery, his stood apart from the other political speeches, free of both clichéd phrases and hidebound dogma.

"The people I meet—in small towns and big cities, in diners and office parks—they don't expect government to solve all their problems," Obama said. "They know they have to work hard to get ahead, and they want to. Go into the collar counties around Chicago, and people will tell you they don't want their tax money wasted, by a welfare agency or by the Pentagon. Go into any inner-city neighborhood, and folks will tell you that government alone can't teach our kids to learn; they know that parents have to teach, that children can't achieve unless we raise their expectations and turn off the television sets and eradicate the slander that says a black youth with a book is acting white. They know those things!"

As Obama told his story, I saw an African American woman nearby brushing away tears. With each point and passage of the speech, delegates all around us were vigorously nodding their heads. Without prompting, folks who an hour earlier could not have picked Barack out of a crowd were joyously waving blue-and-white signs bearing his name.

A few feet in front of Gibbs and me were George Stephanopoulos, now with ABC News, and CNN's Jeff Greenfield, a onetime speechwriter for Bobby Kennedy. "This is a great fucking speech," Greenfield said to George, mouthing the words to cut through the din.

Amid this madhouse, I thought about that night, twenty years earlier, when I heard Mario Cuomo deliver his rousing, career-making keynote in San Francisco. From that moment on, Cuomo was a star, and the constant focus of speculation when presidential politics came up. The reception for Obama in Boston was at least as emphatic.

"Barack doesn't know it, but his life just changed in a big way," I told Gibbs. "It'll never be the same." Though I didn't say it, I had a feeling that the same could be said for Gibbs and me. We were at the beginning of what promised to be a rocket ride with our once-in-a-lifetime client.

Susan watched the speech from a friends-and-family box. When I met up with her afterward, she was effusive. "We were in tears up here!"

The next morning, as we walked the streets of Boston, well-wishers swarmed around Obama. A previously scheduled press breakfast was suddenly overflowing. Back home, the *Sun-Times* screaming headline read, "Obama Delivers!" The *Tribune* published an editorial entitled "The Phenom." "Obama delivered a brilliant, passionate and heartening speech," it read.

All the attention certainly wouldn't hurt us in the Senate race—not that, by then, we needed much of a boost. While Obama was wowing the nation, Republicans were tripping all over themselves trying to find a candidate to oppose him. Former Illinois governor Jim Edgar and several other credible state Republicans opted not to step in the path of our juggernaut. Finally, in August, GOP leaders recruited a candidate from Maryland and conservative talk radio.

Like much of the Midwest, Illinois had a history of moderate Republicanism. Alan Keyes broke that mold. The bombastic, homophobic Keyes was a favorite among right-wing evangelicals for his fiery jeremiads against liberalism in all its forms. The fact that he was African American was particularly enticing to the desperate GOP leaders, who had the preposterous notion that they could match the power of one African American candidate simply by importing one of their own.

Within days of parachuting in to fill the Senate void, the voluble Keyes was roiling the waters, decrying Obama's "slaveholder's position" on abortion and insisting that Obama "countenances even the murder of living young children outside the womb."

The election was effectively over before it started. The first public poll showed Obama with a forty-point lead. By the second poll, his lead had stretched to fifty.

Yet if Keyes was a dead man campaigning in the Senate race, he still had an uncanny ability to get under Obama's skin. Intentionally mispronouncing Obama's first name by putting the emphasis on the first syllable, Keyes was a bubbling, spewing cauldron of pompous, morally superior attacks. The *Sun-Times* pretty well summarized his approach in its account of one of three candidate debates: "Keyes ridiculed Obama as ignorant of the Constitution, naive on foreign policy, out of touch with African Americans descended from slaves and willing to compromise his Christian faith for politics."

As Keyes probably knew, all these were hot buttons for Obama, but the hottest were on race and faith. Barack had written an entire book on his own journey on race, and he took seriously the Christian faith he had consciously embraced as a young adult, even if he didn't read its mandates the same way Keyes did. These frustrations were already evident when the two candidates crossed paths at an Indian Independence Day parade just weeks after the bombastic Keyes arrived in Illinois. News footage captured Obama jabbing the shorter Keyes in the chest with his finger in response to Keyes's demand that Obama honor the pledge he made to Jack Ryan to participate in six debates. "I guarantee we're going to debate," Obama assured him. "Because you've been talking a lot. You've been talking a lot!"

I was shocked when I watched the confrontation on the news. Why in the world would the normally unflappable Obama get into it with a guy he was going to bury at the polls? "I just went over to shake his hand," Barack explained. "But then he started in on debates and got on my nerves. He's an obnoxious guy, man. I just wasn't going to let him punk me."

Obama would go on to win a staggering 70 percent of the vote, nearly an Illinois record, but not definitive enough for Keyes to reach out to him with the traditional concession call before he pulled up stakes and left Illinois. Obama carried all but a handful of small downstate counties and every demographic group and every section of the state. His landslide stood out in a year when Democrats were licking their wounds, losing the presidency and seats in both houses of Congress. It wasn't just the victory that was noteworthy, but how we won.

The previous spring, after the primary but before Ryan's campaign imploded, I sent Obama and the team a strategy memo entitled, "Yes We Can!"

Obama's record of advocacy for the middle class was powerful and important, I wrote,

> but to approach the message in a purely linear fashion, simply checking off issue boxes, would be to rob this campaign of its full power.
>
> Against a backdrop of the paralyzing partisanship and special interest hegemony in Washington, voters are responding to a candidate who has the integrity, temperament and proven commitment to challenge the status quo and get things done.
>
> Barack stands apart from the mess they see, preaching a politics of civility and community, of mutual respect and responsibility. It's a tone distinct from the nasty and personal debate to which voters have become accustomed, and draws to Obama many voters who may not agree with him on specific issues but respond to his character and sincerity.
>
> Our challenge is to maintain that tone, protect that special character and sincerity and always bear in mind that the brain dead politics of Washington is as much our target as Jack Ryan.

This was the essence of Obama's appeal. The core of his "brand." The entire nation had seen and responded to it in Boston. The next test would be how it, and he, would hold up in Washington.

ELEVEN

RELUCTANT HERO

THE DAY AFTER THE ELECTION, we got a taste of things to come.

Fighting through almost no sleep, Barack did two national morning shows, where the hosts informed their viewers that they were listening to a potential presidential candidate and "the next great voice in the Democratic Party." Now reporters jammed into his campaign headquarters to hear from the Man of the Hour, and before he had spent a day in the Senate—before he had hired a staff or cast a vote—he was already fending off questions about just how long he intended to stay.

"We've got to tamp this shit down," he said, before he stepped out to meet the media. "It's way over the top." And he tried. He tried very hard.

Dismissing the notion as "silly," Obama was emphatic. "I can unequivocally say I will not be running for national office in four years, and my entire focus is making sure that I'm the best possible senator on behalf of the people of Illinois."

It was not a misdirection play. In November 2004, the last person on the planet who expected Barack Obama to run for president in 2008 was Barack Obama. It clearly wasn't a lack of ambition or confidence on his part. He was a realist, and the notion of running for president so soon seemed entirely a fantasy. What seemed slightly less implausible was the notion that someone else would want to cash in on Barack's talents and make him their number two. Yet Obama had no interest in running for vice president, even if he were offered the spot. He was not a man suited for the second chair.

"Can you imagine me as vice president?" he asked, with a laugh, in a private conversation. "I can't. I can't imagine wanting that job. I'd rather come back and run for governor after a term than be somebody's vice president. I'm not cut out for that."

Despite Obama's emphatic denial at his press conference, the following Sunday he got the Question again, this time from Tim Russert on a postelection edition of *Meet the Press*. "Before you go, you know there's been enormous speculation about your political future," Russert said. "Will you serve your full six-year term as U.S. senator from Illinois?"

"Absolutely," Barack replied. "You know, some of this hype's been a little overblown. It's flattering, but I have to remind people that I haven't been sworn in yet. I don't know where the restrooms are in the Senate. I'm going to have to figure out how to work the phones, answer constituent mail. I expect to be in the Senate for quite some time, and hopefully I'll build up my seniority from my current position, which I believe is 99th out of 100."

Only two U.S. senators in my lifetime have entered the Senate with such fanfare, Bobby Kennedy and Hillary Clinton, and both for the same reason: no one expected them to stay for long. For Obama, managing these expectations was essential. He didn't want voters in Illinois to feel as if they were merely a launching pad to something bigger. Most important, he didn't want to antagonize his colleagues in the Senate, who would be watching closely to see if this new media sensation had bought into the hype.

Controlling the circus wouldn't be easy, though. After his convention speech made him one of the hottest politicians in America, Obama's well-reviewed but little-read autobiography, *Dreams from My Father*, was reissued, and he was obligated to hit the road to promote it. *Letterman*, *The View*, morning and Sunday shows—he was a ubiquitous presence in the weeks following the election. There was a practical reason for this: Obama actually needed the money. For years he had sacrificed income to public service. The Obamas lived in a four-bedroom apartment in East View Park, a comfortable but modest low-rise condominium complex in Hyde Park. They had a mortgage to pay, and each carried significant tuition debts. So the explosion in popularity meant serious income for the first time in their lives.

Michelle wanted to move to a larger space. Barack had another idea.

"I want Michelle and the kids to move to Washington," he told me. "I'm going to be out there a lot and I don't want to be away from them."

I told him that I thought this was a horrible idea. What message would it send to become an absentee senator, living in Washington and visiting Illinois on weekends and holidays? I suggested he and Michelle have dinner with

Rahm Emanuel and his wife, Amy Rule, who might serve as a model in this matter. Rahm commuted to and from Congress, while Amy and their three kids remained in Chicago.

"The other way doesn't even make sense from a family standpoint," Rahm explained to me and, later, to the Obamas. "He'd have to be here on holidays and weekends, while his family stayed back in Washington. It's a bad idea."

Michelle agreed. She had her own career, friends, and family in Chicago and wasn't eager to move. Instead, they would buy a spacious Georgian Revival mansion in Kenwood, just north of Hyde Park. Barack felt he owed Michelle the home, though he worried about the cost. After a lifetime of thriftiness, he found it difficult to adjust to the fact that he wasn't a struggling legislator and college instructor anymore. His book was a bestseller, and by the end of the year, he had signed a lucrative deal to write three more.

"The price of victory," he said, sighing, though I have no doubt he considered it a fair price, indeed a bargain, for Michelle's extraordinary forbearance and steadfast support in his political endeavors.

One of the other benefits of being shot out of the cannon was that a lot of talented people wanted to jump on for the ride.

Tom Daschle, the former Senate majority leader, had lost his seat in the same election. Now his coveted chief of staff, Pete Rouse, was a free agent. After his nearly thirty years on Capitol Hill, no one knew more about the inner workings of the Senate than Rouse. His seen-it-all, done-it-all wisdom was a highly sought-after commodity. But the gravelly voiced, bespectacled Senate guru was heartbroken by his friend Daschle's loss. They had been together for decades, and Rouse was prepared to follow him out the door. Obama made a hard sell, telling Rouse that he wanted to be an impact player in the Senate, but without being the hot dog some feared. He felt he could make a persuasive speech and digest policy with the best of them, but knew nothing about how to put together a Senate staff or navigate the plays and players that awaited him. He needed a Sherpa to guide him, and Pete was the very best. There was one more thing, Obama told his prized recruit: "You may have heard that I'm planning to run for president in 2008. I can give you an absolute assurance that's not true. I have two kids who are too young for that, and a wife who wouldn't tolerate it. You don't have to worry about that."

So Rouse, who was nearing sixty, put his own plans on hold for this promising newcomer, as he would so many times in the years to come. He became to Obamaworld what George Bailey was to his neighbors in the movie *It's a Wonderful Life*. No matter how much he wanted to leave town, Rouse found that his sense of duty always kept him at Barack's side. Rouse, who made a short-term commitment to help set up the operation, would work for Obama for eight years.

Pete became the lynchpin of an extraordinary Senate staff. Gibbs, though a generation younger, also knew his way around the Senate and the town. In addition to his stint with Kerry and others, Gibbs had been the campaign communications director for Senator Fritz Hollings of South Carolina, though Robert's job there consisted largely of keeping the acid-tongued, irascible Senate elder *out* of the news. Obama also recruited Alyssa Mastromonaco, who had run the scheduling and advance operation for Kerry's presidential campaign. And he apparently forgot that Jon Favreau was the talented young Kerry speechwriter who bore the bad news in Boston when Team Kerry swiped Barack's favorite speech line; Favreau joined the staff as chief speechwriter. Obama was assembling a team of old pros and young talent that could carry him far.

For me, Obama's swearing in was a sublime moment. We had come a long way together since our first conversations back in the summer of 2002, when both of us faced doubts about the future. As I watched from the Senate gallery, I felt I had truly helped do something meaningful. Just the sight of this tall, elegant African American man walking down the center aisle of a chamber filled with white faces represented an important change. After the ceremony, Barack signed my blue ticket in silver marker: "To Axe, Here because of you!"

It was a generous gesture and a memento I would cherish. Yet I knew that our relationship would inevitably change. We began the Senate race as lonely partners in a highly speculative campaign and spoke almost daily for the better part of two years. Now Barack would be in Washington, relying on his superb new staff to guide him on this next leg of the journey. I would continue to provide political advice and would work closely with Rouse, Gibbs, and others, but I would miss the day-to-day interaction of our shared odyssey and the running conversations that veered from professional considerations to the chitchat of friends about sports, family, and life.

As much as I would miss the man and the mission, I would not lack for work in the 2005 and 2006 election cycle. Obama's out-of-nowhere ascension to the

Senate had opened new doors for my firm, now known as AKPD Message and Media, to reflect the names of its four partners: Axelrod, Kupper, Plouffe, and Del Cecato.

I first met David Plouffe in 1994, when, just twenty-seven, he led a Senate race on which I worked, in his home state of Delaware. Two years later he managed a knock-down, drag-out fight to elect Senator Bob Torricelli in New Jersey, and went on to run the Democratic Congressional Campaign Committee. Though still young, he was whip smart, campaign savvy, and would add a Washington presence the firm needed.

Del Cecato was Plouffe's young press secretary at the DCCC when I recruited him to play the same role for Fernando Ferrer during the New York City mayoral race in 2001. John was passionate, hilarious, and creative, and struck me as a guy who could become a good ad writer, so I hired him after that race. My instincts were right. He picked up spot writing quickly, and would become a creative force at AKPD.

While the company was still mine, I wanted to raise the profile of my colleagues. It was necessary to signify to needy clients that when these talented folks provided counsel, they were not the B-Team. Also, we needed a bigger A-Team. As a small, boutique firm headquartered in the Midwest, we had often struggled to land the high-profile races that usually gravitated to Washington-based media consultants, but now the Obama aura had enhanced our stature in the eyes of candidates looking to be the next new thing.

While I was settled in to my other projects, Obama was trying his best to follow Hillary's example and establish himself as a productive and respectful new member of the Senate. He made the rounds of the gray eminences, humbly asking their counsel. And he found an unlikely mentor in Dick Lugar, a well-regarded, five-term incumbent Republican from Indiana. Lugar, the chairman of the Senate Committee on Foreign Relations, worked closely with Obama and took him on as his junior partner in crafting legislation to combat the proliferation of weapons of mass destruction. "I like Lugar," Barack reported. "He's not a showboat. He a very decent, serious guy." He also found Lugar's laconic nature a welcome counterpoint to the committee's verbose ranking member, Joe Biden. "Joe Biden is a decent guy, but man, that guy can just talk and talk," Barack complained to me on one of our regular calls. "It's an incredible thing to see."

A month before Obama took office, the *Sun-Times* had published an investigation revealing that Illinois veterans in large numbers were being unfairly denied disability payments to which they were entitled. After he was named to the Senate Committee on Veterans' Affairs, Barack joined with our state's senior senator, Dick Durbin, in a long campaign to address the problem. He also introduced a bill for the expansion of college Pell grants to needy students. And after reading a piece in the *New Yorker* on the emerging threat of the Avian flu, he wrote legislation to, among other things, fund the development and stockpiling of sufficient vaccine to combat a deadly influenza pandemic. In Obama's first year in Washington, he held thirty-nine town hall meetings across Illinois and, according to the periodic public polls, remained an extraordinarily popular figure in the state.

Yet Barack was frustrated with the slow pace and endless debate of the Senate. On a visit to Washington during his first year, I waited for him outside the Senate chamber while he was delivering a floor speech. His oration over, Barack burst through the door and walked past me. "Blah, blah, blah. That's all we do around here," he muttered. It was clear that Obama would not be comfortable growing old in the Senate. He ruminated again about the possibility of returning to Illinois, near the end of his Senate term in 2010, to run for governor. "Governors don't just talk. They actually can do things," he said. "And, besides, I'd be able to live with my family."

Despite his growing misgivings about the Senate, Obama stuck to the plan, trying to maintain a smooth and low-key debut. Yet he naturally remained the object of immense political interest. He topped the wish lists of candidates and Democratic state parties across the nation looking for a speaker who would boost their fortunes. Gibbs, who functioned as a kind of de facto political director in addition to communications director, deftly arranged the schedule with Alyssa for Obama to campaign for candidates and state parties in as many presidential battleground states as possible. "I just thought it was a good investment," he said. In that same spirit, Obama immediately put his fund-raising power to good use, raising and distributing nearly $1.5 million to candidates.

Despite his best efforts to accept his lowly place in the political hierarchy, Barack found himself inexorably drawn into the spotlight by unexpected and tragic events.

During the August 2005 recess, Obama made his first overseas trip as a senator, accompanying Lugar to Russia, Ukraine, and Azerbaijan to inspect large caches of loose chemical, biological, and nuclear weapons that were dangerous relics of the Cold War. It was a prelude to a new arms-control law the two would introduce jointly. On their way back, the delegation had stopped in London when news of Hurricane Katrina reached them. Barack was watching TV in a hotel bar as CNN broadcast the horrific images of the hell on earth that was New Orleans. As the floodwater rose, desperate residents, many of them poor and black, stood on the roofs of their homes waiting for help that never came. "People in that bar were looking at us in complete disbelief," he reported. "They were floored that negligence on that scale could happen in America."

When he returned to the States, Obama was besieged by media requests. Everyone was interested in what the most prominent African American office-holder in the country thought about the events in New Orleans and the laggard government response—and Barack felt compelled to weigh in. He was wary of being pigeonholed as a "black politician." "I am of the black community, but not limited to it," he would say. Still, he had spent much of his life wrestling with questions of race and identity, and understood the unique place he now held in America's politics. Given the magnitude of the disaster, he felt a responsibility to speak out forcefully on Katrina. It was suggested that Obama head straight to New Orleans, but when the logistical challenges of such a visit were considered, the idea was quickly dismissed.

Alyssa, Obama's savvy scheduler, had a better idea. Former president Clinton and Senator Clinton were headed to Houston, where the Astrodome had become a temporary shelter for thousands of refugees. Former president George H. W. Bush would meet up with them there. What if she could wrangle an invitation for Obama to join them? When Obama, who was soliciting relief funds from Illinois companies, called Clinton to discuss the effort, the former president invited him to Houston.

Obama was eager to dive into the Katrina issue, which he found deeply wrenching, but he was careful not to add to the outcry of racism it had provoked. "I don't think the Bush guys said, 'Those folks are black so take your time getting there to help,'" he told us before making the trip to Houston. "They just (a) blew it; and (b) have no clue about the state of these inner-city communities, where people don't have the wherewithal of wealthy folks to pick up, jump into their Range Rovers, and flee."

As Obama went from cot to cot alongside President Clinton in Houston, warmly ministering to shell-shocked families, George Stephanopoulos was calling Gibbs and begging for Obama to give him an interview. "If you're ever going to do it, this is the right time," George said. "People want to hear from him on this." The decision to appear on the program marked the end of Obama's self-imposed exile from the Sunday shows.

Katrina was a turning point for Barack. However intent he had been on keeping a low profile, there was no avoiding the spotlight now. Obama was an eloquent and thoughtful bridge after the storm, giving voice to the more enduring crisis—the widening gap between the rich and the poor in America—that it had exposed. "I think the important thing for us now is to recognize that we have situations in America in which race continues to play a part; that class continues to play a part; that people are not availing themselves of the same opportunities, of the same schools, of the same jobs," he told Stephanopoulos. "And because they're not, when disaster strikes, it tears the curtain away from these festering problems . . . and black and white, all of us should be concerned to make sure that's not the kind of America that's reflected on our television screens."

In September, Rouse arranged a call between Obama and his inside and out-side advisers on the pending nomination of John Roberts to become chief jus-tice of the Supreme Court. The Left was bitterly opposed to Roberts, a politically astute judicial conservative who, at a youthful (by Supreme Court standards) fifty years old, could shape the Court for decades to come. For Obama, it was not an easy decision. Friends had contacted him to vouch for Roberts. Besides, Obama said, "If I become president someday, I don't want to see my own, qualified nominees for the Court shot down because of ideology." Interesting, I thought, that he would frame it that way. Gibbs said a vote for Roberts would position Obama more in the political center, which could be advantageous in future races. "Not in a primary," I replied. We were all talking around it, but national politics had quickly emerged as a subtext of our discus-sion. Finally, Rouse came down against Roberts, and so, too, did Obama.

"I spent time with Roberts, and came away convinced that he is qualified in every way," Barack said to us. "He's obviously bright. He knows his stuff. But I also have this nagging feeling, based on his opinions, that anytime there's a contest between the powerful and the powerless, he'll find a way to make sure the powerful win. That's how he'll interpret the law. And that's not my vision of how the courts should work, and particularly not the Supreme Court." I didn't think Barack was rationalizing his decision, but I also knew the politics were not lost on him.

The other issue drawing Barack out was Iraq. The situation there was eroding. Public opinion was turning sharply against our involvement, and sentiment for withdrawal of our 160,000 troops was growing. Iraq had become an albatross for those who had supported the war, and the wisdom of Obama's early opposition seemed clearer by the day. He had kept a low profile on the war during his first months in the Senate, in part because he didn't want to appear to be showing up Democratic colleagues who had supported it. "Everyone knows where I was on this from the beginning," he explained. "I think it's best to be a little low-key for a while." By late summer, however, Barack's posture had changed. He felt he couldn't stay quiet any longer. He and his national security adviser, Mark Lippert, a crew-cutted naval reservist, developed a plan for a "phased withdrawal" of American troops, tied to political and security benchmarks.

Barack unveiled his Iraq proposal in a speech to the Chicago Council on Foreign Relations, where he assailed the absence of a coherent strategy from the Bush administration. Just as with Katrina, though, Barack's critique of Bush was more nuanced than a raging antiwar screed. Barack's "phased withdrawal" plan, calling for a significant number of our troops to be out of Iraq by the following year, didn't please those on the left who favored immediate withdrawal; nor did it captivate those on the right who opposed any withdrawal. Yet it thrust Obama back into the middle of an Iraq debate that was likely to shape the 2008 election.

Between Katrina, Roberts, and Iraq, Barack's determination to keep a low profile for 2005 went by the boards. The murmurs about 2008 predictably picked up, and a trip he unexpectedly added to his schedule at the end of the year would only fuel the speculation.

Throughout the summer and fall, Senator Bill Nelson of Florida had asked Obama repeatedly to give the keynote address at the state's Democratic convention in mid-December—and each time, Barack had demurred. It was a weekend speech, and he knew it would mean time away from his family. Besides, he had irritated Michelle by traveling the country several weekends that fall instead of coming home from Washington. So when Gibbs suggested they give the Floridians a definite no, Obama stunned him by replying, "What if I want to go?"

Obama told Gibbs he was eager to "try some themes," and he thought the Florida event would be a great place to roll them out. Left unspoken, because it needed no amplification, was what Florida had come to mean in national politics. No Democrat would recapture the White House without it, which is why three men who were looking hard at 2008 had signed up to speak there. Edwards, Vilsack, and Governor Mark Warner of Virginia were all eager to flash their chops for thousands of delegates at a Disney World resort. By tapping Barack for the prized keynote, the organizers had spared themselves the dilemma of having to choose among the aspiring candidates. The invitation also reflected the growing curiosity and interest Obama was generating all over the country. What was clear to all of us who worked with Obama was that his unexpected decision to risk Michelle's ire and go to Florida reflected growing curiosity and interest of his own.

With Barack's input, Favreau and I worked together on the first of what would be many collaborative efforts in the years to come. Most political speeches today are a series of applause lines, strung together with filler. Barack viewed speeches as carefully constructed arguments. He had learned to animate them with inspiring stories from the lives of people he had encountered, and considered the sound and cadence, as well as the meaning, of words and how they played against one another. Favreau, an accomplished musician as well as a gifted young writer, was innately attuned to the rhythms of language. He and Obama were a perfect match, and the Florida speech was a moving— and suggestive—composition, recalling the themes that animated Obama's maiden voyage on the national stage in Boston.

"We're tired of being divided, tired of running into ideological walls and partisan roadblocks, tired of appeals to our worst instincts and greatest fears," he thundered. "Americans everywhere are desperate for leadership. They are longing for direction. And they want to believe again."

Obama flew back home the same night, leaving a huge buzz of "believers," and a few deflated presidential aspirants, in his wake.

"They may not be able to pronounce his name, but Florida Democrats sure love Barack Obama," wrote Steve Bousquet in the *St. Petersburg Times*. "He was introduced to 2,000 party activists as a 'rock star' Saturday night, and the freshman senator from Illinois lived up to the grandiose billing."

Barack was just thirteen months removed from the Illinois State Senate and had not yet been in Washington for a full year. A 2008 campaign for president still seemed ludicrous and remote. Yet clearly things were changing. It would be easy to ascribe it all to some unseen hand pushing this audacious idea along. Still, it was impossible to miss that one of the hidden hands steering events belonged to the man himself, who continued to say no even as his body language now said, "Maybe."

Attuned to these developments and the shifting political tide, Rouse sent me a memo he wanted to share with Obama. In it, he advised that if there were even a small chance that Barack might change his mind and run in 2008, we should build out his travel in 2006 to include meetings at every stop with influential locals who could be useful down the line.

I agreed with Rouse and the team that this was the way to proceed, and we sent the memo. Barack quickly returned it with a three-word note in the margin that spoke volumes:

"This makes sense."

TWELVE

FROM "NO, I WON'T" TO "YES, WE . . . MIGHT"

JUST A FEW DAYS into 2006, Obama set out for his first trip to a country half a world away that was playing an increasingly prominent role in his political story.

Three years earlier, he had warned against an invasion of Iraq. Now he and a group of congressional colleagues headed there to assess the efficacy of the war effort. Nothing Barack saw on the ground allayed the concerns he had expressed from the start. With the dictator Saddam Hussein gone, the historic rivalries between Sunni, Shia, and Kurd that he had subdued by force were reemerging with a vengeance, challenging the prospects for a viable democratic state.

"It was just what I was afraid would happen," Barack said to me later. "We can send all the troops we want. But if these sectarian factions can't come to a political settlement, we're just spinning our wheels over there—and at a hell of a cost. We're trying to build a house on a bed of sand. It needs a better foundation if it's going to stand."

When he returned, he sat with Russert on *Meet the Press* to discuss his findings. Praising the heroism of our troops, Obama argued for the need to phase down our involvement while increasing incentives for reconciliation. Before he could escape the chair, the dogged host pushed Obama again on his political plans. Confronting Barack with a *Tribune* article assessing his first year in the Senate, Russert noted that Obama had used more ambiguous language than his unequivocal disavowal on the same show a year earlier.

"There seems to be an evolution in your thinking," the host said. "This is what you told the *Chicago Tribune* last month: 'Have you ruled out running for another office before your term is up?' Obama answer: 'It's not something I anticipate doing.' But when we talked back in November of '04 after your election I said, 'There's been enormous speculation about your political future. Will you serve your six-year term as United States senator from Illinois?' Obama: 'Absolutely.'"

Barack shook off the question.

"I will serve out my full six-year term. You know, Tim, if you get asked enough, sooner or later you get weary and you start looking for new ways of saying things," he replied. "But my thinking has not changed."

So you will not run for president or vice president in 2008?

"I will not," Obama said.

Yet things *had* changed, and even as he gave Russert another firm no, Barack was positioning himself to seize the moment if and when it came. He had in hand the memo Rouse, Gibbs, and I had sent outlining a program in 2006 that would keep his options open for 2008.

"If making a run in 2008 is at all a possibility, no matter how remote," we had written, "it makes sense to begin talking and making decisions about what you should be doing 'below the radar' in 2006 to maximize your ability to get out in front of this presidential wave should it emerge and should you and your family decide it is worth riding." We had offered him an opt out, and he had driven right through it, authorizing a series of activities aimed at subtly nurturing the possibility of a candidacy.

Obama already had committed to aggressive travel in 2006 to raise money and build support for Democratic Senate candidates, a strategy designed to burnish his reputation as a "team player" within the caucus and earn chits with his colleagues. Now we set in motion our plan to expand Barack's trips to include meetings with key political players, donors, and local media. We also moved to enhance his political and policy teams, increase his personal fund-raising goals, and seize timely opportunities to spell out an alternative vision for the Democratic Party.

I was skeptical. Hillary was vacuuming up dollars and political commitments, and many other potential candidates already were barnstorming the country, competing for the meager leavings from her table. Most of all, I doubted that Barack, with a young family, would decide that this was the right time to commit to all the hardships of a presidential candidacy.

For my part, I had a bunch of new projects in 2006 that were more immediate and realer than the remote prospect of an Obama presidential candidacy. One of the most satisfying began with a phone call from an unlikely source: my sister, Joan.

Saint Joan, as we sometimes call her, has always been involved in good deeds. An educational psychologist, she is a hero to families around Boston for the guidance and advocacy she has provided for countless kids with learning disabilities. Yet, save for her days as an antiwar protester in college, Joan was never much of a political activist until she took an interest in town government and school board elections in Arlington, the suburb just northwest of Boston where her family lived. Warm, effusive, and relentless, Joan committed her nights and weekends to the school battles and developed into a master field organizer. Her talents had not escaped the notice of aspiring candidates, and now one had stolen her heart.

"Dave, I never do this," she said. "But I just met a guy you have to work for. His name is Deval Patrick and he's running for governor here. I don't know if he has a chance, but he's such a good guy. He's progressive. He's idealistic. He's really inspiring. You would love him."

I knew a little about Patrick and the Massachusetts race. Deval was an African American who had led the Civil Rights Division in the Justice Department during the Clinton years. Friends who had worked with him were effusive in their praise. However, the smart money dismissed Patrick, little known to voters in a state with a relatively small black population, as largely irrelevant to the gubernatorial race. Mitt Romney was retiring after one term to run for president, so, in that sense, the race appeared wide open. Yet Tom Reilly, the state's attorney general, had a huge leg up on the Democratic nomination. If voters preferred an outsider, another rumored candidate, a venture capitalist and education reformer named Chris Gabrieli, could bring significant personal resources to the race. The Beacon Hill insiders were disdainful of Patrick's prospects, as the relative unknown spent a great deal of time and money building a grassroots field operation and meeting with local activists like my sister.

Joan's enthusiastic report on Patrick piqued my interest, and the next day, entirely by coincidence, I got a call from Doug Rubin, a senior adviser for Patrick's campaign. Rubin didn't know my sister; his inquiry about whether our firm would take a meeting with Deval had been prompted entirely by our role in the Obama campaign. "This must be kismet," I told him, relating Joan's call.

The more I learned of Deval's compelling story, the more I was drawn to him. He was a native of Chicago's South Side. His father, Pat, a saxophone player for jazz icon Sun Ra, had abandoned the family, walking out despite the plaintive pleas of his four-year-old son. Deval, his mother, and sister shared a room in his grandparents' small tenement apartment, where some nights he got to sleep in the bunk bed and other nights he took his turn on the floor. Then Deval's life took a dramatic turn when a Chicago public school teacher nominated him for a scholarship at the prestigious Milton Academy in Massachusetts. Milton was a world (maybe a couple of worlds) apart from the one into which Deval had been born. He showed up at Milton dressed in a windbreaker because he had been informed that students were required to wear jackets to class. Notwithstanding the culture gap, Deval excelled and won scholarships to Harvard College and then its eminent law school. As a Justice Department official during the Clinton administration, Deval had proved himself a fierce and able advocate for civil rights, sometimes locking horns with the political hands in the White House who preferred a more muted approach. He went on to break through corporate barriers by becoming the chief counsel first for Texaco and then for Coca-Cola.

Obama knew Patrick well through legal circles. "He's a great guy," Barack told me. "You'll really like him. I don't know what kind of chance he has, though. Seems like a tough road."

Whatever the odds, once Plouffe and I had traveled to Massachusetts to meet Deval, my desire to do the race was unequivocal. He was genuine, passionate, and inspiring. In Deval's campaign, I had found another, exhilarating opportunity to tilt at a windmill and break down a barrier.

For all their superficial similarities and shared ideals, Deval and Barack were very different people. Barack, tall, regal, and blessed with a mellifluous baritone, was more reserved and self-possessed. Deval, half a head shorter with a voice several octaves higher, was naturally warm, open, and accessible. Barack made an early commitment to a career in politics. Deval came to it much later, after his government and private-sector career, and there was a charming innocence to his candidacy. Deval cheerfully endorsed gay marriage before it was fashionable, and a proposed wind farm in the waters off the coast of Cape Cod—an irritant to many of the Cape's prominent denizens, including the revered and powerful senior senator Ted Kennedy. "Look, I believe in these things and I'm going to run on what I believe," Deval explained to us when some of the prickly issues came up for discussion. "If that costs me the job, I can live with that."

Deval and I clicked in every way, collaborating on a series of ads, scripted and unscripted, designed to bring his ideals and vision for Massachusetts to life. Like Barack, he was an eloquent and evocative writer, who drafted his own, soaring speeches, including a stem winder he delivered to the state Democratic convention. "It's time to put our cynicism down," he implored the delegates. "Put it down. Stand with me and take that leap of faith. Because I'm not asking you to take a chance on me. I'm asking you to take a chance on your own aspirations. Take a chance on hope."

Take a chance on hope. In times of disillusionment and doubt, it was such a timely and affirming message. In its freshness, authenticity, and idealism, the Deval Patrick campaign was the spiritual twin of the Obama for Senate campaign. Yet, in its execution, the Patrick campaign was far more advanced. It drew an incisive corps of young insurgents, some of whom were refugees from Howard Dean's failed presidential bid. As such, they had glimpsed the potential of the Internet, and tech-savvy Massachusetts proved to be fertile ground for their new, expansive digital strategies. Plouffe took copious notes that would pay off down the line.

The other big project we took on in 2006 was for Rahm. Nancy Pelosi, vying to become the first woman to serve as Speaker, had drafted Rahm to chair the DCCC and spearhead the party's effort to recapture the House. Rahm's legendary fund-raising prowess, shrewd political instincts, and almost pathological competitiveness made him the perfect choice. After a few weeks of playing hard to get, Rahm cut a deal and accepted the DCCC post, which he knew would consume him for two years and take time away from his young family. In return, he demanded a coveted seat on the House Ways and Means Committee and a place on Pelosi's leadership team if the Dems took back the House.

However reluctant Rahm might have been to take the job, he attacked it with his typical manic energy. He spent months recruiting top-notch candidates in swing districts, love-bombing them with visits, e-mails, and follow-up calls. When Heath Shuler, a former NFL quarterback from western North Carolina, initially refused Rahm's draft appeal because he worried about being away from his small children, Rahm called him repeatedly from his own family events. "I'm at a soccer game with my kids. Just wanted to let you know that," Rahm would say, and hang up. "I'm at a kindergarten play now. Talk to you soon," he'd bark. After ten of these calls, Shuler finally surrendered. Then, after he'd rounded up an all-star slate of challengers, the relentless Rahm spent hours each day overseeing their progress and raising money for an independent campaign to support their candidacies. My firm agreed to help shape strategy and produce party-sponsored ads in a handful of these pivotal districts. As part of the deal, and in a nod to a friendship of more than twenty years' duration, I threw in therapy calls with Rahm at all hours of the day or night, which I knew I would have received in any case.

We took on one other assignment in 2006 that was a labor of loyalty and love—one that would provoke one of the few angry exchanges I ever had with Barack Obama.

My close friend and former business partner, Forrest Claypool, was rattling one of the few pillars still standing from the old Chicago Democratic machine by challenging a longtime incumbent for president of the Cook County Board of Commissioners, a position second in power only to mayor.

It wasn't the first time Forrest had shaken things up. When Daley appointed him to head the Chicago Park District in 1993, Forrest slashed a bloated bureaucracy, fired politically connected slackers, and used the proceeds to enrich park programs. Daley saw the parks as vital civic assets and neighborhood anchors, and tolerated Forrest's reforms despite wails of discontent from patronage-hungry ward committeemen. Then, in 2001, when Forrest decided to challenge a veteran ward heeler with ties to the Daley family for a seat on the county board, the mayor fought unsuccessfully to stop him.

Now, after four years as a reform voice on the board, Forrest was challenging one of Daley's longtime African American allies, John Stroger, for county board president. Forrest saw it as a chance to reform another bloated, underperforming government body. Yet the mayor and his organization were hell-bent on defending their man. Yes, Stroger, seventy-six, was well past his prime, and his prime wasn't all that impressive, but he had earned their fidelity with his own, having supported young Rich Daley for mayor over Harold Washington—the only black ward committeeman to do so—just as he would back Dan Hynes over Obama in the Senate primary two decades later.

I respected Daley and valued our relationship, but I also believed deeply in Forrest, his passion and integrity. I knew the difference he could make to fix an antiquated, corrupt system that, among its other responsibilities, administered the county's health care system for the poor. If he succeeded there, he would be well positioned for higher office in the future. So I worked pro bono for his insurgent campaign, and Forrest slowly gained momentum—with the support of the local newspapers, government reform groups, and a few politicians like Rahm who were willing to buck City Hall. Still, there was one endorsement I felt could make the difference.

I knew Barack admired Forrest and didn't think much of Stroger, and given Stroger's snub in the Senate race, Obama owed him nothing. Yet Obama also believed that to side openly against the highest-ranking African American in Chicago would be a needless affront to the community. Under pressure from both camps, Barack wearied of my repeated appeals to his conscience.

"David, stop it. Just knock it off," he said with irritation, when I called him in Washington to make a last attempt to sway him. "You're not thinking about my interests here. I haven't endorsed Stroger, even though Emil Jones has been pounding on me to do it. It's only out of respect for Forrest, and you, that I've stayed out of it. And by the way, Forrest didn't endorse me when I was running. I didn't push him. He had his own politics, and I understood. So stop pushing me. I don't want to have this discussion again."

Obama's flash of anger was extremely rare, and thus jarring. I had clearly touched a nerve by suggesting that his neutrality was somehow a dereliction of his responsibilities and, more critically, an abandonment of principle. I was in the wrong there. Blair Hull had given twenty-one thousand dollars to Forrest in his first run for office, so, partial as he was to Barack, Forrest had made no endorsement in Barack's Senate race. When I related my conversation with Barack to Forrest, he understood. "That's fair," he said, with a shrug. "I totally get that. He doesn't owe me a thing."

Forrest progressed, even without Barack's backing, and was surging a week before the primary when we learned that Stroger had been rushed to the hospital. Though the extent of his condition was initially shrouded in secrecy, he had apparently suffered a stroke. Suddenly, the dynamic had changed. "It's over," Forrest said glumly. "There is going to be a rallying around John now." Indeed, Daley, Senator Durbin, and other party leaders seized the moment.

They urged a vote for Stroger as he waged his valiant struggle, and confidently assured the public that he would return. He never did. The ailing county board president narrowly won the primary in absentia, only to be replaced on the ticket a few months later by his son Todd, one of the lesser lights on a dimly lit City Council. John Stroger never again appeared in public and died two years later. Obama publicly declared on the eve of the primary that he would vote for Forest, but it was too late. I will never know if an earlier announcement might have made the difference in a tight race, but in terms of his own political considerations, he clearly made a shrewd assessment and, ultimately, the right decision.

Sometime in the spring or early summer of 2006, I got a call from Barack.

"I just had the strangest meeting with Harry Reid and Chuck Schumer," he said. "I didn't know why they were calling me over there. Turns out they wanted to tell me I should run for president."

Though Schumer signaled he couldn't publically oppose Clinton, neither he nor Reid thought Hillary could win. They saw her "yes" vote on the Iraq invasion as an albatross that would sink her, and they worried that their Senate candidates could be sucked down with her in the undertow. As a compelling new face, Barack was untainted by the war or by hostile sentiments aimed at Washington, and had proven to have a broad appeal that could expand the electoral map and redound to the party's benefit in November.

"They pushed me pretty hard to think about it. I still think it's far-fetched, but it was interesting that they felt as strongly as they do," Barack told me. "Interesting" was a euphemism. "Intriguing," perhaps "tantalizing," even "incredible" would have better suited the moment. If two of the most powerful Democrats in Washington thought he was ready to be president, and could win, who was he to dismiss the idea?

Barack was a long way from overtly signifying his interest, but he was certainly creating excitement wherever he went. Both the growing sense of outrage over the rancid politics of the nation's capital and the sputtering war effort were creating a growing appetite for change, particularly among Democrats. Even for the famously chill Obama, this surprising encouragement from unexpected quarters had to be intoxicating. Still, in the spring of 2006, less than a year and a half into his Senate term, the notion seemed implausible.

I was so certain that Obama would not run for president in 2008 that I had begun to plan a hiatus from campaigns. I already had opened informal chats with friends in journalism about writing occasional campaign analyses of the

2008 race, rather than participating in it. Combining my passions for journalism and film production, I also had launched a documentary project about Father Michael Pfleger, the fiery, white Catholic priest of St. Sabina Church on the black South Side. Through sheer force of personality, Pfleger had revived a dying parish and the impoverished neighborhood around it. But his tactics were those of an organizer, and he was as brash in challenging the conservative archdiocese as he was in confronting local street gangs and drug dealers. I was convinced that, despite his accomplishments, Pfleger would be forced to leave the parish he had led for a generation, and I knew this painful drama would make for a great film.

There was another reason I was making alternative plans. Four of my former clients were already at the starting gate for the presidential race: Clinton, Edwards, Vilsack, and Senator Chris Dodd of Connecticut. Edwards, given our rocky past, was a nonstarter. Then there was the odds-on favorite, Hillary, but the idea of working with Mark Penn (her chief strategist) again was unthinkable. I already had informed my partners and staff that I was planning to sit out 2008. The only thing that would change my thinking was if Obama were to run.

In mid-August, Obama took off for a seventeen-day official trip to Africa, with Gibbs and Mark Lippert, Obama's national security adviser, the only staff allowed on what was an official congressional trip. With such a small entourage, the logistics were rocky. The value of the trip, however, was immeasurable. Wherever he went, Obama stirred a huge response, yielding scenes more appropriate to a visiting head of state than a freshman U.S. senator. It was a stature-enhancing tour, and as I watched, I was sure it would further stir speculation about 2008.

"You know, having witnessed this trip, I am beginning to believe this guy is ready to be president," Gibbs told me when they returned. "The reaction he got over there . . . the way he inspired people . . . it was pretty remarkable."

Slowly, subtly, what a year earlier had seemed impossible, had evolved into something more than a pipe dream.

Privately, Barack continued to express healthy skepticism. Self-confident though he was, he was not blind to the audacity of such a candidacy or, more important, the organizational challenges of pulling it off. No less daunting would be the challenge of persuading Michelle that his running for the presidency would be the right path for their young family. Yet after the trip to Africa, Barack was privately a little more forward-leaning. The reception he had received overseas, coupled with the extraordinary media coverage of the trip back home, was an encouraging sign. "With so many folks talking to me about running, I feel like I have an obligation to at least think about this in a serious, informed way," he said to me. "Let's collect some information and sit down after the midterms and see where we are at."

For an Obama candidacy, we reasoned that Iowa stood as the critical threshold. It was the same test Paul Simon had faced twenty years earlier. If Barack, as a progressive senator from a neighboring state, could not make a strong showing in a contest traditionally dominated by liberal activists, he would have no chance to pull off a long-shot candidacy on less friendly political terrain. On the other hand, a victory in these first-in-the-nation caucuses would make all things possible. So as he continued to demur publicly, Barack authorized us to engage in some discreet polling to test the plausibility of an Iowa campaign.

Even before the polling, Obama would have a chance to test his Iowa chops at Senator Tom Harkin's annual Steak Fry, a highly prized event that attracted thousands of hard-core Democratic activists from across Iowa—the type of people who would be important players in the 2008 presidential caucuses. Much like the Florida Democratic convention organizers, Harkin told Obama he needed him to help fend off all the presidential wannabes, most of whom were hungry for the keynote slot. Obama was the perfect compromise: an A-list attraction who had disavowed a 2008 candidacy. But if he accepted, his disavowal of interest might begin to strain the straight-face test. "If we do this, the whole presidential thing is going to kick up like ten notches," I told Gibbs. "Oh, don't I know," he replied. "Be kind of fun to screw with everybody, though."

If Obama was looking for encouragement, he found plenty in Indianola, the site of the Steak Fry. A much larger than usual crowd of about thirty-five hundred activists turned out for Harkin's event and cheered wildly as Barack made a robust case for a renewed Democratic vision that he had refined over his year of political travels. "I'll tell you what," Obama said in his typically understated manner, after returning from his Iowa expedition. "If I did run, I'd have a few supporters there."

When Paul Harstad's hush-hush poll came back at the beginning of October, it confirmed Barack's upbeat assessment. Edwards, who had finished a strong second to Kerry in Iowa in 2004, was well in the lead with 33 percent. Hillary followed with 18—but right behind her, at 15, came Obama, ahead of

2004 caucus winner Kerry and seven other potential candidates all mired in single digits. Without a candidacy or campaign apparatus, and despite being brand new to the national scene, Barack was already in the top tier, with room to grow.

With the encouraging Iowa results in hand, we decided to repeat the polling exercise a few weeks later in New Hampshire. Far from our Illinois turf, we didn't have high expectations, but when the results came back, they showed Obama trailing Hillary by just seven points, with Edwards in third and the rest of the field well behind—this, despite the fact that Obama had spent no time in the Granite State and was virtually unknown to nearly one out of three voters. Holy shit, I thought. This goddamned thing could happen.

After his election to the Senate, Obama had signed a contract to write a second book. It was to be a volume of his reflections on politics and policy. Only there wasn't a great deal of time for reflection. Pressed by his day job, political travel, and the desire to spend time with his family, he had not exactly hunkered down on the project. So throughout the early winter and spring, chapters were flying between Obama and his team. He would hole up in his tiny apartment near the Capitol, writing deep into the night. His policy advisers checked and supplied facts. Favreau contributed edits for language. The political team read for potential land mines—though Obama ignored some of our red flags, having eagerly planted them in the manuscript. That the race to the finish line was such a frantic process made the final product all the more remarkable. The book reflected serious, hard thinking about where we were as a country and where we needed to go.

What animated *The Audacity of Hope* were the stories of people, written with the narrative skill of a gifted novelist. It occurred to me, in reading the manuscript, that Obama approached every encounter as a participant and an observer. He processed the world around him with a writer's eye, sizing up the characters and the plot, filing them away even as he fully engaged in the scene. He has appreciation for irony and a firm grasp on the fact that some things remain beyond our control. It's a quality that contributes to his outward calm, even amid utter chaos.

When Obama signed his lucrative book deal, however, it wasn't with 2008 in mind. But by the time *The Audacity of Hope* appeared, just weeks before the

2006 midterm elections, its publication was viewed by the political world not as a pragmatic moneymaker or a means for Obama to organize and present his views, but as another signal of his political intentions. And the reaction was kinetic.

Though he scrambled to make his deadline, the book was released on October 17 to rave reviews and shot to the top of the charts. Obama was back on the television circuit and touring the nation, where his book signings drew overflow crowds. As folks passed through the line for an autographed copy and a quick hello, many of them urged Barack to take the plunge into the presidential race.

One Saturday in late October, I met Barack and Gibbs in Philadelphia, where hundreds of people had lined up at a local library for a book signing. Obama was taping *Meet the Press* the next day, and I was there to join Gibbs and Barack on the ride to Washington to run through the questions he'd likely face.

The interview was scheduled to promote Obama's book, but there would be an unmistakable subtext. Rigorous as Russert was, *Meet the Press* had become a required proving ground—or killing field—for potential presidential candidates. With Obama's rising stature, Russert would put him through his paces, testing this rookie with the fastballs and hard curves that a serious presidential candidate would be expected to handle.

"One thing you can be one hundred percent sure Tim will do is replay the tape of you on his show from January, when you said you wouldn't run for president or vice president in 2008," I said, as we rumbled down I-95 toward DC.

"Right," Obama said. "Well, I see no point in playing games. I'm going to tell him that I've changed my mind and I'm thinking about it."

Gibbs, who was sitting in the jump seat of the Suburban, shot me a quick glance. We knew that such a statement would be big news, a seismic event that would send the Washington political class into a frenzy.

"Sir, that's fine by me," Gibbs said, "but have you mentioned this to Mrs. Obama?" Robert knew that Michelle was far from sold on the wisdom of a presidential campaign and would not be thrilled to learn about her husband's altered sentiments by watching TV. "Ooh, that's a good point, Robert," Barack said, wincing at the thought. "I'd better give her a heads-up." It probably was a conversation he was less than eager to have. Michelle was barely tolerating the demands of Barack's schedule as a senator and barnstorming campaigner. She was far from ready to sign off on an even bigger and more demanding venture.

The next day, Gibbs and I accompanied Obama to the NBC studios in Washington. Before the show, the garrulous Russert greeted us in the green room, a large sheaf of papers under his arm. They were filled, Gibbs and I suspected, with highlighted passages from Obama's book and likely his public statements dating back to grade school. When the interview began, it was vintage Russert from the first question:

"Let me start with Iraq, because you write about it in your book and you've been talking about it on the campaign a little bit," he said. "This is what you told *New Yorker* magazine: 'There's an old saying in politics: when your opponent's in trouble, just get out of the way . . . in political terms, I don't think that Democrats are obligated to solve Iraq for the administration.' Is there an obligation in non-political terms?"

It was a bracing opener, a tough but fair and exceedingly important question, designed to probe whether Obama was a standard-issue Washington politician, crassly thinking about the next election, or something more. We had anticipated it and Barack didn't flinch or hesitate when it came.

"Yes, and then, you know, if you follow up the quote in that magazine article, what I said is, despite the politics, we have young men and women who are putting their lives at stake in Iraq," Barack explained, pitching his plan for a phased withdrawal of troops. "We're making an enormous investment on the part of the American people, and so we do have an obligation to step up."

For twenty-five minutes they went back and forth, Russert challenging Barack with his own quotes, not merely to set traps but to elicit a deeper understanding of how a President Obama would approach issues ranging from Iraq to North Korea to Darfur. When and where would he commit troops? Would he be willing to negotiate with hostile foreign leaders? Just what had he meant when he wrote that President Bush had a "messianic certainty," or that his own party was "confused"?

Barack's answers were thoughtful and confident. He was passing the Russert Test with flying colors. As the interview turned to the homestretch, Russert prepared the ground for the question that had been hovering over the entire interview.

"You've been a United States senator less than two years," Tim said, leaning in. "You don't have any executive experience. Are you ready to be president?"

Obama was certainly ready for that question.

"Well, I'm not sure anybody is ready to be president before they're president," he replied. "You know, ultimately, I trust the judgment of the American people that, in any election, they sort it through . . . You know, we have a long and rigorous process, and, you know, should I decide to run, if I ever did decide to run, I'm confident that I'd be run through the paces pretty good, including on *Meet the Press.*"

His answer all but demanded the question we had anticipated.

"Well, nine months ago, you were on this program and I asked you about running for president. And let's watch and come back and talk about it."

Russert then played the tape from January, when Barack firmly disavowed a candidacy for national office in 2008. Was that still his position?

"Well, that was how I was thinking at that time," Barack said. "And, and, you know, I don't want to be coy about this, given the responses that I've been getting over the last several months, I have thought about the possibility. But I have not thought about it with the seriousness and depth that I think is required. My main focus right now is . . . making sure that we retake the Congress. After November 7, I'll sit down and consider it, and if at some point, I change my mind, I will make a public announcement and everybody will be able to go at me." Russert raised his eyebrows in surprise.

"But it's fair to say you're thinking about running for president in 2008?"

"It's fair, yes."

The day after the interview, Russert called:

"You know, I've been doing this show for fifteen years, and no one has ever done that before," he said admiringly. "No one has ever simply fessed up and said, 'Yeah, I said that about not running, but now things have changed, and I'm thinking about running. I've changed my mind.'"

Tim might have found Obama's handling of the Question disarming, but not everyone was charmed. While offers of support and encouragement did pour in, there was no shortage of quotes from supporters of Hillary and the other candidates—blind quotes, of course—dismissing Obama's preparedness and, ultimately, his prospects. Also, not everyone was ready to take the idea of an Obama candidacy seriously. *Time* ran a cover story that week by its seasoned political writer Joe Klein, headlined: "Why Barack Obama Could Be the Next President." As soon as the magazine hit the streets, Gibbs grabbed a copy from a newsstand in downtown Chicago. As Robert was paying, the vendor glanced over his shoulder at the headline and scoffed. "Fuck *that!*" the man said with a smirk, as if finding the whole premise ridiculous. When Gibbs shared this story, Barack howled with laughter.

Obama had spent the year raising millions and logging thousands of miles campaigning for Democrats and collecting valuable chits for whatever was to come. Entering the midterm election year as the party's most sought-after surrogate, Barack now emerged from it as its most intriguing prospect.

THIRTEEN

AN AUDACIOUS DECISION

THE NIGHT BEFORE the 2006 election, an exhausted and emotionally depleted Rahm called me in despair. He was convinced, despite all objective evidence, that his Herculean efforts to take control of the House had fallen short. He was inconsolable. "We're not going to make it," he moaned. "I know it. We're going to lose." A day later, he was the toast of Washington, shimmying and clasping hands with incoming Speaker Nancy Pelosi and other House Democratic leaders in a joyous, if awkward, victory dance.

I had a lot of happy options for my Election Night. I could have gone to Boston, where I could personally have congratulated my sister, Joan, for her prescience, as Deval Patrick celebrated a landslide victory in his gubernatorial race. Or I could have taken the short hop up the highway to Milwaukee, where my friend and client Herb Kohl would be rewarded for his excellent service with a fourth term in the U.S. Senate. I decided to spend the night in Washington with Rahm. I knew it would mean a lot to him if I showed up—and I also thought that, just in case the numbers were wrong and the night went sour, I should be there for his very pointed "I told you so!"

I had become accustomed to the campaign cycle and the physical and emotional toll inflicted by the final sprint to Election Day—a blur of urgent calls, quick strategic judgments, last-minute film shoots, and long nights in editing suites. Even when you got a few hours' sleep, your mind never stopped racing. It is an eight-week rush that comes to an abrupt end, and win or lose, you quickly move into recovery mode. You spend what's left of the year decompressing, sleeping in, taking deep breaths, acclimating yourself to the rhythms of everyday life and reintroducing yourself to your loved ones.

Yet there would be no break in 2006, no time at all to recover or unwind. The morning after the election, I got on a plane and returned to Chicago for a meeting that would launch the next election cycle—and phase of my life.

As much out of necessity as a sense of propriety, Barack had postponed any in-depth discussions about 2008 until after the 2006 election. Given his relentless campaign and book promotion schedule, it was unrealistic to carve out the requisite hours for such a monumental subject. Nor could his political operatives bring full focus to the next campaign while we were in the final throes of our current races. With time short for a decision, though, we had agreed to convene the day after the election. So, on the afternoon of November 8, a weary team assembled with Barack and Michelle in the windowless conference room of my office to begin the 2008 conversation in earnest.

I could not recall a single campaign meeting Michelle had attended during his race for the Senate, but the Obamas knew the magnitude of the commitment that would now be under discussion, a commitment that would profoundly impact their family and demand far more of Michelle than the past campaigns. If she were going to be a partner in the campaign, as voters now required of their potential First Ladies, she had to be a full partner in the decision to run. Without her blessing, it would be a nonstarter. Without her total commitment, a blessing wouldn't be enough. And she naturally wanted to hear firsthand what a campaign would entail.

The Obamas had brought two close friends whose counsel they sought in evaluating the decision from a little more emotional distance. Marty Nesbitt was Barack's neighbor, peer, and basketball-playing buddy. He was a successful entrepreneur who had built a nationwide business from off-site airport parking lots. Though he had helped raise money for Barack's previous campaigns, Marty was not a big political player in Chicago. That wasn't his passion. Yet he was passionate about their friendship, and he was there to watch his best friend's back.

Valerie Jarrett was someone I knew better. A lawyer and real estate developer, she had been involved in city government in a variety of positions since the days of Harold Washington. Valerie hailed from one of the city's most prominent African American families. I had always found her to be both smart and pleasant, but she also had earned a reputation around City Hall as a tenacious, bureaucratic infighter. In 1991, as Daley's deputy chief of staff, Valerie hired Michelle Robinson, a bright young lawyer from one of the city's leading firms. Valerie quickly became a mentor and friend to Michelle and her fiancé, Barack Obama, for whom she opened doors to useful political and social circles.

Rouse, Gibbs, and Alyssa had flown in from Washington for the meeting. My partners Plouffe and Kupper were there, as was Steve Hildebrand, an experienced operative who had run Iowa for Al Gore. It was a mighty small group, I thought, considering such a huge undertaking, but if Obama decided to run, this impressive team represented a solid start. Every consultant or staffer in the room had presidential campaign experience, and most shared the chippy DNA of insurgents. Going in, however, few of us believed that Barack would actually run.

"All this hype has been flattering," he began. "But running for the presidency, much less being president, is a serious business, so I want to give this the consideration it deserves."

He spoke of three separate areas of concern on which he would focus in order to make a decision, including the impact on his family and the sheer feasibility of such a race. Then he began making an eloquent case for why it was even worth exploring.

The country, he said, was in a perilous place, confronted by big, long-term challenges such as health care, climate change, and frayed alliances in the world. The special interests were strong and getting stronger, and the middle class was under siege. Against this, we were hamstrung by small, divisive politics that made solving big problems virtually impossible. It was a critical moment in the nation's history. Could he bring something different, something more useful than just fresh and moving rhetoric, to the daunting challenges facing America?

"That's a question I am wrestling with," he said. "Because if the answer is no, Hillary is a very capable person and there are other good folks running."

Most of the conversation was nitty-gritty politics. Having ceded so much early ground to Hillary, Barack questioned whether it was possible to close the gap. Could we raise the money? Hillary's team was boasting of reaping one hundred million dollars for the primaries alone. Could we build organizations to compete in states in which Obama had barely set foot? Obama was particularly concerned about whether we could build out a team to compete with a Clinton organization already a quarter century in the making. "I just don't know if we can attract the kind of talent we need this late in the game," he said, woefully underestimating his appeal to the young campaign warriors who are the backbone of such efforts. The consensus was that it was possible, and Barack made testing that proposition a priority.

Still, as he surveyed the room, few sugarcoated the magnitude of the challenge or the personal sacrifice it would require. Hillary was an imposing, well-financed front-runner, and Edwards remained a significant obstacle in Iowa, where he was popular with the left-leaning caucus crowd. The harder-edged populism he had now fully embraced sold well there. To succeed, we would have to pitch a nearly perfect game and demand total commitment from everybody involved in the effort—and if we pitched the perfect game and won, Gibbs pointed out, well, that would just be the beginning.

"You shouldn't think of this as a one- or two-year commitment," he told Obama. "Because if you get in, I presume you get in because you think you have a reasonable chance to win. So you kind of have to think of this as, possibly, a ten-year commitment, not one."

Everyone in the room believed that Barack had special gifts and a unique ability to inspire a nation desperate for change. The daunting challenges notwithstanding, we agreed that if ever there was a time for such an insurgency, this was it. Nevertheless, we didn't want to leave the meeting without having offered an honest portrayal of the downside of the endeavor for the Obamas. Presidential campaigns are endurance tests. The physical, emotional, and intellectual demands are extraordinary and, quite often, excruciating, as befitting a contest for the world's most difficult job. If Obama ran, the experience would be exhilarating, but it would unquestionably be a relentless ordeal, too. We did not want to be in a position, months down the line, to have either Obama say, "Why didn't you warn us?"

The only outlier in this was Hildebrand, who let his emotions cloud his judgment. He was so painfully eager to see Barack run that he painted a comically idealized portrait of campaign life. When an apprehensive Michelle asked about the demands on her and the children, Hildy's description sounded more like a trip to Disney World than two years of unstinting sacrifice.

"Barack will be able to take some weekends off, at least in the beginning," he said. "And in the summer, it will be great for your girls to come along the campaign trail. There will be fun state and county fairs. They'll love it."

We all stared at Hildebrand in disbelief as he spun this fantasy, and politely worked to paint a more realistic picture of what would be required. Plouffe, in particular, made no attempt to dance around the issue.

"Let's not have any illusions: this is going to be a miserable slog for one year or, if you're lucky, two," he said in his best Joe Friday "Just the Facts" tone. "You, Senator, will be on the road constantly, and away from the kids. There won't be any weekends off. And with all due respect to Hildy, you're not going to want to drag your kids along that often. So there will be a lot of separation."

I was impressed with David's forthrightness, and was sure the Obamas would be, too. Barack didn't really know Plouffe, who had played a very limited role in his Senate race; Michelle had never met him. No one could accuse David of trying to inveigle Barack into the race under false pretenses. He offered a clear, direct analysis unfettered by sentiment, one that would appeal to a politician whose soaring idealism and high principles lived side by side with a pragmatic willingness to do what was necessary in the heat of battle.

As the meeting broke up, Barack assigned Rouse and Plouffe to probe deeper into the logistical challenges of mounting such a campaign: budgeting, fund-raising, available personnel. Alyssa and Gibbs would work on a sample schedule for the first few months of a campaign, and I would undertake a strategic memo on messaging.

Plouffe and Gibbs were convinced that, at the end of the day, Obama would not run. David called me from a cab headed to O'Hare for his flight back to Washington. "I just don't see him pulling the trigger." I wasn't so sure. It was plain that Barack had been giving this endeavor serious thought, and even after our overheated disclaimers, he was continuing our investigation into the process. Michelle was skeptical and, quite naturally, reluctant, but her participation in the meeting and the questions she raised suggested more openness to the possibility of a candidacy than I had suspected.

As I reflected on the possibility, I wrestled with my own ambivalence. Some of it was on behalf of my friends Barack and Michelle: I knew better than they did what a life-changing commitment this could be for them. I also had more personal reservations, born of sheer exhaustion. Having just finished another grueling campaign cycle, I had been looking forward to 2007 and 2008 as transition years into the next phase of my life, whatever that might be. I knew from experience what a presidential race would demand of me. Moreover, the Clintons had been good to me and my family. I could never forget Hillary's willingness to be there when Susan launched her charitable crusade against epilepsy, and I knew that the Clintons would see my role in this Obama insurrection as an unforgivable betrayal.

However, I also believed that Barack offered the country something Hillary could not: a fresh start. At a time of growing cynicism and division, he was a healing figure who was stirring a sense of hope and possibility, a phenomenon I hadn't witnessed since the Bobby Kennedy campaigns of my youth. Also, as in the '60s, it was the young who were responding most enthusiastically. They saw in Barack an authentic, contemporary leader who, like Bobby in my day, was willing to challenge the cramped dogmas that had come to characterize politics. They saw in him a chance to end the wars, both abroad and in Washington, and lift the nation's sights toward higher goals. So did I.

Also, the more I contemplated it, the more I became convinced that Barack could actually win. The "remedy, not replica" theory I had developed around mayoral races was even more germane to presidential campaigns, and no one in the field represented a cleaner break from the divisive politics of George W. Bush than Obama. I was not one for long memorandums. My insights tended to come in stream-of-consciousness riffs, which I would turn into catchphrases or thirty-second ads. Yet given the gravity of the decision ahead and the assignment I had been given, I set out to write a thorough analysis, beginning with what I believed would be the most critical dynamic.

"The most influential politician in 2008 won't be on the ballot," I wrote, in a twelve-page strategic memo I delivered to Obama shortly after Thanksgiving. "His name is George W. Bush."

With few exceptions, the history of presidential politics shows that public opinion and attitudes about who should next occupy the Oval Office are largely shaped by the perceptions of the retiring incumbent. And rarely do voters look for a replica. Instead, they generally choose a course correction, selecting a candidate who will address the deficiencies of the outgoing President . . .

Now we are entering a campaign that will be defined by vivid perceptions of Bush, his record and style of leadership. And that is our opportunity.

Where Bush is hyper-partisan, ideological and unyielding, voters will be looking for the next leader to rally and unify the country around our common interests and mutual obligations as Americans . . .

Where Bush's "Ownership Society" has turned a blind eye to the economic challenges facing many Americans in the new global economy, voters desperately want policies that will put wages, retirement security, health care and educational opportunity at the top of the national agenda.

Where Washington under Bush is a cauldron of special interest favors and inside deals, voters will demand honest, transparent government that puts the nation's interest first.

Where Bush and the Blame Government First crowd have bungled every major challenge since 9/11 while running up massive deficits, voters are asking for smart, frugal and efficient government.

Where Bush's bull-headed policies have created a foreign policy disaster in Iraq and weakened our overall defenses, voters will be asking for a new American foreign policy that is both strong and wise, emphasizing our ideals as well as our might and the multilateralism the neo-cons scorn.

The bottom line is this:

Voters are primed to turn the page and choose a candidate who offers an inspiring, inclusive, confident and HOPEFUL vision for America in the 21st Century.

They want to believe again in themselves, their country and their future. They want to believe again in America's exceptionalism, of which you are both a champion and a reflection.

For all these reasons, you are uniquely suited for these times. No one among the potential candidates within our party is as well positioned to rekindle our lost idealism as Americans and pick up the mantle of change. No one better represents a new generation of leadership, more focused on practical solutions to today's challenges than old dogmas of the left and right.

Obama's lack of high-level government or executive experience was an obvious concern and an inviting target for opponents, I wrote. In a section entitled "The Experience Trap," I argued that if ever there were an election in which Americans would value energetic, new leadership over years of

Washington experience, 2008 would be it. What seemed to be Obama's biggest vulnerability could prove to be an asset.

> Substantive ideas, judgment and *gravitas* are essential. But we should not get into a white paper war with the Clintons, or get twisted into knots by the elites. The insiders will never accept it, but this is a splendid time to be an outsider. That's one of the principal reasons to run now.

Unlike experience, strength is an indispensable quality voters would demand in a president, I wrote, and neither McCain, who endured more than five years of torture in a Vietnamese prison, nor Hillary, who had run a gauntlet of her own during her years in the public eye, needed to certify theirs. Obama's story—the son of a single mother and someone who rose from modest beginnings and youthful challenges to excel—was one reflection of his strength and character.

> But the campaign itself also is a proving ground for strength . . . How you respond to the inevitable challenges you'll face will reveal much about your strength and preparedness for the job.

I also offered Obama my assessment of his most prominent potential opponents:

> Hillary Clinton is a formidable candidate, who should be considered the frontrunner for the nomination because of her strength, intellect, discipline, and, of course, access to an array of assets far in excess of any other candidate.

As a city kid, I am no golfer, but I knew Obama was, so I faked it to make a point about Hillary's advantages.

> She and her team have played this course many times before. They know every bunker, sand trap and the lay of the greens. And she has the best caddy in the business.
> But for all of her advantages, she is not a healing figure . . . The more she tries to moderate her image, the more she jeopardizes herself in the nominating fight and compounds her exposure as an opportunist. And

after two decades of the Bush-Clinton saga, making herself the candidate of the future will be a challenge . . .

Edwards was "not to be discounted," I wrote, because of his strong populist appeal in Iowa and his experience as a presidential and vice-presidential candidate. Having left the Senate soon after his run in 2004, he, too, would offer himself as an "outsider." Nonetheless, Edwards still had a gravitas problem.

In our discussions, the candidate about whom Obama was most wary was not a Democrat, but McCain. Barack had watched McCain's spirited, insurgent "Straight Talk Express" primary challenge to Bush in 2000, during which the Arizona senator had shown significant appeal to independent voters. He was not afraid to buck party orthodoxy, most notably taking on moneyed interests through campaign finance reform measures. He had opposed the Bush tax cuts, which he argued skewed toward the rich and, later, because they were irresponsible in a time of war. The crusty, cantankerous former POW had shown political courage, and if any Republican could escape the stigma of Bush and offer a promise of change, it would be McCain. In his desire to be the nominee, however, McCain had begun to trim his sails, risking his maverick brand.

The GOP hierarchy, which almost always gets its man, seems resigned to McCain. But his nomination won't come without a fight or a cost.

He remains anathema to many activists within the party, from the Religious Right, which is deeply suspicious of his secular politics, to the tax cut purists to K Street. He knows he will have a fight, and this has caused him to make a series of Faustian bargains with the Right. From the dalliance with Jerry Falwell to his embrace of the anti-immigration panderers and gay marriage militants . . . McCain's Straight Talk Express has taken many awkward detours. It will be interesting to see how the irascible Senator, who prides himself on his image of courageous principle, reacts when he's challenged on this down the line.

And at the age of 73, he also will have a problem presenting himself as the candidate of the future.

McCain is formidable, to be sure. But he is not unbeatable.

Finally, I dealt with two issues that related to Obama himself: timing and temperament.

I strongly rejected the counsel of those advising Barack to wait and get some "seasoning" in the Senate before running for the presidency. I pointed out that the most common mistake made by other hopefuls in the past was passing on opportunities—waiting too long rather than running too soon.

You will never be hotter than you are right now. And with the longevity favored by the Washington establishment comes all the baggage. You could wind up calcified in the Senate, with a voting record that hangs from your neck like the anchor from the Lusitania.

For all the virtues and excitement of running for president, I warned,

it also is a relentless, bone-wearying, pressure-filled, degrading and often miserable gauntlet, in which you will be challenged and tested, poked and prodded. Every statement and proposal will be parsed and matched against past votes and pronouncements for inconsistencies. You will be locked in a constant game of Gotcha with a press corps, egged on by your opponents, who will see their role as challengers of the Obama Icon they helped create.

I continued:

At the risk of triggering the very reaction that concerns me, I don't know if you are Muhammad Ali or Floyd Patterson when it comes to taking a punch.

You care far too much what is written and said about you. You don't relish the combat when it becomes personal and nasty. When the largely irrelevant Alan Keyes attacked you, you flinched.

It had to be said. Neither Obama nor any of us knew how he would react to the intense, sometimes absurd scrutiny presidential contenders—and, even worse, their families—get. It is part of the test, and there is no way to simulate the pressures of it, or predict how any candidate, particularly a newcomer like Obama, would handle it. He needed to think about whether he was willing to commit himself to a regimen of irritation and worse.

Plouffe had been doing prodigious work assessing the challenges and logistics of such an ambitious start-up, and his managerial chops were something of a revelation to me. While he was a splendid partner and brilliant counselor, he generally deferred to me as the firm's senior partner on strategic and management issues. So when Rouse first suggested David as the manager, I was hesitant. He was an operational wizard, I thought, but could he take command? "I just don't know if he's a number one guy," I said, proposing that Rouse play the manager's role, with David as his deputy. Yet Rouse, a career government hand still smarting from Daschle's loss, had no interest in managing a campaign. He knew Plouffe from his stint as head of the DCCC, and thought he was right for the job. Maybe I simply hadn't seen Plouffe in that role. I asked Del Cecato, who had worked for him at the DCCC. "Are you kidding?" he replied, stunned by the question. "Plouffe's a brilliant manager. Best I've ever seen."

Our team reconvened in my office in mid-December to review where things stood and to see if Barack had moved closer to a decision. The most memorable and significant moment of that meeting was provoked by a question Michelle asked of him. Fiercely independent and protective of the kids, she was clearly working her way through her own distinct process. She believed in him and shared his convictions, and she recognized that this might be a watershed moment in his career. Yet career advancement alone wasn't a sufficiently good reason to turn their lives upside down.

"Barack, it kind of comes down to this. There are a lot of good, capable people running for president," she said. "What do you think you could contribute that the others couldn't?"

Barack responded quickly. He had plainly reflected on the same question.

"There are a lot of ways to answer that. But here's one thing I know for sure: the day I raise my hand to take that oath of office as president of the United States," he said, lifting his right hand, "the world will look at us differently, and millions of kids—black kids, Hispanic kids—will look at themselves differently."

The room was quiet after he spoke. In all our ruminations, we had talked about the practical challenges that race posed to our ability to win. Yet until that moment, no one had spoken out loud about what his winning would mean. In the eyes of the world, the election of a black man named Barack Obama to the presidency would be an affirmation of America's promise—and to those millions of American kids of whom Barack spoke, it would open up possibilities they could scarcely imagine.

Obama's simple, eloquent point was brought home to me a short time later, when I got a call from a young man named Brad Parker, an inner-city Chicago public school teacher who had grown up with my son Michael. Brad told me about one recent day when he was teaching a section on American presidents.

"One kid raised his hand and asked, 'Why are all these dudes white?'" Brad said. "So we had a discussion about it. And then I told them, 'But, you know, the next president could be our own senator, Barack Obama. And he would change that.'"

Brad said the reaction of these mostly poor, minority kids from the West Side of Chicago was kinetic. "Their eyes were like saucers, they were so excited. The idea that a person of color could be president—they couldn't believe it."

Despite his compelling answer to Michelle's question, Barack said they still had soul-searching to do. He promised to make a decision over Christmas, during his annual family vacation in Hawaii. Still, before he left, Barack asked Plouffe to manage the campaign, were it to move forward. Meanwhile, Michelle and Valerie asked me to dinner at Coco Pazzo, an Italian restaurant near my office, to discuss another and quite sensitive personnel matter.

"We have concerns about Robert," Valerie said. "We don't think he should be a part of the campaign."

That floored me. There was no doubt that Gibbs had some hard bark on him. He wasn't naturally trusting, particularly after his negative experience in Kerry's campaign. While he was ferocious in pursuit of Barack's interests, he was often the bearer of bad news—or the architect of it—for example, when dates were added to Barack's schedule that tugged him away from home. Barack was undoubtedly fine with letting Gibbs take the blame for some of Michelle's unhappiness and frustration, which might have contributed to her doubts about him.

I wondered if either Michelle or Valerie had broached the subject with Barack, who clearly valued Robert. He was an absolutely essential player. Brilliant, incisive, quick-witted, and experienced, he was as good as we could get in the spokesman's role. More than anyone, his hidden hand in shrewd, day-to-day political calls in the Senate office had been crucial in creating the opportunity for Barack. He'd proven an indispensable presence on the road, his loyalty was beyond question, and he had forged a palpable bond with Obama. I couldn't imagine Obama wanting it any other way.

"Look, if Barack runs, it's going to be a war, and Robert is a warrior," I explained. "We cannot do this without him." Michelle and Valerie relented, and I never heard any more about it.

Over the holidays, Susan and I had a chance to talk about the prospect of

Barack's candidacy. She was bullish, both for him and for me. Susan had great appreciation for Hillary, who had been the patron saint of CURE and a source of encouragement when Susan was battling cancer. Still, like many, Susan was virulently antiwar, disgusted by the antics in Washington, and excited by the prospect of Barack as president. I had missed two opportunities to work on presidential campaigns in the '90s because of our family circumstances—she discounted the Edwards experience, having opposed my involvement in that campaign from the beginning—but now, with our kids grown and Lauren's epilepsy stabilized, she felt that this was my time, and perhaps my final chance.

"I always thought if you could have helped Gore, you could have made a difference," she said, ascribing powers to me as only a loving wife could. "It sounds stupid, but I thought that if I didn't have cancer, and you could have helped him in that election, he would have won, and maybe there wouldn't have been an Iraq War. Barack will make a big difference and you know you can make a big difference for *him*."

On January 2, I was working in the small study off my office when Obama strode in unannounced, wearing blue jeans, a black zip-up jacket that seemed too light for the weather, and the ratty old Chicago White Sox cap he prized. He and the family had just come back from Hawaii, and it was time to fish or cut bait.

Everything was pointing to a run, and he seemed to be leaning toward it. The times were urgent. He had gone through real soul-searching about whether he was ready to be president, and he knew he could offer a profile and perspective others would not. He had come to believe that, though the odds were long, we could put together a competitive campaign.

On a personal note, he and Michelle both felt that a campaign now, when the kids were young, might be easier for them than later. "You know, they have their own lives right now—dance and stuff—and they're pretty much oblivious to all of this stuff. Later, it would be harder." And, he noted, if he won and served two terms, he would be just fifty-five when he left office. "There would still be a lot of life ahead of us," he said.

The arguments for doing it were pretty clear, but as a friend, I had to raise one last issue.

"My main concern is that you're not obsessive enough to run for president," I told him. "I've worked with Hillary. I've worked with Edwards. They will drag their asses out of bed at four in the morning day after day after day—even if they're deathly ill—because they *have* to be president. They're driven to be president. I don't sense that in you. You're ambitious, but you don't need to be president in that way. You like to hang with your family. You like to play hoops and watch ESPN. You may be too normal to run for president."

Barack smiled. "Well, you're right, I don't need to be president. It turns out that being Barack Obama is a pretty good gig in and of itself. If I run, I am going to have to find my motivation in the people and the ideas we're fighting for. But I'll tell you this. I am pretty damned competitive, and if I get in, I'm not getting in to lose. I'm going to do what's necessary."

After two hours of conversation, Barack went on his way. In the lobby of my office, he ran into Forrest Claypool, who inquired about the senator's latest thinking on the presidential race.

"It may not be exactly the time I would pick," Barack told him, "but sometimes the times pick you."

He patted Forrest on the shoulder and walked out the door.

FOURTEEN

IN LINCOLN'S SHADOW

Throughout Deval Patrick's improbable march to the governorship, it seemed as if his upstart campaign were destiny's child. Yet on the day he took office, it became absolutely clear that some higher power was at work on his behalf.

Deval had rejected the customary invitation-only inauguration in the Massachusetts House chambers, opting instead to hold his swearing in on the steps of the statehouse. He wanted to signify a new openness and share the moment with the many volunteers who had helped elect him. "They're my VIPs," he said.

Normally, early January in Boston is cold and gray, with temperatures topping out in the midthirties. But on January 4, 2007, the weather abruptly changed and the city was bathed in sun and springlike temperatures. Apparently, the Almighty wanted to signal his blessing on what was most assuredly a new day in the old commonwealth.

Susan and I had come prepared for winter, but we were delighted to unbutton our coats as we sat on the platform behind the podium looking out at the gleeful architects of this seismic political change. I had attended many such ceremonies, all of them happy occasions. Yet this felt very different. Like Barack, Deval had defied conventional politics by appealing to the best in people and trusting them with the truth. His election was deeply affirming, and his inaugural represented much more than the routine transfer of power. It was a joyous, hopeful celebration of community.

Deval understood this, and had labored on his speech throughout the night and into the morning, right up until the final moments before he and his family departed for the statehouse.

"For a very long time now, we have been told that government is bad, that it exists only to serve the powerful and well-connected, that its job is not important enough to be done by anybody competent, let alone committed, and that all of us are on our own," Governor Patrick told the crowd. "Today, we join together in common cause to lay that fallacy to rest, and to extend a great movement based on shared responsibility from the corner office to the corner of your block and back again."

As I took in this sublime scene, I thought about Barack and the weighty decision he would be making within days. What if we could replicate this moment for the whole country? What if we could overcome America's dispiriting politics and rekindle a sense of community and hope? Imagine how sweet it would be to sit on the platform of the U.S. Capitol two years from now and celebrate *that* victory!

Maybe it was an outrageous fantasy. Yet Barack's race for the U.S. Senate had been almost as unlikely. And what about Deval? A year earlier, the Beacon Hill crowd had called his candidacy a joke. Now they were calling him Governor. Each of these compelling men had mobilized grassroots movements that the political establishment could not foresee, even when they were right in front of their eyes. It was exciting to imagine that we might replicate this campaign for hope and change to a much grander scale.

I soon learned—in a decidedly ungrandiose call from Obama—that we would get the chance.

"Axe, I just called Plouffe and told him it's a go," Barack said a few days later. "Michelle and I have talked about it and we decided this may be as good a time as any for our family. And this may be a unique moment in time when someone like me could have an opportunity to make a difference. So let's get to work and see what happens. We have a lot of ground to make up."

When we gathered in Washington the following week, the ground we had to make up seemed most apparent. We had a senior staff of ten, and a whole lot of unmined potential that we needed to tap quickly. The Clinton world would soon shift from a position of bemused dismissal to one of active subversion, working to dry up money from donors and to chill potential supporters who might be willing to support Obama publicly. A news media that had been smitten with Obama would now assume their self-styled role of official hazers.

When we met in the borrowed conference room of a downtown law firm, we didn't waste any time brooding about the tough road that lay ahead. Collectively, the campaign team around the table represented a century of political experience garnered in some of the toughest campaigns and political venues. We were political warriors, not just a band of airy-headed dreamers. Yet we did share the idea that politics should be more than a game waged for the benefit of its players. We believed that politics, at its best, was the vehicle by which Americans could force meaningful change, change that was desperately needed. The never-ending war, a shifting economy that was yielding tremendous gains for some but shrinking security for many more, a health care system careening toward disaster, a climate issue unaddressed and threatening catastrophe—all were defining problems screaming for action. Winning wasn't nearly enough.

Most in the room, including Barack, were too young to remember Bobby Kennedy's iconoclastic campaign of 1968. RFK challenged a war, but also the conventional politics and stale thinking of the times. The young people who signed on back then sought to do more than simply win one man's election. They were out to change the world. Now, forty years later, we had a chance to rekindle that kind of idealism. We weren't daunted by the challenge of taking on the establishment or the prevailing political wisdom in Washington. We were energized by it.

"I have only three rules for this campaign, but I am going to insist on them," Barack said, addressing his team for the first time as a candidate for president of the United States.

The first is that this has to be a grassroots campaign because that's the kind of politics I believe in and the only way a campaign like this, or a candidate like me, can win. Change always begins from the bottom up.

Second, we're going to rise and fall together. When things get tough, and we know they will, I don't want to see us turning on each other. That means no Washington games. No leaking snarky items on one another. And if anybody violates this, they will no longer be a part of this campaign.

Finally, let's have some fun. Running for president is a deadly serious business, but it's also a great privilege to be out there fighting for people, for big, important things and the kind of world we believe in. There should be joy in that pursuit. So let's have some fun. Let's not be timid or afraid.

His final words of inspiration came from a Chicagoan, but an unlikely one. Paraphrasing Joel Goodsen, the Tom Cruise character from the 1983 teen odyssey *Risky Business*, Barack added, "I mean, sometimes you just have to say, 'What the fuck.'"

One of the challenges of being the young black guy without a lot of Washington experience is not having a deep bench of consultants. I had done the media and message work for Obama's Senate race, Paul Harstad had done the polling and focus groups, and Pete Giangreco had done the mail. Yet a campaign of this magnitude would require a larger cast. So, for me, it became a real-life version of the movie *Ocean's Eleven*. Like Danny Ocean, the film's eponymous central character, I set out to assemble a "dream team" of consultants equal to what promised to be a very complex caper.

Having weathered the Edwards debacle, I wanted to recruit a talented team that would not only do good work, but also work well together. I wanted folks who believed in Barack and the cause.

The first call I made was to an old friend, Larry Grisolano. Larry started in campaigns as a teenager in Burlington, Iowa, and had worked for me in the early '90s before establishing a thriving consultancy on the West Coast. He was an incisive strategic thinker and manager. I asked him to come to Chicago to coordinate the day-to-day media and polling operations of the campaign.

Polling and voter research were my next calls. I loved Paul Harstad, who was talented, passionate, and loyal, but given the volume of research required, I thought we would need more than his small shop could handle. So I called another old friend, Joel Benenson, in New York City.

Joel had done a brief stint working for Mark Penn during Clinton's 1996 presidential campaign, but couldn't have been less like him. Raised by a single mother in Queens, Joel came to polling in a roundabout way, working first as a beer distributor, then a journalist, and later as a campaign aide to Mario Cuomo. After his apprenticeship with Penn, Joel opened his own polling firm, and we worked together on several campaigns. His numbers were spot-on, his strategic advice sound, and his sensibilities very much those of an outsider.

As my mother's son, I prized good focus groups, which I had learned could unlock insights that can be difference makers in a campaign. Yet doing them right is the key. So I reached out to David Binder, a researcher from San Francisco whose perceptive focus groups with California voters had helped me work my way through several knotty campaigns. A native of Kewanee, Illinois, David had that quality we call "Midwest nice," a soothing neutrality that allowed him to put any group of voters he spoke to at ease.

I also went through some soul-searching about my own role on the ad-making team. I worried about my ability to write ads and still remain focused on the day-to-day strategy of a campaign that would be fought moment to moment. I asked the advice of my old friend Mark McKinnon, who had been the lead media consultant for George W. Bush. "You need to build an ad team," he said. "You think you're going to want to be writing spots, but you won't have time." I was pondering this on a flight from Chicago to Washington early in 2007, when I turned around and saw, a few seats behind me, the smiling face of Jim Margolis. I first met Jim in 1984 when he was the Illinois state coordinator for Mondale's presidential campaign. Since then, he had become one the top media strategists and ad makers in Washington. Jim was a great talent without all the cynicism and self-puffery that so often comes along with the package. I grabbed the empty seat next to Margolis and asked him if he would be interested in joining the team.

There were plenty of talented consultants to draw on, and given Obama's appeal, we were inundated with offers of help from Hollywood and Madison Avenue, too. We would add other gifted and creative players over time, but Grisolano, Benenson, Binder, and Margolis would become a tight, harmonious strategic core—a devoted Band of Brothers for whom I would be grateful every day.

The other piece we needed to get right was the communications team that would be dealing with the news media. With each passing election, this aspect of campaigning had become more frenetic and demanding. When I was a young reporter, we would write stories for the next day's editions, giving us time to report and the campaigns time to respond to our questions. The growth of cable television along with the emergence of the Internet changed all that. Now news was breaking minute to minute, from both traditional outlets and lone-wolf bloggers whom we'd never even met.

Gibbs would be at the center of managing this maelstrom, but we needed to build a team around him. At Rouse's urging, the campaign hired Dan Pfeiffer, an old Daschle staffer who had been communications director for Senator Evan Bayh before Bayh pulled the plug on his own presidential candidacy. Pfeiffer was hired to travel with Obama while Robert ran the communications operation at headquarters, but they would soon trade places. Gibbs, never much for writing memos, became restless in the office while the boss and the action were out on the road, and Pfeiffer, accustomed to the planning role, easily slipped into the desk job.

Plouffe assumed his new command with the steely determination of a battlefield general. He promoted a genuine esprit de corps among the troops assembling in Chicago—a band of agile, young, cyber-savvy renegades determined to reinvent campaigns.

Still, as much as he encouraged innovative thinking, David also established firm control. When, early on, I was quoted on a campaign matter, Plouffe confronted me. "You have to clear your interviews with the campaign in advance," he said. I was incredulous. I had been dealing with the news media my whole life. Hell, I was one of them! Now I needed clearance for my conversations with reporters I had known for decades? It was particularly galling coming from Plouffe, my former lieutenant at AKPD—but that was the point, of course. David was sending me a message. He was no longer simply a partner in my firm. He was the campaign manager and, as such, the final authority. It was a transition for me, having spent a lifetime bucking authority. The dustup— one of the few we Davids would have—came and went, and I pretty much continued to work in my own fashion. Plouffe gave me a wide berth to direct the message strategy of the campaign, but I took care to keep the campaign posted on my conversations.

Even as we built the team and established our headquarters in Chicago, we also had to move forward with preparations for a February 10 announcement. Alyssa's advance team had scouted several sites, but I was partial to the heavy Old State Capitol in Springfield, with its immense columns and rich history. It was there that Abraham Lincoln, the Great Emancipator, prepared for the presidency and plotted his strategy to save the Union. What better site for Obama to announce his candidacy? And what better town than Springfield, where Barack had forged so many bipartisan coalitions for progress during his years in the legislature? Our team felt we could draw a large crowd there, which was a first, critical test of strength. Also the small-town setting of Springfield would resonate with the people next door in Iowa better than a Chicago backdrop.

Before we got there, however, we had some important matters to resolve. One was to develop a distinctive logo for the campaign. Since the logo would have to travel from print to video, I tasked the folks at Crimson Creative Group, a Chicago edit house where I finished my ads, to come up with options. Colin

Carter, a splendid editor with whom I had collaborated for more than fifteen years, owned Crimson, and had some creative young designers on staff. I was looking for something that would transcend the usual political iconography and would speak to a movement for change, not just a campaign for office. As a starting point, I showed them the blue Harold Washington button from 1983 with the white lines that hinted at a sunrise. "I want something with a feel like this," I told Colin and his team. "Something hopeful. Something that speaks to a new beginning."

A few days later, they came back with a dozen imaginative options. Yet one immediately caught my eye. It was a round insignia with a red-and-white-striped ocean and a white sun rising on a sky-blue horizon. It was exactly what I had hoped for. Even though it employed traditional colors, it didn't look like a political insignia. Without Obama's name or a word of copy, the image conveyed so much. I could see it becoming the badge of the movement we hoped to build. As I circulated the proposed logo, however, I confronted a critical dissenter: the candidate.

"That's awful! It's so corporate!" Obama said, groaning. I pushed back, reminding him of his reservations about the "Yes We Can" tag line in 2004. "Trust me a little," I said. "Well," he said, with a frown. "We're on a short turn-around. I guess we can live with it for a while and see how people react."

Neither of us could have predicted that the sunrise logo soon would become as hip and ubiquitous as Apple's iconic insignia, emblazoned on everything from T-shirts to playing cards to any other tchotchke Plouffe could sell online to support the campaign.

The other and more urgent imperative, as we prepared for the launch, was the speech. Obama's formal announcement was generating enormous interest. It would be intensively covered, and would give Barack an unparalleled opportunity to introduce himself and his candidacy to a huge media audience. In the days leading up to the announcement, I worked on the speech with Favreau and another speechwriter, Wendy Button, whom I had known from my Edwards days. Drafts circulated among the three of us and, of course, Obama. The goal was to get a solid draft to Barack, knowing that he had all the chops to take it to the next level. Besides, the more he owned the words, the more powerfully he would deliver them.

As we discussed the speech, the imperative was clear: this had to be less a declaration of candidacy than a manifesto for change—and not simply a change of parties in the White House, but a fundamental change in the coagulated, self-interested politics of Washington. Obama's own remarkable story would be an important element of the speech, of course, but in the end, the speech would be less about Barack and more about the country; less about "I" and more about "we." Also, while it was essential to bring a strong indictment against the status quo, it was critical to describe an alternative—and far better—future. In place of cynicism and division, our appeal was to hope and change.

As a measure of the elevated attention the media were giving the Obama rollout, *60 Minutes* sent a crew to Chicago a full week before the announcement to interview Barack and Michelle for a piece that would air the day after he launched. The correspondent, Steve Kroft, and his crew gave it the whole nine yards, interviewing Barack in his home and on a drive through the South Side streets he had worked as an organizer and then represented as a legislator. They interviewed him in a van on the way to Springfield and again on the eve of his speech. Yet for all the tape they ran on Obama and all his wisdom and pronouncements, probably the most newsworthy bit came from Michelle, who revealed that she'd agreed to support his decision to run only after he pledged to quit smoking.

For a guy with few discernable bad habits, the cigarette was a glaring exception. It was his one act of complete defiance. He had been smoking since he was in his teens, and Michelle intended to use the campaign as leverage finally to get Barack to quit.

"I hate it," she told Kroft, when the subject of Barack's smoking came up. "That's why he doesn't do it anymore. Proud to say I outed him—I'm the one that outed him on the smoking. That was one of my prerequisites for, you know, entering into this race . . . he couldn't be a smoking president."

When Kroft asked Barack if he had really quit, Barack carefully described himself as a "recovering" smoker, and made reference to chewing Nicorette. Gibbs and I shot each other nervous glances. He might be "recovering," but we knew he hadn't yet "recovered," and after a lifetime of smoking, it seemed doubtful that Barack could quit cold turkey in the midst of the most pressure-filled venture of his life. But Michelle had seen her chance to pin him down on national TV, and she ran with it. "Please, America, watch," she said, with obvious glee. "Keep an eye on him, and call me if you see him smoking."

Maybe if Michelle had offered to pay a bounty to anyone who spied Barack smoking, it would have moved her penurious husband more. He continued to smoke surreptitiously throughout the campaign and beyond, sometimes going to farcical lengths to steal a smoke away from his family and public view. He would finally quit for good a few years later, only after winning the stressful battle for health reform.

Alyssa's team did remarkable work in preparation for the rollout. The setting promised to be as inspiring as the speech. We were overwhelmed by the number of people who signaled their intention to attend. The one thing our team couldn't control, however, was the weather, and on this day, Obama did not have Deval Patrick's good luck. The forecast was for bitter cold, and Michelle, now fully invested in the campaign, wanted to pull the plug on the historic Lincoln site.

"It's not right to ask people, a lot of whom will be bringing their kids, to stand out there for hours in subzero temperatures," she said. "I don't even want to subject *our* kids to that! Let's move it indoors."

Barack was sensitive to Michelle's point, and even more to her feelings. Having worked hard to convince her of the wisdom of the enterprise, the last thing he wanted to do was dampen her enthusiasm on opening day. "Michelle makes a good point," he said, but the rest of us were in a panic. The only alternative was the drab, hangar-like convention center in Springfield, which could accommodate only a fraction of the crowd we expected. It could turn a potentially spectacular announcement into a humdrum affair. So Alyssa and crew shifted into overdrive, purchasing ski caps, hastily embroidered with "Obama '08," twenty thousand sets of hand warmers, and a heater for the podium, all in a concerted effort to keep people warm and Michelle on board. To our relief, she grudgingly relented.

The afternoon before the Saturday announcement, Obama, his family, and senior staff boarded vans for Springfield. Though we all were encased in the multiple layers we thought we would need to ward off the elements, emotionally we were in the capsule and liftoff was at hand. All the months of contemplation and planning were over. Momentum and interest had been building steadily. We were looking forward to a great day. Then we got a call that punctured the buoyant mood.

Rolling Stone magazine had just released a profile of Barack, written by a hot young writer, Ben Wallace-Wells. Headlined "Destiny's Child," it was a generally positive piece, but the text on the magazine's cover—"The Radical Roots of Barack Obama"—portended something else entirely. In researching the piece, Wallace-Wells had spent time in the pews of the Trinity United Church of Christ, where the Obamas were congregants. There he witnessed a sermon by Dr. Jeremiah Wright, Trinity's outspoken and charismatic pastor, whose phrase "the audacity of hope" had provided Barack with the theme for his convention speech and the title of his latest book. On the day Wallace-Wells visited, however, Reverend Wright's sermon was geared less toward raising hope than raising hell.

" 'Fact number one: We've got more black men in prison than there are in college,' he intones. 'Fact number two: Racism is how this country was founded and how this country is still run!' There is thumping applause; Wright has a cadence and power that make Obama sound like John Kerry. Now the reverend begins to *preach*. 'We are deeply involved in the importing of drugs, the exporting of guns and the training of professional KILLERS. . . . We believe in white supremacy and black inferiority and believe it more than we believe in God. . . . We conducted radiation experiments on our own people. . . . We care nothing about human life if the ends justify the means!' The crowd whoops and amens as Wright builds to his climax: 'And. And. *And!* GAWD! Has GOT! To be SICK! OF THIS SHIT!' "

Noting Obama's professed closeness to his pastor, Wallace-Wells extrapolated from there.

"This is as openly radical a background as any significant American political figure has ever emerged from, as much Malcolm X as Martin Luther King Jr."

As we cruised toward Springfield, all I could think of was how our opponents and Fox News would pounce if Reverend Wright were to deliver the invocation as planned. On a day when our message would be about building community and healing the nation's wounds, we would be answering questions about Reverend Wright's contentious remarks. Fair or not, it would be fodder for those who wanted to tap into latent biases and portray Obama as a frightening and divisive figure. I called Barack in his van and explained the situation. He asked to read the story and then called us back.

"Well, we can't afford to let this story hijack the day," he said, without hesitation. The next morning, Reverend Wright led a private prayer with the Obama family and Senator Dick Durbin inside the Old State Capitol. I stood against a wall, and caught Wright's withering glare as he walked by. In his mind, I sensed, I was the political hack who had driven a wedge between the reverend and his most celebrated parishioner. To my mind, there went a man who, however important a role he had played in the Obamas' past, represented a problem we would have to manage carefully in the future.

Outside, the crowd that had begun to gather before dawn had swelled to more than fifteen thousand. This was not your typical political announcement. It was a coming together. And with temperatures near zero, coming together was more than a statement. It was a survival strategy.

"We all made this journey for a reason," Obama told the sea of frozen humanity before him. "It's humbling to see a crowd like this, but in my heart I know you didn't come here just for me—no, you came here because you believe in what this country can be. In the face of war, you believe there can be peace. In the face of despair, you believe there can be hope. In the face of a politics that's shut you out, that's told you to settle, that's divided us for too long, you believe we can be one people, reaching for what's possible, building that more perfect union."

Obama spoke of the lessons he learned as a young community organizer, working to help lift neighborhoods that had been ravaged by steel plant closings. He warmly recalled his years in Springfield, seeking common ground and workable solutions with legislators from throughout a profoundly diverse state.

"It was here where we learned to disagree without being disagreeable—that it's possible to compromise so long as you know those principles that can never be compromised," he said, pointing to the progress he had achieved in Illinois by bringing together disparate factions.

With bridging divisions and forging progress as his mission, Barack Obama stood in Lincoln's awesome shadow and announced his candidacy for president of the United States.

"I recognize there is a certain presumptuousness in this—a certain audacity—to this announcement," he said, conceding the obvious. "I know I haven't spent a lot of time learning the ways of Washington. But I've been there long enough to know that the ways of Washington must change."

That line, which I wrote into the speech, summed up what would be the unique calculus of our campaign. Perhaps in most years past, and possibly again in the future, the fact that Obama was just two years out of the Illinois State Senate would have been disqualifying. Yet in *this* year of pervasive alienation, many Americans would see the absence of years in Washington as a plus.

All of us know what those challenges are today—a war with no end, a dependence on oil that threatens our future, schools where too many children

aren't learning, and families struggling paycheck to paycheck despite working as hard as they can. We know the challenges. We've heard them. We've
talked about them for years.

What's stopped us from meeting these challenges is not the absence of
sound policies and sensible plans. What's stopped us is the failure of leadership, the smallness of our politics—the ease with which we're distracted by
the petty and trivial, our chronic avoidance of tough decisions, our prefer-
ence for scoring cheap political points instead of rolling up our sleeves and
building a working consensus to tackle the big problems of America.

With that, Barack laid out an ambitious agenda for change, from education
to health care to energy; an end to the Iraq War and the dawning of a new
foreign policy in which diplomacy would resume its rightful place in the forefront as a tool of American security.

"I know there are those who don't believe we can do all these things. I
understand the skepticism," he said, as more than a few people around me
nodded their hooded heads.

All of us running for president will travel around the country offering ten-
point plans and making grand speeches; all of us will trumpet those qualities we believe make us uniquely qualified to lead this country. But too
many times, after the election is over, and the confetti is swept away, all
those promises fade from memory, and the lobbyists and special interests
move in, and people turn away, disappointed as before, left to struggle on
their own.

That's why this campaign can't only be about me. It must be about us—
it must be about what we can do together. This campaign must be the occasion, the vehicle, of your hopes, and your dreams. It will take your time,
your energy, and your advice—to push us forward when we're doing right,
and let us know when we're not. This campaign has to be about reclaiming
the meaning of citizenship, restoring our sense of common purpose, and
realizing that few obstacles can withstand the power of millions of voices
calling for change.

My eyes welled up as Barack spoke. I had helped write the speech and advised on the stagecraft. None of what Obama said was a surprise to me. Yet, as
he spoke, I believed. I believed in his extraordinary ability to reason, to lead, to

inspire, and to speak hard truths. More than that, I believed in *them*, the thousands upon thousands of folks crowded into that plaza, folks who had come from near and far on a frigid day to begin the march for change.

"Hell," said a middle-aged man from Indiana who was captured by one of my cameras after the speech. "I'd crawl to Iowa to work for this guy."

This, I thought, was politics as it should be.

FIFTEEN

GROWING PAINS

PRESIDENTIAL CAMPAIGNS ARE a little like stage productions. Traditionally, they begin in semi-obscurity in remote hamlets, as candidates work through their lines and get a feel for their roles. If the play is well received in places such as Keokuk, Iowa, and Berlin, New Hampshire, then, and only then, do the critics take notice.

For Obama and our team, there was no time to take his show on the road. No trial and error in small venues. No discreet rehearsals away from the scrutiny of Washington players and pundits. His production opened on Broadway, under the brightest lights—and with the full battery of critics in attendance, eager to see if he could live up to his inflated advance billing.

The opening scene, the announcement in Springfield, was pronounced an absolute triumph. The launch, with its inspirational speech and large, buoyant crowd, had demonstrated the power and potential of an Obama candidacy. Nobody there could miss the fact that, despite the polar conditions, Obama had drawn not only a large crowd, but a diverse one. We would discover that it included many folks who had never been involved in politics before. Some came because they, like Obama, opposed the war in Iraq. Others were voicing their support for health care reform or new climate change policies. Many others were there because they were feeling the increasing financial squeeze on the middle class.

Beyond any one issue, however, they were drawn to that frozen square by something else as well. They were drawn there by hope, the audacious idea that, against the odds, we, the people, could push back against the bitter, atomizing politics of our time and join together as one American community.

Obama was both a trumpet *for* and a living symbol *of* that hope. He was a natural leading man for those fed up with the cynical, divisive, small-bore politics of Washington, seeking something better for our country.

Once the euphoria of that uplifting moment had passed, we faced the daunting challenge of maintaining its promise against the grinding realities of presidential politics. As with any epic drama, the hero would be tested, as would the idealism that brought so many to Springfield that day. And the journey would begin in Iowa, the first-in-the-nation contest, where the fundamental proposition underlying the campaign would either take root or wither and die.

Shortly after the announcement, we boarded a chartered 757 jet from Springfield to Cedar Rapids, Iowa, with fifty-seven members of the news media in tow. Both the hulking airliner and the media mob were bigger than any upstart challenger might reasonably expect on his first official campaign foray. Yet it was clear from the get-go that Obama was not just *any* upstart.

Early-stage presidential politics in Iowa are usually conducted through "living room conversations." This particular "living room" at Obama's first event, in Cedar Rapids, was a packed high school gymnasium. While many there seemed intrigued by Obama, this was just the beginning of an intense, year-long courtship. Iowans take their outsize role in the nominating process very seriously. They have a rare opportunity not just to *see* all the candidates for president—often several times—but actually to get to *know* them. Iowans are accustomed to being courted by presidential candidates one by one, just as if they were sizing up candidates for the town board. Still, twenty-five hundred Iowans turned out to take their first up-close look at Obama, an unprecedented number for a campaign event eleven months before the caucuses.

Barack gave a shorter, informal version of his announcement speech, and then endured a laborious interview onstage conducted by a prominent local citizen who seemed far more interested in his own questions than Obama's answers. Patience is more than a virtue in a presidential campaign. It's an absolute necessity. When the floor was finally opened up for queries from the audience, Barack got a taste of Iowa politics, and Iowans got a taste of Obama, with (beyond the big applause lines) all the nuances contained in his political views.

Obama received tumultuous applause when he reminded the crowd that he had opposed the Iraq War from the start, but when he told a questioner that he could not promise an immediate bounty for domestic programs once the war ended, because of other, pressing defense needs, he was met with stony silence. He was warmly received when he said teachers deserved much higher pay, but when he added that the increased pay should be tied to greater accountability and higher standards, many in the pro-union audience sat on their hands and rustled uncomfortably in their chairs.

Barack's bet, and ours, was that in 2008, candor was better than pander. While he wasn't above the pleasing line, he understood that you could not wage war against conventional politics by acting conventionally. Also, if we tried the tired game of promising everybody everything they wanted, we would quickly deflate the high hopes his candidacy had stirred.

As Obama was being put through his paces, I was standing near David Yepsen, the rumpled, curmudgeonly, longtime political editor of the *Des Moines Register*. I had known Yepsen for decades. Every four years, during the caucuses, he emerged as the most sought-after expert in American politics. After decades of dealing with an endless parade of aspiring presidents, Yepsen wasn't easily stirred, but on first blush, he seemed impressed with Obama. Barack seemed willing to silence the crowd with unwelcome truths rather than just bring them to their feet with words they longed to hear. "I don't know if this will work," Yepsen said, "but it sure is interesting."

In Ames the next day, five thousand people turned out for Obama at Iowa State University. The sheer size of the crowd was inspiring, and spoke to a hunger for something better and more hopeful than could be found in Washington. Yet the event in Ames brought another glimpse of realities we could not escape: the unrelenting scrutiny of the news media that skewed toward the critical.

In a riff touting his opposition to the Iraq War, Barack ad-libbed a line that caused me to wince. "We have . . . seen over 3,000 lives of the bravest young Americans wasted," he said. *Wasted.* While mostly everyone in that arena felt the war was a mistake, few veterans or their families wanted to hear that the lives of the dead and wounded had been wasted. They had done their duty. They had served and sacrificed for their country. That was not a waste, but heroism.

It was a small yet significant gaffe, the sort that caught the finely tuned ears of reporters and sent them scurrying to Gibbs for further explanation. When we took it to Barack, he was irritated with himself. "I never use that word," he told us. "I just screwed up. It was sloppy." Minutes after the speech, we set up a quick interview with the *Register* to clean up the remark by explaining that it was a regrettable slip of the tongue. We would point any reporter who brought it up to the newspaper transcript, but the offhand comment followed the candidate to New Hampshire the next evening, where he was forced to elaborate on his apology.

The episode was a bracing reminder that every word Barack spoke now would face heightened scrutiny. Being relatively unknown, he would find his every misstep reported and probed to see if it revealed some heretofore hidden attitude or flaw. Obama's rapid ascension from promising prospect to declared candidate meant that he now was aloft on the high wire, in full public view. Reporters and opposing campaigns would seize every opportunity to trip up this unproven talent who had, without paying his dues, commanded such extraordinary attention.

For Obama, who had lived a mostly charmed political life, this ratcheting up of the scrutiny was new and disconcerting. We didn't want to curb Barack's candor or spontaneity, or undermine his authenticity, but the slip in Ames underscored the need for discretion and discipline.

Welcome to the NBA, I thought.

This was the story for much of 2007, as Barack and the rest of us grappled with the sudden g-force that comes with being shot from a cannon. No matter how many campaigns you've worked on, it is still an unsettling experience. We also wrestled with the inherent tension between the spirit of change that had propelled us forward and the conventional, frequently grinding demands of a campaign.

That spirit continued to show itself in the enthusiasm of the crowds and the avalanche of small donations and volunteers that came in the wake of Barack's announcement.

Buoyed by more than one hundred thousand donors, half of whom contributed online, we raised an eye-popping twenty-five million dollars in the first quarter of 2007. This far exceeded our goals and shocked the Clinton world, which routinely listed fund-raising as one of its insurmountable advantages over all its rivals. Always seeking an edge, Plouffe stubbornly withheld the news of our haul until the last minute. He wanted to allow the Clinton campaign to turn over its card first, which they did with predictable braggadocio. Just as Plouffe hoped, allowing them their moment made our matching card more dramatic and unsettling for our opponents.

Rail thin from predawn runs, his piercing, blue eyes habitually framed in red due to lack of sleep, Plouffe never stopped thinking about how to gain an edge. He made himself the hub to which every department reported and, as a result, was the sole person with a grasp of the full scope of the campaign's activities. Though he most often kept his own counsel, when David did speak, he was remarkably direct, holding forth without unnecessary melodrama or unwanted guile. Even though he had spent a great deal of his adult life working in Washington, David burned with a healthy contempt for the myopic politics of the town. Yet he was no gauzy idealist. He was a hard-nosed competitor.

My role was Keeper of the Message and, I believed, the idealistic flame. I had been in my share of political scraps and wasn't averse to throwing a jab (or even a haymaker) when it was required, as I had demonstrated many times. Yet I believed that Barack had a unique chance to lift the country and bring people together by appealing to their common hopes and aspirations. Moreover, he would imperil our campaign if he resorted to conventional political warfare by mining their differences and fears. I also believed, at this moment in history, that America was hungry for that different kind of leader. "Let's never forget that it's not just about winning, it's about why," I would tell my team. "*That's* our edge. We lose that, we *can't* win."

I came to believe that Plouffe and I represented the yin and yang of Barack's personality: the fierce, pragmatic competitor, determined to win; and the genuine idealist, who saw public service as a calling and politics as a means of helping people. As bright and capable as he is, I knew that Barack would never have gotten this far with just one of those qualities—and we, as a campaign, could never succeed without both.

Meanwhile, new recruits were swarming our headquarters in downtown Chicago. They had given up jobs, taken leaves from school, and left behind family and friends to join our cause—often with no promise of pay. The place began to pulsate with a shared sense of mission as well as a healthy injection of youthful mischief. That proved to be one of the benefits of basing the campaign in Chicago rather than Washington: indeed, the chief rationale for that decision was to isolate the staff from the reflexive and numbing cynicism of the chattering class that is inescapable in the capital of conventional political thinking.

The early expressions of interest and support came from not just kids, but from iconic figures like Steve Jobs, the brooding genius of Apple. Obama visited with Jobs at his Cupertino, California, headquarters during an early West Coast swing, which led to one of the strangest interactions I would experience during the course of the campaign.

"He showed me this new phone they're going to be rolling out in June," Barack told me, after their meeting. "If it were legal, I would buy a boatload of Apple stock. This thing is going to be really big. He wants to talk with you about the campaign. Give him a call."

Jobs was not just the visionary developer of trailblazing products, but a marketing wizard, the brains behind the quirky, clever campaigns that turned those products into phenomena. Since we, too, were committed to "think different," I was looking forward to the conversation, but when I called to follow up, it became instantly clear that Jobs was less interested in talking *with* me than he was in talking *at* me.

"What is it that you *do*?" he demanded, with unmistakable edge.

I explained that I was the senator's media consultant, with overall responsibility for the message and advertising of the campaign.

"Yeah, well, I think what your industry does, if you call it an industry, is bullshit," he said. "You guys don't know anything about communication."

In addition to his well-deserved laurels for revolutionizing the way the world worked and communicated, Jobs had a reputation for rudeness and arrogance, which plainly was not unwarranted. I gently pushed back.

"Well, Steve, marketing a candidate for president of the United States is a little different than selling computers," I said.

"That's bullshit," he snarled. "You don't know what you're talking about. What's your communications plan?"

Twenty seconds into my answer, my brush with greatness came to an abrupt end.

"I don't have time for this crap. I'll call you back later," Jobs said. Before I could respond, he was gone. I wouldn't hear from him again until the general election, when his tone was decidedly friendlier.

Jobs's dismissive putdown notwithstanding, Barack was drawing increased support from the grass roots, the Netroots, and even from some tough-minded billionaires, an encouraging sign of early strength. Still, the candidate and the campaign were feeling the full weight of hoisting this ambitious start-up.

It all came to a head in late March, when Barack had his first major face-off with the other candidates at a health care forum in Las Vegas. With the cost of health care rising along with the number of uninsured Americans, health care reform loomed as a major issue for Democratic candidates. Disappointingly, we would fail the first test on this complex and contentious subject.

Our policy team had produced for Obama a dense, thirty-five-page brief filled with the arcana of health policy. What it lacked was a lot of thought about the message we wanted to spread, the quotable lines we wanted to deliver, and the real-life dynamics that were likely to play out on that stage in Vegas. Moreover, while it contained general principles of health reform, it offered no plan.

Hillary was confident and very coherent, drawing on the expertise she had gained leading her husband's ultimately unsuccessful health care campaign. Edwards, running from the left, played to the audience, with a passionate case for reform in human terms. Barack was the odd man out.

Pressed by a questioner from the audience on why there was no detailed plan for universal health coverage on his Web site, Obama awkwardly copped a plea. "Keep in mind that we, uh, our campaign now is, I think, a little over eight weeks old," he said, completely underwhelming the audience.

This was new and depressing terrain for Obama, who was accustomed to excelling. It had taken extraordinary self-confidence to enter the race for president just four years after leaving the Illinois State Senate. Now he was shaken. His unwavering confidence had taken a direct hit.

"Hillary looked like a president up there, and I didn't," he said glumly, when we spoke after the forum. "I am just not a very good candidate right now. But give me some time. I am going to figure this out. I will become a good candidate."

In all the years I had known Barack, I had never seen him like this. Innately resilient, he was unquestionably knocked for a loop now, stirring doubts in himself about his preparedness and justifiable concerns about the campaign's future. While he plowed on, doing everything that was necessary on the road, the anxieties and doubts created by this first face-off with his opponents lingered for months, and the day-to-day demands of the campaign became a grind.

Barack grew weary of reciting the same lines, and occasionally would riff off script—at times brilliantly and at others a little disjointedly. In town hall settings, he preferred to give each question its full due, responding with lengthy, ponderous answers, often saving the most relevant and useful points for last—a bad habit that would resurface time and again. He was frustrated by the endless game of "Gotcha" played by reporters, who also become bored with repetitive speeches and are always looking to stir the pot. He was tired of the travel, missed his family, and constantly lamented the lack of time he had to read and think.

At one point, he grew understandably weary of my constant critiques, and let me know in no uncertain terms. "You know, maybe you should run for president and get up there and answer these questions, David," he said. "This shit is not as easy as it looks!"

In late April we flew to Orangeburg, South Carolina, for the campaign's first debate.

Obama would debate twenty-seven times during the course of the 2008 campaign. While he never fully embraced the prefabricated nature of these affairs, over time he did gain confidence and boosted his proficiency. Still, there wasn't much time for improvement between Las Vegas and now. We had a lengthy prep session in Washington, but there were too many people involved, often offering conflicting advice. For his part, Obama was far more interested in exploring arcane points of fact than memorizing the snappy one-liners that win these events. I didn't come to Orangeburg with high expectations, and I wouldn't be disappointed.

Though we weren't going to stay the night, the debate's organizers provided holding rooms for us at a local motel. Michelle's was on one floor while Barack's was on another. When he emerged from his room, Barack's clothes reeked of an unmistakable odor. He was failing Michelle's no-smoking mandate. "She's either in denial or knows and is mercifully cutting him some slack," I told Gibbs.

The debate would be televised on MSNBC and heavily promoted by NBC, which released a poll the previous evening showing the gap closing nationally between Hillary and Barack. True to my Jewish, glass-half-empty outlook, I could see only the cloud around the silver lining: Barack would now be under even greater scrutiny, pressed by his opponents and probed by the pundits to see if he was worthy of his newly lofty standing in the polls.

When the lights went on, Barack did little to disarm the skeptics. He gave answers without great conviction, as he struggled to adjust to the sixty-second format. He seemed passive, perhaps even a bit intimidated by the occasion or the company. When the moderator, Brian Williams, painting a hypothetical crisis—simultaneous terrorist attacks on major American cities—inquired about the first steps Barack would take, Obama neglected to include that he would pursue the perpetrators. Only after Hillary and others jumped in to make that point did he come back to amend his answer.

After the debate, Obama's terrorism gaffe touched off a fracas between Penn and me in the "spin room," the location of a surreal ritual whereby operatives for each campaign, mobbed by the news media, attempt to put their preferred slant on an event the reporters have just witnessed for themselves. Still, despite our best efforts, there was no hiding the truth. Adam Nagourney and Jeff Zeleny of the *Times* recounted the awkward omission from the terrorism answer, and accurately observed that Obama "seemed subdued throughout."

Objectively, a lot also was still going right for Obama. What was especially encouraging was the openness to the idea of an Obama candidacy in two early states, Iowa and New Hampshire, in which there were few minority voters. None of us was naïve enough to assume that race, which had defined so much of American history, would not be a barrier for some. There were millions of white voters, particularly in the South, who had shifted to the Republican Party over the years almost entirely over issues of race, and many older, working-class and rural white Democrats for whom it would be a factor. Yet our research in Iowa and New Hampshire suggested that there were plenty of white voters who were open to Obama, and responded well to his message and his story.

We also saw among black voters in South Carolina an impulse I had seen among minority voters before. They were drawn to the idea of a candidate from their community, but skeptical that white voters would be. So they were holding back, waiting to see if Obama's candidacy was real. The research suggested that if we won Iowa, it would unlock his support among black voters nationwide, even with the popular Clintons on the other side.

Yet Barack wasn't impervious to all the negative chatter. Although he denied reading political punditry, he somehow was always up-to-date on even the most elite musings. ("You know, I think Andrew Sullivan has a point," a conversation would begin.) And he would hear it from donors, who, sitting in New York or LA, were moved more by a national poll in the *Times* than happy talk from Iowa. Throughout the campaign, Barack would remain remarkably loyal to his team, even when the world was calling for our heads. But he wasn't immune to doubt.

In July, the senior management of the campaign was summoned to a meeting with Barack and Michelle at Valerie Jarrett's Hyde Park apartment. No one saw this as good news. Valerie wasn't deeply involved in the day-to-day workings of the campaign, but protective of her friend, she had an unerring instinct for leaning in when she perceived that things weren't going as planned. Barack told Plouffe and me that he wanted to review "where we were," and consider what changes might be necessary.

Anticipating a challenging conversation, a number of us agreed to meet early at my office to prepare before driving down to Hyde Park together. I worked at home until it was time to leave for the pre-meeting at my office. Then, when I tried to edge my car out of the double parking space I shared with my wife, my car suddenly gunned backward, slamming into the front of her car and into a thick beam. Startled, I quickly shifted the car into drive, and it gunned forward, hitting Susan's car again, before vaulting over a barrier. I didn't want to be late for this critical meeting, so I kept on driving, calling Susan on the way to tell her I "might have nicked" her car. When she came down to see for herself, the parking lot manager was there. "Do you have any idea who might have done this to your car?" he asked. "Yes," Susan said, as she eyed the mangled mess. "I think it was my husband." The manager shook his head in pity.

It turned out that I had cracked an axle on my own car when I jumped the barrier and had put myself and several of the Obama campaign brain trust at risk by driving us to Hyde Park and back. Even without realizing our lives were in danger, though, we found the drive to Valerie's in my wounded Pontiac filled with tension—and the subsequent gathering warranted all of it.

Along with the Obamas, Valerie, and the campaign hierarchy, there was a surprise guest—Chris Edley, the dean of Berkeley's law school, a veteran of the Clinton administration, and an old friend of Barack's. The meeting began with the candidate's review of where he saw the campaign. Obama spoke from copious notes he had written, as was his custom, on a yellow legal pad, raising thoughtful questions about, among other things, how we were utilizing his time. Having just finished his thirteenth swing in Iowa, he wondered whether a continued focus there was strategically right at a time when he was slipping in national polls. He also repeated his familiar refrain that he wanted more time to devote to substantive policy work. Each of us got a chance to respond and report. The fireworks began when Edley, whom few of us knew, took his turn to speak, or more accurately, to lecture. Edley felt we were putting too much of the onus on Barack and were not responsive to his needs.

"Get over yourselves!" he screamed. "He wants time to think through policy, don't fight him, give him that time. He is the candidate. You work for him."

He mined this vein for considerable time, systematically antagonizing everyone in the room except, perhaps, the Obamas, who listened quietly, and Valerie, who told me later that she thought Edley had been "brilliant." There were some modest changes as a result of the discussion, but Edley came and went, and the evening faded into memory as a kind of weird catharsis in the midst of our long march.

The funny thing was that this session happened just as I had begun to sense that things were coming together. Maybe it was because Michelle and the girls had joined him on the July 4 swing, but Barack seemed happier and more energetic than he had in some time. His speeches were tighter and rife with the powerful message of change—not just from Bush, but from Washington—that distinguished him from the pack. While skepticism remained high, even some of the reporters were at least getting the point. *Politico's* notoriously cynical Ben Smith noted the contrast between Obama's appeal and the caustic, hyperpartisan tone in Washington, where, Smith wrote, "Democratic denunciations of the war and the president are growing in volume."

"In some of his speeches, he didn't even mention President Bush," Smith reported after one of Obama's July 4 stops. "He told small-town Iowa Democrats of the huge crowds that had greeted him from Atlanta to Iowa City, and mulled what was drawing the masses to his campaign: Not, he said, his own person, but a desire for change. 'What they're also saying when . . . they come out to these rallies is, 'We don't want to be against something—we want to be for something,' he said repeatedly in Iowa. This is a central gamble of Obama's campaign for president. The loudest voices in the Democratic Party—from Chairman Howard Dean to former Senator John Edwards and Senator Hillary Clinton—have been sounding steady notes of confrontation with the White House. Clinton and Edwards argue that they will win the partisan wars. Obama argues that the country, and even partisans, are tired of partisan warfare."

Exactly right. That was our gamble. The conventional wisdom held that Iowa Democrats were the most partisan of partisans and would reward the candidate who could best take it to the Republicans. Our bet was that there were plenty of Iowans—even Iowa Democrats—who were fed up with the trench warfare in Washington, and wanted a leader who could unite Americans. And the message was beginning to punch through.

Plouffe and Hildebrand had been steadily building the Iowa campaign since February. To run it, they persuaded Hildy's business partner, Paul Tewes, an experienced Iowa hand, to saddle up one more time. They hired Mitch Stewart, a master organizer from neighboring South Dakota, to lead a field operation of young recruits who began arriving in the spring. Legend held that it took Iowans to organize Iowa, but the special kids who were drawn to the state for Obama *became* Iowans. They embedded themselves in their assigned communities and their energy and idealism were infectious. One young man from Colorado became so close to the folks in the town he organized that they would ask him to stay and run for City Council.

Throughout the dog days of summer, visiting with the uplifting kids who were toiling for us in Iowa was the surest tonic for the cynical, dismissive drumbeat of the Washington political class. We believed they would give us a critical edge in a contest that, in the end, would rely on persuading individual Iowans to come out on a cold winter's night and, in front of their neighbors, stand up for Obama. In that process, there was no substitute for building relationships—and while the troops could prepare the groundwork, it often took the candidate himself to close the deal—sometimes going to great lengths to do so.

Once, in between flights on our campaign charter, Gibbs asked Obama to call an Iowa high school student to ask for her endorsement. In Iowa, young people who come of voting age before the general election are allowed to participate in the caucuses, even if they're just seventeen years old. Our Iowa organizers thought the backing of this influential student leader could unleash a raft of caucus attendees from among her classmates. Gibbs got her on the line.

"Hey, this is Senator Barack Obama," Barack said brightly. "I'm calling because I'd really like to have your support."

Obama listened for a moment. "Uh, yeah, sure," he said, before handing the phone back to Gibbs, shaking his head.

What did she say? Gibbs asked.

"She said she was going into a class and asked if I could call her back later," Barack said with a weak smile. "Blown off by a seventeen-year-old kid! You know, this business of running for president can be really humbling sometimes."

To give our troops air cover, we launched our Iowa advertising campaign in late June, a full six months before the caucuses. This is the edge all that early money afforded us: the chance to reach beyond the cloudy filter of the news media and share Barack's appeal with enough volume to make an impact. Harstad and Binder had done extensive research among potential caucus attendees in Iowa, and it confirmed our basic theory of the case. Barack's story was foundational; it authenticated his message. So we began with a series of biographical ads.

The first, "Choices," recalled Barack's early years, the life choices he had made that would illuminate his values and commitments. As a black-and-white archival montage unfolded, the narrator spoke of Obama's years as a young community organizer after college "for local churches, working to help families devastated by plant closings." That one sentence alone was remarkably effective. Iowa was no stranger to plant closings, and Barack's determination to help displaced workers was compelling. That Obama had done the work through churches would help answer the questions that sometimes arose about his faith.

A second ad burnished Barack's bipartisan achievements as an Illinois legislator, and featured one of his Republican colleagues, state senator Kirk Dillard. "Senator Obama worked on some of the deepest issues we had and he was successful in a bipartisan way," Dillard said, as Obama's substantial legislative achievements scrolled on the screen. Some thought it ludicrous to run a testimonial from a Republican in a caucus dominated by partisan Democrats, but it was a refreshing note to Iowans weary of political disharmony in Washington. The ad worked for us, if not for Dillard, who would narrowly lose GOP primaries for Illinois governor in 2010 and again in 2014, flayed by the Right for his display of bipartisanship.

Taken together, the ads were a tapestry, weaving for Iowans a picture of Obama as an authentic and effective agent of change. These ads were right in my wheelhouse. The creative process of interviewing subjects, writing a narrative, choosing words and images that told a genuine story while conveying a larger meaning—and all in thirty or sixty seconds—remained one of my passions. Energizing as this work was for me, though, these ads were among the last I would personally take from conception to air. As McKinnon had predicted, the pace of the campaign meant that I no longer could indulge myself. Increasingly, I would focus on strategy, and simply review scripts and rough cuts of ads. The production would fall to Jim Margolis, his brilliant and prodigious team, and my gifted partner John Del Cecato.

It was hard to let go and even harder to acknowledge that others might have strengths as ad makers equal to or perhaps greater than my own. Yet with Larry deftly managing the process, it was gratifying to watch as so many talents were melded into a coherent and collegial creative team.

Still, no matter how compelling the ads were or how credible and authentic they felt, they remained ads, and voters would always filter them through that lens. In statewide races, where news coverage of campaigns is limited, ads tend to carry the heaviest weight. In presidential races, which are intensively covered by local and national media, voters watch the candidates day to day, and form their own impressions. Events would either reinforce the ads or under-cut them.

We continued pursuing a "lion's den" strategy of telling hard truths in difficult venues. At Gibbs's suggestion, Obama unveiled his plan to require significantly higher fuel efficiency standards for cars and trucks at the Detroit Economic Club, challenging the automakers on their own turf. At an AFL-CIO town hall meeting, he defended his support for charter schools over the vehement objection of the powerful teachers' unions. In the fall, he would challenge Wall Street in a speech at NASDAQ, where he presciently warned that reckless risk taking and market-rigging schemes threatened the economy. Obama was demonstrating what a different kind of politics meant.

For Barack's psyche and self-confidence, there were two turning points that summer, provoked by foreign policy issues that pitted him against Hillary and much of the presidential field along with the Washington establishment.

In a CNN/YouTube debate in Charleston, South Carolina, a questioner asked Obama if he would be willing to meet, within his first year in office, with the leaders of Iran, Syria, Venezuela, Cuba, and North Korea. Obama, without hesitation, responded affirmatively.

"I would," he said. "And the reason is this, that the notion that somehow not talking to countries is punishment to them—which has been the guiding diplomatic principle of this administration—is ridiculous."

Sensing an error, Hillary pounced. "I will not promise to meet with the leaders of these countries during my first year," she said, arguing that foundational diplomatic work would be necessary before any such meetings. "I don't want to be used for propaganda purposes."

The Clinton campaign quickly attacked Barack for naïvely having "committed" to a presidential meeting with such tyrannical figures as Iran's Ahmadinejad and Venezuela's Chavez. Obama hadn't "committed" anything, I shot back, but said he would be "willing" to talk with our enemies, as Ronald Reagan and John F. Kennedy had with their Soviet counterparts during the Cold War. Clinton, I pointed out, had simply shared Bush's view that we should stonewall, which had proven to be a losing strategy.

The next morning, as he was leaving Charleston, Obama jumped onto our regular senior staff conference call—such candidate presence was quite rare—grabbing the phone from Gibbs to deliver a message.

"I don't want anybody backing off, interpreting, or in any way changing the meaning of what I said," Barack ordered. "You guys hear me? I meant what I said. We're right on this, and I'm not going to back up one inch."

Barack was relishing the fight. "You know, this whole exchange really brings into focus why I am running," he said, reflecting on the brouhaha. "These other folks are smart, capable people. But they're just going to tinker at the margins. They're not going to challenge establishment thinking on any of these issues."

A week later, another clash erupted—one to which I unwittingly contributed. In early July, a story in the *New York Times* had caught my eye. It disclosed that the Bush administration had vetoed a raid in Pakistan in 2005 that could have netted Osama bin Laden's top deputy and other high-ranking Al Qaeda leaders. Part of the reasoning behind the administration standing down, the *Times* reported, were concerns that such an operation "could cause a rift with Pakistan, an often reluctant ally that has barred the American military from operating in its tribal areas," where bin Laden and his lieutenants were thought to be hiding.

I found Ben Rhodes, the young speechwriter who was working on a draft of a foreign policy speech Barack was to give in Washington on August 1. A short, intense man whom I called Rocky (to go with Rhodes), Ben was the elegant writer responsible for much of the transfixing, novelistic *9/11 Commission Report*. "You mean to tell me that if we knew where bin Laden was, we wouldn't go in and get him for fear of offending the Pakistanis?" I asked.

"That's been the policy," Ben replied.

"That's fucking outrageous," I said. "One of the reasons Barack had opposed the war in Iraq was that it deflected attention from the mission of dealing with bin Laden and Al Qaeda. He should say something about this." I jotted down a few lines that I wanted to add to the foreign policy speech; Rhodes tweaked them; and Obama, who consistently had argued for a more aggressive posture toward Al Qaeda, agreed with the language.

"I understand that President Musharraf has his own challenges," he would say in the speech. "But let me make this clear. There are terrorists holed up in those mountains who murdered 3,000 Americans. They are plotting to strike again. It was a terrible mistake to fail to act when we had a chance to take out an Al Qaeda leadership meeting in 2005. If we have actionable intelligence about high-value terrorist targets and President Musharraf won't act, we will."

It was a commonsense position, and a pledge on which Obama would eventually make good. Yet the comment touched off a firestorm in Pakistan, where demonstrators burned the American flag and Obama in effigy. The embers, to nobody's surprise, landed in the middle of the campaign, and in particular during a critical Sunday morning debate from Des Moines.

ABC, which would host the debate, released an Iowa poll a couple of weeks before it showing Barack with a one-point lead, in a virtual three-way tie with Hillary and Edwards. It was a better result than our own internal polling, which still had us well behind. We knew that the ABC numbers, coupled with the heated national security back-and-forth, would guarantee Barack a lot of attention.

A few days before the debate, Barack had taken his family to the Iowa State Fair, where the Obamas playfully smashed into one another while riding in bumper cars. The pictures of their joyous romp had been widely seen. I told Obama, when I saw him later at debate prep, that everyone would be after him on Sunday. "The bumper cars may have been the best prep you could have for this debate." As folks laughed, Barack's eyes widened. "You know, that's a pretty good line. I think I'll use that."

In an effort to rouse the candidates and the viewers from their Sunday morning slumber, George Stephanopoulos opened the debate by quoting Joe Biden, another of the candidates, who had said in a recent magazine interview that Obama was "not yet ready" to be president. Starting with Hillary, George asked each of Barack's seven opponents, including Biden, to comment on his assessment. Barack patiently stood by for nearly five minutes, while George gave everyone a chance to whack the piñata. In truth, though, it proved the perfect setup.

"Well, you know, to prepare for this debate, I rode in the bumper cars at the state fair," Barack said with a smile, to laughter and applause. He went on to give a strong, relaxed, confident answer, brushing off the critiques and laying out his differences with Hillary on the foreign policy questions that had bubbled over in the previous weeks.

"I do think that there's a substantive difference between myself and Senator Clinton when it comes to meeting with our adversaries. I think that strong countries and strong presidents meet and talk with our adversaries. We shouldn't be afraid to do so. We've tried the other way. It didn't work.

"I think that, if we have Osama bin Laden in our sights and we've exhausted all other options, we should take him out before he plans to kill another 3,000 Americans. I think that's common sense."

Watching Barack confidently navigate the debate, the first he was widely considered to have "won," I thought about how far we had come since the uncertain performances of the winter and spring. Barack was hitting his stride. Yet the national campaign still lagged behind what was happening on the ground in Iowa. As he repaired to Martha's Vineyard for a late August vacation with family and friends, national polls continued to show Hillary with a large and widening lead. Inside the campaign, we knew it was Iowa or bust. Barack was very concerned about the national polls and the conventional wisdom that suggested we were stalled. While on vacation, he asked Rouse and Valerie to become more involved in the campaign and to provide some "adult supervision."

Rouse's presence was the more easily accepted. He was an organizational whiz and a Washington and campaign veteran who spoke our language of politics and seemed eager to support our efforts. Valerie assumed a more ambiguous role of frequent traveling companion and roving scout for signs that Barack was being ill-served. In fairness to her, it was a role to which Barack and Michelle had assigned her. Still, bright as she was, Valerie had virtually no campaign experience, at any level, making some of her critiques hard to take. Whatever their value, these personnel moves were an understandable response to a dreary chorus of bad news that would only grow worse before it got better.

In early October, Barack, Plouffe, and I flew to Des Moines to deal with a group of restive donors at a National Finance Committee meeting. We scheduled the meeting for Iowa to highlight our prodigious and promising efforts there, but in a bit of unfortunate timing, the *Register* published a poll on the eve of the meeting that showed Barack in third, behind both Hillary and Edwards. While just seven points separated Clinton from Obama, the poll gave the impression that we were backsliding, especially given the unduly robust ABC poll in August that had had Barack a point in the lead. "This should be great fun," I told Plouffe, when news of the poll reached us. In the meeting, the candidate gamely defended the Iowa-first strategy (and his team), acknowledging some early stumbles and lingering challenges, but arguing with conviction that we were still on a path to victory.

Barack's loyalty in the face of those calling for our heads was gratifying. Yet while he defended "the Davids" and our strategy to others, he also scheduled a meeting with the senior team days later— just two months before the must-win

Iowa caucuses—to rigorously test and reconsider all our plans and underlying assumptions.

"We all know we're not where we need to be," he said at the meeting. Sitting on the table in front of Barack was the familiar yellow legal pad, on which he had, once again, meticulously written a series of questions and thoughts. Many were concerned with the campaign's fundamental message. He told us, "We all have to ask ourselves if we are doing the right things, and *everything*, to get us there in the next two months."

We were all under the gun, but I felt it acutely. The message was my portfolio, and when Barack spoke, publicly and privately, of his concerns about the coherence and efficacy of the existing strategy, I took it as a personal challenge. For five years, Barack and I had climbed some improbable heights together, bound by shared values and mutual trust. Now, as the pressure built and time waned, I saw doubt, or at least skepticism, in his eyes.

What made it all the more frustrating was that we had methodically built a strategy in Iowa that was beginning to pay off. As often happens in campaigns, it takes the political community weeks to catch up with shifting dynamics. The vibe in the political community might still have been negative for Obama—but the dynamics on the ground showed that things were moving our way.

Edwards was falling steadily in our Iowa polling, and Hillary, though leading, showed little ability to grow. Also, though Plouffe was typically clandestine about the field reports from Iowa, they were more encouraging by the day. The progress reflected Barack's own good work in the state, where he would spend so much time campaigning that he almost qualified as a caucus attendee himself. Some of it was also the result of the tireless efforts of our devoted organizers. We had laid the foundation with waves of media, and our message was beginning to be heard above the political cacophony.

Yet in the meeting with Barack, I wasn't going to argue about where things stood. As he said, this discussion was about where we needed to go. Larry, Joel, and I had collaborated on a thirteen-page memo with detailed plans that I knew Barack wanted. It was animated by one basic strategic imperative: to close the deal, we had to draw a sharper contrast with the leader of the pack.

So far, Hillary had been the political equivalent of a great baseliner in tennis, playing a steady game and returning everything that came her way. She had pressed her advantage on Washington experience and gamely parried our call for change by embracing the word. Yet the "change" Hillary was offering was not much change at all—certainly not a move away from the raw, divisive politics that had come to define Washington. Rather, she seemed to revel in those politics. ("So if you want a winner who knows how to take them on, I'm your girl," she boasted in one debate.) The change she was offering was not away from Washington's habit of parsing words and passing on tough issues. (She habitually sought safe harbor.) The change she was offering was not away from a system dominated by PACs and corporate lobbyists. (She had taken their money and vocally defended their work.) The only real change she *was* offering was in political parties, and that simply wasn't enough.

"From health care to energy to economic fairness, voters identify the systemic failures in Washington as the major obstacles to progress on the big challenges that face the country and impact their daily lives," we wrote in the October memo. "We cannot let Clinton . . . blur the lines on who is the genuine agent of change in this election."

We had adopted a slogan in September, largely because the Iowa campaign needed time to design and print signs for the state's famed Jefferson-Jackson Day event that would take place in November. Good slogans are the irreducible core of a well-conceived campaign message. Jason Ralston, Margolis's talented second chair, suggested "Change We Can Believe In," which struck us as right on target. (It also reminded me of the tag line I had written for Simon twenty years earlier, "Isn't it time to believe again?") In the memo, we said our task now was to "create a distinct and sustained contrast in all our communications: Barack Obama is the only authentic 'remedy' to what ails Washington and stands in the way of progress. Hillary Clinton is a prescription for more of the same, meaning that our shared goals will once again be frustrated by Washington's failed politics."

Barack poked and prodded our strategy and our plans for executing it—through speeches, debates, interviews, advertising, and, most immediately, his performance at the critical upcoming JJ event, Iowa's traditional proving ground for presidential candidates that would kick off the final sprint to the caucuses. He agreed that we needed to raise the stakes and draw a sharper contrast with Hillary, but he also admonished us not to go too far, rightly pointing out that we could not make an authentic case for change by employing the same sordid, scorched-earth tactics that we had spent so much time attacking.

"I told you guys at the beginning that, win or lose, Michelle and I were going to walk out of this with our heads high, proud of the campaign we had run," he said. "I don't want anyone crossing that line."

SIXTEEN

ECSTASY IN IOWA

My career as an Obama strategist almost ended on a basketball court in Philly a few days later.

We were in town for yet another debate and, as had become our custom before such events, were playing a little pickup basketball with the candidate to keep him loose. It was a mismatched group. Reggie Love, Barack's six-foot-four "body man," the campaign aide who was always alongside the candidate, had played big-time college basketball and football, and was built for it. Marvin Nicholson, our trip director, was six foot eight and another college basketball player. Gibbs was a talented athlete and had played college soccer. Barack, who played on a state championship high school basketball team in Hawaii, was quick and savvy on the court. I, too, had been playing all my life, and had all the components of greatness—except speed, quickness, and jumping ability. So when Barack dribbled past me, headed to the basket, I did what any self-respecting flat-footed defender would do and flailed my arm to stop him. I definitely stopped him. When I raked him hard across the bridge of his nose, he went down hard.

"Holy shit, I just broke the candidate's nose," I told Gibbs, as the Secret Service rushed to Barack's side. Obama had signaled an aggressive posture for the debate. How would it look if he showed up with two black eyes and a bandage across his nose, due to an injury inflicted by his strategist? To my relief, the resilient candidate jumped up after a few seconds and shook off the effects of my matador defense, having suffered no apparent damage.

Hours later, during the NBC debate at Drexel University, it was Hillary on the defensive, the real tripwire for her coming when Tim Russert asked about

Governor Eliot Spitzer's abortive plan to provide driver's licenses to undocumented immigrants in New York. Hillary danced around the issue, palavering at length about Bush's failure to enact immigration reform, without giving a direct answer to Russert's question. She soon found herself besieged by nearly everyone onstage, all eager to take the front-runner down a peg.

It was the first time in a dozen debates that Hillary tripped up. At the very moment when we were arguing that she was nothing more than a status quo Washington politician, her awkward evasions and the critical commentaries that ensued buttressed our case.

My focus, however, was on November 10, the night of the Jefferson-Jackson event in Des Moines.

The Iowa JJ is a yearly event but a quadrennial spectacle, a throwback to earlier times, with each presidential candidate given a fixed time to plead his or her case (without notes or a teleprompter) to a crowd of thousands of soon-to-be Democratic caucus-goers. Held in a cavernous old basketball arena, the JJ had become in recent cycles the most visible, boisterous, and important test for candidates leading up to the caucuses. In 2004, Kerry's strong performance provided the momentum he needed to vault ahead in Iowa. Locked in a close race, Barack would have to give the performance of his life if he hoped to propel his campaign past Iowa.

From the moment Barack signed off on our final-phase strategy for Iowa, I began working with Jon Favreau on drafts for the JJ speech. Obama was in constant motion, so the burden was on us to produce a great draft for him. "We have to take this up one more notch," I told Favs, contributing to his already considerable anxiety about the speech. "We have to raise the stakes. It's not just about Bush. It's about the lousy, phony, self-dealing politics of Washington that stands in the way of solving these big, pressing problems. Changing presidents isn't enough if we don't change the game. We have to make that case and, by implication, draw the contrast with Hillary. Yes, she's an experienced player of the Washington game, running a state-of-the-art campaign. That's exactly what we *don't* need right now."

The speech had to convey urgency and lay some responsibility on Iowa voters themselves. At this precarious moment in our history, it was, as another client of mine had said, up to them to "take a chance on hope." The speech needed to serve up enough red meat to feed an arena filled with carnivorous Democrats hungry for victory, while still delivering the message that winning alone was no longer enough.

We were told that each candidate at the JJ would have just eleven minutes to speak, and would be held to it. Favs and I traveled with Barack in the days before the speech, in case any last-minute revisions were to be needed, but he made only minor edits—unusual for a speech of this magnitude. The task of memorizing it amid the organized chaos of the campaign was more than enough to occupy him. After every long day on the road, he would head to his room to study and practice. On the campaign RV or when he was waiting in a holding room for some event, he would randomly recite lines to reassure us and himself that he was getting it.

When JJ weekend rolled around, the whole Democratic community (office-holders, donors, activists) seemed to descend on Des Moines. The JJ was seen as the surest indication of the campaigns' caucus day potential, making it a major organizational test to rally the troops beforehand to fill seats for the dinner and speeches. That meant, in part, buying tickets in large numbers and distributing them to your supporters—if you had the money *and* the supporters. The proposition was simple: the more folks you could wrangle, the greater your chances of engendering a big, enthusiastic response inside.

The highlight of the day was a raucous march from our campaign headquarters to the arena, several blocks away. It was led by a smiling, playful Barack and Michelle, who danced along to the beat of a local drum corps, followed by a sea of delirious young supporters. It was an irresistible, inspiring scene that reflected the spirit we had seen building as we toured the state to growing and enthusiastic crowds. These were not conscripts. They were believers, who saw at the end of the march the chance to change their country.

Dinner tables were set up on the main floor, surrounding a large stage, but the bulk of the crowd takes its seats in the huge balcony that rings the arena. By the luck of the draw, Barack was assigned the last speaking slot, following Hillary. House Speaker Nancy Pelosi was the emcee, introducing each candidate as "the next president of the United States," so as to show no favoritism. Even though Edwards, who was the leadoff speaker, was still very much in contention in Iowa, there was a definite sense that he was on the evening's undercard. Clinton and Obama were the main event.

Sometime after 10:00 p.m., Hillary climbed onto the stage to tumultuous applause. Penn and her strategists knew that voters judged her to be most experienced and battle-tested. So, from the very beginning of her remarks, she hammered at those points relentlessly:

"We are ready for change," she said. "But, you know what? Change . . .

change is just a word if you don't have the strength and experience to make it happen. We must nominate a nominee who's been tested, and elect a president who is ready to lead on day one."

Barack and Michelle sat at a table about twenty feet away, listening with an air of studied calm to his rival's presentation. He had been given the option of waiting in a holding room before his speech. "No, I want to see Hillary," he said—and, perhaps, he also wanted her to see *him*.

As Hillary spoke of change, it was clear the change she offered was not in style or tone. She presented herself as a veteran of the Washington wars, a proven gladiator who was best equipped to beat the Republicans at their own game.

"Now, we're getting closer to the Iowa caucuses. They're going to be earlier than ever before. And I know as the campaign goes on, that it's gonna get a little hotter out there," Hillary continued. "But that's fine with me. Because, you know, as Harry Truman said, 'if you can't stand the heat, get out of the kitchen.' And I'll tell you what, I feel really comfortable in the kitchen."

With that, Hillary launched into a long call-and-response, smacking the Republicans hard in every stanza, and then cuing her supporters to chant the made-for-JJ tag line "Turn Up the Heat."

"I'm interested in attacking the problems of America, and I believe we should be turning up the heat on the Republicans; they deserve all the heat we can give them," she said.

"Turn up the heat!" her sign-waving supporters shouted in unison, with all the spontaneity of a Politburo meeting.

Standing against the bleachers as Hillary spoke, I thought she had done a fine job of executing her strategy, but she also had played right into ours. There could not have been a starker example of "textbook politics." Her speech was a steady diet of red meat for a partisan crowd, without a whole lot of nutritional value. The Republicans were responsible for all America's problems. Now, to solve them, we had to "turn up the heat" on them. It might have seemed like an ideal refrain in an arena full of activist Democrats, but even in that boisterous room, folks were weary of the overheated, partisan food fight that had broken out in Washington. They knew it wasn't just the Republicans, but our entire political system, that was askew. Many liked Hillary, but saw her as a polarizing figure. By stressing her Washington experience, toughness, and preparedness to fight, Hillary seemed to be promising more of the same.

Well, she's done her part, I thought, as I waited for Barack to begin. Now I hope to God we do ours.

From the moment Nancy Pelosi returned to the stage to welcome Barack, our supporters, more numerous and frenetic, were primed to explode. Large banners bearing the word "Hope" were strewn from the railings surrounding the balcony, and the mere mention of Obama's name created pandemonium. We added to this a little shtick of our own. I had recruited Ray Clay, the old Chicago Stadium announcer, to record an additional introduction to lead Barack to the stage in the same hyperbolic fashion Clay had once used to usher Michael Jordan to the court during the player's glory years with the Bulls.

"And now," Clay roared in his signature growl, "from our neighboring state of Illinois, a six-foot-two force for change—Senator Barack Obama!" By the time Barack sprinted up the stairs, hugged Pelosi, and seized the mike, the creaky old arena was rocking. After a brisk stroll around the perimeter of the stage to acknowledge the cheers, Obama quickly quieted the crowd.

If Hillary had appealed to them as partisans, Barack addressed them as Americans, signaling from his opening remarks that these were no ordinary times.

We are in a defining moment in our history. Our nation is at war. The planet is in peril. The dream that so many generations fought for feels as if it's slowly slipping away. We're working harder for less. We've never paid more for health care or for college. It's harder to save and it's harder to retire. And most of all we've lost faith that our leaders can or will do anything about it . . .

. . . And that is why the same old Washington textbook campaigns just won't do in this election. That's why not answering questions 'cause we're afraid our answers won't be popular just won't do. That's why telling the American people what we think they want to hear instead of telling the American people what they need to hear just won't do. Triangulating and poll-driven positions because we're worried about what Mitt or Rudy might say about us just won't do. If we are really serious about winning this election, Democrats, then we can't live in fear of losing it.

This party—the party of Jefferson and Jackson; of Roosevelt and Kennedy—has always made the biggest difference in the lives of the American people when we led, not by polls, but by principle. Not by calculation, but by conviction. When we summoned the entire nation to a common purpose—a higher purpose. And I run for the presidency of the United

States of America because that is the party that America needs us to be right now.

It was Barack at his best. Hillary had made a standard political speech. Barack was making a reasoned and resonant argument for deeper and more fundamental change. As he spoke, I noticed supporters of the other candidates nodding their heads in agreement and joining in the applause. We had won the day.

As Barack finished to a rapturous ovation, Gibbs and I exchanged a hug and a high five, before catching up with Barack and Michelle as they exited the arena. "Fucking home run," I blurted. "Yeah, I thought it was solid," he said, a term to which I long ago had come to realize meant "really good" in Obama's understated parlance. As we spoke, a gleeful Harstad, who had been sitting in the balcony with the troops, stumbled over. It was clear, from the moment he threw a congratulatory arm around me, that Paul had begun the celebration a little early. "This was a really big night for us," he said, hanging unusually long on the word "really." "He reaaaallly nailed it!"

Whistling past the graveyard, Penn told reporters that Obama had packed the arena with kids who would never attend the caucuses. Their response was meaningless, he said. But that was a loser's lament. Barack *had* nailed it, clearly and compellingly defining the race in his terms. While we remained in a three-way tie in Harstad's polling, Barack's JJ speech infused our Iowa campaign with a new sense of energy and purpose that would sustain us for the final sprint of the campaign.

When Hillary spoke that evening, she told the crowd, "I'm not interested in attacking my opponents. I'm interested in attacking the problems of America." It was consistent with her usual posture as the strong, confident presumptive nominee. Yet after that evening in Des Moines, it was clear that we had entered a new reality. The presumptive front-runner was in jeopardy—and she knew it.

On November 18, the *Times* reported that the Clinton campaign had called a Code Blue in Iowa, doubling the size of its operation there and vastly increasing Hillary's presence in the state. On December 1, the *Des Moines Register*'s latest poll revealed why the Clinton campaign had gone into emergency mode. In October, Hillary was leading by seven. Now Obama had passed her and was winning by three.

The next day, when Hillary met with the media, it was clear that she was ditching the above-the-fray strategy. "Now the fun part starts," she said. "We're into the last month, and we're going to start drawing a contrast, because I want every Iowan to have accurate information when they make their decisions." Three weeks after declaring that she did not want to attack her primary opponents, Hillary was about to do just that—and she sounded downright gleeful about the prospect. Even the campaign-hardened press seemed taken aback by the ardor with which she bared her teeth—Hillary unchained!

In campaigns, the most discouraging thing is to be ignored by your opponents. So from my vantage point, Hillary's challenge was good news. She wasn't going after Biden or Dodd, or even Edwards. She was attacking *us*, and everyone understood why. Moreover, there was an air of desperation to the shift. The eagerness with which she descended from her front-runner's perch to declare open season on Obama only validated our critique that she was a reflection of scorched-earth Washington politics rather than an answer to it.

True to Hillary's vow, the Clinton camp commenced its version of "shock and awe," launching attacks that veered from the legitimate, such as Barack's practice of voting "present" on some controversial issues in Springfield; to the absurd, such as highlighting a pair of schoolboy essays in which Barack wrote of wanting to be president. "What's next? I didn't play well in the sandbox in kindergarten," Obama joked. The goal was to paint him as more of an ambitious, calculating politician than an agent of change—to characterize Obama in the same way he had so effectively characterized Clinton. Yet soon the tenor of the attacks would take on a more personal edge, courtesy of a prominent Clinton supporter in New Hampshire.

Billy Shaheen, husband of the state's former governor Jeanne Shaheen, was the cochair of Hillary's campaign in New Hampshire, where public polls showed Obama was closing the gap. So it was big news when he unloaded on Obama for the teenage drug use that Barack himself had disclosed in *Dreams from My Father.* That admission, Shaheen said, would make Obama a fatally flawed nominee.

"It'll be, 'When was the last time? Did you ever give drugs to anyone? Did you sell them to anyone?'" Shaheen said during an interview with the *Washington Post.* "There are so many openings for Republican dirty tricks. It's hard to overcome."

The next day, we were in Washington, where Barack had Senate business. I joined him because we planned to use a flight to Des Moines to go over strategy for a debate later that day. As the gate swung open at the entrance of the charter terminal, I saw a young man running up to our car. Trying to catch his breath, the kid blurted out, "Senator Clinton would like to speak to Senator Obama." Hillary's charter plane was parked right next to ours.

"What do you think this is about?" Barack asked.

"She'll tell you how sorry she is for Shaheen's remark and assure you that she and her campaign had nothing to do with it," I said. "Then they'll leak that she personally apologized."

Gibbs and I climbed into our plane and grabbed window seats so we could watch the show. Hillary climbed down the steps of hers with her longtime traveling aide, Huma Abedin, and greeted Barack on the tarmac. The conversation seemed to begin calmly enough, as Hillary spoke and Barack listened. Then, when Barack responded, Hillary became very agitated, jabbing her finger at him and speaking in an animated fashion. The exchange went on for ten minutes, as Huma and Reggie toed the ground and gazed skyward, looking as if they wanted to be just about anywhere but on the tarmac bearing witness to this unfriendly encounter between their bosses. At one point, Barack put his hand on Hillary's shoulder in what appeared to be an effort to calm things down, but she brushed it away. "What the hell is going on over there?" I asked Gibbs. "I don't know, but she doesn't look too happy," he said.

Finally, Barack and Reggie returned to the plane. Barack flopped down in a seat, a look of disbelief on his face, as he reflected on what had just gone down. Hillary's initial points were exactly as I had predicted. She apologized. She said she'd had no idea Billy was going to attack the way he had and certainly hadn't approved it. Then, when in accepting her apology, Barack said each of them still had to take responsibility for the actions and tone of their campaigns, Hillary got angry. She recounted a catalogue of affronts she felt she had endured from us. It wasn't Hillary's words that struck Barack, but her demeanor.

"For the first time in this campaign, I saw fear in her eyes," he said.

I spent the last six weeks before the caucuses traveling with Barack on what was a combination rock tour and political revival. Some events were ear-splitting, arena-filling extravaganzas, such as the three-state journey from Iowa to South Carolina to New Hampshire with Oprah Winfrey, which drew a combined sixty thousand people.

Yet much of our time was spent moving around the small towns of Iowa in

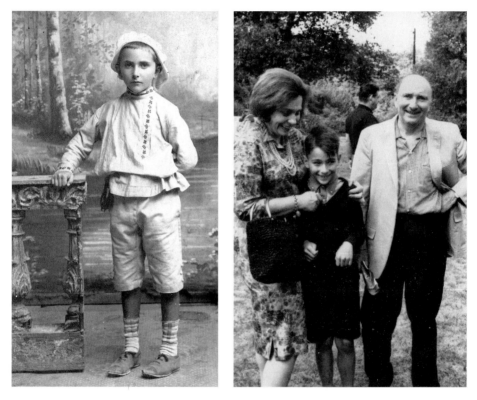

LEFT: My father, Joseph Axelrod, as a boy in Bessarabia, today a part of Ukraine, circa 1918. A few years later, he and his family fled violent anti-Semitism and set sail for America.

RIGHT: They were all smiles here but there weren't many laughs between my father and mother, Myril, whose marriage broke up when I was a kid.

LEFT: Driven from the start, my mother found success, first as a journalist and later as a pioneer in the art of focus groups, plumbing the depths of public attitudes.

BELOW: Twelve days before the 1960 election, John F. Kennedy spoke to a rally in Stuyvesant Town, the New York City housing development where I grew up. For me, it was a life-shaping event.

ABOVE: Already a political junkie at the age of nine, here I am at the 1965 inauguration of Lyndon B. Johnson with my mom and sister, Joan.

RIGHT: Boy reporter. When I completed a six-month internship at the *Villager*, my editors at this venerable community weekly in New York City put together a mock front page to mark the occasion.

Reflecting The Treasured Traditions Of This Cherished Community

TheVillager

GREENWICH VILLAGE, THURSDAY, NOVEMBER 22, 1973   VOL. XLI, NO. 33—15 CENTS

Axelrod In Snit Quits Job

By Doris Diether

Diether, David End Love

Hoopsters of Village
Mourn Passing Of Axelrod

Two days after college, I began working at the *Chicago Tribune*. In this reporter scrum, I questioned Jane Byrne, whose improbable election as mayor of Chicago catapulted my career as a political writer.

Tired of merely writing about political actors, I jumped into the action in 1984, managing the upset victory of U.S. senator Paul Simon of Illinois. I was twenty-nine.

I never worked for a more charismatic or entertaining politician than Harold Washington, the first black mayor of Chicago, shown here in a billboard photo I staged for his reelection campaign in 1987.

In 1992, I turned down a job with Bill Clinton that I thought would take too much time from my family. When Clinton came to Chicago in the final weeks of the campaign, he signed a poster for my son Michael.

LEFT: Devastated by our daughter's lifelong battle with epilepsy, Susan launched Citizens United for Research in Epilepsy. It's now the largest private funder of epilepsy research in the world.

In 2004, I helped engineer the election of Barack Obama to the U.S. Senate. Here we were shooting an ad in a closed steel mill near where Barack once worked as a community organizer on Chicago's South Side.

LEFT: For inspiration, Obama kept an iconic photo of a triumphant Muhammad Ali on the wall of his tiny campaign office.

BELOW: By the summer of 2004, Obama was drawing huge crowds, as his then-six-year-old daughter Malia could see through the window of our campaign RV.

On the road. Sitting in the bleachers at a campaign rally in 2008, chatting with Shailagh Murray of the *Washington Post*.

"Stop the Drama. Vote Obama." Weary of the marathon battle with Hillary Clinton, communications director Robert Gibbs and I visited reporters in the back of our campaign plane, clad in T-shirts bearing that message.

As the campaign wore on, the "O Team" gained notoriety. This *Newsweek* cover, late in the primary season, featured Valerie Jarrett and me flanking the soon-to-be nominee.

I was shocked to pick up the *New Yorker* and find myself alongside Chief of Staff Rahm Emanuel, peeking around the corner as the president-elect interviewed candidates for White House dog.

Hours after he learned that the grandmother who raised him had passed away, Obama tearfully spoke of her before a huge rally in North Carolina on our final campaign swing.

Capping off inauguration night at the White House, with Susan and the new president. The next morning, we would show up for work to face an economic crisis, two wars, and a determined Republican opposition.

When I was leaving for the White House, Lauren presented me with this picture she had painted of it, with the Chicago skyline reflecting in the North Lawn fountain, to remind me of home. It was the first thing I saw every day when I walked into my office.

ABOVE: Sundays were rarely a day off. Here I joust with former host David Gregory on NBC's *Meet the Press*.

LEFT With the nation in crisis, we met daily with the president's economic advisers, led by Larry Summers, a powerful personality at the core of a sometimes fractious team.

Obama's decision to take on health care reform touched off a titanic year-long struggle. Here I am, making a point in the Oval Office with the president; Chief of Staff Rahm Emanuel; our health care point person, Nancy-Ann DeParle; and legislative director Phil Schiliro.

The president drops into my office, adjacent to his, during one of my daily meetings with the White House speechwriters. Those sessions, where we hashed out themes and messaging, were a highlight of my day.

The debate over strategy in Afghanistan would consume much of our first year in the White House. Here I am in Kabul, with Obama; General Stanley McChrystal, the allied commander; and Hamid Karzai, the mercurial Afghan president.

On the runway in Louisiana, where we traveled on Air Force One to survey the damage of the BP oil spill in the Gulf of Mexico in June 2010. The leak was one of many headaches leading into what would be a disastrous midterm election.

Defying the odds, we were in control of the 2012 election for most of the year, with one glaring exception. Despite multiple debate prep sessions like this one, the president still fell into a trap in his first encounter with Mitt Romney.

On the road to the 2012 Democratic National Convention, September 1, 2012.

"The Davids." Through two campaigns, David Plouffe and I were strategic partners. A brilliant manager and visionary tactician, Plouffe was the perfect counterpoint to my more instinctive style.

Iowa gave Obama's campaign life in 2008. Four years later, we would end our campaign where our presidential odyssey began.

The Axelrods. Leaving campaigns was an adjustment. Spending more time with Susan, Lauren, Ethan (left), Michael (right), and his wife, Liz (not pictured), has been a rich payoff.

a campaign RV outfitted with couches, tables, a kitchen, and televisions tuned to ESPN, not cable news, by order of the candidate. There was always food around. When we weren't taking our meals in a back office or gymnasium locker room, before or after events, we would eat in the RV. Generally, it was lean chicken or fish and vegetables for Barack, who was determined to eat healthily, and worked out hard every day; and pizza, cheeseburgers, and fried chicken for those of us whose survival was less crucial to the future of the country. In between meals, there was an endless supply of snacks, which was deadly for me, and my wardrobe, on which one could too often find visual evidence of the day's samplings. A habitual nosher, especially when I am tense, I would gain twenty-five pounds by the end of the campaign—and I wasn't exactly svelte when it started.

All this contributed to my sometimes cartoonish image as a rumpled, paunchy, food-stained savant. Susan hated that portrayal, regarding it as demeaning, but it was a source of endless fun for my colleagues, especially the fastidious and elegant candidate. Barack could spot a stain on my clothes from twenty paces, and loved to rib me about it. It didn't help my cause when, one day on the road, I tried to multitask by snacking and answering e-mail at the same time, perhaps becoming the first person on the planet to disable his BlackBerry with a Krispy Kreme donut.

Much as I enjoyed the jovial camaraderie and the rolling smorgasbord of snacks, I did have a few essential functions on the road. With a full press corps in tow, a lot of plays had to be audibled on the spot when breaking news demanded a rapid response from the candidate. That might mean crafting a "topper," or an insert for his next set of remarks. It also meant briefing Barack, on the fly, for one of the many interviews he would do along the campaign trail and doing interviews myself, usually to fill the voracious appetite of cable news.

I was an on- and off-the-record resource for the reporters who were following us. My goal in these conversations was to advance our message and ignore whatever contretemps du jour had seized their attention at present—and, generally, I succeeded. Yet in one such scrum, late in December, I wound up making unintended and decidedly unhelpful news.

Benazir Bhutto, the former prime minister of Pakistan, had been assassinated the previous day, apparently the victim of Islamic extremists. A reporter said Clinton supporters were pointing to Bhutto's murder as an example of the volatility of the world, underscoring the need for a tested, experienced president like Hillary. Almost mechanically, I followed our basic strategy of turning such questions back to the issue of judgment and Iraq.

"Barack Obama had the judgment to oppose the war in Iraq," I said in response. "And he warned at the time that it would divert us from Afghanistan and Al Qaeda, and now we see the effect of that. Al Qaeda is resurgent. They're a powerful force now in Pakistan . . . There's a suspicion they may have been involved in this. I think his judgment was good. Senator Clinton made a different judgment . . . So that's a judgment she'll have to defend."

There were some two dozen reporters there, and almost all of them got my point. Yet one, Jessica Yellin of CNN, drew a slightly stronger inference than I had intended, giving the Clinton campaign an opportunity to suggest that I had blamed Hillary for Bhutto's death. It required me, later that day, to clarify to CNN what I meant, which added another dimension to the dispute and gave the network's anchors new angles to discuss. Wolf Blitzer asked Hillary and Barack about it in separate interviews. Suddenly I was the story.

"I believe our policies in Iraq have had a direct impact on events in Pakistan and Afghanistan, but I would not suggest there is a straight line relationship between the events of today in Pakistan and anyone's particular vote," I said. "What I was pointing out was the difference in judgment at the time. Obama thought that the war would have a negative impact in Afghanistan and Pakistan, and that seems relevant right now . . .

"I certainly wasn't suggesting Senator Clinton was complicit. She made a bad judgment on this war, and the war helped exacerbate problems in Afghanistan and Pakistan. And that's certainly something I would stand by."

It was a needless brushfire, which smoldered for some time. When Ted Kennedy called Bill Clinton in January to complain about the tactics Hillary's campaign had deployed against Barack, the former president argued that we were the ones guilty of unscrupulous attacks. "Axelrod said Hillary killed Benazir Bhutto!" he complained.

The Bhutto imbroglio was another reminder of just how easy it is, in the wildly reactive world of a presidential campaign, to trip a wire and, at least for a moment, send the media coverage spiraling off in unhelpful directions. Barack recognized the absurdity of the whole scene, and strongly defended me when he was asked about it in a television interview. Privately, however, he cautioned me about going too far. "I'm telling you what you always tell me. Don't give them a chance to write stuff like this."

For the most part, however, the final weeks of the Iowa campaign were as exhilarating as any I had experienced in politics. From the JJ on, Barack was on fire, inspiring the belief that real, meaningful change was within reach— in not just our policies, but our squalid, debilitating politics. It didn't need to be said that our candidate's improbable rise was a living symbol of that hope and change. Overflow crowds greeted us, in large towns and small, for events that now felt less like political rallies than wholesome, joyous community celebrations. At each stop, Barack, his voice raspy from overwork and overexposure to the winter chill, reminded Iowans about the enormous power they wielded to change history's course.

As the days ticked down, thousands of supporters poured in from across the country on their own dime, happily trudging through the Iowa snow to augment the young corps that had been working the state without relief for months now. Susan and my youngest son, Ethan, home for the holidays from Colorado College, relocated to Des Moines to pitch in for the final stretch. Four years earlier, as a high school student, Ethan had spent a summer volunteering for Barack's Senate campaign, working as a press assistant in the relative tranquility of our small campaign office. Now he and Susan would man the phone banks amid the pandemonium of our dilapidated Iowa headquarters.

My old friend Bettylu Saltzman, who had introduced me to Barack with such extravagant predictions about his future, encamped in Des Moines with her husband, Paul, for the final push. Though in their seventies, the couple bundled up and went door to door for Barack, as did many other old friends from Chicago.

Throughout December, Harstad's polls still had Iowa as a tight three-way race. Yet under Iowa's idiosyncratic caucus rules, where supporters of candidates who failed to attain a prescribed "threshold" of support among caucus attendees could switch their support to one of the "viable" candidates, Barack held a slight edge. This hurt Hillary, who might have been beloved by her own supporters but, with higher negatives than either Barack or Edwards, wasn't a popular second choice.

Our goal from the start was to expand the size of the caucus by attracting new participants, with an emphasis on young attendees. Now, in the final days, it seemed clear that all those efforts would pay off. We were getting encouraging reports from our Iowa directors, Paul Tewes and Mitch Stewart, with the army of organizers they had been banking for months. If at this point you had dropped the scraggly faced, slovenly dressed, sleep-deprived pair on a street corner in Chicago, they probably would have been arrested for vagrancy. Nobody on our team was letting up.

In late December, I got a call from John Kerry, who said he wanted to endorse Obama. "I really think Barack is the right guy," Kerry said. "I saw something special in him four years ago when I asked him to give the keynote." While Kerry had chosen Edwards as his running mate four years earlier, it was clear that there had been an alienation of affections. I learned later that before Kerry gave Edwards the nod, he had exacted a promise that if the ticket lost, Edwards would give Kerry first dibs on the 2008 race. Almost immediately after the polls closed in 2004, however, Edwards started maneuvering for the 2008 nomination. It was the kind of betrayal politicians don't soon forget, and Kerry clearly hadn't.

The day after Kerry's phone call, a sketchy poll showed the Iowa race as a virtual tie between Clinton and Edwards, with Obama a distant third. It was a preposterous result, but given the insatiable appetite of the news media, word of Obama's sinking prospects didn't take long to spread. This prompted another call from Kerry, this time more agitated.

"Jesus, man, what's going on out there?" he demanded. "I just saw this poll with Barack in third!"

"Well, Senator," I said, "I can only tell you that nothing we see, from our polling or the hard counts from our organizers, suggests that we're going to finish third. We're going to win this thing."

Kerry wasn't convinced.

"But, Jesus Christ, I mean, it's hard for me to jump in there if he's in third place. I really need to think this over. I'll call you back."

I liked and respected Kerry, my admiration extending back to the 1970s, when, as a decorated veteran of the Vietnam War, he became one of its most powerful and eloquent critics. Yet in his concern over the poll, I saw the anxious indecision that probably had cost him the presidency four years earlier. It stood in stark contrast to the inspiring courage he would show years later, as Obama's secretary of state.

Days later, on New Year's Eve, the final *Des Moines Register* poll was released. The *Register*, which had an excellent record for accuracy, kept its polls under wraps with the same ferocity that Plouffe hoarded fund-raising numbers. It routinely released them to the world only hours before their physical publication, keeping the entire political world on edge. No leaks. No tips. The

Register poll earlier in the month had given us a huge psychological boost, but this one would set the tone for the caucuses, just three days away.

I can't recall where I was when I got the news. I just remember hearing the elation on the other end of the line when the call came from headquarters with the numbers: Obama 32, Clinton 25, Edwards 24. Barack had lengthened his lead from three to seven points. The stories would all be about his momentum, which would only serve to inflate its effect. "I wonder how long it will be before we hear from Kerry," I asked Gibbs. It wasn't long. On New Year's Day, Kerry called Margolis and Marvin Nicholson, his old body man, and offered to fly in to barnstorm for Obama.

Kerry's offer of support prompted an impromptu caucus of our own. I joined Plouffe, Margolis, Gibbs, Marvin, Tewes, Stewart, and John Norris, a longtime Iowa hand who had been a huge force for Kerry, under the bleachers at a rally in a Des Moines high school. As we huddled in the darkness, Tewes and Stewart were vehemently opposed, arguing that a ritual laying on of hands by an establishment figure such as Kerry was not the way to close the Iowa race. Margolis and Norris weren't as sure, seeing value in Kerry's blessing. I was a little miffed at Kerry's fickleness, which colored my view. Plouffe, as usual, kept his counsel, hearing out all the arguments before voting no.

After the event, we took it to Barack, who asked the Iowa team for their thoughts. "I'll call Kerry and tell him we appreciate the offer, but the timing isn't right," he said. It was the right political call, but there seemed to be an unstated, but obvious additional message there for Kerry: the ship had already sailed.

I had been through hundreds of Election Days, and the pattern was familiar. You wake up before dawn, with great anxiety and little more to do. Before long, you're calling around, desperate for any tidbit on turnout or weather, or some scuttlebutt that almost certainly winds up meaning nothing. Yet caucuses are different because they take place in the evening, at the same, specified hour, and end quickly; there is no real window for scuttlebutt. Instead, I filled my time reviewing the speeches for that night and the following day in New Hampshire, talking with Larry about upcoming ad strategy and doing interviews with reporters. My son Ethan, whom I had barely seen, was at his post, sitting next to Susan in the windowless cavern that was headquarters, from where thousands of reminder-to-caucus calls would be made to our supporters throughout the day.

When the verdict came in, it came quickly. The first signs were overflowing crowds at caucus sites, far eclipsing anything seen before. In all, more than 239,000 Iowans would caucus for Democrats, a 90 percent increase over the turnout in 2004.

Shortly after 7:00 p.m., the networks released entrance polls, as opposed to the exit polls taken during elections. The survey of Iowans on their way into the caucuses projected Obama in first place, with 38 percent of the overall caucus vote. Stunningly, Edwards apparently had edged Hillary for second, a disastrous outcome that suddenly put her candidacy in jeopardy. With the New Hampshire primary just five days away, we had seized all the momentum, and it would be hard for her to recover in time to reverse it. Suddenly you couldn't help but feel this heady notion that if we won in the Granite State, the nomination fight might effectively be over after just two contests.

The numbers revealed just how effective our strategy to mobilize the young had been. For the first time, there were as many caucus attendees under the age of thirty as over the age of sixty-five. We had built a broad coalition, carrying Democrats, who made up three-quarters of the caucus-goers, while also running up big margins among the Republican and independent voters who had decided to caucus on our side. We carried every income group, from rich to poor, uniting Iowans behind common dreams rather than dividing them against one another. And in an ominous note for Hillary, we carried women as well as men.

By the time the entrance polls popped, I was already doing TV interviews from the auditorium in downtown Des Moines where Obama would greet his supporters. As the magnitude of the results sank in, I regretted having that duty when I could have been sharing this sublime, surreal moment with the inspiring miracle makers back at the office. I wanted to celebrate it with Plouffe and the gang of apostates who had walked through fire together, enduring the smug contempt of Washington insiders and the ill-timed jabs of doubting friends. And I wanted to share it with Ethan and Susan, who would insist on staying at headquarters until the last calls were made.

I had hooked up with Barack six years earlier, at a time when my idealism was being challenged by the cynical, dispiriting exercise that politics had become. I didn't exempt myself from those harsh judgments, but my partnership with Barack was founded on a shared belief that we could do it a different and better way. Now I saw this big, hopeful, unifying campaign as the triumph of politics as it should be.

Before Barack spoke that night, I frantically searched for Ethan and Susan. When I saw her across the room, our eyes locked and filled with tears. She ran toward me and we shared a big, tight embrace. I wiped her face and smiled. "I'm so damned proud of you," she said. Then, together, we drank in the moment, amid the euphoria of the delirious crowd.

"They said this day would never come," Barack told them, his voice bearing the strain from a year of nonstop campaigning. "They said our sights were set too high. They said this country was too divided, too disillusioned to ever come together around a common purpose.

"But on this January night, at this defining moment in history, you have done what the cynics said we couldn't do. You have done what the state of New Hampshire can do in five days. You have done what America can do in this New Year, 2008.

"In lines that stretched around schools and churches, in small towns and in big cities, you came together as Democrats, Republicans and independents, to stand up and say that we are one nation. We are one people. And our time for change has come."

SEVENTEEN

THE EMPIRE STRIKES BACK

JUST HOURS AFTER the Iowa triumph, we were airlifted out of Des Moines and headed to New Hampshire, with a huge media contingent in tow and all the hubris of a conquering army on its way to dictate the terms of surrender.

We had been tied with Hillary in the last poll Benenson conducted in New Hampshire, just before the New Year. Yet now, five days before the primary, we had all the momentum, and political history suggested that the race would open up in our favor, leaving Hillary with little time to mount a comeback. Edwards was running a distant third in New Hampshire, and nothing had happened in Iowa to alter his standing. Biden and Dodd were out of the race on caucus night. Bill Richardson and Dennis Kucinich were finished, and their decisions to drop out were only a matter of time. It was now a two-person race, and we were poised to deliver the knockout punch.

We arrived in Portsmouth before dawn and rolled up soon after to an old Pan Am airline hangar filled with several hundred supporters. Barack, tired and hoarse from the frenzied last days of the Iowa campaign, delivered a version of his post-JJ stump speech, with the added hint that New Hampshire could strike the decisive blow of the election season.

"Last night the American people began down the road to change, and four days from now, New Hampshire, you have the chance to change America," he told them.

We followed up with a second event in the state capital, Concord, where an enthusiastic crowd of more than a thousand stood in a quarter-mile line just to jam into a high school gymnasium to hear Obama speak. It all looked good. So why did I feel so bad?

"There's something about this that doesn't feel right," I told Plouffe. "We're getting rock-star treatment, but it doesn't feel right. We're not connecting the way we did in Iowa."

I quickly became concerned that, despite all our momentum, we were taking way too much for granted in the Granite State. Maybe it was that Barack had spent relatively few days in New Hampshire compared with the eighty-nine we devoted to Iowa, where people really came to know him. We had scuffled and struggled and earned our win there. Now it felt as if we were doing victory laps. Where, days earlier, we felt and acted like the scrappy challenger, now we were the fat and sassy front-runners.

Wounded, perhaps mortally, Hillary was no longer regarded as the "inevitable" nominee. Now that yoke was ours, and *she* became the scrappy, sympathetic challenger. This sudden role reversal played out in unfortunate fashion during a debate on the Saturday before the primary. When one of the moderators wondered aloud whether Hillary simply wasn't as likable as Obama, she responded with a mocking pout: "Well, that hurts my feelings." Barack then inexplicably interposed himself in her glowing moment: "You're likable enough, Hillary," he barked, without even glancing at her.

The faint praise came off as a rare ungracious note. Barack seemed, for an instant, dismissive and, well . . . unlikable. Hillary, on the other hand, parried an uncomfortable question about her perceived shortcomings with grace, good humor, and even charm.

When we raised the matter with Barack afterward, he was surprised and frustrated that a debate in which he had generally performed well would be remembered for what he regarded as a throwaway line. "Seriously? That's the story?" he asked in disbelief. Yet that "throwaway line" was replayed often in the following days, and it emerged as a potential red flag for some voters, particularly women, who were getting their first good look at Obama.

There was another moment in the debate that was less noted but far more revealing. In an answer in which she touted the change she had fought for over the course of her career, Hillary added, "We don't need to be raising the false hopes of our country about what can be delivered."

With one ad-libbed comment, Hillary had identified the main fault line of her campaign. Her message was clear: she understood the limitations posed by a bitterly divided and corrupted Washington, where political survival and self-interest were paramount. You can't change that game, she implied; to get things done, you had to know how to play it.

As soon as she said it, I recognized the opportunity that Hillary had handed us. She was too much a part of the system in Washington ever to change it—and without changing the politics of Washington, real solutions to big problems would never come.

Several public polls had us surging, and our internal numbers the weekend before the primary had us up by eleven points. The evening after the debate, that lead had slipped to eight, with some erosion among women, but we didn't think much of it. An eight-point lead was still substantial, and certainly the Clintons weren't behaving as if they felt positive about her chances.

While we were barnstorming the state on the Monday before the primary, we heard that Hillary had "broken down" in answer to a question at a campaign event in Portsmouth. In New Hampshire, the news instantly recalled the 1972 Democratic presidential race, when putative front-runner Edmund Muskie teared up in response to nasty inferences about him and his wife in the Manchester *Union Leader.* The incident was widely believed to have ended Muskie's presidential bid, and now pundits and pols, some of whom weren't even alive at that time, were wondering if Hillary's show of emotion might similarly spell the end for her.

Yet this wasn't 1972, and we didn't have to wait for the evening news to see the footage. Within minutes of the incident, it was posted online, enabling us to view it as we rode in the RV. What we saw was a little different from how it had been first portrayed to us. Sitting in a diner, with undecided voters around her, Hillary became emotional when a woman asked her how she endured the sacrifices and pressures involved in running for president while keeping herself so put together.

"It's not easy, it's not easy," she said, pausing for a moment, before delving deeper into her feelings. "And I couldn't do it if I just didn't, you know, passionately believe it was the right thing to do. You know, I have so many opportunities from this country, I just don't want to see us fall backward." Hillary's voice caught, and her eyes moistened. "You know, this is very personal for me. It's not just political, it's not just public. I see what's happening, and we have to reverse it . . ."

Barack and I had the same immediate reaction. Far from looking vulnerable, Hillary had come across to us as disarmingly honest, open, and *human.* Now, as she struggled for her political life, she seemed to connect more genuinely with the struggles of others. We both thought it was a poignant and powerful moment. "I don't like this," I told him. "I actually think this could really help her. She looked more appealing here than she has in this entire race."

Campaigns are always about momentum. Whoever has it last tends to win. We had it coming into New Hampshire, but my gut—which, in my anxiety, was growing more substantial all the time—was telling me that, in the final seventy-two hours, Hillary had recaptured the momentum. Despite our leads in public polling, she was moving up and we were moving down. Yet even though all of us, including Barack, sensed the shifting dynamics, we were still counting on our post-Iowa bounce to sustain us.

My sister did nothing to quell my fears. Joan, who had been shuttling up from Massachusetts for months to volunteer in New Hampshire, was working precincts over the final weekend in some of the white, working-class areas in Manchester. "It's okay, not great," she reported. "A lot of folks are taking our literature, politely thanking us, and shutting the door without committing. That's never a good sign."

On Election Night, as Barack and Michelle awaited the victory celebration alone in their hotel suite, the first returns came in to the nervous folks in our boiler room, the primary night nerve center, a few floors below. While the first wave of exit polls had suggested a comfortable win, the last run, as the polls closed, showed the numbers tightening. I had been scheduled to do press at the site of our Election Night event. While my sister was driving me there, I picked up the late exit polls. "Better take me back to the hotel," I told her. I returned and headed straight to the boiler room.

When the first, actual returns came in, Matt Rodriguez, our state director, looked stricken. "This can't be right," he said as he reviewed the early data. The numbers from the white, working-class precincts of Manchester were considerably better for Clinton than we had projected. Joan's instinct had been right. "If this holds up, we're not going to win," Rodriguez said glumly. "We're underperforming pretty badly in Manchester." We gave it time, hoping a wave of young voters in college towns such as Hanover would offset the deficit. They did not; we would lose by three.

Stung but not surprised, I called Favreau and told him that he had better read through the victory speech and excise all references to victory. Under the circumstances, they might seem a bit off-key. I ribbed Joel, whose polls generally were deadly accurate, on his final New Hampshire forecast that had us up by eight. "What was the margin of error on that, plus or minus ten?" The ashen pollster was not amused. Though his pre–New Hampshire poll would become the source of good-natured teasing for years to come, gallows humor only went so far in the moment. Plouffe waved Gibbs and me into a quiet corner and said grimly, "I guess we'd better go upstairs and tell him." "Who wants to go first?" I said, pushing the others forward as the elevator door opened on Obama's floor. We knocked on the door and asked Barack to come into the hallway. It didn't require clairvoyance to discern the purpose of our visit.

"All right, what's going on?" he said, searching our stern faces.

"We think we're going to come up short," Plouffe said.

"By how much?" Barack asked.

"Two, maybe three. She made a big move at the end," Plouffe replied.

"What do we think happened?" Barack asked, a reasonable question, given our poll and others that had had us in the lead heading into the final stretch. We spent several minutes analyzing this: the debate; her emotional answer in the diner the previous day; our Olympian style of campaigning; the seemingly more competitive Republican primary, which might have prompted some potential Obama supporters among independents to pick up a GOP ballot instead on behalf of John McCain, who was facing a stiff challenge from former Massachusetts governor Mitt Romney.

After a few minutes of postmortems, the conversation shifted to what the results in New Hampshire would mean going forward. Barack leaned against the wall and smiled wanly. "This is going to go on for a while, isn't it?"

In just five days, we had run the gamut of emotions from soaring victory to stunning defeat. As we left the hotel for his concession speech, the candidate had a message for us. "Folks are going to be looking at me and all of you for clues. If we look deeply wounded, that's how they will see it. So let's be upbeat. I mean, let's remember: a year ago, we would have been thrilled to be where we are."

When, a few minutes later, he entered a jam-packed gymnasium, Barack looked and sounded like anything but a defeated candidate. "I am still fired up and ready to go!" he began, eliciting a hearty roar from the crowd. After a gracious and unambiguous nod to Hillary for her victory, he gave the same challenging speech we had planned before the results were known.

"We have been told we cannot do this by a chorus of cynics. And they will only grow louder and more dissonant in the weeks and months to come. We've been asked to pause for a reality check. We've been warned against offering the people of this nation 'false hope.' But in the unlikely story that is America, there has never been anything false about hope."

It was an extraordinary performance, graceful yet defiant. Even in defeat, Barack looked like a winner, cheered on by an overflow crowd that interrupted him with applause at every turn.

I did my rounds with a news media eager to probe for the meaning of Hillary's come-from-behind win, and then stayed up much of the night asking myself the same questions. I stewed about things we could have done to close the relatively small gap. I had seen it coming, but couldn't have—or hadn't—done anything to stop it. Now the Clintons had new life, and the Empire would surely strike back. Had we missed our moment?

Early the next morning, we piled into an SUV for the hour ride to Boston for what had been intended as a triumphant postprimary fund-raiser. It was clear on the ride down that Barack also had been up much of the night. While he plainly wasn't happy, he was far from discouraged. "You can see what people were thinking," he said, waxing philosophically. " 'Here's this young, untested guy who was a state legislator just a few years ago. We're not ready to say, after two contests, that he's ready. We want to see more.' I get that, don't you? It makes sense."

Barack picked up on this theme in Boston. Without a note in front of him, he launched into a brilliant, passionate case for change, delivering among the most inspiring speeches of his campaign.

"I know this is going to sound like spin, but I really think yesterday's results were good for us," he told the intimate gathering of supporters crammed into the dining room of a private club on the top floor of an office tower. "Because we were a little like Icarus, flying too close to the sun. This was never meant to be easy. Change—real change—never is. You have to stay close to the ground, and work for it, and struggle for it and fight for it. And I am here to tell you why it's worth that struggle; worth that fight."

A year earlier, I had written that I didn't know whether Barack could take a punch. Here was the answer. Knocked down, he didn't wallow in disappointment or point fingers of blame. He not only got himself up, but he lifted everyone around him. I would see that quality many times in the coming months and years, and so would the American people—which might have been the point. At the end of the day, whether by intent or instinct, the voters of New Hampshire had cautioned, "Not so fast, Mr. Obama! Run the course. Show us more. Take some hits, and then we'll judge whether you are ready."

We finally rolled out Kerry's endorsement the day after the Boston event. As it turned out, it was far more valuable to us in defeat than in victory. To have a senior Democrat, the party's past nominee, step up and embrace us at that moment helped prod the media off a negative story line.

Still, there is no substitute for winning, and winning in Nevada, just a week away, would be a tricky pass. Hillary had a strong lead in polls there, though that was not the whole story. In Nevada, as in Iowa, delegates to the convention would be chosen not by statewide popular vote, but by district caucuses. This arcane formula meant that with our superior ground game in the far-flung regions of the state, we could win more delegates, even as Hillary turned out more people overall because of her strength in populous Las Vegas.

That's how it played out. Yet in the game of perceptions, it took a lawyer, not our volunteers in the field, to salvage the day.

The problem for us was that while Hillary's victory was clearly visible, ours was not—not to a news media lacking expertise in Nevada's abstruse caucus rules. Whatever spin was accepted that night would wind up defining the vote. So the only drama that mattered came *after* the caucuses, when we thrust Jeff Berman, a reclusive, gray-bearded Washington lawyer and our chief delegate hunter, onto a conference call with hundreds of reporters to explain how we had claimed a win. They hung on the line, rapt, as Berman went through the numbers and Nevada caucus rules with the chief Associated Press delegate counter, to whom news organizations looked for authoritative numbers. "You're right," the AP man finally acknowledged, reversing himself and unofficially awarding Obama a one-delegate edge over Hillary. Technical as the discussion was, Berman's timely intervention helped muddy the coverage of what would have been viewed as a clear win for Hillary, her second in a row. "We'll keep letting them spin the victories, and we'll keep taking the delegates," I told the reporters on the call, most of whom were smart enough to appreciate that I was spinning them even as I mocked Hillary's spinners.

No such gamesmanship would suffice the next week, in South Carolina, where with its large black population, anything short of victory would be a potentially mortal blow.

As the primary approached, Edwards sent emissaries to talk with Plouffe and me about a possible deal to get him out of the race and onto our side. Edwards was done and knew it, and he was tempted to drop out rather than lose his native South Carolina—and Hillary's camp was desperate to escort him out the door. "They figure they're a lot more likely to win with John out of it, instead of splitting the white vote," the Edwards man told me, repeating the familiar racial calculus that hovered over the South Carolina primary. "But John doesn't want to hurt Barack so he is willing to hang in there. But he wants to know that there would be a place for him with Barack down the line." I recognized a squeeze play when I saw one, and immediately scrambled up some vague assurances.

"Sure," I said. "John is a talented guy, and I'm sure there would be a place for him."

"Well, between us, Hillary is offering attorney general, but what John really wants is to be on the ticket again."

Stunning as it was, you had to admire the unmitigated chutzpah of it. Here was a guy who had finished out of the money in the first three contests, yet he was playing his cards as if he held a full house, aces over kings.

"Well, I can take that to Barack, but I'm pretty sure that's not going to fly," I said.

That was an understatement. When we raised the idea with Obama, it not only didn't fly. It crashed.

"Seriously?" Barack said, with a quizzical smile. "He wants me to commit the vice presidency to him to stay in the race? Forget about it. Just tell them that I think highly of John, but that he'll have to make his own decision."

The proposition of a different, more hopeful politics would be tested in South Carolina, a pillar of the old Confederacy, where the heavy cloud of race hung over the primary. After a particularly nasty debate, in which Barack and Hillary threw away their scripts and went at each other in caustic, personal terms, Hillary left the state to her husband, who tried to rally white voters on her behalf with "she gets you" appeals. Gibbs was convinced that Bill Clinton was trying to tap into the ugly impulses in southern politics that he had done so much to allay during his political career. "This guy had risen above the Old South," Robert said. "Now their backs are to the wall, and look at what they're doing. Campaigning right out of the Lee Atwater handbook!" referencing a southern political operative who was legendary in the 1980s for brazen racial appeals that helped solidify Republican control of the South.

Gibbs, who had worked in South Carolina before, quietly teed up one of our supporters, a crusty former state party chair named Dick Harpootlian, to go after Clinton for his tactics. Famous for getting in the faces of his opponents, Harpootlian lived for moments like this. "I realized, as soon as I talked to him, that I had launched a missile without a particularly sensitive guidance system," Robert told me. Harpootlian eagerly adopted Robert's edgy analogy as his own, publicly accusing Clinton of "reprehensible tactics reminiscent of Atwater." Bill Clinton was born when the Jim Crow era was still a reality in Arkansas, so it drove him absolutely nuts to be compared to the race-baiting Atwater. Red-faced and furious, Clinton responded with an unusual, lengthy, and much replayed public screed aimed at us and the news media. Wagging his finger at a group of reporters, he stalked away after telling them, "Shame on you."

Clinton's outburst only fueled the tension, which made an NBC poll, released the day before the election, all the more titillating to a press corps for whom race was the shiniest of objects. It showed Obama's white support in South Carolina had dropped ten points in a week, and was now hovering near single digits. Tim Russert, in an interview on the *Today* show, called the development "rather dramatic." The press swarmed. At Barack's event later than morning, I ran into Ron Fournier, a veteran Associated Press political reporter who had followed Clinton from Little Rock to Washington. "You guys are in trouble," he said. "I know the South. These white folks just aren't going to vote for your guy."

Cornell Belcher, who was polling for us in South Carolina, was more optimistic. Harpootlian was utterly confident. Plouffe had dispatched Steve Hildebrand to help marshal the field operation in South Carolina. I ran into Hildy that night at a rollicking final rally in Columbia, and he was even more robust in his forecast. "We're going to win this thing by eighteen points," he said. It sounded absurd, but even accounting for some irrational exuberance, we appeared to be in a far better position than public polling and the conventional wisdom suggested.

We had thrown everything we had at South Carolina and had done everything we could. Yet I was still worried because, having spent a lifetime around the politics of race, I knew we were challenging some deeply ingrained attitudes.

Rather than stew, I used Election Day productively and set up a film shoot for the late afternoon with Michelle, who was in South Carolina for the final days of the primary. While we were filming, I got an e-mail from Stephanopoulos with the initial exit polls and a subject line that read something like "Wow." When I opened them, I understood the note of surprise. "I can't believe this," I said. "What?" Michelle asked. "I just can't believe these exit polls I just got!" I replied. "What? What? What do they say," she said, showing some exasperation. "They say we're winning by thirty points." Michelle slugged my arm, and not in a playful way. "Don't ever scare me like that again," she said.

The exit polls weren't far off. When the vote came in, Obama won by twenty-eight points, collecting nearly 80 percent of a huge African American turnout, but also a quarter of white voters, including a third of young voters.

There was an innocent beauty to caucus night in Iowa, but for me, South Carolina was even more powerful. Just a day earlier, pundits were writing us off, predicting that the primal pull of race would trip us up at the end. Now the people of South Carolina had emphatically defied that cynical calculation. The thousands of supporters who jammed into our victory party were there to celebrate *that* victory, too. Some burst into spontaneous chants of "Race Doesn't Matter!" which way overstated the reality. Still, here in the heart of the old Confederacy, an African American had taken a big step forward, buoyed by blacks *and* whites, making this win especially sweet.

Upon leaving the state before the polls closed, Bill Clinton capped his tough week with an appalling postmortem. "Jesse Jackson won South Carolina twice, in '84 and '88, and he ran a good campaign. And Senator Obama's run a good campaign here."

His point was abundantly clear. No big deal. The black guy had won the black primary. The dismissive remark didn't require a response or any significant spin. Everyone could see it for what it was. The media blowback for both Clintons was fierce, and the hard feelings between the forty-second president of the United States and the man who would become the forty-fourth would take years to heal fully.

One Democrat of importance was monitoring these events closely.

For some time, Ted Kennedy had been inching toward an endorsement of Obama. He had been a warm mentor to Obama in the Senate. He had said in the fall that he was looking for a candidate who would inspire him, which we took as a welcome sign. With Kennedy as the foremost champion for civil rights in the Senate, it seemed almost irresistible for him to play a leading role in electing the nation's first black president. If Kennedy had any reluctance,

Bill Clinton unwittingly had pushed him our way a few weeks earlier when he called and asked Teddy to support Hillary. As Kennedy related it, Clinton argued that Obama hadn't paid his dues. "He just got to town, dropped his bags, got someone a cup of coffee, and now he thinks he should be president," Kennedy recalled Bill Clinton saying, a comment to which Kennedy took offense. "He thought it was coded language," one of his aides told me. "It really outraged him."

The endorsement would come on a Monday in Washington. Before it did, Caroline Kennedy, who had lobbied her uncle to back Obama, delivered her own endorsement in a touching piece that appeared in the Sunday edition of the *Times*.

"I have never had a president who inspired me the way people tell me that my father inspired them," wrote Caroline, forever frozen in our memories as a five-year-old gripping her mother's hand as her father's horse-drawn casket rolled by on its way to Arlington. "But for the first time, I believe I have found the man who could be that president—not just for me, but for a new generation of Americans."

As one of the many Americans whose passion for politics was ignited by JFK, I teared up when I read Caroline's closing lines.

On Monday, Teddy, Caroline, and Patrick Kennedy joined Barack at American University in Washington. For all the tragedies and setbacks he had endured, there was no one who relished the process more than Ted Kennedy. He believed deeply in public service as a calling, and plainly loved the theater of politics. It was a joy to watch him in action.

Taking the podium by storm to officially enter the fray, the seventy-five-year-old Lion of the Senate instantly had an arena full of college students in the palm of his hand when he cocked his head slightly and roared, "I feel change in the air." Within two years, Teddy would be gone, the victim of a brain tumor. Yet on this day, he was filled with youthful energy and idealism.

Recalling the arguments that were made against his brother, JFK, Kennedy went right at the critics who were saying Obama wasn't ready.

"What counts in our leadership is not the length of years in Washington, but the reach of our vision, the strength of our beliefs, and that rare quality of mind and spirit that can call forth the best in our country and the best in the world," Kennedy said.

It was an amazing, gratifying moment. Barack and I had spoken about striving to rekindle the spirit and urgency of the 1960s, when young people marched and organized in the belief that they could change the world. The Kennedys ignited that belief and embodied that spirit. Now, here was the last of the Kennedy brothers—stooped and gray but still a powerful figure—wholeheartedly endorsing Barack and our campaign as heir to that tradition. Though he was just a child during that era, Obama had been an avid student of its history and he was visibly moved by Kennedy's warm embrace.

"You know I am usually pretty chill about these things, but I have to say, that was humbling," Barack said afterward. "To have Ted Kennedy essentially hand you the torch like that. With Caroline sitting there. You can't help but feel a responsibility to be worthy of that."

Though I had worked for his son in Rhode Island, I didn't know Kennedy well. Still, I knew that, even in a bitterly divided Senate, he remained a beloved and respected figure on both sides of the aisle. I knew that he had always inspired extraordinary loyalty among his staff. What I quickly learned was that for all his elevated stature, Kennedy was as far from a prima donna as could be. He responded to every request, asked for little, and gently offered constructive advice when he thought it might help and encouragement when he knew it was needed. A few weeks later, he would chase me down by phone on the birthday we shared to wish me well.

One small moment from that day gave me some insight into Caroline. Backstage, she noticed Gibbs wearing a fleece with our campaign logo and asked where she could buy one. He laughed and said we would be happy to furnish her with one. "Oh no," she said emphatically. "You guys have enough to do! Just tell me where I can order it." Here was a woman who, almost from birth, was regarded as American royalty. Yet she displayed no trace of entitlement and had a healthy and hilarious disdain for those who did. She would become a great friend.

I viewed Ted Kennedy's rousing embrace, coming on the heels of the landslide in South Carolina, as a pivotal moment in the campaign. It wasn't that his backing or Caroline's would automatically translate into votes—our polling was pretty clear that people were inclined to make their own judgments—but the association with the Kennedy legacy gave fresh luster to our message of hope and possibility. While the endorsement of a forty-five-year Washington veteran might not have screamed of "change," Ted Kennedy's weighty imprimatur was a powerful rejoinder to those who questioned whether Barack had the experience to be president.

From the beginning, we knew that once the actual nominating process began, it would either come to a quick resolution or become a long, hard slog. And the verdict was in. We had missed our chance for an early knockout in New Hampshire and survived Hillary's ferocious comeback. Now we were in for an extended battle for delegates, a race to see who could reach the magic number needed to clinch the nomination. It had become a math-laden marathon for which we were better prepared.

So confident were they of a knockout, that Hillary's folks had focused intensely only on the early states. Thinking like an insurgent, General Plouffe, in contrast, had created separate operations—one for the first four states, under Hildebrand's command; and another for all the rest, run by a quiet, intense young Peace Corps veteran and master organizer named Jon Carson. While the political world was fixed on the early contests, Carson prepared for the long march, studying all the vagaries of the delegate selection processes, which varied widely state by state. Some were primaries, with delegates elected congressional district by congressional district. Others, as in Iowa and Nevada, selected their delegates through local caucuses, which put a premium on the enthusiasm of your supporters, since participating in caucuses is a much greater time commitment than simply casting a vote at a polling place. Under the party rules, it was hard to walk away from primaries with a huge margin of delegates, even if you won the popular vote by a comfortable margin. Yet caucuses could be a treasure trove for the well-organized.

Capitalizing on the huge influx of the young and young at heart from every corner of the country who had come together online, Carson had a strong corps of volunteers in every state, which would be particularly crucial in caucus states. As soon as one of the early primaries or caucuses ended, he would scoop up our best-performing organizers and give them just enough gas money to get to an upcoming state to help direct this wealth of determined volunteers.

With the first four contests behind us, we were hurtling toward Tsunami Tuesday on February 5, a slate of primaries and caucuses so big that "Super" was no longer extravagant enough to describe it. More than half the delegates to the convention would be chosen that day, in twenty-two states in every region of the country plus American Samoa—and with California and New York among them, the conventional wisdom in Washington was that Clinton, better known and with decades of associations and chits to call in, was well fortified for this far-flung competition.

Plouffe, Carson, and an army of folks out to change the world had a surprise waiting for them.

The expanded battlefield meant a much more complicated advertising challenge. Thanks to an extraordinary influx of money—fifty-five million dollars would come in during February alone—we would run ads in nearly every Tsunami Tuesday contest. Grisolano was our cartographer, mapping media strategy on an office wall lined with whiteboards indicating which ads were destined for which state. Margolis and his GMMB team had melded well with Del Cecato and my AKPD crew, with all becoming a cohesive creative force. We would add other top-flight ad firms, as well. Working with some of the talented Democratic ad makers against whom I had competed for years felt like playing in an all-star game.

I loved the team, one or more of whom I was in touch with from the time I woke up each day—assuming I actually slept—to late at night, going over scripts and polling data, trying to find any edge we could. They were brilliant, funny, irreverent, and deeply committed. In a situation that could have been convulsed by jangling egos, we hung together. Still, it wasn't points on the air that would allow us to survive the tsunami, but sneakers on the ground.

The weekend before the big vote, we held a rally in Boise, Idaho—not a regular stop for a candidate on the Democratic political circuit. There were fourteen thousand boisterous supporters waiting, a number that represented just about 1 percent of Idaho's population. "This is unbelievable," a wide-eyed local activist told me, as he surveyed the jam-packed arena. "Four years ago, five thousand people caucused for the Democrats in this entire state. Look at this place!"

It was an auspicious auguring—and on Tuesday, we rolled.

Hillary wound up taking nine states, including the glamour twins of New York and California, which allowed her to claim a narrow lead among the sixteen million Democrats who voted that day. Yet we won thirteen contests, including six of the seven caucus states, carrying them by an average of more than forty points.

In Idaho, for example, we netted twelve delegates more than Hillary. That one, tiny state wiped out the entire delegate advantage she rolled up in beating us in the much larger state of New Jersey.

By investing in these caucus states, which Hillary had largely ignored, we were able to eke out an overall thirteen-delegate edge among the nearly seventeen hundred at stake that day. And as we looked down the roster of the nine remaining state races in February, which generally fell in places where we had significant demographic and organizational advantages, we saw we had a chance to run the board and pad our lead.

The Saturday after Tsunami Tuesday, the dominos began to fall for us. We handily won the Louisiana primary, overwhelmed Hillary in caucuses in Nebraska and the state of Washington, and, for good measure, won 90 percent of the vote in the U.S. Virgin Islands. The following day, we pulled off a coup by winning the Maine caucuses Hillary had been favored to carry. Two days later we racked up wins in Virginia, Maryland, and Washington, DC, putting Barack in the lead by one hundred delegates. The once-mighty Clinton campaign was broke and sputtering.

Yet as we rolled up victories, the relentless campaign—thirteen months on the road and counting—was taking a toll on us as well. Even Barack, whose steady temperament was one of the campaign's great strengths, was getting cranky. His irritation spilled out during a campaign stop in Milwaukee after I informed him that we had added an advertising shoot at the end of the day. It was necessary because, with the elongated race, we had to keep up with the demand for fresh scripts and footage, but I still felt like an accountant telling a client who was expecting a refund that he needed to write another check. Barack clearly felt the same way. "Come on, man," he pleaded. "I'm ninety minutes from Chicago. I thought I was going to get home in time to see my kids. And now you want me to do ads instead? Give me a break!"

Despite his grumbling, Barack did the shoot and performed impeccably, reading scripts and warmly interacting with students and others in a series of B-roll shots the ads required. That warmth didn't extend to me on the ride home. Anyone who could find another way back to Chicago did, leaving me to deal with the sullen candidate. As Obama read through some papers, I caught up on my e-mail, including one with an irritating story about Elizabeth Edwards attacking our health care plan. Her husband had just dropped out of the race, and it struck me as gratuitous for Elizabeth to continue weighing in. It brought back old memories, bad ones.

"Goddamn it," I muttered.

"What's wrong with you?" Obama asked, without looking up from whatever he was reading.

"Oh, it's Elizabeth Edwards out there attacking us," I said. "They just got out of the race. What's the point?"

Barack shrugged. "Forget about it," he said. "They've had a pretty hard time lately. It's not worth worrying about."

It impressed me that, even in an irascible mood, Barack was able to rise above an annoying provocation—and I felt slightly embarrassed that I had not.

Barack wasn't the only Obama who found the run-up to Wisconsin challenging. The day before the primary, Michelle had made some unwelcome news while campaigning in Milwaukee. "For the first time in my adult lifetime I'm proud of my country . . . because I think people are hungry for change," she told a crowd of supporters, setting off an immediate firestorm.

Before the primary season officially began, Fox News and other conservative outlets had run wild with a claim that Barack, as a child in Indonesia, had been educated in a madrassa, which, to many Americans, meant a radical Islamic school in which anti-Western values were routinely taught. With Gibbs and our research team on point, we were able to beat back that calumny—and we had frustrated other efforts to peel away white voters by portraying Barack as an angry, alien black man. Now Michelle's comment provided fodder for the right-wing commentators eager to portray the Obamas as outside the American mainstream.

It was a momentary tempest, but the criticism hit Michelle hard. Driven to excel, she had worked her way from modest beginnings on Chicago's South Side to Princeton and then Harvard Law and an admirable career of her own. She had performed in stellar fashion for us in Iowa and South Carolina. Now she had become a target. She felt exposed and vulnerable and was unhappy with the support she was receiving from the campaign team. While she let us know about it in no uncertain terms, her frustrations would boil over in the months to come.

It is the nature of presidential campaigns that each success brings heightened scrutiny. The process gets harder and more demanding, and thus, inevitably, more exasperating the longer you go. Every misstep or inconsistency is blown up instantly. The trivial can seem cataclysmic, at least for one news cycle. As a crusty alderman I once covered put it when I asked him about a colleague who was pondering a race for higher office, "Just remember, the higher a monkey climbs a pole, the more you can see his ass."

Now we were indisputably the front-runner, and everyone was looking up.

Much has been written about how hard it is for politicians to deal with defeat. Yet success presents its own challenges, inviting hubris and the safe harbor of conventional thinking. If there was a lesson we should have taken from New Hampshire, it was that when you're up, you can become too eager and begin to cut corners. Yet with ten straight wins and a solid delegate lead, we were desperate to end the nominating contest. John McCain had wrapped up the Republican nomination, and would have free rein to focus on us, while we were still tussling with the unsinkable Hillary. Bill Clinton had signaled to reporters that she would have to win the March 4 primaries in both Texas and Ohio to remain a viable candidate—and we had decided to move heaven and earth, and a whole lot of money, to slam that door.

With uphill fights in both states, Plouffe authorized prodigious spending for television and mail to try to muscle our way through—the political equivalent of Shock and Awe. Yet trying to gain traction with older white, working-class voters, who would have a decisive say in both primaries, we wound up launching some decidedly un-awe-inspiring attacks.

The North American Free Trade Agreement, or NAFTA, was a signature achievement of the Clinton administration, passed in 1993 over the vehement objections of organized labor and liberal Democrats. Hillary had argued then, and for years after, that NAFTA benefited the economy by opening new markets for American goods. However, fourteen years later, NAFTA still was anathema to many in rust belt states such as Ohio, where companies had shut down manufacturing plants, lured by cheap labor and lax regulation to Mexico and China. From his Senate race on, Barack had taken a nuanced view, embracing the need to boost trade, but opposing NAFTA because it lacked sufficient labor and environmental protections. In Ohio, where our polling showed that NAFTA could prove a big liability for Hillary, we were, to put it charitably, a little less nuanced. A mail piece featuring the picture of a closed plant quoted Hillary as calling NAFTA a "boon" to our economy, which was actually one newspaper's paraphrase of remarks ascribed to her back in 2006.

The second issue we pressed was the health care mandate. Hillary had pummeled Barack for omitting it from his heath care proposal, arguing that his plan would fall far short of universal coverage. While her position resonated with activists on the left, our polling showed that it was deeply unpopular with many voters. So we sent out a hard-hitting piece declaring that Hillary would force "everyone to buy health care, even if you can't afford it."

The pieces were factually defensible, and Barack stood behind them publicly. The tactics followed the tried-and-true rules of engagement that my colleagues and I had executed over hundreds of campaigns—and Hillary's team was hardly firing blanks at us. Still, Shock and Awe was a long way from Hope and Change. Hillary was *supposed* to be the experienced practitioner of such "textbook" politics. We were not. The attacks we wielded against her would look even more dubious in the full blush of history, given that Obama, as president, would embrace the health care mandate and become a stalwart promoter of trade treaties.

Sensing a chance to knock us off our white horse, Hillary seized on the mailings with a theatrical outburst during a press conference in Ohio. "Shame on you, Barack Obama," she shouted, waving the mail pieces. With all the righteous indignation she could muster, Hillary fingered us as practitioners of the black arts favored by Bush's hard-hitting political guru Karl Rove, and accused us of aping the anti–health reform arguments of the insurance industry.

Her campaign also got widespread attention with a late ad in Texas that went right at the question of experience. The ad asked voters whom they wanted in the White House when the 3:00 a.m. call came alerting the commander in chief to a crisis somewhere in the world. Its message, ironic given the role Hillary would later play in an Obama administration, didn't make a huge impact on voters when we tested it, but the media loved it and played it so incessantly that many voters in Ohio, where the ad never aired, said they had seen it.

The cumulative result of all this, at least by the gauge of my gut, was the same dyspeptic feeling I had in the days before New Hampshire. We were out of sync, playing Hillary's game instead of our own, and playing it not as well.

That became apparent on primary night in San Antonio, where we had gone hoping to claim one victory. The first hit came in from Rhode Island, where Hillary, as expected, routed us. Then came Ohio, where she whomped us by a commanding ten points. The exit polls in Texas, which predicted a close race with Hillary holding a slight edge, proved accurate, as she won by three points. Our only solace was that Texas had a hybrid system, with caucuses and a primary on the same day. As usual, we won the caucuses, and by such a large margin that, overall, we netted more delegates than Hillary that night. Still, as energetically as I tried to spin our delegate numbers, there was no hiding the fact that we had gone in for the kill and Hillary had escaped. "She's like Freddy Krueger in *Nightmare on Elm Street*," I told Plouffe. "She just won't die!"

The plane ride back to Chicago was as quiet as any we had ever taken. Barack and Michelle were glum and unsmiling. As we were leaving the plane, he said, "I am going to want to meet with the team at the headquarters."

That afternoon, we approached the meeting with all the enthusiasm of convicts heading into a sentencing hearing. Barack walked in the conference room after us, the now-familiar yellow legal pad under his arm. It had been a frustrating couple of weeks, for sure. The missiles we had launched at Hillary had fallen short, and by firing them, so had we. We were disappointed in the results and in ourselves. The future looked bleaker than it had a few days before. Obama's vulnerabilities among older, working-class white voters had been further exposed—and these voters would dominate the next major primary seven weeks ahead in Pennsylvania, a state James Carville once described as Philadelphia and Pittsburgh with the state of Alabama wedged between them.

There were a number of reasons for our bad day, the biggest of which was that we had put far too much time and resources into Ohio instead of doubling down on Texas, where we had a better chance to win. We also had gotten careless, taking cynical shortcuts that undermined Obama's message and brand. That, I felt, fell on me. Though Plouffe was the campaign manager and leveraged great influence and authority over the apportionment of resources and the overall direction of the campaign, I was the strategist with ultimate responsibility for the media and message. In my haste to go in for the kill, I felt I had made some poor judgments.

Whenever campaigns stumble, all fingers tend to point at the message and the message keeper. That comes with the territory, and while our long friendship and close collaboration were generally assets, Barack seemed to feel freer to criticize me, because I was not just the message maven but the most familiar member of his team. On this day, however, it was quickly clear that Barack was not there to brood on our failures or assign blame.

"We all know we had a bad day yesterday," he told the twenty or so senior staff in the room. "I can think of a dozen things I personally could have done better. And I bet each of you could do the same. So I'm not here to point fingers. We're all in this together. What I want to do is discuss what we've learned from it, and whatever changes we need to make so we can do better next time." Barack's prologue immediately lifted the pall that had hung over the room, and kicked off a productive two-hour discussion, during which we worked through a number of issues and everyone got a chance to share his or her observations.

As he was leaving, Barack turned to reassure his team. "Now I want you to know I am not yelling at you guys." After a few more steps, he added a parting thought: "Of course, after blowing twenty million bucks in two weeks, I could yell at you. But I'm not yelling at you." With that, he smiled and walked out the door.

It was a graceful, uplifting moment. We had come in deflated and anxious, and Barack had picked us all up. Everyone in that room would have run through a wall for him—which was a very good thing, because we were about to hit a big one.

EIGHTEEN

TO HELL (OR AT LEAST ALTOONA) AND BACK

IT COULD HAVE BEEN called "Wright's Greatest Hits," a carefully edited video of some of the reverend's most incendiary sound bites. Three decades of his sermons were mashed into a few explosive minutes of outrage, a missile directed right at the heart of our campaign.

With losses in Ohio and Texas, and another tough battle looming in Pennsylvania, the jarring video was an unwelcome intrusion in a race that already had become a grinding slog.

"We bombed Hiroshima, we bombed Nagasaki, and we nuked far more than the thousands in New York and the Pentagon, and we never batted an eye . . . and now we are indignant, because the stuff we have done overseas is now brought right back into our own front yards," Wright thundered, in one of the most incendiary clips, recorded after the 9/11 attacks. "America's chickens are coming home to roost."

In another, he railed against the historic injustices African Americans had faced.

". . . God Bless America? No, no, no, not God Bless America. God *damn* America—that's in the Bible—for killing innocent people. God damn America, for treating our citizens as less than human. God damn America, as long as she tries to act like she is God, and she is supreme. The United States government has failed the vast majority of her citizens of African descent."

It was sharp, provocative language of the sort that might be heard from pulpits of many black churches. Yet this wasn't just any church or any pastor. It was Obama's church and the pastor whom he had portrayed as a central influence in his life. Whether these selected moments of rage and indignation reflected the central message in the sermons from which they were plucked, let alone the entirety of Reverend Wright's life or ministry, was immaterial. There was no room in this heated presidential campaign for interpretation or nuance or allowances for ministerial hyperbole. It was trouble.

Videos of Reverend Wright first started appearing on the Fox News TV show of right-wing shock jock Sean Hannity, who had made Reverend Wright a focus throughout the campaign. Two days after the Mississippi primary, however, the story went mainstream when Brian Ross, an investigative reporter for ABC News, ran the now infamous tape on *Good Morning America*. I was convinced it had been leaked to Ross by an opposing campaign. Later, Ross disclosed that, having been denied an interview with Reverend Wright, he was informed by the church that DVDs of all Wright's sermons were available for purchase. It was a good investment for ABC. The condensed reel Ross put together from the videos sent the political world into an immediate uproar.

When Obama first announced his candidacy, there were many in and out of the media who questioned whether the country was ready to embrace the idea of an African American president. Now the Wright tapes had rekindled those questions, threatening to undermine Barack's image as a positive, unifying figure. In his writings, Barack had introduced the world to Reverend Wright as the pastor, mentor, and father figure who brought him to Christ. The "audacity of hope" was a line inspired by one of Reverend Wright's sermons. But here he was, from the same pulpit, delivering fiery jeremiads filled with bitterness and vitriol and anti-American slanders.

No one needed to be told we were now in crisis mode.

At headquarters I ran over to our research department. After the blowup in *Rolling Stone* on announcement day, I had asked them to collect any existing videos of Reverend Wright so we could anticipate potential problems. I never received a report and was too preoccupied to follow up. Now I wanted to hear the sermons from which these outrageous remarks had been lifted, in the hope that they had been distorted or used way out of context. With Wright having preached at Trinity for three decades, it was a labor-intensive project, and our young research director sheepishly acknowledged that the initial project had fallen through the cracks.

I responded with a few comments that made Reverend Wright's seem tame. *Someone* had found time to cull through these sermons and to blindside us with a tape that could potentially take down our campaign. If we had known about these jeremiads, we certainly would have encouraged the church to remove the tapes from their gift shop. We might even have encouraged the Obamas to remove themselves from the church. At the very least we would have been prepared for the onslaught we now faced.

There wasn't a heck of a lot of time that morning to dwell on this lapse, however. We had our hands full fielding a flood of obvious but fair questions. Was Barack in the church when Reverend Wright delivered any of these broadsides? If so, did he challenge Wright in any way? If he missed these particular sermons, had he seen the tapes? What did he think about them? Will he continue as a member of Trinity? The subtext of all the inquiries, though, was the biggest challenge: How could Barack reconcile the bitterness and contempt for America exhibited in the stinging language of his pastor with the healing message of his campaign?

Within hours, the storm was raging, but Barack wasn't quite up to speed on its impact. He had been busy all day in Washington, with a flurry of Senate votes that would run past midnight. We had talked only briefly on the phone—just long enough to ascertain that he did not recall hearing any of those particular salvos from Reverend Wright. We had made much of Barack's church membership, in part to reassure those who questioned his faith. Yet like many Americans, he was more of an Easter and Christmas worshiper than a regular attendee. "The truth is—and I don't know how we want to handle this—I wasn't there every Sunday. I was there for holidays and some Sundays, but not every Sunday. Rev. could get torqued up sometimes. I mean, he's a *preacher*. But I would have remembered hearing *these*." With Barack mired in Washington, a fuller discussion would have to wait until his return to Chicago the following day.

As if this flap weren't problematic enough, a separate controversy was bubbling up at the same time, about another provocative figure in Obama's life.

Tony Rezko had been one of Obama's early political patrons, a fund-raiser and conduit to some of the entrepreneurial players in Chicago's black community, where Rezko had extensive real estate dealings and political connections. Now Rezko was on trial, having overplayed his hand as one of Blagojevich's top fund-raisers, and reporters were drilling down into the nature and extent of the reform-minded Obama's relationship with an accused extortionist and bagman. The Chicago papers were particularly focused on a curious set of real estate transactions in which Rezko bought a small lot next to Obama's Kenwood home and later sold a sliver of it back to Obama for a side yard.

It was a rare and foolish misjudgment on Obama's part to enter into the transaction with Rezko, as he publicly and privately acknowledged. Yet the *Tribune* and *Sun-Times* editorial boards had more questions for Obama, and in a spectacularly unlucky piece of timing, we scheduled the meetings for the day he returned from Washington.

Having been tied up in the Senate into the early morning hours, Barack didn't arrive at campaign headquarters until the afternoon—and with the Wright story cascading out of control, there was little time to prep for the Rezko probe. The land deal was an embarrassing story, but the Wright tapes had unleashed the raw fury of race. Obama spent an hour rewriting a draft statement about Wright's sermons, making sure to condemn the offensive words, but also putting them in the context of Wright's history as a former marine and widely regarded clergyman.

Even without the prep, Obama emerged from two long editorial board sessions on Rezko relatively unscathed—but not from cable TV interviews later that evening, in which he got a full blast of the frenzy that the Wright tapes had touched off.

Late that night, Barack called me.

"I want to do a speech on Wright and the whole issue of race in America," he said. "We have to try and put this in a larger context or it's just going to go on and on." Barack had been eager to give a speech on race during the campaign in Iowa, but we strongly discouraged him. Race was not inhibiting our support, I had argued, so why bring it up? Now circumstances had changed dramatically. Obama wasn't calling to discuss *whether* he should give the speech, but *when.* "I want to do it no later than Monday or Tuesday. And I'll have to write it."

I didn't argue. As I had sat there watching the Wright tapes recycling hour after hour on cable, I hadn't come up with any better plan. Yet it was approaching midnight Friday, so the timing seemed impossible. Obama was scheduled to campaign in Indiana on Saturday. We had a film shoot around Chicago on Sunday that we absolutely needed for advertising and a long day of campaigning in Pennsylvania scheduled on Monday. When would he have time to write a speech of such importance and magnitude? "Just set it up," he said. "I can work with Favs. I know what I want to say."

The next morning, I shared the plan with our senior staff and advisers. It was the first Favs had heard of it, and the color quickly drained from his face. He was ghost white. "Are you shitting me?" he said. He and I huddled that afternoon to talk about the speech, but quickly realized that this was not one we could map out ourselves. Barack had spent much of his life wrestling with the issue of race. This speech had to flow from his head and heart. We couldn't proceed without him.

Late Saturday night, after returning from Indiana, Barack spent more than an hour on the phone with Favreau, conveying his thoughts. "What was most impressive wasn't the language," Favs said later. "It was the power of the argument, as he laid it out, point after point, off the top of his head. He had clearly thought it through."

On Sunday, while we were shooting ads at the closed steel mill near the South Chicago neighborhood Barack had helped organize as a young man, Favs sat in a Starbucks banging out a preliminary draft. That evening, after putting his kids to bed, Barack finally began to work in earnest on perhaps the most critical speech of his life. He sent back partially completed revisions in the middle of the night. We were leaving for Philly in about five hours.

After a full day of campaigning, we arrived at our hotel in Philadelphia at 9:00 p.m., just fourteen hours before the speech. Working on little sleep, Barack headed to his room to write, and I headed to the hotel bar to drink. It was filled with reporters who had descended on the city like buzzards, circling to see if our campaign would survive. In truth, I wondered that, too. I had believed from the very start that Barack's race would not prove to be an insuperable barrier; that he would be judged by the majority of voters on the basis of his character, his capabilities, and his authentic message of change. Now Reverend Wright's fulminations had put those assumptions—so fundamental to the entire campaign—to the test.

I woke up at about three o'clock on the morning of the speech and reflexively checked my BlackBerry. Just a few minutes earlier, Barack had sent his final draft. I stood there in the dark, completely blown away. In the intervening hours, under an extraordinary array of pressures, Barack had polished and pruned and pulled together all the necessary strands, weaving them into what would be one of the most thoughtful, honest, and inspiring speeches on race ever delivered by an American political leader. Normally, I had edits and quibbles. This time, I only sent him a brief reply: "This is why you *should* be President!"

What stood out most, however, were the candid and deeply personal passages about his relationship with his pastor, the church, his family, and the African American community. It occurred to me, in reading them, that having spent so much of his early life struggling to find his racial identity, Barack could not and would not renounce it now, even if the price he paid was the chance to be president of the United States. So even as he would separate himself from Wright's bitter words, he refused to disavow the man or deny the complex realities of race in America.

The next morning, Barack's supporters anxiously filed into the auditorium at the Constitution Center, as the cable networks prepared to carry his remarks live. Four days earlier, this speech wasn't even scheduled. Now it was a major national event, with astronomical stakes. Yet the man at the center of the drama was completely at peace with the moment.

"Hey, this is how I feel," Barack said, as we stood in the greenroom, waiting for the signal for him to move toward the stage. "I'll give this speech, and people will either accept it or they won't. And if they don't, I won't be president. But at least I'll have said what I felt *needed* to be said. And that, in itself, is worth something."

Yet the speech and the speaker proved as big as the moment. In riveting language, Barack told the story of America's historic struggle with race, and spoke honestly about his own journey. He explored the corrosive legacy of discrimination at the core of his aging pastor's rage, and the resentment felt by some whites over programs meant to redress "an injustice that they themselves never committed." While Barack spoke bluntly about the work Americans, black and white, had to do to repair the breach, he also celebrated the meaningful progress in American society that Reverend Wright had ignored.

"The profound mistake of Reverend Wright's sermons is not that he spoke about racism in our society," Barack said. "It's that he spoke as if our society was static; as if no progress had been made; as if this country—a country that has made it possible for one of his own members to run for the highest office in the land and build a coalition of white and black, Latino, Asian, rich, poor, young and old—is still irrevocably bound to a tragic past. What we know—what we have seen—is that America can change. That is the true genius of this nation. What we have already achieved gives us hope—the audacity to hope—for what we can and must achieve tomorrow."

As I stood watching at the side of the stage, my apprehension quickly dissolved into a mix of awe, pride, and gratitude. Everything about the modern presidential campaign grinds you down, and leads you to a series of small, unsatisfying tactical maneuvers. This moment, though, had genuine meaning. This moment was worthy of the great men who had met down the street more than two centuries earlier to envision the union.

From my vantage point, I could see friends and supporters, many of them African American, in the front rows, dabbing their eyes. I knew Marty Nesbitt as Barack's best buddy and fellow jock. Tears were flowing down his cheeks as he heard his friend speak so evocatively about his own journey and the black experience. After the speech, I caught up with many of the reporters who had come expecting to bury Obama. They all recognized that something extraordinary had happened. By taking on the explosive issue of race so directly and personally, Barack had transformed his own political crisis into an occasion for national reflection. The world, and even those of us closest to him, got new insight into how he would deal with the crushing pressures and complex challenges of the presidency. Our opponents had hoped the Wright tapes would tear him down and destroy his candidacy. Instead, he had never looked more presidential.

The crisis had passed and we had survived, but there was no respite, no time for rejoicing. Now we had to return to the grinding realities of a nominating fight that felt as if it would never end. The delegate numbers were moving inexorably in our favor. Hillary's campaign was deeply in debt and suffering from organizational disarray. Penn, caught up in a lobbying controversy, would soon be forced to resign. Still, the national polls remained tied or showed Obama with slight leads; and coming off wins in Ohio and Texas, the indomitable Hillary was not about to give in.

If the speech in Philly was a high point, much of the rest of the campaign for Pennsylvania was an unmitigated disaster, marked by several unforced errors. One was mine. I had the bright idea to send Barack to campaign in that bastion of working-class America, the bowling alley. I love bowling. When my daughter, Lauren, was young and shunned by kids her own age because of her disabilities, she and I would pass hours together at the local bowling alley. Spending as much time as I had there, I remembered that while one person is bowling, everyone else is sitting around waiting a turn. It's a perfect setup for a politician looking for hands to shake. The image of Obama in a bowling alley would cut against the elitist caricature his opponents wanted to hang on him. Unless, of course, the candidate stopped shaking hands and actually tried to *bowl*—and racked up a grand total of 37, as Barack would do in Altoona. Lauren, as a seven-year-old on her worst bowling day, would have knocked down more pins!

It's a funny thing about politics. You can deliver incisive speeches, do thoughtful interviews, or pass meaningful laws, yet little of it penetrates the public consciousness. Yet when you bowl a 37 in front of the cameras, it's not only big news, but also fodder for late night comedians and (worst of all, for a proud jock like Obama) ESPN. So my little bowling alley gambit was a complete gutter ball. Instead of connecting with working-class voters, Barack became a butt of their jokes.

Obama compounded the problem a few days later when he chose to hold forth on the psyche of working-class, white Pennsylvania voters in answer to a question at what he believed was a closed-door fund-raiser in San Francisco.

"You go into some of these small towns in Pennsylvania and, like a lot of small towns in the Midwest, the jobs have been gone now for twenty-five years and nothing's replaced them," Barack said. "And they fell through the Clinton administration, and the Bush administration, and each successive administration has said that somehow these communities are gonna regenerate and they have not. So it's not surprising then that they get bitter, they cling to guns or religion or antipathy towards people who aren't like them, or anti-immigrant sentiment, or anti-trade sentiment as a way to explain their frustrations."

This was a common problem. Barack would get into a room of wealthy supporters and, thinking he was among friends, offer remarkably candid, if impolitic, observations—except this time there was a blogger for the *Huffington Post* in the crowd, recording the entire disquisition on her digital recorder.

"For crying out loud, he sounds like Margaret Fucking Mead interpreting the natives to a freaking anthropology conference," I screamed when I read the quotes. I understood Barack's analysis and the perspective from which he was offering it. He was not trying to *demean* the white working class; he was actually trying to *defend* them. He was putting himself in their shoes. However, his description of Americans clinging to guns and religion as a reaction to their economic marginalization came off as patronizing and insulting.

Irksome as it was, the San Francisco gaffe also produced some collateral damage. Campaigning at Haverford College in Pennsylvania, Michelle decided she had heard enough and took a hard swing at those who branded Barack an elitist. "There's a lot of people talking about elitism and all of that. Yeah, I went to Princeton and Harvard, but the lens through which I see the world is the lens that I grew up with," she said. "I am the product of a working-class upbringing. I grew up on the South Side of Chicago in a working-class community." Then, with more than a little edge in her voice, Michelle added: "Now when is the last time you've seen a president of the United States who just paid off his loan debt? But, again, maybe I'm out of touch."

It wasn't so much *what* she said, but *how* she said it. The footage quickly made the rounds on cable and the Internet, and it didn't take a political genius to see that it was harmful. Michelle is a warm, whip-smart, and often hilarious person, but when she's angry, she can be stinging and come off as sarcastic. Her remarks seemed to me more diatribe than discussion. This normally highly polished professional woman looked peeved and out of sorts. With her comments in Wisconsin—"for the first time in my adult lifetime I'm proud of my country"—and now this, Michelle was playing into a Fox News game of transference: if Obama himself isn't scary, maybe you can raise doubts by depicting his pastor and his wife as angry militants.

If people thought Michelle seemed angry on the campaign trail, they should have seen her afterward with us. She was livid—and with plenty of justification. Perhaps she had slipped with her remarks, but we were the ones who had thrown her out on the trail with inadequate staffing, preparation, and support. The result was that a remarkable woman, a woman who would become one of our greatest assets, was now regarded as a liability. It would shake her confidence in the campaign team, and that had repercussions. It spun up Valerie, who was sensitive to her friend's feelings and saw herself as Michelle's personal advocate within the campaign. Also, it would distress Barack, who revered his wife and felt more than a little guilt over the sacrifices he had asked her to make for his career. He didn't like being a target; he hated how she had now become one.

Hillary would win Pennsylvania by more than nine points, but in what was becoming a familiar pattern, she won only a few more delegates than Obama, and not enough to cut into our increasingly insurmountable lead. Her only remaining path to victory was to fight to the end, hoping to expose in Obama a fatal flaw that might persuade the three hundred or so still-unpledged superdelegates—members of Congress and party officials—to tilt the nomination her way. Despite our miscues, national polls were working against that scenario, many of which reported that Hillary's negatives among general election voters were at an all-time high, far exceeding Barack's.

"If Senator Clinton thinks she has a legitimate chance to win the nomination, she has every reason to stay," I told reporters on the back of our campaign plane, as we escaped Pennsylvania on primary night and headed home. "But if her only strategy is to try and tear down Senator Obama, I think that's going to make a lot of Democrats uncomfortable." Gibbs and I did the press "gaggle" decked out in T-shirts we'd bought in Philly: "Stop the Drama. Vote Obama."

The next day's drama was mostly internal when Barack called another "yellow pad" meeting at his home. I learned later that Valerie and Rouse had met with Barack and Michelle before we arrived. They concluded that Plouffe, Gibbs, and I exercised too much power over the campaign, and that the decision-making group had to be expanded. Moreover, they wanted more "discipline" in our message operation. If I had known about the pre-meeting meeting, I would not have been blindsided when Barack announced that there would be an additional "strategy" call every evening, led by Anita Dunn.

Anita was a smart operative, a partner in Squier's old firm whom I had recruited to join the campaign as a senior adviser in our communications shop. Still, I was irritated by Barack's gesture, which came without forewarning and was interpreted by everyone in the room as a shot at me. We knew we couldn't win Pennsylvania. Our mission had been to keep the race close while holding down Hillary's margin and delegate bounty, and in that we had mostly succeeded. By my accounting, we had moved from quixotic challenger to the doorstep of the Democratic nomination on the strength of the strategic messaging I had developed from the start. Barack's periodic complaint, particularly in low moments in the campaign, was that my style was instinctive and undisciplined. Yet I certainly hadn't suggested the "clinging to guns and religion" line or unleashed Reverend Wright—and I wouldn't have sent Barack to a bowling alley if I had known he was going to roll a 37!

Our campaign had experienced blessedly little of the palace intrigue that had crippled Hillary's and so many others'. When there were issues, we aired them openly. In the main, that would be true until the end. So this maneuver, cooked up in furtive sidebar conversations, was an unwelcome aberration. I seethed in silence, and the new arrangement wound up amounting to little change in my role. Still, the drawn-out battle in Pennsylvania and this grueling campaign had drained something out of everyone.

There would be seven more state elections, but the May 6 primaries in Indiana and North Carolina were Clinton's last real opportunity to tilt the race by casting doubt in the minds of still-uncommitted party leaders about Obama's electability. Indiana's demographics played to her advantage, while North Carolina, with its large African American base, was ripe for us. A loss there would be a serious blow.

The run-up to these contests brought additional turbulence, as Reverend Wright resurfaced on a national media tour. It culminated in a preening, provocative performance at the National Press Club, in which he took delight in reprising some of his most controversial statements, and dismissed Obama's race speech as the prattling of a politician, as opposed to the truth telling of a man of the cloth.

When I reached Barack on the road, he didn't quite process the tone and scale of Wright's act, and issued an antiseptic statement disavowing the minister's remarks. Later, when he got to his hotel that night and watched the footage, and the breathless coverage it generated, he absorbed its full impact.

When I caught up with him the next morning, he wasn't looking for advice.

"I know what I have to do," he said grimly

It was the final straw. Barack had tried hard to defend his pastor, even as he condemned some of his words. Now he didn't hold back. "[I]f Reverend Wright thinks that that's political posturing . . . then he doesn't know me very well. And based on his remarks . . . well, I may not know him as well as I thought, either." Days later, the Obamas withdrew their membership from Trinity.

It felt as if we had been running on fumes for months. The car was moving forward, but without much pep. Then a gift dropped in our laps that allowed Barack to refill his tank and ours.

In the midst of the Pennsylvania primary, McCain had tried to force his way back into the campaign narrative by calling for a federal gas tax moratorium in response to record high gas prices. Hillary soon embraced McCain's proposal, which seemed to many like Politics 101. With gas prices nearing four dollars a gallon, logic dictated that you do something, *anything*, to appear to be responding to the problem.

When Barack was asked about the gas tax idea, however, he gave a different answer. He had voted for such a policy as a state legislator, and it had turned out to be a scam. The savings rarely reached consumers because they were quickly gobbled up by the oil industry. Such bogus palliatives failed to address the true causes of fuel price spikes, like manipulation of the oil markets and the absence of a comprehensive national energy policy, Barack said.

Rather than embracing a formulaic Washington gimmick, Obama was telling hard truths. We inserted language on the gas tax debate into Barack's stump speech, and he went from there, riffing so compellingly that we turned it into a sixty-second ad.

As this dispute was playing out, the *Washington Post*'s Dan Balz grabbed me at the back of a rally in North Carolina and asked, "Are you sure you guys know what you're doing on the gas tax? Everyone in Washington thinks you're nuts." Yet our numbers showed that it was having exactly the impact we had hoped for. People accepted the gas tax debate as less about relief at the pump than a parable about honesty, character, and leadership.

Emblematic of "Change You Can Believe In," the gas tax debate put us on the offensive again. I was feeling great until I got a call from Harstad, who had been polling in Indiana on the eve of the primaries.

"I have some numbers, and the news isn't particularly good," he said. "We've been slipping a little every day in Indiana, and in tonight's calling, we were twelve points down."

Twelve points? We were playing for a win in Indiana, or at least a close race.

Sensing my mood, Harstad offered a hasty disclaimer: "It could just be a bad night of calling, and if you look at the full sample of the last three days, we're still relatively close. But I thought I should tell you."

I wished he hadn't. Despite Harstad's very sensible admonition about the reliability of one night's calling, and the visible signs of enthusiastic support right in front of me in the jam-packed Indianapolis mall where Obama had just spoken, I was completely overwhelmed by a sense of impending doom—and I apparently didn't hide it well. When I walked into Obama's holding area after the speech, he was in the midst of a big laugh with his friends Valerie, Marty Nesbitt, and Eric Whitaker, who were riding along to help keep their friend's spirits up. As soon as he saw my face, Obama stopped laughing.

"What's wrong with you?" he said.

I foolishly reported on Harstad's call. In part, I didn't want a repeat of New Hampshire, and a downbeat knock on his door if things went bad. I also didn't want to suffer in silence. Yet after the gauntlet of the past two months, Barack had been enjoying himself and he wasn't in the mood for bad news.

"Get the fuck out of here," he said, waving me off, only half in jest. "You're a big downer."

As I walked into the hotel, I ran into Shailagh Murray of the *Washington Post* and Richard Wolffe of *Newsweek*, two of the more seasoned members of our traveling press corps. Shailagh was a delight, as smart and perceptive as any journalist on our plane, without any of the ego such qualities would imply. Richard, a Brit, approached me suspiciously when he first came to interview me about the campaign, but over time, we had come to trust each other. Both Shailagh and Richard had great senses of humor. Shailagh's came with a big, lusty laugh. They had become my frequent companions on the road. So when I walked in, they quickly sensed my distress.

"What's wrong?" they asked in unison.

We took a quiet table in the bar, where I swore them to secrecy and shared the details of Harstad's call. "We're fucked," I said glumly. "You're nuts!" Shailagh replied. "You're not losing this state by twelve points. You might even win. You guys are in good shape."

When we hit Raleigh for Election Day, the world seemed brighter. The mood on the ground was buoyant, with Obama signs and supporters everywhere. That night, we would win an overwhelming fourteen-point victory in North Carolina, and despite the funky Monday night calling, we battled Hillary to a near draw in Indiana. It was almost over. We'd have to endure another month of the primary campaign, but once the last states voted on June 3, Barack Obama would be the Democratic nominee.

Favs and I had worked on a speech that shifted the focus to the general election and John McCain, in the hope of sending a strong signal that the primary was effectively over.

"This fall, we intend to march forward as one Democratic Party, united by a common vision for this country, because we all agree that at this defining moment in our history, a moment when we are facing two wars, an economy in turmoil, a planet in peril, a dream that feels like it's slipping away for too many Americans, we can't afford to give John McCain the chance to serve out George Bush's third term. We need change in America. And that's why we will be united in November."

On the way home to Chicago, Barack was clearly relieved by the results, so much so that he broached the selection of a running mate. He had quietly tapped a small group of outside advisers to begin a vetting process that would eventually evaluate some thirty prospects. Yet Barack already had a notion.

"You know, I'm thinking Joe Biden might be a good choice," he said. Barack ticked off his reasons. A native of Pennsylvania who still had close ties there, Biden could help us in a must-win state that had given us problems. He had a strong connection to the struggling middle class, which was central to our economic message and our chances. A Washington veteran of thirty-six years with expertise in foreign affairs, the silver-haired Biden would be a reassuring figure in our capital and others. Finally, Barack said, Biden had been a candidate for president himself.

"I was impressed with how Joe handled himself in the debates," said Barack. "He was strong, smart, and much more disciplined than I expected. This national media nonsense is harder than it looks. It would be good to have someone who has gone through that experience."

But before that process could move forward in earnest, there were still primaries to endure. Hillary absolutely crushed us in Kentucky and West Virginia, and beat us soundly in South Dakota, states filled with white, rural voters—some undoubtedly less than enthused about a black man in the White House. Pugnacious to the end, she tried to sway the still-dwindling number of unpledged superdelegates, arguing that Obama's weakness with white working-class voters was a fatal flaw. She waged a procedural battle to reinstate delegates she had won in Michigan and Florida, two states that had been sanctioned for breaking party rules about when they could hold their primaries.

Sometimes her zeal got the better of her, as when, in an effort to illustrate that competitive June primaries were not unusual occurrences, she made a ham-handed point that raised the hackles of everyone in Barack's inner circle: "My husband did not wrap up the nomination in 1992 until he won the California primary somewhere in the middle of June, right? We all remember Bobby Kennedy was assassinated in June in California."

It was a bizarre, off-key comment, for which she quickly expressed regret. Still, it enraged me. Those of us who cared about Barack shared a fear for his safety. As the first African American candidate for president, Barack had been assigned Secret Service protection earlier than any candidate in history. The threat stream against him was high, which is why the agents insisted he wear protective gear under his clothes in large crowds. Whatever Hillary's intentions—and I don't believe they were malicious—her thoughtless comment was inexcusable.

These were just the last gasps of a campaign that had finally run its course.

As the final primary votes were cast on June 3, we flew to St. Paul, Minnesota, where Obama would claim victory, in the same arena where the Republicans would hold their national convention in three months. The moment demanded a largeness of spirit; his mission now was to unify Democrats.

Beyond the satisfaction of doing the right thing, we needed to bring the

Clintons, wounded and seething, back into the fold. The draft we sent Barack reflected that imperative, lavishing praise on Hillary as a worthy opponent and a critical future ally in pursuit of progress for the country.

Seventeen thousand delirious supporters filled the arena, including Susan, who joined me while in the Twin Cities to visit friends; fifteen thousand more stood outside watching the speech on a giant video screen. Though I had worked with Favs on the words, it still was exhilarating, almost surreal, to hear Barack speak them.

Sixteen months have passed since we first stood together on the steps of the Old State Capitol in Springfield, Illinois. Thousands of miles have been traveled. Millions of voices have been heard. And because of what you said—because you decided that change must come to Washington; because you believed that this year must be different than all the rest; because you chose to listen not to your doubts or your fears but to your greatest hopes and highest aspirations, tonight we mark the end of one historic journey with the beginning of another—a journey that will bring a new and better day to America. *Because of you, tonight I can stand here and say that I will be the Democratic nominee for the President of the United States of America.*

We had made history, navigating the most challenging route a candidate had ever taken to the nomination. We had harnessed the power of the Internet in ways that had never before been done to build a grassroots campaign of millions, many of them new to politics. Finally, together we had beaten back the Washington cynics who'd said "No You Can't" to the prospect of change and the chances of a young black man who had insisted that "Yes We Can."

Much as I admired him, I hadn't known at the start just how Obama would hold up under the constant and weighty pressures of a presidential campaign. Yet he had weathered them all, displaying the uncommon wisdom, grace, and toughness the presidency required.

For inspiration, Barack had hung in his Senate office that same iconic portrait of Ali, an improbable victor, standing triumphantly over Liston, a feared, formidable, and defeated champion.

Now Obama had taken on the Democratic Party's undisputed champions, the relentless tag team of Clinton and Clinton.

And he had emerged with the crown.

PART FOUR

NINETEEN

FROM BERLIN TO BIDEN

It TURNS OUT that Unity can be hard to reach.

On June 5, two days after their marathon ended, Barack and Hillary held a clandestine meeting at the Washington home of Senator Dianne Feinstein to begin burying the hatchet—and preferably not in each other! The first order of business was dealing with a troubling problem before it got out of hand. Many of Hillary's supporters, if not Hillary herself, believed that a near tie for the top spot entitled her to the vice-presidential nomination. They argued that she would only add to the historic nature of the ticket and boost Obama with a proven, tenacious fighter to dog the Republicans throughout the fall.

Barack was eager to begin the healing, but he also wanted to halt any momentum toward an Obama-Clinton ticket. Barack sent a gentle but clear message to Hillary at the Feinstein summit by telling her that he was considering a range of people and that he wanted to spare her the full, intensive vetting process unless he reached the point of actually choosing her.

Obama respected Hillary and knew firsthand that she was a tough, indefatigable campaigner, battle-tested on the national stage. But the wounds of the long primary were still fresh and a lot of our supporters were adamantly opposed to her selection. Her nomination would have the feel of a co-candidacy, a factor that would be compounded by the larger-than-life spouse who would, inevitably, figure into the deal. And while half of the voters had favorable feelings about Hillary, almost as many did not. We all felt it was baggage that we didn't need.

After the Feinstein Summit, there was an array of contacts and discussions between Hillaryland and our campaign. Plouffe quickly established lines of communication, eager to figure out how we could begin to tap into Hillary's vast fund-raising network. The Clintons, in turn, wanted help in retiring their campaign debt. The day after Hillary dropped out, I called Neera Tanden, her longtime policy maven and my old friend. It was the beginning of a courting process. I wanted to reestablish our relationship and, after a respectful period of time, recruit Neera to our team. I also reached out to Patti Solis Doyle, Hillary's ousted campaign manager, whom we asked to prepare and run the campaign operation for the eventual vice-presidential nominee. I felt a bond with Patti, who was from Chicago, and admired her. It was also appealing to have a prominent Hispanic woman in the leadership of our campaign. One ancillary benefit was that, given her recent, painful history with Hillary, Patti's selection would send a signal to the tea leaf readers that Clinton was unlikely to be the choice for VP.

At the end of June, and after much negotiation, Barack and Hillary met with her key donors in Washington, where she urged them to fall in line. The next day, they held their first public event together, in Unity, New Hampshire. Jim Demers, a longtime New Hampshire political operative and our state campaign cochair, had pitched Unity not just because of its irresistible name, but also due to the fact that Obama and Clinton had each received 107 votes there. It was the perfect embodiment of neutral ground. Plus, New Hampshire would be a swing state in the fall.

The only problem was that Unity the town was almost as hard to reach as unity between campaigns that had battled long and hard. The tiny hamlet is nestled in a far corner of the state, bordering Vermont. There is no major airport nearby. Reaching it would require a seventy-minute plane ride from Washington to Manchester, followed by an hour-long ride in the campaign RV. That's a lot of togetherness for folks who had so recently come together and whose bonds were tenuous. Yet on the flight from DC, Hillary and Barack sat next to each other and seemed to be engaged in intense, friendly conversation. Then, when we hit the road to Unity, Hillary regaled us with stories of her travels with John McCain, laughing heartily about some vodka-drinking episode on an official trip in Estonia.

In the spirit of the moment, I thought I would try to make amends of my own. When I got a few minutes alone with Hillary, I told her that it was never my plan to be working against her, that I admired her and appreciated the kindness she had shown my family. Beyond that, I told her that I could not have imagined a more able or determined opponent. "McCain's going to seem like a day at the beach after you," I said. I thought it went well, but later I realized that I probably sounded like the phony, cloying Eddie Haskell from the old *Leave It to Beaver* show, buttering up Mrs. Cleaver. Also, my words must have rung a little hollow after I had dedicated the previous eighteen months to thwarting her ambitions. Hillary sat impassively as I spoke, and later compared our conversation to a "root canal."

Yet I wasn't simply blowing smoke. Hillary was as game, smart, and experienced an opponent as Barack could draw, and she had pushed him in ways that made him a much better candidate. After sparring with her for fifty rounds, McCain seemed less daunting than he had at the beginning, when Barack speculated that beating the Arizonan would be our most difficult challenge. Had McCain been the McCain of 2000, that might still have been true, but the crusty senator was no longer the bold iconoclast of 2000 who nearly upended George W. Bush by challenging orthodoxies of both parties. As I had forecast in my initial strategy memo, in order to lead his party, McCain had had to fall in line and make peace with President Bush and appease the right-wing elements of the GOP that were so critical in the nominating process, striking Faustian bargains that would benefit us in a general election.

The hawkish McCain was predictably an outspoken supporter of Bush's war policies, which gave us one clear contrast. As the 2008 campaign approached, however, McCain also had muted his past objections and embraced the Bush tax cuts. He would argue during the campaign that our economy had "made great progress" during the Bush presidency, an opinion few Americans shared.

For voters in Benenson's polling and Binder's focus groups, McCain's reversals and circumlocutions dimmed his luster as a maverick who would change Washington. Even McCain, so engaging and open during his 2000 campaign, seemed uncomfortable with his cramped, new 2008 model. "I hate my new friends," he confided to a mutual acquaintance. His ambivalence showed on the stump, where he often seemed a little irascible, like the grumpy, old neighbor shooing the locals away. "Hey, you kids, get off my lawn!" Gibbs would croak every time he saw McCain fulminating on TV.

Barack had come roaring out of his long contest with Hillary better known and liked than McCain. Growing economic problems and disenchantment with Bush had created atmospherics that were very much in our favor. It would be a "change" election, and Obama looked and sounded much more like change than the veteran Washington pol who had been forced to embrace the eight years of the Bush presidency in all its dubious glory. Also, even before the massive registration and mobilization efforts we planned, the electorate promised to be more diverse than ever. Benenson's model suggested that if we properly defined the choice, we were looking at a 53–47 win, which would be a landslide by contemporary standards. It was an amazing prospect, given where we began.

Still, tempting as it was to become intoxicated by our own brilliance and good fortune, no one was doing victory laps. Barack Hussein Obama was still a black man with an alien-sounding name. He still was just four years out of the Illinois Senate. He still lacked experience, particularly in the areas of foreign policy and defense, which could be exploited by McCain. Finally, given the stakes, the other side, led by a man whose tenacity had been proven under the most brutal conditions, was not going to surrender and start chanting, "Yes, we can!"

In campaigns, there are two things that keep you up at night: the things you don't know and the things you do. Campaigns can turn on totally unanticipated events. This is a given of presidential elections. Then there also are crucial, *anticipated* events that demand assiduous planning and execution: the selection of the vice-presidential candidate, the convention, and the candidate debates. In 2008, we added one more.

For more than a year, we had been talking about sending Obama on a major trip abroad to burnish his image as a potential world leader and commander in chief. We shelved it during the primary campaign because we felt we couldn't afford the time out of the country and feared that Bill Clinton, with all his global clout, would find ways to undermine it. Even now, the foreign trip was a high-risk, high-reward venture. Done right, it could help close the stature gap with McCain, the war hero and POW whose one big advantage was his national security experience. Yet if we stumbled, it would only underscore Obama's newbie status and raise questions about his abilities in this critical arena. Pulling off an international trip worthy of a world leader without all the assets of one was an audacious challenge. Enter the Little General.

On first blush, you wouldn't mistake Alyssa Mastromonaco for a logistical wizard and mover of men. Short and freckle-faced, Alyssa looked younger than her thirty-two years, but she'd come to Obama with critical experience, having directed Kerry's presidential campaign scheduling team. From the announcement in Springfield on, Alyssa had aced every task we had thrown at her. So her assessment was critical in persuading the candidate and the team that this gamble was worth taking. Now, after assiduous discussion and planning, she and our foreign policy advisers mapped out an ambitious, eight-country tour that would take Obama from the thorny Middle East to the major capitals of Europe. "We can do this," Alyssa said. "It won't be easy. There are lots of moving parts. But we can do it."

Obama's journey began with two stops, the details of which we couldn't announce in advance: Afghanistan and Iraq. It was an official trip, on which only Senate staff could join. From a campaign standpoint, though, it could not have turned out any better. The pictures, including one showing Obama touring Iraq by helicopter with General David Petraeus, were pure gold. Even better was a development we hadn't anticipated. The day before Obama arrived in Iraq, prime minister Nouri al-Maliki embraced Obama's proposed timetable for the withdrawal of American troops. It was big news, and elevated Obama's image on the world stage beyond anything we could have planned.

As we watched Obama land in Jordan from Iraq in a military helicopter, Gibbs was ready to declare victory before the campaign-sponsored tour began. "Okay, can we just cash in our chips now and go home?" he asked, as the whirring Osprey set down. "It can't get better than that!"

But it did. Barack was accorded first-rank treatment at every stop, greeted by heads of state and government as if he were already in office.

In Israel, Obama deftly navigated the full gauntlet of government and opposition leaders. He made a moving visit to the Holocaust memorial, Yad Vashem, and visited Sderot, a village in the Negev that had been the constant target of shelling from Hamas in the Palestinian-held Gaza. We also squeezed in a visit to Ramallah, in the West Bank, where Barack met with the president of the Palestinian Authority, Mahmoud Abbas. Israel's venerable president, Shimon Peres, received Barack with particular flourish, all but endorsing him in a warm public statement before their meeting. The visit would help quell the concerns of some American Jews, who feared that a black man with an Islamic-sounding name and a Farrakhan-hugging minister would not feel a sufficient bond with Israel. I was a top adviser, and many of Obama's early mentors and supporters in politics were Jews. Yet the questions persisted. "I know what he *says* about Israel," I was asked more than once by anxious Jews back home, "but does he feel it in his *kishkes*?" Though the questions would persist into his presidency, on this trip, Barack more than passed the *kishkes* test.

At the same time, Barack also passed a presidential-level endurance test. In retrospect, what we asked of him was beyond crazy. To get the maximum return out of his week abroad, we jammed as much as possible into his daily schedule. Following an exhausting tour of Afghanistan and Iraq, he hopscotched across Israel and the West Bank, from one tricky pass to another, a journey culminating in a late-night dinner with Israeli prime minister Ehud Olmert. "I could fall asleep standing up," he confided to opposition leader Bibi Netanyahu earlier in the day. When he finally got to sleep, he had completed the day without a single misstep. With every new adventure, I was learning more about my friend and his prodigious capabilities.

One of the signature commitments Obama had made during the campaign was to rebuild our alliances throughout the world after eight years of Bush's unilateralism. Barack believed that the solutions to the greatest problems of our time (terrorism, human rights, poverty, and climate change) required global cooperation, and the economic integration newly wrought by technology absolutely demanded it. We wanted one public speech on the trip in which he could address the people of Europe and the world about our common interests and interwoven destiny. Berlin, which was so central to the convulsive changes of the twentieth century, seemed the perfect setting for it.

Alyssa, half German herself, had shown her Teutonic steel by arm-wrestling with the authorities there for a permit to speak at the Brandenburg Gate, where former presidents Kennedy and Reagan had made historic speeches during the Cold War. When Barack heard about this plan, he was incredulous. "You think we're setting expectations a little high? Let's find another spot." We did, though the new site was hardly modest: the Victory Column, in the center of the historic Tiergarten, about a mile or so from the gate.

A few hours before the speech, Gibbs and I took a walk through the Tiergarten, a beautiful, leafy park rife with history. It was there that the people of Berlin rallied to resist a postwar Soviet blockade of food aimed at starving them into submission. (In his speech, Obama would recall the American- and British-led airlift that sustained Berliners through that siege, just three years after the end of World War II.) The Victory Column stands in the center of the park, an ornate, nineteenth-century granite-and-sandstone tower topped by a bronze sculpture of Victoria, the Roman goddess of victory. Obama would walk down a long, dramatic runway to a speaker's platform that extended into the plaza surrounding the column. It was an awesome setting, but I wondered how in the world we were going to fill it. We had proven our ability to draw huge crowds in America, but now we were across the ocean, counting on people who would never vote in an American election.

I needn't have worried. A few hours later, when I returned with Obama for the speech, the plaza was overflowing. So was the boulevard beyond it, with people stretching back blocks toward the Brandenburg Gate, some hoisting handmade signs with the Obama logo, or the words "Yes We Can!" Riding past this assembly with Barack and Ben Rhodes, I was blown away by the sheer size of the crowd. "Boy, the Germans are a lot nicer than my grandparents made them out to be," I said. Yet it wasn't just Germans. People had come from all over the Continent to see Barack, a stunning outpouring of affection after all the anti-American sentiment that had welled up in Europe during the Bush years.

"The day I raise my hand to take that oath of office . . . the world will look at us differently," Barack had said back when Michelle challenged him to articulate what he could uniquely bring to the campaign. As I surveyed this remarkable crowd, more than two hundred thousand strong, I fully appreciated just how right he had been. Whatever our foibles, America remains a beacon for much of the world. The folks who turned out in Berlin also yearned for change, and welcomed a new American leader, a black man, whose expansive and inclusive views along with his inspiring personal story spoke to a universal ideal that gave them hope for the future.

The speech Barack gave had to strike a delicate balance, urging greater global cooperation without disparaging America or attacking Bush on foreign soil. If he appeared to cast his country or his president in a negative light, it would backfire at home. To assure that this wouldn't happen, I had read multiple drafts from Rhodes, a young writer and student of history every bit as gifted as Favreau. Barack, with his edits, had taken the speech to another level. By the time Obama walked down the runway, I had every confidence it would be one of his best ever, a speech that could have been delivered in the shadows of Kennedy and Reagan at the historic Brandenburg Gate.

Framed by the stirring story of the Berlin Airlift and, more than forty years later, the demolition of the wall that had divided East and West, his speech made a passionate case for the new spirit of collaboration between peoples that was required to tackle the huge challenges facing an ever-shrinking and interconnected world.

"Partnership and cooperation among nations is not a choice; it is the only way, the one way to protect our common security and advance our common humanity," he said. "That is why the greatest danger of all is to allow *new* walls to divide us from one another. The walls between old allies on either side of the Atlantic cannot stand. The walls between the countries with the most and those with the least cannot stand. The walls between races and tribes; natives and immigrants; Christians and Muslims and Jews cannot stand. These now are the walls we must tear down."

In time, the challenge of overcoming ancient rivalries, of rising above parochial political concerns and advancing democracy in places with no history or institutions to support it, would prove far more daunting than we had hoped or imagined on that glorious day in Berlin. Stubborn realities would intrude, often frustrating the vision of meaningful global cooperation Barack articulated in the Tiergarten. Yet on that day, looking out at the vast, cheering crowd from a discreet perch behind Barack, I believed, as Obama surely did, that anything was possible.

The trip almost came off without a hitch but for a couple of exceptions. One was a phony theory peddled by the right-wing echo chamber suggesting that Obama canceled a trip to an American military base in Germany to visit with servicemen and -women wounded in Iraq and Afghanistan because he couldn't bring cameras with him. The second problem was never aired publicly, but it had long-term repercussions.

Maureen Dowd, the talented but tart columnist for the *Times*, was traveling with us and was granted a brief interview with Obama. When we brought her to the front of the plane for the interview, however, Obama proceeded to blister her for a previous column she had written. No one got under Barack's skin more than Maureen, whose penchant for delving into the psyches of her subjects was particularly irritating to the self-possessed Obama. Normally polite under any circumstances, he was patronizing and disrespectful to Maureen in a way that I had rarely seen. This was not well received by Dowd who, like most journalists, was accustomed to firing off salvos, yet decidedly uncomfortable when fired upon herself. After that awkward encounter, she seemed to take particular delight in psychoanalyzing Barack and belittling him in print, which only deepened his contempt. Maureen, who is as gracious and loyal to her friends as she is rough on the high and mighty, would become a friend of mine in Washington, which became a minor source of tension with Obama. "Why are you friends with her?" he would demand after Maureen sent one of her acid darts his way.

Meanwhile, I was delighted to see that the stories from back home reported that McCain's team was "seething" over Obama's elevated treatment by world leaders and the international media. The footage of Obama amid the frenzied, adoring crowds would later be used in a McCain ad portraying Barack as the Paris Hilton of politics, basking in unearned celebrity. It was the preposterous contrivance of a campaign rendered powerless in the face of the torrent of positive coverage Obama was receiving on the trip.

By the time Obama traveled overseas, the VP selection process was well under way. A team of lawyers had spent weeks quietly vetting potential candidates, under the direction of Eric Holder and Caroline Kennedy, with strong input from Plouffe and our campaign attorney, Bob Bauer. I asked Harstad and Binder to conduct some very discreet polling and focus groups. In addition to testing various contenders, I wanted to know what people were looking for in Obama's running mate. Not surprisingly, they wanted more of what Barack didn't have. Governors were considered appealing for their executive experience, but more than that, folks were looking for someone with a little gray hair. They thought Obama represented sufficient change by himself, and preferred as his backstop a candidate with long experience in Washington and a deep résumé on national security.

Plouffe and I would brief Barack periodically. He wasn't dismissive of the political considerations, but knew that if he won the White House, this would have been his first and most significant personnel decision. He was intent on finding someone who could not only help us win the election, but also bring value to the administration. Above all, he wanted someone who would be ready to take over if disaster struck. Though I never asked him about it, it seemed to me that a sense of his own mortality loomed somewhat large in the mind of the first African American to be this close to the presidency. He knew he could be choosing a future president.

In the end, the process winnowed down to four, and then three. The names that emerged were Biden, Senator Evan Bayh of Indiana, and Governors Tim Kaine of Virginia and Kathleen Sebelius of Kansas, though Sebelius didn't make the final cut. In the political calculus, we concluded that we could pass on Hillary, but not for another woman.

In the midst of the search process, Harry Reid, the Senate majority leader, called to make a surprising recommendation. Reid floated the name of Robert

Gates, Bush's defense secretary, who had made a strongly positive impression after succeeding the terminally arrogant Donald Rumsfeld. Gates certainly had the gray hair, Washington experience, and national security credentials, but he was a Republican, and despite Obama's vow to end the red state/blue state divides, there wasn't much public appetite for such a fusion ticket. It was an intriguing suggestion, but never seriously considered.

I also got a call from Caroline.

"I'm here with Uncle Teddy," she said. "He wants to talk to you." Kennedy was home in Hyannis Port, where he was recovering from brain surgery to remove a malignant tumor. After a few minutes of small talk, Kennedy raised the vice-presidential search. The names of the front-runners had now leaked, which was natural, given the amount of vetting that had to be done.

"Joe Biden is a great guy," Teddy said, in his familiar, though slightly labored, Bah-ston accent. "I can't say a bad word about him." Next he turned to Evan Bayh. Bayh's father, Birch, also had served in the Senate and had once saved Kennedy's life, pulling him from the wreckage of a small plane in which they had been flying. "His father is a great friend of mine. Great guy," Kennedy said. "I just don't know the son very well." Since Kennedy had served with the younger Bayh for nearly a decade, I assumed he was making a point. "And I just don't know Governor Kaine much at all. I'm sure he's a good man. I just don't know him."

Kennedy then got to the point of the call. "Have you thought about John Kerry?" he asked. "He's smart, he's experienced, he has debated before and did very well." Kennedy's loyalty was impressive. The support he gave to his longtime ally from Massachusetts at a critical juncture in 2004 helped Kerry win the Iowa caucuses and the nomination. Now, fighting a mortal illness, Kennedy was calling from his sickbed to tout Kerry again. Yet choosing the last presidential nominee for the second spot seemed odd, and the idea never went anywhere.

Obama held a series of clandestine interviews with the finalists during the first week of August, and then asked Plouffe and me to do the same. So as Barack and his family took off for a vacation in Hawaii, David and I headed east in a small chartered jet for a whirlwind day of meetings with all three candidates.

The favorite was still Joe Biden, for all the reasons Barack had laid out in May. Biden had come through our polling project on top. Barack had interviewed him a couple of days earlier, in Minnesota, and had been impressed.

Biden asked for no formal portfolio as vice president but very much wanted to play the role of consigliere, advising the president on all key decisions. "I want your advice, Joe," Obama replied. "I just want it in ten-minute, not sixty-minute, increments!" The shot was playful, but the concern was real. Biden had shown admirable restraint in the debates, but he still could not shake his penchant for talking in a long, rambling fashion.

Plouffe and I landed midmorning in Wilmington, Delaware, and were greeted at the charter terminal by Biden's wife, Jill, and his son Beau, who was the attorney general of Delaware. The Biden family story was well known. Shortly after he was elected to the Senate in 1972, Biden's first wife, Neilia, and his daughter, Naomi, were killed in a car accident. Beau, then three, and another son, Hunter, who was two, were seriously injured in the crash. Biden kept vigil by their bedsides, and considered renouncing his Senate seat in order to care for the young boys. Instead, he would commute each day to Washington from Wilmington, becoming Amtrak's greatest patron. In 1977 he married Jill, a vivacious schoolteacher, who added stability to the family. Together, they added a daughter, Ashley.

In the brief drive to our secret rendezvous with Biden, I was charmed by Jill and Beau, and struck by their close and seemingly easy relationship. They asked about our families, and spoke about theirs with a warmth and old-fashioned wholesomeness that—and perhaps this reflects only on the odd world of politics—seemed remarkably normal and unconstrained by their prominent places in the public eye. A few minutes after we arrived at the home of Biden's sister, Valerie Owens, the senator drove up in a pickup truck wearing a baseball cap and sunglasses, in keeping with the clandestine nature of our meeting. Before Beau drove off and left us to our interview, Biden kissed him good-bye. "I may come by later to see the kids," he told his son, an Iraq War veteran and rising star in Delaware politics. Maybe because I lost my dad so young, I was touched by this simple expression of love between a father and his grown son. "There's something special about this family," I told Barack later when I was debriefing him on our trip.

In our interview, Biden did nothing to dispel our concerns about his verbosity. Even as we expressed that concern, he would respond in ten- or fifteen-minute bursts, coming up for air only long enough to inquire, "Do you understand what I'm saying here?" or "Am I making sense?" Yet when you cut through the hail of words, Biden *was* making sense. He was genuinely impressive, disarmingly candid, and just plain likable.

"You know, I ran for president because I thought I would be the best president, and I still do," he said honestly, leaning in for emphasis. "But what, one percent of the people in Iowa agreed with me? And I was done. Barack got the nomination and now I want to help him win this election and govern. I like being a senator, but this is such an important election and such an important time. It's just so important that he succeed."

In what amounted to a two-hour monologue, Biden talked about the world, the middle class, the challenges and opportunities America faced, and how he might be helpful to Obama as a running mate. I was so transfixed that we were halfway back to the airport in Biden's truck before I realized I had left my briefcase sitting by the poolside table where we'd met.

Our next stop was the Greenbrier resort in West Virginia, where Evan Bayh, his wife, Susan, and their young twin sons were vacationing. Bayh, barefooted and in shorts, greeted us in his suite. He once was the Boy Wonder of Indiana politics, elected to statewide office at the age of thirty and governor two years later. He had benefitted from his father's name, but shared little of his warmth or populist bent. Bayh was an avowed centrist who had won five statewide elections as a Democrat in a conservative state by hewing closely to the low-tax, small-government line. Now fifty-two, and in his second term in the Senate, Bayh was ready to move on. He had briefly explored a campaign for president, but found little traction.

Bayh had an impressive résumé and came from a state that would be in play for the Democrats for the first time in forty-four years. Still, I was struck by how low-key, even flat, he seemed. Maybe it was that we had just spent two hours with Joltin' Joe, but I was a bit concerned by how little emotion Bayh displayed when he spoke, be it about family or the critical issues facing the nation. He presented himself more like an MBA interviewing for a senior management position at Whirlpool. Next to that of Biden, who spoke energetically, in big, historical terms, Bayh's vision of the vice-presidential role and the times we lived in seemed decidedly small. As we made our way back to the plane, Plouffe and I agreed: Bayh would be a safe but uninspiring choice.

Our last stop was Richmond, Virginia, where we visited Tim Kaine. The round-faced, bright-eyed governor had an impressive story. He had served with Jesuit missionaries in Honduras, graduated from Harvard Law School, and then spent many years as a civil rights lawyer, primarily representing victims of housing discrimination in Richmond. He was elected to the City Council and then as mayor, and went on to win races for lieutenant governor and governor despite his personal opposition to both the death penalty and abortion. He was able to overcome the predictable attacks from the opposition and from within his own party, in part because he radiated a palpable sense of decency and integrity.

"I know it's pretty unlikely that I'm going to be the pick, but it's flattering to be considered," he said as we sat down in the living room of the governor's mansion. "I think it would mean so much for Barack to win this race. I'm happy to do anything I can to help. Even this."

Kaine had already proven his commitment. He was the first sitting governor outside Illinois to endorse Obama, just days after he announced his candidacy in 2007. If affinity and shared values were the sole basis on which Barack was going to make the vice-presidential decision, he might well have selected Kaine.

"The problem with Tim is that we're too much alike," Obama said when Plouffe and I reported back from our journeys. "I don't know how many young, liberal, Harvard-educated civil rights lawyers with very little Washington experience the market will bear." On the other hand, Barack wasn't going to choose someone with whom he had little affinity, knowing they could be partnered for years to come. That made Bayh unlikely. Barack also repeated his concerns about choosing anyone who had not experienced the unique pressures of a national campaign. "There's not going to be a lot of time to adjust," he said. "I'm afraid that if someone is experiencing this whole, crazy circus for the first time, it would be too much to ask."

I felt confident that Barack was going to end his VP search where he began, with Biden, but his choice would remain shrouded in mystery a while longer. Plouffe and the social media team had a clever idea to boost our database of supporters, promising anyone who signed up that they would be the first to hear the news of Obama's VP choice. He was absolutely determined to thwart leaks until our text message went out to our supporters the morning of August 23, two days before our convention was to open.

At the appointed hour, I was part of an elaborate scheme, flying a charter from a small commuter airport outside Chicago, holing up in some fleabag hotel outside Philly, and waiting for the Eagle (or, in this case, the text message) to land before fetching Biden and his family from their home in Wilmington for a flight back to Springfield for the announcement.

Afterward, I hit the road for a four-day journey to the convention with Barack.

In a nod to our grassroots campaign, we had decided to move Obama's acceptance speech on the final evening from the arena to the football stadium where the Denver Broncos played. The open-air speech would be an electric moment, of which more than seventy-five thousand of our supporters would be a part. It would be an extraordinarily memorable night, though the candidate, recalling his announcement in subzero temperatures, was less than enthused when Plouffe and I pitched the idea.

"All right," he said reluctantly. "But if it rains, you two guys will be standing next to me holding the umbrellas."

It wasn't the weather that worried me. It was what Barack would say once he got to the rostrum—because as we hopscotched the country just days before he would accept the nomination in Denver, we still didn't have a speech. The draft we had was far too long and lacked an organizing phrase that would provide coherence and an emotional connection. We were going to have to pull together another big speech on the fly.

Late on Tuesday night, less than forty-eight hours before the speech, the muse finally arrived—and not a minute too soon. One of our convention night themes was "Renewing America's Promise," and I suggested that we organize Barack's acceptance speech around that same idea. This is what our campaign and so much of Obama's career had been about: standing up for that core American promise of a fair shake and opportunity for anyone willing to work for it. "Renewing America's Promise" extended to our global leadership as well, where the Bush-Cheney-Rumsfeld approach had left our alliances in tatters.

"I think this can work." Barack said, offering Favreau some language and structural guidance. "Favs, you're going to have to rework this thing overnight and get me a new draft in the morning." It was already close to midnight. The next morning, a bleary-eyed Favreau emerged with a solid draft in hand.

Later that day, after our flight to Denver, I was looking it over in my hotel room as the convention was getting under way on the TV. When the roll call nominating Obama began, I put the speech down and watched. For weeks we had been pushing for Hillary to make the motion nominating Obama by acclamation, but some of her supporters were insisting on recording all her delegates.

The roll call began, but an hour or so in, there was a dramatic stir. The crowd, cheering with anticipation, parted as Hillary entered the hall and made her way to the New York delegation. Sheldon Silver, the New York Assembly Speaker and delegation chair, warmly acknowledged every New Yorker but the state mascot before finally relinquishing the mike to the state's junior senator. When he did, Hillary read slowly and resolutely from a statement she held in her hands.

"With eyes firmly fixed on the future, in the spirit of unity, with the goal of victory, with faith in our party and our country," she said, "let's declare together, in one voice, right here, right now, that Barack Obama is our candidate and he will be our president."

The hall erupted in a raucous demonstration, as Hillary, smiling through this difficult and bittersweet moment, called on the hall to suspend the vote and nominate Obama.

Maybe it was simply the codification of the victory we'd fought so hard to secure, but the ritual was truly moving. The image of Hillary, flanked by delegates on the convention floor, making such a strong and emphatic motion was an inspiring symbol of the party unity we had sought and needed.

It was an incredible accident of scheduling that Obama's speech the next day, August 28, would fall on the forty-fifth anniversary of Dr. King's momentous March on Washington. The date had been set years in advance by the Democratic National Committee, long before anyone could imagine the nominee would be a black man. Now it had special meaning.

Without King and the movement he led, Barack would not have been poised to accept the nomination for president. It was a debt that was impossible to ignore. The cold political calculus, however, dictated that we not overdo it. It was obvious that his nomination represented a huge milestone in the social history of the country, but we didn't want to suggest that this was the central rationale for his candidacy. The tribute ultimately found a home among the soaring closing passages in which Barack paid homage to America's promise.

> . . . It is that promise that, 45 years ago today, brought Americans from every corner of this land to stand together on a Mall in Washington, before Lincoln's Memorial, and hear a young preacher from Georgia speak of his dream. The men and women who gathered there could've heard many things. They could've heard words of anger and discord. They could've

been told to succumb to the fear and frustrations of so many dreams deferred. But what the people heard instead—people of every creed and color, from every walk of life—is that, in America, our destiny is inextricably linked, that together our dreams can be one.

"We cannot walk alone," the preacher cried. "And as we walk, we must make the pledge that we shall always march ahead. We cannot turn back."

Barack had collaborated with Favs on these lines. Now, as he read them aloud in the hotel suite for the first time, just hours before he would deliver them to the world, his voice caught and his eyes filled up. He paused, looked down, and took a deep breath. "Give me a couple of minutes, guys," he said before disappearing into the bathroom. He returned several minutes later and settled back in behind the rostrum. "I'm sorry," he said quietly. "I guess the enormity of this just hit me. I hope I hold it together out *there*!"

It was a striking moment. Obama wasn't given to such displays of emotion, even in a small room of his closest aides. In all our collaborations, I certainly had never seen him falter while rehearsing a speech, but I had no difficulty understanding why his emotions had spilled over now. No one said much or, indeed, had to. In the frenzy of a campaign, you become consumed with minute-to-minute tempests and the thousand tasks at hand. Then there are a few unforgettable moments when you feel privileged and grateful to be a small part of history.

TWENTY

THE TEST

ON THE DAY AFTER Obama's speech, we left Denver on a high. Our risky gamble, moving the final night outdoors, had paid off big. By throwing open the convention doors we had kept faith with the grassroots supporters who had propelled us to that moment. The symbolism was powerful, as was the show of organizational strength in filling the enormous stadium.

The swing voters from Binder's focus group in the heartland capital of Kansas City declared Obama's speech a success, allaying their lingering concerns that Obama was too partisan or reflexively liberal. The positive reaction was certainly supported by our postconvention polling, which indicated that Obama had forged ahead in the race, departing Denver with a solid four- to five-point lead.

I called Barack in his car on the way to the airport and shared some of the good news. "It was a home run," I said, with gushing enthusiasm. He was pleased, but hardly gushing. "Well, they get their shot next week," he said. "We'll see how they do."

We were triumphant and riding a media wave.

It lasted all of a few hours.

Knowing that we had scored big, McCain didn't wait for the GOP coronation to lay claim to the spotlight. When I got off the phone with Obama, my BlackBerry started blowing up with reports that McCain was about to unveil his running mate. We had war-gamed a variety of possible nominees, including McCain's vanquished primary rival, the former Massachusetts governor Mitt Romney. Our list even included a Democrat, Senator Joe Lieberman of Connecticut. It seemed improbable that the Republican base would embrace

Lieberman, who was pro-choice and a leading voice on environmental issues, but the hawkish Lieberman had been McCain's wingman on foreign policy issues and was one of his closest friends. If McCain wanted to signify his independence, a fusion ticket with Lieberman would certainly do the trick.

In all, we had ordered opposition research reports on more than half a dozen potential candidates and had discussed exactly how the campaign would react to each of them. By the time I boarded our campaign jet, the identity of the nominee was leaking. Her name wasn't even on our list. "Where the hell did *this* come from?" I shouted into the phone when one of our press staff called to share the news that McCain would name Governor Sarah Palin of Alaska. "She's been governor for what? Two years?" I barely knew of Palin, and had never heard her speak. I vaguely remembered that she had toppled the Republican establishment in Alaska to win the governorship, but I knew little more. Our collective ignorance about the governor and her politics dictated caution. "Let's not say too much until we get our bearings here," I instructed the team, particularly cautioning against hitting her years of experience, given the obvious retort about the length of Obama's résumé.

I raced up to the front cabin, where Obama and Biden were settling in for the flight to western Pennsylvania, from where they would set off on a joint bus trip together with their wives. I grabbed Barack and shared the news.

"Really? That's kind of surprising," he said, in typically muted tones. "Why do you think he did that?" Before I could share my thoughts, Barack answered his own question. "I guess the best way to blunt the 'change thing' is to put a woman on the ticket. An outsider. It'll create some buzz. I get it." He paused for a second, and then resumed his monologue. "But I'll tell you something. I think I'm reasonably smart, and it took me a good six months to figure out how to handle this whole national campaign thing. Now maybe she's the greatest politician since Ronald Reagan, and she can come out of Alaska with a year or two as governor and deal with all the pressure and scrutiny. But I would give it about three weeks before we make a judgment. Let's see how she handles all of this."

Obama's analysis was consistent with the concerns that had driven him to choose Biden, who had been around the track and knew what a presidential campaign required. As if on cue, his newly minted running mate joined our huddle.

"What's up?" Biden asked.

"McCain picked Sarah Palin for VP," I told him.

Biden's face went blank. "Who's Sarah Palin?"

Much of the rest of the country was asking the same question—and just like that, our triumphant convention was yesterday's news. Obama's instant analysis was dead-on. McCain didn't look remotely like change at a time when Americans were demanding it. Desperate to alter the calculus, he and his campaign had stretched to find an intriguing new character who could compel a revision to the prevailing story line. In the long run, McCain's choice would prove to be a Faustian bargain. At the age of seventy-two, with a history of melanoma, McCain knew there was more than a trivial chance that whomever he selected could become president. Yet here he was, the candidate who promised to put "Country First," tapping a person of dubious qualifications as his second in command. Ultimately, it would prove a costly gamble, but for the moment, Palin's selection ignited his campaign exactly as his team had hoped, and roiled the waters for us.

First, there was the obvious. She was a "she," the first woman ever on a Republican ticket. "Hillary left eighteen million cracks in the highest, hardest glass ceiling in America. But it turns out the women of America aren't finished yet, and we can shatter that glass ceiling once and for all," Palin said on the day of her announcement. Some of the Republicans in the crowd groaned, but as I watched, I could admire the play. We asked Hillary to issue a statement reminding her supporters that McCain and Palin were running on a distinctly different platform from hers, but she refused, perhaps flattered by Palin's tribute.

Palin was also a self-styled reformer, about as distant from the mess in Washington as you could get. She had begun her political career as a small-town mayor, but soon took on Alaska's Republican establishment over spending and ethics, winning a David-and-Goliath battle to oust the state's Republican governor. It was, as we would say in my newspaper days, a hell of a yarn: a fearless, plainspoken, working-class "hockey mom in Alaska," rattling the cages of the high and mighty. It had particular appeal at a time of widespread anger and cynicism about Washington. As I watched their joint rally in Ohio, I understood her allure and recognized that she had an intriguing backstory.

Yet what would become clear was that the power Palin wielded was less about gender or reform than class and culture. She was a world apart from Hillary. No Ivy Leaguer, Palin had bounced around five colleges before earning a degree in journalism from the University of Idaho. A former high school athlete, beauty queen, and sportscaster, she had married her high school sweetheart and was the mother of five, including a toddler with Down syndrome. Her teenage son was about to deploy to Iraq. She was a social conservative and a hunter who ate red meat and relished dishing it out in folksy barbs ready-made for Rush Limbaugh's radio show. Her pitch was for the disaffected, non-college-educated white voters with whom we had struggled so mightily in the primary. If Obama represented the changing face of America, Palin wound up energizing those who resented that change. The East Coast establishment might disdain her as unlettered and ill-prepared, but that would only make her more appealing to millions of Americans who felt they had been getting the raw end of the deal.

"I've learned quickly, these last few days, that if you're not a member in good standing of the Washington elite, then some in the media consider a candidate unqualified for that reason alone," she said in her acceptance speech at the Republican convention. The line touched off a cascade of boos that lasted for half a minute before Palin could continue with her harangue. "Here's a little news flash for those reporters and commentators: I'm not going to Washington to seek their good opinion. I'm going to Washington to serve the people of this great country."

The speech was filled with references to Palin's rural roots and values, and laced with biting lines that portrayed Obama as an exotic poseur detached from the traditional values and life experiences of everyday Americans.

"I guess a small-town mayor is sort of like a 'community organizer,' except that you have actual responsibilities," Palin said, in one of the speech's more memorable lines, which touched off pandemonium in the crowd, but particularly irritated me with its disdain for people who do noble, selfless work. "I might add that in small towns, we don't quite know what to make of a candidate who lavishes praise on working people when they're listening, and then talks about how bitterly they cling to their religion and guns when those people aren't listening. No, we tend to prefer candidates who don't talk about us one way in Scranton and another way in San Francisco."

The "we" she was speaking for turned out in droves at McCain–Palin rallies in the days after their convention. They weren't coming to see the old pol at the top of the ticket, the guy who had spent much of his life in Washington forging compromises with folks like Ted Kennedy. They were coming to see his provocative running mate, whose connection to them was undeniably visceral. Palin had delivered a desperately needed energy boost to the McCain campaign.

While McCain suddenly was drawing his biggest crowds, we largely steered away from big rallies, still wary of the "celebrity" attack McCain had leveled against us in the wake of Obama's overseas trip. Our reticence was a mistake. As I watched the news, I recognized that the contrast between his scenes from the campaign trail and ours fed the narrative that McCain had all the momentum—and the narrative wasn't entirely wrong. A week after the convention, Benenson's polling, now concentrated in the battleground states we thought to be in play, showed that our lead, which had topped out at five points the day of Barack's acceptance speech, had shrunk to just one. When voters were asked what they had seen lately that would make them more inclined to vote for McCain, one-third of them had the same answer: Sarah Palin.

I called a meeting on Sunday morning, September 14, at my company office to consider additional steps to blunt the McCain-Palin momentum. Barack decided to join us, but seemed subdued, even a little distracted. Finally, as we were wrapping up, he explained why. He had spent an hour on the phone the previous night with Bush's Treasury secretary, Henry Paulson. Paulson had informed him of major events that would unfold that very night, bringing with them severe negative impacts on the markets and the economy. "I can't share the details with you, but it is going to be a big story and will require the government to intervene in some way," Obama said. "I told Hank we would be as supportive as possible as they try and contain this. And I'm telling all of you, there are times when—what's the old expression?—'good government is good politics.' Well, this is one of those times. In any case, it's the right thing to do. So I want all of you to abide by that."

We sat quietly as Obama shared the news, or at least as much of the news as he felt he *could* share. It was a sobering reminder that we were engaged in something more than a competition. There were dramatic, real-life consequences to the decisions of our leaders that transcended the political considerations of winning or losing. I was not surprised that Obama, even in the heat of battle, fully grasped that perspective. He might not have been president yet, but he was clearly thinking like one.

The next morning, I woke up to the news that Lehman Brothers, one of the world's leading financial services firms, had filed for bankruptcy. You didn't need an MBA to grasp the magnitude of the story. Hundreds of billions of dollars were tied up in Lehman, and its failure would drive the market down.

Worse, Lehman's demise clearly foreshadowed larger problems within the system. What we didn't yet realize was how much this event and its aftermath would shape the remainder of the campaign as well as Obama's presidency.

As Obama headed to Colorado for a campaign event, I watched McCain at his own rally in Florida address the bleak news of the day and ad-lib a line that would go down in presidential campaign lore as Exhibit A in the category What Not to Do. "You know," said McCain, "that there's been tremendous turmoil in our financial markets and Wall Street and it is—people are frightened by these events. Our economy, I think—*still, the fundamentals of our economy are strong.*"

I couldn't believe it. He had said the same thing before, and we had used it in ads. Now it seemed so off-key that it bordered on satire. It wasn't just that Lehman had gone belly-up, the stock market was tanking, and forecasts were universally bleak. By all the measures most people used, the economy had been in turmoil long before that. The country had already lost more than six hundred thousand jobs in 2008. The unemployment rate had climbed more than a point. Wages were falling and home foreclosures were skyrocketing as the bills came due on the easy-money subprime mortgages that were at the heart of the financial crisis. McCain's comment reinforced concerns as to whether he had any clue about the lives that everyday people were leading. Only a guy who couldn't recall how many homes he owned would measure this economy and conclude that its fundamentals were strong.

By the time Barack landed in Colorado, we had drafted an insert for the speech he would deliver to more than thirteen thousand supporters at a rally at the Pueblo fairgrounds, a welcome return to large-scale campaigning. Energized by the crowd, the magnitude of the news, and the political opening he'd just been given, Obama took aim at McCain's lame response.

"I don't think John McCain gets what's happening between the mountain in Sedona where he lives and the corridors of power in Washington where he works," Barack said. "Because if he did get it, he would have different policies. Why else would he say that we've made great progress economically under George Bush? I mean, that's not what somebody who gets it would say. Why else would he say that the economy isn't something he understands as well as he should? Why else would he say, today of all days—he said this just this morning—that the fundamentals of the economy are still strong? Now, Senator McCain, what economy are you talking about?"

When we spoke later, Barack was genuinely mystified by McCain's gaffe.

"Why would he say that?" he asked. I suspected that McCain had been hoping to offer reassurance to an anxious country, but it had proven to be a serious mistake. For days after, McCain tried to clean up his mess, but only succeeded in making it worse. He initially opposed then later endorsed an emergency plan announced by the Federal Reserve to shore up American International Group, a firm that insured many financial institutions against wholesale losses and that now found itself in danger of collapse. Also, he said that if he were president he would "fire" the head of the Securities and Exchange Commission, something the president lacks the authority to do, as the media quickly pointed out.

As McCain flailed, Barack kept up his attacks on the Bush-McCain economic policies, while taking care not to shoot down potential emergency steps that might be necessary to avert an even larger disaster. He spoke several times with an informal group of top economic advisers, including former treasury secretaries Robert Rubin and Lawrence Summers and former Fed chairman Paul Volcker. While there were plenty of political points to be scored in resisting any rescue plan for the bankers, Barack feared the crisis might take down the entire economy. So, true to his word to Paulson, he refrained from any criticism—beyond opposing any blank check for the banks.

All this took place as we prepared for the first of three presidential debates, scheduled for the following week. The debates, like the convention and the VP choice, were among the standard tests any nominee had to pass—or at least not fail. This first head-to-head contest, however, would take on added meaning in the midst of a national crisis.

I knew the informal debate prep process that I had led in the primaries wouldn't cut it in the fall. This time it would require singular focus and a well-organized effort to prepare the candidate adequately. To lead that process, I had recruited two seasoned pros, Ron Klain and Tom Donilon, who between them had decades of experience preparing Democratic candidates for national debates.

Three days before the first debate, we headed to a Tampa area resort for "boot camp." As we drilled inside a darkened, cloistered, makeshift auditorium, we knew all hell was breaking loose in Washington. Desperate to keep the subprime mortgage contagion from toppling the financial sector, Paulson and Bush had proposed providing up to seven hundred billion dollars to buy the bad mortgage debt that was weighing down the banks' balance sheets. The stakes for the economy were huge, but six weeks before a national election, they were asking members of Congress to perform an unnatural act: to risk their careers to bail out a bunch of Wall Street bankers from their own misbegotten schemes. Even with cooperation from Democrats now in charge of Congress, it wasn't clear that any rescue plan could get the necessary votes.

Our fear was that McCain might opt for a Hail Mary by breaking with Bush to oppose the plan. It would be risky, not to mention totally irresponsible, but a grand populist gesture might help him restore his independent and iconoclastic image of bygone days. On the flight to Tampa, Obama told us that he had received a call from Oklahoma's Republican senator Tom Coburn, the friend with whom he had collaborated on government reform legislation. Coburn proposed that Obama call McCain to suggest a joint statement of principles regarding the crisis. If they held hands on the solution, he reasoned, neither would suffer the fallout—or at least they would share the brunt of it. After mulling it over for a day, Obama placed the call.

We had set up our debate camp in Tampa, a pivotal market in the largest battleground state, so that Obama could do a little campaigning between prep sessions. When McCain finally returned the call, he caught Barack in the car on the way back from one of these events. As soon as their conversation ended, Barack called to report that McCain had proposed a suspension of the campaign so that the candidates could return to Washington to work on a solution. "I told him that the last thing they probably needed right now was a couple of presidential candidates tromping around Washington in the middle of all this," Obama said.

Obama thought they had agreed to reflect on the options, but within minutes, McCain announced that he was suspending his campaign to join the negotiations in Washington. It was another bizarre twist in McCain's herky-jerky approach to the crisis. The good news for us, and for the country, was that he wasn't torching the idea of a bailout, but his announcement also meant that the first debate, just two days off, was now in limbo.

As Barack told McCain and, later, the reporters who were waiting at the hotel for his reaction, he saw no point in a suspension and now viewed the debate as more important than ever. "It is going to be part of the president's job to deal with more than one thing at once . . . it's more important than ever that we present ourselves to the American people and try to describe where we want to take the country and where we want to take the economy."

Later, as we continued debate preparations, Josh Bolten, the president's chief of staff, called Plouffe to give him a heads-up that McCain had asked for a White House meeting the next day with Bush, Obama, Paulson, and congressional leaders. Bush called Obama a few hours later and was almost apologetic. While the president wasn't convinced of the utility of a White House confab, he felt he had no choice but to comply with McCain's request. "And we don't have any choice but to go," Barack concluded.

I stayed with the debate team in Tampa while Barack returned to DC. When he reported in after the meeting, he painted a surreal picture of what happened inside that room. As he recounted it, the discussion started off fine, with Paulson detailing the state of the financial market. Then the meeting took a bizarre turn when, in a portent of things to come, John Boehner informed the group that his caucus wasn't on board. Obama, who had been designated by the Democrats to speak for them, had offered qualified support for the Bush-Paulson plan. Now, taken aback by Boehner's reticence, he said, "Well, I guess if you have another plan, we could start over." At that point, Bush, aware that the clock was ticking on this fiscal time bomb, chimed in: "We're not starting over." Almost as shocking was that McCain, who had called for the meeting, came up almost empty. "He spoke for maybe sixty seconds," Barack recalled. "It was *his* meeting, and he didn't have anything to say!" When the parties adjourned, Paulson was on one knee, begging Nancy Pelosi not to walk away from his plan. "Guys, I'm just telling you," Barack said without a trace of humor, "based on what I just saw, we'd better win this election or this country is screwed."

Rather than return to Florida, Barack met us the next day in Oxford, Mississippi, where, with or without McCain, he would appear on national TV. While McCain was still unwilling to commit to the debate, we promised the organizers that Obama would show up regardless and would be happy to chat with Jim Lehrer, the moderator, for the prescribed time. Still, we were eager for a debate.

It wasn't until hours before the debate that McCain signaled he would show up. His uncertain posturing only added to the impression that he was behaving erratically throughout the crisis. Barack was confident and, despite the truncated boot camp, felt prepared. For all McCain's supposed mastery of foreign policy—which was to be the focus of the entire evening until the financial meltdown demanded attention, as well—Barack was eager to challenge him over the costly decision to invade Iraq, for which McCain had been an unrepentant cheerleader. The banking crisis provided an opening to attack the Bush economic policies to which McCain had attached himself.

Through all my years in politics, I have never enjoyed the minutes just before debates. As we waited alone in the hold for this one to begin, the air felt particularly heavy, almost suffocating. I was slightly nauseated, and presumably looked it. "How do *you* feel?" I asked the man who momentarily would have to stand and deliver in front of fifty-three million Americans? "Just give me the ball," Barack said, taking an imaginary shot at a basket.

As expected, the first question was about the proposed bank bailout—and as planned, Barack laid out his principles for a rescue plan that would help distressed homeowners, protect taxpayers, and ensure that their tax dollars didn't line the pockets of the bank CEOs. Then he made the broader argument for a new direction.

"We also have to recognize that this is a final verdict on eight years of failed economic policies promoted by George Bush, supported by Senator McCain, a theory that basically says that we can shred regulations and consumer protections and give more and more to the most, and somehow prosperity will trickle down. It hasn't worked. And I think that the fundamentals of the economy have to be measured by whether or not the middle class is getting a fair shake."

Everyone on our debate team had heard the "final verdict" line so many times in prep sessions that we could have recited it in unison with Obama. When he delivered the opening answer just as he had practiced it, we all breathed easier. Barack was doing everything we had hoped for and more. He was relaxed and confident, in command of his arguments and the facts.

It wasn't that McCain performed poorly in the debate. He seemed honest and generally candid, and while his shots at Barack were occasionally off-key, he also showed flashes of the disarming, self-effacing humor that had once charmed Americans. When, in a bit of awkward direction, Lehrer insisted that Obama turn and face McCain with his criticism, the snow-haired senator interrupted, "Are you afraid I couldn't hear him?" Yet at this late date, charm and humor could take him only so far. McCain was playing a bad hand, forced to defend policies in which the American people had long since lost faith.

There were thirty-nine days until Election Day, and the rest of the campaign would have its twists, turns, and moments of high anxiety. The financial storm provided a real-life test of the candidates' presidential mettle, and, looking back, I believe the outcome might have been sealed during the eleven-day period that began with Lehman's collapse and ended with this first debate in Oxford, Mississippi.

How fitting that this watershed moment would come on the Ole Miss campus, where nearly a half century earlier, deadly riots had erupted when the first black student arrived to enroll.

With his solid debate performance and his steady, measured handling of the Lehman crisis, Barack had passed an important audition with voters who, while predisposed his way, had fretted about his lack of experience. When we had met in my office the day before Lehman's collapse, the race was essentially tied. Now Obama had moved into a six-point lead, a deficit McCain would be hard pressed to close.

TWENTY-ONE

WINNING THE BIG ONE

OBAMA'S HUNCH WAS RIGHT.

When McCain named Sarah Palin as his running mate, he had hoped her quirky *Northern Exposure* charms would cover his exposed Right flank—and for the first weeks they had. Yet the magic was short-lived.

Palin would remain a star to the conservative Republican base that saw her as a feisty truth teller, standing up for traditional values against an approaching liberal apocalypse. Her stumbling performance in interviews, though, had fueled a larger discussion about her qualifications for higher office—and McCain's dubious judgment in choosing her.

She had exceeded expectations in her one televised debate with Biden, with a warm, winking performance that might have amused the harrumphing elites but played well with the average American.

As McCain's prospects faded, however, the charming, disarming Palin of the debate stage would give way to a candidate with an unmistakable edge. Palin ramped up the ferocity of her attacks, to the delight of the angry throngs who streamed out to greet her.

We didn't realize it then, but those edgy supporters were a portent of the future. Some chanted vile epithets about Obama, and they all seemed to share an enmity toward a government they viewed as overweening, wasteful, and corrupt. They resented taxes, reviled gun control, and eagerly parroted right-wing tripe questioning whether Obama was even a citizen eligible for the presidency much less a loyal American. If Obama's ascent was a source of pride to many Americans, to these Americans he was an alien symbol of unwelcome and frightening change. Later, they would form the core of what would come to be known as the Tea Party movement, an uncompromising force that would make consensus in Washington that much harder to achieve.

Even McCain, who would tangle with these very forces in the years after the election, seemed at times caught off guard by the vehemence of the crowds at his own rallies.

"We're scared," a middle-aged white man told McCain at a rally in Minnesota. "We're scared of an Obama presidency."

McCain vigorously shook his head in response. "I have to tell you, he is a decent person and a person that you do not have to be scared as President of the United States," McCain responded, to a hail of boos and catcalls from his own crowd.

When I read about the dustup, my first thought was that McCain's team knew that the personal tone of their attacks was driving up his negatives. We were polling almost daily now, and that trend was obvious. When I saw the video, however, I viewed his reaction as more heartfelt than tactical.

"And we want a fight, and I will fight. But we will be respectful. I admire Senator Obama and his accomplishments. I will respect him," he said, shouting over the objections of his supporters. "I want everyone to be respectful and let's make sure we are because that's the way politics should be conducted in America."

In subsequent days, McCain would denounce Obama as a crypto-Socialist and accuse him of plotting to turn the IRS into a "giant welfare agency," but this one moment, when he stood up to the ugliness instead of feeding it, would be McCain's finest of the campaign.

Everything was now breaking our way. We were as well fortified as any campaign had been in a long time, with a huge edge in money and the grassroots foundation we had built over a nearly two-year, fifty-state primary battle. Plouffe had done an extraordinary job of managing this massive effort. We had marshaled a historic voter registration drive, adding more than a million Americans to the rolls, the majority of whom were young or minorities (or both), many situated in the handful of battleground states that would decide the election. The huge and active community we had built through e-mail and Facebook was the source of more than cash (although that benefit was substantial); it was a font of volunteers and an invaluable tool for viral, friend-to-friend persuasion and mobilization.

Everywhere Obama went, he was greeted by enormous, adoring crowds. The "celebrity" rap was no longer threatening, and, indeed, I felt as if I were traveling with a rock star. Having done so much TV on Obama's behalf, Gibbs and I now were widely recognized as members of the band. Basking in Obama's reflected glow, I found it surreal when folks chanted *our* names; demanded hugs, pictures, and autographs; and thanked us for the roles we played.

The outpouring of hope and idealism that greeted Obama wherever we traveled, and the millions who sent dollars or signed up to help, was deeply inspiring. We had taken on the cynics and we were winning. But there was a troubling aspect to it, as well.

At every rally, Obama would look out on a sea of people, many of whom held posters or wore T-shirts bearing his stenciled, stylized portrait, under which appeared the words "Hope" and "Change." The heroic image, drawn by a street artist named Shepard Fairey, had become almost as ubiquitous as our sunrise logo. The posters, T-shirts, and other items bearing it had become bestsellers in Plouffe's online souvenir store, which would earn the campaign millions of dollars. They also lent a cult-of-personality quality to these events. While it was inspiring, in an era of such cynicism, that so many were willing to invest such hope in Obama, it also made me uncomfortable.

Obama must have felt that way, too. As we approached one of the enormous rallies that greeted us in the final weeks, Barack looked out the window of the RV and surveyed the sea of humanity. "You know," he said, "we may be the victims of our own success. The expectations are so high. It's going to be really hard to meet them."

For as our fortunes soared, the economy was sinking.

In the first weeks of October, the stock market plunged, in part because Washington had dithered, but principally because the massive scope of the financial crisis was becoming clear. Mortgage foreclosures were epidemic. The September employment report recorded 159,000 jobs lost, the largest drop in five years, and every indication was that October would be even worse. The need for change was more obvious than ever. So the exultation greeting Obama at every stop was leavened by the growing realization of what winning actually would mean. On one flight, Barack peeked over the top of the *Wall Street Journal* and said, mostly in jest, "Are we sure we *want* to win this thing?"

As Barack crossed the nation, Biden did the same. He was an ebullient, effective campaigner, with a disarming, and occasionally disconcerting, penchant for speaking his mind. It was one of those disconcerting moments that provided the campaign with what was one of its last little bumps on a long, rugged campaign trail. Speaking at a fund-raising event in Seattle in late October, Biden appeared intent on making McCain's case about Obama's lack of experience when he warned supporters to "gird their loins" for an international crisis early in the Obama administration. "Mark my words, mark my words. It will not be six months before the world tests Barack Obama like they did John Kennedy," Biden predicted. "The world is looking. We're about to elect a brilliant 47-year-old president of the United States of America. Remember I said it standing here if you don't remember anything else I said: watch, we're gonna have an international crisis, a generated crisis, to test the mettle of this guy." The McCain team, desperate for any small edge, jumped all over Biden's ominous prediction.

Barack was livid. "Why the hell would Joe say that?" he fumed. "It plays right into their argument. It was sloppy." Obama delivered that message personally to Biden, who later made it clear that he was not thrilled with the private chastening. "It's not as if he never makes mistakes," Biden told me, his feelings obviously ruffled. For Biden, a proud and accomplished pol who was used to charting his own course, the role of supporting actor required a major adjustment.

One sad note disrupted our exhilarating march. In late October, Barack got word that his grandmother, battling cancer, was slipping away. Toot, as the family called her, was the only parental figure Barack had left. He had planned to see her after the election. Now, less than two weeks from winning the presidency, Barack would break away from the campaign and return to Hawaii to say good-bye to the woman who provided the ballast in his tumultuous early years.

When Barack returned to the campaign after a thirty-six-hour absence, he was stoic about what had to be a profoundly sad journey. As moving and evocative as Obama could be in giving voice to the struggles of others, he was reserved and reticent about revealing his own emotions. "I'm glad I got a chance to see her," he said quietly. I remarked that it was sad she might not see him elected president. "She knew, but she wasn't terribly impressed by all that," he responded. "She honestly cared more about what kind of husband and father I am."

Gibbs, who had accompanied him on the trip, said that Barack went for a solitary walk in the neighborhood where he had grown up, but had shared little on the flight home. "I felt like he was not just saying good-bye to her but to the life he knew that was about to change forever," Robert said.

As Obama began the final day of campaigning, his sister, Maya, called to tell him that Toot had died. The campaign would release a statement, but given his grandmother's central role in his life, the media clearly was going to clamor for more. On the way to an event in Charlotte, I sat down next to Barack. "You know, there is going to be a lot of interest in this and—" Before I could finish, he cut me off. "I know," he said. "I'm going to talk about her at this event. Don't worry about it."

I stood in the back of the crowd at an outdoor rally at UNC-Charlotte, where tens of thousands had gathered to hear him despite a light rain. "Some of you heard that my grandmother who helped raise me passed away early this morning," he began. "I'm not going to talk about it too long because it's hard a little to talk about . . . I want everybody to know, though, a little bit about her."

Occasionally glancing at notes he had scribbled, he spoke of his grandparents and their quintessentially American story: the Depression and war, the GI Bill and the journey west in search of a better life. Then he riffed. "She was somebody who was a very humble person and a very plain-spoken person," he said. "She was one of those quiet heroes that we have all across America who . . . they're not famous. Their names aren't in the newspapers, but each and every day they work hard. They look after their families. They sacrifice for their children and their grandchildren. They aren't seeking the limelight. All they try to do is just do the right thing. And in this crowd there are a lot of quiet heroes like that—mothers and fathers, grandparents who have worked hard and sacrificed all their lives. And the satisfaction that they get is seeing that their children and maybe their grandchildren or their great-grandchildren live a better life than they did. That's what America's about. That's what we're fighting for."

I couldn't make out Barack's face from a distance. Only later, when I watched the video, could I see that it was covered with tears. Somehow, a man so restrained in private had found communion in the crowd. Yet after the speech, we hiked up a hill, back to a waiting caravan of vehicles. Head down, hands in his pockets, Barack walked alone.

Election Day was a blur. I cast my vote in the lobby of the huge lakefront high-rise where I lived, which was a precinct unto itself. Turnout was heavy, the election judge told me. "We're going to run out of ballots at this rate," she said.

While I had been traveling around the country, Susan and a rotating corps of friends had spent the entire fall at our vacation house in southwest Michigan, working precincts for Obama. When McCain abandoned Michigan in early October, the campaign asked Susan and her team to shift their focus to South Bend, Indiana, a half hour from our home. Yet Susan continued to spend much of her time knocking on doors in Benton Harbor, one of the most down-on-its-luck communities in all of Michigan. Over the years, so many had given up on Benton Harbor, an overwhelmingly black community divided by a narrow river and a shameful class chasm from St. Joseph, the white, solidly middle-class town next door. But Susan refused to turn away. "I've never seen such need," she told me. "I visit these run-down homes, with mattresses on the floor and babies wandering around, and I can imagine Barack walking up those broken steps and caring about these people. I can't imagine John McCain walking up those steps."

In the past, voter turnout in Benton Harbor had been abysmal. Every night, when we talked on the phone, Susan related her conversations with people there. "They're excited about Barack, but they keep asking when the election is and where they have to go to vote. These people aren't watching the news or reading newspapers. They're just trying to get by each day. I worry they won't show up." A little after noon on Election Day, Susan called from Obama's tiny storefront field office in the beleaguered town. She was choking up. "They're doing it, Dave. They're coming! Benton Harbor cast as many votes by noon as they did the whole election four years ago!"

In the campaign's Election Day war room, a phalanx of staff manned phone lines and computers, taking in turnout figures and then actual returns, while the analytics kids crunched the numbers and matched them with our projections. The legal team commanded thousands of volunteer lawyers across the nation, directing them to problem spots to protect our vote. The machinery was humming.

Network exit polls, or rumors of them, streamed in throughout the day and early evening. Then we began to get real numbers. I was with Susan, who had raced home from Michigan, when I got word that the Associated Press was calling Ohio in our favor. Ohio was the ball game. Without it, McCain couldn't win. I wrapped Susan up in my arms, closed my eyes, and hugged her so tightly I worried for a second that she couldn't breathe. "Now you'll never have to say you never won the Big One!" she whispered. I put one hand on Susan's wet, smiling face and, in a straddle that was by now familiar to her, reached with the other for my cell phone to call Barack, who was still at home.

"That sounds pretty encouraging," he said, when I gave him the Ohio report. Suddenly my mind flashed to a story from Election Night four years earlier, when Bob Shrum congratulated John Kerry on the basis of exit polling that showed him a winner. "May I be the first to say 'Mr. President?'" the beaming strategist famously asked his client. With that, Shrum also became the *last* person to call Kerry "Mr. President," as the exit polls turned out to be wrong. "I'm not going to congratulate you yet," I told Obama, who laughed off my disclaimer. "Whatever. I'll see you later," he said.

Susan peeled off to a reception, and I headed to the war room to wait for the official results. Plouffe and I and a few other senior leaders of the campaign gathered in a small conference room with three TVs. The numbers were now rolling in, and battleground state after battleground state was falling our way. Virginia was in the bag, and even Indiana was trending Obama. Neither had gone Democratic since the LBJ landslide of 1964. The outcome was clear and decisive, but by agreement, the networks would not call the race until 8:00 p.m. Pacific Time, when the polls closed in California. As that hour approached, we stared at the TV screens, unwilling to avert our eyes for a second lest we miss the historic moment. The sound was up on CNN. "This is a moment that a lot of people have been waiting for. This is a moment that potentially could be rather historic," said Wolf Blitzer, the anchorman who, with his bristly whiskers and swept-back hair, appeared aptly named. Then the moment came: "And CNN can now project that Barack Obama, forty-seven years old, will become the president-elect of the United States."

At that point it was hardly a surprise, but when I actually heard the words and saw Obama's face superimposed next to the presidential seal, I was overwhelmed. My lips quivered and my eyes brimmed with tears. I had grown up studying the presidents as distant, Olympian figures. In the long history of the country, there had been just forty-three, all of them white men. Now my friend, this extraordinary black man from the South Side of Chicago, would be the forty-fourth! When we teamed up six years earlier, Barack was a little-known state legislator, one loss away from leaving politics and, quite probably, living a productive life in relative obscurity. Now he had made history and inspired a sense of hope the world over. I was overcome by feelings of pride in him, in myself, in my fellow campaign warriors, and in the country for thumbing its collective nose at the cynical political class and saying, "Yes, we can!" Frank Capra or Aaron Sorkin might have written such an improbable script, but what an extraordinary privilege to have lived one!

As each network made the call for Obama simultaneously, the room erupted in high fives, hugs, and kisses. Plouffe, whose face had been a grim mask of determination for much of the past twenty-one months, was smiling like a Cheshire Cat. We emerged from the room to a loud ovation from the staff. I thought how much I would miss these kids who, with their blend of irreverence and idealism, had provided a source of energy and emotional renewal each day. "We'd better get over there with him," Plouffe said. Barack and his family were encamped with a few close friends in a suite across the street at the Hyatt, waiting to make the short trip to Grant Park, where 240,000 people were waiting to hear from the next president of the United States.

Walking out of the building, Plouffe was working his BlackBerry furiously. "We've still got some states out. We'd like to run this margin up a little bit," he declared. We had won by a landslide, but that wasn't good enough for my old partner. He wanted to run up the score.

Even in the minutes since the polls closed, it seemed the security ring around Obama had tightened. The elevator to Barack's floor at the Hyatt was turned off, so we had to get off a floor below and take the stairs. Inside the stairwell, rifle-bearing Secret Service agents nodded at us as we walked by. Outside the suite, Obama's gentle giant of a trip director, Marvin Nicholson, wrapped us up in warm embraces and then opened the door and led us in. Barack was sitting on the couch with Michelle and the girls, watching the news coverage, which now included spontaneous celebrations breaking out in streets around the United States and the world. "Can you congratulate me now, Axe?" he said, laughing while reaching for my hand. "I think it's safe."

I had imagined this moment a thousand times. Yet when it arrived, it wasn't so much elation I felt as a sense of awe. The last time I had seen Obama he was still a candidate. Now he was the president-elect, and even as we laughed and traded congratulations and thanks, there seemed to be a sobriety about him, as if he were already focused on the new burdens he had assumed with his triumph.

Before we took off for the park, Barack suggested a victory photo with Plouffe, Gibbs, and me. When I saw it later, I couldn't help but recognize that Gibbs and I, bloated after two years of eating our way across America, looked like nothing so much as doughy Michelin Men flanking the lean, athletic Obama and the emaciated Plouffe.

Led by the Secret Service and Chicago police, we caravanned down a closed Lake Shore Drive past a makeshift security fence that separated us from the massive, cheering crowd. A stage was set up in the south end of the sprawling downtown park that is Chicago's front lawn. In 1968 it had been the scene of bloody rioting during the Democratic National Convention. The searing images of police and protesters battling under clouds of tear gas defined the bitter divisions of the times. On this night, forty years later, the same park had become a moving mosaic of national unity, filled as far as the eye could see with people of all backgrounds joyously waving American flags.

It was a sea of people with shared hopes but very different stories. Some of the faces were familiar to me. I saw Reverend Jesse Jackson, flag in hand and tears streaming down his cheeks. He could be a shameless hustler and relentless self-promoter, but the reverend also was a trailblazer who had devoted his life to civil rights. He had been there with Dr. King the night he was slain and had, himself, run two symbolic races for the White House. Now the image of the new First Family—a splendid, *black* family—introducing themselves to the nation, had the reverend genuinely overcome. I saw Lane Evans, a former congressman from Rock Island, Illinois, whom I had covered back in 1982, when he was an idealistic young legal aid lawyer running a seemingly quixotic race for a House seat owned by the Republicans for decades. A soft-spoken, principled liberal, Lane had been one of the few downstate politicians to stick his neck out and endorse Obama in the 2004 U.S. Senate primary. Now, just four years later, Parkinson's disease had robbed him of his ability to walk, speak intelligibly, or serve in office, but not of his spirit or belief. So there he was in his wheelchair, braving the bedlam to be a part of it. His face was a frozen mask, but as his old friend spoke to the crowd, his cheeks were moist with tears.

"If there is anyone out there who still doubts that America is a place where all things are possible; who still wonders if the dream of our founders is alive in our time; who still questions the power of our democracy, tonight is your answer," Obama proclaimed, in a speech laden with appeals to unity and bipartisanship. "It's been a long time coming, but tonight, because of what we did on this day, in this election, at this defining moment, change has come to America."

Though familiar with the words, I truly felt their full weight as I stood in Grant Park and heard America's new leader warn the nation of what lay ahead: "[E]ven as we celebrate tonight, we know the challenges that tomorrow will bring are the greatest of our lifetime."

For us, the end of this extraordinary saga was just the beginning of another—the full demand of which we could not yet fully appreciate as we celebrated into the night.

TWENTY-TWO

THE DOGS THAT CAUGHT THE CAR

THROUGHOUT THE CAMPAIGN, Barack told me that he felt better prepared for the challenges of the presidency than he had for the often absurd and trivial demands of running for it.

It took enormous self-assurance—even audacity—to leap into the presidential race as a relative newcomer on the national scene. Now, having survived that crucible, Obama seemed absolutely confident in his ability to handle the job. Yet he also had a sober grasp of the enormity of the challenges ahead, and knew he needed a team equal to the task.

Maybe if times had been different, Obama would have cast a wider net for his cabinet and staff, reaching for a band of smart outsiders to help him effect the change he had promised. However, no president in our lifetime had entered the job facing as many serious challenges—and this helped frame his thinking.

As steward of the economy, he would need a seasoned team, prepared from day one to grapple with a financial crisis that was spiraling out of control.

As commander in chief in a time of war, he would need an experienced national security team that could garner the confidence of the Congress, the nation, and the military itself.

Also, as a president relatively new to the Washington he had just spent two years flaying, he would need a chief of staff who knew his way around the town.

Confident of victory, Obama had begun thinking about his team well before the election.

For chief of staff, he wanted someone with significant White House or administration experience along with the toughness and savvy to deal with Congress. It had to be someone with enough fluency in economics and familiarity with the financial sector to help shepherd the president's plan to address the economic crisis, and sufficient grounding in national security to help him wind down two wars—all this and the skill set to manage a complex organization. From the start, he had one candidate in mind.

"I'm thinking about Rahm for chief of staff," he said, during one of our flights in the final weeks of the campaign. "He's got the right experience. He's smart and tough. And he's a friend. I really don't have a great second option."

When I sounded out my old pal Rahm Emanuel, however, I detected some reluctance. "Fuck, no," he screamed into the phone. "Absolutely not. I'm not fucking doing this, David. Tell him not to call."

Having brilliantly orchestrated the Democratic takeover of the House, Emanuel was on a heady trajectory. Now a member of the powerful Ways and Means Committee, he also had vaulted to fourth in rank within the Democratic caucus, already functioning as its political brain. If you raised his name in any parlor in Washington, you would hear the same conventional wisdom: "He's going to be the first Jewish Speaker of the House someday."

Rahm was sitting pretty. His life had settled into a comfortable, albeit fast-paced rhythm. His family was happy in Chicago. He was unbeatable in his district. Having spent nearly six years in the Clinton White House, he knew how demanding the chief of staff's job was, even in times of peace and prosperity. He knew that the coming years promised to be neither. To a guy comfortable with his life and allergic to failure, Obama's offer was a perilous proposition. His last comment, though, was a giveaway.

For all Rahm's take-no-prisoners approach to politics, he also takes public service seriously. He was the son of an immigrant and believed that when the president of the United States asked you to serve, you just didn't say no. Whatever his misgivings, he knew that if asked, then he couldn't refuse, which is why he pleaded with me to tell Barack not to put him in that position.

I knew Barack needed Rahm, which meant the country needed him. So I didn't regard it as any kind of betrayal when I told Obama, "I think he'll do it. You should give him a call."

It took a few weeks of agonizing, but Rahm succumbed. He assumed I would be joining him in Washington, as did Obama, but I was going through some agonizing of my own. I loved working with Barack, believed in him, and felt thoroughly invested in his success. The past two years had been the most exciting and gratifying of my career, and the thought of jumping off now was hard to imagine. Gibbs and many of the friends with whom I had shared the adventure would be moving on to the White House. While I could consult from Chicago, I knew I couldn't have any day-to-day impact at a distance. As someone who still believed in the potential of politics, I knew the opportunity to serve at the highest levels of government was virtually impossible to refuse.

Yet I had real misgivings. Lauren was thriving at Misericordia, and it wouldn't be fair to move her. Susan couldn't move to Washington while Lauren lived in Chicago. Moreover, her epilepsy research foundation, CURE, was growing by leaps and bounds, and her duties there required her to stay put. If I took the job, we would be living apart for the first time in thirty years. To avoid conflicts of interest, I would also have to sell the businesses I had built over a quarter century; businesses that had been an emotional hub for me.

Odd for someone who had written and spoken the word "change" thousands of times, but in truth, I didn't much like it in my own life. When I was just out of college and starting at the *Tribune*, I decided I should move out of Hyde Park, so I leased an apartment on Chicago's North Side. Before spending a night there, though, I changed my mind, forfeiting my first month's rent and begging my landlord for my old apartment. He took advantage of my idiocy by tacking an extra twenty-five dollars a month on my rent.

I cherished the ability to come and go as I pleased, to be the master of my own life. I had always worked long, hard hours, but on my own schedule. I was never a clock puncher or a paper pusher. Even when I was a reporter, no one much cared if I filed my stories from City Hall, a bowling alley, or a saloon— and I filed from all of them—so long as I broke news. Also, reporting, at least in my day, was one job in which you actually were rewarded for questioning authority, a great fit with my personality. I didn't see myself as a good company man. As a consultant, I took comfort in the knowledge that I could choose my clients and choose to quit those who offended me, which I did more than once. I was loath to surrender that freedom, which I told Barack as I tried to explain my misgivings.

"I've always set my life up so I could tell anyone I wanted to go fuck themselves," I said during one of our long plane rides near the end of the campaign. "And I know that you can't tell the president of the United States to go fuck himself."

Barack pondered my dilemma and conceded my point. "No, you really can't. But you're someone who believes in public service. You have a chance to work for a president who's your friend at a pretty important time for the country. You can make a difference. Isn't that what this is all about?" He paused, and added, "Oh, and one other thing: You *can* tell me to go fuck myself, just don't do it in front of anyone else!"

Despite all this, Susan pressed me to go to Washington. "If you don't, you're going to regret it for the rest of your life," she said. I knew she was right. "Go. I'll come out a week a month. Maybe you can come back some weekends. We'll get through it." With her blessing, I told Barack I would come for two years. That was all I felt I could ask of Susan and, after going flat out for the previous two years, all I could physically and emotionally endure. Barack was fine with it. Plouffe, whose wife, Olivia, had given birth to their second child two days after the election, wanted to take a couple of years off before joining the administration. "In two years, Plouffe can take your spot and you can go back to Chicago and work on the reelect," he said. If that was slightly presumptuous, it was no time to quibble.

I had another reason for my two-year plan that I didn't share. We had won the election in a deeply divided country by a remarkable six-point margin, a large enough victory to sweep sizable Democratic majorities into both the House and Senate. We had captured dozens of seats in Republican-leaning districts. Now, with expectations sky-high for Obama, we were taking over in the midst of an epic economic crisis that would get worse before it got better. It was a situation that seemed certain to result in big losses in the midterm elections, which are often unkind to sitting presidents, and I knew that Washington would be even less forgiving of whoever was sitting in my chair. I had witnessed friends unceremoniously dumped by the White House in the wake of Clinton's rough 1994 midterm election. I wanted to make sure that I left Washington of my own volition and wasn't booted out of town as the fall guy for the disappointing election performance that seemed nearly inevitable.

Susan and I took a week's vacation in Mexico, most of which I spent brooding about whether I had made the right decision. While we were there, the *Times* ran a story about how the administration intended to enforce strict ethical guidelines among its members, including on issues such as the payment of household staff. Susan reminded me that we had paid cash to Anna, the immigrant Polish woman who occasionally cleaned our house. I called Bob Bauer, our crack campaign lawyer, who thought it could be a deal breaker. "Maybe I'm *not* going," I told Susan, barely masking my relief. It turned out that Anna, a U.S. citizen, had been assiduous in reporting the income and had worked few enough hours to exempt us from reporting. We had not done anything improper. I received that news with more than a little ambivalence, and returned home ready to plunge into my new life.

Obama had chosen John Podesta, who served as Clinton's last White House chief of staff, to lead the transition process that began months before the election. Working alongside Podesta, a fixture in DC since the Carter administration, was Pete Rouse, whose tenure there was just as long. Rahm, who had worked closely with Podesta and Rouse before, slid seamlessly into the staffing discussions. He was particularly worried about one personnel issue. Obama had made it clear that he wanted Valerie Jarrett at his side in the White House. She was fiercely loyal, and he felt she brought an invaluable perspective as an African American woman to an operation dominated by white men. She would also serve as a conduit to the First Lady. Though Michelle rarely involved herself in the workings of the campaign, her concerns were usually channeled through Valerie. Rahm, however, was wary of having someone on his senior staff by day who socialized and even vacationed with the Obamas on nights, weekends, and holidays.

"I don't want to manage the president's best friend," Rahm confided. "It's a disaster. I saw these situations when I was working for Clinton, and it doesn't work. It's a bad idea." So when Dick Durbin, our senior senator, approached Valerie about possibly replacing Barack in the Senate, Rahm became the most enthusiastic promoter of the idea. While Valerie was intrigued by the prospect, Barack discouraged the notion. "It sounds attractive now, but when you're spending the next few years stomping around county fairs downstate, trying to get yourself elected, you might have a different view," he told her. "I liked it. I'm not sure you will." Still, Barack was a devoted friend to Valerie, and as long as she was intrigued by the notion, he wanted a window on the thinking of Governor Blagojevich, who would make the Senate appointment.

Obama and Blagojevich weren't close. Burning with class resentment, Rod saw Obama as an undeserving Ivy League elitist who had won the political lotto. Obama viewed Blagojevich as a vacuous lightweight and a demagogue to boot. Rod was unlikely to want to do the president-elect any favors, at least not without a price. Rahm, desperate to keep Valerie out of the White House, opened his own private channel with one of the governor's closest political advisers.

Soon after this trial balloon took flight, Barack persuaded Valerie to abandon the Senate notion and instructed Rahm to give Blagojevich's office several other names he recommended as possible successors. Yet Rahm waited forty-eight hours before delivering that message and quietly continued engaging his go-between about the idea of appointing Valerie to the Senate. When Blagojevich's man inquired what the governor would get in return, Rahm demonstrated the savvy that had made him one of the few senior members of the Clinton administration to depart the White House without ever having been subpoenaed. "He would be 'thankful and appreciative,'" Rahm replied.

As tapes would show when they were played later in federal court, Blagojevich was unimpressed by Rahm's quid for his quo, having hoped for something more tangible, such as a cabinet post or a lucrative outside job. "I get nothing?" he thundered, on a wiretapped conversation. In another taped conversation with an aide, Blagojevich was even blunter. "I mean I, I've got this thing and it's fucking . . . golden," he said. "And I, I'm just not giving it up for fucking nothing."

Rahm wisely broke off his discussions. By December, Blagojevich was arrested at his Chicago home. He would be indicted on an array of charges, including the attempted sale of the Senate seat. I was in my doctor's office taking a stress test before my move to Washington and I almost fell off the machine when I learned that Rod had been pinched. The Illinois governor would be stripped of his office and, later, convicted of federal charges that sent him to prison for fourteen years, an outrageously long sentence, meted out by a judge who'd wearied of Rod's preening. I recalled my last substantive conversation with Blagojevich when he was urging me to join his gubernatorial campaign in 2002. "Come on, we're going to raise more than anyone ever has for this thing," he said. "It'll be great." My instincts, like Rahm's, had been honed by Chicago politics. I walked away. Hearing the news about Blagojevich, I was relieved that I had made the right choice, though saddened that a guy I liked and with whom I had once worked had sunk so low. Rahm's name and his advocacy for Valerie rated press coverage during the scandal, but there was never any indication of wrongdoing on his part.

Despite Rahm's unabated concerns, Valerie would come to the White House and—like Rouse and me—carry the title of senior adviser. Having negotiated a large portfolio, she would gain supervisory authority over the Office of Public Engagement and the Office of Intergovernmental Affairs, two White House agencies charged with building political and public support for the president's initiatives. She would also become the president's liaison to the business community, a rocky piece of real estate to hold in an administration that would cross swords with Wall Street.

After the election, the transition team was headquartered in secure offices in a federal building in downtown Chicago. It was in the plaza below where, six years earlier, a little-known state senator had made his stand against the impending war in Iraq. Now, as president-elect, Obama was forging the national security team he would need to end it.

Long before the election, he had sent out a feeler to Secretary of Defense Robert Gates about staying on in the new administration. Barack respected Gates and felt his institutional credibility and knowledge would be critical to implementing the Iraq transition and the strategic change in Afghanistan. As a lifelong Republican and a fixture in every Republican White House since Reagan's, he would also confer a spirit of bipartisanship in national security. Six days after the election, Obama and Gates met at a fire station at Reagan Airport and sealed the deal.

The big surprise was Barack's choice for the other major national security position. "I think I am going to ask Hillary to be secretary of state," he told me. I was stunned. I knew that, despite their battles, Barack respected Hillary. During our travels after the primaries, he had once mentioned that he would like to find a role for her, perhaps on the Supreme Court. There were obvious plusses to having Hillary inside the tent rather than in the Senate, where she might become a competing force—but secretary of state? That's not just inside the tent, but center ring. I knew Barack revered Lincoln and had devoured *Team of Rivals*, Doris Kearns Goodwin's riveting history of that era. Still, how could he make this former rival the top foreign policy appointee when she had run ads questioning his preparedness to be commander in chief?

Barack was unconcerned and undeterred. "Well, we were friends before we were opponents," he explained. "She's very smart. She's tough, and I believe that if she's on the team, she'll be loyal. We have an economic crisis that is going to be taking up a bunch of my time, at least in the near term. I need someone who is instantly recognized and respected around the world in that spot. When she lands someplace, they'll know her. They'll know they're not getting the B-Team." Barack also believed that the choice would convey a powerful message about our democracy when two opponents, having battled so fiercely, could unite after the election for the good of the country.

Hillary initially turned Obama down. "She said she's tired, which I, of all people, understand," he reported. "But I wasn't going to let her off the hook.

I asked her to sleep on it." Eventually, Hillary relented, and the warm partnership they built would become one of the inspiring subplots of my time in the administration.

Barack's other major focus was on forging a strong economic team, the urgency of which was clearer by the day. The October job numbers, reported a few days after the election, were catastrophic, with another 240,000 jobs lost—we would learn two months later that the actual number of jobs lost was actually 423,000. In November, we would lose another half million, the worst monthly loss in thirty-four years.

Between campaign stops in New York in mid-October, Obama held a private meeting at the W Hotel, where we were staying. He filled me in later that evening. "I just met a guy I think you would really like," he said. "Very smart, thoughtful, unassuming guy. He spent time overseas as a kid, so we had that in common. Plays basketball. But what I liked the most about him was that he spent the whole hour trying to persuade me why I shouldn't hire him."

If that was Tim Geithner's mission, he failed miserably. Geithner, just a couple of weeks younger than Obama, had spent much of his career in public service. An expert in global finance, he had worked in the Treasury Department during the Clinton administration, rising to assistant secretary for international affairs. Now, as head of the New York Fed, he was as deeply involved as anyone in the efforts to stem the financial crisis. Rahm and others had urged Barack to consider Geithner for treasury secretary, and the president came away from their meeting favorably impressed.

Another candidate for treasury secretary was Geithner's old boss Lawrence Summers, a renowned economist who held the job during the final years of Clinton's presidency. Afterward, he returned to Harvard, where his rise and fall as university president had been a major national story. After five productive but controversial years, Summers was forced to resign after a speech in which he cited research on gender differences that, he believed, helped explain the lack of diversity in science and engineering programs. He made the point as part of an argument in favor of promoting such diversity, but Larry, who can be brusque and abrasive, had given an opening to the many faculty members he had rubbed the wrong way.

Having read about the Harvard controversy and Larry's role as treasury secretary in deregulating a financial sector that was now imploding, I wasn't particularly well disposed toward him. So when I first met him during a campaign meeting of Obama's unofficial economic advisers, I was pleasantly surprised. Robert Rubin, Summers's venerated predecessor as treasury secretary, took issue with Obama's focus on the middle class, arguing that Obama should cast himself as a "pro-growth Democrat," without making what Rubin regarded as class distinctions. Summers challenged him. "Bob, it really is a problem that the middle class is being squeezed," said Summers, who had written as much in his columns in the *Financial Times*. "We need growth, but the growth we've been getting isn't producing the kind of gains for people in the middle it once did. It seems to me that this is a problem and we ought to be addressing that."

Larry wanted his old job back. Given the magnitude of the problems we would be facing, his experience and powerful intellect appealed to Barack, but Obama also liked Geithner's freshness and his unassuming style. Barack and Rahm arrived at a Solomonic decision: appoint Geithner as treasury secretary and ask Summers to serve as director of the National Economic Council and the president's chief economic adviser. On paper, it would be a step down for Summers. This was a *staff* job, not a cabinet position, and Larry was taken aback by the suggestion. Then Rahm sweetened the pot, assuring Summers that he would succeed Ben Bernanke as chair of the Federal Reserve when his term expired in 2010. With that, Larry agreed to accept the lower-profile appointment.

Obama filled out the team with two more economists, Peter Orszag as budget director and Christina Romer as chair of his Council of Economic Advisers. Orszag, a wunderkind in the Clinton administration, was an expert on the economics of health care. Romer, a professor from UC Berkeley, was known for her writings on the Great Depression, which seemed increasingly relevant. The CEA chairmanship had been coveted by Austan Goolsbee, the University of Chicago economist who had advised us since the Senate campaign. But Barack was hell-bent on diversity, and Goolsbee had to settle for a seat on the CEA under Romer.

On December 16, the new economic team gathered in Chicago for the first time to brief the president-elect, Biden, and the senior staff on the new economic realities we would inherit. Before the larger meeting, some of us were given a preview of the group's forecast, and it was jaw-dropping. "Here's the problem, folks," I said. "The American people know it's bad, but they have no idea it's *this* bad. They haven't had that 'holy shit!' moment where someone tells them the full extent of the problem. Somehow we have to get that news out so we establish the baseline we're walking into and lay the foundation for the steps we'll need to take."

The briefing with Obama, in a packed, windowless conference room of our transition headquarters, was, if possible, even starker.

It opened with a presentation by Romer, whose cheery, Julia Child–like affect seemed rather incongruous given the bleak news she was delivering. She displayed a series of charts, all with lots of lines heading downward. Romer compared the projected trajectory of the current economy with previous recessions in the United States. "In short, Mr. President, this is likely to be the deepest recession we've faced since the 1930s."

Summers picked up the narrative, elaborating on the impact of these trends charted by Romer. He described a massive projected loss of economic activity, and its impacts. "Given what Christy described, Mr. President, we will see a significant decline in output that will mean the loss of millions of additional jobs," he said. "And unless we intervene aggressively and replace some of that lost output, there is a one-in-three chance of a second Great Depression."

A second Great Depression? Never had any of us anticipated a cataclysm of that magnitude. For all the lofty plans we had made, it was clear that we would be arriving in Washington as a triage unit, with the immediate and all-consuming priority of keeping the American economy from going under.

Summers added an unhappy historical note about recessions triggered by financial crises. Because of constricted lending, he said, recovery tended to be slower and more challenging than the usual "V-shaped" comebacks associated with other recessions.

When it came to bad news, Geithner was not to be outdone. Despite the initial steps by the Bush administration and the Fed to undergird the financial industry, he said, that industry's desperate attempt to spin off failing subprime mortgages into other complex financial offerings was dragging down banks and financial institutions worldwide. "The banks are very fragile," reported our future treasury secretary. "No one is lending, and there is a real chance that the system could collapse."

Orszag, who probably would have preferred a happier occasion to mark his fortieth birthday, anchored the grim presentation. "Between the money we'll need to spend to stimulate the economy and the revenues we will lose because of the decreased output and higher unemployment, the short-term deficits are going to grow," he said.

As I absorbed the impact of their words, two things occurred to me. One was that this was the first meeting I had attended in which everyone referred to Barack as Mr. President. The second was that it was a hell of a time to have acquired that title. I was sure I wasn't the only one periodically gazing over at Obama to see how he was processing the news. If he was panicking or even taken aback, however, I couldn't detect it. Just as we had seen during the most stressful moments of the campaign, Obama appeared calm, confident, and focused. "Well, it's too late to ask for a recount, so we had better figure out what we're going to do about this," he said with a thin smile, the best he could muster under the circumstances.

For the next several hours, we discussed what was the first essential step to stem the bleeding. Summers and the group argued for a stimulus plan, a quick and substantial regimen of government spending to pump capital back into the economy. The consensus was clearly the bigger the stimulus, the better the result. Romer, however, noted the political problem I had reflected on earlier, and while it was amusing to hear this very proper professor rehearse my "holy shit" language, the challenge was not. How do you sell a massive spending plan to a country that had not yet grasped the magnitude of the crisis and that was already outraged by ballooning budget deficits?

We had promised to tame Bush's record deficits, swollen by the cost of the wars and two substantial tax cuts. Now we were going to ask the Congress and the public to accept, as our very first act, a major, unfunded spending program that would only add to those deficits. There had already been talk in Washington of a record three-hundred-billion-dollar stimulus in the fall, to be voted on after the election, and that had stirred great angst. Two months later, we were discussing one that might be three times as large.

Obama asked Rahm what he thought was achievable in Congress. "Seven hundred fifty to eight hundred fifty billion, max," he said. "And that will be a hard lift. But I'll tell you, they will never accept anything with a *t* in front of it. They're not going for a trillion."

Summers said the nature of the spending was less important than the volume. While some initiatives, such as food stamps, were particularly effective because people would immediately spend the money, any dollar pumped back in the economy would help spur jobs and growth. "Well, let's think carefully about the components of this package," Obama said. "I want to make sure we invest in things that help in the short run but also have long-term benefits and fulfill some of the commitments we've made. Because my guess is that this is the last new spending we're going to be able to do for some time." He suggested as examples clean energy projects and information technology for health care. A major infrastructure program would be included to address the backlog of "shovel-ready" projects around the nation. To win Republican support and provide some relief to the middle class, tax cuts would also have to be part of this package.

Could it have been just six weeks since that sublime evening in Grant Park? It seemed like ancient history as we discussed emergency measures needed to save the American economy from collapse. It was a mission that would consume much of our time and political capital for months to come and, inevitably, shape the contours of the Obama years.

As we left the conference room, Obama commented, with no apparent self-pity, on the dismal hand we had drawn. "I'll tell you one thing," I said in response. "We're going to have a one hell of a tough midterm election." Yet that must have seemed like an eternity away as well as the least of our problems right then. He looked at me and just walked away.

On January 4, I flew to Washington with the president-elect to build up support for his stimulus. His family had arrived the previous evening, so his daughters could get situated in their new school. The Bush administration had sent a jet from the presidential fleet to pick us up in Chicago. It was my first exposure to such travel, with well-appointed planes configured for comfort and work, and staffed by a wonderfully attentive navy crew. Barack spent some time at the desk in the office/cabin reserved for the president. When we landed, one of the long, black armored presidential limousines was waiting at the foot of the stairs. Settling into the plush backseats, our eyes were drawn to the phone between us, adorned with direct-dial buttons labeled with the names of Bush's top aides. Barack glanced over and smiled. "This has been some trip, hasn't it?" he said, a reference not just to the journey from Chicago to Washington, but from obscurity to the pinnacle of power.

We had spent the last two years condemning George W. Bush's policies as a failure of epic proportions. Yet from the moment the election's outcome was known, he and his team were gracious, cooperative, and open. Maybe part of it was due to Obama's working closely with Bush and Paulson after Lehman's collapse. Mostly, I suspected, Bush had a respect for the meaning of the transition period. After all, he was not just the president, but also the son of a president. Transitions were a critical rite of democracy, and George W. Bush was intent on managing this one properly.

That became even clearer a few days after our arrival in Washington, when, at Obama's request, Bush hosted a White House luncheon for Obama and the three living former presidents Clinton, George H. W. Bush, and Jimmy Carter. At the same time, all of our counterparts on Bush's senior staff invited us to lunch to provide a rundown on their operations and answer any questions.

I had visited the White House several times during the Clinton years, but still felt a sense of awe as I entered, thinking about the larger-than-life leaders who had served there and all the history they had made. The imposing oil portraits in heavy wood frames and even the musty, museum odor of the place reeked of history. The other striking thing about this citadel of American power is its size. Small! Very small! The halls are narrow, the office spaces cramped and limited in number, which made the West Wing the most select real estate in Washington, and it felt surreal that I would have such a prominent spot there, with my office right next door to the president's.

Ed Gillespie, the counselor to President Bush, was waiting for me in the lobby. Ed, a former chair of the Republican National Committee, played the same strategic communications role in the White House that I would assume less than two weeks later. He spent hours with me, going over the nature of his routine and life in the White House. It was a generous gesture and an invaluable primer.

When we were done, we walked down a tight staircase and past two Secret Service agents and into the Oval Office. I had never before stepped inside. It was like walking onto a movie set. Standing across from us was Obama and his four living predecessors. Has there ever been such a gathering, I wondered?

The curved, windowed door to one side of the president's desk opened, and Dana Perino, President Bush's press secretary, led a phalanx of photographers into the Oval Office to capture the moment. Gibbs, who would take her job, trailed along. As the cameramen clicked away, the two Bushes flanked Obama, with Clinton and Carter to the younger Bush's left. All were smiling, but the taciturn Carter, perhaps revealingly, stood a few steps apart from the group. When the cameramen were gone, Barack motioned Gibbs and me over to meet the elder President Bush. "Mr. President, this is Robert Gibbs and David Axelrod. These guys helped get me elected." George H. W. Bush smiled his warm, crooked smile and pumped a fist in the air. "Nice going, boys," he said.

The next day, Summers and I appeared before a closed meeting of the Senate Democratic Caucus in the ornate Capitol room named for Lyndon B. Johnson. A few of the senators had been my clients, and I knew others, but this was my first command performance before the entire boisterous crew. Many were palpably smart. Others left you wondering how in the world they had ever reached such heights. Running this circus was Harry Reid, who spoke like the small-town Nevada lawyer he once was, but who managed the show like a firm ringmaster.

We were there to advocate for Obama's stimulus plan, which we had dubbed the American Recovery and Reinvestment Act after research revealed that people didn't like or even understand the word *stimulus* but supported almost anything "American." I briefed the group on the polling and strategy for the plan, while Summers conveyed the urgent need for its implementation. The size of the emerging proposal, just shy of eight hundred billion dollars, worried some senators. Others were annoyed that one-third of it would come in tax cuts, which they viewed as an ineffective sop to Republicans—even though these breaks would be targeted to the middle class and working poor. Larry made a powerful case and respectfully answered all their questions, including some contentious ones, displaying a patience that belied his prickly reputation.

I would return to the Senate Democratic Caucus periodically over the next few years, often to absorb a beating from allies distressed by the impact of the economy and Obama's decisions on their reelection prospects. What I quickly learned is that if you go to the caucus expecting to be challenged, poked, prodded, and even slapped around a bit, you will never leave disappointed.

I went home to Chicago the following weekend to see Susan and to deal with lingering details of my move. Before returning to DC on Monday morning, I stopped off to speak at a fund-raising breakfast for Misericordia, the wonderful community for people with special needs where Lauren lived. I shared some reflections on the campaign and thoughts about the challenges ahead. When I finished, Lauren came onstage for a surprise presentation. One of her favorite activities was painting, and she was very good at it. Our vacation house in Michigan was decorated with her nature scenes. The painting she presented me on this day, however, was a new subject: the White House. Lauren had painted the Chicago skyline reflecting in the North Lawn fountain, so I would never forget home. I hung that painting in the White House, where it was the first thing I saw each day when I walked into my office.

The day before the inauguration, I went to the Blair House, the official guest residence across the street from the White House, where the Obamas were staying. I was there, along with Favreau and Michael Sheehan, the speech coach, for a rehearsal of the inaugural address. Barack was late for the session, and when he finally arrived, he waved us off. "Sorry, guys, I'm a little tired," he said. "Let's do this later, if we can." I didn't think much of it. He had been on the run constantly.

That evening, Susan and I were having drinks with Joel Benenson, the pollster, and his wife, Lisa, when Rahm called me on my cell phone. "Can you call me right away from a hard line?" he asked, giving me his number. Rahm sounded a bit agitated, but that was hardly unusual. What was unusual was his request for me to use a more secure phone line. We were at the Benensons' apartment, so I used the phone in their bedroom.

"I'm going to tell you something you can't share with anyone, not even Susan," he said. "We've been talking to Chertoff all day, and there is a serious threat on the inauguration." Michael Chertoff was Bush's secretary of homeland security so the nature of the threat was clear. Rahm said that four young Somalis from the United States, who had been radicalized overseas, might have slipped back into the country, and there were concerns that they might target the inaugural ceremonies. While he didn't go into detail, Rahm said there was sufficient worry that contingency plans were being made to disperse the crowd quickly. If that were necessary, he explained, the Secret Service would alert Obama, who would proceed to the podium and inform the assembled crowd to follow directions and leave in an orderly fashion.

"I can't read the speechwriters into this," Rahm said, "so I want you to write a brief statement for the president-elect. Meet him right before the ceremonies in the Speaker's office and give it to him. He'll put it in his pocket in case it's needed."

As instructed, I kept quiet, and as Rahm requested, I wrote out the emergency instructions for Obama. I couldn't sleep that night, one of the first I would spend in the apartment Susan had rented for us six blocks from the White House. All night long, I tossed and turned, listening to police sirens and wondering if they were related to the search for the fugitive Somalis. In the morning, I was booked for a series of TV interviews, during which Susan and our son Ethan would join the Obama and Bush families at the traditional ecumenical worship service at St. John's Episcopal Church, across Lafayette Park from the White House. I was frantic. What if an attack happened *there*? I desperately wanted to tell them to stay away, but that would have violated Rahm's edict. As I watched my wife and son disappear through the door, I worried that I might have made a terrible mistake, one I would regret for the rest of my life.

I wended my way through a fortressed Capitol to the Speaker's office to wait for Obama, who, in accordance with tradition, would ride to the ceremony together with the outgoing president. Bush came into the room first, and I thought I would take the opportunity to thank him for the generosity he and his team had shown us.

"Mr. President," I said.

"Yeah, Axelrod," he replied. It made sense, after all the exposure I had gotten, that he would recognize me, yet it surprised me nonetheless.

"I was on television this morning—" I began to say, but he cut me off.

"I don't watch TV," he barked, with a wave of a hand.

"I know, sir, but I wanted you to know what I said. I said that you handled this transition like a true patriot, and we really appreciate it."

Bush shrugged and put his hands on my shoulders.

"Axelrod, I've been watching you," he said, in that familiar Texas twang. Given the many unkind things I had said about the Bush administration over the past two years, I wasn't sure what would come next. "I've been watching you, and I think you're all right. You're going to do just fine. Listen, you're in for the ride of your life. Just hang on and really enjoy it, 'cause it'll go by faster than you can imagine."

I believed then, as I do today, that the decisions Bush made in office—the war, the tax cuts, the derogation of policy making to industry lobbyists—were epically wrong, and that America will be living with the consequences for generations. Yet I will never forget his kindness to me in that moment. It gave me a window into George W. Bush as a person and an understanding of why so many who had worked for him were unwaveringly loyal.

A few moments later, the president-elect walked into the Speaker's office. After he greeted the luminaries assembled there, I cornered him and handed him the sheet of paper with the emergency instructions. He tucked it into his pocket without even looking at it—and thankfully, he would have no reason to read it later.

"Thanks for an incredible journey," I said. "It's been a great partnership."

He smiled and extended his hand. "And it's only just begun."

PART FIVE

TWENTY-THREE

NEXT DOOR TO HISTORY

THE MORNING AFTER THE INAUGURATION, I cast my bleary eyes on the White House and my first full day as a presidential aide. The buoyant memories of the long, historic day and night were fading fast. Now I was late for my first senior staff meeting with the man I had known for years as Barack, but from this moment on would call only Mr. President.

What made my late arrival particularly embarrassing was that I didn't have far to travel. Rahm had assigned me the room adjacent to the Oval Office, which was the small but coveted space he occupied during his years as senior adviser to President Clinton. In those days, there was an interior door that led directly into the president's private dining room and, beyond it, the Oval Office. Yet this back door to the inner sanctum had long since been walled over.

The rest of the senior staff was already in place when, delayed by a call, I hurried into the Oval to join them. These meetings took place in a seating area opposite the president's desk. There were two chairs with coffee tables near the fireplace and a couch on each side. The conversation was already under way when I slipped into the chair across from the president. As soon as I sat down, Rahm locked disapproving eyes on me and motioned vigorously with his head until I got the hint and moved to the couch. It turned out that the chair I had grabbed is traditionally reserved for the vice president—even when the VP isn't in attendance.

I was entering a new world, and I needed to adjust to it.

Just the ritual of waking up before dawn and putting on a suit was for me an unnatural act. Ever since my new suit was ruined covering a tornado on my first day at the *Tribune*, I had seldom worn one. My new uniform felt confining.

Far worse, though, was that, after the inaugural week, I would be waking up alone. The apartment Susan rented us had a balcony overlooking the Washington Monument. It was a swell view, but most of the time I was gazing at it on my own. The encrypted national security phone installed in my apartment; the card I carried in my wallet instructing me on where to go to be evacuated in case of attack; the Secret Service detail assigned to me after a deranged gunman was found with my name and address in his notebook—all added to the sense of how profoundly my life had changed.

In those first days, as I sat behind a desk staring at a card filled with my appointments, I missed my family, friends, and freedom—the life I had left behind. Yet with all hell breaking out around us, there was little time for brooding or doubt. The challenges confronting us were monstrously complex. Even in more placid times, there is no easing into life in the White House. It operates at full bore, every hour of every day.

My days would begin with Rahm's senior staff meeting at 7:00 a.m., in the chief of staff's office in a corner of the West Wing.

We would start by going over the president's schedule and breaking news before each of us was given the floor to share issues of concern. Still, it was unquestionably Rahm's show. He generally came armed with a long list of ideas, questions, and follow-ups. Some he formulated during sleepless nights, others during his predawn swim. Not surprisingly, Rahm's meetings could sometimes take on the raucous quality of a Jewish family dinner. When the group veered into too much levity, though—and I was a frequent culprit there—Rahm would bang the table with the stub of his right middle finger, severed on a meat slicer at Arby's when he was a seventeen-year-old fast-food worker. "Okay, okay, okay, okay," he would yell. "Let's get focused here."

Rahm is a pile driver who values, above all else, getting things done. He wants to put "wins on the board." Given the multiple challenges we were facing, that was exactly the kind of chief of staff the new president needed. Yet Rahm's approach underscored a fundamental tension between a campaign that promised to change Washington and a White House that had to deal with the town as we found it.

Everything I saw in my years there merely confirmed Obama's campaign critique: most members of Congress are fundamentally concerned with winning and holding on to their seats and to power. The special interest lobbyists who fund their campaigns leverage far too much influence. The partisanship is intense. The entire community is obsessed from day to day with who's up and who's down, and the politicians with scoring points for the next election more than solving problems for the next generation.

It was all true, but now we were there, in the middle of multiple crises. We weren't going to change politics overnight, but almost overnight, we damn well had to pass a stimulus bill to save the economy. We had to ask Congress to authorize more help to shore up a Wall Street that was in maximum disfavor. We had to petition for more money to fight the wars we'd come there to end, until we could end them. Finally, the president had a long and ambitious list of additional priorities that he put on a fast track.

Obama had hired Rahm because he needed someone who could skillfully navigate the Washington that is, not the Washington as we hoped it could one day be. We banned lobbyists from key administration jobs, kept public logs of everyone who visited the White House, and affected stricter ethics guidelines than any administration had before. Yet we couldn't force Congress to play by our rules; nor could we afford to walk away from the process in bouts of pristine righteousness.

So Rahm would grow impatient whenever Gibbs and I objected to a tactic that we felt violated a commitment or the spirit of the campaign. "I'm goddamned sick of hearing about the fucking campaign," he would scream. "The campaign is over. We're trying to solve some problems here!" As close as we were and will always be, the next two years would test our friendship.

One early, illustrative confrontation came over the issue of congressional earmarks, the time-honored but sometimes tawdry practice of allowing members to add pet projects to the budget. Earmarks had become symbolic of wasteful government, and Obama had campaigned vigorously against them. In the first weeks of the administration, however, we received word that Congress would soon be sending over a spending bill to keep the government operating that included nine thousand separate earmarks. When the president said that, in keeping with his pledge, he was inclined to veto the bill, Rahm was uneasy.

"You could do that Mr. President, but it might cost you your Recovery Act," he said. Rahm added that the bill and the earmarks were important to Harry Reid, the Senate majority leader. Furthermore, in discussions about the passage of the Recovery Act, Rahm had assured Reid that the leftover spending bill would be signed. Harry would view a veto as a breach of trust, Rahm explained. Gibbs and I argued that signing the bill would be a breach of trust with the American people. The president listened to the arguments and, though clearly pained by the prospect of green-lighting the earmarks, agreed to sign the bill. With the economy cratering, he believed there were bigger things at stake.

Such was the constant tug and pull between the principles we hoped to establish (principles we had run on) and the progress we absolutely had to make. While I worked to ensure that we didn't trample those principles, I also recognized that symbolic battles over reform wouldn't halt the spiraling recession or put food on anyone's table—other than, perhaps, those of the lobbyists hired to fight those battles. I appreciated Rahm's focus on the bottom line, and so did the president, and I came to realize that in this imperfect world, some of the things we'd campaigned against, such as earmarks, were essential tools with which leaders marshaled votes.

Rahm and I would clash over other things, the biggest of which was the use of the president's time. Rahm wanted Obama out in public constantly. "If you leave a vacuum, someone else will fill it," he said more than once. I was concerned that overexposure and too many B-level press events would turn the president into a play-by-play announcer for the government rather than the narrator of a far larger story. "Rahm, this is a long game. We don't have to win every news cycle," I told him once, when he proposed an event I thought unworthy of Obama's time. "Oh, yeah? Well, I do!" Rahm replied, and stormed out of my office.

I would not have wanted to be in the White House without Rahm, particularly given the crushing array of challenges we faced when we walked in the door. Yet the very same qualities that made him an indispensable force would occasionally drive me nuts.

There is no handbook for the senior adviser role I played, and every person who has held the job has brought with him or her a different set of strengths. A big part of my role was to monitor polling, guide our message, and try to keep us true to Obama's principles and campaign brand. Apart from providing advice to the president and others who spoke publicly for the administration, I exercised control primarily through the speechwriting process I oversaw.

Every day I could, I carved out an hour to meet with the president's speechwriters. As they filed into my office, I would always greet them with genuine enthusiasm and the same salutation: "Hello, Wordsmiths!" Led by Favreau, who was twenty-seven when we arrived at the White House, the team was talented, creative, and versatile. I relished these sessions and came to love this young corps of writers as if they were my own kids.

On major speeches, such as the State of the Union or a significant policy announcement, Favs and I would begin with the president, whose thoughts about what he wanted to say and how he wanted to say it were generally well ordered and already elegantly expressed. Still, the president didn't have the time to set a direction for the day-to-day speeches. So that job fell to me.

Typically, I would begin my meetings with the Wordsmiths by going over the schedule of upcoming presidential speeches, statements, and scripts. I'd explain the strategic imperatives and then riff on how I would approach each one. Favs and the writer chosen for each assignment would then probe the subject while others chimed in with their ideas. Out of that free-for-all process, we produced remarkably cohesive speeches. Not only were these sessions fun, but they gave me my best chance to try to orchestrate consistent themes that were faithful to the president's message and that could be heard through the gale force distractions that regularly blew in Washington. My days were largely spent navigating one political morass after another, and as the Wordsmiths were passionate believers, my time with them was nourishment for the soul.

Gibbs and I also would speak a dozen or more times a day. His office was on the other side of the Oval, closer to the pressroom, where his restless charges in the press corps were penned in and waiting to be fed dollops of news.

There is an expectation that presidents in the modern era must react to whatever news is breaking—and in an age when cable TV, Twitter, and online media outlets all can seize the national debate in a flash, there is a new freneticism to that process. In today's media age, Teddy Roosevelt's stout "bully pulpit" has been atomized. Americans now get their news from countless varied sources. Presidents must try to steer their agenda through a tumultuous environment in which anyone with a cell phone camera has the potential to hijack the story of the day. Managing this media chaos during a campaign was bracing enough. Now the stakes were infinitely greater.

Robert and I would take turns shuttling back and forth to consult on how to handle the tempest of the moment or, not quite as often, genuinely meaningful news. If the issue couldn't wait for our daily senior staff meetings, one or both of us would poke our heads into the Oval to see if the president was free so we could read him in.

One role I carried over from the campaign was that of the "public face."

Even before we took office, I was defending our economic plans on the Sunday television shows, jousting with hosts who served up edgy questions hoping to knock me off my talking points and goad me into acts of news I didn't want to commit. Every comment I made had greater consequences now that I was speaking for the president of the United States, and I spent many sleepless nights gaming out the likely questions I would get and the answers I would give. Ten minutes before every show I would invariably be seized by a bracing sense of impending peril. Often I did these interviews from Chicago or from the North Lawn of the White House, so I became practiced at carrying on lively exchanges with a TV camera as the voices of disembodied interlocutors came at me through an earpiece. I also carried the administration's message to more unorthodox venues that had become important forums in the new media age. During my White House years, I found myself sitting across the desk from Jay Leno, David Letterman, and Jon Stewart.

There were regular scheduling meetings in Rahm's office, at which the president's itinerary for the coming weeks would be plotted. I would then spend considerable time with the scheduling and communications team as they worked to marry message with execution. What recovering small business could we visit to underscore hopeful signs about the economy on a day when we expected a downbeat monthly jobs report? Which clean-energy start-up would provide the best backdrop to tout the benefits of the investments we had made? As we considered such questions, there was the overlay of future battleground states and markets.

I also tried to keep close tabs on what members of the cabinet were saying and doing, as I knew their actions and pronouncements would reflect on the president. This led to the occasional row, including an early dustup with Eric Holder, the new attorney general. In a speech delivered just a few weeks after taking office, Holder described America as a "nation of cowards" when it came to confronting deep-seated issues of race—which provoked the predictable firestorm. America had just taken a remarkable step forward by electing the first black president, one who was busy trying to rally the nation behind tough measures to confront multiple crises. It was a terrible time to divert the country's attention with a provocative speech on race relations.

I liked Eric, but he was a lawyer and not a politician, so I asked for a meeting at which I suggested adding someone to his communications staff who could help advise him on these nuances and protect him from unnecessary errors that might splash back on us. Holder listened politely, but soon was complaining to others that I was trying "to stack the Justice Department with political people."

I was furious. During the Bush administration, Karl Rove had come under justifiable fire and congressional scrutiny for his involvement in the highly political hirings and firings of U.S. attorneys. I was determined never to interfere at Justice in that fashion, and I never did. A few days later I cornered Holder after a White House meeting and let him know my strong feelings about his insinuation. The discussion, which began in an open corridor of the White House, became so heated that Valerie shooed us into a private office to finish it.

One great challenge of the White House is that while you are trying to affect policies that speak to the concerns of the American people, you rarely leave the building to meet those people. Working in the White House, a colleague once said, is like working in a submarine—and it's hard to get a read on the pulse of America when you're looking at the country through a periscope. I tried to remedy this by hosting a meeting every Wednesday night at my apartment with key White House communications players and my campaign strategic team. Benenson, Binder, and Grisolano would offer readouts of and insights into their research, and we would fill them in on the administration's plans. These meetings became a lifeline that helped me keep in touch with the world beyond the White House gates.

That said, I can't remember a time during my two years in the White House when I looked at my watch wondering when the day would end. Instead, I regularly found myself asking where the day had gone. I worked at the office well into the evenings, often catching a late dinner with a reporter, colleague, or member of Congress. When I arrived home, almost always after ten, I would spend an hour or two catching up on papers and news stories I had missed and reading materials for the next day. Some nights ended with late calls from the president, who'd want to chew over the events of the day. After a scant few hours' sleep, the whole cycle would start all over again.

It was a relentless, bone-wearying, pressure-filled grind. However, after the initial shock to my system, I found it thoroughly addictive and engaging. In what other job could you deal with issues of war and peace, an economic crisis, pirates, pandemics, and natural disasters—sometimes all in one day? Where else could you have the opportunity every day to play a small role in history?

During those two years, we would pass more meaningful legislation than any new president had in half a century: a vast expansion of college aid for needy students; new consumer protections for credit card holders; a long-sought law tightening regulation of tobacco; the Lilly Ledbetter Fair Pay Act, strengthening the tools for women to fight for equal pay; and the abolition of the Don't Ask, Don't Tell law prohibiting gays from serving openly in the military. Obama would forge a breakthrough agreement with the auto industry for higher fuel efficiency standards and end a ban on potentially lifesaving stem cell research. Also, he would put two splendid women on the Supreme Court—including the first Hispanic, Sonia Sotomayor—making America's highest court more reflective of the nation it serves.

For all that, though, three historic undertakings loomed so consequential and consuming that they would define not only my two years in the White House, but the Obama presidency.

TWENTY-FOUR

NOTHING BUT BAD CHOICES

THROUGHOUT THE LONG CAMPAIGN, Obama was preparing to assume office in a time of war while facing an ongoing terrorist threat. We expected *that*. Now we also faced a once-in-a-century economic disaster that would hover over us for years, through long, grinding days and short, sleepless nights. Obama had inspired a battered and disillusioned nation to believe that there were better days ahead. Yet there was no magic wand to wave to deal with this calamity; no easy or painless answers—just a series of necessary but unpopular choices.

To break the downward cycle and jolt the economy, we would have to fight for the massive emergency spending bill we had begun plotting back in Chicago in December. To keep capital flowing while the financial crisis deepened, we were forced to buttress some of the very bankers whose greedy schemes had brought down the economy. Also, within months of taking office, the president would have to decide whether to save the American auto industry from its own strategic mistakes or allow it—along with communities across the industrial Midwest—to collapse. All this would only add to the record deficits Obama has pledged to bring under control.

Bemoaning our dismal hand, I wondered out loud how it would have been to arrive at the White House in *good* times. Obama smiled. "Don't kid yourself, brother," he said. "If these had been good times, we wouldn't be here!"

So we dug in, drawing down on the popular new president's goodwill to try to resuscitate the rapidly failing economy, spending money we didn't have and bailing out those who had helped inflict this catastrophe on the rest of us.

I knew that each of these decisions would rankle millions of Americans, neither rich nor poor, who already were deeply alienated in the modern-day economy. The explosion of technology coupled with globalization had lifted productivity and corporate profits to new heights and created lucrative opportunities for the highly educated. It also had cost millions of Americans good jobs and put downward pressure on wages. The Great Recession would only accelerate these trends. Many Americans were working harder to meet their responsibilities, and falling further behind. Now they watched in dismay as, all around them, the people and institutions that had failed to meet *their* responsibilities were being extended lifelines by the government.

Some of their ire was directed at the poor, who were the beneficiaries of modest public assistance. Increasingly, though, their anger was aimed at Wall Street and the folks at the top, who they felt had rigged the game in their favor to the detriment of the country. This wasn't lost on Obama. It rankled him to ride to the rescue of high-flying financiers and oblivious auto executives. He had campaigned to reform the irresponsibility on Wall Street and in Washington, and had promised to tackle the Bush deficits. Yet with the economy crashing, the inescapable truth was that for President Obama to meet *his* responsibility, he would have to take steps that some who voted for him would view as an abrogation of those principles.

In doing so, Obama would come under withering criticism from all corners—from his supporters who yearned for heads to roll; from a financial community that felt it was above penalty or even rebuke; and from a united Republican opposition content to sit back and blame the new president for failing to promptly clean up an epic disaster that their policies had helped to create over many years. He was caricatured as fickle and feckless.

I was a witness to a different and truer picture. I saw the president make a series of politically toxic decisions to rescue the financial industry and the larger economy from a far more devastating crisis. I saw him reject seductive answers that had strong, populist appeal for fear of retarding recovery not just for Wall Street, but for the entire country. I saw him thinking past the crisis to how we would rebuild the economy, using the leverage of recovery funds to promote higher educational standards, new energy industries, and more efficient health care delivery. And, yes, I saw him take on powerful forces to promote fair, open, and transparent markets in which the interests of consumers and the economy would be protected.

I also saw him steer the country past a second Great Depression and on an undeniable path to recovery.

Larry Summers and the economic team believed it was essential for the government to move quickly with a stimulus plan, the bigger the better. The proposed package would include tax cuts for the middle class and the working poor, a basket of accelerated investment tax credits for business, aid to state and local governments, expanded food stamps and unemployment benefits, and funding for backlogged infrastructure projects to revive a moribund construction industry. True to Obama's Chicago mandate, it also would include an array of investments in education, health care, and clean energy technology, which would spark activity in the short run but also plant seeds of longer-term progress and growth.

Obama and Biden would hit the road to promote the plan's regional benefits and the 3.5 million jobs we said it would "save or create." All of us who spoke for the new administration ran the gauntlet of TV talk shows to advocate for the rescue plan. Rahm worked the phones and shuttled back and forth across Pennsylvania Avenue and the Capitol Rotunda, bargaining, cajoling, and pleading to wrangle votes. This meant beating back Congress's reflexive instinct to lard the bill with indefensible pet projects, and balancing the more progressive and expansive ambitions of House Democrats with the concerns of a handful of Senate moderates, Republican and Democrat, over massive new spending.

Still, to Americans alarmed by record deficits and suspicious of government's motives and capabilities, the plan would be polarizing, sending Democrats to one corner and Republicans to another. By its very nature, the package, a potpourri of tax cuts, state aid, social spending, and infrastructure projects, created the image of the typical pork-lined Washington bazaar. To a cynical public, it looked less like "Change We Can Believe In" than "Dollars We Can't Afford," which was another way of saying business as usual. Also, it gave an early opening to Republican leaders looking for a wedge to peel away support from the popular new president.

More than any substantive position of the campaign, it was Obama's pledge to end the bitter partisan wrangling in Washington that had drawn frustrated Americans to his side. Yet it quickly became clear that the Republicans in Congress would hardly greet us with flowers, chocolates, and a new spirit of cooperation. A week after taking office, Obama asked for a meeting with the House Republican Caucus to plead his case for the Recovery Act. Then, just before he left the White House to brief them, the Associated Press reported that Republican leaders were already urging their caucus to oppose the plan. The president was heading off to present his case to a kangaroo court. "This shit's not on the level, is it?" he asked as he walked out the door.

The Recovery Act would pass the House without a single Republican vote. In the Senate, three Republicans supported the emergency measure, enabling its passage. One of those Republicans, Arlen Specter of Pennsylvania, left the party a few months later, having become a pariah in his caucus for breaking ranks.

Could we have done more to secure Republican support? There is no doubt that in our haste to pass the plan, Rahm and our team worked more closely with the Democratic majorities in Congress. However, the near-unanimous Republican opposition was not in a fit of pique about being insufficiently consulted. Their opposition to the plan was a political strategy, hatched right from the start (one that would become a running story line throughout the Obama years). Mitch McConnell, the Senate Republican leader, explained as much in a newspaper interview a year later. "It was absolutely critical that everybody be together because if the proponents of the bill were able to say it was bipartisan, it tended to convey to the public that this is O.K., they must have figured it out," said McConnell, boasting of the party discipline he had enforced.

We naïvely assumed that in a time of national emergency, Obama might find governing partners across the aisle to meet the crisis. After all, only a few months earlier, when Bush and Paulson were begging for bipartisan support to buttress the financial system, Obama and the Democratic leaders in Congress had answered their call. Now we were facing monolithic Republican opposition, and it was galling. Maybe this was what Hillary was talking about when she chided us during the campaign for "raising false hopes."

By any fair measure, the Recovery Act would make a palpable and positive difference. Within months, the economy would be growing again, the hemorrhaging of jobs ended, and hiring resumed—albeit at a maddeningly slow and uneven pace. Whatever the macroeconomic indicators, though, trillions of dollars in wealth had been washed away in the storm, and Americans were not feeling that progress in their own lives. Having sat out the effort, the Republicans seized on the public's sour mood. They would depict the Recovery Act as an emblem of profligacy—proof that Obama, who had run for president pledging fiscal responsibility, was just another spendthrift, big-government liberal. "Where are the jobs?" became the irksome mantra of the Republicans, though more than a few of them eagerly showed up smiling for the cameras at ribbon cuttings for Recovery Act projects in their districts. "These guys are shameless!" Obama said, flabbergasted after reading one such story.

As the months went by, the Washington media, wont to filter everything through the prism of politics, began to question the wisdom and efficacy of the Recovery Act. Even after its positive effects were becoming evident, one of Washington's most respected journalists parroted this ludicrous notion that had emerged from the GOP playbook.

"What are you going to do about the Recovery Act?" she asked me.

"What do you mean?"

"It's a failure."

"A failure?" I asked, incredulously. "Why?"

"Well, only thirty-eight percent of voters support it!"

It was a parable of life in our nation's capital, where success is measured not by what you accomplish, but how voters *feel* about it at any given moment. Breathless and ubiquitous cable TV coverage and social media have created a permanent campaign mentality that treats every day in Washington as Election Day. The industry I helped build is now ready to mobilize at a moment's notice, with ads, e-mails, and all the tools at its disposal to make incumbents pay for impolitic decisions, even when they are a courageous response to an urgent national need. For Obama, who draws a tight distinction between the demands of campaigning and the responsibilities of governing, the permanent campaign mode was a source of constant frustration.

"You know, I love this job," he said, as we were waiting for a town hall meeting in Los Angeles during the first months, when he was wrestling with the economic crisis. "I love diving into problems. But dealing with some of the people you have to deal with and the whole cable thing wears you out. I'll be honest—four years of this might be enough. I won't be run out. But if we can turn the economy around and get some things like health care done, I could see walking away from it."

I knew it was the weariness of the moment talking. It was hard to imagine this highly committed and intensely competitive man "walking away." A few weeks earlier, Obama had told Matt Lauer of NBC that his failure to turn the economy around within three years would make his presidency a "one-term proposition." Those words would come back to haunt him. Progress would come, but painfully slowly. Many corporations responded to the recession by "streamlining" their operations, meaning the permanent elimination of jobs.

Even when the economy began to grow again, wary executives hoarded their cash rather than investing in new employees.

I had spent much of my life studying polls, and continued to devour them every day in the White House. Now I became a voracious reader of other numbers: the weekly unemployment claims, durable goods orders, manufacturing reports, the University of Michigan Consumer Sentiment Index, and an array of other arcane economic statistics and indexes that I scoured for any hint of good news. Of course, we all approached the monthly jobs report with a combination of anticipation and dread. Pummeled with a constant stream of bad news, you could leave yourself susceptible at times to unwarranted optimism. When Treasury officials bragged about the success of one of their early initiatives, Obama had a tart reply: "Let me say, you guys did a great job. Take a moment, give yourself a pat on the back, and figure out a way to put eight-point-four million people back to work!"

In early planning for the administration, I had suggested that we add a daily briefing on the economy to the president's schedule, similar to the traditional national security briefing he would receive each day. Led by Larry Summers, these became the hub for rigorous strategic discussions.

Larry had a reputation for intellectual superiority, which didn't bother me, because he actually was as smart as he thought. While his sometimes imperious style was a source of tension within the president's economic team, I appreciated Larry, even when we disagreed, which was not infrequently. Larry playfully dubbed Rahm and me Tammany Hall, for injecting real-life political considerations into these economic discussions. He also worked to understand those considerations. His broad sweep and mastery of economics made him an indispensable asset to the president, though Obama, never intellectually overmatched, occasionally forced Larry to pause and utter some sentences rarely heard from him before, such as "I never thought of that!" or "I'll have to get back to you."

Even more interesting was the dynamic between Summers and Geithner, his onetime protégé. For the most part, they agreed on policy matters and worked together effectively, but there was no consensus between them on one of the most vital and vexing questions we faced: how to stabilize the banks so they would start lending again.

The fragility of the banks was a dark cloud hovering over the prospect of recovery. Obama didn't have much patience for the bankers and speculators whose ruthless and reckless pursuit of personal gains he blamed for much of the crisis. He understood how angry the American people were at Wall Street for its costly excesses. Riding to its rescue was unquestionably bad politics, but he also knew that the country needed a flourishing financial sector, first to survive and then grow. "We have to fix this," he told me, in the midst of the storm. "If we don't, the whole thing falls apart."

The responsibility for fixing it fell squarely on Geithner's shoulders. At first blush, they weren't particularly *big* shoulders. A slight man with an impish face and tousled hair, Geithner wasn't an imposing figure in person or on television. Together, he and Summers looked a little like Laurel and Hardy. Yet Tim was a smart, strategic thinker who proved far tougher and more resilient than his boyish looks suggested—and he would need to be tough for the bruising battles ahead.

Geithner's first major pronouncement on the banking crisis in early February fell well short of market expectations. It didn't help that, on the eve of Tim's speech, the president promised at a televised news conference that his treasury secretary would be "announcing some very clear and specific plans for how we are going to start loosening up credit once again." Encouraged by the president's comment, the frantic financial community anticipated aggressive steps to buy the toxic assets that littered their balance sheets. Instead, Geithner, nervous and unimposing, merely announced a general framework for action. The stock market plummeted upon the news. It was a striking reminder that, in our new roles, a few ill-chosen words could send armies marching and markets crashing. For the new secretary of treasury, it was a disaster. Weeks into the administration, the political community was already placing sell orders on Geithner. "I don't think Tim's going to make it," Valerie confided, echoing the prevailing view in Washington.

The environment was so ugly that Tim asked me to call his wife, Carole, who had stayed behind in New York with their high school–age son. "She doesn't get all of this and she's really upset," he said. "Can you just reassure her?"

Meanwhile, we still needed an answer on the banks, which was late in coming, in part, because of squabbling among our economic advisers. Summers and Christy Romer, who generally didn't mix, were now allied in the view that we should buy the toxic assets and take over the worst of the failing megabanks, which the two believed were terminally ill. Geithner, who was less fatalistic about the underlying health of the banks, argued against "nationalization" on policy grounds. He also believed that such an approach would eventually run up against political impediments because it would require far more taxpayer money than Congress had authorized the administration to spend. While the team argued, the stock market continued to tumble and lending remained frozen. The bank crisis was a lead weight on the recovery, and the famously chill Obama was tired of waiting.

Determined to maintain his bond with the American people, the president had asked for ten representative letters each day from among the tens of thousands the White House received for him. The letters would be included in the thick packet of homework the president took back to the residence each night. After his children went to bed, he would cap off his already long and difficult day by reading dispiriting notes from struggling Americans who desperately feared for their families. Some had lost their jobs or homes. Others, small businessmen, were starving for loans. So many of them would detail their struggles and then plaintively ask the president, "Where's my bailout?" Often he would respond by hand. Occasionally, he would phone the letter writer. Sometimes he would call me late at night. "I'm telling you, man, these letters just tear you up," he said during one such conversation.

Moved by these stories of distress, Obama had had enough of the endless debate among his economic advisers. "We all look like we have our heads up our asses," he told them. "I'm not going to be the president who sat here and fiddled while Rome burned. I'm tired of reading letters from people who are desperate for help and are looking to us for answers we don't have."

On Sunday, March 15, he summoned his economic advisers to a meeting, determined to force an answer on the banks. Despite the president's obvious frustration, Geithner, Summers, and Romer continued to argue for several hours on the path forward. Finally, the president stood up. "I'm going to get a haircut and have dinner with my family," he announced. "I'll be back at seven. When I get back, I want a consensus."

With the president gone, all hell broke loose. The problem, Tim argued, was that most banks were paralyzed because they didn't know the full extent of their exposure to toxic assets. His bet was that the "stress test" audits would reveal to the banks and the world that most were in better shape than the markets feared. Once you wiped away the uncertainty, the banks would raise the private capital they needed to gird themselves against future crises. Larry and Christy remained skeptical and continued to favor aggressive action that would require more significant government intervention. Rahm clearly, repeatedly, and colorfully offered a dose of political reality, warning that we were not going to get "another fucking dime from Congress" for the banks. "Well, that's no good," Summers finally concluded. Geithner, red-faced with exasperation, exploded: "Well, welcome to my world, Larry!"

When the newly shorn president returned, the group had reached a grudging consensus. It was risky and depended on Geithner's hopeful hunch about what the stress tests would reveal. If he was wrong—well, I pictured our administration like the wayward *Apollo 13* space capsule: instead of reentering the atmosphere and landing, we could skid off into the abyss, taking the economy with us.

Nationalizing the banks—and seeing the televised images of fired financial executives walking out of their offices with their belongings in cardboard boxes—would have better addressed the country's fury, but Obama bought Geithner's argument that such a step would carry significant economic risks and require more taxpayer dollars than Congress and the American people were willing to provide. Understanding the lousy politics, Obama placed a big bet on his embattled treasury secretary—and it would pay off, stabilizing the banks in a way that allowed the government to recoup taxpayers' loans with interest.

Before that marathon Sunday meeting in the Roosevelt Room wound down, I raised another issue that struck me as a symbolic disaster.

The *Washington Post* had reported over the weekend that AIG, the giant insurer of banks at the heart of the financial meltdown, was poised to pay its executives $165 million in bonuses, despite record losses and a $170 billion in emergency government loans. I was outraged, and I was not alone. The bonuses would touch a raw nerve with a public already incensed by the avarice and recklessness they had seen. "This is going to be a huge problem," I said, arguing that the president had to strongly condemn the bonuses, a sentiment he shared.

The White House had scheduled an event for the next day, the focus of which was on getting credit flowing again to small businesses. It would provide the president a natural opportunity to condemn the bonuses publicly, and he agreed to a statement that was direct and to the point: "[T]his is not just a matter of dollars and cents. It's about our fundamental values. All across the country, there are people who are working hard and meeting their responsibilities every single day, without the benefit of government bailouts or multi-million dollar bonuses." Contrasting AIG and the financial community with the struggling, responsible small business owners at his side—one of whom was keeping his doors open by working without pay—Obama concluded: "All they ask is that everyone, from Main Street to Wall Street to Washington, play by the same rules. That is an ethic that we have to demand."

Over the Treasury Department's objections, I had included a line calling on Geithner to explore every avenue to block the AIG bonuses. Treasury's objections had been rather vague, but soon after the president spoke, I learned that Geithner had known about the bonuses well in advance. Worse, he and Summers had quietly lobbied against an amendment to the Recovery Act that would have significantly restricted the payment of bonuses at AIG and other firms receiving Troubled Asset Relief Program, or TARP, funds. They believed any retroactive steps would violate existing contracts. Their quiet lobbying, however, flew in the face of the president's strong denunciation of the bonuses. It made the president look like a phony, posturing to a receptive public while his operatives took the opposite tack out of view.

I was livid, and confronted Geithner and Summers at one of Rahm's morning meetings. Dancing around their subterfuge, they argued that it would be irresponsible, even illegal, for the administration to support "clawback" provisions denying the Wall Street players bonuses to which they were contractually entitled. Tim dismissed doing so as "Old Testament justice" that would satisfy the public bloodlust at the cost of the economy. "This would be the end of capitalism as we know it!" he barked.

"I hate to break the news, Mr. Secretary," I replied, "but capitalism isn't trading very high right now!"

Within months, Geithner's stress test and recapitalization plan had helped stabilize the banks. Yet, to the frustration of the president and to millions of Americans seeking loans for their homes and businesses, the capital was still not flowing. The financiers, gun-shy after their near-death experience and discouraged by independent government supervisors who had dropped the ball before the crisis, had tightened their standards for loans in response.

Obama came to a morning meeting in the summer of 2009 with two clips from the same newspaper, one discussing the paucity of credit and the other announcing billions more in bonuses for Wall Street.

"I can only imagine how people feel about this," Obama told us. "I know how I feel about it. Loans are down and now the bankers are doing well again—thanks, in part to us—and they're *still* not lending!"

It would be an ongoing struggle.

So, too, would be housing. This was ground zero for the crisis. Millions who had taken easy-money loans were now in default, and with the rash of foreclosures, home values plummeted. Many Americans who had thought of their homes as their nest eggs now found them worth less than their outstanding mortgages. Plus, with massive layoffs, millions more were facing foreclosure. In the past, it was new home construction that helped lead America out of recessions. This time, the housing industry was down and out.

Obama returned to the issue again and again, and Treasury responded with an alphabet soup of programs called things such as HAMP and HARP. They set aside fifty billion dollars to help distressed homeowners refinance their loans at record low interest rates, part of an array of emergency measures undertaken to spur the economy. Yet much of the money never went out, and progress came at a glacial pace. Eventually, the aid would help millions, but the housing programs overpromised and underdelivered, as the president reminded us often.

"I get these letters every day from people who should qualify for the mortgage mitigation program but are still turned down by the banks," Obama complained at one economic briefing.

"Mortgages are like unemployment," Geithner responded. "It will trail."

As we raced to pass the Recovery Act and restart lending, a third crisis was bearing down.

With credit markets frozen and car sales at their lowest level in a quarter century, the automotive industry was forced to shed four hundred thousand jobs in 2008. The iconic American companies GM and Chrysler, two pillars of Detroit's Big Three, were reeling. Under pressure from foreign competitors and hobbled by dated product lines, heavy debt, and labor obligations, GM and Chrysler were buckling even before the recession. Now they were teetering toward an outright collapse.

The Detroit executives evoked about as much sympathy as their counterparts on Wall Street—particularly after traveling to Washington on private jets in the winter of 2008 to ask Congress to bail out their mismanaged companies.

At our quiet urging, Bush had agreed to provide just enough loans from the TARP fund to keep GM and Chrysler alive for a few more months. With that life support now coming to an end, Obama had to decide what, if anything, to do.

In the first weeks of the administration, Obama formally assigned Steven Rattner, a prominent New York private equity investor, and Ronald Bloom, who'd helped advise labor on the restructuring of the American steel industry, to head an auto task force that would work through the knotty issues at each company and make recommendations on how to proceed. Rattner and Bloom looked like an odd couple. Bloom, the old union man, was a no-frills guy. Rattner, a former *New York Times* reporter, looked every inch the successful financier he had become. They were backstopped by a brilliant, young White House staffer, Brian Deese—who became so steeped in the workings of the auto industry that I would forever after call him Diesel.

By late March, after months of work and with the clock ticking, Rattner, Bloom, and Deese joined the daily economic briefing to report back to the president. For forty-five minutes, they put forth their findings and recommendations, which would require another sizable investment from the government—perhaps as much as eighty-eight billion dollars—to rescue GM and Chrysler. The government would buy a majority interest in GM as the company restructured; but Chrysler, the more fragile of the two companies, would need a partner to survive. Chrysler had announced a tentative partnership with Fiat two months earlier, but the details needed considerable work.

Behind schedule and frustrated by the lack of time to deal with such weighty considerations, Obama adjourned the meeting until that evening. "I am not going to decide the future of the American auto industry on the basis of a half-hour discussion. I have more questions."

The president had been late for the auto meeting because of a prolonged national security session on ominous stirrings in North Korea. In the hours following the auto session, Obama would have a meeting on classified Bush-era documents related to torture and would host an online town hall meeting on the economy and another meeting on the retooling of U.S. strategy in Afghanistan and Pakistan. It was a typical day at the office for the president of the United States: confronting a parade of critical and complex matters, each of which demanded intense preparation and focus. Obama managed it with remarkable agility. Still, the pace was brutal and took its toll.

"I'm tired," he confided during a brief lull after the meeting on Afghanistan and Pakistan. "It's getting to the point where I am concerned I'll make bad decisions."

Yet decisions had to be made—and as we gathered that evening in the ornate Roosevelt Room, across the hall from the Oval, everyone felt the weight of the matter at hand. Without government intervention, there was no question that GM and Chrysler would go bust—and very quickly. And their collapse would create a wave of failures up and down the supply chain that fed the auto giants.

On the other hand, there was no guarantee that, even with government assistance, the auto companies would survive. We could be throwing good money after bad, and quite a lot of it. The Republicans, already on the march, would undoubtedly howl about the government taking a major stake in a private business. "Socialism!" they would proclaim, in horror. Yet the opposition was broader than that. Even Michigan appeared to have given up on what had long been its economic underpinning. Fresh polling data showed that a majority of voters there opposed any federal aid for the auto companies. Nationally, the numbers ran three to one against a bailout. I wasn't urging the president to walk away, but I wanted him to understand what he was walking *into.*

Gibbs, who functioned as both an all-purpose adviser and press secretary, spoke powerfully about specific towns in the industrial Midwest that, wholly dependent on the auto industry, would be wiped out by the collapse of GM and Chrysler. Robert, who was familiar with the region, having served as communications director for Michigan senator Debbie Stabenow, told the president, "Sir, these towns aren't experiencing a recession. They're already experiencing a depression. This would be more than they can bear."

The president drilled deeper into the details of each company's case and prospects for success. After ninety minutes, he made his decision.

"David, you raise the polling, and I get that. I understand it," he said. "People look at these automakers, who have made a series of bad decisions over a long period of time, and ask why the American taxpayer should throw them a lifeline. But if GM and Chrysler go down, it's not just their workers who will lose their jobs, but you'll see job loss right down the supply chain. We could lose a million more jobs, in the middle of what already is the worst recession since the thirties. And we'd lose two iconic American companies. I mean, we *invented* the auto industry. That's a big deal. No blank checks. But if we can leverage our help to force them to reorganize, streamline, and modernize their companies so as to make them competitive again, we have to try."

It was a fateful decision. In a process shepherded by Obama's auto task force, both companies went through bankruptcy, shed debt and failing product lines, renegotiated labor agreements, and replaced their management teams with aggressive new leadership. Chrysler formed a strategic alliance with Fiat, which, ultimately, took ownership of the firm. Within two years, the companies began growing again, restoring shifts at existing plants and building new ones. The American auto industry was resurgent.

Like most of the president's early decisions on the economy, this one was fraught with uncertainty and political risk. Republican critics responded on cue, mocking GM as "Government Motors." The criticism was muted, however, by the time the 2012 presidential election rolled around—especially in Ohio. The auto boom would be a factor in Obama's capture of that pivotal state, where one in eight workers is engaged in some way in the auto industry, and folks remembered the bet he had placed on them.

The slow pace of recovery complicated another goal of Obama's. "Before we're done, we have to do something about the deficits," he had told me early in the term. "I don't want to leave the next president the kind of mess they handed to us." We had campaigned on deficit reduction, but falling tax revenues and the additional spending contained within the Recovery Act had swelled the 2009 deficit to $1.4 trillion. The objective fact was that we needed to spend *more* money in the short run to add momentum to the flickering recovery while adopting a plan to curb debt in the long term by increasing revenues and trimming the potentially explosive growth of Social Security and Medicare. "We need to work the accelerator and brakes in the right sequence," Obama said.

Americans were desperate for jobs and growth, but panicked about deficits. Republicans had found their footing and invigorated their base by attacking Obama for overspending, and would oppose any proposal to reduce deficits by raising new revenues. Meanwhile, Democrats were loath to embrace any long-term solution that would tamper with Social Security or Medicare, which Americans regard as insurance programs for which they have already paid. It was hard to make the case for curbing the growth of benefits, even in the future, at a time when so many were worried about making ends meet. Besides, from time immemorial, the uncompromising protection of Social Security and Medicare had been a political winner for Democrats, and few were eager to stray from that position, even if some changes might be required to shore up the programs for the long haul.

One day, in a senior advisers' meeting, Obama wondered why these issues languished when demographic changes in an aging country screamed out for some adjustments. Why hadn't the politicians acted? I was taken aback. "Because hard things are hard," I told him. It is a hugely unpopular idea to trim the growth of benefits, I said, and politicians don't opt to do hugely unpopular things. "Hard things are hard" became an ongoing joke after that, though the inherent wisdom of that mantra became clearer by the day. When I left the White House in 2011, I would give the president a desk plaque that read, "Hard Things Are Hard!"

Another "hard thing" Obama undertook in 2009 was a landmark financial reform law. Even before the crash of 2008, Obama had called for new rules adequate for the twenty-first century to prevent the bilking of consumers and the gaming of financial markets. Yet the crash made the need for such reforms painfully and unavoidably clear.

It was no coincidence that this rewrite would be the most comprehensive since the 1930s, the last time financial manipulation had brought down the economy on such a large scale. Now, with all the intricate new financial instruments and technology that had eluded oversight and regulation, there was an obvious need to protect consumers. Furthermore, there was a need to address the "too big to fail" dilemma to ensure that no single bank's collapse could threaten the entire system or compel another widespread taxpayer bailout. Since the industry itself barely had a handle on all its machinations, writing the rules was a brutally complex undertaking. When Obama unveiled them in June 2009, Wall Street responded by deploying an army of lobbyists to help shape, if not stop, many of these reforms in a battle that would last more than a year.

It was infuriating but not surprising. Now back on their feet, the financiers would spend a fortune fighting the reforms the crisis demanded. It was one more irritant that would make Obama's relationship with Wall Street and the larger business community an ongoing challenge. It was a matter of politics and principle. The president could hardly do the things required to bail out the financial industry from a mess of its own creation without, at the same time, strongly condemning their excesses. Beyond that, he had run on the promise to level a playing field that had been badly skewed under the "anything goes" policies of the Bush years. All this would come to a head in a *60 Minutes* interview in December 2009. In it, the president denounced firms that had taken emergency government loans to navigate the crisis while paying out billions of dollars in executive bonuses.

"I did not run for office to be helping out a bunch of fat cat bankers on Wall Street," he said, in a quote that would be played back to me for years afterward by aggrieved financiers who felt he had tarred the entire industry with a broad brush.

Yet he had run promising a fair shake for everyday Americans, so one key provision of his financial reform package called for the creation of an independent Consumer Financial Protection Bureau to protect people from deceptive or unscrupulous practices by the issuers of credit cards, mortgages, and other loans. "We've had for 60 years a system of bank regulation under which the regulators view bankers as their constituency," Summers said. "There is a good argument for an agency that has the consumer as its focus."

Obama was enthusiastic. The crisis had laid bare the vulnerability of financial consumers, some of whom had shared their experiences with him on the campaign trail or in the letters he read at night. However, he didn't need their testimony. He had his own. When I gave the president a copy of *The Big Short*, Michael Lewis's riveting book about how mortgage scams had led to the financial crisis, Obama thumbed through it with a knowing smile.

"I lived this story," he said. "I remember very well. Because of our student loans, Michelle and I could never catch up. So, some months, we paid our bills with credit cards. I went to refinance our condo and I was kind of surprised when they said, 'You can get cash, too.' So all of a sudden, my condo is worth fifty thousand dollars more and I can take forty thousand dollars in cash as a loan? I did it, but it seemed too good to be true. It was a racket."

The idea of a consumer financial protection agency was first proposed by Elizabeth Warren, the Harvard law professor and bankruptcy expert. Warren's writings on the economic struggles of the squeezed middle class and the abuses of the financial industry had made her a hero to the Left, and a burden to Wall Street. Their antipathy only grew when Warren was named by Democrats in Congress to lead an oversight panel on the bank bailout program. From that perch, Warren had asked tough and sometimes embarrassing questions both of bankers and of government officials, including Geithner. Neither he nor Summers, who knew Warren from Harvard, were big fans. Meanwhile, I thought her background and sensibilities made Warren a splendid candidate to lead the new consumer agency, if Congress created one, and I told the president so.

I invited Warren to lunch in June 2010, as a final vote loomed on the financial reform law, and she wasn't the least bit coy about her desire to lead the new consumer bureau. "I can do this or something else. But just between us, I'd rather do this than look over Tim Geithner's shoulder for the next ten months," she said pointedly. Elizabeth was tough and didn't make any effort to hide it.

I delivered that message to the president, who was equally direct in his response. "Tell her to keep her mouth shut. She may well be the choice, but we can't surface that now." Understanding what an irritant Warren was to Wall Street and its allies in both parties, Obama didn't want to signal that Warren was his candidate before the law passed and the agency was created. Afterward, he did appoint her to help organize the consumer bureau, a job she performed with great enthusiasm and skill, recruiting first-rate talent and laying a strong foundation. Still, after gauging the politics of the Hill, Obama concluded that Warren couldn't win the Senate confirmation required to be the bureau's permanent director. The president feared that such a battle could damage the bureau and complicate other administration priorities. It was a decision that disappointed many on the left. The president, though, had an alternative notion. "Why doesn't Elizabeth think about going home to Massachusetts to run for the Senate?" Obama asked. Scott Brown, the Republican who had taken Ted Kennedy's seat in a special election after Kennedy's death, was up again in 2012. "She could win that."

I took the suggestion to Warren, a neighbor in my Washington apartment building, who at first greeted it warily. Senate and Massachusetts Democrats lobbied her hard, and Warren warmed to the race. With Obama at the top of the ticket, she easily defeated Brown, taking her seat alongside the very senators who had resisted her appointment to lead the consumer bureau.

The episode was a parable about Obama and his approach to politics, dating back to his years in the Illinois legislature. He is both idealistic and pragmatic, progressive in his goals but practical in pursuing them. He liked Warren and valued her leadership for the consumer protection bureau, but he wasn't going to sacrifice its creation or the larger financial reform law, or invite rearguard actions to undermine it after its passage, by surfacing her name too early or keeping her in place for too long. The Left was eager for the fight. Obama was playing for meaningful gains.

Ironically, Summers fell victim to that same sense of pragmatism. Despite his yeoman service, and Obama's deep respect, Larry was twice passed over for the Fed chairmanship he had been promised when he agreed to serve in the White House. The first time, in the spring of 2009, Obama yielded to Geithner's recommendation that he reappoint Bernanke in order to reassure the jittery markets. Four years later, when Bernanke retired, the president passed over Summers again, concerned that opposition from the Left, including Senator Warren, would make the nomination too heavy a lift, jeopardizing other priorities.

Obama had shown a willingness to make such sacrifices and strike hard bargains in order to achieve his larger goals, but he drew bright lines when he felt such concessions would undermine fundamental principles.

As the financial reform bill was winding its way through Congress, Obama instructed his team on his negotiating posture with Congress and insisted he would veto any bill that didn't include the consumer bureau and the so-called Volcker Rule, which would bar banks and financial institutions whose deposits were federally guaranteed from gambling their own funds in the risky financial markets. "I'd rather bring a vote on a strong version and lose, having held up a principle," he said. "Politically and substantively, I'd rather lose and fight the good fight. Let's get an improvement on the status quo."

The Dodd-Frank Wall Street Reform and Consumer Protection Act finally passed in the summer of 2010 after a long, bruising fight. While these historic reforms wound up pleasing neither Wall Street nor its critics, they did deliver that much-needed "improvement on the status quo" that Obama had sought, with a sweeping law that would make the markets more transparent and the banks more accountable.

The Republican-leaning business lobby would seize upon his tart lines to paint Obama as antibusiness, which struck a nerve with a president who felt he had taken great risks to right their ship in the midst of the raging storm.

On one occasion, while I was still working at the White House, a top aide told Obama that he had just returned from a meeting in New York with financiers and corporate chiefs where he had his head handed to him. "They say they have a fifty-page list of concerns," he said. "They asked me, 'Where's your list of accomplishments?'"

The president shrugged. "How about saving the economy? That's my list. One page. How about that?"

TWENTY-FIVE

WHY WE DO THE WORK

WHEN THE GREAT DEBATE over America's health care system began, I didn't need a primer on its problems. I had lived them.

In my early days as a reporter at the *Tribune*, I had signed up for an insurance plan that seemed perfectly adequate. Susan and I were young, healthy, and fit, and we believed the health maintenance organization we had selected provided all the coverage we would need. Then, in 1982, when Lauren's seizures began, we learned very quickly how wrong we were. We had no prescription policy, so our insurance didn't cover all the expensive medications Lauren required. Even as the plan's designated specialist spoke of surgically removing a part of our child's brain, the HMO refused to pay for a second opinion. Finding better coverage was out of the question. Now that Lauren had a preexisting condition, no other insurer would take us.

Susan had quit her job to stay home with the baby, whose constant seizures and frequent hospitalizations made a steady work schedule impossible. I was making a decent salary at the newspaper, about forty thousand dollars a year, but with annual out-of-pocket medical expenses of ten thousand or more, we were routinely shuffling bills and taking on debt. Even as we dealt with the heartache of Lauren's struggles, we grappled with the huge financial burden that came along with them—and we *had* insurance. I often wondered, as I sat in emergency rooms, how folks who *didn't* have coverage dealt with these pressures.

What wouldn't I have given then for minimum coverage standards that included prescription drugs? Or for a law that would have prevented insurers from turning us down because of Lauren's preexisting condition? Back in the 1980s, though, a health care law like that seemed a pipe dream.

Obama had his own searing story. When his mother was diagnosed with ovarian cancer at age fifty-three, she was denied the disability pay she needed for her medical and living expenses. "She spent the last months of her life worrying as much about the medical bills as she did about trying to get well," he recalled with sadness and anger.

As a state senator from liberal Hyde Park, Obama had sponsored an amendment to the Illinois Constitution guaranteeing every resident the right to health care, but it went nowhere. During his Senate race, Obama stopped short of universal coverage, sticking instead to a plan that insured children, the poor, the temporarily unemployed, and the elderly. He did not advance a plan in the U.S. Senate because, coming from a junior senator who didn't even sit on the committees that had jurisdiction over health care, it would have been viewed as grandstanding.

We presented a comprehensive plan in the 2008 campaign, but we pummeled Hillary for including in hers a mandate requiring every American to obtain coverage. Then, in the general election, our research suggested that even our more moderate plan could be turned against us. So we ran a series of ads that infuriated some of our strongest supporters, denouncing both "government-run health care" and the excesses of the insurance industry. Finally, we beat up John McCain for proposing to tax health care benefits Americans got through their employers.

Yet the public policy case for action was hard to ignore.

By the time Obama took office, the number of people without coverage was nearing fifty million. Health care costs claimed a much higher share of our economy than in the other industrialized nations, almost all of which have some form of universal coverage. Also, despite the belief most Americans held about the superior quality of care in the United States, we lagged far behind most of those other countries in health outcomes. The cost of health care to consumers had been rising sharply for years, placing huge and growing pressures on families and businesses. As our budget director, Peter Orszag, drilled home in our internal deliberations, health care was the fastest-growing item in the budget and the greatest driver of long-term debt. The status quo would not hold.

In my role as the new president's political adviser, however, I knew what a perilous mission health reform would be.

Americans, in principle, were concerned about the growing number of uninsured and abuses by the industry, and they were reeling from the rapidly rising costs. Still, 85 percent had coverage, and they were leery of government plunging more deeply into health care, fearful that this would further raise their costs and limit their choices in order to cover the uninsured.

That resistance wasn't new.

For generations, health care reform had been the siren song of American politics, attracting presidents who wanted to solve the problem only to smash them against the rocks of furious industry lobbying and fickle public opinion. With Hillary as the skipper, Bill Clinton was the last to run up against these rocky shoals when he pushed a plan for universal coverage during his first years as president, in the early '90s. It was widely seen as one of the factors leading to Clinton's disastrous 1994 midterm elections, in which Republicans seized control of the Senate and, for the first time in forty years, the House of Representatives.

Given my own family's experience, I desperately wanted to see the system reformed. Yet, at least until the president made his decision, my job was to advise him candidly of the high political cost of taking it on and the long odds of success.

Adding to my anxiety were the details of the comprehensive plan he would advance if he decided to move forward. A team of health care experts had been hammering out a proposal since the election. It included both the mandate, which they said was essential to guarantee that healthy people join the insurance risk pool, and a new tax on high-cost health care plans offered by employers. Both, they argued, were indispensable elements of reform.

The tension over what to do about health care came to a boil at a meeting we held in the Roosevelt Room in early March 2009. The debate was centered on two huge questions: First, should we tackle health care in the first year of the administration? Second, if we tackle it, should we shoot for the whole package of comprehensive reform or settle for a more modest improvement?

"You're going to have to do something because Nancy and the House Democrats will insist on it," said Rahm, who spoke with the authority of a man who, just months earlier, was on Speaker Pelosi's leadership team. He argued for a more modest approach, the better not to expend our political capital on one vexing issue. The vice president, who knew more than a little about the workings of Congress, agreed that large-scale reform was too ambitious given everything else on our plate. He felt we needed to be squarely focused on the economy.

Fearful of how a contentious health reform battle would play out in the middle of an economic crisis, I suggested that the president defer it and place the focus on another of his causes: education reform. Ensuring every American got the education and training they needed was a sacred value and essential to long-term economic growth and competitiveness, I argued, and was the best answer to the burgeoning gulf between the wealthy and everyone else. Of all the major issues, it also had the best chance to attract some bipartisan support.

Then a woman I didn't recognize spoke up. "Mr. President you've made a commitment and you have to keep it," she said with a sharpness and finality that I didn't appreciate.

The speaker was Jeanne Lambrew, who had coauthored a book on health reform with Tom Daschle, Obama's first choice to lead the Department of Health and Human Services. When Daschle withdrew from the nominating process because of a personal tax controversy, Jeanne stayed on, working for his replacement, Kathleen Sebelius. I would later learn just how smart and committed Jeanne was, but at that moment, I viewed her as a meddlesome and presumptuous interloper.

"Look, I don't know who you are because, so far as I know, you weren't involved in our campaign," I said. "So let me tell you exactly what commitments the president made. He promised not to have a health care mandate. He promised not to tax health benefits. That's what he promised, and now you folks want him to break those promises."

The president, sitting in the slightly taller chair reserved for him at the center of a long, wooden conference table, took it all in. I could tell by the questions he asked and the comments he made, however, that Jeanne's bold thrust had been unnecessary. He was already on her side. He felt a commitment to move forward, boldly and swiftly. After spending two years telling the country that we needed leaders who would make decisions for the next generation and not just the next election, he was going to embrace that principle.

"I understand the risks," he told me later. "But what are we going to do? Are we going to put our approval ratings on the shelf and admire them for eight years? Or are we going to spend down on them and try to get some important things done for the future? If we don't take this up in the first two years, there's a good chance we won't get it done at all. We'll end up kicking the can down the road, and millions more people will go without insurance and the whole thing will implode."

Half of me wanted to stand up and cheer. This was exactly why I loved

Obama, who saw the winning of elections as the gateway to do meaningful things, not as a final destination.

To pass through that gateway, Obama had proven himself to be a shrewd politician, willing to make the necessary compromises. Without that quality, he would have been just another smart guy teaching law back at the University of Chicago. It was he who insisted during the primary that we omit the mandate from our campaign plan, arguing that it was unfair to force people to buy insurance unless and until we could make it affordable. It was a respectable policy argument, but I knew the politics were not lost on him. He had not been shy about flaying Hillary for her mandate, just as he'd green-lighted our health care ads against McCain. However, now he *was* the president, and he wasn't going to duck what might be his best opportunity to tackle what no other president had done. He was determined to help the desperate folks he had met along the way and all those whose anxious letters he was now reading each night. Their stories truly haunted him. The crisis of the uninsured and underinsured was an affront to American values and a threat to our country's solvency.

Obama's sense of urgency also reflected his understanding that there was zero chance he would be greeted by a *more* hospitable Congress after 2010, and he knew that presidents rarely became more powerful and influential over time. He was likely at the zenith of his power and popularity and was intent on fighting to accomplish as much as possible before the midterm elections. Health reform; tough, new financial regulations; a cap-and-trade bill to combat climate change; immigration reform—everything was on the table.

"Whenever I leave here, in four years or eight, I just want to leave knowing I did everything I could," he said. "We may not solve all these problems, but I want to know that we tried."

The half of me that wasn't poised to cheer was just worried. As much as I admired Obama's resolve, I knew that we really hadn't run on any of those issues except in the most general of ways, and if we had, we may not have won. Now, in the midst of an economic calamity, we were going to take a sharp turn and focus on some of the most divisive questions in Washington. Yes, they were issues that screamed out for solutions, but they hadn't been solved yet for a reason.

A rationalist in an often irrational business, Obama believed that if we just did a good job of explaining the health care plan to the American people, they would respond. I wasn't so sure. He also underestimated the reluctance of many politicians in Washington to stick their necks out on an issue that had traditionally been a killing field. For these reasons, to pass the bill, we would have to employ some of the time-honored techniques of legislative commerce in Washington that he had attacked as a candidate.

If I was concerned, Rahm was despondent.

More than most, he understood the limits of Congress. Moreover, the Clinton years had schooled him on the peril of big endeavors, particularly ones that put the White House at odds with both powerful Washington forces and widespread public sentiment. "David, I don't know how we're going to land all these planes," he said, sitting at his desk, staring at a pile of papers in front of him. Nonetheless, the president had made his decision, and Rahm went to work.

It was better to partner with Congress from the beginning, he concluded, and let them draft the plan with our input. Also, he was determined not to let "Harry and Louise" ride again—that fictional couple whose skeptical ads for the insurance industry had helped kill the Clinton plan. "We need to keep the insurance industry people off the battlefield for as long as possible," Rahm said at one of our early morning meetings. "We can't let them strangle this in the crib." This would set up another juncture where the idealistic promises of the campaign collided with the real politics necessary to get things done.

As a candidate, Obama had promised to give all the heath care stakeholders a "seat at the table," suggesting fancifully that the negotiations could be aired on C-SPAN so all of America could witness the process. As it turned out, the insurance industry and drug companies did have a seat at the table, but the discussions were discreet and out of public view, to facilitate the frank, bottom-line bargaining that characterizes any big piece of legislation. If the insurance industry considered the proposed regulations too burdensome, even the promise of millions of new customers wouldn't keep them in the fold. For PhRMA (Pharmaceutical Research and Manufacturers of America), the calculus was even simpler: it wouldn't accept any plan that allowed American consumers to import prescription drugs from overseas, where they are often sold at a fraction of their U.S. price.

Although Rahm deliberately kept the president at arm's length from some of the details, to give him the latitude to disown them, Obama understood that getting the job done would require difficult and unpopular trade-offs. If passage of comprehensive health reform required some bitter pills along the way, he had resolved to swallow them, as long as the larger goals (extending coverage to tens of millions of Americans and broadly reducing overall costs) were not compromised away.

Even with the industry groups sidelined, however, health reform's opponents found their footing as details of the House and Senate bills surfaced. The Senate was marking up a bill that would cost almost nine hundred billion dollars over ten years to help insure some thirty-one million Americans who lacked coverage. The House bill, more generous in its subsidies, had a price tag of more than a trillion. Each day's stories from Capitol Hill left the impression of a huge, new social welfare program that would swell already intolerable deficits. It mattered not that, with the savings and new revenues the bills would generate, they would actually *lower* the deficits. That sounded like Washington math. Few believed it.

"They're going to add these numbers up," said an exasperated Rahm. "Seven hundred billion for the banks and auto companies, eight hundred billion for a stimulus they still don't believe in, and now another trillion to buy someone else health care."

Cautious at first, the Republican leaders saw opportunity. They were buoyed by a memo from Frank Luntz, a Republican pollster and language Svengali. Noting that Americans did believe there was a health care crisis, Luntz advised the GOP to embrace reform—but only "the right kind of reform that protects the quality of healthcare for all Americans." In the Orwellian world of Luntz, this was not a primer on how to pass or improve health reform. It was a blueprint on language to *defeat* it. He advised Republicans to rail against a "Washington takeover" of health care and a one-size-fits-all system that would rob Americans of their choice of doctors and access to timely care.

Fear too often trumps reason. There was plenty of support for a law that would ban the worst practices of the insurance industry and bring down costs. Yet given widespread public disdain for Washington, our promises of relief were not considered as credible as the scary warnings against the intrusion of a meddling, incompetent government. Moreover, all the news coverage focused on the plight of the uninsured. Many came to see health reform as something that would help others, but at a cost to them. By June, we were losing momentum. Democrats on Capitol Hill grew increasingly wary of the politics, and there were signs that the president's own standing was beginning to take a hit.

Around that time, I brought him some data that showed how we were suffering politically as a result of the ongoing debate. "I'm sure you're right," he said, after giving me a respectful hearing. "But I just came back from Green Bay, Wisconsin. I met a woman there who was thirty-five years old, had a job, a husband, and two children, and health insurance. But she also has stage-three breast cancer, and now she's hit her lifetime caps, so her insurance company is refusing to pay her bills, and she's terrified that she's going to die and leave her family bankrupt."

By then, I felt Obama's hand in the small of my back, gently ushering me to the door of his office. As he opened it, he paused for a moment. "That's not the country we believe in," he said. "So let's just keep on fighting."

Obama desperately wanted a bipartisan bill to come out of Congress, and it wasn't just a matter of getting the votes to make health reform the law. He knew that to pass the biggest piece of social legislation in half a century on a straight party-line vote would only exacerbate the deep divisions in the country and undermine public confidence.

The Senate Finance Committee was working to mark up and pass its version of the law by the August recess, and the ranking Republican member of the committee, Chuck Grassley of Iowa, had in the 1990s supported a law with an individual mandate and health insurance exchanges as a GOP substitute for the Clinton plan. The bill that was emerging in the Senate now looked very much like the one Grassley had supported then, so Obama invited Grassley to the White House as part of his ceaseless lobbying effort—and, at least as the president related it, they found plenty of common ground.

"I said, 'Chuck, we agree on ninety-eight percent of this stuff. Can you support a bill?" Obama reported after the meeting. "He said, 'Not unless you can get another ten Republicans to stand with me. I can't be out there alone.'" "Another ten" was a polite way of saying no. We were having trouble finding even one Senate Republican to support our plan. McConnell had locked up his caucus and would squeeze even harder as the year went on.

Inside the White House, doubts were growing about our ability to pass sweeping reform legislation. Worried that a long, costly fight could hurt Democrats come midterms while ultimately yielding nothing, Rahm recommended scaling back to a plan that would cover fewer people, but garner more votes. Obama asked his legislative director, Phil Schiliro, to rate the chances of passing the larger bill.

"Depends how lucky you feel, Mr. President," Phil replied.

Obama smiled. "Can I say this? I always feel lucky. Let's go all in. When your name is Barack Obama and you're the president of the United States, how can you not feel lucky?"

Still, Obama was frustrated by the traction that his opponents were getting. It drove him up a wall when a group from the consulting firm McKinsey and Company came in and outlined the unconscionable waste, fraud, and market manipulation that had made health care in America the most expensive in the world. Why didn't people understand that his reform package could save enough to help millions obtain coverage and, in the long run, cut health care spending? "We haven't communicated this well," he told me. "They think it will raise their costs and the deficits."

His frustration frustrated *me*, with its implication that this was all a failure of the messaging that I had devised. I had warned from the beginning how difficult this would be. Health care was the Fort Knox of messaging. Forgive me for not having picked the lock!

The predictable carping had begun in political circles: Why was an operation that had been so deft in winning the presidency now so hapless in selling Obama's chief priority? Perhaps because, in the campaign, we had recognized the political pitfalls and dodged the most challenging aspects of health reform. Now that we had taken up the cause, our fears had proven to be justified.

I wasn't sure, even as he spoke in March of spending his political capital on health reform, that the president fully grasped what a difficult sell this would be. He was so confident in his ability to communicate, and was convinced that, with the need so obvious, the benefits would eventually become apparent. It might have been valiant to dismiss the political concerns that Rahm and I and others had raised months earlier, but they hadn't been unfounded.

"Despite our best efforts to explain, many Americans are simply finding it too hard to square adding a trillion dollars as part of a strategy to cut costs," I wrote to the president in an August memo. "They suspect that this is about spending and taxing more to take care of someone else. And even if they see universal coverage as a laudable goal, they think it's irresponsible to undertake it now—a liberal indulgence we can't afford. To them, our determination to plow forward on an expedited timetable in the midst of a fiscal crisis is not sensible. It aligns us with the Washington they disdain—the dogmatic politics they thought we were going to change."

Washington is a terrible place to be when the story line has turned against you. The town is one big echo chamber, and if you're the target—as the White

House often is—the din becomes deafening and deflating. The resident experts are always generous with their advice, which in this case, not surprisingly, was to limit our losses by taking what we could get and moving on. Before heading out west in mid-August for a set of town hall meetings, though, the determined president laid down the principles we needed to communicate, and exhorted all of us to forge ahead.

"Here's what I want to go out there and say. This law will help the vast majority of people who have health care. It will help all of those who have insurance to make sure that if someone gets sick, you don't get screwed. And I want to make sure that anyone who wants insurance can get it at a price they can afford. If we can make that case, we win. If we can't tell that story, we lose.

"I know things are tough right now and a lot of the pundits are saying that the presidency is at stake and all of that," he continued. "I don't care about any of that. I'm not thinking about reelection. There will be plenty of time to worry about that. I don't want to let down. I don't want to give up. It's important for the country and the future and many, many people. That's why we're here. It's to get important things done. So I don't want anyone losing heart. We're doing the right thing."

But doing the right thing isn't often the easiest politics.

Throughout the country, members of Congress were assaulted by angry mobs at town hall meetings, railing against runaway spending and a "government-run" takeover of health care. Though the Republicans no doubt fanned the flames, much of the impetus was coming from an edgy new force in our politics, the Tea Party, which began as an organic protest movement but would quickly be enhanced by deep-pocketed Republican oligarchs intent on wresting the Congress away from Obama and the Democrats. Their vitriol was reminiscent of the angry crowds that had turned up at McCain-Palin rallies less than a year earlier. Now, in Obama's initiatives, they were convinced they had found evidence of the dark, socialist impulses they had imputed to him all along.

The ugliness and personal tone of the protests betrayed a truth we were loath to acknowledge publicly. For some in the crowd, their ire was rooted in more than disagreements over policy. It was rooted in race: a deep-seated resentment of the idea of the black man with the Muslim name in the White House. The facts notwithstanding, to them, health reform was just another giveaway to poor black people at their expense.

Speaking with the authority of a former president and a lifelong southerner, Jimmy Carter decided to weigh in on the nature and tone of the protests. "When a radical fringe element of demonstrators and others begin to attack the President of the United States as an animal or as a reincarnation of Adolf Hitler . . . those kinds of things are beyond the bounds," he said during a speech at Emory University. "I think people who are guilty of that kind of personal attack against Obama have been influenced to a major degree by a belief that he should not be president because he happens to be African-American."

I appreciated Carter's candor, but cringed when I read his remarks. I didn't doubt that race had added an element of fury to some of the protests that summer, and even to the defiance of some in Congress. I also knew that Lincoln had been depicted as an ape. Roosevelt had been denounced as a dictator. Clinton was the fulcrum of relentless personal attacks from the Right, as was George W. Bush from the Left. If we appeared to be dismissing opposition to Obama's policies as racism, it would enrage all those who had honest concerns about his legislative priorities, including millions who had voted for him.

The day after his comments, President Carter sent me an e-mail acknowledging these challenges. "Please express my regrets to the President if I have created an additional problem for him," the Georgian wrote. "I have lived with these people for 85 years, been their governor and their President. I have made it clear in all my statements that it is ok to debate important issues, even to claim falsely that Obama supports death squads to kill old people. But some of the ad hominem and extremely vitriolic attacks go beyond a tough political debate. I'll do anything to help him, but cannot deny what I am convinced is true."

"Mr. President, I never doubted your sincerity or your intentions," I wrote in reply. "I know very well the vantage point from which you spoke. But race is the catnip of the media. They didn't believe Obama could win because of it and, given the current story line that he is stumbling, they tremble with excitement at any suggestion of it as a defining factor now. It is not a diversion we need."

Whatever was behind the serial maelstroms that erupted over the summer, the beating we took from them dominated the news coverage, compounding a sense that health reform and its chief proponent were sinking.

We had to do something dramatic if we hoped to be heard over the mob. I suggested a joint address to Congress as soon as it returned after Labor Day. A prime-time speech would be broadcast by the networks and watched by tens of millions of Americans. It would be our best opportunity to explain plainly and clearly the benefits of reform to *all* Americans, not just the uninsured: an end to the ban on preexisting conditions and lifetime limits on care; savings to consumers that included a cap on out-of-pocket expenses; the requirement that every insurance plan cover routine preventive care; and the creation of an affordable, competitive market for people to buy insurance. Such a speech would also allow us to knock down health-rationing "death panels," exploding deficits, and the other menacing myths our opponents had created and embellished.

On the evening after Labor Day, as I stood on the floor of the House chambers listening to the president's address to Congress, I kept refreshing my BlackBerry for bulletins from Tempe, Arizona, where Binder was conducting dial groups with forty-nine swing voters. The news was encouraging. The president's speech had accomplished what we needed it to by assuaging people's concerns and winning them over to our side. Even so, as if to affirm Carter's analysis, the speech was marred by a stunning moment, when the president refuted yet another pernicious piece of fiction—that the law would cover illegal immigrants—and one of the Republican House members, Joe Wilson of South Carolina, shouted back at him, "You lie!"

Obama's forceful performance gave us a respite. Yet within weeks, any benefit had faded and we found ourselves once again bogged down in the grinding realities of the legislative process and the hyperpartisanship that gripped Washington and beyond.

Fighting against this factionalism, we still held out hope to get at least one Republican vote for health reform in the Senate. We might need it if anyone of the Senate's sixty Democrats flaked, making it impossible to break a Republican filibuster to block a vote on the bill. Ben Nelson, a conservative Democrat from Nebraska, was no sure thing. So we pinned our hopes on Olympia Snowe, a moderate Republican from Maine, who had a long history of independence and had broken with Mitch McConnell by supporting the Recovery Act. She was working on her own amendments to the plan, and was still hinting at supporting it.

"I would take the Snowe plan in a heartbeat!" the president said. "We'll *call* it the Snowe plan. Hell, she can live here in the White House! Michelle and I will get an apartment." Obama would continue to court Snowe throughout the fall and winter, but she would dither until the end, whipsawed between her desire to make progress and the relentless hammering by McConnell. "You can't blame her for hesitating," Obama said, even as he worked to win her over. "If she bolts on this, it won't be pleasant in that caucus. They're not pleasant people."

In November, the House passed its plan, which was more generous in its benefits than the plan emerging in the Senate; benefits paid for by taxes on the wealthy. It also included a government-run "public option" to compete against private insurers in the health care exchange. All these were nonstarters for Nelson and some of the more conservative members of the Senate.

Finally, in early December, the Senate debate began. On a Sunday afternoon, Harry Reid asked the president to make his case to Senate Democrats at the Capitol. When we got back into his limousine to return to the White House, he was reflective. "Why is everyone so scared?" he asked quietly, glancing out the window. "They're scared because these are the best jobs they've ever had and they want to keep them," I said. He looked at me. "But what good is it to be up here for thirty years and never get anything meaningful done? I don't get it."

It was a revealing moment that helped explain the disconnect between Obama and so many in Washington. He hated life in the Senate, with its endless talk and abstruse rules that seemed designed to frustrate solutions instead of promoting them. The idea of staying there and "doing nothing" was as incomprehensible to him as casting votes that might cost them their seats was to his former colleagues.

The president continued to make his case nine days later, when the still-unsettled Senate caucus visited him at the White House.

"Why did we get into this business in the first place?" he asked them. "Not to see our names in the lights, not to go to White House parties. It was to help people . . . so this is it. This is the moment. This is why you want to be here, so that forty years from now people will look at us as people look back today at those who passed civil rights. I didn't mention Teddy the last time, but I do think about if he were here today, he would say, 'This is the moment and we have to seize it.'"

With the final showdown nearing, a single Democrat, Nelson of Nebraska, was holding out, and Republican Snowe had yet to declare. Rahm sent a pair of

Senate staff veterans, Rouse and Jim Messina, the deputy chief of staff, to Capitol Hill to reel in Nelson, a conservative former insurance executive who was often an outlier in his own party.

Unless we could round up one of the two, McConnell and the Republicans could, and would, simply block a final vote. Rahm was glum. "McConnell warned everyone that he'd pull the chairmanships of anyone who votes for cloture," he told us. "They're whipping the vote. It's over, that's it." Phil Schiliro, the legislative director who had been trapped for a year between the president's determination and Rahm's reticence, snapped back. "It's not over!"

That night, Rahm and I ran into Vicki Kennedy, who was working the bill on her own, tapping old friendships to try to advance her late husband's legacy. "I met with Olympia for an hour today, and she really seemed eager to be for this," Vicki said. "Tonight, she sounds different. Something's changed." Then, as Rahm studied his BlackBerry, he pulled me aside. "Doesn't matter," he said. "We've got Nelson."

Rouse, Messina, and the Senate grandees had bargained with Ben Nelson for thirteen hours. The final deal included a special provision that Nelson had demanded to help Nebraska offset the tab for expanded Medicaid, as the new law would require. When news of the "Cornhusker Kickback" spread, it caused a huge firestorm that would taint the process. In the meantime, we had our sixtieth vote. The president was already en route to join his family in Hawaii when the Senate passed the bill at dawn. "Congratulations! Your determination—not your luck—made this possible," I wrote. "We're all very proud. But before you type it, I know we just have to finish the job."

When I wrote those words, I had no idea how hard finishing the job would be.

The hostility between Republicans and Democrats in Washington is readily apparent. What's striking, when you spend a little time there, is the outright contempt between the House and Senate, even among members of the same party.

It was the system the Founders envisioned: a "People's House," burning with popular passions; and the more reflective Senate, to provide needed ballast. Yet as Obama discovered when he returned to Washington, it is an ingenious system unless you have to negotiate differences between them over something as volatile and complex as health reform. If playing Dr. Phil to warring factions of his own party was what it would take to reach agreement, though, then that seemed a small price to pay after all we had been through.

For several days and nights in early January, House and Senate Democrats met in the Cabinet Room in the White House, working to harmonize their plans. Meanwhile, voters in Massachusetts were preparing to force these two warring blocs to come together.

Ted Kennedy had died the previous August. Even before the holidays, I had begun hearing disturbing rumblings about the special election in January to fill his unexpired term.

David Simas, my deputy and a Massachusetts native, was wired into the Bay State's politics. He had warned me that Martha Coakley, the state attorney general, was taking the race for granted, while her Republican opponent, Scott Brown, was running a strong campaign and closing in on her. Traveling the state in a pickup truck and projecting an easy, working-class affability, Brown, a state senator, had deftly captured the anti-Washington zeitgeist, using the machinations around health reform as Exhibit A in his case for change.

Coakley hadn't exactly displayed that same common touch. When a reporter asked whether attending photo opportunities with local officials was the best expenditure of her time, she committed an unpardonable sin. She said: "As opposed to standing outside Fenway Park? In the cold? Shaking hands?" Unlike her opponent, Coakley had taken a pass on campaigning outside the storied ballpark, where Boston's beloved Bruins had played a New Year's Day game outdoors against the Philadelphia Flyers.

The president strolled into my office just as I was hearing the details, and inveterate ESPN watcher that he is, the cultural meaning of the gaffe was not lost on him. "Nooooo!" he cried in disbelief, grabbing my shirt for emphasis. "She didn't say *that*?" At this point, the president of the United States began jumping up and down in exasperation. "She's going to lose! She's going to lose!"

It wasn't the prospect of Coakley's loss that had the president hopping mad. It was what he feared her defeat would mean for health reform.

We had exactly 60 Democratic votes in the Senate, including the interim senator appointed to fill Kennedy's seat until after the special election. If she lost the seat, we would only have 59, dooming any chance of bringing a compromise House-Senate bill back for a vote. Moreover, the symbolic damage would be incalculable. "There is no doubt that a defeat on Tuesday is an unmitigated disaster," the president said. "If we lose Ted Kennedy's seat on the eve of the health care vote, it will send Washington into a frenzy, and it will take months to clean up." Rahm was darker and more succinct: "If we lose Coakley, we're done."

The president appeared for Coakley on the final weekend, but we couldn't save her from herself. Obama was furious. He had worked his tail off to make health reform a reality. Now, at the eleventh hour, an indifferent candidate and our inability to prop her up had put the whole deal in jeopardy. "I just wish everybody would do their jobs," he said pointedly.

Washington would be gunning for Obama now, expecting admissions of failure—perhaps a midcourse correction. Yet the president was more defiant than defeated. "These guys are so cynical," he said of McConnell and the Republican leadership. "They would take the country over the side just to score some points . . . and they shouldn't be rewarded for that."

So, on the day after we lost Ted Kennedy's seat, when everyone in town was reading last rites over our health care bill, Obama began plotting the miracle of its resurrection. There was no possibility of bringing a different piece of legislation to the Senate floor now; McConnell had the votes to block it. We would have to persuade House Democrats to accept the Senate bill that many of them loathed. If they held their noses and moved forward, we would clean up some of the technical, finance-related issues in the bill through a process called budget reconciliation, which would require only 51 votes. "We only have two hundred votes in the House right now to pass the bill," Schiliro reported. "We need two eighteen."

"We may have to pivot for a few months. We have to put the focus on jobs and take it off of health care, while we regroup," Obama said.

Obama conferred with Reid and Pelosi. The Speaker was as committed as the president to passing health reform, but she wasn't about to get out in front of her Democratic caucus too quickly by endorsing the Senate plan. Pelosi intended to get us there, but first she would poke and prod us as well as the Senate to demonstrate to the firebrands in her caucus that she had done everything she could and there was no alternative course.

I was asked to appear before a grumpy Senate caucus in early February. They had been polite and reasonably well behaved earlier in the day when they heard from the president, but they plainly didn't feel they owed me the same consideration and instead demanded to know our strategy to pass the bill. When Reid called on Minnesota senator Al Franken, the retired *Saturday Night*

Live star decided to put on a performance. "I am just livid! I am doing a slow burn over here!" he said, with a forced flourish that revealed why he had been a comedian and not a dramatic actor. "Both the president and you come here, and neither of you has told us how we're going to get health care done . . . When is he going to show some leadership?"

Now I was livid, too. Health reform would have been dead long ago but for the president's leadership, I told Franken, reciting everything Obama had done to bring the issue to the brink of final passage. As we continued to spar, Harry Reid sat quietly, staring at the floor. Harry was in close communication with the White House and approved of our play, but he was content to let his caucus vent its frustrations—and far better on me than him.

Franken wouldn't let up. "Then why doesn't he just walk on over to the House of Representatives and demand a vote on the Senate bill?"

"Senator," I said through slightly gritted teeth, "if you have a piece of paper with two hundred eighteen votes on it, give it to me and I'll walk it over to the Speaker right now. I don't think she has such a list."

As is customary in turbulent moments, many Washington savants were calling for the heads of Obama's team as well. In early February, Steve Clemons, a widely read Washington blogger, wrote a piece entitled "Core Chicago Team Sinking Obama Presidency." Leslie Gelb, a former correspondent for the *Times* and certified establishment Wise Man, chimed in with a piece entitled "Replace Rahm."

If I was mildly dismayed by this, Rahm was furious. He had done heroic work to help pass key pieces of the president's agenda in 2009 and to keep all the balls in the air. Now health care was faltering, just as he had warned, and he was bearing the brunt of the blame. In the aftermath of the Massachusetts election, Rahm continued, at the president's direction, to hold discreet discussions with members of Congress about a smaller health care package that we could pass. Yet, Obama wouldn't relent as long as he saw a path to the more comprehensive bill. He was worried a retreat could influence the remainder of his presidency, and other presidencies to come.

"I'll tell you what's keeping me up at night," the president said one day during this period. "What health care has exposed is whether we have the opportunity to do big things anymore . . . On bipartisanship, people want it, but the question is, how much are we willing to compromise before what we do in the name of bipartisanship becomes meaningless?"

I had been deeply concerned about taking on the health care fight at the beginning, but now that we were here, I saw the president's point. A smaller health care bill would be seen for what it was, a surrender, a sign of weakness, not strength. I admired the president's determination, and felt we had to play this out.

In the midst of these internal and existential struggles, Dana Milbank, a *Washington Post* columnist, wrote a defense of Rahm—but it was help Rahm could have done without. "Obama's greatest mistake was failing to listen to Emanuel on health care," Milbank wrote, detailing Rahm's advocacy for a smaller health care bill. "Had it gone Emanuel's way, a politically popular health-care bill would have passed long ago, leaving plenty of time for other attractive priorities, such as efforts to make college more affordable. We would have seen a continuation of the momentum of the first half of 2009, when Obama followed Emanuel's strategy and got 11 substantive bills on his desk before the August recess."

I didn't believe that Rahm was Milbank's source or that he would separate himself publicly from the president in this fashion, but he had many loyal friends in whom he had confided too much. One or more of them had taken it upon themselves to tee up Milbank on behalf of Rahm. Rahm understood the damage the effort had caused the president.

"I decided I am going to resign," Rahm told Gibbs and me. "This isn't working for the president. I can't go out for him and can't function inside. Our friendship has changed. I'm going to see health care through and then I'm leaving."

I told Rahm to take a deep breath. The Milbank column was bad, even inexcusable, but his value to the president was such that he couldn't leave—and certainly not on this note. I was fairly sure that Obama would feel the same way. I saw Rahm a few hours later, after he returned from his talk with the president. "I tried to resign, but he wouldn't let me," he reported, groaning. "He said, 'Oh no. You're not resigning. Your punishment is that you have to pass health care!'"

Later, the president gathered his senior advisers, urging us to remain united. "Rahm made a mistake, but the problem is Washington," he said. "This is what I hate about this town. Small people try to stir up the intrigue and pit people against each other. I want everyone to know that I have your backs, and I hope you have mine. And I want you to stand up for one another."

Rahm apologized to the group. "I let you down," he said. "I didn't mean to, but I did."

My turn came next. I got a call from Mark Leibovich, a reporter for the *New York Times*. I liked Mark, a smart, funny writer with an appropriately biting perspective on the nation's capital. I enjoyed reading his pieces when they were about others. I wasn't thrilled when he said his next story would be about me, particularly when he added, "I'm sorry."

Leibovich was going to write the piece with or without me, so I agreed to sit down with him. I had a fresh shipment of deli food from Manny's in Chicago stowed at the White House, and I invited Leibovich to join me in tackling it. I figured we could bond, Jew to Jew, over corned beef sandwiches and the *Flintstones*-size turkey legs that were a Manny's specialty. It was a terrible mistake, furnishing the writer with vivid color for a story about a guy who ate too much, slept too little, and was buckling under the pressures of Washington. It didn't help when the president walked into my office in the middle of lunch and found me with an enormous turkey leg in my hand. "What is this, King Arthur's Court?" he quipped, providing another great line for Leibovich, who, as it turned out, was there to feast on me.

Under the headline "White House Message Maven Finds Fingers Pointed at Him," the story's lead set the dispiriting tone: "David Axelrod was sitting at his desk on a recent afternoon—tie crooked, eyes droopy and looking more burdened than usual. He had just been watching some genius on MSNBC insist that he and President Obama's other top aides were failing miserably and should be replaced." It went downhill from there, including quotes from my sister and a friend from Chicago hinting that I was near collapse.

I read the story while in Phoenix, trying to enjoy some rare days off with Susan and the kids, who suffered the fallout as I sulked away the remainder of our rare, brief vacation time together. I was accustomed to shots at my strategy, and my eating habits were well-trod ground, but the image of a guy utterly defeated irritated the hell out of me.

I wasn't back at my desk in the White House for long before the president walked in and sat down. Casually stretching his arms and legs, he said, "So, how you doing?" I knew why he was asking and told him I was fine. "I saw that story," he said. "It's Washington bullshit. Don't worry about it. Let's just get health care done, and all this will get better."

And little by little, the prospects of getting health care done *were* improving.

Part of that comeback had to do with two widely covered events, in which the president directly confronted his opponents, answering their questions face-to-face in front of TV cameras. The first was at a House Republican retreat in late January. Before the president appeared, we pressured the caucus to open the event to cameras, and what unfolded was a candid, unscripted, and riveting exchange of views. Obama clearly got the better of it and came back to the White House with an idea.

"Why don't we invite everyone down here, Republicans and Democrats, who are involved in the health care issue and have a health care summit? We can televise the whole thing, get all the questions on the table, and give this thing a thorough airing?"

After ten months of closed-door negotiations and backroom deals, the seven-hour summit on February 25 at the Blair House was a welcome disinfectant; a small gesture to make good on Obama's pledge to work through health care on C-SPAN. It wasn't that many watched it. It was that they knew they could.

Meanwhile, Pelosi, slowly and skillfully steered her caucus to the only logical conclusion: that the Senate bill, however imperfect, was now the only path forward.

Coakley's defeat had widely been read as the death knell for health reform. Paradoxically, it might have saved it by breaking the deadlock between House and Senate Democrats. The House would have to accept the Senate bill they hated—without a public plan or some of the more generous emoluments—or there would be no health reform law at all.

There was, of course, the inevitable last-minute drama—this over the perennially vexing issue of abortion—but after a few tense hours, a compromise was reached, and on March 21, the House gathered for a rare Sunday session to consider the Senate bill.

That night, the president, vice president, senior advisers, and all the men and women who, for over a year, had led the health care effort, gathered in the Roosevelt Room to watch the vote on TV. As the vote wound down, I left the room and went across the hall to sit alone in my own office. When I heard the cheers from next door, I began to cry—not little sniffles, but big, heaving sobs. Suddenly the political calculations and ups and downs of the previous year seemed irrelevant. I thought about Susan and Lauren and the horrific struggle we had endured to save our child and pay for her treatments. I knew that because of what had happened on this night, because of what we had done, because of the president's determination against all odds, other families would be spared that ordeal. It was emotionally overwhelming.

Because politics was my arena, I understood, perhaps better than Obama, the steep price he had paid for this historic achievement. His standing with moderate, swing voters had taken a hit. Elected as an apostle of change in Washington, he had compromised when he had to, employed the traditional tools of the trade to achieve his goal, and jammed the law through on a straight party-line vote. In doing so, he had ignited a blazing grassroots opposition that would cost him his House majority and bedevil him for the remainder of his presidency. Yet, on this night, all of these calculations seemed beside the point. He had spent his political capital on a worthy cause, and had brought about real, substantive reform that would save and improve lives and strengthen the country for generations to come.

When I composed myself, I went and found my friend, the president, and thanked him on behalf of my family and all those who, in the future, would never have to confront the trials we had known. He put his hand on my shoulder and smiled.

"That's why we do the work," he said.

TWENTY-SIX

WAR AND PEACE PRIZE

HE WAS THE ANTIWAR candidate turned wartime commander in chief, the constitutional scholar struggling to balance our values and rights with our security in a new age of terrorism. He would be the winner of the Nobel Peace Prize who sent tens of thousands of additional troops into battle.

In the two years I worked at his side in the White House, I watched him carefully parry with the military to define, and confine, America's mission in Afghanistan. I saw him confront the daily reality of terrorism and explain to a roomful of skeptical civil libertarians the limitations those threats, and practical politics, imposed on him as commander in chief. And I was in the audience in Oslo as the reluctant Nobel Prize winner reconciled his vision for a more peaceful world with his belief that there are times when evil must be met with force.

It is an inspiring strength of our democracy that, by a vote of the people, the unquestioned authority over the military is handed to the civilian president. At any hour of the day or night, he might be called upon to make decisions about the deployment of manpower or weaponry that almost certainly will cost someone (or many someones) their life. Sometimes those missions are covert. Often they present scenarios he couldn't have imagined when he was crisscrossing the country auditioning for the job.

Yet what you learn when you work for the president is that while the military is scrupulously nonpartisan and will respond faithfully to the orders of the commander in chief, the Pentagon is as political a player as you'll find in Washington. Its leaders understand how to deploy their institutional leverage to influence policy and corral presidents: the strategically placed leak, a discreet call to a friendly congressman, or less-than-supportive testimony on Capitol Hill from a general or admiral, his uniform festooned with a bedazzling array of medals and ribbons.

That concern was partly why Obama had asked Robert Gates to stay on the job as defense secretary. Gates, a fixture for four decades in the country's national security establishment, had brought a more thoughtful sensibility to the Pentagon after the bombastic and divisive Donald Rumsfeld. Yet there was more to it. Obama was pursuing a quantum shift in policy—ending the war in Iraq and refocusing our efforts against Al Qaeda in Afghanistan, banning torture as a means of interrogation, and closing the detention center at Guantánamo Bay. He was wary of military intervention as a first resort and eager for a surge of diplomacy. Obama understood that he would need more than a respectful salute from the military to accomplish his goals. He needed their support.

To the military, Gates represented continuity. He was an able and methodical manager, low-key and rational in his judgments. All this appealed to Obama, who shared many of the same qualities. "He's really solid," the president said of the defense secretary, early in his term, an assessment I would hear him repeat often. At least to me, Gates expressed equal admiration for the president. In the summer of 2010, after Gates agreed to re-up for an additional year, we chatted before a White House reception. "We really appreciate your sacrifice," I told Gates, a short, gray-haired man with the reassuring mien of a trusted, small-town banker. Drawing closer, Gates smiled. "I love working with this president," he said.

When Gates had agreed to continue as defense secretary, though, it was a commitment and not a contract. If he objected to the direction the president was taking, he could happily return to the bucolic splendor of his rural home in the other Washington across the country. Obama thought highly of Gates and valued his counsel, but he also *needed* Gates, as the secretary well knew. The respectful but wary tango between the commander in chief, his defense secretary, and the military leadership was a running story of my years in the White House—and much of it centered on the vexing challenge of Afghanistan.

Iraq was as central to Obama's candidacy and election as any other single issue, but soon after he was sworn in, we would begin winding down our involvement there. The Bush administration had signed an agreement, partly at the insistence of the Iraqis, mandating the withdrawal of all American troops by the end of 2011. Obama would hold the United States to that agreement, which closely matched the plan he had proposed as a candidate. Soon after taking office, the president announced a precise schedule for that withdrawal, ending our combat mission by the summer of 2010. It was a compromise based on the advice of his commanders, extending the U.S. combat role a few months longer than he had proposed as a presidential candidate. The decision to lengthen the mission by a few months was publicly supported by John McCain and other hawks on the right, and openly criticized by our allies on the left. Still, all our troops would be home by the end of 2011, certainly a welcome relief for a war-weary country, for the servicemen and -women who had borne repeated tours of duty, and for their families. From my parochial perspective, it would also give Obama a huge promise kept for his reelection in 2012.

Afghanistan was a whole different story.

It began as a mission to rout Al Qaeda and bring Osama bin Laden to justice, but unraveled after the Bush administration shifted the military focus some fourteen hundred miles west, to another war in Iraq. Now, seven years later, bin Laden and Al Qaeda's core leaders were still at large, the Taliban was resurgent, and the United States and its NATO allies were deeply mired in Afghanistan. Some six hundred Americans had already died there, and thousands more had been injured, in an effort to help prop up the government of Hamid Karzai, the country's mercurial and corrupt, if democratically elected, leader. The allied mission, already costing more than three billion dollars every month, was adrift without an obvious strategy or endgame.

Obama was resolved to change that.

He knew that this would initially mean a greater commitment of U.S. troops to stabilize the country, train Afghan soldiers, and step up the assault on Al Qaeda. He had said so as a candidate. Yet he also was determined to define the mission and limit its duration. He felt the wars had already cost the nation dearly and had inflamed anti-American sentiment in Muslim countries and beyond. "This can't be an open-ended commitment," he said. "We can't afford it and the American people won't tolerate it."

This triggered a months-long debate in the fall of 2009 about the size and scope of the mission, which played out in nine dramatic meetings in the cloistered White House Situation Room. The sessions revolved around a strategy proposed by General Stanley McChrystal, a newly appointed commander of

U.S. forces in Afghanistan. Before the president ever saw the plan, its details began leaking, setting the fault lines for the debate.

Before the formal review began, an agitated Joe Biden called me into his office. "Our objective in going there was to destroy Al Qaeda, so why are we plunging into COIN here?" the vice president said, predicting that the McChrystal plan for an expansive counterinsurgency, reported in the media, would become a sinkhole from which we could not escape. Biden believed that fewer troops, focused on Al Qaeda and counterterrorism efforts, was the smarter and more responsible strategy. "The president has asked me to play the bad cop on this and I am ready to do it."

I shared Biden's concern. We had campaigned against nation building and open-ended engagements. McChrystal's plan might mean leaving troops in Afghanistan throughout Obama's presidency. Still, very properly, when the meetings began, I was just a silent observer, there because I would have to help explain and defend whatever decision the president made.

Determined not to repeat the mistakes of the past, the president came to the first meeting in mid-September with a raft of probing questions about the length, scope, and goals of the mission—questions he would need answered before making any decisions about additional troops. What was necessary to defeat Al Qaeda? What was achievable in Afghanistan, given the weak and corrupt government there? What was the strategy for neighboring Pakistan, more than a passive player and increasingly a safe haven for both the Taliban and Al Qaeda?

Before he could get the answers, though, the president was treated to a lesson in the complex politics of dealing with the military.

Testifying before the Senate Armed Services Committee, Admiral Mike Mullen, the nation's top military man, was asked about McChrystal's report, which was classified and had not been released. McChrystal had yet to put a number on his request for more troops, Mullen told the committee. "But I do believe that, having heard his views and having great confidence in his leadership, a properly resourced counterinsurgency probably means more forces and, without question, more time and more commitment to the protection of the Afghan people and to the development of good governance." Six days later, the classified McChrystal memo was leaked. The front page of the *Washington Post* screamed, "McChrystal: More Forces or 'Mission Failure.' "

Whether it intended to or not, the Pentagon had jammed the commander in chief.

Even the slow-to-boil Obama was furious. He called in Gates and Mullen and, according to Rahm, was very blunt about his feelings: "McChrystal's report is leaked and published. We meet for two and a half hours on Sunday and have a good discussion on the way to go, and then you go out and run way out in front of where you know I am? I can only conclude one of two things, Mike. Either you don't respect me as commander in chief or you all have been very sloppy. Neither is justifiable."

"It got very quiet, for like five seconds, which felt like an hour," Rahm recalled. "And then Gates said, 'We respect you, Mr. President. The mistakes are ours.'"

What was supposed to have been a secret review was now a public debate. When the president met with congressional leaders at the White House in early October, the Republicans pushed him to embrace McChrystal's plan, including the additional forty thousand troops he was rumored to be requesting.

"You're the commander in chief. This is your decision, and I don't envy you," said Obama's vanquished general election opponent, John McCain. "I appreciate that you need a strategy, but I do think time is not on our side."

After a few others chimed in, echoing the same point, Obama had heard enough.

"John was right that this is *my* decision," he said, with unmistakable edge. "And I assure you, John, we will not make it in a leisurely manner. But it's important to get it right. If we're going to debate on spending and deficits, there are consequences to the decisions we make. And the allies have to buy in to what we might be expecting them to do, and they will be looking for a plausible story for how this ends."

In meeting after meeting with his war cabinet, the president pressed for a sharper definition of the mission. "The goals need to be realistic and narrowly tailored to serve our national interest, and they need to be achievable," the president told them. Yet, even as he elicited agreement on scaled-down objectives, Gates and his commanders clung to the McChrystal plan and troop request. Obama was frustrated: "If we can't describe closure, if we can't describe the end point, it's an open-ended commitment," he complained. "No one can describe closure here."

I had no doubt that Gates, Mullen, and the commanders were earnest in their recommendations and more attuned than anyone in the room to the wages of war. Even so, presidents have to weigh their decisions against a broader array of considerations. It is the tension between the civilian and military roles—a tension that occasionally boiled over.

After a meeting on October 26, from which many of us were excluded, Rahm told me that he had confronted Gates. "I said, 'Bob, you're boxing the president in. You know that forty thousand is just the beginning and in ten months or a year you'll be asking for more. There's no end to it.' And he just stared at me. 'Well, then you guys better think of something.' I said, 'Us guys, Bob?' I've never seen such a campaign waged against the president of the United States."

Three days later, the president made an unannounced midnight trip to Dover Air Force Base to greet a military plane carrying the remains of fifteen servicemen and three Drug Enforcement Agency agents killed in Afghanistan. He stood at attention and saluted as their flag-draped coffins filed by, then spent hours consoling their families. It was almost dawn when he returned to the White House. I asked Gibbs, who had accompanied him, what the president had said on the way home. "Nothing," Robert told me. "He just looked out the window and said nothing."

Obama knew that a surge of troops in Afghanistan would ensure that there would be many more flag-draped coffins and heartbroken families before he could bring the troops home. "It was very, very sobering," he said. "It reminds you that there are real, grave, human consequences to these decisions. It's not just about moving pieces around the board."

In the midst of the deliberations, I got a call from Colin Powell, who spoke with the wisdom of a man who had been on both sides of such debates, as a military commander and civilian authority.

"Just remember that he's the commander in chief and they ain't," he said. "They want more troops. They'll *always* want more troops. History has shown that this is not always the right answer. My advice is that you take your time."

On November 11, Veterans Day, the war council went through the force options, including a new Gates variation, which called for thirty thousand to thirty-five thousand additional troops, down from the forty thousand McChrystal had requested. The president, however, was focused on not just the size of the force but also the timing of its deployment. Obama had been shown a graph of the proposed troop buildup and its projected drawdown. The chart assumed a process that would last some six to eight years and cost fifty billion per year, far lengthier and costlier than he believed wise or doable. Even if it made sense and he agreed, there was no guarantee he could bring Congress along for such a plan. "I don't know how I am going to describe this as a surge," he said, "if in five years from now, we're only where we are now in terms of troop levels. I want to look at an option that is not open-ended, and puts troops in for eighteen to twenty-four months and then begins thinning them out." Holding up the chart, he said, "Why can't we move the bell curve to the left, get the troops in and out sooner?"

The accelerated pace would project greater force in faster to stem the Taliban's progress, train the Afghan military and police to the best of our capacity, and allow us to intensify operations against Al Qaeda. An aggressive timetable for the drawdown of our troops would also put pressure on Karzai and the Afghan army to get serious about defending their own country. "Karzai needs to know that this is a no-kidding deal," the president said.

By the end of November, the president had made his decision. He would accept the military's revised manpower request, identifying the defeat of Al Qaeda as the core mission and establishing more modest and achievable goals for Afghanistan. Most important, they had agreed on an accelerated timetable—not just to send the troops, but also to bring them home. "It creates an inflection point," he told me. "It puts this war on a path to end." Before Obama finalized it, however, he had to be absolutely certain that his commanders were on board.

"I want to make sure everyone is on the same page, and if not, they state a clear alternative," he told his war cabinet at the ninth and final meeting of what was being called the AfPak review, which went late into the night. "We need to leave here with a unified military and civilian position. Our goal is not perfection in Afghanistan. It is to stabilize key population centers and transfer to Afghan forces. If you don't think we have a chance to achieve the goal I've set out, say so now. If people think that a two-year timetable is not possible, let me know. If we're not all in, now's the time to say so . . . I don't want to be in a position years down the road, where someone says, 'We're not there yet. We need more.'"

One by one, they embraced the plan without reservation. "I will, and the military leadership will, support your decision," Mullen assured the president. For all the controversies that would follow, Obama has kept his promise to bring our troops home: there were nearly 180,000 Americans serving in Iraq and Afghanistan when he took office; at the end of 2014, that would be down to just over 10,000—though the emergence of the brutal Islamic State of Iraq and Syria, or ISIS, would compel him to reengage American forces there.

On December 1, Obama flew to West Point to announce his decision on Afghanistan before an audience of young soldiers. After the speech, the president plunged into the crowd, painfully aware that some of the cadets joyously jostling to shake his hand would lose their lives as a result of the order he had just unveiled.

Susan called me after the speech. As a mom, she was heartsick over the sacrifice that the surge of troops would mean. "I hate this war," she said, "but tell him I thought he did the best he could."

I passed her message on. "Tell her the commander in chief probably hates it as much as she does," he said.

Still, Obama didn't shrink from his responsibilities as commander in chief. For all of Bush's bluster, Obama hit Al Qaeda with a fury his predecessor had never mounted. On his watch, drone strikes in Pakistan, Yemen, and Somalia systemically eliminated many of Al Qaeda's top leaders.

He didn't need any more evidence that Al Qaeda was a threat, though there was plenty in the constant stream of intelligence that greeted him in his national security briefing each day.

Throughout my years in the White House, Obama would have to guard against both large-scale, command-and-control-style attacks such as those on September 11, 2001, and the growing threat of "homegrown" acts of terrorism. Even on Christmas Day.

When Congress finally adjourned on Christmas Eve after the Senate passed its version of the health care bill, the president flew west to Hawaii to join his family's vacation and I headed to my place in Michigan for some badly needed rest. That blessed peace lasted all of several hours. On Christmas Day, an e-mail arrived from Bill Burton, the deputy press secretary, who'd traveled with the president to Hawaii: "Wanted to make sure you all saw and read this report of an explosion on board a plane landing in Detroit from Amsterdam today. I'm flagging because I know these events of interest sometimes go unnoticed. . . . . but I assume that this will be a story of size once the reports are out. With a fire on board and injured passengers, according to initial reports."

"Story of size" didn't quite capture the full impact of it, as we would learn in phone calls throughout the course of the day.

Just before the plane landed in Detroit, a young Nigerian named Umar Farouk Abdulmutallab had tried to detonate plastic explosives packed in his underwear, but the device failed to trigger properly and, instead, burst into flames. Whisked away after the plane landed safely, the scalded would-be bomber admitted that he had been dispatched by Al Qaeda in the Arabian Peninsula. There had been vague "chatter" in the intel stream for weeks about the potential for a Christmas Day attack. I surmised that this was, in fact, it. It would be reported that just two months earlier, Abdulmutallab's father had volunteered concerns about his son's "extremist" views to a CIA agent at the American embassy in Abuja, Nigeria, but that information had languished on someone's desk. While his name had been added to a larger terrorist database, he was not included on a No-Fly List that would have tipped authorities before he was allowed to board the plane. In other words, we got lucky.

Obama had been fully briefed, and stayed in constant contact with his team over the weekend. We decided to put Janet Napolitano, the director of homeland security, at the top of several Sunday morning news shows to update the nation on the incident and the ensuing investigation. Gibbs would appear on several shows as well. He asked me if we should also put the president out on Saturday night, so Americans could hear from him directly. "No," I said. "Napolitano is going to be out tomorrow. She can deliver the message. Let's give the poor guy some time with his family."

It was a huge mistake, and one we would never repeat. When big things happen, people expect to hear from their president. It doesn't matter how many hours he had been working on the phone or in briefings. People want to see the president of the United States and *know* that he's in charge. Obama didn't face the cameras until the following Monday, prompting criticism that he had been disengaged. Napolitano's Sunday show appearances only compounded the problem.

On Saturday night, we held a call to prepare Napolitano. On the call, I confronted her with Republican charges that the security apparatus had failed. Napolitano, a bit defensive, said something about the system "working." We all jumped on the answer. John Brennan, the president's Homeland Security adviser, said "human error" might have come into play. This much we knew: there'd been a terrorist with a bomb on a U.S.-bound plane, and the only thing that had prevented a catastrophe was the bomb's malfunction. It was hard to argue that the system had "worked."

The next morning, the usually sure-footed Napolitano took the interviewers' bait. "Once the incident occurred, the system worked," she said on one show, while using similar phrasing on others. "Everything happened that should have" after the plot was foiled, she said.

Once the incident occurred? But *why* had the incident occurred in the first place? And what could have been done to prevent it? Napolitano and the administration became piñatas for a bipartisan line of stick-carrying critics.

It wasn't until Tuesday, when the president addressed the incident for the second time in as many days, that the administration publicly acknowledged a "systemic failure." Obama ordered a comprehensive review of how the No-Fly List could be strengthened. He also wanted the establishment of a clear protocol for the interrogation of terrorism suspects for intelligence purposes before they were read their rights and charged. In this case, however, none of it mattered. Abdulmutallab provided valuable intelligence to his civilian interrogators, was tried and then convicted in the district court, and was sentenced to four lifetime sentences in a federal supermax prison.

Obama was determined to carry out his responsibilities to protect the American people against these ongoing threats. At the same time, he also was committed to reversing and reforming some of the controversial antiterrorism tactics the Bush administration employed after 9/11. Unwinding the country from this history would prove maddeningly difficult.

He pledged as a candidate to ban the use of torture, which he did almost immediately after taking office. He moved, over the objections of the intelligence community and after much internal debate, to release classified documents detailing acts of torture and other "advanced interrogation techniques," and the legal rationale behind them, that had been employed by Americans against suspected terrorists. Yet to the chagrin of many of our supporters, other documents remained classified when he felt they would endanger American troops and personnel. The president also refused cries from the Left to prosecute Bush administration figures for their role in this dark past, choosing to spare the country what he felt would be a divisive, backward-looking trauma.

Few issues were more vexing than closing the prison camp at Guantánamo Bay, Cuba. While the Bush administration had released several hundred detainees from Gitmo, more than two hundred detainees, scooped up overseas for suspected involvement in terrorism, were still being held there. Some had been there for years, foreign nationals languishing in "preventive detention," unable to be tried because of a lack of legally admissible evidence, but deemed too dangerous to release.

Obama and the military wanted to clear these cases and close Gitmo, whose existence not only raised serious constitutional issues but had become an anti-American propaganda gold mine for Al Qaeda and its supporters.

So the president signed an executive order the day after his inauguration to begin an orderly shuttering of Guantánamo, to be completed within a year. But before long, congressional Republicans seized on the issue, stirring "not in my backyard" panic about the prospect of Gitmo detainees on American soil. That panic eventually consumed many Democrats as well. His efforts frustrated, the president turned to developing a sounder legal regimen for the indefinite detainees, but this didn't satisfy a group of leading civil libertarians Obama invited to the White House in 2009. Some represented organizations such as the ACLU; others, clients at Guantánamo. All believed that this "preventive detention" was an affront to our constitutional principles, and looked to a president, rooted in their community, to do something about it.

"We didn't choose the field we're playing on, and we will continue to try to change it," Obama told the group. "But, to be frank, I don't think it helps when I'm equated to Bush in your press releases.

"We have different roles," he explained. "You represent clients, and you are doing exactly what you should. I am the president of the United States, with the responsibility to protect the American people. Do we just release them and take the chance they blow you up? There's only so much a democracy can bear."

You come to expect the unexpected in the White House. It's part of the daily regimen. Yet on October 9, I woke up to some truly startling news. "And word from Norway this morning that President Barack Obama has won the Nobel Peace Prize," blared the newscaster from my clock radio. It had been a typical too-brief night's sleep and I wondered if I was dreaming. I bolted up and grabbed my BlackBerry to confirm the news, which I greeted as more of a surreal challenge than a cause for celebration.

Obama had been in office for less than a year. He had banned the use of torture, worked (if unsuccessfully) to close Guantánamo, and pushed for new limits on nuclear weapons—but what, exactly, was he getting the award *for*? Whatever the rationale, my guess was that Obama was being honored for his galvanic, groundbreaking election, which had inspired so many around the world. Still, I anticipated a deluge of questions about the president's deserved-

ness from a cynical media and what would certainly be an incredulous opposition.

When Gibbs woke him up with the news, the honoree was also nonplussed.
"Gibbs, what the hell are you talking about?" the president demanded.

"You won the Nobel Peace Prize," he said.

"Are you kidding me?"

"I promise you, sir, that I wouldn't wake you up to play a joke," Gibbs replied. "You've won the Nobel Peace Prize."

"Gee," Obama said, absorbing the unlikely news. "All I want to do is pass
health care."

Later that day, he told us about Malia and Sasha's disarming reaction. "They
came in this morning and Malia said, 'Good news, Daddy. You won the Nobel
Prize and it's Bo's birthday,'" she said, in reference to the family dog. And Sasha
said, "Plus this is a three-day weekend!" At our urging, Obama shared his
daughters' comments with reporters, as he acknowledged the surprise honor
with the proper mix of gratitude, humility, and more than a touch of bewilderment.

What made this unsolicited award even more complicated was that it came
in the midst of the president's deliberations about what to do in Afghanistan.
He knew the final decision on a troop increase would come shortly before the
Nobel ceremony in December. The president of the United States might be
stepping out of his war council to accept the Peace Prize. "I want to stress my
role as commander in chief," he told us, thinking ahead. "I don't want to give
our friends on the other side a chance to run this One World stuff against us."

Occupied with his decision on Afghanistan and the critical speech at West
Point announcing the surge of thirty thousand more troops, which would take
place just nine days before the Nobel ceremony, the president wouldn't focus
on his Nobel address until after the West Point speech was delivered. Having
just been consumed by the debate over the need for war, the president understood the case he wanted to make. A few hours after we arrived, Obama delivered an elegant, well-reasoned speech that, like the man himself, blended
genuinely high ideals with cold-eyed realism.

"As someone who stands here as a direct consequence of Dr. King's life
work, I am living testimony to the moral force of non-violence," he said. "But
as a head of state sworn to protect and defend my nation, I cannot be guided
by [those] examples alone. I face the world as it is, and cannot stand idle in the
face of threats to the American people. For make no mistake: Evil does exist in

the world. A non-violent movement could not have halted Hitler's armies. Negotiations cannot convince Al Qaeda's leaders to lay down their arms. To say that force may sometimes be necessary is not a call to cynicism—it is a recognition of history, the imperfections of man and the limits of reason."

That night, at a warm and intimate Nobel dinner, I was seated next to Gro Brundtland, a physician and public health crusader who, in 1981, became the first woman to serve as Norway's prime minister. Brundtland was a warm and witty dinner companion who shared the lessons she had learned through three stints at Norway's helm. "If you're going to lead, you have to make decisions, some of them hard, and you can't look back," she said. "And you have to make them with the long term in mind. If you're just worrying about the politics of the moment, you'll never get much done." Glancing at Obama, she added, "He seems to understand that."

He certainly did. Few of the decisions he had made would satisfy the politics of the moment. But at home and abroad, Obama was playing a longer game.

TWENTY-SEVEN

THE STUBBORN WORLD

THE ENTIRE WORLD STOOD with America after the 9/11 attacks, but the war in Iraq and the bellicose, go-it-alone Bush-Cheney foreign policy had squandered much of that goodwill, straining our relationships even with long-standing allies.

That's why, as powerful as the scenes were in Grant Park and across America the night Obama was elected, I was moved to tears as I watched the footage of the joyous, spontaneous celebrations that broke out in other countries. As Obama predicted back in 2006 when we discussed whether he should run, it would speak volumes to the world if a relatively young African American, who came from little, could be elected president of the United States. His election also spawned the hope that a president whose father was from Africa and who had spent part of his childhood in Indonesia would have a richer sense of the world and its interconnectedness. So while he worked to shore up the economy and end two wars, Obama was also focused on mending old partnerships and building new ones to address common problems, from terrorism to nuclear proliferation to climate change. To that end, he would visit twenty-five countries on four continents during the two years I was there.

Some of the early trips were consumed by the economic crisis—G20 and G8 meetings, at which Obama argued for coordinated action among the world's leading economies to stem what had become a global recession. Others were NATO meetings, where he shared his strategy for winding down the war in Iraq and refocusing the war in Afghanistan. Everywhere he went, he lobbied relentlessly, leader to leader, for America and its allies to coordinate punitive economic sanctions in order to curb Iran's nuclear ambitions—sanctions that ultimately gave us the leverage to force Iran to the negotiating table.

One of the extraordinary benefits of my job was a ringside seat on many of these journeys. I watched a president eager to change the equation on the world's knottiest problems only to confront obstacles, such as age-old tribalism and parochial politics every bit as intractable as those he faced at home.

The fifty-kilometer stretch of road from Riyadh to Jenadriyah was how I had always pictured Saudi Arabia, parched and brown, a difficult climate in which to make things grow—that is, until we arrived at the sprawling horse farm of Abdullah ibn Abdilaziz, the king of Saudi Arabia. As we approached, the terrain suddenly changed from brown to green, the result of the elaborate irrigation system used to keep grass growing for the enjoyment of his majesty, his guests, and, perhaps most important, his thoroughbred treasures. Abdullah, then eighty-four, was the country's sixth king since his father founded the modern Saudi Arabia, a country beneath which sits nearly one-fifth of the world's oil. That bounty, coupled with the monarchy's shrewd, iron-fisted rule had made the House of Saud a regional and global power.

So many of the world's troubles emanated from this region. Osama bin Laden was a Saudi national, as were fifteen of the nineteen hijackers who struck America that September day in the name of Islam. The president's mission on this journey was to reach out to the mainstream Islamic world, and in doing so, to isolate the extremists. So it made sense to begin in Saudi Arabia, home of Mecca, birthplace of the Prophet Muhammad. On this journey, Obama also hoped to breathe life into the stalled efforts to forge peace between Israel and the Palestinians, a conflict that had defied the entreaties of generations of American presidents and was a continuing source of tension in the region.

We were greeted with a welcoming luncheon for U.S. and Saudi officials dining in what the Saudi royals told us was a "tent." That would be like Americans calling the Grand Canyon the "Little Hole in the Ground." We weren't exactly squatting under canvas or eating food cooked at a campfire. The "tent" was, in the parlance of less exalted worlds, a huge and elegant banquet hall. The president chatted amiably with the king at the head of a long square table. I was seated next to one of the king's many sons. Like most of the men in the family, he had significant governmental responsibilities.

"I liked President Bush," the son said, speaking of Obama's predecessor.

"He was a good man. We would smoke cigars together. But my father told him on Saddam Hussein, 'He can be the ring on the American finger.' But President Bush said, 'He's a liar. I don't trust him.' My father told him, 'Don't stay in Iraq for long. That will lead to trouble. And don't dissolve the army. They will come back to attack you.' But he didn't listen.

"We have great hopes for this president," my seatmate continued. "He is here in the first year in the Middle East! He speaks with understanding."

It was more than just Obama's words that convinced him of that. Though Obama was a Christian, his ethnicity and his familiarity with Islam, while a source of dark, disgraceful inferences for our political opponents back home, was, for these people, a sign of hope. As we were leaving a brief ceremonial meeting with the king following lunch, the president spotted Abdullah's chief of staff holding his son, an adorable, dark-skinned child with kinky, flowing hair. "I used to have a haircut just like yours," Obama told the wide-eyed little boy, delighting his father and everyone within earshot.

There was power in such gestures, gentle signs that this was a new era and a different kind of American president. Still, as he would quickly learn, the intractable realities of the Middle East, defined by ancient rivalries between Sunni and Shia, Arab and Jew, would not yield easily to his charm, gestures, or persistence. The president met with Abdullah for three hours, leaving without the sought-after commitment for a renewed peace initiative between Israel and the Palestinians. Even kings have to be mindful of domestic politics.

After all the meals and meetings ended that evening, guests were escorted to elegant cottages, where large gift-wrapped packages awaited us on our beds. We might not be leaving the Middle East with peace, but the king didn't want us to go home empty-handed. I ripped open the wrapping on mine to find a green alligator-skin briefcase stuffed with an assortment of jewels, necklaces, earrings, and watches. They had to be worth hundreds of thousands of dollars and would have had me all set for birthdays, anniversaries, and even Valentine's Days for several lifetimes. It was considered bad form to refuse such gifts, but the next morning, the State Department protocol police scooped up the jewel-filled attaché cases to be inventoried and stored back home. "Aww, can't we keep a *few*?" Valerie joked with a smile as she surrendered her loot.

The centerpiece of the trip was scheduled for the next day, in Cairo, where Obama would deliver a much-anticipated speech directed at the Islamic world. Determined to start a new dialogue and to repair the rift created by the war in Iraq, Obama had contemplated such an address from almost the moment he took office. He and Ben Rhodes had traded multiple drafts, and the president had spent much of the thirteen-hour overnight flight from Washington to Riyadh honing his words. Before delivering it, though, he would visit another of the region's longtime rulers, Hosni Mubarak.

Obama was a college student when the former military commander became president of Egypt in 1981, following the assassination of Anwar el-Sadat. Mubarak had maintained tight control of his country ever since, while mostly upholding Egypt's peace treaty with Israel, and maintaining a vital alliance with America.

While Obama was meeting privately with Mubarak, our delegation waited in a reception hall of Al Qubba Palace. The secretary of state was chatting up a tall young man. "That's Mubarak's son Gamal," Hillary explained a few minutes later. "Everyone assumes that he'll be taking over at some point."

Soon we were ushered into a large bilateral meeting between the presidents and their respective delegations. Obama touched on a variety of issues, including the need to support a durable bulwark against Al Qaeda in Afghanistan, and to present a united front against Iran's nuclear ambitions, an easy sell, given Egypt's hostile relations with the Shia regime in Tehran. The president's strongest appeal, though, was for a concerted push for peace between Israel and the Palestinians.

Mubarak, once an appealing, energetic leader, was now eighty-one and showing his age. Our visit was his first major event since the devastating loss, a few weeks earlier, of his twelve-year-old grandson. Whether it was grief or the burdens of almost three decades in power, Mubarak seemed weary and unfocused as he listened to Obama's appeal to their shared interests. "Help us find progress in this peace process and we will reduce the influence of Iran in this part of the world," Obama told him.

How many American presidents and their envoys have made similar appeals over the years? I wondered. The old man leaned closer and, in a gravelly voice, offered observations about the region he knew so well. It felt like a scene from *The Godfather*, an aging don sharing the weary wisdom accumulated over a lifetime of turf wars.

"Netanyahu says he would accept two states in the end," Mubarak said of the Israeli prime minister. " 'We want to live in peace,' he says. I told him that he has to be flexible. I told him, '*We* have peace, but the Palestinians don't trust you. Do something big!' "

"We will work for this," Mubarak told Obama. "But the Middle East is so complicated."

After a symbolic visit to one of Cairo's historic mosques, we made our way through empty streets to Cairo University. Cairo was a ghost town, shut down for Obama's speech, which was broadcast live on state television and monitored closely throughout the Middle East. As I took a seat among the Egyptian dignitaries near the front of a gold-ceilinged reception hall, there was a palpable sense of anticipation. It would have been a major event if *any* American president had spoken there. That it was *this* president at this moment raised hopes that there might be greater understanding, possibly even genuine friendship someday, between America and the Islamic world.

When Obama punctuated his opening salutation with the traditional Muslim greeting, *Assalamu alaykum*—"Peace be upon you"—the Egyptians around me burst into smiles and applause.

"I've come here to Cairo to seek a new beginning between the United States and Muslims around the world, one based on mutual interest and mutual respect . . . ," he told them. "But I am convinced that in order to move forward, we must say openly to each other the things we hold in our hearts and that too often are said only behind closed doors."

He then delivered on that pledge by acknowledging U.S. government actions that had inflamed the Islamic world: the war in Iraq, our use of torture as a tool of interrogation, and the open-ended detention, without trial, of some at Guantánamo Bay. He also pushed back against the defamation of America that had become the mantra of Islamic extremists.

"Now, much has been made of the fact that an African-American with the name Barack Hussein Obama could be elected president," he said, a point that was lost on no one there. "But my personal story is not so unique. The dream of opportunity for all people has not come true for everyone in America, but its promise exists for all who come to our shores—and that includes nearly seven million American Muslims in our country today . . ."

The audience repeatedly interrupted Obama's speech with enthusiastic applause. The clerics relished his every invocation of the words of the Koran. Veiled women in the audience heartily applauded the president's plea for women's rights, a sensitive issue in the Middle East. The audience warmly received the president's call for a Palestinian state, and heartily cheered when he denounced Israel's development of Jewish settlements in occupied territories as a barrier to peace. Yet the hall was conspicuously quiet when the president made a passionate case for Israel's right to exist.

For the speech to be honest and credible, we felt it was essential both to stress our unbreakable bond with Israel *and* to include a statement condemning new Jewish settlements in the West Bank and in East Jerusalem. Opposition to new settlements had been U.S. policy for decades, but the president's blunt restatement of that position in Cairo and his determined outreach to the Islamic community was seized upon by some critics to cast doubt on Obama's commitment to Israel's security and, ultimately, its survival. It was a canard, belied by the unprecedented military aid and unwavering support in international forums the president would give to Israel. And he viewed his persistent call for a resolution to the longstanding siege between the Israelis and Palestinians as a boon to both.

Obama also gave voice to the democratic aspirations of people across the Middle East, who had found inspiration in his election. "America does not presume to know what is best for everyone, just as we would not presume to pick the outcome of a peaceful election," he said only a few hours after we had sat down with the despotic Mubarak. "But I do have an unyielding belief that all people yearn for certain things: the ability to speak your mind and have a say in how you are governed; confidence in the rule of law and the equal administration of justice; government that is transparent and doesn't steal from the people; the freedom to live as you choose. These are not just American ideas; they are human rights. And that is why we will support them everywhere . . ."

Many of the Egyptian officials around me shifted uncomfortably as the president implicitly challenged their domestic politics, where opposition parties were marginalized or banned, the rule of law was administered at the discretion of the rulers, and speech was anything but free. Yet his remarks prompted a rousing response from the auditorium's balcony, where the university's students were seated. "Barack Obama, we love you!" one of them shouted.

Looking back, I am sure the student who shouted in approval was also in Tahrir Square two years later, when the Arab Spring swept Mubarak from power. Perhaps he was even the young man I saw on television proudly hoisting the handmade sign reading, "Yes We Can Too." Yet that inspiring moment faded into the harsh reality that, as Obama noted presciently in Cairo, elections alone don't ensure democracy. The democratically elected Muslim Brotherhood proceeded to subdue civil institutions, trample minority rights, and impose its theocratic agenda on the country, while Egypt's problems continued to grow. Soon, a counterrevolution brought to power a new strongman in the Mubarak tradition, with whom America would necessarily have to deal. Across the region, the hopeful Arab Spring unleashed darker forces, as the impulse for democracy warred with ancient ethnic rivalries.

As Mubarak said, "The Middle East is a complicated place."

After Cairo, the president stopped in Germany, where he would pay his respects to victims of the Holocaust with a visit to Buchenwald, the site of one of the most notorious Nazi concentration camps.

We were joined there by Elie Wiesel, the Nobel Prize–winning author and human rights activist. As a teenager, he had been a prisoner at Buchenwald and witnessed his father die there. His unforgettable memoir, *Night*, was my most searing vantage point on the unspeakable horrors of the Holocaust, as it had been for generations since it was first published in the 1950s. "I've been back there only once for fifteen minutes, years ago," Wiesel told us, his eyes brimming with tears. "It's difficult."

While we were together, Rahm asked Wiesel whether it bothered him to share a stage with Angela Merkel, the German chancellor, as he would at Buchenwald later that day. "No," he said, without hesitation. "The children of murderers are not murderers. We cannot carry the sins of the parents forward."

Millions had died in the death camps. Others survived with souls forever scarred. Yet this kindly, thoughtful scholar emerged from the nightmare and years of reflection with a kind of spiritual wisdom that, combined with his gift for narrative, had made him the conscience of the world. Having nearly lost his life at Buchenwald, the wispy-haired, sad-eyed Wiesel had spent much of the rest of his life shining an unsparing light on acts of inhumanity.

"You don't know this, but you changed my life," the president told Wiesel, who was sitting beside him in the limousine on our way to the ceremony. "You came to Occidental College in Los Angeles when I was a student there. I still remember the lecture. You brought some much-needed sobriety to my life. You made me realize that it was time to think about something more than myself."

I was surprised at how fluent Obama was in Holocaust literature. He engaged Wiesel most deeply on the works of Primo Levi, an Italian scientist turned resistance fighter who wound up a prisoner in Auschwitz. Levi recounted his experiences in a series of books and poems before taking his own life in 1987.

"I spoke to Primo a few days before he died," Wiesel told us. "I begged him to let me come spend time with him. I told him I would clear my schedule. He said, 'It's too late.' And I knew he was gone. Primo died at Auschwitz. He lived for another forty years, but he died at Auschwitz."

We transferred from the car to Marine One, the president's helicopter, for the rest of the trip. Wiesel looked out the window as we glided above the heavily wooded German countryside, its lush beauty so incongruous with the death camp the Nazis had built there.

"I think of how you arrived here the first time, piled into a boxcar," I said. "Now you're returning by helicopter with the first African American president of the United States. Maybe history has a sense of justice."

Wiesel smiled and shrugged. "I don't know if history has a sense of justice. But it certainly has a sense of humor."

Of all the people I had the honor to meet during my years in the White House, none moved or impressed me more than Wiesel, who would become a loving friend and mentor. Somehow, when I am with him, I feel closer to God.

Having come of age at a time when the prospect of nuclear annihilation was a day-to-day reality, I have always been fascinated by the relationship between the United States and Russia. The showdown between Kennedy and Khrushchev over Soviet missiles in Cuba was one of the defining memories of my childhood.

Obama was only a year old when that scary drama took place, and was living in Hawaii, as remote from the action as you could be and still be in America. Dmitry Medvedev, who became president of the Russian Federation in 2008, was born three years *after* the Cuban missile crisis. Both were young men when the Berlin Wall fell and the Soviet Union dissolved. Their political sensibilities and careers had been shaped in a post–Cold War world.

Yet when Obama took office, relations between the United States and Russia were as chilly as at any time since the Cold War. At the beginning of his first term, President George W. Bush claimed to have looked into the eyes of then President Vladimir Putin, the ex-KGB officer who has led Russia since 1999, and got "a sense of his soul." Bush liked what he saw. Relations between Bush and Putin soured over time, however, reaching their nadir when Russia invaded the former Soviet Republic of Georgia in the summer of 2008. Now Obama hoped to find in Putin's successor a partner with whom he could deal.

The United States needed Russia's help to curb Iran's nuclear ambitions and to contain North Korea's penchant for belligerence. Also, a range of other issues—from the battle with Islamic extremism to the integrity of supply lines for U.S. troops in Afghanistan—required cooperation between the two countries. Moreover, almost a half century after the Cuban missile crisis took the world to the brink, the question of what to do with American and Russian nuclear arsenals was still unresolved.

As a senator, Obama had focused on the mortal threat that "loose nukes" posed in the age of terrorism. Yet any serious effort to curb nuclear weapons had to begin with the countries that held 95 percent of them, the United States and Russia. The Strategic Arms Reduction Treaty, or START, a nonproliferation treaty between the two nations, had gone into effect at the end of 1994 and was about to expire. At a time when Obama hoped to rally the world around sanctions against Iran's nuclear program, he felt it behooved the United States and Russia to set a good example.

Obama and Medvedev met for the first time in early 2009 at a G20 summit in London. I was struck then by how young and boyish the forty-three-year-old Medvedev appeared. Yet it was his height—even wearing substantial shoes, he was only five foot four—that made the biggest impression on me. I wondered if his diminutive stature was one of the virtues the vain and vertically challenged Putin, just five seven himself, saw in his handpicked successor and placeholder.

Appearances aside, the new Russian and American presidents had much in common. Both were cool, pragmatic lawyers largely unburdened by the passions of the Cold War era, and they quickly developed a comfortable working relationship. Medvedev couldn't ignore Putin, who wielded more power than his new title of prime minister suggested, but at this first meeting, the Russian president still had enough leeway to agree to pursue a nuclear treaty slashing offensive weapons. He also opened the door to cooperation on Iran and other fronts. "You were right about Iran's capacities and we were wrong," Medvedev conceded, establishing the candor that would come to characterize their relationship. After the seventy-minute meeting, both men spoke hopefully about a fresh start and a reset in relations.

A few days later, in Prague, we were reminded of the urgent need for global action to curb the development and spread of nuclear weapons.

While we were there, I woke up with a start when the phone rang in the middle of the night. "Sir," the official-sounding voice on the other end began, "this is the Situation Room. I'm calling to let you know that the event we had been anticipating has happened. You might want to get to the skiff."

I gathered my wits about me and quickly processed the message. North Korea had fired a missile, in contravention of warnings from the United States and the global community. Our intelligence had been closely monitoring the situation and for weeks had been predicting the inevitability of this latest act of belligerency. I threw on a T-shirt and sweatpants and headed for the hotel room designated as the Secure Compartmented Information Facility, or SCIF (the "skiff" my caller mentioned), a secure location—in this case tents specially designed to thwart outside surveillance—where classified communications and discussions could be held. Gibbs was assigned to roust the president. I had left my room so hastily that my hair was standing straight up in the air. When Obama arrived, perfectly groomed, and saw me, he also saw his perfect, unwitting foil. "Axe, I see you decided to dress up as Kim Jong-Il for the occasion," he said, a reference to the North Korean leader with the famously bizarre hairstyle.

Even as I unwittingly provided this moment of levity, the scene was intense. And it gave added meaning to evoking the dream of a world without nuclear weapons, and pledging the U.S. to concrete steps toward that goal, including a New START treaty with Russia.

Three months later, when we arrived in Moscow to advance those talks, the rapport between Obama and Medvedev was apparent. During a nearly four-hour meeting in an ornate, gold-trimmed Kremlin hall, good-natured jousting punctuated their talks. When the subject turned to Moscow's selective barriers against the importation of American pork in response to the H1N1 virus, Obama said, "I appreciate that you have loosened the restrictions on some states—including my own state of Illinois," he said. "I'm sure it was a coincidence!" Medvedev grinned broadly. After the meeting, the two men signed a preliminary agreement sketching the outlines of the "New START," as it would be called, that would yield deeper cuts in the nuclear arsenals of both countries to levels not seen since the early part of the Cold War.

The morning after signing the preliminary arms agreement Obama met with Putin. Their meeting ran long, and it was a sobering harbinger of a turbulent future. The first hour, the president reported, was devoted almost entirely to Putin's energetic litany of complaints about the indignities he felt the West had heaped upon Russia since the breakup of the Soviet Union. If Medvedev was looking past the Cold War, Putin seemed consumed by it. "You are a highly educated man," Putin told the president edgily. "I come from the security sector." Later, I asked the president for his assessment of Putin. "He's smart, tough, clear about his interests, and without a trace of sentimentality."

In the fall of 2009, we traveled to Asia, with Obama's first visit to China as the centerpiece of the trip. Given Asia's meteoric growth, Obama sought to make our engagement in that region a key element of his foreign policy. And in the interconnected world of the twenty-first century, no global relationship was more important or complex than the one with this rising superpower. China is a fierce, sophisticated, and sometimes unscrupulous competitor, but with more than a billion people, it is also a huge and growing market for American goods. A notorious currency manipulator, gaming the system to favor Chinese exports, it is also the largest holder of American debt among foreign nations, which makes confrontations over currency and other economic issues tricky. China has cast a troubling shadow over our allies in the region and has expanded its presence to every corner of the world. It seeks the international community's embrace while routinely violating human rights. Yet it is a necessary ally in forging global responses to challenges such as the ones posed by North Korea and Iran. For the United States, China is a very complicated piece of business.

On our way there, we were reminded that China is a police state and that we shouldn't consider our communications secure. There would be hidden surveillance cameras in our hotel rooms, including the bathrooms. I felt nothing but pity for the poor security officer whose job it would be to monitor me showering. While we were there, police swarmed the floors of our hotel. Gary Locke, the secretary of commerce who would later become ambassador to China, returned to his hotel room to find two men rifling through his things.

Our first stop was Shanghai, where Obama was to hold a town hall meeting with students. Chinese authorities were unenthusiastic about such an unbridled exchange and made organizing the event as difficult as possible. Ben Rhodes, who was assigned to oversee the session for the national security team, had engaged in heated negotiations over the ground rules. By the time Obama and our delegation arrived, Rhodes discovered that his BlackBerry was unusable; it remained jammed by forces unknown for the duration of our stay.

In Beijing, the president and our delegation held a bilateral meeting with

Chinese president Hu Jintao. "Bilats" with the Chinese, I learned, are less free-wheeling exchanges than exercises in responsive reading. The leaders come prepared with written answers to anticipated questions and rarely stray from the script.

The meeting took place in the Great Hall of the People, a massive and elaborate edifice. Obama decided to lighten the mood with a little icebreaker. "I'm told this magnificent hall was built in just ten months," he said. "You'll have to give me the name of your contractor. It sometimes takes that long to get a kitchen done in our country." Our side of the table chuckled, but Obama's quip apparently didn't translate. Hu and his team stared at him, a great, impassive wall of Chinese. After that, we engaged in what was a generally productive, if stilted, meeting.

At the end of our visit, we were treated to the Chinese version of a state dinner. I was seated next to a minister of science and technology who regaled me with tales of the high-speed rail in which China was investing aggressively. China had already built many such lines between major cities. We had been trying, through the Recovery Act, to encourage high-speed rail between ours, but as with so many worthy endeavors, it was running into political resistance over spending.

The highlight of the evening was a musical revue that included the soulful stylings of the People's Liberation Army Military Band, playing, in honor of America's first black president, Stevie Wonder's "I Just Called to Say I Love You." We also heard from happy Uighurs, joyous Tibetan snow queens, and festive Mongolian folk singers, a cross section of China's oppressed minorities. In China, all minorities are valued and respected, the master of ceremonies assured us.

Across the table, a jet-lagged Larry Summers was sound asleep and almost falling off his chair as one of China's leading opera singers was reaching his crescendo. Favreau shot me an e-mail: "It looks like SOMEONE'S in need of a second stimulus." I burst into laughter, which quickly turned into heaving snorts as I tried to contain myself. My outburst drew about the same stony reaction from our Chinese hosts as the president had with his contractor joke. Though nothing was said, they clearly disapproved and wondered what I could possibly have found so hilarious in this stirring aria.

Not a triumph for American diplomacy.

TWENTY-EIGHT

"BRUTAL"

IN THE SPRING OF 2010, I was summoned to a meeting with the Speaker of the House.

I genuinely admire Nancy Pelosi. Watching her shepherd the politically fraught health care bill through her chamber was an awesome thing to behold. She loved to get things done, and was as deft and fearless at navigating the crosscurrents of Washington as anyone I met there.

Yet Pelosi didn't need my pat on the back, and wasn't calling me over to offer hers. She was worried about the upcoming midterm elections, and was unhappy about the president's rhetoric.

I had continued to frame the president's speeches in the language of change, taking aim at excessive partisanship and special interest power that everyone in America except those in Washington recognized as obstacles to progress. The rhetoric, it seemed, didn't sit well with our allies on Capitol Hill.

"We can't run against Washington," she insisted. "We *are* Washington!" I was relieved that no one was videotaping our meeting. It would have made one hell of a Republican ad.

Pelosi wanted us to put the focus squarely on the Republicans, not the entire town. Yet I was reluctant to turn the president, who had run promising to end gridlock, into the point man in the partisan wars. When Pelosi took her case to Obama, however, he was more sympathetic. He appreciated that his string of legislative successes had been achieved only with the help of Pelosi, Reid, and congressional Democrats.

"I think Nancy's right," he said, dialing back some of my less measured language. "Democrats are not the reason things are all gummed up here. We shouldn't give people the impression that the two parties are equally culpable."

And that was only one dilemma. Overclaiming success was the other.

We had made historic achievements up to that point, playing by Washington's rules and pushing our partisan advantage in the Congress. There was undeniable progress on a variety of fronts.

The health care battle was finally behind us. The war in Iraq was winding down, or so it seemed, and a decision had been made about the path forward in Afghanistan that would lead to an end to that conflict, too. Also, by April 2010, it looked as if the economic recovery was fully engaged. The job numbers were steadily moving up, the unemployment rate inching down.

Still, I was focused on the political realm, where the numbers and news weren't nearly as good. The damage from the recession was so vast that it would take years to recover the more than eight million jobs lost. Benenson's polling and Binder's focus groups revealed a nation in which anxiety still ran high and a siege mentality had taken hold, as most Americans were still struggling to keep their heads above water.

Moreover, Obama had been elected promising something more ambitious, a wholesale change in our political culture—and by this measure, he was failing. The country was no less divided. The debate seemed no less riveted in ideology. And the perverse effect of our aggressive challenge to so many institutions was that the lobbyists, hired to protect the special interests, had never fared better. Eager to move his agenda, but denied cooperation from the other party, we had accommodated and abetted the status quo.

Soon enough, a growing debt crisis in Europe caused a pullback in the nascent economic recovery. The jobs picture returned to a dispiriting cycle reminiscent of the administration's early months: minus 125,000 in June and minus another 131,000 in July. As the election season approached, any hint of recovery seemed a distant memory, and any effort to blame this backsliding on Europe was clearly futile. You might as well have been talking Greek to exasperated American voters.

Then, in late April, Carol Browner, the president's chief adviser on energy and environmental issues, brought another headache to Rahm's morning meeting.

"There's oil gushing out of the broken well at the bottom of the Gulf of Mexico," she said, explaining that a deep-sea oil rig owned by BP had exploded. "This could be a real mess."

Carol's report was brief, to the point, and duly noted. Government agencies were activated, but even as we listened, none of us could have imagined just how much damage that calamity would do the Gulf Coast and to the administration.

I learned quickly that, for all the sophisticated technology required to haul oil up from beneath the seafloor miles below the surface, it turns out no one had a clue how to stop an underwater gusher that would foul the Gulf waters, wildlife, and livelihoods of people in four states. An underwater camera, positioned near the leak, became an inky testimony to futility, playing around the clock on cable TV.

It is a fact of modern political life that when such disasters strike, even those Americans who say they believe in smaller government, or no government at all, quickly break glass and call the government, demanding relief. The media fans their expectations and turns such events into tests of leadership. The fact that there was no easy or immediate remedy to stop the gusher notwithstanding, folks wanted action. So as the oil continued to flow, the president increasingly bore the blame. Opponents began calling the leak "Obama's Katrina," and even our friends piled on. "Man, you got to get down here and take control of this!" said James Carville, the Democratic political consultant, and New Orleans resident, who unleashed on us during a national TV interview about a month after the initial explosion. "Put somebody in charge of this thing and get this moving! We're about to die down here!"

With each passing day, the gusher dominated the news and the attention of a White House grappling with a looming midterm election that seemed increasingly daunting for Democrats.

"I have to tell you that for the first time I feel really let down, and it breaks my heart," the president told me in late May, after weathering an hour-long press conference on the leak. "I should not have had to stand up there explaining for an hour because we let this story get away from us. It shouldn't have happened."

Dan Pfeiffer, the White House communications director, was disconsolate after the president questioned us about a barrage of bad press.

"I don't want to be defensive," Dan said, slumped in a chair in his small office near the main entrance to the White House, looking like a man tempted to sprint through those doors and never return. "But it's tough to persuade people you're doing well when there is oil pouring out of a hole, and it's hard to persuade people you're doing great on the economy when unemployment is at nine-point-nine percent!"

For the president, there was no escaping the story, even at a seemingly benign White House event for the Make-a-Wish Foundation.

"There was a little kid with glasses, sitting in a wheelchair," Obama told a few of us in the Oval. "So I lean over to talk to him and he says, 'When are you going to get that hole filled?' And I'm thinking, Come on, kid. Give me a break! Then he says, 'You know if you don't fix that soon, you're going to have a lot of political problems.' I mean, he was like nine years old! Can you believe that?"

He could only laugh about the kid, but the advice was no joke—and by June, Obama, who was leading oil spill meetings that resembled a war cabinet, was blunt about the toll the ongoing siege and stalled recovery were taking. "We have to get back to where we were a month ago," he said. "We are back to where we were a year ago. There is a feeling of chaos in the world."

The president summoned Rahm and me to the small, private dining room next to his office to vent about the oil spill problem.

"So how do we get out of this mess?" he asked us, as he ate an impeccably healthy lunch. "We have to cauterize this thing because it's paralyzing. It's corrosive to the morale of this White House. It's corrosive to *me*!"

Rahm laid out a cohesive plan, already under way, to recover damages from BP, repair the coast, and reform oversight of deep-sea drilling.

In subsequent weeks, the president would summon BP executives to the White House for a tongue-lashing over their apparent negligence, compelling the oil giant to pony up twenty billion dollars for reparations to the coast and the fishermen and hotel and restaurants owners whose businesses were damaged by the disaster.

Still, the paramount challenge remained the one a nine-year-old boy could identify, and it was still the hardest to solve.

One day, at the height of our distress, I sought a few moments' escape at Ike's, a little deli in the basement of the Old Executive Office Building, across the street from the White House. As I was walking in, I noticed Steven Chu, the secretary of energy, sitting alone at a table in the corridor, doodling on a napkin.

"Steve, what are you doing here?" I asked.

"I think I've figured out how to shut down this well," he said, lifting up his napkin to share his work. Chu, a Nobel Prize–winning physicist, then launched into an impenetrable monologue on how to detect the well pressure and all the implications of that. I stopped him in midflow.

"Whoa, whoa, whoa," I said, holding up my palm. "I barely made it through high school physics. But have you shared this with anyone who can do something with it?"

Chu wound up leading an all-star team of scientists that augmented the BP team and, ultimately, played a huge role in capping the leak. Still, the intervening months had been a symbol of government futility that, when added to the economic reverses during the summer, robbed us of the forward momentum we had hoped for with the job growth in the spring.

Just as we were close to plugging the leak, I got a message from a media star who wanted to talk about oil.

"Listen," Donald Trump said when I called him back. "That admiral you have down there running this leak operation seems like a nice guy, but he doesn't know what he's doing. I know how to run big projects. Put me in charge of this thing, and I'll get that leak shut down and the damage repaired."

I thanked the Donald and assured him of our optimism that a solution was close at hand. Either way, I promised to check back with him within a few weeks. By the time I did, the leak had finally been plugged.

"Yeah, yeah, it looks like you have that one under control," Trump acknowledged, quickly moving on. "But I've got another thing for you. I build ballrooms. Beautiful ballrooms. You can go to Tampa and check one of them out for yourself." Not being much of a dancer, I didn't quite know where this was heading. "I see you have these state dinners on the lawn there in these shitty little tents. Let me build you a ballroom you can assemble and take apart. Trust me. It'll look great."

In the midst of all this dismaying news, another unwelcome and unexpected problem unfolded in June, in the pages of *Rolling Stone*. For some inexplicable reason, General McChrystal and his team had granted extraordinary access to an edgy reporter named Michael Hastings, during a trip to Paris, where they had gone to brief NATO leaders on developments in Afghanistan. Hastings, who had spent time with them there and in Afghanistan, was perfectly positioned to pick up on all the towel-snapping fun of McChrystal's team, including derisive comments made about Vice President Biden, or "Bite-me," as one of the general's aides called him; and about Jim Jones, the president's national security adviser, whom another aide labeled "a clown." While the president was spared such harsh descriptors, another McChrystal aide revealed his disappointment upon meeting the president in the spring of 2009. The headline on the *Rolling Stone* piece, "The Runaway General," wasn't chosen idly. Though the general himself was shown as more circumspect, he was present for much of the inappropriate banter, and he made a number of embarrassing remarks.

Obama liked and admired McChrystal, and he feared that a change in command at a time when the war effort was at a critical juncture would be a setback. Yet he felt that many of the derisive comments reported in the piece represented a challenge to civilian authority and could not be allowed to stand. Despite Gates's recommendation that McChrystal be allowed to hang on, Obama accepted the general's resignation, replacing him with David Petraeus.

"This is not a good thing," he told us, after meeting with McChrystal for twenty minutes in the Oval Office. "It is not a good thing. It was the right thing to do. But I don't want anybody exploiting this or making it seem as if we're triumphant about it. If I find anyone doing that, I will land on them like a ton of bricks."

We had a few big wins before Congress left town. The president signed the Dodd-Frank financial reform law, and the Senate confirmed Obama's second Supreme Court pick, Elena Kagan, the former Harvard Law School dean who had been our solicitor general. In Kagan, Obama saw a leader who could match wits with Chief Justice Roberts. "Roberts thinks strategically about these decisions," he said. "Elena will, too. I think she can be a real leader on the Court."

These substantive gains did little, though, to lift the pall hanging over the White House, and the relentless pressures were beginning to tear at our team. We appeared wounded and inept, and nothing titillated Washington more than the sense of blood in the water, particularly when the blood belonged to the smart-asses who had defied the Washington establishment to get there.

As the message strategist and frequent voice of the administration, I felt particularly vulnerable, a condition exacerbated by the fact that I was physically exhausted and mentally drained. Some days, I was so beat I felt as if I were having an out-of-body experience. I would speak during a meeting or interview and my voice sounded as if it were coming from some other person. All I could do was listen carefully as I spoke, hoping my words made sense or, at the very least, sentences.

In trying to meet the president and Pelosi's mandate, I had written a strategy memo in the spring and refined it for summer, urging the president and

Democrats to posit the fall elections as a choice between moving forward or returning to the failed policies of the past. Still, the plain fact is that it is hard to turn a midterm election into anything other than a referendum on the party in power. Anticipating a huge drop-off in voter turnout, most of it among young and minority voters who had come out in droves for us in 2008, the prospects for the fall were dismal.

As Congress got ready to leave town, Pelosi called me in for another two-hour lambasting. "The most accomplished first two years of any president, and no one knows what he's done," said Pelosi, who obviously took pride in what they had achieved together. "It's a communications failure."

No one was feeling the pressure more than Rahm. He had been more responsible than anyone for producing the Democratic majority in the House. He had personally recruited dozens of new members in 2006 and had lived and died with each of their races. They were his protégés and his friends. Now, as he looked out at the political landscape, Rahm could see that many of his recruits would be casualties come November. The DCCC chairman who had elected them was in danger of becoming the chief of staff who helped preside over their defeats. The fifty-four thousand jobs lost in August, and myriad polls, added to the fear of big losses in the midterms.

That pressure revealed itself at one of Rahm's early-morning meetings in August, when I raised two potentially explosive issues. One was a New York City controversy over whether a Muslim group could build a mosque near the site of what had been the World Trade Center. The other was a movement in Congress to amend the Fourteenth Amendment to the Constitution, which confers citizenship on any child born in the United States. We had a press conference scheduled for the end of that week, and I said it was likely the president would want to weigh in on both if he were asked. That didn't sit well with Rahm.

"Then we're cancelling the press conference," he said, panicked at the prospect of Obama taking stands on these freighted issues that would rile swing voters. "How many bricks do you think this load can stand?" he demanded. His consternation only grew when we raised the issues with the president.

"I'm happy to take these questions," he said, as I had predicted. "The Fourteenth Amendment? The amendment that guarantees equal protection under the law? We're going to tamper with that for politics? It's offensive. And folks want to build a mosque on private property and they can't? That's offensive, too. This is not who we are. I would love to get those questions. These folks out there play to people's fear and anger. This is not who we are. Or it is a part of who we are, but it's the worst part."

While the press conference was cancelled, we proceeded with an off-the-record luncheon for some of the print reporters who covered the White House. Predictably, the mosque question came up.

"This country was built on the principle of religious freedom," Obama responded. "That we would tell people that they could not build a house of worship, with their money, is deeply offensive."

"That's really interesting, Mr. President," said Margaret Talev of *McClatchy*. "Are we the only ones who know you feel this way?"

The question stung Obama, who assured the reporters that he would be addressing the matter soon. On our way back to the Oval, the president said, "We have a Ramadan dinner here tomorrow night for leaders of the Muslim community. If you guys don't find some outlet to address this before then, I am going to do it there."

Rahm was livid, convinced that the rest of us were encouraging the president. He thought it was unnecessary for Obama to wade into choppy political waters that would create problems for other Democrats. Yet the president was determined, and did make a statement at the Friday night dinner. "You guys did this," Rahm fumed, storming into Gibbs's office where a number of us had gathered. Predictably—at least predicted by him—Rahm was pummeled over Obama's statement by his former colleagues, home for the break and nervous about their prospects.

By the time the story broke, I was in Italy for a long-planned vacation with Susan. Soon after arriving, though, I was flat on my back, knocked down by a parasite or stomach virus that lingered for our entire stay. Susan enjoyed gourmet Italian meals at the villa in Tuscany where we were staying, and brought back dry toast and ginger ale for me. The only virtue of the vacation debacle was that it forced me to discipline my diet.

When I returned, the president was reflecting on our quandary.

"I've been too isolated, too shut off," Obama told me. "I need to go out there and be myself. Reagan was an actor and he was good at reading scripts. That's not me . . . I just don't know how we change this sour mood, this blanket of pessimism out there. I know I can't do it myself. But it's what I continue to think about."

In early September, I got a call from Bill Daley giving us a heads-up (a five-minute one) that his brother was about to announce that he was not running for reelection as mayor of Chicago. "He's done," Daley told me. "Twenty-two years as mayor is enough." It made sense. Rich's standing had suffered in recent years. His wife, Maggie, was in ill health. Still, it was hard to imagine him giving up a job he loved so much.

I also knew instantly that Daley's decision likely would change my world, too.

Ever since Rahm was elected to Congress, we had discussed the possibility that he would one day run for mayor. It was a job tailor-made for him. Successful big-city mayors, particularly Chicago mayors, have to be tough, larger-than-life characters with an ability to cut a swath from the neighborhood streets to the downtown boardrooms. Rahm is exactly that kind of person.

Minutes after Bill's call, Rahm appeared at my door. "You heard about Rich?" he asked, hands on his hips. "What do you think?"

I knew Rahm wasn't asking me for my astute analysis of Daley's decision or tenure. "You have to run," I said. "This is the right time."

The race was the following February, with filing in late November. To set up a campaign and meet the filing requirements, he would need to leave by early October at the latest. He would take a few weeks to make a decision. Yet standing in my office that day, Rahm already knew in his heart that he was going home. It was the job he had long coveted as well as the escape from the White House that he needed.

One thing none of us could escape was the omnipresent drumbeat of unsolicited counsel coming from all quarters. That cacophony reached surreal proportions in late September, when I traveled to New York with Obama for the annual opening of the United Nations General Assembly. UNGA week is always a scene, mixing world leaders, politicians, and cause-oriented celebrities. Rupert Murdoch and Mayor Mike Bloomberg had made a practice of co-hosting a dinner during the week for an eclectic handful of invited guests. At a rooftop reception afterward, I got a full blast of advice from a cavalcade of stars. Barbra Streisand was one who summoned me over for an urgent consultation.

"He needs to speak to people in simple, easy-to-understand ways," said the chanteuse, who famously sang that "people who need people are the luckiest people in the world." On this night, though, she offered a slightly different take on "people." "I hate to say to say it, but people are stupid. Bill Clinton really knows how to speak to them."

Then I was confronted by Marianne Williamson, the self-styled spiritual author and Democratic activist from LA, who had written an array of books on love, miracles, and healing of the soul. Yet she didn't approach me on a mission of love or healing.

"Do you know how betrayed and devastated we are?" she demanded. "Do you know how *let down* we feel?"

Just to get my bearings, I asked her who "we" were. "The Left!" she said. "Just remember. We got you elected! And then you give us a health care plan without a public option? It's so disappointing."

At the end of the evening, Mayor Bloomberg added his two cents—or whatever the corresponding number is for a billionaire.

"You know what his problem is? You have to like people to be successful. You have to connect," the mayor said, opining on the president. "I saw him greet people at the golf course. You probably told him to do it. But he doesn't *feeeel* it. You have to have that!"

I have a lot of respect for Bloomberg, whose public works and private philanthropy have made a real difference for his city and far beyond. But "warm" and "fuzzy" were not the first words that came to mind when describing New York's brusque and sometimes imperious mayor, which made his critique of Obama more than a bit ironic.

During the dinner, Murdoch, who was seated beside me, insisted that the president had to move on immigration reform. "We have to do something about immigration. We have to protect our human capital," he said, a common and valid lament of the business community about highly skilled, young professionals, trained in American institutions but denied the right to stay and work in the United States.

"But the solution has to be comprehensive," I said. "We can't just attack a piece of the immigration problem. And, you know, there's one big thing that you can do to help, and that is to keep your cable network from stoking the nativism that keeps us from solving this."

Murdoch shrugged. "You'll have to talk to Roger about that."

"Roger" was Roger Ailes, the impresario Murdoch had hired to create and build the Fox News network, which, by catering to a conservative viewership, had become one of the greatest profit centers of Murdoch's News Corp empire. As it happened, I already had a coffee set up with Ailes for the next day. Even though Fox had kicked the living hell out of us, often in ways I found patently dishonest, I enjoyed Ailes, an old political warhorse and masterful storyteller.

Back in 1988 he was the architect of one of the most brilliant and diabolical ad campaigns in the history of presidential politics, helping to bring Vice President George H. W. Bush back from seventeen points behind to defeat Governor Michael Dukakis of Massachusetts.

A working-class son of small-town Ohio who came of age in the 1950s and '60s, Ailes still speaks the paranoid, antigovernment language of that era's John Birch Society, and he built a wildly successful television network to appeal to people of like mind.

"The problem with liberals is you all want to intellectualize things," he told me, fulminating about Obama's position on the New York mosque. As he spoke, it struck me that Ailes was one of those people whose form reinforces their image. Short and squat, he very much *looks* like a bulldog. "You never connect with people. Where's his heart? Does he know what it means to be an American? Does he care?"

Even considering the source, it was a stunning question, coming just two years after Obama was swept into office by passionately articulating a shared vision of America—the country, he often said, that had made his story possible. He had connected plenty well *then*.

Having been beaten up by the Left, Right, and center, I returned to Washington to hunker down for the final run-up to the midterm election. Every scrap of data suggested that we were going to be routed, and the White House was, not surprisingly, on edge.

In this emotional tinderbox, it didn't take much to set off sparks. In mid-September, an authorized biography of Carla Bruni, the wife of French president Nicolas Sarkozy, created a five-alarm fire. The book alleged that Michelle Obama, sharing with Bruni her feelings about the role of First Lady, had said, "It's hell. I can't stand it." Michelle heatedly denied it.

Concerned that Bruni's claim, if unchallenged, could become a troubling story line for both Obamas, Gibbs swung into action, hammering every Frenchman he could get on the line for hours until that country's government formally disclaimed the quote. It was heroic duty, as the president himself would acknowledge, but when we arrived for the morning meeting, Valerie startled us with her report. "The First Lady is very disappointed in how the Bruni story was handled." I was sitting next to Gibbs, which was like watching the formation of a volcanic eruption. He was understandably proud of the effort he had put in the day before, not to mention the positive result, and was absolutely stunned to be told that he had fallen short. "Excuse me?" he said. Valerie repeated her claim. I wanted to grab Robert and put my hand over his mouth because I knew this was about to get ugly. Flushed and angry, he directed his remarks to Valerie, and the First Lady in absentia, in words that were unmistakably clear, if imprudent. Then he stormed out of the room.

A week before the election, I sent the president a seven-page memo analyzing the morass we had now found ourselves in, and how we could get out of it.

"More than any issue, the fundamental appeal of our campaign was to bring a renewed sense of responsibility to Washington," I wrote. "That meant overcoming withering partisanship and ideology, and bringing people together around commonsense solutions to stubborn problems. It meant reining in the power of special interests that tilted policies in their own favor at the expense of the middle class and the country. It meant disciplining the budget. It meant doing business in the light of day, so the American people could see how decisions were being made, and participate in them."

We had put a premium on getting things done, which was his ultimate responsibility. In doing it, though, we appeared to have ignored, if not flouted, our campaign commitments. We would have to reset, I said, and return to a focus on our core themes.

As he prepared for what promised to be painful postelection interviews, however, the president was not in an apologetic mood. He might acknowledge errors in style and approach, he said, but he believed in the programs and policies he had pursued. He was proud of historic achievements, such as health reform, which would pay huge dividends to the country and everyday people for generations to come.

"I've read some of the commentary, and here's the problem," he said. "They want me to say the policy was wrong. That it was a mistake to do what we did. And I'm not going to say it because I don't believe it. And so they'll never be satisfied."

On Election Night, a few of us gathered in my office to monitor returns, which turned out to be not as bad as had been predicted, but far worse. As state after state reported, Democratic member after Democratic member was swept away, delivering the House to a new tea-flavored Republican majority. In all, sixty-three seats were lost.

Obama called and started ticking off the names of some of his favorite young House members who were in tough races. "What about Patrick Murphy in Pennsylvania?"

"Gone," I said.

"Boccieri in Ohio?

"Gone."

"Perriello in Virginia?"

"Gone."

"The sad thing is that we're losing all these promising young guys who were the future of the party," he said glumly.

At midnight, after reading the coverage, he sent me a succinct e-mail: "Brutal."

The only thing that consoled me was history, the knowledge that the sainted FDR did even worse in the 1938 midterms, when Democrats lost seventy-one seats. Two years later, he was reelected by a wide margin. I even recognized a perverse benefit in what Obama would publicly acknowledge as our "shellacking." The Republican Party was now firmly in the thrall of its right-wing.

The same forces that had energized the GOP for its House takeover would play an outsize role in the 2012 presidential nominating process. This meant the nominee would have to pass their litmus test by pledging to support draconian budget cuts and oppose any tax increase, even on the wealthiest Americans. He or she was likely to oppose immigration reform, making it harder for Republicans to capture swing states with large blocs of Hispanic voters in the general election. And the Republican nominee would line up with the social conservatives on issues such as the right to choose, giving us a chance to replicate the large advantage we held with women voters in 2008. The result was bad for governance and bad for the country, but from a strictly political point of view, not necessarily bad for our chances of winning reelection.

"I think the seeds of your reelection may have been planted yesterday," I told the president the day after the carnage. He looked at me for signs of temporary dementia, perhaps brought on by stress.

Obama was less concerned about reelection than the upcoming lame-duck session of Congress. Many essential items had been put on hold for the midterms. Unchastened by the beating we had taken, and perhaps spurred on by the realization that his hefty Democratic majorities would expire in eight weeks, the president arrived for work the day after the debacle toting an ambitious wish list for the rest of the year.

As official Washington was hanging black crepe on the White House, Obama was rallying his team.

"Okay, we got our asses kicked," he said. "But we have stuff we have to get done here, so I want to focus on that."

If Congress failed to act to extend the Bush tax cuts for the middle class, every American would face a steep tax increase on January 1, placing an unwelcome new burden on them and the still-fragile economy. Obama and Democrats had promised to end the tax cuts for people earning more than $250,000 a year, a popular position. Yet Republicans were dead set against any such decoupling.

Beyond taxes, Obama was desperately fighting to ratify the New START nuclear arms treaty with Russia. He wanted votes on the DREAM Act, to make the children of undocumented immigrants eligible for citizenship upon completing military service or some college; and repeal of the "Don't Ask, Don't Tell" policy banning from military service gays and lesbians who weren't willing to keep their sexuality secret—a change for which the president had been working since taking office. He wanted to pass new laws to help ensure food safety, and favored a children's nutrition law that had been championed by the First Lady. "First, it's a good law. Second, I want to go home at night," he said wryly.

I thought it was nuts. What about the midterm election did he not get? Yet Biden, it seemed, who had spent much of his life in the Senate and had good relations across the aisle, was bullish. Obama had sent him to the Hill in October to try to get some of our judicial appointments unstuck, and Biden used the opportunity for a broader discussion with McConnell. The truth was that Biden, a proud, lifelong politician, was a far better conduit for such deal making than Obama, and he came away convinced that we could reach a sweeping agreement with the opposition. For their own reasons, the Republicans wanted to get the New START done, and didn't want to get blamed for raising taxes. "But they're never going to decouple the high end from the middle class," the VP said of the Bush tax cuts. "And if we force the issue, I would bet over time more than a few of our own folks will get wobbly."

After days of back-and-forth, the contours of a deal emerged. It would require the president to swallow a two-year extension of the entire Bush tax cut, including the portion for the wealthy. It would include a one-year payroll tax cut for every American and a one-year renewal of extended unemployment insurance for millions of Americans, who otherwise would have lost it on January 1.

The final stumbling block was the extension and expansion of estate tax exemptions, which were set to expire as well. Under the Republican proposal, more multimillion-dollar estates would be sheltered from taxation. Yet the Republicans were refusing to continue refundable tax credits for low-income workers. "One principle we can defend is that taxes shouldn't go up on anyone right now," Geithner said. "To raise taxes on millions of Americans while we sweeten the pot for the wealthy? It's a terrible deal. Almost indefensible." Obama agreed. "I'm not going to give new tax breaks to folks at the top, and see taxes go up on folks at the bottom. Unless we get those refundable tax credits, it's no deal."

When the Republicans caved on the tax credits for the working poor, the president announced the deal, which touched off an immediate firestorm among the Left, who felt Obama had given up too much.

I was asked to call a few commentators to explain the deal, including Keith Olbermann, whose hour-long show was a mainstay on the left-leaning MSNBC. When I reached out to him by e-mail, though, the tempestuous host wasn't interested in chatting.

"You can kiss the base goodbye," he said, in a terse reply.

"I think when they learn what is in this package, the base will think differently," I answered.

"Oh THAT'S the problem?" he shot back. "The people who elected you are too stupid to figure out what's going on?"

At the end of the week, Bill Clinton dropped by the White House for lunch, during which the presidents went over details of the package. When Clinton blessed the deal, Obama suggested the two of them make a joint statement. They wandered into the press office, looking for someone who could open the door to the White House Briefing Room. "We want to talk to some reporters," the president explained to a junior staffer who was hoping to catch up on some work on what was supposed to be a lazy Friday afternoon. Gibbs came along and asked the presidents to stand by while he rustled up the press corps. When he did, Obama spoke briefly, turned the lectern over to Clinton, and departed for an event with the First Lady. Clinton continued for nearly half an hour, brilliantly and cogently making the case for the deal.

Some reporters wrote after Clinton's exegesis that Obama had diminished himself by ceding his lectern to his predecessor. Obama waved that off. "I don't care about that stuff," the president said. "He was doing the Lord's work in there."

As Biden forecast, the deal paved the way for other votes that had been frozen. The DREAM Act failed, albeit with 55 votes, but the president got everything else on his list—New START; the food safety and nutrition bills; the defense authorization bill to fund the ongoing war efforts; and, to our mild surprise and great relief, the repeal of "Don't Ask, Don't Tell," a major milestone in the social history of the country.

Despite unhappiness among some on the left and right over aspects of the tax deal, the lame-duck session, historic in the scope of what it achieved, was met with relief from most Americans, who were just happy to see something get done on a bipartisan basis. Coming after a devastating election, the deals proved a surprising close to what had been a challenging year, and Obama's poll numbers would soon reflect this.

By then, I was a lame duck as well.

In September, anticipating the outcome of the election, I made public what I had planned from the beginning, announcing that I would be leaving the White House in early 2011 without specifying an exact date. In my own mind, I wasn't sure. I knew Plouffe was coming to replace me, and he would arrive in January. Yet as dizzying as the White House merry-go-round could be and as spent as I was, it was still hard to jump off the carousel. For two years I had been in the middle of everything, in close and constant contact with the president, grappling with extraordinary, sometimes excruciating issues and battling on his behalf on television and in the halls of Congress. Like any addiction, it's not good for you in the long run, but it's damned hard to kick.

The president resolved that problem for me.

"You have to get out of here early in the year," he said, as we chatted in his dining room in mid-November. "You need some time to clear your head. Hell, I'd like to do it myself. But I can't go. You can. And I need you rested and ready for the campaign. You're the closest to me, to how I think. I need you firing on all cylinders."

He had handled the matter well. After all, this just codified what we had agreed to two years earlier. Still, it was uncomfortable. On the same day, he told me that he would be naming a new press secretary, which seemed inevitable after the Carla Bruni flap. Robert and I bore the scars of a thousand battles, inside the White House and out. Rahm was gone. Now it felt as if the president were clearing the decks for a new team. "Next to me, you get beat up the most. Gibbs is next," the president said.

I stayed a month into the year, long enough to help guide the State of the Union speech process and to overlap briefly with Plouffe. On my last weekend, some friends threw a large going-away party, which was a wonderful coda to my Washington years. The president came and milled around for a couple of hours with a crowd of my White House colleagues, government leaders, and quite a few news media folks with whom I had become close. Having been raised in journalism, I still—for all the lofty company I had been keeping since my arrival in Washington—felt most comfortable with reporters.

Then there were my speechwriters, the brilliant, spirited kids whom I would miss the most. They presented me with a leather-bound, gold-embossed book entitled, *Hello, Wordsmiths*. It was a volume of major speeches on which we had collaborated, annotated with alternately touching and hilarious commentary. On an inside page, I saw an inscription in familiar handwriting that caused my eyes to well up. The president had written, "This book is a testament to our collaboration and how you've always been there to help me find my voice."

PART SIX

TWENTY-NINE

FROM THE OUTSIDE
LOOKING IN

For four years, two on the campaign trail and then two in the White House, I had been in constant motion, on call 24/7. Then, on February 1, 2011, when I left Washington and returned to Chicago, I had no schedule and only the vaguest sense of what I would be doing in the coming weeks and months. The sole trapping left of my former life was the Secret Service, and that would end quickly. As a courtesy, my splendid detail leader, Cleveland Brown, accompanied Susan and me on the flight home. Soon enough, I thought, as Cleveland whisked us past airport security, I would be back in long lines with everyone else, slipping off my shoes, emptying my pockets, and walking through metal detectors.

Contributing to an eerie sense of otherworldliness was the weather. Chicago was about to welcome us with a blizzard. Ours was one of the last flights to land before the airport shut down. I found the snowstorm comforting, a fitting "welcome home" to the Windy City. Throughout my time in Washington, I had referred to myself as a "Chicagoan on Assignment." It was my way of signifying that my heart and soul were firmly planted on the shores of Lake Michigan, where I would eagerly return after my tour of duty. Now that day had come, and the whole town was at a standstill due to one of its signature winter storms. And so was I.

After a short break, I would begin to travel the paid speaker's circuit. I would return to my old offices in the loft building in River North, by the elevated train tracks, renting workspace from my old firm. But during my first weeks home, and without much to do, I would occasionally catch Susan staring at me with all the focus of an intensive-care doctor, apparently checking my vital signs to gauge how I was tolerating this sudden separation from all the action back in DC. "I just worry you'll be bored," she said. I wasn't, exactly. It was good to be home with her and enjoy the newfound freedom to do whatever I pleased. Still, I found that, too often, I was incessantly checking my iPhone, perusing my e-mail, and glancing at Web sites for breaking news—habits that were hard to break.

The most difficult adjustment, though, wasn't so much that I missed the action as much as I missed the main actor. Throughout the previous seven years, I had been in close touch with Obama. In the White House, I would see or speak to him several times a day. Unrealistically, as it turned out, I had expected that contact to continue. "Don't worry, I'll be calling you at least once a week," the president had assured me when I went to the Oval to say good-bye. Yet as days and weeks passed, I rarely heard from him. My e-mails to him, which once fetched quick replies, often went unanswered. Suddenly, after serving for years as Obama's principal adviser, my advice was not being solicited and was, perhaps, unwanted. The silence stung—and I found it depressing.

It had been a while since I had seen Obama when I returned to Washington in late spring. He had just spent the previous few weeks mired in a dreadful budget standoff. It ended with a deal that merely postponed some tough choices that needed to be made, which of course left everyone involved looking bad, especially the president.

I was in town for the over-the-top celebrity weekend that had become the White House Correspondents Dinner. As usual, the dinner called for the president to deliver a comedic speech that skewered him and others. I had contributed a few lines to his routine, and came by the White House to go over the speech with him and his speechwriters.

It was a Saturday afternoon, and the White House was largely empty. The president had just returned from a tour of tornado-devastated communities in Alabama. "I met a little boy down there, maybe ten years old, who was standing with his dad," he told me as we ate lunch in his dining room. "And as the dad told me the story of how their house was blown away around them while they huddled to survive, I could see this kid's lip quivering. He was trying so hard to be brave, you know, for the president. So I just kind of wrapped him up in a hug and told him it was going to be all right."

It was a nice, warm conversation of the sort I had often shared with Obama over the years.

While we were speaking, there was a knock on the door. The president's assistant peeked in and passed him a note, which he acknowledged with a quick nod. "Can you step out for a minute?" he asked me. "There's a national security briefer here who has to go over something with me." I didn't think anything of it, and waited outside the Oval with Favreau and some other speechwriters. When we reconvened to go over the speech, Obama laughed his way through the comedy routine until we got to a joke about one of his prospective opponents, Tim Pawlenty, the former governor of Minnesota. "Poor Tim Pawlenty," the line went. "He had such promise, but for that unfortunate middle name, bin Laden." It was a self-deprecating joke, coming from a president whose middle name was Hussein. But Obama wanted it removed. "Bin Laden," he said. "Bin Laden . . . that's so hackneyed . . . so *yesterday*. Let's think of something else." I thought it was funny, but he was the guy who had received the 365 electoral votes, so we changed the joke. Even without it, the routine played to rave reviews.

I woke up early the next day to prepare for an appearance on *Meet the Press*, and turned in early that night. I had barely put my head on the pillow when Susan burst in. "You'd better get up," she said. "I think they've killed bin Laden." I scrambled out of bed and looked at my iPhone, which was overflowing with urgent e-mails from the White House imploring me to turn on the TV to hear Obama's remarks.

As I watched the president announce to the nation that bin Laden was dead, killed by an elite unit of Navy SEALs, I thought about our visit the day earlier. Now I understood why he'd wanted the bin Laden joke eliminated. He already had given the order that would eliminate bin Laden! *"That's so hackneyed . . . so yesterday."* Obama undoubtedly knew when we met that if the risky mission had failed, it would trigger huge recriminations that might doom his reelection prospects. "Amazing," I told Susan. "He was completely calm. As normal as could be. Not a hint that anything out of the ordinary was going down." This is one of Obama's greatest strengths. He can be painfully deliberative in making decisions, assuring himself that he has thought things all the way through. Once he decides, however, he won't wring his hands or second-guess himself. He is willing to live with the consequences, an indispensable virtue in a president.

Given the complexity of the mission, the uncertainty as to whether bin Laden was even in the compound, and the divided counsel of the president's advisers, Obama's decision to authorize the raid—made without Pakistan's knowledge let alone its approval—was a courageous one. "Honestly, I didn't have the balls to tell him to go for it," Biden confided to me later. "And neither did many others around the table, regardless of what they say now. It was a big, big call."

When I visited the president a few weeks later, I mentioned the iconic photo that had been released of him and his team watching a feed of the mission, just as one of the two U.S. helicopters crashed in bin Laden's compound.

"Were you thinking about Jimmy Carter?" I asked. Carter's failed mission to rescue American hostages in Iran in 1980, in which U.S. choppers crashed in the desert, was a harbinger of his doomed candidacy for reelection.

"How could you not?" Obama said. "But mostly I was thinking about those SEALs and getting them out of there."

But the afterglow of the successful mission was short-lived. Washington became mired in a high-stakes standoff between Obama and House Republicans over the once-routine act of raising the nation's debt limit. The Republicans essentially handed the president an ultimatum: agree to deeper budget cuts than he thought wise or fair, or face the first-ever default on the nation's debt, which would have catastrophic implications for our fragile economy.

Faced with this stark choice—a lousy deal or economic disaster—he chose to save the economy. But this episode only showcased Washington politics at its worst—gridlock, brinksmanship, and an unsatisfying "solution" that merely kicked the can down the road. Many of our supporters were outraged because, after fighting for "balance," the president had been forced to accept a cuts-only package. The Tea Party had thrown a tantrum and, in the minds of many of our supporters, had won; the hostage takers had walked off with the ransom.

A few days after the debt ceiling resolution, Susan and I returned to Washington for the president's fiftieth birthday party at the White House. The combination picnic and dance party was, for a beleaguered Obama, a welcome interregnum in a downbeat summer. After the beating he had been taking, it was nice to see the guy I used to call Barack happy and relaxed, amid a sea of friends, family, and a smattering of celebrities. When we left after midnight, the president was still cutting a rug in the middle of the crowded dance floor, Michelle in one hand and a martini in the other.

The next morning, he might have felt like reaching for another libation. Standard and Poor's, dismayed with the debt resolution, downgraded America's credit rating for the first time ever. That decision, along with burgeoning debt crises in Italy and Spain, triggered the steepest drop in the stock market since the height of the financial crisis.

All in all, things were a mess.

I thoroughly understood the strategy of trying to transcend Washington's dispiriting partisan divides, not least of all because it was a fundamental principle that had drawn many independent voters to us in 2008. I recognized that we needed to signify seriousness about deficits and spending. Yet by almost single-mindedly pursuing those objectives for much of the year, we had largely lost the sense of advocacy for the middle class and middle-class values that had been the lynchpin of our message. After the debt ceiling debacle, Obama's image as a leader had taken a major hit.

The president called me while vacationing on Martha's Vineyard in late August, clearly angry over his lost summer. "I'm going to spend the next couple of weeks thinking about where we go from here," he said. "We're not going to play defense from now until next November."

I agreed, and took the opportunity to send him a blunt memo summarizing my thoughts on what had gone wrong these past few months.

"People need to know what you are fighting for beyond the bloodless, ministerial task of cleaning up the balance sheet," I wrote.

You were elected, first and foremost, because you brilliantly and passionately described the central challenge of our time: the erosion of the middle class and the "American Dream"—a phrase that is now in disrepute because it feels to so many Americans like an unobtainable cliché . . . Your message ultimately carried for two reasons: One is that it was rooted in the idea that we are a better and stronger country when everyone gets a fair shot and a fair shake; when hard work and responsibility is rewarded, and all of us are accountable. The second is that it recognized that there are things we must do together as a country to ensure a brighter future . . .

You have been way ahead of the curve on the impact on the middle class of revolutionary changes in the economy and the unsavory tilt of the playing field in this new Gilded Age. Much of what you've done as President has been aimed at addressing these challenges, and at restoring the economic security so many Americans have lost. But we are not consistently telling that story. We are not consistently communicating the values of fairness and responsibility. We are not consistently describing the vision of an America where hard work once again pays off, and opportunity is widely available, or how everything you're doing is aimed at achieving that goal . . .

Despite everything, however, I'm convinced we can win this election. It won't be easy. But the research is clear. Our values and vision beat theirs.

We just have to be seen as *fighting* for [people], day-in and day-out, and identify those who stand in the way.

September 2 was my thirty-second wedding anniversary—a gratifying, if unremarkable milestone—but it became a memorable day for another reason. Plouffe called me with news of the monthly jobs report. He was never one to be carried away by irrational exuberance, but on this occasion he sounded downright glum.

"You won't believe this," he said. "In this whole, vast country, guess how many jobs were created last month?" I didn't hazard an answer, but assumed from Plouffe's tone that the news wasn't good.

"Zero!" he said.

"Zero?" I asked. "You mean exactly none?"

"I mean we didn't lose a job, that's the good news," he said. "And we didn't gain a job. That's the headline. Zero is the number. It's implausible. Ridiculous! I'd rather have lost a few jobs. You can imagine the fun they'll have with this one. We're Mr. Zero!"

It wasn't shocking that job creation had stalled in light of the debt ceiling follies and general economic unease that gave employers pause. The "zero" was just a cruel end to a lousy month, in which Obama was made to look weak and ineffectual.

Even before getting a zero, we had planned for a nationally televised speech to Congress on jobs and the economy, to regain the initiative and restore confidence that Obama had a plausible plan and the gumption to fight for it. I also viewed this as the first speech of the 2012 campaign—a chance to show strength and advocacy and to burnish our economic values.

When I got the first draft, however, it struck me as all wrong. The language was grandiloquent and featured a long, historical windup about how we got into this fix, followed by a detailed discussion on deficits and a robust defense of government. I could imagine eyes glazing over and minds closing across the nation. *Here we go again.* We had a chance for a reset before a television audience of tens of millions of Americans desperate for action and a champion—and I worried that we were about to squander it.

"This is a Joe Friday moment," I wrote in an urgent memo, invoking the laconic 1950s TV detective. "[The American people] don't want a lot of analysis or explanation or rhetorical flourishes. (In fact, in this cynical environment, rhetorical flourishes will work against us.) They want good, solid ideas—in plain, simple English—about how he plans to spur job creation right away. They want to know that the guy in charge isn't out of bullets . . ."

I rewrote the top of the speech to reflect my advice and better capture the mood of the country. Favs polished it and rewrote its body in language to match—punchy, insistent, and rife with an authentic sense of advocacy that people hadn't heard too often since 2008. Obama skipped the usual windup and plunged right in, with an arresting open that cut through the cynicism and captured the mood of the nation.

"Tonight we meet at an urgent time for our country," he began. "We continue to face an economic crisis that has left millions of our neighbors jobless, and a political crisis that's made things worse. This past week, reporters have been asking, 'What will this speech mean for the President? What will it mean for Congress? How will it affect their polls, and the next election?' But the millions of Americans who are watching right now, they don't care about politics. They have real-life concerns.

"The people of this country work hard to meet their responsibilities. The question tonight is whether we'll meet ours. The question is whether, in the face of an ongoing national crisis, we can stop the political circus and actually do something to help the economy." Here he was interrupted with a burst of sustained applause. "The question is whether we can restore some of the fairness and security that has defined this nation since our beginning."

Delivered with passion and purpose, Obama's performance was more than the presentation of a plan, though the plan was helpful. It was a clear and powerful reaffirmation of the values on which he had run for president and would animate our reelection campaign. It was plainly clear for what and whom he was fighting.

I was thrilled with the speech, and happy when he phoned later that night. "I don't often say it, but I just wanted to thank you," Obama told me. "You did a good job working with Favs in shaping the speech." After spending the better part of the year in the wilderness, cut off from Obama and the action, his call meant a lot to me. I was thrilled to be back in the game—maybe not at center stage all the time, but still a vital resource at critical moments.

As the strong reviews poured in for the jobs speech, I could finally see the way back—most critically, of course, for the president, but also for me.

THIRTY

RESURGENCE

WHEN THE PRESIDENT'S TEAM gathered in the ornate White House State Dining Room, on September 17, 2011, for the first major strategic meeting of his reelection campaign, the setting was far grander than the small conference room where we had held the first Obama for America strategy meeting in early 2007, but there was little of the romantic, tilting-at-windmills exhilaration I remembered. Back then we knew the odds were long, but we were energized by the challenge, and thrilled to have the chance to try to change the world. Now, after three of the toughest years any president had faced, we were just as determined, but far more subdued.

"I know we're probably underdogs," the president said in kicking off the meeting. "But I intend to win this race. There's too much at stake here."

I had come to the meeting on a mission.

After a year dominated by Obama's fruitless efforts to find common ground on deficits with the Republicans in Congress, the president needed to come out swinging for his vision of an economy driven by a growing, thriving middle class. The compelling jobs speech before Congress was a good start, a hint of the power of his economic message and a reminder of his extraordinary gifts as a messenger. Even so, we had to build on it.

Obama had devoted his entire life to the vision of that jobs speech. Yet his focus had become muddled in the minds of voters, diluted by competing messages, a slow economic recovery, and some unpopular decisions, such as the Wall Street rescue forced on him by the financial crisis.

I intended to convey that sentiment in no uncertain terms. "I'm going to go in there and be really blunt," I told Grisolano before the meeting. "And if he throws me out on my ass, so be it. To win this thing, we need Barack Obama to *be* Barack Obama."

To dramatize the point, I put together a short video reel of some of Obama's public moments throughout the years. The first was footage of his magnificent convention speech in 2004, in which he so eloquently gave voice to the hopes and struggles of hardworking Americans he had met while traveling in Illinois. There were some highlights from the 2008 campaign, as well, including the Jefferson-Jackson Day speech that was such an inspiring and authentic manifesto for change on behalf of the middle class. I finished with more recent footage, documenting a restrained president sharing the details of his deficit reduction policies and what they would mean for some distant fiscal year. It was a clinical and bloodless performance, lacking both passion and a sense of advocacy. The contrast was striking—not just in how much Obama had aged during this seven-year journey of ours, but also in his cramped tone.

It was not the Obama we knew, but it was increasingly the one the public was seeing. "We need you to be *that* guy again," I said, referring to the earlier Obama, passionate and purposeful. "The guy who is out there urgently fighting for people and their values, for a country in which folks can still work hard, get ahead, and hope for better for their kids."

This was the issue of our time. This was our North Star. It provided the strongest economic contrast with the Republicans. In response to the crisis, they offered the same old laissez-faire, trickle-down theory—an absolute killer at a time when the yawning gap between the rich and everyone else was growing and the excesses of Wall Street were viewed as the prime cause of our nation's economic woes.

Obama listened impassively, but he was plainly frustrated by my suggestion that he had lost his focus. "I talk about the middle class all the time," he protested, insisting that the media had simply lost interest in a familiar theme. He knew where his heart was, as of course did I. We had shared so many conversations: about the letters he received from anxious Americans, about his life path, and about his disdain for those who mistook their own vast and growing fortunes for the nation's progress. However much he agonized about the problem in private, though, it was not enough to sprinkle mentions of the middle class formulaically in speeches—not remotely the same as waging a day-in, day-out campaign on the issue. That, I told him, was what we needed from him now.

I had never met a brighter person or one more capable of inspiring others.

Yet Obama was inclined to divide his roles, viewing campaigning as one thing and governing as something entirely different. When he was campaigning, he worked hard at connecting with people, invoking shared values, and defining the choice before them. He yielded, albeit grudgingly, to the need for short, message-laden sound bites that reporters would use and voters would remember. As president, however, he had taken to heart Mario Cuomo's dictum that you "campaign in poetry and govern in prose"—and followed it to a fault.

That was most conspicuous during press conferences and interviews. As a candidate, he came to view questions as opportunities to burnish his message. As president, he eschewed that discipline, too often giving long, complex answers—sometimes running seven or eight minutes—and, finally, ending with the point he should have emphasized from the start. During my White House years, he would bristle whenever we tried to push campaign-like discipline on him. "I'm not a candidate now. I'm the president," he would say whenever I complained about the length and construction of his answers. "And people want to know the details."

In drawing this stark line between campaigning and governing, Obama had misread history and his role in it, I would argue to him. Even as they compromised on the details of governance, the truly transformative presidents—be it the Roosevelts or Ronald Reagan—never stopped campaigning or communicating their basic message or core values. JFK's press conferences were exercises in elegant message efficiency. Bill Clinton self-consciously slid to the center after the disastrous midterms of 1994, but he never stopped talking to, or for, his working-class base.

Getting Obama into a campaign frame of mind was the key, and the nearly five-hour meeting in the State Dining Room proved a good start. "We're in campaign mode now," the president said at the conclusion of the meeting. I was heartened to hear this, and as he traveled the country in subsequent weeks, challenging the Republican Congress to pass his jobs bill, Obama appeared ready to embrace it. More and more, he returned to being the advocate for working people. In a meeting with us a few weeks later, he said, "If Congress won't act on this jobs bill, I'm going to take every step I can on my own. We can't wait!" That simple line, "We can't wait," became a mantra for him on the stump, conveying the sense of urgency he shared with the American people.

Obama's mood was brighter when I visited him in the Oval Office in late October. As I was coming in, Michelle was just leaving. She had been in Chicago a few days before, where she had given a truly inspiring speech to the campaign staff. I told the president that FLOTUS had done a great job.

"She always does," he said, beaming at his wife.

"Raised a little money, too," she said, with joking self-reverence.

"And," I added, "she told the kids at headquarters that she's going to jump into the campaign with both feet!" Obama laughed, knowing what a reluctant campaigner Michelle had always been.

"She already is. She just made them believe she's excited about it!" he said, as the First Lady smiled and walked out the door.

"I feel a little better out there," the president said as he settled in behind his desk. "I think this 'We Can't Wait' thing works well. And I'm working on the stump, trying things out. It's not like 2007, where I could test stuff out in New Haven. We're on Broadway every day now. But I am doing some stuff out there that I think works."

In one sense, he was wrong—Barack Obama had been on Broadway since 2004—but he was right about this: things *were* improving. Still, in a conversation a few weeks later, he conceded that he felt constrained by the economic message, and for that he faulted his political advisers. "You want me to be authentic. You want Obama to be Obama. Well, there are other things I believe are really important to the future of this country. I'm pretty sure you guys would say they're *off message*, but maybe part of being *authentic* is saying them. I mean, I don't want to go down knowing I hadn't said everything I wanted because we were afraid to be honest."

Here was the recurring tension between Obama the idealist and Obama the politician; between the man who understood that in order to serve and make a difference, you had to be elected, and the one who sometimes resented the compromises that the process required and the advisers who enforced them.

He repeated that lament at another of our large campaign strategy meetings in November, provoking more than a little anxiety among his team. "There are things I feel strongly about," he said, "things I'll want to work on in my second term. Some of them may make you guys nervous. But Axe keeps saying I should be 'authentic.' So maybe I should go out there and just let it rip."

"Given our situation, sir, I'm not sure we're in a position to go all *Bulworth* out there," Gibbs quipped, referring to the dark comedy in which Warren Beatty plays a despondent senator, on the verge of losing reelection, who goes on a boozy bender of truth telling.

To show respect for the president's concern while setting the matter aside for a while, we suggested he write down those things he wanted to talk about on the trail, for discussion at our next meeting.

A week later, the president returned to the group with the yellow legal pad, covered with his meticulous scrawl—for pages and pages. It was not just a list of important issues on which he felt he had been insufficiently forthright, but expansive thoughts on each. He had apparently been up until 2:00 a.m. preparing for this session. "Maybe we overshot the runway when we suggested this exercise," I murmured, after glimpsing his notes.

The president's list didn't surprise me: immigration reform, climate change, Guantánamo, poverty, the Israeli-Palestinian conflict, and of course gay marriage, something that had vexed him for years. They were difficult issues, rife with controversy and political challenge, that he had hoped to tackle and resolve before his presidency was done. Yet his efforts so far had revealed just how difficult that would be.

On some, he had been stymied by Congress: immigration reform and the DREAM Act, to give legal status to the children of illegal immigrants; "cap and trade," to curb the emission of greenhouse gases at the root of climate change; and the closing of the detention center at Guantánamo Bay. Those efforts hadn't satisfied his own party activists, who were intent on holding Obama to the letter of his campaign promises and who scolded him for not making each of these issues the same, single-minded priority that health reform had been.

He had fought for refundable tax credits for the working poor and vastly expanded college aid for needy students. Yet here he was, the first black president, a man who began his career in the inner city as a community organizer, and poverty had *grown* on his watch. He regretted not having made its eradication more of a visible national priority.

From almost his first day in office, he had pushed the Israelis and Palestinians for a two-state solution, but his efforts, like those of presidents before him, had been run aground by the intractable politics of the Middle East. He was frustrated with both sides, but felt he had pulled his punches with Netanyahu to avoid antagonizing elements of the American Jewish community.

Gay marriage was a particularly nagging issue. For as long as we had been working together, Obama had felt a tug between his personal views and the politics of gay marriage. As a candidate for the state senate in 1996 from liberal Hyde Park, he signed a questionnaire promising his support for legalization. I had no doubt that this was his heartfelt belief. "I just don't feel my marriage is somehow threatened by the gay couple next door," he told me. Yet he also knew his view was way out in front of the public's. Opposition to gay marriage was particularly strong in the black church, and as he ran for higher office, he grudgingly accepted the counsel of more pragmatic folks like me, and modified his position to support civil unions rather than marriage, which he would term a "sacred union." Having prided himself on forthrightness, though, Obama never felt comfortable with his compromise and, no doubt, compromised position. He routinely stumbled over the question when it came up in debates or interviews. "I'm just not very good at bullshitting," he said with a sigh after one such awkward exchange.

By 2010 he had told reporters that his position was "evolving," and in 2011 the administration announced that it would no longer fight in court to uphold the Defense of Marriage Act, a controversial Clinton-era law absolving federal and state governments of their obligation to recognize gay marriages sanctioned in states where they were legal. Yet if Obama's views were "evolving" publicly, they were fully evolved behind closed doors. The president was champing at the bit to announce his support for the right of gay and lesbian couples to wed—and having watched him struggle with this issue for years, I was ready, too. Jim Messina, the campaign manager, was nervous about the impact of such a step. "We've looked at this and it could cost you a couple of battleground states; North Carolina, for one," he said. By year's end, however, Obama was no longer interested in analysis. "I just want you guys to know that if a smart reporter asks me how I would vote on this if I were still in the state legislature, I'm going to tell the truth. I would vote yes."

As Obama ran through all the issues on his legal pad, I doubted there was anyone in the room who disagreed personally with the positions he took. As weighty as they were, though, none of them rose to the top of the list of concerns in a country where the economy was still weak and the middle class was under siege. Going *Bulworth* on a range of "hot-button" issues was not only risky; it would detract from our ability to drive the winning economic argument. While some of these issues (gay marriage, immigration reform, climate change) had important, targeted appeal, we simply couldn't afford to make them the focus of the campaign to the exclusion of our economic message.

I suspected that Obama, who seemed relieved just to get all these nagging concerns off his chest, received exactly the political counsel he expected. What he didn't expect was that his private ruminations would quickly leak. Only days after our meeting, two reporters working on a campaign book, Mark

Halperin and John Heilemann, inquired about the president's *Bulworth* list, on which they were shockingly well informed. While their account wouldn't appear until after the election, the breach of trust was truly distressing.

"Why would anyone on our team do that?" Obama asked, more hurt than angry. I was just angry. "Because that's how people in this town certify their own importance," I told him. "You should read these folks the riot act at the next meeting and walk out." I was late for the next session, and by the time I arrived, the president already had come and gone, after delivering a dressing-down to the group for what he viewed as an unforgivable show of disloyalty. As a result, he told them, he would no longer participate in such meetings. For the rest of the campaign, our strategy sessions were restricted to a handful of key players.

It only compounded our frustrations when nervous party insiders, many of whom had not supported Obama in the first place, lobbied publicly and privately for the president to boost the ticket by asking Hillary Clinton and Joe Biden to swap places. As secretary of state, far from the political fray, Hillary now polled far better than Biden or, for that matter, the president—and, or so the argument went, would add some needed pizazz to the ticket.

I thought it was preposterous.

Obama and Biden had forged an extraordinary working relationship. The president had handed his VP the nightmare assignment of managing the Recovery Act, and he had done a remarkable job, ensuring that it came off better than anyone had a reason to expect. Obama also assigned Biden to work with the contentious factions in Iraq to make sure they could form a functional government. Also, Biden was an invaluable back channel to his old Senate colleagues, with whom he had friendly relations dating back decades. Buoyant and unfiltered, Biden's rhetorical flights sometimes landed him in unexpected places, giving our press shop occasional heartburn. Yet he was as warm and caring a person as I have ever known in politics and a very savvy and effective public official.

Obama appreciated his vice president, and the feeling was mutual. One day Biden called me into his stately office, down the hall from the Oval. "Do you remember that conversation we had at my sister's house in Delaware?" he asked, recalling the interview in which he told Plouffe and me that he felt he would be the better president. "Well, you know what? I was wrong. The right person won. He's an incredible guy, and I am proud to work with and for him."

Swapping Clinton for Biden would have been seen as weak and disloyal, I argued, when some in the campaign suggested we had an obligation to test it in polling. When we did, it made no difference. The subject never came up again.

In early December, Obama traveled to Osawatomie, Kansas, the town where, in 1910, Teddy Roosevelt gave his rousing New Nationalism speech, railing against the excesses of the Gilded Age and calling for bold new steps to restore fairness and broad opportunity to the American economy. Now we were living in a new Gilded Age, in which rapid technological advances had generated fantastic wealth and concentrations of power, but also vast disparities in opportunity. So Osawatomie was a fitting place to throw down the gauntlet and set the terms of the upcoming election.

"Now, in the midst of this debate, there are some who seem to be suffering from a kind of collective amnesia," the president said. "After all that's happened, after the worst economic crisis, the worst financial crisis since the Great Depression, they want to return to the same practices that got us into this mess. In fact, they want to go back to the same policies that stacked the deck against middle class Americans for way too many years. And their philosophy is simple: We are better off when everybody is left to fend for themselves and play by their own rules. I am here to say they are wrong." The audience jumped to their feet, interrupting the president for sustained applause that went on for half a minute.

"I'm here in Kansas to reaffirm my deep conviction that we're greater together than we are on our own. I believe that this country succeeds when everyone gets a fair shot, when everyone does their fair share, when everyone plays by the same rules. These aren't Democratic values or Republican values. These aren't 1 percent values or 99 percent values. They're American values. And we have to reclaim them!"

The rousing speech was widely covered and thoroughly analyzed. Some commentators cast it as the president's play to the populist Occupy Wall Street movement that had sprung up organically in the fall of 2011. Yet the values and themes Obama struck in Kansas were the same principles that had driven him since his days as a community organizer in the shadow of closed steel mills on Chicago's South Side. If Occupy Wall Street was an unfocused expression of rage, Obama was arguing for commonsense rules and policies to promote fairness, balance, and a broader prosperity. His speech in Kansas not only captured the zeitgeist of the country, but also set up a critical contrast with the candidate we were likely to face in the dawning election year—Mitt Romney.

Romney had been a runner-up to McCain for the nomination in 2008 and had continued to build an imposing fund-raising and political network. He was a former Massachusetts governor, untainted by Washington—and, at least on its face, Romney's profile as a very successful businessman with the know-how to create jobs offered an attractive rationale for his candidacy in a country still reeling from recession.

Yet in a race focused on economic values, Romney would also be the perfect foil. He had faithfully subscribed to Bush's economic policies and continued to preach the same gospel of deep tax cuts and deregulation. While Obama took steps to save the American auto industry, Romney, whose late father, George, was a former auto executive and governor of Michigan, argued against government intervention in an op-ed famously titled, "Let Detroit Go Bankrupt." Also, as a corporate takeover specialist, Mitt Romney had made his fortune by downsizing companies, outsourcing their jobs, and stripping employee pensions and benefits—all while parking some of the money it generated in offshore tax havens. To his core, Romney was a devout believer in unfettered capitalism and trickle-down economics.

Before Romney could face us, however, he would have to tango with the Tea Party and win over social conservatives concerned about some disturbing acts of moderation in his past. But none of his primary opponents were making an effective case against him, and we wanted Romney's road to the nomination to be as long and bumpy as possible. So, more than a year until Election Day, we decided to take that job on ourselves.

In a conference call with reporters, I unloaded on Romney as a serial flipflopper; a moderate sheep in a conservative wolf's clothing. It was a signal for the Right, reinforcing their latent concerns about Romney's fealty. But the strategy was also a calculated risk. While Romney's moderate past was a potentially fatal flaw for the ideologues that vote in Republican primaries, it would appeal to swing voters in a general election. We were gambling that he would have to thoroughly disown his past positions to get the nomination. And that would make it harder for him to stake out centrist positions in the fall without being ridiculed as a double flip-flopper.

And, as we hoped, Romney responded by working that much harder to court the Right. His team apparently wasn't worried about a future race against a president they believed to be doomed by a struggling economy. But the long, bloody and expensive primary battle, which would stretch deep into the spring, would prove exceedingly costly to Romney.

"I'm feeling strong," Obama said, in a late-night call after his State of the Union address in January 2012, which reprised many of the themes of the Osawatomie speech. "I'm getting that 'What the fuck' feeling back!" As usual, Obama had scanned his iPad for elite commentary on his largely polemical speech, and his indifferent reaction to the critiques he found underscored how true that was. "They say, 'Where are the big ideas?' They just want me to light myself on fire."

There were other reasons for optimism.

The unemployment rate, which had stood at 9 percent or higher for thirty months straight, had finally dropped into the 8s in October. January would be the third straight month of significant job growth, reducing the rate even farther, to 8.3 percent. The auto industry, saved by the president's actions over the objections of Republicans such as Romney, was hiring again. Obama had brought the last troops home from Iraq in December and was making slow, steady progress on his goal of ending our war in Afghanistan. And bin Laden was still dead. We weren't hanging "Mission Accomplished" banners, but when the president declared in his speech, "the state of our Union is getting stronger," it was becoming a little harder for Republicans to evince scorn.

While the Republican candidates continued to spar over immigration, birth control, and just how small and insignificant they could make government, our campaign spent the winter and early spring methodically planning for the general election. The innovation hub at our Chicago headquarters was swelling with a T-shirted, iconoclastic army of young whiz-kids—data analysts, software designers, social media savants—who were inventing new products and programs to expand the reach and efficiency of all aspects of the campaign. From fund-raising and field organizing to rapid response and media placement, they were pushing the horizons of Big Data and the Internet to provide us with a critical edge.

And every so often, things would happen that recalled the enormous stakes.

In May, a few days before Obama's formal launch as a candidate for reelection, I got a call from the president that put all the campaign rigmarole in perspective. He had just returned from a quick, unannounced trip to Afghanistan.

"I visited the hospital, and they said, 'We have a young guy who was really badly hurt. But we think he can hear and understand and that it would mean a lot to him for you to say hello.' So I go in, and this guy was wrapped up from head to toe—just a mess. And I told him how proud we were of him, and how we were all praying for him and hoped he would be back with his family soon. And I didn't know if he was hearing me or not. But I turned to leave, and the doctors called me back. And this kid held up his arm and grabbed my hand. It was all I could do to keep from crying."

As thoroughly as I was engaged in the daily scrum of the modern campaign—the efforts to build a better campaign mousetrap and the cheeky repartee in the media and on Twitter that filled my days—the story of the president's encounter with that soldier made it all seem trivial.

A few days later, I stood with Plouffe at the campaign kickoff, staring at thousands of empty seats in the upper bowl of the Ohio State University basketball arena. "Wouldn't have been an empty seat last time," Plouffe fretted. It was another sign that 2012 would be different, less a lofty movement than a grinding battle to define the race.

The next day, Biden, on *Meet the Press* as part of our campaign launch, changed the subject in an unwelcome way. Asked about the volatile issue of gay marriage, he said, "I am vice president of the United States of America. The president sets the policy. I am absolutely comfortable with the fact that men marrying men, women marrying women, and heterosexual men and women marrying one another are entitled to the same exact rights, all the civil rights, all the civil liberties. And quite frankly, I don't see much of a distinction beyond that."

It was galling because, as Biden surely knew, we had been discussing the timing of the president's own declaration of support for gay marriage. We had talked about making the announcement the following week, during an interview on *The View*, the women-oriented daytime talk show. Now, in a moment of candor and ebullience more than calculation, Biden had beaten us to the punch. He was asked a direct question about his own view, and the blunt-to-a-fault VP had answered with the truth.

I tried feebly to finesse his crystal-clear declaration with a tweet that insisted Biden had merely restated the president's position. "What VP said—that all married couples should have exactly the same legal rights—is precisely POTUS's position," I wrote, trying to parse the un-parsable. By the end of the week, the president had tired of taking a beating for lagging behind his vice president and summoned ABC's Robin Roberts to the White House to make his own position as clear as Biden's. While some on the president's staff and campaign team were furious with the VP for his lack of discipline, Obama was not. The president was certain that Biden hadn't intended to show him up, and refused to come down hard on his teammate for taking a position the two men shared.

"I would have preferred doing this on my own terms, but it is what it is," he told me the night before his interview with Roberts. "I know Joe screwed up, and when I have lunch with him tomorrow, I'm going to talk to him about it. It was sloppy. But, you know, I can't be too hard on him. He was speaking from a bigheartedness."

As in 2008, my role in our newly launched campaign was the message overseer. That meant providing guidance to our folks engaged in battle every day and working with my *Ocean's Eleven* team, back and humming, to flesh out the story we'd be telling in our advertising. We knew we would be under constant attack on TV, not just by Romney but by third-party groups that—thanks to a recent Supreme Court ruling—had been unshackled to spend to their heart's content. Our mission was less to defend the president than to ensure that people understood the choice. That meant aggressively defining Romney, his record and views—and doing that before he had a chance to repackage them for the general election. We persuaded the president that we should front-load our ad buy, taking the risk of having a lighter TV presence than originally planned for the final months of the campaign.

"Every impactful ad I can think of in presidential elections over the past thirty years aired before Labor Day," I told him. "That's when the Swift Boat ads ran against Kerry. Roger Ailes ran most of the ads that sunk Dukakis in the summer of eighty-eight. People don't know Romney. We have to fill in the picture and do it with force before the end of summer. We can always raise more money. We can't raise more time."

After a month of positive advertising about the president's leadership, we launched a new flight in June recalling Romney's economic record as governor. If, as he had been suggesting, he had the secret sauce to repair the economy, how had it worked out in Massachusetts? The answer from our research team: not so well. Under his tenure as governor, the state fell from thirty-sixth to forty-seventh in job creation. When Romney left office, Massachusetts ranked number one in having more per capita debt than any state in the nation.

Our ad makers had a field day taking the Romney record apart. In order to spotlight their good work, we decided to stage a press conference and rally at the State House in Boston, featuring local officials who could attest to Romney's weaknesses as governor. Our communications folks urged me to attend mostly as bait for the national news media. Yet it wasn't just reporters I lured.

In setting the rally on the State House steps, our team had neglected to calculate that Romney's national headquarters was just a few blocks away. As I walked over, someone casually mentioned that there might be a few protesters. I was confronted by what was more like a mob: a herd of young Romney workers who had angled on over to "welcome" me personally to Boston—even if they didn't get my name right.

"Tell the truth, Axelfraud!" they shouted, as I took to the podium. The hecklers were only about fifteen feet away, forcing me to shout over them. I kind of enjoyed this theater of the absurd. But the whole thing looked ridiculous on TV—as the president reminded me when he called that night.

"I see you had an interesting day," he said dryly. "It didn't look like a very good expenditure of your time."

If the event was a flop, our ads were successful in establishing some initial doubts about Romney, his public record, and the image he was selling as an economic savior. There were larger and more damaging questions to come about his business record. Romney had made a fortune as the founder and chairman of Bain Capital, a private equity firm that bought underperforming businesses, forced management and operational changes to wring out greater profits, and then sold them, often at a tidy profit. Those changes often involved wage and benefit reductions for workers, bankruptcy filings to reduce pension obligations, and the outsourcing of plants to low-wage nations. While these practices had helped enrich Romney and his partners, workers—including many who had devoted much of their lives to a company—were sometimes left in the lurch. It was ground zero for an economic values argument.

A super PAC supporting Newt Gingrich had released a vicious video attacking Romney on Bain during the primaries, and we began to revive the issue with the media in May, as a prelude to ads we planned to air in June. Yet Bain, a company with a bipartisan set of partners, had a lot of powerful friends on both sides of the aisle. Without warning and apparently much forethought, Bill Clinton sprang to Romney's defense at the end of May. "I don't think that we ought to get into the position where we say, 'This is bad work. This is good work,'" Clinton said on CNN, before praising Romney's "sterling business career."

We were furious, and conveyed that message through Clinton's staff. When the former president arrived in Chicago a few days later for a meeting of his Clinton Global Initiative, he summoned Messina and me to his hotel. "Guys, I am really sorry," he said. "I just kind of wandered into that one. You know, the truth is, I'm a little rusty." Clinton muted his commentary after that.

No one is immune to gaffes, as Obama would demonstrate a few days later. Nearing the end of a press conference in the White House Briefing Room about worse-than-expected jobs numbers, the president served up a choice sentence that would quickly find its way into Republican ads.

"The truth of the matter is that, as I said, we created 4.3 million jobs over the last 27 months, over 800,000 just this year alone. *The private sector is doing fine.* Where we're seeing weaknesses in our economy have to do with state and local government."

It was a fair point, poorly stated—but the potency of poorly stated points was not lost on us, having hung "the fundamentals of the economy are strong" around John McCain's neck in 2008. Few Americans believed the "private sector" was "doing fine," and Romney quickly pointed to the remark as evidence of a president disconnected from the reality of the American economy.

"I'm sorry to make your job more challenging," Obama said, in a call a few days later. "I hate being sloppy. That was sloppy." I told him we should never have thrown him out there to answer questions when he was sleep-deprived after an exhausting West Coast trip. "I was a little tired," he acknowledged. "But no excuses. It was a screwup and it was mine."

Romney seized on the theme of Obama as a naïve crypto-socialist, and many on Wall Street, eager for one of their own in the Oval Office, were all in. Shortly after Romney clinched the nomination, he arrived in Washington to a hero's welcome at the Business Roundtable, an elite group of CEOs formed in the 1970s to lobby against regulation and corporate taxes. "The president and his folks just don't understand how the private sector works," he said with a pitying smile, as the crowd nodded in agreement.

The scene was galling. Obama had taken the difficult steps necessary to save an economy that, thanks to a lack of rules, had been sabotaged by egregious abuses of the market. Now the Dow was up 70 percent, corporate profits were robust, and the CEOs cheered lustily as Romney smarmily chided Obama for his lack of understanding.

I wasn't the only one irritated by Romney's performance. The president was clearly peeved when he called me that night. "I saw him over there, all full of swagger," Obama said, after watching an account of Romney's speech. "A homecoming of the plutocrats!"

No one doubted that Romney knew "how the private sector worked." He had the fortune to prove it. Yet if his storied career in private equity made him a favorite at the Business Roundtable, it wouldn't, as more details of his business practices emerged, garner the same applause from most Americans outside that room. Only a week later, the *Washington Post* ran an explosive investigative piece on Bain's business practices.

"During the nearly 15 years that Romney was actively involved in running Bain, a private-equity firm that he founded, it owned companies that were pioneers in the practice of shipping work from the United States to overseas call centers and factories making computer components, according to filings with the Securities and Exchange Commission," the *Post* reported, noting that China and India were among the beneficiaries of the outsourced jobs.

"Pioneers" in outsourcing! The *Post* had added new findings and important validation to our research, including a filing by one Bain-owned company offering "a range of services that provide our clients with a one-stop shop for their outsource requirements."

It would be a devastating story, particularly in battleground states such as Ohio and North Carolina, which had suffered deep job loss to outsourcing. What made it worse was that Romney had been barnstorming the country for a year promising to get tough on China, giving us a raft of videotape with which to hang him.

"Romney's never stood up to China. All he's done is send them our jobs," closed one ad we rushed on the air. Another began with Romney sermonizing during a primary debate about the need to get tough on China. "The Chinese are smiling all the way to the bank, taking our jobs and taking a lot of our future, and I'm not willing to let that happen," he earnestly promised. "He made a *fortune* letting it happen," the ad responded, presenting the facts from the *Post* story.

The hypocrisy was breathtaking, and it went to the heart of Romney's campaign. He was going to be the jobs president, the businessman who knew how the private sector worked. Yet now he looked more like a businessman who had worked the system at the expense of American jobs.

After pounding away at other aspects of Romney's business practices, we shifted to his policy proposals, including a familiar-sounding fiscal plan: heavy tax cuts skewed to the wealthy and paid for with deep spending cuts and greater burdens for the middle class. In one ad, we flayed him on the impact of his college aid plan, replaying Romney's priceless counsel to America's youth to "borrow money if you have to from your parents" to pay for an education.

With separate and discrete tracks of advertising, we spoke directly to women, replaying some of Romney's harsh positions on a woman's right to abortion, contraception, and equal pay. We launched Spanish-language media in May, to run through the election, stressing the differences in position on education, job training, and health care.

By the end of July, Romney would be "underwater" in Benenson's battleground state polling, with a majority expressing a negative opinion of him, and Obama would break into a four-point lead, hitting the magic mark of 50 percent.

We were helped along by two developments, one orchestrated by the president and the second coming from a surprising source.

The president had announced in mid-June an executive order deferring deportation proceedings against hundreds of thousands of students and military personnel who were the children of undocumented immigrants. Though not the permanent answer he still sought through the DREAM Act and more comprehensive reform, it brought relief to some young people and produced the expected outcry from Republicans that would only drive Hispanic voters and young people farther away from the GOP.

Then came some news that was far more meaningful than any mere boon to the campaign. The Supreme Court had been considering the constitutionality of the Affordable Care Act, and given the conservative bent of the Court's majority, the outcome was in doubt. We had spent many hours pondering the political implications if the justices were to throw out Obama's signature accomplishment. Would it galvanize our base and sympathetic swing voters? Or would it become a symbol of overreach and failure? Yet for millions of people without coverage, people with chronic illnesses like my daughter's, the stakes were even greater.

On the day the Court was to rule, the loud din that normally engulfed our campaign headquarters in Chicago was reduced to an anxious murmur as hundreds of workers and volunteers crowded around television screens, awaiting word from Washington. I watched with Jim Messina in his office. We had waged the health care battle together in the White House, where Jim was the deputy chief of staff. Now health care and maybe even our election chances hung in the balance.

I was glancing out the window when Messina let out a pained grunt. "That's it," he said glumly, staring at his computer and a tweet from CNN. "They killed it."

Before I could ask much or absorb the meaning of what he had said, we heard loud cheers and applause from the sprawling bull pen outside his closed door. "Then why the hell is everyone so happy?" I asked as we scanned the coverage. We quickly discovered that CNN had gotten it wrong. The law had been upheld—and by the vote of Chief Justice Roberts, no less.

Messina's eyes welled up with tears. Jim was a hard-core political operative, an occasional mercenary with whom I had issues in the past and would again in the future. Even so, we were both proud of the health care law and deeply invested in its survival. We gave each other a big, relieved hug, and then plunged into the celebration outside.

Later that day, the president called.

"I call a lot when things are bad. Just wanted to chew on some good news for once," he said. "I plan to win, but whatever happens, I feel like we've locked something in that will help a lot of people. And that feels good." Before he hung up, he cheerfully shared a data point that he had picked up on one of his regular tours of his iPad. "The one poll I've seen lately that makes me feel good is that sixty-five percent say I would do a better job of dealing with extraterrestrials! Can't beat that!"

It was classic Obama, a sense of what's important coupled with a wry detachment that helped him survive some of the most trying and tumultuous years in American political history. A few days later, at a Fourth of July pool party on the White House Lawn, Kathy Ruemmler, the White House counsel, asked the president if he "didn't every once in a while just want to punch someone in the face."

"No, not really," he said. "There was an old critic who said, 'Everything is either a comedy or a tragedy, and the difference is whether you are on the inside, or on the outside, looking in.' I try to remember that, and step outside on those tough days and see the absurdity of some of these scenes. Plus, we've been at this a long time—lots of ups and downs. You just get used to it."

The next day, we were heading out on a two-day bus tour through Ohio and Pennsylvania. The president was looking over his remarks and practicing his opening. "You know, I'd like to start by saying, 'This is my last campaign. And so I've been thinking lately about my first campaign, and why I got into this business in the first place.'" As he spoke, I recalled the first time I met

Obama, a newly minted law graduate. He saw politics as a calling, as a way to give people a fighting chance. Now, as he sat in the forward cabin of Air Force One reserved for the president of the United States, he was summoning that same spirit as he prepared to make his case to folks at venues ranging from big-city rallies to small-town squares to rolling farms. This is the guy, I thought, as I watched him throw away his notes and speak from his heart. This is the guy I know.

Though he lacks the grab-your-elbow, stare-into-your eyes shtick of a Bill Clinton, Obama enjoys people and relishes escaping Washington and getting into the factories, diners, and taverns where folks are interested in more than the Gallup daily tracking poll. He called following the trip, still jazzed by the chance to mix with regular people and by the encouragement they offered.

"I told the senior staff today that we dodged a lot of bullets in the past couple of weeks—immigration, health care, jobs numbers that could have been worse. Like Churchill said, 'Nothing is as exhilarating as the sound of bullets whizzing past your head.' All we have to survive now are four more jobs reports, maybe a European crisis or two, three debates, and the occasional gaffe. And then we're home free!"

Throughout August, we held a narrow but steady three- to four-point lead in our own polling. Our gamble to front-load our media had paid off. Now, even with the burdens of a fragile economy and the onslaught of ads blaming us for it, I liked our chances as we rounded the turn into the final stretch.

If the front end of presidential campaigns is dominated by advertising, the back end is focused on the big set pieces—conventions and debates, orchestrated extravaganzas that take place when most Americans are just beginning to focus on their choices.

Romney got a little buzz heading into his convention by choosing Paul Ryan, the conservative House budget chairman, as his vice-presidential nominee. It was a surprising pick. I expected Romney to reach out for a moderate. Instead, he picked the author of the radical, tax-cutting, Medicare-voucherizing Republican budget that Obama had consistently flayed to such great effect. The choice tied Romney closer to the unpopular Republican Congress. Still, it was clearly a genuine meeting of the minds. Romney shared Ryan's economic views, and the young, attractive, and telegenic congressman was a favorite of the social conservatives and Tea Party activists who would fill the seats in Tampa.

When the Republican convention began, however, a day late due to a Democratic-leaning hurricane named Isaac, Romney seemed something of an afterthought at his own coming-out party. Ryan got a warmer reception from the delegates, many of whom were committed to primary candidates Romney had dispatched in bruising fashion. Chris Christie, the imposing governor of New Jersey, spent sixteen minutes at the podium sharing his own life story before he even mentioned the Man of the Hour. Also, full-throated denunciations of Obama produced far more enthusiastic responses than any tributes to Romney. Yet the biggest head-scratcher came on the night of Romney's acceptance speech.

I was alone in my office watching the preliminaries on cable when a very evocative and moving biographical video aired that presented Romney as a loving father and husband, a leader in his church community, a generous and caring person. Where has *this* guy been? I wondered. And why hadn't they run this video in prime time, to introduce Romney to the largest possible audience? We ran a similar video in 2008 and would again in 2012. It's free advertising, and the networks would surely have run all or part of Romney's.

Instead, when the prime-time hour kicked off, I watched as Clint Eastwood strode out to the podium. Using a nearby chair as a surrogate for Obama, Eastwood proceeded to ad-lib a routine that was by turns offensive and incomprehensible. TV occasionally punctuated the bit with cutaways of an unsmiling Ann Romney, Mitt's wife, who apparently shared my bewilderment at how the convention planners could have squandered this precious time on this bizarre piece of performance art.

I got up and walked next door to Grisolano's pizza- and beer-littered office, where a bunch of the media team was taking in the show. "Is it just me, or is this a fuckup of monumental proportions?" I asked, wondering if I was missing something. They all howled with laughter. Though Romney would follow with a decent speech, he would be upstaged in media coverage by Dirty Harry's onstage meltdown. Our postconvention poll showed no bump in support for Romney; but Obama's personal ratings had actually gone *up*.

Compared to the Republican train wreck, our convention in Charlotte the next week ran like a Swiss watch—even though an old master played with the clock.

Two months before the convention, I suggested an unusual candidate to deliver the nominating speech. No former president had ever put a sitting president's name in nomination. Yet who better than Bill Clinton to take apart the Republican economic argument?

Clinton eagerly agreed. But now, twelve hours before his prime-time appearance, we still hadn't seen a draft of the speech.

A little concerned, I asked two of our senior people and old Clinton hands, Bruce Reed and Gene Sperling, to see if they could pry a draft from their former boss—but they promptly disappeared into Clinton's Bermuda Triangle, going radio silent for hours before, finally, responding to one of my countless e-mails: "getting closer." I finally had to pay a small ransom, offering Clinton a little more time in the program to accommodate his case.

Ninety minutes before the start of the scheduled speech, the draft finally arrived. Smart, punchy, colloquial—it was classic Clinton, a joyful gutting of the Republican economic plan along with a strong endorsement of the president's. Favs and I made a couple of small suggestions and sent it back. And at about twenty-seven minutes, it would fit well within the window of the hour of network coverage we had planned.

Or so I thought.

From the moment Clinton took the stage, smiling and clapping his hands in response to a tumultuous welcome, he was an artist at work, deploying telling statistics and folksy aphorisms to lethal effect.

"We simply cannot afford to give the reins of government to someone who will double down on trickle-down," he said. "Think about this: President Obama—President Obama's plan cuts the debt, honors our values, brightens the future of our children, our families and our nation. It's a heck of a lot better."

Standing at the side of the stage, I found it a thrill to watching one of the greats at work—so much so that it took me a while to realize he was ad-libbing half his speech.

From my vantage point, I could see the large teleprompter in front of Clinton that was scrolling along with his text. At some point I realized that the prompter was stopping frequently, sometimes for minutes, while Clinton rolled on. Before long I realized that he hadn't cut his speech at all. He had simply memorized long passages that weren't included in the draft he sent us. But who cared? Clinton was so good that the networks stayed with him for the duration, through fifty rollicking minutes.

Of course, he had barely finished before the talking heads began speculating about whether Obama could rise to Clinton's standard in his acceptance speech the next night. "I don't care about that crap," said the president, who rose to the challenge the following night. "He did exactly what we hoped."

We left Charlotte with our polls showing we had a 51–46 lead. Obama's approval ratings were his highest of the year, and Romney's were once again underwater. We had not just survived one more critical test, but passed with flying colors.

Ten days after the convention, Stephanie Cutter, the deputy campaign manager who oversaw our communications shop, and Ben LaBolt, our press secretary, walked into my office and shut the door. Stephanie was a brilliant and seasoned campaign veteran, who had seen just about everything. But what she was about to report was a gaffe beyond anything she had experienced. "There's a story breaking and we wanted to know what you think we should say," Stephanie said. They explained that a videotape had surfaced showing Romney at a closed fund-raiser. On it, he disparaged 47 percent of Americans as tax-shirking loafers content to live lives of perpetual dependency. It was almost too good to be true. "What do you think we should we say?" Stephanie asked. "Not much," I replied. "When your opponent is blowing himself up, just get out of the way."

The full tape was even worse than they had described, including Romney's coda: "And so my job is not to worry about those people—I'll never convince them that they should take personal responsibility and care for their lives."

It was stunning to see him blithely dismiss half the country as slackers. It made everything in our ads ring even truer. A year earlier, I had described campaigns to reporters as "like an MRI for the soul—whoever you are, eventually people find out." Now people were staring at Romney's soul scan, and it was a disturbing image.

Hours after the tape surfaced, I got a late-night call from the president, who was not at all surprised by Romney's sentiments, but amazed that he would voice them in front of others. "Man," Obama said, "we'd better not lose to *this* guy! I mean, you can't make this stuff up!"

Seven points up with seven weeks to go—a year earlier, you could have made a fortune in Vegas betting on that scenario. Yet before we could drop the balloons and toast our good fortune, we would have our own MRI moment.

THIRTY-ONE

TURBULENT RIDE, SMOOTH LANDING

THROUGHOUT MODERN CAMPAIGN HISTORY, the first presidential debate has been a perilous turn for sitting presidents.

It's not all that surprising. Presidents haven't debated for four years, while the challenger is generally well practiced, having run a gauntlet of candidate debates and forums on the path to nomination. Presidents have spent almost four years on a pedestal. Now the challenger, standing just a few feet away, is on equal footing, poking, jabbing, and treating the Leader of the Free World with little of the deference to which presidents become accustomed. The mere act of standing toe to toe with the president of the United States elevates the opponent and levels the playing field. So, on my campaign calendar, I had one date circled in red: October 3, the evening in Denver when Obama and Romney would debate for the first time.

Obama's mentality had changed since the last time he walked onto a debate stage. By the fall of 2008, after the long primary contest with Hillary, Obama had accepted, albeit grudgingly, that these events are performances. The goal is to drive a message relentlessly, land a telling quote or two that underscores the contrast with your opponent, and in a way that connects with the American people. Obama, who stumbled at first, had mastered this skill over the course of the 2008 campaign. Now he had tumbled back to viewing the debate as a teaching moment.

He pored through the 364-page book on Romney's record and then produced a voluminous follow-up memo that demanded more information and answers. He followed the same pattern when we presented him with a thick book on his own record. By complying with his requests for endless research, we were abetting the president's worst instincts.

Our fears were confirmed in mid-August, when we held our first informal mock debate at Democratic National Committee headquarters in Washington. To play our opponent, we had recruited John Kerry, who, as a fellow Bay Stater, knew Romney well and would be adept at channeling him. Kerry also understood the mentality of a presidential challenger, having proven a strong debater in his three encounters with George W. Bush in 2004. Knowing the candidate and the terrain, he would make a formidable sparring partner for the president.

In their first session, it was Kerry who looked like the champion and the president a not-ready-for-prime-time contender. Knowing that Romney had shown a penchant for needling opponents in his primary debates, Kerry frequently baited the president into a series of defensive answers and snarky attacks that betrayed Obama's irritation with both Romney and the format while doing little to advance our arguments. "Don't interrupt me," Obama snapped at one point, when Kerry had cut in hoping to provoke just such testiness.

It was only the first practice, five weeks before the real debate, but the consensus of our prep team—led once again by Ron Klain, a brilliant and seasoned debate strategist—was that we needed to do a lot of work. "No surprises for first outing, but too much time spent on Romney's side of the field," Plouffe e-mailed after the session. "Too much defense throughout."

So we worked the president. We held informal sessions in which we fired off likely questions and tried to hone his answers, his timing, and his overall demeanor. We provided him with a few "zingers"—witty lines aimed at neutralizing Romney's attacks—but not too many barbs, lest he sully himself in the process. At times, Obama delivered compelling answers, but too often he retreated into a defensive posture, explaining a program or problem in mind-numbing detail without evoking the fundamental contrast with Romney on economic values and vision. He was decidedly a work in progress but we consoled ourselves that we had a three-day debate camp at the end of September when he could refine his approach and lock in his answers.

If there were harbingers of impending disaster, one might have been our drive from the airport to our debate prep site at a resort in Henderson, Nevada. Henderson, a burgeoning suburb with easy access to the Vegas Strip, had been devastated by the mortgage crisis that began in 2008. Now, as we wound our way through the sprawling city, we passed what appeared to be mostly abandoned subdivisions with browned lawns and rows of foreclosure signs—sober reminders of the crisis that had dominated so much of the president's term, and the lagging recovery that he would be forced to defend.

If the scene outside the hotel was dispiriting, what unfolded inside of our cordoned-off ballroom over the next three days was truly alarming. Practice was not making perfect. Too often and too easily, Kerry could knock Obama off his game, prompting the president to eschew the pithy answers he had rehearsed in favor of long, detailed, and defensive discourses. While there were moments when Obama movingly invoked the stories of the people he'd met in office, he regularly retreated into dreary recitations of tedious facts.

When a candidate is well prepared, the debate prep team can almost always anticipate every answer, sometimes mouthing the exact words as they are being delivered. Yet twenty-four hours before the first presidential debate, none of us could predict with certainty how the president would answer *any* question. Obama had absorbed reams of material, but it was not clear that he had also absorbed our counsel. Openly disdainful of the artifice the process demanded of him, he refused to indulge us by rehearsing his answers again and again until he had memorized them.

All the problems and pitfalls were in evidence during our final run-through, on the night before the Denver debate. Many of the notes I typed as I watched the final practice foreshadowed what was to come: "Threw away the contrast," I wrote after one answer. "Wonkfest," after another. "Wants to wonk it up on Medicare cost curves," I noted after an answer on health care. "No humanity" was the distressing synopsis of another exchange. As Obama and Kerry sparred, the team sat stone-faced, trying not to betray our increasing anxiety, but it seemed clear that our man wasn't ready.

As had been customary through two elections, Klain asked the speech coach, Michael Sheehan, and me to go over the night's practice session with Obama before he turned in. When we got into the makeshift tape screening room where Michael would offer performance pointers, the president said, "I think that went pretty well, don't you?" I could have nodded affirmatively on the theory that it was too late to affect much of a change. Instead, I opted to tell him the truth.

"There were some good moments, but there's some stuff we need to clean up," I said. Before I could launch my critique, however, the president indicated he'd already heard enough. "Motherfucker's never happy," he harrumphed, bolting up and heading briskly out of the room. "Well, that went well, don't you think?" I said to Sheehan, as we stared in shock and dismay at the double doors through which the president had just exited.

That was a first. Obama and I had been working together for a decade, through some pretty hairy moments, but he had never before lost his temper in this fashion. He had certainly never attacked me quite so harshly, especially in front of others. I had no doubt irritated him, but there was more to it. My sense was that the president knew he wasn't ready. His mind-set, his reluctance to embrace this game, had been wrongheaded from the start, and now it was clearly hurting him.

Nothing was said about our testy exchange the next day on the flight from Vegas to Denver. The unnerved folks on our debate team passed the time trying to reassure themselves that, somehow, it might work out. "Trust me, he's a gamer," I told Klain, who stared back at me poker-faced. We all knew the truth. It would take an act of Providence or some major gaffe by Romney for us to have a good night.

A few minutes before the debate began, Plouffe and I visited the president in his hold in a locker room in the University of Denver's hockey arena. Four years earlier, in another locker room before the first presidential debate, a focused, confident Obama said, "Just give me the ball!" Now, in Denver, he appeared distracted, even disinterested—and immune to our last-minute pep talk. "Let's just get this over with and get out of here," he said. These were not exactly the parting words you hoped to hear as you sent your candidate out to do battle.

The debate fell on Obama's twentieth wedding anniversary, and we had the idea that he should give a nod to his widely admired wife at the beginning of his opening statement.

"There are a lot of points I want to make tonight, but the most important one is that 20 years ago I became the luckiest man on earth because Michelle Obama agreed to marry me," the president said, in one of the few practiced bits he had committed to memory. "And so I just want to wish, Sweetie, you happy anniversary and let you know that a year from now, we will not be celebrating it in front of 40 million people."

It turns out that intimacies delivered in front of forty million people are difficult to pull off. Obama's attempt appeared somewhat phony and forced.

Worse, Romney's debate prep had forecast this very exchange, so Mitt was, as they say in baseball, "laying on the pitch."

"And congratulations to you, Mr. President, on your anniversary. I'm sure this was the most romantic place you could imagine—here with me," he cracked, when it was his turn to speak. If Obama's awkward line seemed canned, Romney's came off as spontaneous, charming, and self-effacing.

After reading all the stories about the "47 percent" tape, Americans being introduced to Romney for the first time might have been expecting Mr. Burns, the misanthropic corporate executive from *The Simpsons*. Instead Romney was, from start to finish, warm, confident, and well prepared. He flawlessly delivered line after line, tweaking the president frequently without overstepping any boundaries. We watched as Romney, who had spent most of his campaign pandering to the Right, brazenly yet deftly repositioned himself as a moderate on issue after issue. "I don't have a $5 trillion tax cut," Romney said unabashedly, walking away from what had long been a centerpiece of his economic plan.

The president performed about how he had in prep, occasionally scoring message points, but mostly following the questions and Romney's parries down rabbit holes. When he explained for a third time the rationale behind the cost-cutting commission empaneled by his health care act, there were audible groans in our staff room. While he defended his record to a fault, indulging in esoterica, Obama was remarkably passive, seldom challenging Romney or, especially, Romney's cynical reinvention of himself. Worse, the president looked disengaged, in stark contrast with a challenger who was in command of the moment.

"We're dead," Klain said ten minutes into the debate. We were all staring at dial group findings streaming across the bottom of the CNN screen that showed Romney's answers getting consistently higher ratings than the president's. Our own dial groups, while marginally better, would also give Romney a decided edge. The chatter among political reporters on Twitter was painful to read: Romney was aggressive, Obama was halting. Some on our team simply shut their computers in despair.

I braced myself for the postdebate pandemonium of the "spin room," where I would try to redirect reporters' attention to Romney's blatant distortions of his own record. It was a futile effort, as if I were trying to ticket Romney for double-parking when everyone wanted to know about the president's car wreck. The greatest outcry emanated from our own supporters, particularly progressives who were livid that the president hadn't strafed Romney over Bain Capital or hit the giant "47 percent" target Romney had on his back. Lawrence O'Donnell of MSNBC pulled me out of a scrum of reporters. "You might want to get on our air," he said. "They're ripping your guy apart."

In truth, I didn't want to go on the air. I just wanted to get out of there. When I finally escaped, my cell phone rang. It was Marvin Nicholson, the president's body man. "The boss wants to speak to you," he said.

Obama was on his way back to the hotel, but he had already scanned the early reviews on his ubiquitous iPad.

"So I guess the view is that we didn't have a very good night," he said.

"Yes," I replied. "I think that's pretty much the consensus."

"I just didn't feel that way up there," he said. "I knew we hadn't won big in any way, but I felt it was at worst a draw."

I couldn't help but think about all the ways in which we had failed him— the brutal assault of briefing papers; our reluctance to butt heads with the president by insisting on drilling specific answers until they were second nature. Back at the hotel, we tried to regroup, rewriting the president's remarks for the following day to demonstrate the fight that had been missing during the debate. "We have to come out swinging and show we have a pulse," I told Favs as we worked up a new script.

We had long planned a rally in Denver the morning after, to build on the debate's momentum. Now, absent any momentum, we instead had to reassure worried supporters. I grabbed Obama as he was leaving the hotel for the event. "Everyone's going to be taking their cues from you," I said. "You need to come out on fire or it will just prolong the story line."

"I know, I know," he said, as he took off down the hall and headed to the waiting motorcade. It turned out he did know. He came out with all the energy, and many of the arguments, that had been missing the night before.

"When I got onto the stage, I met this very spirited fellow who *claimed* to be Mitt Romney," the president said, launching into the satirical trope we had prepared about the stranger who had debated the president the night before. "But it *couldn't* have been Mitt Romney, because the real Mitt Romney has been running around the country for the last year promising $5 trillion in tax cuts that favor the wealthy. The fellow onstage last night said he didn't know anything about that."

The crowd ate it up. Just the sound of laughter was somewhat soothing, but only so much. A reporter e-mailed me midway through Obama's speech to ask the obvious: "Where was this guy last night?"

We had nearly two weeks until the next debate, and I knew it would be an endurance test. I remembered the frenzy that erupted after Reagan flubbed his first debate with Walter Mondale, briefly breathing life into Mondale's moribund campaign—at least in the minds of a news media eager for a contest. I believed the same thing was happening now.

Still, we almost certainly couldn't afford a second straight rout. We needed a return to form, just like the one Reagan executed on his way to a forty-nine-state landslide.

By the next day the president had read and heard enough to understand that the first debate had been a lost night. One commentary in particular had caught his eye. "What Matt Bai wrote in the *Times* really kind of made sense," the president said of a blog post headlined "Obama's Enthusiasm Gap." In it, the columnist wrote about Obama's reticence to perform, linking it to a "lack of neediness" that drives most politicians. "It turns out, though, that craving validation is a useful political trait. It makes you want to explain yourself and prevail in the argument," Bai wrote.

It was interesting that the president embraced this commentary, among the many he'd read, to explain his failure. And it reminded me of the conversation in 2007 when I told Obama that he might not be "pathological enough" to run for president. Now, as he contemplated his rare stumble on a large stage, I heard his competitive instincts kicking in. "I'm not going to let him beat me again," the president said. "Ever! I'm disappointed that I didn't make a stronger case to the country."

The day after the debate, I got an unexpected call from Bill Clinton. Generally, when things go badly wrong, you receive a lot of unsolicited strategic advice. Yet President Clinton's was different and welcome.

"Listen, everybody is beating up on the president," he said. "But only a few of us know what it's like to be up on that stage. It's not easy. I hope everyone cuts him a little slack. He'll be all right."

Klain took the debate particularly hard and offered to resign, a gesture Obama quickly and properly refused, and when the debate group reconvened with Obama the following week, the president was shouldering all the blame. "I know everyone in this room feels a responsibility," he said. "But this one was on me." He promised to be ready for the next encounter, a town hall–style debate, now just one week away.

As we flew to Williamsburg, Virginia, for our second debate camp, I sensed that the president had genuinely reengaged. Biden had done well in his debate with Paul Ryan. But Obama understood that only he could put to rest any lingering doubts brought on by Denver. Our early prep sessions were encouraging, with Obama performing well in the first night's run-through.

It sure felt as if we were in a better place and that, with continued practice and improvement, he'd be ready in three days' time. However, the next night, when Kerry returned to the attack, the wheels came off. Once again Obama allowed himself to be baited into long explanations rather than delivering prescribed lines and messages that would resonate with the audience. He dealt peevishly with Kerry's interruptions, whining that the moderator needed to intervene. Benenson, Plouffe, and I watched the mock debate on a closed-circuit feed in a nearby room so that we could share our thoughts openly. "Holy shit," Benenson said, succinctly capturing our collective sentiment over this recurring nightmare.

Klain didn't even bother having Obama sit through the usual critique. Where would we even begin? Instead, when Obama retired, we held a long brainstorming session to figure out how, in the day we had left, we were going to pull the president back from the abyss. "We need an intervention," someone suggested.

The next morning, a small group of us—Klain, Plouffe, chief of staff Jack Lew, and I—sat down with the president to give him our honest assessment. "You're treating this like it's all on the level," I said. "It's not a trial or even a real debate. This is a performance. Romney understood that. He was delivering lines. You were answering questions. I know it's a galling process, but it is what it is. It's part of the deal. You've done it before. We need you to do it again."

The president responded to our candor with a rare and disarming admission. "I know I am not hitting this, guys," he said. "I'm a lawyer. I was trained to argue facts. When I stop in diners or taverns or factories, I'm talking to people. In speeches, I'm talking values. But my inclination here is to argue fact. And I know that's not the exercise. I know I am letting folks down.

"I'm just out of sync," he continued. "It's like the movie *Tin Cup*. You know, the guy develops a slice and he can't straighten out his swing. Finally the caddy—I think it was Cheech from Cheech and Chong—says, 'Put your hat on backward . . . do this . . . do that. And put your tees in your left pocket. Okay, *now* swing.' And the guy hits a long, perfect drive. He didn't change anything, really, but his head.

"It's in my head now, and I need to straighten it out."

After the others cleared out, I lingered to offer a little encouragement. "We'll get there," I said, hoping, but without real conviction, that I was right. I thought about our exchange backstage in Boston before Obama made his national convention debut eight years earlier. "Don't worry, I *always* make my marks," he reassured me back then, without betraying a hint of anxiety. Yet he hadn't made his marks in Denver, and now he was confronting an unfamiliar and unwelcome feeling of vulnerability.

"I'm doubting myself," Obama conceded. "And I have to get past that."

When he left, we reconvened the debate team to consider what had become an exercise in triage. Obama did have some terrific moments and great lines during our sessions; our problem was that he couldn't be counted on to repeat them. Bob Barnett, a prominent Washington attorney we had assigned to prep Kerry as part of our team chimed in with a sensible suggestion, perhaps gleaned from years of experience prepping Hillary. "I don't know any way to do this but to take the same question over and over until he locks in the same answer."

When Obama returned for the final day's exercises, the difference was palpable and positive. Proceeding topic by topic, he worked over and massaged his answers while incorporating our suggestions. He promised this time to deploy his best lines and hit Romney's "47 percent" slander, and he repeated all the exchanges until everyone was satisfied that he could replicate them on the real stage the next night.

As much as we try to orchestrate these debates, planning well in advance how to address the major themes of the election, news events intrude and can roil the discussion. A month earlier, on September 11, the U.S. ambassador and three other Americans had been killed in a terrorist attack on our diplomatic compound in Benghazi, Libya. It quickly became a right-wing meme that the White House had tried to obscure the true nature of the attack and possible Al Qaeda involvement in order to preserve the president's national security bona fides through Election Day. It was an absurd charge.

From a political perspective, if the Republicans wanted to spend the last two months of the campaign talking about terrorism instead of the economy, I would have welcomed it. After bin Laden's death and Obama's aggressive pursuit of Al Qaeda, national security was a huge advantage, and the tragic events in Benghazi weren't going to change that.

Obama knew and liked the ambassador, Christopher Stevens, and was genuinely offended by the suggestion that the White House would put politics first in the midst of such a tragedy. The allegation was particularly galling because it was Romney's campaign that had sent a press release trying to capitalize on Benghazi even before we learned the fate of the Americans there.

So as Kerry was channeling Romney bearing in on Benghazi, Obama responded with righteous indignation. "Well, let me first of all talk about our diplomats, because they serve all around the world and do an incredible job in a very dangerous situation. And these aren't just representatives of the United States, they are my representatives. I send them there, oftentimes into harm's way. I know these folks and I know their families. So nobody is more concerned about their safety and security than I am. So the suggestion that anybody on my team would play politics or mislead when we've lost four of our own, governor, is offensive. It's offensive to me as a president. It's offensive to me as commander in chief."

It was powerful, strong, and genuine, and we rehearsed it again and again until the president had it locked in. "If this comes up, it will be a hell of a moment," I said, confident that it would, given the demand welling up in the right-wing blogosphere. If Romney didn't take the Benghazi shot, he would be flogged by his base.

By Monday night, our panic had subsided. In twenty-four hours, the improvement had been nothing short of miraculous. This time the president was going in with a game plan. He was armed with answers, clever lines, and useful pivots. It's possible he even wanted to be there. When I saw him the next morning, Obama removed a piece of paper from his pocket. "When I went back to my room last night," he said, "I outlined about a dozen questions and exactly how I'm going to deal with them. Figured I would review it on the way up to New York." What a difference a day made!

A few hours later we were hanging out in our holding rooms at Hofstra University, the debate site, when the president beckoned Plouffe and me. "I just wanted to tell you guys, I feel really good about this," he said, his handwritten primer sitting on a nearby table along with a golf tee we had presented him that morning as a reminder of Cheech's advice in *Tin Cup*. "We prepared well. I know what I have to do. We're going to have a good night."

Maybe we could have survived another bad night, but after what we had just heard, I told Plouffe that I was pretty sure we wouldn't find out.

"You don't get to be president of the United States by accident," I said. "You get there because when you're tested, because in those really hard moments, you come up big. Either he will or he won't. But he always has."

Our space at Hofstra was cramped, and the tension was palpable. Our contingent was larger than usual, given the high stakes. Even Kerry, who had skipped Denver, was there. Klain paced the room obsessively. Then, a few minutes into the debate, Klain's once-grim visage morphed into a flushed smile.

Obama looked confident as he rose from his stool and approached the first questioner, a college student who was concerned about entering an uncertain job market. "Number one, I want to build manufacturing jobs in this country again. Now when Governor Romney said we should let Detroit go bankrupt, I said we're going to bet on American workers and the American auto industry and it's come surging back," the president began. Economic values, message, and contrast all in one answer—exactly as Obama had practiced. Our crew was no longer groaning or slamming laptops in dismay, but rather hooting and hollering in delight.

When Romney responded by touting his five-point plan, the president pounced.

"And Governor Romney's says he's got a five-point plan? Governor Romney doesn't have a five-point plan. He has a one-point plan," the president said, in an answer he had first surfaced on the plane ride to Williamsburg. "And that plan is to make sure that folks at the top play by a different set of rules. That's been his philosophy in the private sector, that's been his philosophy as governor, that's been his philosophy as a presidential candidate. You can make a lot of money and pay lower tax rates than somebody who makes a lot less. You can ship jobs overseas and get tax breaks for it. You can invest in a company, bankrupt it, lay off the workers, strip away their pensions, and you still make money. That's exactly the philosophy that we've seen in place for the last decade. That's what's been squeezing middle-class families."

It was pure message without the stultifying minutiae—and it presaged a complete role reversal. It was the president who was fully engaged and on the offensive against a challenger who suddenly looked defensive and ill at ease. I smelled a rout.

By the time the night was over, Binder's focus group of fifty-two Des Moines–area swing voters would award us the debate by a whopping thirty points.

There would be a third debate, dedicated to foreign policy, a week later in Boca Raton, Florida. Yet it now lacked any of the high drama of the first two encounters. The president had confronted an obstacle he had never before faced: self-doubt. And as this doubt surfaced, it had spread to the rest of us like an epidemic. When he vanquished it in the second debate, it simply never returned. Our preparations at Camp David for the final debate were blessedly uneventful.

"We've figured out how to do this," Obama said aboard Air Force One as we headed to the final showdown with Romney in Boca Raton. "We didn't prepare right for the first one, and I just wasn't in the right psychological place.

"I really felt like I let everyone down. I didn't go out and fight for them. I'd go to these rallies and see these young volunteers who are working their hearts out, trying to keep their chins up. But I knew I had let them down, and I wasn't going to let them down again. I think this was just a wake-up call to remind me who and what I'm fighting for."

And hours before his last encounter with Romney, the race well in hand, Obama reflected on the campaign and the country.

"You know, it's a crazy country and a crazy process," he said. "But what we end up with are a Mormon and a black guy who, it turns out, are pretty good reflections of our politics. He represents the America of the 1950s, and believes that the country does well when guys like him are in charge. I represent the America that is."

Throughout the year and particularly in the final weeks before the election, I was acutely aware that, after three decades in the trenches of American political campaigns, those days for me were coming to an end. Even during the most agonizing, pressure-filled days of the campaign, I was suffused with a sense of good fortune and deeply appreciative of the life I would be leaving behind.

There is nothing quite like that final coast-to-coast barnstorming of a presidential campaign, when the frenzied pace and pandemonium delivers the excitement of a rock-and-roll mega-tour. The "road show" becomes a world unto itself, and the ultimate bonding experience for those who share it. And there was a renewed sense of mission that was palpable in the final weeks. You could feel it in the warm, enthusiastic crowds that greeted us everywhere, reminiscent of 2008, if not quite as large. As we traveled, I was like a retiring baseball player in the fall of my final season, appreciating every last moment of a glorious rite I knew I would never experience again.

I felt the same way every time I walked into our bustling campaign headquarters and found it overflowing with inspiring, joyful, sleep-deprived kids who had come from all over America to be a part of our effort. I would miss the high-energy collaborations and the ceaseless banter with my gifted and creative colleagues. We were a tight team, bound together, day and night, by this urgent, heady mission, all of us working toward a single goal and a single day when America would choose its leader and its course.

Along the way, I spent hours with reporters who were misled by public polls and the Romney campaign into believing that the race was closing. In a moment of exasperation, I wagered my mustache of forty years to Joe Scarborough on his eponymous morning TV show. After the election, I would parlay my winnings into a larger deal to raise money for CURE. It cost me the 'stache, shaved off on national TV, but raised $1.2 million for epilepsy research. Susan was thrilled with the money and, to my surprise, the chance after all those years to glimpse my naked lip.

Only Mother Nature would disrupt our sprint to the finish line. When a colossal hurricane named Sandy slammed into the Eastern Seaboard on October 29, Obama's official responsibilities trumped his campaign schedule. With more than a hundred dead and fifty billion dollars' worth of destruction, Sandy pushed the election news off the front page. While the storm and its aftermath didn't determine the outcome of the election, the pictures of the president and Governor Chris Christie, a GOP stalwart, working together as they toured the ravaged New Jersey coast was a heartening show of bipartisanship for a country that, of late, had seen far too little of it.

When the president resumed campaigning on the final weekend before Election Day, Bill Clinton joined us for a Sunday rally in New Hampshire. Clinton had campaigned so aggressively in the closing days that he barely had any voice left. On the ride to the event, Clinton gazed out the window at the passing countryside and remarked on how much he loved New Hampshire. What went unspoken was that the state had revived not only his political fortunes in '92, but Hillary's in '08. Plouffe, pugnacious to the end, couldn't resist. "We feel the same way about Iowa!" he said with a big grin.

So it was only fitting that Iowa, which four years earlier had given life to our campaign, would be where this final race would come to an end. Bruce Springsteen joined us for the final day, and before the Obamas made their last appeals to a massive crowd in the late evening chill, the troubadour offered his sage and world-weary perspective on the distance we had traveled.

"I've lived long enough to know that the future . . . it's rarely a tide rushing in," he told the crowd between songs. "It's often a slow march, inch by inch, day after painful, long day . . .

"President Obama last time ran as a man of hope and change and you hear a lot talk about how things are different now . . . Things aren't any different. They're just *realer*. It's crunch time now. The president's job, our job—yours, mine; whether you're a Republican, a Democrat, independent; rich, poor; black, brown, white; gay, straight; soldier, civilian—is to keep that hope alive and to combat the cynicism and the apathy; and to believe in our power to change our lives and the country and the world that we live in."

Springsteen had captured the moment. This wasn't the beautiful, innocent rapture of 2008. Our idealism had been tested and tempered by four hard years of wrenching problems and brutal politics. It was *realer* now. Progress had come, but not as a "tide rushing in." The gains we had made were the product of a "slow march, inch by inch, day after painful, long day." And for all he had done, Obama could never match the outsize expectations he had first stirred in Iowa.

On the plane home to Chicago, Obama stopped in the senior staff cabin for one last bit of campaign analysis from Plouffe, Gibbs, and me. Based on all our data, we believed we would win 332 electoral votes. I was hoping North Carolina might even give us another 15. Either way, tomorrow figured to be a very good day. The president listened and nodded, as if he had heard such confident expressions from us before.

"Okay, but I don't want the three of you knocking on my door with long faces again tomorrow night to tell me you were wrong," he said, shifting his gaze between us as he recalled that moment in the hallway of a Nashua hotel, almost five years earlier, when we had to tell him we had come up short in the New Hampshire primary.

"He didn't sound like he was kidding," Plouffe said with a nervous smile after Obama left the cabin.

"No," I said. "I don't think he was."

One of the enduring mysteries of the 2012 election is how the Romney crew so thoroughly missed the reality of what was happening on the ground. Even on Election Day, the Romney team was still preparing its victory party— complete with a barge loaded with fireworks to light up Boston Harbor. It wasn't that Romney and his team weren't smart people, but that they seemed so detached from minority communities and younger generations that they wholly underestimated their commitment to the country and its election process. That is why Team Mitt was shocked when the numbers rolled in.

When Messina, Plouffe, and I arrived at the president's hotel suite that night, there was no trace of the serene Obama who awaited us on Election Night in 2008; this time, he was pumped, and he greeted us with fist bumps and high fives.

He was a president who believed he had made tough decisions at a critical time, only to find himself dismissed as a shooting star whose fire had burned out, a certain one-termer. Now he had won and won decisively—not just with 332 electoral votes but by a margin of almost four points in the popular vote. "In some ways, this one's sweeter," he told us. "Because it was harder. And there was so much on the line." He felt the differences between his vision and Romney's were so stark; the stakes were even greater than 2008.

There was a mob of delirious supporters waiting for him a few miles down the road, and he was eager to celebrate with them, but we had heard nothing yet from Boston. "How long do we have to hang here?" Obama wondered about the protocol of waiting for Romney's concession. "If he doesn't call soon, we should go. I don't want to leave those folks just standing there."

While we were waiting, I sat down with Plouffe in a quiet corner of the suite. He was never one for sloppy emotion; that was my province. Yet, after ten years of partnership and collaboration, it was an incomparable moment for both of us, one I knew we would never again share. We spent a few minutes reflecting on what we had accomplished together. "It's been a pleasure, brother," I told him, extending my hand. "I'm proud that we'll always be linked together in history. The Davids!"

Shortly before midnight in Chicago, Romney called. We gathered around Obama as they spoke. Obama said the appropriate things, congratulating his opponent on a hard-fought race and wishing Romney's family well. He was unsmiling during the call, and slightly irritated when it was over. "He said, 'We were surprised. You really did a great job of getting the vote out in places like Cleveland and Milwaukee.' In other words, black people," the president said. "That's what he thinks this was all about."

Before we left the suite, he wanted to make one more call. "Can someone get Bill Clinton on the phone?" Four years earlier, they had gone after each other hard, and it had taken time for those wounds to heal. Yet now they had become true allies, even friends—and maybe most important of all, they were peers, among a handful of living men who had known the burdens of the American presidency.

"Bill," the president said. "I'm just calling to say thanks. You were the MVP of this campaign."

When we reached the event site, I scrambled out of the motorcade to look for Susan. For the second straight Election Night, we had crossed signals and been separated. We finally met up in the tangle of staff and friends who were penned off at the side of the stage where Obama would speak. Susan said that she had encountered the president and First Lady backstage and shared a warm embrace.

"I'm happy for David," said the man who was our friend long before he was our president. "He's going out a winner!"

I winced a little when Susan shared Obama's words. The winning was sublime, but "going out" was a jarring reality. On this night, surrounded by the White House colleagues and campaign warriors with whom I had marched for six long years, it was hard to accept that the moment had finally arrived and this vital, intense part of my life was ending.

I had much to look forward to in my new life. I had already agreed to launch an Institute of Politics at the University of Chicago, where I would have the chance to inspire a new generation—one desperately needed—to consider careers in the public arena. And I was excited about spending more time with Susan, our family, and wonderful friends, whose company I had sacrificed so often for too long.

I contemplated just where this long journey had left me. I certainly wasn't the wide-eyed little boy on a mailbox anymore. I was hardened and sobered by enough battles to know that democracy is more than fluttering flags, swelling music, and inspiring words. It is a tough, messy business, always demanding and often disappointing. Still, as I gazed up at my friend the president, who had made such a difference, I knew that there was no other work I could ever do that would mean so much.

EPILOGUE

MY MOTHER DIED IN January 2014 at the age of ninety-three. She left this world just as she lived—on her own terms. Four days before she passed, I got a call from a hospice doctor. "Your mother has made a decision," he said. "I told her that if she stopped taking her heart medication, she would die within a few days. And that's what she wants to do. She's very much at peace with her decision. If you would like to say good-bye, you should get out here right away."

Congestive heart failure and old age had taken their toll. Mom was weak and often confused, but just aware enough to hate what her life had become. She had willed herself to live long enough to see Obama's second inauguration, and had hoped to attend. Yet, tethered to walkers, wheelchairs, and oxygen tanks, she was in no shape to travel. My sister staged an "Inaugural Gala" in Mom's building, so she could wear her gown and brag about her son one more time.

When I arrived at her assisted-living apartment in a Boston suburb, she was as upbeat and bright as I had seen her in years. "I've had a great life, Dave," she explained, having blessedly forgotten or simply overlooked long periods of personal unhappiness, including a difficult marriage and our own tenuous relationship. "I've done everything I wanted to do. It's just too hard now. It's time."

We spoke for hours about her life and mine, about her grandkids and how pleased she was with their progress in life. Never one to forget a grudge, Mom asked for a piece of paper so that she could sketch the seating arrangement at the rehearsal dinner before my wedding, thirty-four years earlier, and point to the exact spot where Susan's uncle stood when he toasted "my wonderful niece and the nebbish she's marrying."

It was one of the best talks we ever had, and as mom slipped away, I passed the time looking through the files and memorabilia she had maintained for some seventy years. There were yellowed newspaper clippings and magazine stories she had written in the '40s and '50s, articles from trade newspapers announcing her appointments as she climbed the ladder in advertising, and seemingly every note of thanks or commendation she had ever received from editors, clients, and bosses.

Those files revealed so much. I could see in them the prodigious drive that had made her a professional success, but that had also robbed me as a child of her focus and attention. All her talent was reflected in those pages, but also her painful insecurity and insatiable need for approbation. It was impossible to escape the plain fact that, for better and worse, she had passed the good and bad on to me.

Yet, nearing sixty, I was looking back at my mother's life through a more discerning lens, with greater understanding and less resentment. Those last days also were a stark reminder of the fleeting nature of time, something that seems infinite when you're young and in such a hurry to get somewhere that you're incapable of appreciating life's sublime gifts.

I value those gifts more now. Susan is alive and healthy, and I'm grateful every day for her and the life we share. Once, we dreamed of a day when Lauren might be happy and healthy, too. Today, miraculously, she is, having been seizure-free for fourteen years. Every day, that makes me smile. Our boys, Michael and Ethan, who were tested and sensitized by their sister's struggles, have become fine men, with successful careers of their own. Mike married the lovely Liz, and baby Maelin came along in 2014, casting her new grandparents in her enchanting spell.

With the years come perspective, and that extends to my journey in politics. I can see the gray better now, not just in my hair but in the world around me.

It makes me smile to think of the cocksure audacity it took for me to walk into a publisher's office as an eighteen-year-old kid and assert confidently that I was equipped to share my insights about politics in the pages of his newspaper. I'm so glad I did, and so lucky he believed me, or at least took a chance on me. Reflecting back on my life, I'm reminded of the sage line: "I'm not young enough to know everything."

Back then, I sure thought I did.

When I arrived on the South Side of Chicago, four years after the bloody '68 Democratic National Convention, I saw little need for nuance. I felt the prevailing political machine was corrupt and racist and run for the benefit of the insiders and I pretty much wrote from that righteous but limited perspective.

I wasn't wrong. It just wasn't the whole story. The machine was greased by patronage jobs and "sweetheart" contracts and by elected officials (even judges) often slated more for their loyalties than their abilities. It was a feudal structure dominated by white ethnic ward bosses, and it left the burgeoning black and Hispanic communities on the outside looking in. Yet when JFK needed votes for the Civil Rights Act, he could count on Mayor Richard J. Daley to deliver them—and the mayor, in turn, could count on largesse from Washington with which to build his city.

As a kid columnist, I reflexively sided with the earnest, upright do-gooders who believed that all patronage was inherently evil and that every public dollar should be awarded on the merits—and then only after rigorous public debate, rather than the bartering that sealed backroom deals between politicians. I still tend to see it that way, but I'm a little less certain and sanctimonious about it at sixty than I was at eighteen.

As a White House aide, I had argued for the elimination of earmarks, the open-ended funds from which individual members of Congress could direct dollars to projects in their district. It was a system that had been egregiously abused and had become an obvious symbol of corruption in Washington. Obama had campaigned against it, and I agreed it had to go. Yet, in my years in Washington, I learned how few tools a president and congressional leaders now have at their disposal to corral support for their initiatives. So I see the wisdom of allowing legislators greater ability to target resources within their communities. Had we at once "reformed" the system yet made it less workable and responsive?

I'm not young enough to know for sure.

Back in the day, I learned that some of the beguiling rogues I covered took genuine pride in governing and ministering to their constituents, and some of the "reformers" I put on a pedestal had little feel for people or, far worse, lectured about ethics as they lined their own pockets. Most of the folks I've met in politics are neither pure saint nor unrepentant sinner. It was a joy to hear Dan Rostenkowski reminisce about the writing of Medicare or how he helped save Social Security from insolvency or the 1986 tax reform law he negotiated with Ronald Reagan. "The question I always asked is whether it was good law," Rostenkowski would say. Yet he ended his career on the wrong side of the law, mostly for penny-ante crimes such as trading in postage stamps from his office and pocketing the cash. Raised in the culture of the old Democratic machine, Rosty went down like a two-bit grifter. It would be easy to write this as his epitaph, and there was a time when I would have. Yet he also was one of the most effective and impactful legislators of his time, an ebullient politician who loved the process of horse trading and knew how to work across party lines to get vital things done for the country. I'm a little nostalgic for that.

For years, Rosty would drive home to Illinois each weekend with Bob Michel, a Republican from Peoria who would become House minority leader. It's a quaint memory today, when the idea of senior members of the two parties sharing a meal, much less an eleven-hour car ride, would be regarded as a treasonous act. Yet Rostenkowski and Michel were of a different generation, raised during an era when Americans served side by side to save the world from fascism, an experience that bound this big, diverse nation as one. They were friendly adversaries who had different views on many things—which is, after all, why there *are* two parties—but neither ever questioned the other's intentions and certainly never his patriotism or love of country.

Another of Rosty's friends was George H. W. Bush, with whom he briefly served in the '60s on the House Ways and Means Committee. Decades later, the two of them, Bush as president and Rosty as chair of that powerful tax-writing committee, helped fashion a budget plan to reduce the yawning gap left by Reagan's supply-side fiscal policies. Many analysts credit the deal with paving the way for the prosperity of the '90s, but it also touched off a right-wing rebellion within the Republican Party that helped sink Bush and led to Michel's ouster as GOP leader in the House.

That *putsch* was orchestrated by a crafty young conservative from Georgia, Newt Gingrich, who frowned upon Michel's moderation and his fraternization with folks on the other side of the aisle. It was a watershed event, setting in motion the mad cycle of polarization that turned the aisle between parties into a jagged divide, one that today is increasingly difficult (or, far too often, impossible) to cross.

Gingrich doesn't shoulder all the blame. Today's cable and Internet-driven media, in which Americans increasingly seek "news" from sources that affirm, rather than inform, their views; the trend toward partisan gerrymandering of congressional districts, making primary elections the only risk faced by most incumbents; the mind-boggling explosion of special interest and ideologically driven money in campaigns—all have conspired to make conflict in Washington more rewarding for politicians than compromise.

Obama's "hope and change" campaign of 2008 was about many important things, from ending the war in Iraq to reclaiming the American dream. Above all, though, it was about fixing the broken politics of Washington. "E Pluribus Unum—out of many, one," he liked to say, invoking the national motto. Obama preached the gospel of one America, a diverse nation with shared concerns and a common destiny. Together, he promised, we could overcome the grip of partisanship and special interest influence that had hijacked our national politics. It was a vision he painted with inspiring passion and genuine conviction. Given who he was and the life he had led, Obama stood as a living symbol of the possibility for greater harmony and progress.

The huge and enthusiastic crowds Obama drew—the resounding vote on Election Day that reached well beyond the Democratic base—offered genuine hope to a country hungry for change. Yet it must have been a terrifying prospect to Republicans in Washington, who are in the business of winning elections and had reason to fear that this was only the beginning. If Obama could forge the kind of bipartisan solutions he had promised as a candidate, he could remake American politics for a generation. They weren't going to let that happen. So while most of Washington celebrated on the night of Obama's inauguration, key House and Senate Republicans skipped the parties to meet with Gingrich and plot a strategy of relentless resistance.

In his first two years in the White House, Obama accomplished more than any president since LBJ. Not only did he staunch the bleeding of an economy on the brink of disaster and pass health care reform, but he also saved the American auto industry, passed landmark Wall Street reform, raised fuel efficiency standards in cars and trucks, struck down the ban on gays in the military, expanded college aid and reformed student loans, paved the way for new clean energy sources, and passed the Lilly Ledbetter Law to combat pay discrimination against women. He also began to make good on ending America's longest-running wars, negotiated a new arms control treaty, and rallied the world behind withering sanctions that would bring Iran to the negotiating table over its nuclear program.

Yet his legislative victories were possible only because of the strong Democratic majorities that Obama had helped sweep into Congress. The Republicans stuck to their game plan and refused Obama cooperation from the start, compelling him to pass every major bill on party-line votes, thus denying him the claim to bipartisanship that both the president and the country desired.

The Republicans knew the recovery would be long and arduous, and decided it was far better to blame the president's policies than to be complicit in shaping them. Mitch McConnell openly boasted about the strategy of obstruction and thrilled the GOP base when he vowed that defeating Obama would be his top priority. Then things got worse. When Republicans took over the House in 2011 after the Tea Party stormed the election, everything ground to a halt. Small-government conservatives were edged out by no-government conservatives, and Americans witnessed bitter, partisan retrenchment that took the country to the edge of a catastrophic default on its debt. The frenetic action of the first two years surrendered to a more virulent strain of gridlock than any we had witnessed before.

Throughout my years with Obama, I publicly deflected questions about whether the vehemence of his opposition was rooted in race. "I'm sure some people voted for the president because he is black and some people voted against him because he is black," I would say, with the authority of one who had spent a lifetime working with minority candidates to knock down racial barriers that blocked higher offices. "The election of the first black president was a dramatic step forward for America, not a magic healing elixir." I simply didn't want to fuel the discussion or appear to be setting the president up as a victim.

Still, the truth is undeniable.

No other president has seen his citizenship openly and persistently questioned. Never before has a president been interrupted in the middle of a national address by a congressman screaming, "You lie!" Some folks simply refuse to accept the legitimacy of the first black president and are seriously discomforted by the growing diversity of our country. And some craven politicians and right-wing provocateurs have been more than willing to exploit that fear, confusion, and anger.

Obama feels this, I'm sure, though it's not in his nature or interest to dwell on it. He remains calm, deliberative, and ultimately rational, which are virtues in a president and commander in chief and were welcome qualities after the bombast and bluster of the Bush-Cheney era.

Even so, over the years, that same preternatural cool has increasingly worked against Obama in public opinion and commentary. Calm has too often been read as detachment; deliberativeness as uncertainty. Americans, sometimes, like it when their presidents want to punch someone in the face—or at least sound as if they do. In politics and diplomacy, the ultimate rational man bent on solving thorny problems is frequently destined to frustration and disappointment in these games where the other players too often measure their moves by much different yardsticks.

This is the way it is with all people, I've learned. A person's strengths almost always have a flip side. Obama's strengths are prodigious, but he's not perfect or exempt from blame for some of the disappointments I hear expressed about him ever more frequently these days.

The day after the Affordable Care Act passed, a slightly hungover but very happy president walked into my office to reflect on the momentous events of the night before.

"Not used to martinis on work nights," he said with a smile, as he flopped down on the couch across from my desk, still bearing the effects of the late-night celebration he hosted for the staff after the law was passed. "I honestly was more excited last night than I was the night I was elected. Elections are like winning the semifinals. They just give you the opportunity to make a difference. What we did last night? That's what really matters."

That attitude and approach is what I admire most about Obama, the thing that makes him stand apart. For him, politics and elections are only vehicles, not destinations. They give you the chance to serve. To Obama's way of thinking, far worse than losing an election is squandering the opportunity to make the biggest possible difference once you get the chance to govern.

That's what allowed him to say "damn the torpedoes" and dive fearlessly into health care reform, despite the obvious political risks. It is why he was able to make many other tough calls when the prevailing political wisdom would have had him punt and wait for another chance with the ball.

Yet there is the flip side to that courage and commitment.

Obama has limited patience or understanding for officeholders whose concerns are more parochial—which would include most of Congress and many world leaders. "What are they so afraid of?" he asked after addressing the Senate Democrats on health reform, though the answer seemed readily apparent: losing their jobs in the next election! He has aggravated more than one experienced politician by telling them why acting boldly not only was their duty but also served their political needs. Whether it's John Boehner or Bibi Netanyahu, few practiced politicians appreciate being lectured on where their political self-interest lies. That hint of moral superiority and disdain for politicians who put elections first has hurt Obama as negotiator, and it's why Biden, a politician's politician, has often had better luck.

While Obama has been willing—if only grudgingly—to surrender to the demands of a campaign, with its focus on one central issue and its occasional need for theatricality, he refuses to be scripted in the critical arena of governance. Yet the truth is, governing requires some of the same discipline, and the ability to make progress often rests every bit as much on performance as policy.

During the 2012 campaign, we focused relentlessly on economic values and the plight of the middle class, which is one big reason we were able to survive a difficult election. For Obama, the case was entirely genuine. Given who he is and the life he's led, no one I know believes more strongly in an America where everyone gets a chance, and where anyone who works hard can get ahead. More than once, he's told me that he sees extreme economic polarization and the decades-long assault on economic mobility as the most pressing challenges of our time.

When the polls closed, however, Obama turned back to his entire punch list of priorities: climate change, immigration reform, a sharper focus on poverty and discrimination. As with health reform, he also sees these as issues of transcendent importance, moral imperatives, and he wasn't going to leave office without doing as much as he possibly could to meet them—even if they didn't rise to the top of the polls as immediate public concerns. The steady demands of an uncertain world, rather than the economic challenges of everyday Americans, also claimed a great deal of the president's time on the public stage after the election. Putin's aggressive territorial plays, and the convulsive politics of the Middle East, frustrated Obama's vision of a more peaceful and cooperative world and forced him to reengage on the dusty battlefield of Iraq.

Obama would return to economic issues at times and continue to work on an array of solutions. Yet, without the persistent, passionate, and almost singular focus of the campaign, few Americans would identify the daunting economic issues they face as the president's driving concern.

I deeply admire the president's determination to defy the small, poll-driven politics of our day to tackle big things. However, the gap between the singular focus of the campaign and his varied and ambitious agenda afterward undoubtedly sapped some of his political strength, leaving Americans wondering if he was truly focused on their concerns. You can't take politics entirely out of the process.

I don't speak with the president as much anymore. With the campaigns over, our once-frequent conversations have slowed to a trickle. I miss them. And when I hear the thundering hooves of the Washington pundits and pols on a stampede to run him down, I feel for him. Hell, I bleed for him. The brutal midterm election of 2014 was another painful rebuke. Yet I know this:

There are people who are alive today because of the health coverage he made possible. There are soldiers home with their families instead of halfway across the world. There are hundreds of thousands of autoworkers on the assembly line who would have been idled but for him, and the overall economy is in better shape than it has been in years. There are folks who are getting improved deals from their banks and mortgage lenders thanks to new rules in place and a new cop on the beat. There are gay and lesbian Americans who are, for the first time, free to defend their country without having to lie about who they are. There are women who have greater legal recourse when they're paid less than the man doing the exact same job alongside them. There are families who can afford to send their kids to college because there is more aid available.

Oh, and yes . . . just as he predicted in my conference room back in those wonderful, heady days when we first considered an audacious run for the presidency, millions of kids in our country today can dream bigger dreams because Barack Obama has blazed the trail for them.

Elections matter. He's proven that.

Yes, I deeply regret that we couldn't change the rancid politics of Washington. It's a bitter irony that the election of a president on a mandate for that change touched off such a ferocious counterreaction that it wound up only exacerbating the problem. Obama couldn't bridge that divide; now divided government seems to be our fate for the foreseeable future. Will Americans tolerate ever-escalating partisan warfare or will they demand something better?

For it's not just the politicians who bear responsibility for the current climate, but a passive citizenry that, in its disgust, has walked away from politics altogether. When just 10 or 20 percent of eligible voters turn out for party primaries, leaving them to the most strident forces and self-interested oligarchs who bankroll campaigns, the 80 or 90 percent who stay away share some of the blame for the results.

I spend a lot of time with young people now, bright, public-spirited kids from across the political spectrum who give me hope for the future. They treat each other respectfully, even when they don't agree. They care deeply about the community, the country, and the world around them. They want to have an impact, but they're not sure that politics is a viable path on which to do that.

With the benefit of my years and what passes for wisdom, I remind them that whatever they may care about—be it national security, the environment, education, or human rights—government will play a leading role for good or bad. Its receptivity to new ideas and innovation will, to a large extent, be determined by decisions that are made in Washington, state capitols, and city halls.

Congress is going to meet with you or without you, I tell them. Don't turn away in disgust and leave those decisions to someone else. You don't like politics today? Grab the wheel of history and steer us to a better place. Run for office. Be a strategist or policy aide. Work for a government agency or a non-profit. Become a thoughtful, probing journalist. Get in the arena. Help shape the world in which you're going to live. At a minimum, be the engaged citizen a healthy democracy demands.

A lot has happened to our country and the world since I heard JFK's call to a New Generation of Leadership. It's noisier, messier, and thus harder today to make this case to the newest generation, but it has to be made because it has never been more important.

I can say this without reservation because, a half century later, I'm still a believer.

ACKNOWLEDGMENTS

When I began working on this book, my sage editor, Ann Godoff, was characteristically blunt about the nature of the enterprise. "This is going to be really hard," she said. Knowing nothing, I shrugged off her admonition. After all, I had written all my life—newspaper and magazine stories; speeches and memos; thirty-second ads. Surely, this couldn't be that much more difficult?

I thought about that exchange often during the ensuing months, when the task of writing acknowledgments seemed like the distant peak of a very tall and seemingly unscalable mountain. I could not have reached it without the indispensable help of many people.

Ann herself was a rich source of wonderful insights and the firm taskmaster an old journalist needed to make his deadlines. I am grateful to her, Ben Platt, and the skillful folks at Penguin Press for their support, confidence, and patience.

Tim Skoczek was a fine young White House communications aide when I persuaded him to join me in Chicago and act as my all-purpose right-hand man on this project. I'm sure there were many days when he questioned the wisdom of his decision. For almost four years, he spearheaded the voluminous research this book required, read and reread every word, offered valuable advice, and lived through all the anxious moments with me. This book is his as well as mine.

I am grateful to my terrific assistant, Chenault Taylor, for keeping the world at bay while I labored on this project—and for putting up with my "shoot the messenger" moodiness when she occasionally could not.

Conor Reynolds played an integral role in the research and fact-checking that went into this book. Mike Rice, Austin Burke, and Michele Friedman at

VR Research did the impressive legwork required to find my family's histori-cal records.

I appreciate the understanding and support of my colleagues at the Insti-tute of Politics at the University of Chicago for my frequent absences as I worked on this book, and I am thankful to NBC News for granting me a sab-batical from my chores there to complete it.

Robert Barnett, my attorney, was a helpful and experienced counselor and guide through the world of book publishing, which was new to me.

In the midst of writing, I spent a week in Newton, Massachusetts, where my mother lived and died. During her final days, I reconnected with an old friend who lived nearby. Mark Starr was a mentor of mine at the *Chicago Tribune* in the 1970s, and best man at my wedding. He took a job as the Boston bureau chief for *Newsweek*, and we lost touch. When I saw him after my mother died, Mark, now retired, said he had some free time and offered to read my copy, as he had done so many times when I was a kid reporter. His good suggestions and moral support at critical junctures were a great gift.

Others read drafts and offered helpful advice as well. I am grateful to Larry Grisolano, Peter Cunningham, Joel Benenson, Jon Favreau, Shailagh Murray, Sam Smith, Forrest Claypool, David Plouffe, Robert Gibbs, Stephanie Cutter, Tommy Vietor, and Kathy Ruemmler for taking the time to offer their thoughts and, more than that, for their wonderful friendship. Particular thanks to Doris Kearns Goodwin, Governor Deval Patrick, George Stephanopoulos, and Mike Murphy for their kind words.

When I began, Ann suggested that I write everything, without regard to length. "We can always cut," she said. I am pretty sure she came to regret that direction. Ann was helpful—perhaps even a little desperate—in scaling back my expansive recollections to keep this book on track. Lost in that necessary process of pruning, however, was mention of the many great clients and price-less talented colleagues who deserved recognition in these pages but fell victim to the knife. I hope those folks, too numerous to list here, know how much I love and appreciate them. They, too, are very much a part of my story.

In the final days of running through edits, my staff and I were meeting at my apartment when Susan entered the room. Susan had put many things on hold for me while I finished this project, as she had done so many times in our thirty-five years of marriage. "No one will be happier than my wife when this book is done. She's borne the brunt of it," I said. Susan smiled. "I always do. Just read the book!" This project, like almost everything of value I have done in my life, would not have been possible without Susan's love and support. She held our family together through so many storms, yet still found time to change the world. The foundation she launched at our kitchen table, CURE, is now the largest private funder of epilepsy research. It is impossible to fully express my love, gratitude, and admiration for Susan, or the incredible luck I've had to share my life with such a lovely, remarkable woman.

Writing an autobiography can be painful, I learned. It reminded me once again of the sacrifices I imposed over the years on my children—Lauren, Michael, and Ethan. Now that they are adults, the most blessed times of the year are those special occasions when we are all together. They, along with my daughter-in-law, Liz, and new granddaughter, Maelin, provide a joy no campaign could offer.

There is one more person who made this book, and so much more, possible.

Barack Obama has been a great friend and a dream client. He is not perfect, as no one is. But he is a thoroughly admirable person, who personifies the spirit of politics and public service in which I believe. For that, and our long association, I will always be grateful.

INDEX

PHOTO CREDITS